# THE COMPARATIVE STUDY OF POLITICS

*David F. Roth*
*Frank L. Wilson*
PURDUE UNIVERSITY

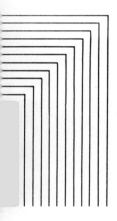

# THE
# COMPARATIVE
# STUDY
# OF
# POLITICS

HOUGHTON MIFFLIN COMPANY     BOSTON
*Atlanta   Dallas   Geneva, Ill.   Hopewell, N.J.   Palo Alto   London*

Library of Congress Catalog Card Number: 75–31002
ISBN: 0–395–20103–9

320.3

*To those whose lessons we shall always value, to those who gave so that our lives might be more meaningful; to Mom and Pop Ziff, to Dad, Louis Roth, and to Granny, Madame Anna Chin.*

*D.F.R.*

*To Erin, Sara, and John.*

*F.L.W.*

# CONTENTS

*Maps of the six countries appear between pages 257 and 266*

# II
# POLITICAL
# ACTORS

# III

## POLITICAL
## PERFORMANCE

## 9  *The Government and Society*  387

## 10  *Political Stability*  439

# 11   *The Challenges of Change*   474

# PREFACE

There have been many attempts to develop introductory courses in comparative politics. Some have chosen to limit their discussions to one region, most frequently Europe. Others have incorporated non-European nations into this same descriptive case format. Some preferred to apply limited theories of comparative politics to case studies, often stripping the cases of much of their relevance rather than adding to the governmental descriptions of previous works. Others attempted the theoretical approach. These professors took problem areas, e.g., parties, interest groups, or political functions, and discussed them in terms of the findings to date. None have effectively welded theory with case material. This book attempts to give the students an insight into comparative politics by selecting nations that reflect three types of political endeavor: *liberal-democratic, communist,* and *third world.* We have used two diverse examples of each: Britain and France; the Soviet Union and China; Mexico and Nigeria.

In discussing these three types of political systems we used a logical model, commencing with the history and social background of the actors within the system, and then turning to the policy and political performance arising from that system. The important topics of military intervention, instability, economic and social performance, and change are all introduced by highlighting the theoretical findings (middle-range theory) in each of these areas. These are then applied to each of the problems and to each of the nations discussed. It is hoped that the students will gain thereby a familiarity with (1) the political workings of these three system types, (2) the diversity within the types, and (3) the application and challenges of middle-range comparative politics theories.

We deal extensively with the issues of political development and change. By comparing countries that are considered "developed," such as Britain, France, and the Soviet Union, we hope to demonstrate the developmental process of the past and to suggest that it is still incomplete even in a country—such as Britain—that has been evolving its modern political and social institutions for over a millennium. In addition, the discussions of Mexico, Nigeria, and China suggest three radically different paths to development followed by contemporary third world countries. China uses both single party control over the bureaucracy and total social mobilization. China, in contrast to Mexico and Nigeria, is a unique nation whose norm is change rather than political stability. Nigeria is attempting to develop through military control of the bureaucracy. And Mexico is seeking the same objective with a single party structure.

It is hoped that students will be challenged by the problems presented—the unfinished, exciting business of comparative politics. The findings on the causes of military intervention and political instability and on the paths to socioeconomic development should allow introductory students to find the exciting changes of the real world of even more interest and perhaps more understandable than before this course.

We would like to acknowledge the patient and invaluable advice of a number of scholars who read and commented on all or part of the manuscript. We express special thanks to Keith R. Legg, University of Florida; Richard P. Longaker, University of California, Los Angeles; and Gerald G. Watson, University of Northern Colorado, who reviewed our entire manuscript two or three times at various stages of development. Their extensive comments and suggestions have contributed significantly to the quality of this book.

Special gratitude is also owed to our colleagues at Purdue, Robert Melson and Rolf Theen, whose criticism and encouragement were particularly helpful. Others whose comments alerted us to errors and omissions were Richard Baum, University of California, Los Angeles; Frederick Homer, University of Wyoming; Floyd F. Merrell, Purdue University; Josephine F. Milburn, University of Rhode Island; Philip E. Morgan, Emory University; Philip B. Taylor, Jr., University of Houston; and Robert G. Wesson, University of California, Santa Barbara. We happily acknowledge that this book is much better for their assistance. We are also grateful to Dotty Eberle, Rita Lynch, Diane Amos, and many others who helped us with the preparation of this manuscript. Of course, this book would not have been possible without the encouragement and concern of the editorial staff of Houghton Mifflin Company.

David F. Roth
Frank L. Wilson

# THE COMPARATIVE STUDY OF POLITICS

# *Introduction*

When you have been away from an American town for a while and ask what has happened in politics you are told who has been elected to what office, or appointed to which job. It will not be hard to discover whose political star is rising or falling, and who is working with or against whom. Jones, it appears, has broken with Smith and run against him in the last election. Smith, we are told, alienated the Negro vote on the school issue, and lost trades union support by his stand when the municipal employees struck. We may hear that Jones now has the support of the State Democratic machine, and has a good chance for the Governorship. Smith has strong friends in Washington and rumor says that he will soon be taken care of with a Federal job. And so on and on.[1]

The author of these words, Harold Lasswell, points out that if politics were nothing more than this, a well-informed journalist or newspaper-reader would know all there is to know about it and there would be little need for more detailed study. But the study of politics encompasses far more than such surface phenomena as governmental institutions, officeholders, rising and declining political fortunes, and readily observable political groups. It also involves study of the cultural and historical values that shape contemporary attitudes, and the social divisions that influence individual and group action; explanation and perhaps prediction of the behavior of those engaged in political activities; understanding of the formal and informal processes of setting public policy; evaluation of policy; and explanation and prediction of political and social change.

1. Harold Lasswell, *Politics: Who Gets What, When, How* (Cleveland and New York: World, 1958), p. 181.

Political scientists analyze political phenomena in order to understand the political process. Toward that end, they apply principles borrowed from the natural sciences: rigor, objectivity, reliability, generalizability, and predictability. But because laboratory experimentation cannot reproduce the political process, persons interested in politics make the world their laboratory. Observation of the political experience of different countries is an excellent way to gain a better understanding of politics. This is the heart of *comparative politics:* the study of individuals and groups in the political processes and performances of different political systems.

Thus, one of the reasons for the study of comparative politics is the hope that the examination of different political systems will lead to a better understanding of the nature of the political process: how and why decisions are made, who participates in making them, and the effects of such decisions. Understanding of politics is immeasurably enhanced by observing its workings in different settings and with different historical backgrounds, participants, and rules.

The study of foreign political experience also helps us to understand our own country's politics. For example, only awareness of certain foreign political party systems enables Americans to recognize the organizational weakness and disunity of their own political parties. Foreign political experience may also provide models for policy and procedural reforms applicable in our own country. Many features of the American political scene have been adapted from foreign models: the principle of separation of powers and the checks and balances system from the writings of the French philosopher Montesquieu; the civil service system from the practice of the Prussian bureaucracy; social security and unemployment insurance from European programs; and so on.

The study of comparative politics is also justifiable on the grounds of knowledge for its own sake. The variety of political experience is endless and can be fascinating to those interested in "what's going on." We live in an increasingly small world. An event apparently limited to one part of the world can have worldwide effects. It is worth knowing why a presidential election in France may be crucial for the future of American relations with Europe, while a presidential election in Mexico, though interesting, is unlikely to lead to many changes within or outside Mexico. It is important to know that the dissolution of Parliament by the British prime minister is not the same as the dissolution of the legislative body by the Nigerian military. Rarely can we gain genuine insight into such matters from our newspapers or news magazines without a solid background in the basics of comparative politics.

The term "comparative politics" suggests both a *subject matter* — multinational and cross-cultural political experience — and a *methodology* — comparison of different political systems for the purpose of finding similarities and explaining differences. However, much of the existing work in the field of comparative politics focuses on single countries, making only limited comparisons to other countries. Descriptions of political events and acts, such as the decision to participate in a war or the passage of legislation in a deliberative body, are rich in detail and highly suggestive for the development of propositions about the nature of politics. They also have the virtue of depicting an entire political system rather than mere segments of it.

But these "atheoretical" approaches are only a first step in political analysis. In attempting to develop a truly comparative political science, scholars have found that the single case study is not always adequate as a basis for generalizations. However, broad multinational comparisons are difficult; a great deal of effort and skill is required to master the political process in one country, let alone those of several countries. Another important obstacle to multinational comparisons has been the lack of meaningful tools of analysis, which are as basic to political scientists as are weights, measures, and instruments to the natural scientists.

In order to provide a rigorous and universal framework for political analysis, some political scientists have borrowed from engineers and natural scientists the notion of *systems analysis*.[2] In general, systems are goal-seeking entities with complex but interrelated subparts. They are seldom free from outside influences; usually they are interdependent with other systems, just as their parts are interdependent. The airplane, the human body, a heating system, and a stereo set are examples of systems. A *social system* is characterized by enduring patterns of human relationships. Religious groups, economic networks, and the pattern of international relations among countries are examples of social systems. Such systems pursue certain goals and perform specific tasks to meet human needs.

The systems approach to the study of politics is best illustrated by Figure I.1. In brief, the systems approach treats the political process as a political system operating within an environment composed of such other social systems as the religious system, the economic system, the international system, and the social class system. The interrelationships between the environment and the political system have a definite pattern: demands and supports emanating from the environment (inputs) are transformed into policies and decisions (outputs) that allocate authoritatively the society's scarce resources. These decisions may in turn affect and reshape the environment, thus altering subsequent inputs (feedback).

There is considerable debate among political scientists about the usefulness of the systems approach when applied rigorously as a model of the political process. Problems arise when one attempts to define clearly the boundaries of the political system vis-à-vis other social systems — which is necessary if meaningful observations are to be made on the interrelationship between the political system and its environment. It is also claimed that the systems model does not offer any insights into the heart of the political process, the transformation of

2. David Easton, *A Framework for Political Analysis* (Englewood Cliffs, N.J.: Prentice-Hall, 1965).

FIGURE I.1
*The Political System*

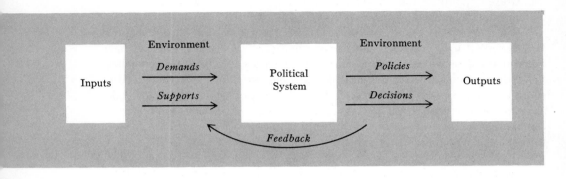

*Source: David Easton, "An Approach to the Analysis of Political Systems,"* World Politics
*IX (April 1957): 384.*

inputs into outputs. That is, it does not help us to understand how inputs, in the form of demands and supports, are transformed into policy decisions and actions; it simply tells us that there is some kind of interaction and interdependence between inputs and outputs.

However, the systems approach is widely used in a less rigorous fashion as an organizing framework for the study of politics. It is especially useful in facilitating the comparison of politics in countries with different backgrounds, institutions, and levels of development because it is not unique to a particular culture or kind of institutional framework. It permits the organization of data from diverse political units and makes possible cross-national comparisons of political experiences.

It is the generalized application of the systems approach that will be used in this text. The systems concept will serve to organize the subject matter and provide a framework for comparisons of the political process of six different countries. We will discuss the environment, history, societal composition, and cleavages of each of the nations, and will then examine the system's actors (individuals and groups involved in politics), noting how they perceive their environments, formulate policy demands, and translate such demands into policy decisions. We will then examine the processes of making policies and aspects of their outcomes: social, economic, and political performance, stability, and change. We will familiarize ourselves with a series of concepts, problems, and generalizations in comparative politics in order to explore how they operate in six political systems with widely different institutions, ideologies, and backgrounds. These comparative case studies will, we hope, shed light not only on the concepts and problems in question, but also on the general nature of politics. The study of problems in comparative politics — such as the promotion of public participation in politics, maintenance of political stability, legitimacy, socioeconomic change, and political performance in assuring the quality of life — manifested in six countries should offer rich insights into the complexities of sociopolitical processes.

# Six Case Studies: Britain, France, the Soviet Union, China, Mexico, and Nigeria

For Americans, the study of comparative politics has traditionally meant the study of *foreign* governments, and particularly of those deemed of greatest importance to the United States — the major European powers. In the past two decades, the interest of Americans has spread beyond democratic Europe to encompass communist political systems and those of the Third World, or developing, countries. The motivations for this broadened outlook are various: American economic interests have spread beyond Europe; non-European areas have come to play a larger part in American foreign policy; the communications revolution has brought even remote sections of the world to the attention of the American public, stimulating curiosity about them; and, finally, the proliferation of new and seemingly exotic states outside of Europe has aroused interest in the Third World.

While it is still necessary to understand the operation of Western democracy, the student of comparative politics can no longer be familiar only with the traditional European countries. Thus this text will compare and contrast three general types of political systems — liberal democratic, communist, and Third World or developing political systems. This typology of political systems is neither neat nor analytically precise. We are, in a sense, mixing apples and oranges, since the first two types of political systems are defined by the nature of their ideologies and political frameworks, while the third is defined by its degree of social, political, and economic development. The term "Third World" also suggests the tendency of these developing countries to avoid close political alignment with either the United States or the Soviet Union. By comparing liberal democracies, communist regimes, and Third World countries, we can consider the great variety of contemporary political experience and also identify features common to all political systems. To emphasize the diversity that exists *within* each type of political system, we will study two countries in each category. The liberal democracies are Britain and France; the communist states are the Soviet Union and the People's Republic of China; and the Third World nations are Mexico and Nigeria.

Roughly one-fourth of the world's nearly 150 independent states can be classified as essentially liberal democratic. The term "democracy," as it is commonly used in the Western world, denotes government based on popular sovereignty, or, in Lincoln's words, "government of the people, by the people, for the people." It assumes election of the government by the people through free and contested elections. Democratic government is by definition limited in power — usually by a constitution that restricts the amount of power at its disposal — and in scope — for example, by competition with groups it does not control, such as labor unions, social clubs, and churches. This concept of democracy is a product of Judeo-Greco-Christian tradition.[3]

Since the democratic experience is characteristic of countries as dissimilar as Costa Rica and the United States, no single country typifies the liberal democratic political system. We will note many differences between Britain and France; they in turn differ from other liberal democracies. However, case studies of these two countries will provide a basis for further comparisons with other liberal democratic countries. For example, study of the French political parties, though they are by no means typical of parties in all liberal democracies, will facilitate comparisons with other democratic parties that will make the latter more understandable. Likewise, examination of Britain's difficulties in dealing with disorders in Northern Ireland will illustrate the problems that confront all democracies in coping with organized violence.

The Western concept of democracy emphasizes the defense of individual liberty and freedom, defined in essentially political terms: freedom of the press, assembly, speech, and religion; the rule of law; and the equality of all citizens before the law. Needless to say, these ideals are often imperfectly achieved in Britain, France, the United States, and other liberal democracies. Communist countries also espouse democracy; indeed, they claim to be more democratic than the "bourgeois" liberal democracies. The communist concept of democracy recognizes the importance of political equality, but insists that it is possible only as a consequence of social and economic equality. In the communist states' pursuit of "social justice" (social and economic equality), limited government may not be possible. In fact, government is viewed as a major tool for achieving social justice and equality. If the search for social justice conflicts with individual liberty — if, for example, the desire to end social and economic inequities affecting many people collides with the property rights of a few individuals — preference is given to the community goals. To be sure, all communist states fall far short of achieving democratic goals, even when these goals are defined in their own terms. However, it is important to remember that most, if not all, of the liberal democracies also fail to fulfill their ideals.

The second set of case studies focuses on two communist states, the Union of Soviet Socialist Republics (Soviet Union) and the People's Republic of China, which will serve as examples of the sixteen functioning communist political systems.[4] While the communist states are few in number, they include two of the world's greatest powers and govern roughly one out of every three

3. The Judeo-Greco-Christian tradition is also compatible with nondemocratic forms of government, as is attested to by the authoritarian pasts of the European countries and the recent fascist authoritarianism of France, Germany, and Italy.
4. The sixteen communist countries are Albania, Bulgaria, Cambodia, China, Cuba, Czechoslovakia, East Germany, Hungary, North Korea, Outer Mongolia, Poland, Romania, the Soviet Union, North and South Vietnam, and Yugoslavia.

people in the world.[5] For a decade or more after World War Two, the communist world was dominated by the Soviet Union. The Russians played a major role in the development of the political systems of the eight communist states in eastern Europe, in most cases imposing on them the Soviet model of government. Even in the communist world, however, there is a great diversity of political practices. Yugoslavia began early in the 1950s to make important modifications in its political framework, and less dramatic political evolution occurred in other east European communist states as a result of the de-Stalinization movement of the late 1950s. In the seven non-European communist political systems, the Soviet model was never successfully implemented; in most cases, no attempt was made to apply the Soviet political structure in toto. As a result, the Soviet pattern of politics is no longer the standard brand of communist political organization.

China represents a sharp contrast with the Soviet Union and an alternative path to the implementation of communist ideals of social justice. China's growing importance in world politics and its success in developing a new model of communist development make it important to gain an understanding of Chinese politics. While most European communist regimes have emphasized economic development and industrialization even at the cost of social justice and economic equality, China has sought to balance social goals and economic development. These two sets of goals often conflict, and the attempts of the Chinese to wrestle with this dilemma account in part for the seemingly erratic behavior of their political system. Though Chinese methods have varied from those of other communist states, China shares common problems with the rest of the communist world: the maintenance by the Communist party of a monopoly on political

---

5. Communist countries are frequently labelled *totalitarian,* a term originally used to describe the supposedly absolutist and monolithic nature of rule in Nazi Germany and in the Soviet Union under Stalin. The most widely known definition of totalitarianism is that given by Carl J. Friedrich and Zbigniew K. Brzezinski in *Totalitarian Dictatorship and Autocracy* (Cambridge, Mass.: Harvard University Press, 1956). They list six traits of the totalitarian regime: (1) Absolute dominance of an official and totalist ideology (2) Rule by a single mass party led typically by one man (3) Terroristic police control (4) Monopoly of control by the party of all mass media (5) Monopoly of control of all means of effective armed combat (6) Central control and direction of the entire economy. So defined, totalitarinism is an abstract "ideal type" against which real-world examples can be measured. Some commentators have questioned whether the totalitarian model is an accurate description even of Stalin's Russia or Hitler's Germany. It clearly does not describe fascist Italy, despite the fact that Mussolini himself coined the term. As for contemporary communist countries, internal divisions and conflicts, the leashing of terror, the emergence of autonomous or near-autonomous economic and social groupings, and the sudden removal of supposedly all-powerful dictators (including Nikita Khrushchev in 1964) demonstrate that Friedrich and Brzezinski's concept of totalitarianism is not entirely applicable. Thus, the ideal type of totalitarian model coincides only approximately with real-world examples, just as the liberal democracies correspond imperfectly with ideal models of democratic rule.

The term "totalitarian" has been misused during the Cold War to distinguish "bad" totalitarians from "good" democrats. It should be used without negative connotations to describe the communist regimes' aspirations to complete monopoly of political power and total control of society and economy. The term will be used in this text to refer neutrally to the *total scope and control* of government sought, but not achieved, by communist regimes.

and social power, organization and control of the economy and society by the party, and the implementation of Marxist ideology.

We have described the democratic and communist political systems as distinctive political orders characterized by specific political philosophies. The developing Third World, however, is characterized by political systems confronting the task of political, social, and economic development, rather than by systems with distinctive political structures or ideologies. For the most part, these developing countries are located in Africa, Latin America, Central Asia, Southeast Asia, and the Middle East.

Most Third World countries are in the process of transformation from basically traditional political systems into modern states. *Political development* is defined here as the emergence of mass participation in politics and the elaboration of political institutions capable of responding to or directing such mass participation.[6] Political development also involves the dispersal of social and political decision-making powers among specialized structures (structural differentiation). In place of a single political entity — such as a tribal chieftain — responsible for a broad range of issue areas, there evolve special agencies, bureaucracies, and individual roles to perform specific tasks within a relatively narrow scope. Political development also entails the transformation of traditional political values and orientations into rational, analytical, and empirical values and orientations (secularization of political culture).[7] Finally, political development implies the capacity of the government to realize its policy objectives (effective political performance).

Political development does not mean the replacement of the traditional past with a completely unrelated present. Rather, it is a process of building on the past in a manner that permits the retention of many traditional features. Indeed, we will note throughout this text the persistence of the past even in revolutionary systems in which tremendous efforts have been made to eradicate its influence.

The approximately one hundred countries that may be categorized as part of the Third World are at various stages of development and nondevelopment and are characterized by widely different political forms and philosophies. Most Third World countries are governed by a single dominant party regime or by military rulers. Mexico is an example of single-party rule, Nigeria of military rule. Mexico and Nigeria also exemplify the general problems of political development and can profitably be contrasted with each other and with other types of political systems.

Mexico has progressed further along the path of political development than have most developing nations. While age is not always a decisive factor, Mexico has been an independent nation since 1821 and has for the past sixty years been undergoing a social and political revolution. Our examination of Mexico will

6. See Samuel Huntington, *Political Order in Changing Societies* (New Haven: Yale University Press, 1968).

7. Gabriel A. Almond and G. Bingham Powell, Jr., *Comparative Politics: A Developmental Approach* (Boston: Little, Brown, 1965), pp. 22–25, 105, *passim.*

enable us not only to identify problems of development common to much of the Third World, but also to discuss ways in which one country has confronted, and sometimes overcome, these problems.

Nigeria, by contrast, is a recently independent country (1960) just beginning the process of political development. Nigeria is the most populous of the African states and has a promising base for economic development with large oil deposits. Its struggles to overcome the legacy of colonialism, the tensions of an ethnically divided country, and social and political disturbances deriving from modernization will suggest the challenge confronting the more than seventy countries that have gained independence since 1945. It also resembles many other Third World countries in that it is currently ruled by a military regime.

Comparison of Mexico and Nigeria will highlight the crucial problem of developing effective and legitimate political institutions capable of meeting growing popular demands for governmental services and action. Among the other challenges of development that we will consider are the need to develop a sense of unity among the different, and sometimes hostile, ethnic and cultural groups that find themselves joined within the geographical confines of a single new state; the need to respond to rising popular expectations of progress in economic and industrial development, social reform, and political modernization; the role in political development of such intermediary groups as political parties and interest groups; and the threat of military intervention in politics.

In describing these three types of political systems — democratic, communist, and developing — we make no pretense of offering a typology that will illuminate the study of comparative politics as a whole or pave the way to a general theory of politics. Our typology is not rigorously defined in that it excludes some political systems and permits others to be assigned to two or more classifications simultaneously. Traditional political systems, such as Nepal, Afghanistan, Saudi Arabia, and Liberia, do not fit readily into any of the three categories. On the other hand, India may be considered both a democratic and a developing political system, and several non-European communist political systems might also be classified as developing. The purpose of this typology is to suggest that the six comparative case studies in this text may be considered as examples of the way politics is organized in other countries as well.

Each chapter begins with a general examination of some concepts, problems, and theories germane to political phenomena, which are then applied in detailed case studies of the six countries. Our goals are to familiarize you with some of the major ideas prevalent in comparative politics and to provide you with a fairly comprehensive survey of politics and government in the six countries.

In Part I we look at some of the general background features of politics. One important result of the interest in systems analysis is that it has sensitized political scientists to the importance of examining interaction between the political system and the environment in which it operates. We focus on two aspects of the environment: the influence of past experience and sociocultural factors. In Chapter 1, we survey briefly the political effects of historical heritages. All political systems, even revolutionary regimes that seek to break deci-

TABLE I.1

*Area and Population Density*

| Country | Area (thousand square miles) | Persons (per square mile) |
|---|---|---|
| United Kingdom | 94.2 | 599.4 |
| France | 210.0 | 247.0 |
| China | 3,691.5 | 230.0 |
| USSR | 8,599.3 | 29.5 |
| Mexico | 761.0 | 80.9 |
| Nigeria | 356.6 | 166.5 |

*Source: Charles Lewis Taylor and Michael C. Hudson,* World Handbook of Political and Social Indicators (*New Haven: Yale University Press, 1972*), *pp. 299–302.*

sively with the past, find themselves constrained by the political options imposed by history. Chapter 2 deals with the social environment, concentrating on the effects on the political system of class, regional, cultural, and ideological social cleavages within the political unit. Chapter 3, the final introductory chapter, is a brief survey of the basic political institutions of each of the six countries, designed to explain the institutional framework within which politics takes place.

In Part II the object of study is political actors — individuals and groups involved in politics. The first type of political actor we examine is the individual citizen (Chapter 4). Most modern political systems, whether democratic or dictatorial, strive to maximize the political participation of the masses. However, the purposes and modes of encouraging such participation differ dramatically from one type of regime to the next. And the methods and significance of mass participation also vary widely. In Chapter 5 we look at two of the most influential sets of group actors in politics: interest groups and political parties. Once again, interest groups and parties exist in most political systems, but their activities and goals differ markedly from one system to the next. In Chapter 6 the leadership and bureaucracy are examined. Among the concerns of this chapter are the social backgrounds of those recruited as political leaders, the styles they adopt as leaders, their political resources and limitations, and the problem of controlling the bureaucracy. The final set of actors we examine is the military (Chapter 7). In some countries the military takes virtually no active part in politics; in others it completely dominates the political process. Why and how the military becomes politicized, how it acts in politics, and how to control it are the questions explored in this chapter.

Part III deals with political performance. The way in which policy decisions are made and the content and effectiveness of these policies determine the political system's performance or output. In recent years, there has been increased interest in assessing the ability of political systems to meet the changing needs and demands of their people and to provide stable and efficient government. In making such assessments, observers have usually defined in accordance with their own biases the priorities and values to be sought by alien political systems. In the case of Americans, this tendency has often meant that foreign governments are evaluated by the criterion of whether they perform the same tasks in the same manner as does the American government. Our approach seeks to avoid this kind of bias by encouraging the evaluation of political performance in terms of the goals and priorities established by each regime.

In Chapter 8 the policy-making process is closely examined. Often the constitutional description of this process is an inaccurate explanation of how and why decisions are actually made. This chapter emphasizes the informal and sometimes extralegal forces and institutions that determine the policies of each political system. Chapter 9 explores the role of government in the social and economic aspects of a nation's life. Among the issues considered are the reasons for the expanding role of government in society, the manner in which social and economic goals are determined and pursued in different political systems, and standards for evaluating government performance in achieving these goals. Chapter 10 looks at the question of political stability: what it is, how it is achieved, and how it is maintained. In Chapter 11 we look at the issues and processes of political change, examining different styles of change (revolutionary versus evolutionary), stages of political development, and future trends.

# I

## BACKGROUND TO POLITICS

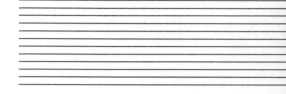

# I

# *Historical Sources of*

# *Contemporary Politics*

## Introduction

In George Orwell's *Nineteen Eighty-Four,* the "Party's" slogan is: "Who controls the past controls the future; who controls the present controls the past." The Party makes certain that the record of the past is "correct." Newspapers, books, and other documents are constantly altered to correspond to changes in the leadership's position.

> Day by day and almost minute by minute the past was brought up to date. In this way every prediction made by the Party could be shown by documentary evidence to have been correct; nor was any item of news, or any expression of opinion which conflicted with the needs of the moment, ever allowed to remain on record. All history was a palimpsest, scraped clean and reinscribed exactly as often as was necessary. . . . Books, also, were recalled and rewritten again and again, and were invariably reissued without any admission that any alteration had been made.[1]

Though it lacks the thoroughness of Orwell's fictional state, the Soviet Union is a real-world example of a regime seeking to control the past by rewriting history.[2] In Stalin's days, the alteration of official history was crude and undisguised. One Soviet citizen recounts:

1. George Orwell, *Nineteen Eighty-four* (New York: Harcourt, Brace & World, 1946), p. 41.
2. See Cyril E. Black, ed., *Rewriting Russian History,* 2d ed. (New York: Random House, 1962).

I was finishing my last two years of high school during the purge trials [the early 1930s]. During that terrible period, it seemed that every day we would have to open our books and take the scissors to a picture of someone who had been highly respected up to that time. If there was anything about the person in the text itself, we would cross it out with heavy black ink. It had to be very heavy, so that no later student would be able to make out the type underneath.[3]

Despite such efforts to control the content of written history, the historical process leaves marks on a country that even revolutionary regimes have difficulty erasing. Any political system is strongly influenced by the legacy of past political, social, and economic experiences. A nation's history does not determine the nature of contemporary politics, but it undeniably affects the political process, often in a very profound way. As a consequence, an important aspect of comparative political analysis is the evaluation and comparison of the accumulated political history of the countries under consideration.

## THE IMPACT OF HISTORY ON POLITICS

It is not impartial historians' explanations of past events that affect contemporary politics, but the way the people of a country remember or interpret these events. Most Americans, for example, regard the War of 1812 as a battle for freedom of the seas forced on their ancestors by the seizure of American sailors for service on British warships. However, an impartial historian might conclude that the war was precipitated by an American attack on Canada motivated by frontiersmen's desire for free land and by their belief that the British in Canada were responsible for Indian harassment of settlers. The latter, more accurate version has little moderating impact on the inaccurate popular version. The War of 1812 provided the new nation with honored victories, heroes, and "The Star-Spangled Banner." What counts is not history in the abstract but history as it is perceived.

Contemporary political systems are shaped by the past in a number of ways. In this chapter we will focus on four historical legacies: political institutions, political and social problems, political symbols, and political ideas and values. the term *political institutions* is used broadly to encompass customary practices; such political forces as parties, militaries, and bureaucracies; and formal governmental offices. Each generation creates new institutions in response to current needs, but a surprising number of political institutions inherited from the past are adapted for contemporary use. In the United States, for example, our inherited institutions include the Constitution and the governmental bodies it created, the two largest political parties, the bureaucracy, and a host of customs and precedents. Political institutions often persist even when there occurs a sharp break with the past. Many countries that achieved independence after World War Two have retained institutions developed by their former colonial masters. The bureaucracy, the military, and the educational system are among

3. Susan Jacoby, "Reforming Soviet Education," *Saturday Review/World,* 12 February 1973.

those institutions most often retained. Furthermore, such nations often choose as the national tongue the language of the former colonial power, rather than an indigenous language. Even if the old regime has been overthrown by violent revolution, aspects of the past sometimes persist in new forms. Old organizations acquire new names and tasks; political customs are observed by the new leaders; and past experience serves as a model for future political action.

Each political system has a legacy of *social and political problems* that it must manage or resolve. For example, the failure of American political leaders after the Civil War to assure equal treatment for blacks created a legacy of racial antagonism that contemporary leaders are still struggling to overcome. Many countries inherit populations composed of diverse racial, religious, and linguistic groups. The integration of such a culturally pluralist state is often aggravated by a history of conflict among the various cultures now joined in a single political entity. As we shall see in Chapter 2, the British are still struggling with the conflict between Protestants and Catholics in Northern Ireland, which goes back to the Anglo-Norman invasion of Ireland in the twelfth century. Similarly, political systems may inherit societies characterized by deep class cleavages originating in the past. The caste system in India, for example, has been inherited from past social orders and thrives despite governmental efforts to eliminate it or moderate its socioeconomic effects.

Many countries' past economic and social development patterns have bequeathed unbalanced economic growth, widespread illiteracy, overcrowded cities, overtilled farmland, unequally distributed wealth, and malnutrition. This is the case in many areas of the developing world whose colonial past has left a heritage of economic exploitation and social inequities. In short, each political system is faced with problems originating in the past — sometimes the very distant past — that it must attempt to resolve.

A third way in which history affects present political configurations is through a legacy of *political symbols*. Political symbols are persons, events, slogans, legends, artistic achievements, institutions, and objects that engender emotional or affective reactions of national pride and unity. Many of these symbols are derived and acquire their emotional potency from a country's past experiences and struggles. A flag or national anthem, an honored tradition or political office, a revolutionary incident, or a dramatic reform may stir powerful feelings of patriotism and national identity. Such symbols are important to the political system in its efforts to maintain or create loyalty to the political unit and to motivate mass support for the regime's goals.

The manipulation and, in some cases, creation of political symbols offers political leaders important resources to use in pursuing desired policies that are likely to be unpopular or to entail important sacrifices. Winston Churchill invoked the past achievements and struggles of the British people to mobilize support for the tremendous sacrifices necessitated by World War Two. At the same time, Mussolini was mobilizing the Italian people in pursuit of his foreign policy goals by recalling the glories of ancient Rome and promising to create a new Roman empire. More recently, American political leaders evoked

A country's history and traditions help to shape contemporary politics. In Britain, the Queen's annual address to Parliament no longer contains the monarch's own ideas or words, but the continuation of this centuries-old tradition emphasizes the continuity and stability of the state. In France, a long tradition of protest and revolt provides examples that are often seized upon by contemporary dissatisfied groups and individuals. Student protesters during the Events of May 1968 patterned their actions on earlier periods of revolt; in the future, a new generation may draw upon the Events of May 1968 as a model for their rebellion. In most Third World countries traditional culture provides a welcome thread from the past. But in China it is seen to be an inhibition from the past. With ideological objectives, the status-laden ideas of Confucius were associated with existing harmful bureaucratic trends and were attacked by the regime, as illustrated in these anti-Confucius posters being read by a group of Chinese workers.

images of past American resourcefulness and willingness to endure trials in order to encourage sacrifices during the energy crisis of 1973–1974.

In general, the longer the political unit's existence the richer the symbolic resources of its history. China, Japan, the European countries, and other nations have long histories as distinct political units, and the heroic episodes and martyrs of the past serve as powerful stimuli to national unity and purpose. Some nations, especially the recently independent countries of Africa, have little written history capable of providing political symbols. Those historical symbols that do exist are often perpetuated through tribal folklore and legends, and are in many cases based on tribal experiences rather than the common experience of all citizens of the modern political unit. It is not unusual for such tribal symbols to serve as disintegrative rather than integrative forces, since they often stem from conflict among tribes now joined in the same political unit. In several new countries, efforts are being made to seek historical roots as a means of finding symbols that will generate national identity and pride. The study of earlier civilizations and of native art and folklore thus often contributes to the political integration of new states.

A fourth legacy of the past is *political ideas and attitudes*. These ideas may be widely held and clear-cut political belief systems or they may take the less explicit form of individual political values, feelings, and knowledge. *Political belief systems* have been described as the sets of beliefs by which individuals navigate and orient themselves in the sea of politics.[4] Such systems include beliefs about the nature of politics, its aims, and its purposes. Certain belief systems are based on clearly stated, rational, and deductive principles and elicit a high degree of emotional commitment; such belief systems are often labelled *ideologies*. Examples of explicit and well-developed ideologies are the Marxist-Leninist principles of communism and the tenets of a variety of different strains of democratic socialism. Less clearly defined belief systems are grounded more in pragmatism than in deductive reasoning. These pragmatic belief systems are usually composed of implicit rather than explicit principles and arouse less emotional commitment than do ideologies. Among the most important contemporary examples of pragmatic belief systems is the pluralist liberalism of many Western democracies, which posits that representative democracy functions best through the interaction of interest groups, government bureaucrats, and elected public officials.

Both ideological and pragmatic political belief systems are often inherited from the past. Each nation's unique historical development provides a rich heritage of political thinkers and ideas. In the United States, Alexander Hamilton, James Madison, and Thomas Jefferson developed a core of political ideas that has since been enhanced by a variety of political philosophers and practitioners. Even when a belief system is imported from abroad, it is often interpreted in the light of the recipient country's own past experience with similar belief systems and integrated with the ideas of native political thinkers. For

4. Giovanni Sartori, "Politics, Ideology, and Belief Systems," *American Political Science Review LXIII* (June 1969): 398–411.

example, some of the ideas of Italian fascism were imported into Germany in the early 1920s, and were then transformed in the light of German experience into Hitler's National Socialism.

In addition to the political belief systems that establish political aims and priorities, individuals have political feelings, values, and information that influence their political behavior. The general political attitudes and orientations of the population are referred to as the *political culture*. An important aspect of the political culture is the people's emotional feelings about the political world: whether or not they feel a strong bond of loyalty and affection to the political regime, for example. Another facet of political culture is people's evaluation of the government's performance and their likes and dislikes relative to the political scene. On the basis of these attitudes, the individual adopts certain expectations of government in terms of performance and certain political duties, such as voting or taxpaying, to be expected in return. While there is little evidence to suggest that these attitudes determine the individual's actual political conduct, there is a strong feeling among political scientists that these attitudes do influence what the individual does politically.

In a more general sense, a country often inherits from the past social values with important political consequences. For example, many Western countries have acquired from their Judeo-Roman-Christian backgrounds a political culture that emphasizes the individual. The state is seen as a means to assure the individual a full opportunity to express himself or herself. Individual liberty and freedom are regarded as supreme political values to be guaranteed by the state. The value placed on individual rights explains in part the pluralist nature of most Western countries — including Britain, France, and the United States — and their emphasis on the protection of liberty and freedom. In cultures in which emphasis on the community and the collective good prevailed in the past, the individual must give precedence to the attainment of collective goals. Personal ambitions and rights may be valued much less than the community goals and thus may be abridged by the state in pursuit of those goals. In the Soviet Union and China, attempts are made to develop the collective traditions of the past in order to foster the community spirit considered important for the achievement of a communist society.

The political culture is normally passed from one generation to the next, which means that the attitudes and values of the past tend to be conveyed into the present. Of course, the individual's political ideas change throughout his or her life in response to political experiences, but basic orientations often persist. Thus, the attitudes of previous generations — based on the political events of their lifetimes — may indirectly influence the political conduct of contemporary citizens. The difficulty of altering this process by means of conscious efforts to shape political attitudes can be seen in the case of postwar Germany. The Allied occupying forces in the western zones of Germany sought to alter the political culture in the direction of increased emphasis on public virtues, lessened interest in private virtues, and thus a greater sense of democratic civic responsibility. The results of these deliberate efforts to control political socialization have not been encouraging: West Germans remain uninterested in politics and largely passive toward government. In communist countries attempts are being made to create a new political order supported by a new political culture. This effort has involved the use of methods of socialization that Westerners are prone to label as extreme, for the purpose of developing political attitudes more consistent with the Marxist-Leninist or Maoist concept of the good citizen. The enduring nature of ingrained political attitudes has prevented even the sometimes brutal tactics employed in the creation of the "new Soviet man" and in the Chinese Cultural Revolution from eradicating completely the legacies of the czars and dynasties.

The pertinence of history to contemporary political patterns makes it imperative that comparative political studies take note of historical backgrounds. Space limitations prevent us from giving comprehensive histories of the six countries we are examining, but in the sections that follow we will briefly sketch the origins of the current regimes and note some general historical trends.

# Britain and France: Contrasts in the Development of Liberal Democracies

## BRITAIN: HISTORY AND TRADITION ENSHRINED

*The Evolutionary Nature of Political Development*  In the parliaments of most countries, members sit as a body facing the speaker's podium. But members of the British House of Commons sit on two banks of benches facing each other. Some claim that this seating pattern is responsible for the British two-party system: with one party on each side, there was no room for third or fourth parties.[5] Whatever the validity of this claim, the unusual seating pattern has a historical source. The Commons' first permanent meeting place was the Chapel of St. Stephen in Westminster Palace. As in most English churches of the time, St. Stephen's pews faced each other. When it burned down and Commons moved to a new location some three hundred years later, the face-to-face seating arrangement was retained. Similarly, after the bombing of Commons in World War Two, the chamber was rebuilt with facing banks of benches.

This gradual growth and subsequent careful preservation of tradition is characteristic of the British pattern of political development. Modern British democracy is the product of at least seven hundred years of gradual evolution. We may designate as the beginning of democratic evolution the year 1215, when

5. It is interesting that the shape of the seating pattern is believed to have an impact on legislators' behavior. In 1975, the British government ordered the redesigning of the seats in the Northern Irish regional parliament, changing from facing banks of seats as in Commons to a horseshoe shape that would presumably foster understanding and compromise among Ulster's warring political groups.

FIGURE 1.1
## Some Important Landmarks in British History

| | |
|---|---|
| 1066 | Norman conquest of England, the last successful invasion of the British Isles |
| 1215 | King John signs the Magna Carta |
| 1265 | First Parliament meets |
| 1536 | Act of Union binds England and Wales |
| 1542 | Henry VIII assumes title of King of Ireland |
| 1642–1649 | Civil War ends in execution of Charles I and establishment of a military dictatorship under Oliver Cromwell |
| 1660 | Restoration of the monarchy under Charles II |
| 1688 | "The Glorious Revolution" deposes James II for attempting to reimpose Catholicism on England |
| 1689 | Bill of Rights accepted by William and Mary on their coronation assures political supremacy of Parliament |
| 1707 | Act of Union binds Scotland to England |
| 1721–1742 | First "prime minister": Sir Robert Walpole |
| 1832 | Great Reform Act extends suffrage to middle classes |
| 1867 | Reform Act further extends right to vote |
| 1911 | Powers of the House of Lords abridged |
| 1945–1951 | Postwar Labour government enacts sweeping social and political reforms |

King John was compelled by his barons to sign the Magna Carta, guaranteeing them certain privileges. While the Magna Carta's immediate effect was to make possible a powerful and independent aristocracy, it has come to symbolize the limitation of the powers of the king and the supremacy of law. The seventeenth century was a high point in the battle to limit the powers and prerogatives of the monarch. The Puritan Revolution (1642–1649) culminated in the trial of King Charles I by Parliament and his subsequent execution for treason. After a dozen years of military dictatorship under Oliver Cromwell and his son, the monarchy was restored when Parliament invited Charles II to assume the throne. But the power of Parliament was again demonstrated by the Glorious Revolution of 1688–1689 in which the monarch, James II, was deposed because of his Catholicism. Parliament later assured its inalienable supremacy over the monarch in the Bill of Rights, which was accepted by William and Mary as they assumed the throne in 1689. The Bill of Rights did not guarantee individual freedoms but was a contract between the Crown and Parliament limiting the powers of the Crown.

The confirmation of Parliament's supremacy did not mean the advent of democracy, since Parliament was dominated by the nobility, the wealthy, and the Church of England. It took two more centuries to democratize parliamentary rule in Britain. It is difficult to specify the exact date of the emergence of British democracy, since the evolutionary process continues today, but a convenient reference-point is the adoption of the Parliament Act of 1911, seven centuries after the Magna Carta. This law established the supremacy of the House of Commons over the House of Lords; in the event of conflict between the two houses, the decision of Commons (whose membership is determined by popular elections) would ultimately prevail over that of the Lords (whose membership is based on aristocratic birth).

Another example of the evolutionary nature of constitutional development in Britain is the movement toward universal adult suffrage and honest elections for Commons. Originally, the House of Commons was composed of two knights from each county and two citizens elected by a highly restricted portion of the middle-class population of each borough. In the nineteenth century, however, the Industrial Revolution caused rapid changes in population distribution. Certain boroughs, called "rotten boroughs," lost most of their populations but retained representation in Commons. New industrial centers and cities that had experienced very rapid population growth had little or no representation. The result was extreme malapportionment of seats in the House of Commons. While important new industrial centers like Manchester, Leeds, Birmingham, and Sheffield had no representatives in Commons, some 51 boroughs with a combined total of less than fifteen hundred voters sent more than one hundred representatives to sit in Commons.[6]

The Great Reform Act of 1832 corrected these inequities, abolishing most of the rotten boroughs, granting some industrial centers their first representation in Commons, and increasing the representation of other cities. The Reform Act also enfranchised middle-class males, thus doubling the size of the electorate. In 1867 another Reform Act was passed, reducing property requirements for the vote and extending the vote to the lower middle class, rural tenant farmers, and some urban workers; the size of the electorate thus doubled again. In 1872 the secret ballot was introduced, freeing voters from possible intimidation. Further reforms in 1884 and 1885 corrected malrepresentation due to uneven distribution of seats relative to population. Then, after World War One, the Representation of the People Act of 1918 granted universal suffrage to males over twenty-one and to women over thirty. In 1928 a new law lowered the minimum voting age for women to twenty-one. The Representation of the People Act of 1948 adjusted the distribution of seats according to population shifts and established the principle of one citizen—one vote by abolishing procedures that had permitted certain upper-class citizens to vote several times. Finally, the voting age was lowered to eighteen by the first Labour government of Harold Wilson; eighteen-year-olds voted for the first time in the general elections of 1970.

This recapitulation of historical highlights makes it clear that British democracy is not the product of revolution, nor even of very rapid change. Instead, democratic procedures were adopted step by step over a long period of time. The process of building democracy was for the most part orderly, but it was often prodded forward by periods of great political and social turmoil. The movement that ultimately resulted in the Great Reform Act of 1832 gained

6. Kenneth Mackenzie, *The English Parliament* (Harmondsworth, England: Penguin Books, 1965), p. 99.

impetus from a bloody riot in 1819 that occurred when a crowd gathered in Manchester to petition Parliament for redress of local grievances. Women found recourse to violence in seeking the right to vote: in 1912 Emmeline Pankhurst, a suffragette leader, and her associates carried out a well-planned campaign of breaking windows, saying, "The argument of the broken window pane is the most valuable argument in politics."[7]

*Respect for Tradition*   Though this is an age in which the impulse to modernize and demystify has brought inherited values under scrutiny, the British still retain their awe for the traditions of their past. Many of these traditions revolve around the monarch and the royal family.

The British monarch is a powerful living symbol linking the British of today with a rich past and a royal future. The monarchy prevails because it has adapted to the modern world and to democracy while retaining its value as a symbol of national unity and continuity. As one observer notes, "Modern societies still need myth and ritual. A monarch and his family supply it; there is no magic about a mud-stained politician."[8] While the queen has no political power today, the illusion of power is carefully maintained by observance of traditional ceremonies. This is well illustrated by the following description of the queen's annual address to Parliament:

> It is a very formal occasion. She drives to Westminster [where Parliament sits] in a State Coach with an escort of Household Cavalry. The peers attend in their robes, and the peeresses in the gallery wear their tiaras. The Queen robes in the Robing Room and wears the Crown. She sits on the Throne and summons the Commons, who attend at the Bar headed by Mr. Speaker with the mace. She reads the Queen's Speech announcing the intentions of the Government during the session. The whole thing is a "circus" though, like most British ceremonies, it has purpose. It draws attention to the importance of Parliament in the national life.[9]

The queen's speech is prepared for her by the Government: not one word in it is her own. To an outsider it might seem more reasonable for the prime minister to deliver this annual message, since it describes the Government's plans rather than the queen's personal wishes. But a British scholar explains: ". . . we must not forget our history, for history has consequences. The Queen and her predecessors have sat in Parliament for seven hundred years. For all we know the Queen and her successors will go on sitting in Parliament for seven thousand years."[10]

Most of the British population continues to revere the royal family. The strength of this popular allegiance is demonstrated by the massive public interest in the 1973 marriage of Princess Anne and the 1969 investiture of Charles as

7. George Dangerfield, *The Strange Death of Liberal England, 1910–1914* (New York: Capricorn Books, 1961), p. 170.

8. Ian Gilmour, *The Body Politic* (London: Hutchinson, 1969), p. 313.

9. Sir Ivor Jennings, *The Queen's Government,* rev. ed. (Harmondsworth, England: Penguin Books, 1965), p. 67.

10. *Ibid.,* p. 68.

Prince of Wales. While no serious proposals have been made in recent years to abolish the monarchy, there has been some criticism of the cost of maintaining the royal family. Including direct and indirect costs, approximately 15 million American dollars are allocated from public funds to maintain the royal standard of living. It is likely that the monarchy will adapt to changing circumstances — perhaps by sacrificing some of its grandeur due to economic pressures — but the monarchy will remain the living embodiment of a rich and glamorous history.

The British Empire is an important aspect of this glorious past. Over a period of some four hundred years, Britain built an empire that ultimately became one of the largest in the history of the world. British imperialism is correctly explained in Marxist terms as the inevitable search for markets and resources inherent in the advanced stages of capitalism. But other motives operated as well. Some colonies were established by religious dissenters seeking the opportunity to practice their beliefs; some were acquired out of a genuine commitment to the civilizing mission Rudyard Kipling called the "white man's burden"; still others fell into British hands as spoils of war. The empire was a source of national pride, as well as political and economic strength, and made what might otherwise have been an insignificant island nation into a world power.

The empire that took four hundred years to build has crumbled in the thirty years since World War Two. Of the seventy-four states that gained independence between 1943 and 1973, forty were former British dependencies. What is left of the empire is the Commonwealth of Nations, a loose association of thirty-three sovereign states. While its member nations do enjoy some mutual trade advantages and engage in some political consultation, the Commonwealth does little more for Britain than provide a faint glimmer of past glory. Adaptation to the loss of the empire has been a difficult process. Years ago, an American diplomat said that Britain had lost an empire but had not found a role. This remained true at least until 1973, when Britain belatedly gained membership in the European Common Market.

*A Deferential Society*   There is no single factor that accounts for the relatively peaceful evolution of British politics. A partial explanation may be that much social discontent was manifested as religious rather than political dissent. The Methodism of John Wesley, Puritanism, Congregationalism, and other nonconformist religions diverted social and political unrest into religion, thereby reducing possible sources of support for political dissent. Another partial explanation is the absence of political absolutism since the seventeenth century. By that time the powers of the monarch were limited, but by no means inconsequential, and served as an obstacle to the perpetuation of a new absolutism by Parliament, prime ministers, or military figures.

Another important factor in the evolutionary nature of British political development is the ability of those holding power to recognize growing demands for change and to respond to them so as both to deflect demands for more radical change and to preserve their own political power. The Conservative party, long the most important and successful political party, was particularly adept at this. Driven by a powerful will to rule, the Conservatives were quick to accept and enact reforms proposed by others. In many cases the Conservatives, though they represented the most privileged sectors of the population, took the initiative in carrying out far-reaching social and political reforms before they had even been proposed by supposedly more reform-minded sectors of society. The Conservative party's interest in reform was not simply a means of perpetuating its hold on political power, but also an outgrowth of British aristocratic notions of *noblesse oblige,* or the responsibility of the governing class to concern itself with the general well-being of all people. As a result of this philosophical commitment to the social duties of the upper class, Conservative governments often led the way in social reform. For example, the Conservative government of Benjamin Disraeli (1874–1880) enacted a series of innovative social reforms including legal protection of the right to strike, definition of workers' rights, establishment of sanitation services, slum clearance and reconstruction, and regulation of food and drug standards. This was not an isolated instance; other Conservative cabinets, prodded by electoral considerations and/or noblesse oblige, have manifested the party's willingness to pursue social and economic reform.

Furthermore, the propensity of the conservative forces to accept change was complemented by the willingness of liberal forces to negotiate and compromise their demands for change. In Britain few have advocated violent revolution to achieve their ends. Rather than insist on rapid change, the socialist and liberal forces have adopted a gradualist approach to their social and political goals. Commitment to evolutionary development is well illustrated by the Fabian Society, long the voice of radicalism and socialism in Britain. The emblem of the Fabian Society is the turtle, symbolizing the belief that the British road to socialism was one of slow but steady progress through reform. Thus, at the leadership level there has been agreement (or "elite consensus") on the part of those favoring radical change and those representing the status quo that change should occur through compromise within the existing order.

On the part of the general population there has rarely been much interest in political agitation. This is partly attributable to general political apathy and the availability of other outlets for social discontent (the dissenting religions and, later, the labor movement). Another possible explanation is broad popular confidence in the country's political leaders. Among the few mass political movements prior to the twentieth century was the Chartist movement (1838–1850). The Chartists advocated universal suffrage as a means of achieving democracy and social equality. To promote their goals they organized strikes and demonstrations and circulated petitions. The widespread support of the Chartists is attested to by their submission of a petition bearing over 3 million signatures — a tremendous accomplishment in the nineteenth century. Chartism eventually died out when general prosperity and new factory reform laws improved conditions for the working class. Thenceforth, mass working-class activities were directed toward economic issues by the trade union movement and remained on the margins of politics until the twentieth century.

Thus, change in British politics has more often resulted from the acquiescence of powerful and privileged groups than from mass action. This pattern of gradual reform from above, rather than revolt from below, has developed into a tradition of peaceful coexistence and even cooperation among sectors of society with different values — a tradition that continues to affect British political life. For example, the British Conservative party, because of its concern for the needs and interests of the lower classes, continues to enjoy the confidence and electoral support of a sizable sector of the British working class. The working class expresses its support for the party of the "natural" ruling class by voting for Conservative candidates. At least one-third of the working class regularly votes for the Conservative party. The political effect of this phenomenon has been to make the Conservative party, the direct descendant of the king's party and the aristocratic party of old, the most effective electoral party. Working-class loyalty to the Conservatives persists today because, as the authors of a study of this voting phenomenon argue, the deferential working-class voters "do not perceive a conflict between their support of the Conservative party and the demands of class loyalty or well-being: they do not see themselves as sacrificing material for symbolic rewards in supporting the Conservative Party. On the contrary, the deferential ideology holds that the material interests of ordinary people are best advanced by entrusting the direction of a delicate economy to whose who are uniquely qualified to manage these esoteric matters; the Labour party is often credited with good intentions but condemned as intrusive and incompetent."[11] With support from all sectors of society, the Conservatives have dominated British politics, heading the government for over sixty years of the ninety years since 1885.

By no means all elements of the lower classes manifest this social and political deference. However, even among those sectors of the lower classes that are more motivated by egalitarian and secular democratic values, the tradition of accommodation to different class interests, rather than violent class conflict, affects contemporary political behavior. The British aristocracy and lower classes, as well as business groups and labor unions, work together quite readily to resolve their differences without trying to destroy their opponents. Each side has a variety of viewpoints and interests to defend, and each recognizes the other's right to exist and to defend its interests. Both sides emphasize accommodation and compromise rather than seeking total victory. This tradition of mutual forbearance is solidly rooted in a history of cooperative adjustment of interests and demands by rival classes or groups.

The strength of political attitudes favoring deference and compromise prompts some commentators to say that Britain has a "traditionally modern"

11. Robert T. McKenzie and Alan Silver, *Angels in Marble: Working Class Conservatism in Urban England* (Chicago: University of Chicago Press, 1968), p. 248.

or "deferential-civic" political culture.[12] The value placed on tradition, the deference characteristic of a hierarchical society, willingness to compromise, and strong emotional attachment to political institutions and symbols all characterize Britain's historical legacy of political attitudes. Together with more modern political attitudes, such as the predisposition to be informed about politics and to take part in the political process, these traditional attitudes give Britain a political culture conducive to the success of liberal democracy.

## FRANCE: TRADITIONS OF POLITICAL TURMOIL

*Regime Instability* In marked contrast to the evolutionary political development of Britain, France's political history is punctuated by frequent abrupt changes in the nature of its political system. Since 1789 France has been governed by three monarchies, two empires, five republics, a fascist state, and several provisional governments. On the average, a complete change in the constitutional order has occurred approximately every fifteen years.[13] This extreme instability has been accompanied by considerable political turmoil, manifested in frequent civil disturbances and occasional revolutions. The following list of major civil disturbances since 1870 illustrates the tumultuous nature of French politics. (Asterisks indicate episodes that led to the fall of a regime.)

| | |
|---|---|
| *1870–1871 | Loss of the Franco-Prussian War and the abdication of Emperor Louis Napoleon followed by the Commune riots |
| 1887–1889 | Boulangism (attempted right-wing coup led by popular military "man on horseback," General Georges Boulanger) |
| *1898–1902 | Dreyfus Affair (prolonged scandal over military's framing of a Jewish officer, Alfred Dreyfus, for allegedly spying on behalf of Germany) |
| 1917 | Army mutinies and worker disorders provoked by the length of the war, economic hardships, and heavy casualties in ill-advised offensives |
| 1934 | Attempted fascist coup and rioting by fascist leagues |
| 1936 | General strike and occupations of factories by workers in anticipation of socioeconomic reforms when Radical-Socialist-Communist "Popular Front" won parliamentary elections |
| *1940–1944 | Collaborationist Vichy government versus the Free French Resistance |
| 1947 | Communist-led general strike |

12. See Richard Rose, "England: The Traditionally Modern Political Culture," in *Political Culture and Political Development,* ed. Lucien W. Pye and Sidney Verba (Princeton: Princeton University Press, 1965), pp. 83–129; and Gabriel A. Almond and Sidney Verba, *The Civic Culture* (Boston: Little, Brown, 1965).

13. Unless an active participant in politics, the individual French citizen was likely to be unaffected by a change in regime. The basic criminal and legal codes remained unchanged; tax schedules changed only gradually, if at all; the bureaucracy the citizen confronted in day-to-day affairs also went unchanged.

| *1958 | Military-inspired coup by Algerian settlers and military units, possibly encouraged by Gaullists |
|-------|--------------------------------------------------------------------------------------------------|
| 1960 | Revolt of settlers and military in Algeria against de Gaulle's decision to grant independence to Algeria |
| 1960–1963 | Guerrilla-type operations by the right-wing Secret Army Organization (OAS) in opposition to Algerian policy |
| 1961 | Attempted putsch by military in Algeria over Algerian independence |
| 1968 | Student riots and general strike, nearly topple the regime |

This legacy of political instability poses a threat to all French regimes because it offers precedents for the replacement of a regime as a means of confronting crises. In the United States and Britain, political scandal provokes voters to throw the rascals out of the office in the next election; in France scandal frequently provokes the overthrow of the whole rascally system.

Frequent changes of regime indicate a lack of consensus on basic issues, such as the nature of political institutions and the goals of politics. In the United States, few question the Constitution or the principles of the American Revolution of 1776. In contrast, there is still disagreement among French citizens over whether the French Revolution of 1789 was a good thing. And there is division on basic constitutional issues as well. Two patterns of organizing politics have competed throughout recent French history. One pattern, emphasizing the need for strong executive leadership, was embodied in the monarchies, the Napoleonic empires, and the current Fifth Republic. The other pattern confers full power on the parliament, with the expectation that it will delegate power to a "government" of a prime minister and a cabinet only so long as that government retains the confidence of the parliamentary majority. This pattern was embodied in the Third (1871–1940) and Fourth (1946–1958) Republics.

Those advocating the strong-executive pattern claim that firm leadership is essential to a country divided among as many political groups as is France. They point to the experience of the Third and Fourth Republics to illustrate the ineffectiveness and political instability they regard as inherent in the strong legislative system. During the seventy-year life of the Third Republic, there were eighty-eight distinct governments and over fifty prime ministers. During the twelve years of the Fourth Republic, there were twenty-seven governments and in the six-year period 1947–1953 seventeen cabinets were formed and dissolved. Under such conditions, it is argued, government is unable to act on the key issues confronting the country. The failure of the Third and Fourth Republics in times of crisis is also invoked to buttress the claim that France needs strong executive government.

Supporters of the dominant-legislature format claim that it is the only democratic alternative. They argue that the strong-executive pattern lends itself to demagoguery, authoritarianism, and the abuse of individual rights and liberties, and cite the two empires and the wartime fascist Vichy regime as examples of the disappearance of democracy under the strong-executive pattern.

FIGURE 1.2
## Some Important Landmarks in French History

| | |
|---|---|
| 1789–1794 | French Revolution abolishes the monarchy (the *ancien régime*) and establishes the First French Republic |
| 1799–1815 | Rule of Napoleon Bonaparte, initially as "first consul," later (1804) as emperor of the First French Empire |
| 1815–1830 | Restoration of the Bourbon monarchy |
| 1830–1848 | July 1830 Revolution forces the abdication of Charles X and establishes the monarchy of Louis Philippe |
| 1848–1851 | Revolution of 1848 establishes the Second Republic |
| 1851–1870 | Coup d'état of Louis Napoleon overthrows the republic and establishes the Second Empire |
| 1870–1940 | Defeat in the Franco-Prussian War brings about collapse of the empire and establishment of the Third Republic |
| 1940–1944 | Defeat by Germans leads to the fascist Vichy Republic of Marshal Pétain and Pierre Laval |
| 1944–1946 | Provisional government of Charles de Gaulle |
| 1946–1958 | Fourth Republic |
| 1958– | Revolt of military and settlers in Algeria precipitates fall of the Fourth Republic and establishment of the Fifth Republic |

They admit the past failures of the legislative pattern but consider its defects remediable. They further argue that the strong legislative pattern is most appropriate to France's democratic values and traditions.

Each school of thought has its own set of political symbols and values. Those favoring the legislative pattern — generally people from the Left — identify with the issues and heroes of the Revolution of 1789, the Revolution of 1848, and the Paris Commune of 1871. Their rallying-point for marches and demonstrations is the Bastille — the place where the Revolution of 1789 began. Those who support the executive pattern — generally from the Right — have as heroes Joan of Arc and Napoleon Bonaparte. Their rallying-point is the Arc de Triomphe, a monument to Napoleon's victories. Each side also identifies with a distinct series of political issues and past battles.

There are weaknesses in both patterns of organizing politics. The executive pattern has undeniably given rise to threats to individual liberties by authoritarian and quasi-authoritarian leaders. Even the Fifth Republic, the executive-dominated regime that has shown by far the greatest respect for democracy, has resorted to the arbitrary exercise of power on occasion. And the legislative pattern proved an abysmal failure during the Third and Fourth Republics, when the regimes simply could not act in times of national emergency. It would seem logical that a combination of elements from both patterns might produce a system characterized by an effective executive constrained to observe democratic procedures. In fact, the Fifth Republic was conceived as an attempt to blend these two patterns; in practice, however, it has evolved toward the executive pattern as a result of the political style of the presidents and their supporters' dominance of the legislature. Clearly, the debate over the pattern of organizing politics is not an esoteric dispute divorced from practice. It is perpetuated by periodic shifts in political institutions to coincide with whichever side has temporarily defeated or outmaneuvered the other. Rather than attempting compromise, each side has preferred to wait for the opportunity to put its pattern into operation in its pure form.

*The Delinquent Community*  French political culture offers some useful insights into the nature of political turbulence. France's history of turmoil is explained in part by the attitude of the French toward authority.[14] The French citizen generally places great emphasis on personal liberty and political equality, and on the individual's right to total independence. Rather than participating actively in governmental decision-making, he or she prefers to confer power on an aloof authority figure and retain the right to protest or oppose that leader's decisions. Since participation in the give-and-take of politics might entail a commitment to accept compromise outcomes, the typical French citizen protects the right to oppose such outcomes by adopting a stance of noninvolvement. By granting authority to a remote but powerful figure, the individual maintains equality vis à-vis his fellow citizens, since they too are uninvolved in making decisions. He maintains his individualism and liberty in relation to the authority figure by seeking to avoid the consequences of any decision he opposes. This attitude toward authority has been described as characteristic of a "delinquent community" because of the individual's avoidance of involvement and insistence upon the right to protest and secretly subvert any disliked policy decision.[15] Thus, the French citizen grants authority either to the aloof president or emperor or the equally aloof deputy, permitting them to rule but retaining the right periodically to revolt and overthrow them and their political institutions.

The notion of authority inculcated in the home and school teaches children to defer when necessary to the authority of parent or teacher but to evade it whenever possible.[16] In the political realm, this predisposition translates into a permanent state of potential insurrection against authority and the prevailing regime. Rather than trying to change policy in a positive manner, the individual simply opposes it and seeks to evade its effects. This spirit is well described by Alain, one of France's most influential political philosophers: "The true power in the voters should be defined, I believe, rather by resistance to the authorities than by reformist action. . . . The important thing is to construct every day a little barricade or, if you like, to bring each day some king before the

14. This paragraph is based on the arguments of Jesse R. Pitts, "Continuity and Change in Bourgeois France," in Stanley Hoffmann *et al., In Search of France* (New York: Harper & Row, 1965) and of Michel Crozier, *The Bureaucratic Phenomenon* (Chicago: University of Chicago Press, 1964), pp. 213–236.

15. Pitts, "Continuity and Change in France."

16. On French socialization patterns, see Charles Roig and Françoise Billon-Grand, *La Socialisation politique des enfants* (Paris: Armand Colin, 1968).

court of people." [17] These attitudes lead to disdain for politics, protest, and obstructionism. A sociologist describes their consequences:

> To this government, . . . the citizen refuses the dignity of statecraft. . . . The government is made up of incompetents, swindlers, or fools, who are usurping the function of the state. The government is that which prefers someone else. The government is that which threatens the family property through taxes. The government is that which threatens the established order through partisan legislation. The government is that authority which must be checkmated or exploited through seduction, silence, and systematic obstruction. The government replies in kind through police spying, blackmail, bribery, and undercover deals with citizens who threaten to be difficult.[18]

Political attitudes such as these make it easy to understand why France is more disposed to resist authority than to rally in support of the political system.

The negativism inherent in French views of the political system in no way detracts from national pride and patriotism. The French make a distinction between the *pays légal* — the legal political institutions, which merit their scorn — and the *pays réel* — the real France they love and serve. Indeed, their distaste for politicians is enhanced by the feeling that the political system and leadership are unworthy of France. Politicians may be corrupt and institutions faulty, but, in de Gaulle's words, "France cannot be France without *grandeur*." Contempt for the failings of the *pays légal* fuels the search for frameworks more worthy of the *pays réel*.

*Plurality of Political Tendencies*   Another legacy of the past that affects contemporary politics is France's extreme political pluralism. Unlike the British pattern of politics, which has for more than a century been distinguished by two large political camps, the French political system has always been characterized by a large number of small political factions that compete with each other for public office. The French political spectrum runs from fascists, monarchists, and Bonapartists (who wish to restore the Napoleonic empire) on the far Right to anarchists, Trotskyites, and Maoists on the far Left. Even during the French Revolution of 1789 there was no united revolutionary movement but, instead, a large number of loose factions, which eventually turned on each other with the same violence they had earlier directed at the monarchy.

Many of these political groups have elaborated ideologies that shape their political actions and interpretations of the world: communism, socialism, fascism, liberalism. Others profess vaguer principles of political action, such as anticommunism, anticlericalism, or antigaullism, which prove to be equally firm obstacles to interparty cooperation despite their relative lack of rigor. These political belief systems often persist as guidelines for political action long after the problems that inspired them have lost their political significance. For example, division over the Catholic church's role in politics continued to cause political cleavage long after the issue had been resolved by the curtailment of

17. Cited by Philip M. Willams, *Crisis and Compromise: Politics in the Fourth Republic* (Garden City, N.Y.: Doubleday, 1966), p. 5.
18. Pitts, "Continuity and Change in France," p. 260.

the church's influence. Many French leftists still refuse to believe that a practicing Catholic can be a leftist or even a supporter of republican government. This attitude stems from a battle fought over fifty years ago, when Catholics opposed the republic because it had severed the tie between church and state. Thus political disputes of the past are perpetuated even though issues and personalities change.

French political leaders have often shown great skill in compromising their ideological beliefs when circumstances have demanded it. But compromise is not considered as heroic or desirable a style of political action as loyalty to abstract principles and ideologies. Fidelity to ideological principles thus hinders compromise and may ultimately undermine those compromises that are successfully negotiated. Under the Third and Fourth Republics, for example, the coalition governments were based on delicate compromises among several parties. Most were eventually overthrown when one or more of the individuals involved responded to the promptings of his ideological convictions.[19]

*A Legacy of Instability* The French know their history well, and frequently seek models for contemporary political acts in the past. The most striking recent evidence of the weight of history is the student riots and general strike that paralyzed France during May–June 1968. The crisis resulted from social and economic unrest among workers and students. Paradoxically, however, the youthful instigators of the "Events of May" — who, like other radicals, distrusted anyone over thirty — consciously patterned their revolt on the Paris Commune of 1871 and drew inspiration from other revolutionary episodes in French history. This evocation of the past — indeed, this attempt to re-create the past — by the most radical elements of society illustrates the importance of historical precedents in France. It also illustrates the self-perpetuating nature of political turmoil. The revolutions of the past acquire glamour and heroic connotations even if they ultimately failed. The mystique and camaraderie of previous revolts make revolt an attractive solution to present and future crises. No doubt a future generation of revolutionaries will one day employ the model of the Events of May 1968 to fashion a new revolt.

## CONTRASTING PATTERNS OF DEMOCRATIC DEVELOPMENT

While there is no single path to democracy, it is generally agreed that historical events affect the likelihood of successful democratic development. As one scholar has written, historical events start "a process which increases (or decreases) the likelihood that at the next critical point in the country's history democracy will win out again.[20] France is an example of a country whose

19. See the arguments of Duncan MacRae, Jr., *Parliament, Parties, and Society in France, 1946–1958* (New York: St. Martin's Press, 1967), pp. 328–329.
20. Seymour Martin Lipset, *Political Man* (Garden City, N. Y.: Doubleday, 1963), pp. 28–29.

democratic development has been hindered by past political turmoil and the related political culture. Britain, on the other hand, has had a history supportive of democratic development and stability.

The contrast between the two countries is striking. Britain's long-standing consensus on its institutions is the antithesis of France's continued division over the basic political questions of institutions and procedures. In Britain political leaders have been willing to compromise, whereas French leaders' commitment to principles and ideologies has given compromise a bad image. British social hierarchism and deference to authority are directly at odds with the individualism and strident egalitarianism of the French. In Britain political development has been characterized by reform from above; revolt or protest by the masses has characterized French history.

These contrasts may help explain why the British pattern of democratic development and change has been consistent with stability and the French pattern with turmoil and instability. However, it would be wrong to conclude that the British pattern is the only valid pattern of democratic development or that it is superior to the French pattern. Though the French pattern has resulted in greater turmoil, there is greater consistency between democratic norms and the French value of egalitarianism. Furthermore, the British pattern is by no means the only successful alternative to the French pattern. There are other, equally successful paths to democracy that lack the social inequality inherent in the British pattern.

# China and the Soviet Union: Historical Continuity and Change in Revolutionary Countries

For communists, history is the projection of contemporary political beliefs onto the events of the past. Such a philosophy of history justifies rewriting history to coincide with current needs and problems. Interpretations of history thus change with the political purposes of skillful political leaders. Yet the effects of history cannot be fully controlled or eliminated even in revolutionary societies. The exploitation of historical values and patterns for current purposes itself tends to perpetuate them, and thus limits future options unless the state is prepared to carry out the unending revision of history portrayed by George Orwell in *Nineteen Eighty-Four*. Since neither the Soviet Union nor China has engaged in such a massive effort at minute-by-minute "verification" of history, both countries' revolutions have been shaped by historical legacies. Marxism, a foreign ideology, was blended with indigenous historical forces and shaped by the personalities of local leaders. The result has been two political systems that differ from each other and from the visions of Marx.

## HISTORICAL BACKGROUND TO
## CONTEMPORARY SOVIET POLITICS

World War One provided clear evidence that czarist Russia was in an advanced stage of decay. On the home front, shortages of food and other essentials quickly resulted as the economy proved too disorganized and inadequate for the rigors of war. On the field of battle, Russian troops suffered a series of major defeats caused by poor organization, poor communications, and the ineptitude of the officers. Gradually, popular support for the czar eroded as military defeats continued and famine spread. Then, in March 1917, food riots in Petrograd touched off a general strike and a mutiny. Within days the czar abdicated and a provisional government was formed, under the leadership first of Prince Lvov and later of Alexander Kerensky.

The Kerensky government was based on a coalition of the moderate socialist Mensheviks and Socialist Revolutionaries. The more radical Bolsheviks[21] had little part in the March revolution and remained unallied with the Provisional Government, criticizing its failures and pledging to provide "Peace, Bread, and Land" when they came to power. The Provisional Government proved no more successful on the battlefield than had the czar, and the economic situation continued to deteriorate. Land reform and other desperately needed social changes were postponed while the Provisional Government struggled to continue the war against the Axis powers of Germany and Austria-Hungary. "Peace, Bread, and Land" became increasingly attractive and, under Lenin's direction, the Bolsheviks grew rapidly in strength. They directed their efforts at winning control of the soviets, small mass-based councils that were playing an increasingly important but unofficial role in governing Russia. In June 1917 there were only 14 Bolsheviks in the National Congress of Soviets, out of a total 1,115 delegates. But by September the Bolsheviks had acquired a majority in the soviets of key political centers: Petrograd, Moscow, Kiev, Odessa, and other large cities. When the second Congress of the Soviets was held in November 1917, the Bolsheviks claimed 390 of the 650 delegates present. At that point Bolshevik supporters seized the seat of government, the czar's Winter Palace, and other strategic locations, in most cases encountering nothing more than token opposition. Within a few days power had passed into the hands of Lenin and his followers, ushering in the communist era.

While the communists have retained a monopoly on political power in Russia since 1917, the nature of their rule has changed dramatically on several occasions. These changes probably had a more profound impact on the lives of both the political elite and the citizenry than did the several changes of regime in France since 1870. There have been four distinct eras in Soviet politics since 1917, each with its own pattern of political, economic, and social interactions:

21. Lenin's followers adopted the nickname of Bolsheviks, or majoritarians, to contrast themselves with the Mensheviks, or minority, when they won a majority of votes at the 1903 congress of the Russian Social Democratic Labor Party. Lenin's group lost their majority soon thereafter and did not regain it until after the Revolution, but the nickname was retained for its propaganda value.

FIGURE 1.3
## Some Important Landmarks in Russian History

| | |
|---|---|
| 1237–1240 | Mongol (Tatar) conquest of Russia begins 200 years of Mongol rule ("the Tatar yoke") |
| 1480 | Ivan III frees Muscovy from Mongol rule |
| 1712 | Peter the Great moves capital of Russia to St. Petersburg (now Leningrad) for a "window to the West" |
| 1861 | Emancipation of serfs by Alexander II |
| 1905 | Revolution forces Nicholas II to grant token reforms, including establishment of a parliament (the Duma) |
| 1917 | March Revolution overthrows monarchy and establishes moderate socialist government |
| 1917 | November Revolution brings Lenin's Bolsheviks to power |
| 1917–1921 | War Communism |
| 1921–1928 | New Economic Policy (NEP) |
| 1924–1938 | Death of Lenin in 1924 leads to struggle for power, Stalin emerging on top and then ruthlessly consolidating his control |
| 1953 | Death of Stalin |
| 1957 | Consolidation of power by Khrushchev |
| 1964 | Khrushchev ousted and replaced by Brezhnev and Kosygin |

War Communism (1917–1921), the New Economic Policy (1921–1928), the Stalinist rule of terror (1928–1953), and the post-Stalinist era (1953–present).

War Communism was a period of intense struggle to consolidate Bolshevik political power and crush antirevolutionary forces. Civil war was raging, and the new Bolshevik government faced multiple challenges: antirevolutionary forces ("Whites") allegedly seeking the restoration of the old czarist regime; foreign military forces from the United States, Czechoslovakia, Britain, and France; separatist forces among minority nationality groups formerly part of the Russian empire (including Poles, Lithuanians, Finns, Estonians, and Latvians); and various rivals to the Bolsheviks' claim to total power (including Mensheviks, left-wing intellectuals, and others). Because the danger of a restoration of the old regime by White and foreign armies was genuine, the Bolsheviks could portray the civil war as a patriotic and democratic struggle against foreign invaders and reactionary autocracy. They were thus able to rally support from many sectors of society with no genuine commitment to communism.

The challenge of the civil war also permitted rapid consolidation of the dictatorship of the proletariat. By December 1917 the Bolsheviks had organized their own secret police force (known then as the Cheka) to combat "counterrevolution and sabotage." As the civil war intensified, the Cheka resorted to terror and forced labor. After Lenin was seriously wounded by an assassin in

August 1918, "terror became a deliberate instrument of policy."[22] The Cheka engaged their own assassins and carried out large-scale executions of suspected counterrevolutionaries.

The Bolsheviks quickly nationalized all industries and sought to impose rigid central controls on the economy. The peasants, who had rallied to the Bolsheviks because of their promise of land, were soon threatened with the loss of their newly acquired land to state-run collective farms. In the meantime, the Red Army seized grain and other produce to sustain the civil war effort. All the while the Communist party was elaborating its own institutions and consolidating its political monopoly. Proclamation of the Russian Socialist Federal Soviet Republic (RSFSR) in July 1918 and the promulgation of a new constitution were early steps toward the consolidation of political power.

After the last White armies were defeated, pressures for a relaxation of the revolution's pace grew rapidly. Repression of peasants and others, which had been justified by life-and-death struggle with reactionary and foreign armies, could no longer be sustained. In early 1921 a series of measures brought the New Economic Policy (NEP) into being. Under the NEP forced requisitions from the peasants were replaced with taxes, and pressures for collectivization of land were abandoned. Economic controls on industry and trade were also relaxed. While the state retained ownership of key industries, private trade and enterprise were permitted to develop. The terrorism of the secret police was curtailed and limited dissent was tolerated within the Communist party and even outside it. In short, the whole tone of politics changed profoundly from the days of War Communism, although political power remained solidly in the hands of the communists. Symbolic of the change was the adoption of a new name — the Union of Soviet Socialist Republics (USSR) — and a new constitution in 1924.

The NEP ended in 1928 with the launching of Stalin's "Third Revolution" (the first and second being the March and November Revolutions of 1917). Stalin was dedicated to rapid industrialization so as to enable the Soviet Union to "overtake and surpass" the advanced capitalist countries. He marshalled the country's human and material resources to industrialize in accordance with guidelines established in the five year plans. Forced industrialization made it necessary for workers and peasants to accept subsistence-level existence and to make sacrifices of time and energy. Workers were encouraged to greater production by economic and honorific rewards for "Stakhanovites" (outstanding workers) and by threats of punishment for workers who failed to meet expectations. Peasants were compelled to join collective farms, whose product could be more easily controlled and acquired by the state. Many peasants resisted collectivization, and several million died in the conflict and the resulting famine. Countless others were exiled to Siberia or to forced labor camps. The struggle over collectivization also served to drive the surplus rural population to the cities, where it was needed to expand the industrial work pool. The costs in human

22. Edward Hallett Carr, *The Bolshevik Revolution 1917–1923,* vol. 1 (New York: Macmillan, 1951), p. 168.

sacrifice were great, but the goal was achieved: in less than twenty years, the Soviet Union was transformed from a backward country to a military and industrial superpower controlling an "empire" larger than was ever dreamed of in four centuries of czarist autocracy.

Another aspect of the era was Stalin's drive for absolute power. The secret police expanded its activities and sought out potential, as well as actual, dissenters. Forced labor was instituted as a means not only of developing remote areas but, more importantly, of isolating and destroying suspect groups or individuals. The Communist party's control was extended as all possible competitors for social and political influence — whether churches, social clubs, or families — were weakened. Within the party, Stalin ruthlessly purged all those who could conceivably be regarded as rivals to his personal power. Outside the party, terror was used as a means of political control. The arbitrary and indiscriminate nature of Stalin's terror is well described by Sidney and Beatrice Webb in a discussion of the purge of the intelligentsia:

> Nobody regarded himself as beyond suspicion. Men and women lived in daily dread of arrest. Thousands were sent on administrative exile to distant parts of the country. Evidence was not necessary. The title of engineer served as sufficient condemnation. The jails were filled.[23]

The toll was heavy: millions were arrested; hundreds of thousands were executed or died in prison labor camps.

The present post-Stalinist era represents another distinct period. Terror has been leashed and openly renounced as an instrument of government. The pace of industrialization has eased as the Soviet economy has matched or exceeded the production of rival capitalist countries. The party's political monopoly is still unchallenged, but in practice other groups have been able to influence certain decisions. Though the party leader is still the paramount political figure, his rivals no longer risk liquidation or exile in Siberia. While political dissent is still risky, it is no longer entirely squelched by terror.

Despite the dramatic changes that have taken place in Russia since the dissolution of the old czarist order, there are important historical continuities that have affected the nature of Soviet politics. One such legacy is that of *centralized autocracy*. Russia has never experienced limited government. Russia achieved independence from autocratic Mongol rule only through the equally autocratic domination of the czars. Even in the sixteenth century, when absolutist monarchies prevailed all over Europe, the Russian czar was regarded as the epitome of autocracy and absolutism. While the British nobility proved an effective check on monarchial power, the Russian nobility was weak and dominated by the czar. Whereas other European monarchs were limited by the existence of a large independent ecclesiastical power, the Russian Orthodox church was clearly subordinate to the czar and served as a mainstay of czarist power.

23. Sidney and Beatrice Webb, *Soviet Communism: A New Civilization*, vol. 2 (New York: Charles Scribner's Sons, 1936), p. 553.

Any opposition that did develop was checked by a ruthless and effective secret police. As early as 1826 an independent secret police force answerable only to the czar had been endowed with the power to arrest, try, and condemn political malcontents. The secret police operated a network of spies and *agents provocateurs* who infiltrated suspect groups and provoked them to undertake illegal actions that would justify brutal suppression. Exile to Siberia and forced labor camps were widely used as punishment for those who dared to oppose the czarist order.

A second legacy is the *nationality problem*. The czars built their empire by means of expansion into territories surrounding the homeland of the Great Russian people, rather than by the acquisition of overseas colonies. The Russians succeeded in dominating dozens of other nationalities, and incorporated them into a single large country spreading across Europe and Asia to the Pacific. The Russian push eastward to the Pacific is comparable to the "manifest destiny" that pushed American civilization westward. The result was a country possessing one-sixth of the earth's land surface and more than two hundred distinct nationalities, some with long histories of independence. The conquered peoples were frequently restless under Russian domination, leading some to refer to the Russian empire as "the czar's prison of nations." The persistent discontent of these minority nationality groups continues to create problems of integration and control for the contemporary communist leadership, as we shall see in Chapter 2.

Straddling both Europe and Asia, Russia has historically exhibited considerable *ambivalence toward the Western world*. On the one hand, Russians were traditionally taught by the Eastern Orthodox church to condemn the West as heretical and inferior. This attitude was accompanied by fear of the incursion of deviant philosophies and culture as a result of contact with the West. On the other hand, Russians admired the technological and cultural achievements of the West and sometimes sought to import Western ideas and methods. In the nineteenth century the dilemma of Western influence became more acute. Russia recognized its need for modern technology and increased industrial capacity if it was to remain militarily competitive with the West. But its leaders also acknowledged that Western liberalism and erosion of absolutism would undermine Russian autocracy if contacts were permitted to multiply. The same dilemma plagues the czars' communist heirs as they seek means to relate to the ideologically hostile capitalist world.

Another legacy is the virtual *absence of private enterprise*. Agriculture was the dominant sector of the economy until the twentieth century, but Russia had little experience with farming by landowning peasants. Until 1861 the bulk of the population was composed of "Crown peasants" and serfs, bound to the land by feudal ties and virtually owned by their masters. Czar Alexander emancipated the serfs in 1861 and provided the newly freed peasants with approximately half the land then under cultivation, to be paid for in annual installments over forty-nine years. The few peasants fortunate enough to receive the better land prospered and acquired more land from the less successful. Many of the rest soon became tenant farmers on the land of the wealthier peasants or on the large estates of the nobility or Crown. Thus, there was no tradition of an independent landholding peasantry. Instead, the peasants' social and economic experience had more frequently been with the *mir,* a village form of communal self-government. While the mir was by no means socialist or democratic, it did provide a historical precedent for the communal farms introduced by the Bolsheviks. Similarly, there was no tradition of private ownership in industry. The industrialization that took place during the last decades of czarist rule was directed and financed by the state. Railroads and heavy industry were built with funds from the government and from foreign investors. Thus, communist efforts to control the economy are in keeping with precedents established under the czars.

The final legacy is that of *political dissent and revolt.* Despite the absolutist nature of czarist rule, opposition did develop and express itself. Russia has a long history of peasant rebellions and the struggles of national minorities for cultural autonomy. There is also a tradition of opposition and revolt among the better-educated stratum of czarist society, the intelligentsia. Throughout the nineteenth century revolutionary groups planned alternative societies, plotted the overthrow of the czar, and occasionally acted to undermine the regime. They engaged in isolated uprisings, acts of violence, and assassinations. These revolutionary movements constituted a heritage of thought and experience that influenced Lenin and other Russian revolutionaries of the twentieth century. As one of Lenin's biographers notes:

> Himself the heir of a long, fascinating and rich revolutionary tradition, Lenin also became the recipient of a ready-made revolutionary doctrine from the West, namely, Marxism. The fusion of Western Marxism, elements of the Russian revolutionary tradition, and Lenin's own peculiar psychology resulted in the formulation of a revolutionary doctrine that — in conjunction with objective historical forces — resulted not only in the October Revolution of 1917, but also in the inspiration of various political movements opposed to liberal democracy throughout the world.[24]

The tradition of intellectual dissent is currently being manifested by sectors of the Russian intelligentsia, as we shall see in subsequent chapters.

## CHINA: REVOLUTION'S ENCOUNTER WITH TRADITION

In China the leaders of 800 million people are seeking to alter fundamentally pre-existing social and economic institutions. To understand this bold venture, we must examine China's history for traditions and practices that have been objects of change and that have shaped change. China's modern history is divisible into three segments that define moments of change: the prenineteenth-century establishment and reinforcement of tradition; the nineteenth-century impact of Europe and decay of tradition; and, finally, the twentieth-century

24. Rolf H. W. Theen, *Lenin: Genesis and Development of a Revolutionary* (Philadelphia: Lippincott, 1973), p. 14.

Age of Decision, characterized by the decline of traditional social and political institutions and tensions over the selection of their successors.

The modern period inherited an institutionalized monarchy and a legal–philosophic system dating back to the Chou dynasty (circa 1122 B.C.). In the centuries following the Chou dynasty, several major political and social changes occurred, each leaving its mark on the early modern period of Chinese history. During this time the Chinese "nation" was frequently plagued with feuding minikingdoms. The Han dynasty (206 B.C. to A.D. 222) centralized authority, abolished slavery, and established the Confucian ideology. According to Confucian thought, the ideal social structure was founded on a set of prescriptions for the relations of ruler and subjects, neighbor and neighbor, father and son, husband and wife, brother and brother. These regulations, based on the norms of filial piety (veneration of parents) and loyalty to the ruler, went so far as to describe the modes in which persons should walk, talk, and sit consistent with these status relationships. If the individual learned these relationships and applied them with sincerity, the result would be an improved government and a society in harmony with its government. According to Confucius, education and sincerity were essential for good government. This outlook led logically to the creation under the T'ang dynasty (A.D. 618 to 906) of a bureaucracy whose personnel was recruited on the basis of examinations in Confucian principles. This recruiting procedure created the world's first modern bureaucracy — that is, a bureaucracy based on merit or achievement as opposed to political obligations. However, the results were not always as Confucius might have expected. Greedy and corrupt bureaucrats prided themselves more on their status (equating it with virtue) than on the quality of their service. By the midnineteenth century, the Confucian bureaucratic system had become a conservative obstacle to social change. It glorified the past and ignored the need to adapt to a constantly changing present. The "modernity" of its method of recruiting bureaucrats by means of competitive examinations was countered by its atavistic and antimodern outlooks toward contemporary problems.

Confucianism, the official ideology of prerevolutionary China, has had a lasting effect on the political culture. It encouraged familial loyalties and private, as opposed to public, interests. This tradition is in sharp contrast to those of industrialized societies in which public education has inculcated a set of civic virtues and norms. Confucianism taught that one's loyalty was owed first to the central authority, particularly the emperor and the bureaucrats. The family, headed by the father, was the overwhelming de facto focus of attention, and family interests always took precedence when they conflicted with the interests of friends.

The lasting political effects of the Confucian emphasis on the family transcend simple social deference. One scholar argues that Chinese familial relations are the source of hostile political manifestations. Within the family, he argues, the father is supreme, and children cannot express anger at him. As a result, they look for distant and less threatening forms of authority to attack. Contemporary examples of such remote and safe objects are landlords, rich peasants,

FIGURE 1.4
*Some Important Landmarks in Chinese History* _____

| | |
|---|---|
| 2000 B.C. | Hsia dynasty |
| 1500 | Shang dynasty |
| 1122 | Chou dynasty — age of feudal states, Confucius, Taoist school, legalist school, warring states |
| 211 | Ch'in dynasty |
| 206 | Han dynasty |
| 222 A.D. | Six-dynasty Period |
| 589 | Sui dynasty |
| 618 | T'ang dynasty — development of bureaucracy based on Confucian examination system |
| 907 | Sung dynasty |
| 1127 | Southern Sung dynasty |
| 1278 | Yuan dynasty — Genghis Khan and Kubla Khan conquer parts of China |
| 1368 | Ming dynasty — Chinese period resumes |
| 1644 | Ch'ing (Manchu) dynasty — sustained contact with West begins in mid-19th century |
| 1908 | Fall of Manchu dynasty |
| 1912 | Republic of China is formed — Sun Yat-sen becomes the first president |
| 1912–1949 | Years of chaos — Chiang Kai-shek wins nominal control — Japanese war and communist revolt ensue |
| 1949 | Communists win control of China's mainland — the Mao era begins |
| 1958 | Great Leap Forward |
| 1965–1969 | Great Proletarian Cultural Revolution |

American aggressors, or even Communist party officials during the Cultural Revolution.[25]

This family-based social structure produced behavior that inhibited modernization of the Chinese economy and society. The system of "feudal bureaucratism" was characterized by a set of landowning families who composed the majority of the "literocracy" and civil servant class.[26] This social elite enjoyed many privileges, refused to engage in manual labor, and also became associated with many abuses: the *corvée,* or compulsory unpaid labor for landlord and state; exorbitant rents in kind of 50–70 percent of the tenant farmers' crop; private armed bands; and the use of violence to control the peasants. The combination of a privileged and powerful gentry and the noncompetitive and deferential teachings of Confucianism inhibited the emergence of a capitalist class. Land was highly valued, and the landowners who controlled political power tended to prevent the growth of a potentially powerful competing bourgeois class in the cities by personally managing such state industries as communications, salt, and iron.

25. Lucian Pye, *China: An Introduction* (Boston: Little, Brown, 1972), pp. 82–99.
26. Han Suyin, *China in the Year 2001* (New York: Basic Books, 1967).

FIGURE 1.5

## Population Density in Communist China

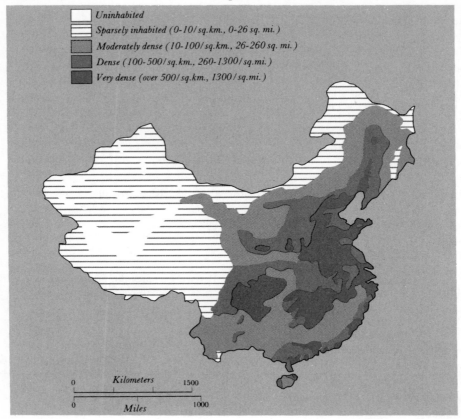

Source: Winberg Chai, The New Politics of Communist China: Modernization Process of a Developing Nation (Pacific Palisades, Cal.: Goodyear Publishing Company, 1972), p. 73. Copyright © 1972. Goodyear Publishing Company. Reprinted by permission of the publisher.

Wealth, opportunity, education, and political power formed a self-contained system in prerevolutionary China. The values of this system were sincerity, loyalty, reliability, and steadfastness.[27] Within this world there was a clear demarcation between subjects and officialdom. Subjects did not seek or demand rights, merely favors and sympathy. The ruler was a patriarch, and the same kind of filial relationship that existed between father and son prevailed between ruler and subject. While the early modern era inherited these values and institutions, it was the arrival of Europeans in the nineteenth century that ushered in the second segment of this era, which witnessed the decay of tradition.

27. Pye, China, ch. 3.

*The Decay of Tradition*   Early Chinese perceptions of foreigners were a function of their relations with neighboring southeast Asian states, which China treated as tributaries. European states were expected to conform to this system. Some, such as Holland, Portugal, the Papacy, and Great Britain, did so and were listed in 1818 as regular tributaries. During the same period others — Spain, France, Sweden, and Denmark — were listed as mere trading countries. These early interactions caused the Chinese to see others as benefitting from their trade with China but acknowledging its superiority with tribute missions.

This system was to disintegrate when foreign private traders began residing in Canton in order to build up the triangular trade between India, China, and England. The British demand was primarily for tea; the Chinese wanted raw cotton and, increasingly, opium from India. During the late eighteenth century 1,000 chests of opium a year were being imported from British India. In 1838 the annual total had grown to 40,000 chests, each chest containing 133 pounds.[28] By the 1830s there were an estimated 2–10 million habitual opium smokers in China, many of them government officials. While the British profited from the trade, the court at Peking also drew official and unofficial revenues from the foreign trade.

Periodic efforts were made to control China's growing opium problem. One early effort triggered the First Opium War and resulted in China's defeat by the British. In 1839 the Ch'ing government ordered a crackdown on the opium trade by the Canton provincial governor. But the British responded with force, sending warships to attack the Chinese defenses all along the coast from Canton to Shanghai. The defeat led to punitive demands against China, formalized in an 1842 treaty.

This treaty marked the beginning of a series of "unequal treaties" with foreign trading powers providing for the opening of additional Chinese ports to foreign traders. The treaties granted foreigners preferential trade conditions, fixed the tariff rates the Chinese could impose on imports, and asserted the doctrine of "extraterritorial rights," which, among other things, prevented the Chinese from punishing foreign merchants or sailors who committed crimes in Chinese ports.

There followed a series of reactions to these treaties. Within a decade of the first unequal treaty, the Taiping Kingdom, a rebel government, moved from province to province to build its "kingdom of kings." Inspired by the classic *Rituals of Chou* (200 B.C.), they envisioned a new utopian society founded on the ideal of brotherhood and a primitive economic communism. Land was to be redistributed. All persons were to contribute their possessions and services to a common treasury and in turn to receive their support from it. The rebellion lasted more than a decade before the imperial armies, with the aid of Western weapons and advisors, defeated the last of the Taiping forces in 1864.

European penetration and the Japanese defeat of China in the Sino-Japanese War (1894–1895) were a constant source of shame to Chinese aware of their

28. John K. Fairbank, Edwin O. Reischauer, and Albert Craig, *East Asia: The Modern Transformation* (Boston: Houghton Mifflin, 1965), pp. 136–144.

historical greatness. On May 2, 1895, K'ang Yu-wei led a group of some 1,200 provincial graduates in the Ten-Thousand-Word Memorial. This protest movement advocated rejecting peace with Japan, moving the capital inland to allow for prolonged warfare, and instituting a series of reforms. Proposed reforms included a stronger centralized government to cope with the threat from abroad, a parliament, Western dress, and even equality of the sexes. The movement's goal was a blend of East and West, with emphasis on maintaining Eastern ethics and importing Western science. A few years later K'ang gained access to Emperor Kuang Hsu, and was able to enact a number of reforms during a period known as The Hundred Days. Between June and September 1898 the Emperor, under K'ang's influence, issued some forty reform decrees. Reactionary forces led by the dowager empress, soon revoked these reforms. But the need for change did not abate and their reverberations continued.

Reactionaries took a more violent, less intellectual approach in the Boxer Rebellion (1898–1900). The rebellion had its origins in the activities of secret societies, a political form recurrent in Chinese history. Motivated by fears that China would be divided up by foreigners, fueled by social unrest as a result of severe floods along the Yellow River and widespread famine in Shantung during 1898, a secret society called The Righteous and Harmonious Fists came to the forefront of history. The movement was hostile to foreigners, and in particular to the Chinese Christian converts it considered symbolic of the ill effects of Western imperialism on China. After the siege of Peking and the destruction of many foreign missionaries, Western powers joined to defeat the Boxers.

The inability of the Chinese government to resist foreign demands stimulated more opposition to the Chinese imperial tradition. After the deaths of the emperor and the dowager empress in 1908, conditions were ripe for the 1911 republican revolution. In its ultimate effort to survive, the Ch'ing dynasty had made concessions that contributed to China's readiness for revolution: students were sent abroad to study, elections for 21 provincial assemblies were held in 1909, and the warlord General Yuan Shih-k'ai was asked for assistance in maintaining order. The students who returned supported Sun Yat-sen's call for the overthrow of the monarchy and the creation of a republic. The elections resulted in the accession to power of landowners, businessmen, journalists, and educators, who used the forum of the provincial assemblies not to support the regime but to overthrow it. In 1911 they contributed to the revolutionary climate by declaring provincial autonomy against the Ch'ing dynasty. This act prompted the dynasty's appeal to General Yuan Shih-k'ai to restore order. The general did enter the fray, but joined the opposition and demanded the abdication of the remaining Ch'ing family. It has been suggested that this revolution abolished feudal imperial rule only to make way for the emergence of feudal military warlords who fought among themselves and against the republicans for control of China.[29] Only the outbreak of World War One gave China a brief respite.

29. Han Suyin, *China in the Year 2001*.

However, with the Europeans fighting each other thousands of miles away and its own economy rapidly modernizing, Japan saw an opportunity to enhance its economic interests in China. In 1915 the Japanese presented China with a set of twenty-one demands that, if consented to, would have made China a virtual colony of Japan. The October Revolution in Russia altered the international political system and prompted the United States to make secret agreements with Japan. In exchange for Japan's invasion of Siberia, the United States recognized Japanese interests in Shantung Province and special rights for Japan in Manchuria. Chinese intellectuals heard of these secret treaties through the Peace Conference of Versailles in 1919 and 3,000 Chinese students and intellectuals demonstrated in protest on May 4, 1919. As the protest movement spread to two hundred Chinese cities and towns during the following eighteen months, over 20 million students, professors, workers, shopkeepers, and merchants participated.[30] One participant, Mao Tse-tung, saw this revolt as a crisis of conscience that was political rather than economic in nature. A small group of Marxist intellectuals, including Mao, promoted a spontaneous nationwide united front of laborers, peasants, and intellectuals.

Politically, the heirs of Sun Yat-sen were divided. A broad coalition, consisting of the left and right wings of the Kuomintang party under Chiang Kai-shek and the communists, existed through the early 1920s. In 1926 there were still three communists in top cabinet posts, Moscow having ordered the Chinese communists to stay in the coalition government. Chiang Kai-shek, like Sun Yat-sen before him, had called on the Russians to help organize the Kuomintang party and the armed forces. This Stalin did. Mao and other Chinese communist leaders did not agree with Stalin's decisions, believing that they could have been more effective by organizing the peasants — who were very dissatisfied — and by building their own military force. As Chiang's military organization became successful, strong demands were made by the left and right Kuomintang and the military to eliminate the communists. Chiang did so by means of a coup in April 1927, consolidating his control over the party and government. Nevertheless, Stalin, who was involved in a struggle with Trotsky, considered it wise to maintain support of Chiang and the Kuomintang. But spring 1927 brought more bloodshed between communists and right-wing Kuomintang. In short, during the crucial formative years of the Chinese Communist party, Stalin frequently supported the political enemies of the Chinese communists in the interest of maintaining Russia's good relations with the Chiang Kai-shek regime. He did so even when it was clear that Chiang and his followers were bent on exterminating the Chinese communists. While other factors contributed to the current dispute between China and the Soviet Union, their early relations were not conducive to establishing trust and cooperation.

The struggle between the Kuomintang and the Chinese communists was to last nearly thirty years. More often than not, it took the form of a military conflict rather than an ideological war for people's minds. Among the events

30. Fairbank *et al., East Asia,* pp. 665–670.

of this turbulent period, "the Long March" stands out as a political symbol and source of legitimacy and integration for the current communist regime. On October 16, 1934, some 100,000 Chinese communist men and women, led by Mao Tse-tung, burst from Kuomintang encirclement and began a march that ultimately took them some 6,000 miles. This trek by foot lasted an entire year and passed through eleven provinces. But more significant than the geographic distance and hardships was the exposure of millions of Chinese to the movement's ideals. In addition, the Long March shaped the leadership structure. The march was the source of their discipline and dedication, the spirit behind the contemporary sacrifices they have deemed necessary for the modernization of China. This epic march was also the wellspring of the simplicity and idealism that have been hallmarks of the leadership through the 1960s and into the 1970s. Commitment to the guerrilla ethos over that of the technocrat is another product of the Long March that characterizes contemporary China. Aside from the development of a creed and ethos, the Long March was instrumental in the survival and ultimate victory of the communist movement in China. By the powerful technique of demonstration, Mao communicated in deeds (i.e., by redistributing land and restructuring leadership and policies in territories under communist control) the theories of a communist state. This was the key factor in gaining adherents to the successful communist drive for the control of China during the late 1940s.

*The Age of Decision*  The climax came in the years after World War Two. The communist forces succeeded in defeating the American-trained and -equipped forces of Chiang Kai-shek. On October 1, 1949, Mao Tse-tung proclaimed the establishment of the People's Republic of China and raised the red flag in Peking, marking the end of the decay of traditional China and the beginning of the Age of Decision. The choices that then faced China involved issues common to many Third World nations following their independence from colonial masters: What new political institutions must be created? Should governmental efficiency and centralization be preferred to mass involvement? How can the military be restrained from wresting political control from the civilians? And, unique to China, there was the issue of priorities: Should economic development precede or occur simultaneously with the creation of a communist society?

At this stage Chairman Mao promulgated a vision, whose features were abolition of state power, the necessity for perpetual revolution, leadership by the working and peasant classes, the strengths of Chinese cultural traits, and the sanctity of labor. But even more important was a compulsive concern for social justice, equality, and economic modernization. Conscious of history, Mao recognized that ideas unaccompanied by action cannot in themselves be realized — that the construction of a new society is closely associated with the realistic need for economic capacity. There followed, between 1949 and 1952, a period of reconstruction and transition during which a basis for change was laid through governmental organization and the educational base. Land reform was completed during this period and China's planning commissions and party membership structures were organized. Most important, China stood up to a foreign power for the first time in its modern history in the Korean War (1950–1953).

Between 1953 and 1957, the First Five Year Plan laid the foundation for industrialization, the modernization of agriculture, and the socialization of the economy. Progress was so encouraging that the leaders enthusiastically proposed the Great Leap Forward toward the first communes in 1958. The transition had negative effects on agricultural and industrial production. Morale problems and political reactions ensued and the 1961–1965 period was one of consolidation, adjustment, and transition.

With the emergence in 1965 of the Great Proletarian Cultural Revolution, a new phase in socialist construction commenced. While interpretations of the Cultural Revolution vary, it undeniably had political as well as strong socio-cultural effects. One political consequence was the removal of political leaders who had temporarily eclipsed Mao's control. Perhaps of greater moment was Mao's idealism and concern for maintaining the purity of the revolution. It had become apparent that social justice and equality would not be achieved in a single battle or crusade. Mao considered the temptation to exploitation and privilege to arise from status and from the contradictions between mental and physical work and between urban and rural life styles. Policies to rectify these conditions enacted during and after the Cultural Revolution included new measures to further equal status, education for peasants and factory workers, workers' and peasants' councils to participate in managing factories and communes, and a requirement that students, economic managers, and party cadre experience physical labor on factory or farm.

In reviewing the three segments of the modern period, one notes the complexity of contemporary revolutionary China. The family, though no longer the main social unit, remains an important source of individual development and identity. Its influence persists at the apex of the political hierarchy in the veneration of the national father figure, Mao Tse-tung. The Confucian hierarchy and loyalty to authority persist but are being modified by decentralization of authority, institutionalized critiques of the uses of authority, and recruitment from formerly nonparticipating classes. Education remains an important value and means to advancement; while its prerevolutionary function was individual enhancement, contemporary education focuses on collective advances. The new form of education is founded on such norms as social justice, cooperation, group achievement, and respect for the idea that the "ancient must serve the present."

# Mexico and Nigeria: Colonialism and Its Aftermath

Mexico and Nigeria have both experienced colonial rule. The impact of their former colonial masters, Spain and Britain, is readily apparent in contemporary politics. Mexico's history as a colony is longer, Spain having ruled for over three centuries (1519–1821) while the British ruled Nigeria less than one hundred years (1861–1960). Although there were distinguished civilizations in the pasts of both Mexico and Nigeria, the colonial era marks the beginning of the modern states of Mexico and Nigeria as we know them today. The existing miniking-doms were replaced under colonial rule by centralized political control, modern bureaucracies, Western religious ideas, and European economic structures and values.

## MEXICO: TOWARD A MODERN STATE

Mexico has a long and tumultuous political history. The highly developed civilizations of ancient Mexico — especially the Mayan, Toltec, and Aztec — are sources of great pride for contemporary Mexicans. These civilizations were, at their heights, the most advanced and artistically expressive societies in North America. The fall of the Aztecs to Spanish conquerors who sought to spread Roman Catholicism and to exploit the New World's natural resources ushered in a new era for Mexico.

The Spaniards integrated the separate Indian kingdoms, reinforcing the traditional hierarchical systems while imposing a new hierarchy of their own. Spanish religious domination was also imposed by force. While Catholicism was often guilty of intolerance, it also served as an integrating mechanism binding together the various Indian tribes. The same thing is true of the spread of the Spanish language, which gradually came to serve much of Mexico as a common tongue. Another form of integration was the intermarriage of Spaniards and Indians, which produced what is today the largest racial group in Mexico, the *mestizos* (people of mixed Indian and Spanish blood).

Mexico won its independence from Spain during the Wars of Independence (1810–1821), and the newly independent nation then entered a long period of political turmoil and violence. This turmoil lasted well into the twentieth century and has left a multifaceted legacy that profoundly affects contemporary Mexican politics. One aspect of that legacy is a tradition of *authoritarian political rule*.[31] The pre-Conquest political order of the Aztecs was rigidly authoritarian. After the invasion of the Spaniards, the divine right to rule passed from the native priest-king to the distant monarch of Spain. The Crown administered New Spain through a viceroy in Mexico City who by proxy ruled by divine right, which Spanish monarchs claimed came from God.

After the end of Spanish colonial rule, the emerging Mexican state, like most other newly independent Latin American countries, patterned itself on the American political model, with a president and a congress. However, the political formula that worked well in the United States did not prosper in Mexico. The president soon came to exercise all meaningful political power and the congress was reduced to a sham. The congress persists to the present but the

31. By "authoritarian political rule" we mean the arbitrary and absolute exercise of power by a single individual or a small group of individuals.

FIGURE 1.6
## Some Important Landmarks in Mexican History

| | |
|---|---|
| 1325 | Aztecs overcome Toltecs |
| 1519 | Arrival of Hernán Cortés and the Spanish conquistadores |
| 1810–1821 | Wars of Independence |
| 1836 | Texas revolts from Mexican authority and establishes a republic |
| 1846–1848 | Mexican-United States War, in which Mexico loses lands north of the Rio Grande River |
| 1857–1861 | The Reform, led by Benito Juárez |
| 1861–1867 | Maximilian, Austrian archduke on Mexico's throne, defeated by Benito Juárez |
| 1876–1911 | Rule of Porfirio Díaz |
| 1910–1917 | The Revolution |
| 1917 | New constitution provides for social reform |
| 1929 | Founding of the Partido Revolucionario Institucional |
| 1934–1940 | Presidency of Lázaro Cárdenas — important social and economic reforms |

tradition of personalistic authoritarian rule by the president has also persisted, and congress is relegated to an unimportant political role.

After independence, the divine right rationale for authoritarian rule was discredited. Thenceforth, leaders sought to base their authority on personal appeal, military strength, or a combination of the two. Personalism inevitably led to demagoguery, as aspiring leaders tried to tie their futures to winning causes and succumbed to excesses of vanity when they achieved power. One practitioner of such personalist rule was Santa Anna, the general who stormed the Alamo. During a tumultuous political career that spanned over thirty years, Santa Anna was president of Mexico on eleven different occasions. In office he was vainglorious: in 1842, for example, he organized a spectacular state funeral, with parades, speeches, poems, and cannon salutes, to mark the interment of the lower portion of one of his legs, which had been severed several years earlier during a brief battle with the French.

A type of authoritarian leader during the unstable era of Mexican politics is the *caudillo,* a military leader who acquires political power and establishes a dictatorship based on the personal loyalty of his followers. Santa Anna was one of many such. In fact, with the exception of Benito Juárez during the Reform (1855–1872),[32] nearly all Mexico's political leaders were military officers until the twentieth century. One of the most successful caudillos was Porfirio Díaz,

32. Benito Juárez, the Oaxaca Indian who led the Reform (1855–1872), occupied the presidency for three terms, interrupted by a civil war over the role of the church in politics and by the brief rule of Maximilian. He was an immensely popular leader who based his rule on liberal democratic principles, carried out major land reforms, attempted to check the power of the military, and sought to reduce the economic and political prerogatives of the church. The Reform was one of the few bright spots in the generally dismal nineteenth-century history of Mexico.

who governed Mexico from 1876 to 1911. Díaz had a distinguished record of combat against domestic conservatives and French expeditionary forces. He came to power in a military coup d'état and established a conservative regime that emphasized economic growth and domestic stability. Such an outlook was no doubt necessary in a nation plagued by bandits and politically ambitious generals. However, order was pursued in a ruthless manner by Díaz's private army of thugs and the newly formed national gendarmerie. Furthermore, economic progress under Díaz favored a privileged few, almost exclusively whites of Spanish descent. Reforms intended to mitigate the sufferings of the Indians and mestizos were quietly abandoned. Meanwhile, the comfort of Díaz and the wealthy was assured by opening the Mexican economy to exploitation by foreign capitalists. The excesses of "Porfirismo" ultimately led to the Revolution of 1910 and the establishment of the current Mexican regime.

Regionalism persists in Mexico despite governmental efforts to achieve centralized control from Mexico City. In practice, most Mexican political leaders have found it difficult to implement centralized control. Regionalism is the product of many years of inadequate communication between the capital and remote sections of the country, and of the variation in cultures fostered by different climatic and economic conditions.

One political manifestation of regionalism is the tradition of *caciquismo,* a type of political rule administered through local political bosses (*caciques*). Though the caciques are in effect agents of the central government, they remain free to do virtually as they please within their fiefdoms as long as they maintain order and collect the assigned taxes. Caciquismo is a direct outgrowth of the Spanish type of colonial rule, under which local leaders or chiefs were granted extensive prerogatives by the viceroy in return for keeping the population quiet. The caciques used their powers to pursue the interests of their lieutenants, the wealthy landholders who supported them, and themselves. This tradition became even more firmly entrenched after independence, due to the instability of the central government. Constant changes of president and the resultant fragility of presidential power gave even greater latitude to the caciques. Caciquismo has proved to be a lasting legacy from the colonial era, manifested in a modified form in the political and social power exercised by the governmental party's local leaders. Problems resulting from the irresponsible personal rule of local political bosses continue to plague contemporary Mexico.

Regionalism and caciquismo have also retarded the development of a sense of national community and nationhood. Emphasis on regional goals and regional policies pursued by local political bosses have undermined efforts to build a Mexican national community. Even the national leaders have as a rule been unconcerned with national political integration. Since their ascendancy has been based on personal appeal and military prowess, rather than a well-established set of national political rules and loyalties, they have had little incentive to promote the sense of nationhood. Leaders who have felt the need to arouse national loyalties have usually done so by fomenting extreme nationalism directed at a foreign enemy. Because of its proximity and the threat it posed to Mexican independence, the United States has been the usual target of such nationalism. In the absence of a stable governmental framework and a consensus on national goals, anti-Americanism has been one of the few devices that leaders could employ to stimulate a sense of Mexican national community.

A third legacy to contemporary politics is the problem of vast *social inequities*. The social class structure that evolved during the colonial era was based primarily on race. At the top of the class structure were the whites: first Spaniards from Spain (*peninsulares*), then Spaniards born in Mexico (*crillos*). Before independence, the social caste distinction between these two classes of whites was usually huge, the *peninsulares* enjoying the privileged political, social, and often economic positions. Next were the mestizos, those of mixed caucasian and Indian blood, and below them were the Indians. On an even lower level were people of other mixed racial backgrounds and Negroes. While many efforts have been made to break down this class structure, it remains a basically accurate description of relative social ranking. The class structure is now complicated by occupationally based classes: the working class; the so-called middle sector, composed of merchants, civil servants and others; and peasants. But Indians remain on the margin of Mexican society, and the few lineal descendants of the landed aristocracy still possess a disproportionate share of personal wealth and social prestige.

While the Indian is still only marginally involved in Mexican society, Indianism — the cult of the Indian — is, paradoxically, an important feature of contemporary political culture. The accomplishments of the ancient Mexican civilizations constitute an impressive heritage that arouses national pride and patriotism and permits Mexico's leaders to link modern achievements and aspirations with a glorious past. As might be expected, the cult of the Indian has resulted in the liberal invention of new myths to glamorize these civilizations. Despite pride in the past achievements of the Indians, the Indians of today remain neglected, as we shall see in Chapter 2.

A fourth historical legacy to modern Mexico is *reverence for the Revolution*. While the history of Mexico is full of political revolts, coups, and civil wars, "the Revolution" is the name proudly given to the revolt that began with the attempt to oust Porfirio Díaz in 1910. The issue that united the various anti-Díaz forces was opposition to the re-election of the aging dictator in the July 1910 presidential election. Whatever the real outcome of the balloting, the Díaz regime announced that Díaz had defeated the Anti-Re-electionist ticket headed by Francisco Madero.

After several government efforts were made to suppress continued opposition by the Anti-Re-electionists, Madero in October 1910 issued a statement, known as the Plan of San Luis, declaring the elections null and void and proclaiming himself provisional president on the grounds that he would have won an honest election. Madero was joined by other anti-Díaz forces, notably Pancho Villa and Emiliano Zapata and their followers. After scattered guerrilla action that did not really threaten Díaz's hold on power — the Madero forces held only the border town of Cuidad Juárez — Díaz resigned in May 1911. Madero and the revolutionary forces entered Mexico City in June, and Madero was formally installed as president in November.

With Díaz out of the way, the heterogeneous revolutionary forces began to fight among themselves over the control and future course of the Revolution.

The dissolution of a traditional system and subsequent failure of alternative political institutions to take root often produces a contest for power that is subject to no legitimate rules and is characterized by violence. Such was the case in Mexico until 1917, when Venustiano Carranza, a former senator under Díaz, developed a winning coalition that enabled him to fend off rival groups and begin to create the foundations for realizing the promise of the Revolution. It was Carranza's successor, Alvaro Obregón, who began to institutionalize the revolutionary coalition by means of land distribution and labor reform which became the basis for important coalitions with peasant and labor groups. The social and political commitments of Obregón's revolutionary successors have varied. Some have pursued the promise of social justice through expansion of educational opportunities, land refrom, and the amelioration of the laborer's lot. None has hesitated to preserve the unity of Mexico through the use of force as well as conciliatory flexibility.

The Revolution provided Mexico a rich legacy of political institutions, ideas, and customs. In 1917 Mexico adopted the world's first socialist constitution. The Revolution is the source of the presidential system that grants the popularly elected president great power but limits him to one six-year term. (The rallying cry of the revolt against Díaz was "effective suffrage and no re-election.") The memory of the Revolution serves to remind contemporary leaders of their obligations to pursue social and economic reform. Finally, the Revolution has given modern Mexico its major party, the Partido Revolucionario Institucional or Institutional Revolutionary Party (PRI). One student of Mexican politics has correctly noted:

> . . . the term "revolution" had been wrenched out of its ordinary context. *The* Revolution is now a glittering edifice contrived of all the notions of the Party planners. The Party has become the revolution, and, as its spokesmen say quite openly, but not altogether exactly: "The Revolution *is* Mexico." [33]

A final legacy of Mexico's past is *violence*. The turbulence of Mexican politics has resulted in the liberal shedding of blood. Throughout the nineteenth century, when political power shifted rapidly from one leader to the next, it was the custom to label the vanquished "bandits" and to shoot them. Furthermore, there was a tendency on the part of dissidents who temporarily lacked the strength to oust the current leader to resort to banditry and violence. The Revolution perpetuated political violence. Its first decade was devoted to civil war: first to eliminate counterrevolutionaries and secure the Revolution and then to fight over the definition of the Revolution and leadership of the govern-

33. Lesley Byrd Simpson, *Many Mexicos* (Berkeley and Los Angeles: University of California Press, 1960), p. 295.

ment. The first president of the Revolution, Francisco Madero, was arrested by his own palace guard and murdered. The peasant leader Zapata, disgruntled at the slow pace of agrarian reform, was murdered as he began to reorganize his followers. During the first two or three decades of the Revolution, an estimated 1 million Mexicans lost their lives due to acts of violence or starvation brought on by economic disorder. The latest chapter in this violent tradition is the 1968 shooting of unarmed demonstrators and onlookers in a confrontation between antigovernment protestors and the police and army at the Tlatelolco apartment complex in Mexico City. While the actual number of fatalities resulting from this tragedy has never been made public, it is estimated that approximately three hundred people lost their lives.

Because it is a blend of widely divergent political attitudes and norms, the Mexican national political culture can accurately be labeled *transitional.* The political attitudes and values held by some individuals are clearly traditional in nature and not conducive to the development of a modern economy or of Western democracy. In other cases, the political norms seem supportive of economic development and Western democratic government. One traditional attitude with political implications is *machismo,* the aggressive assertion of maleness. In politics machismo often results in unwillingness to compromise, concede, make peace, or admit error; such patterns of behavior are often considered signs of weakness or lack of virility. Other aspects of the prevailing political culture are the product of conscious attempts by Mexican political leaders during and since the Revolution to reshape attitudes and values. Thus the government pushes for greater literacy, encourages political participation, and promotes veneration of the heroes and ideals of the Revolution.

A large sector of the population — estimated at close to 25 percent — does not partake in any way in the national political culture. This group is composed of most of the Indian population and part of the rural mestizo population. Among these people, the concept of national identity — recognition of the existence of a Mexican nation and government — is very poorly developed. Perhaps 5 to 10 percent of the total population is scarcely aware that the government exists. The others are apathetic about politics due to poverty, illiteracy, or despair. One Mexican social scientist refers to the have-nots who do not participate in the economic, social, or political life of the nation as "the marginal population."[34] Much of this marginal population lives in remote villages, whose isolation gives rise to localism and separatism. The village or tribe is the primary object of the individual's loyalty and the only meaningful political unit. Outsiders, whether agents of the national government or members of neighboring tribes or villages, are regarded with suspicion and sometimes hostility.

The number of marginals is diminishing due to the government's efforts to penetrate the hinterland with educational programs and to integrate the Indians and rural population into the national unit. However successful such

34. Pablo Gonzáles Casanova, *Democracy in Mexico* (New York: Oxford University Press, 1970).

programs prove to be, the demise of parochial political attitudes and orientations is still far in the future. Furthermore, the involvement of these socially and economically deprived sectors of the population in the political system may cause difficulties for the regime if they demand changes in the existing social, economic, and political structures. At present this parochial population creates little difficulty for the regime. If the political and social mobilization of this population were to outstrip the ability of the government to meet its demands, political corruption and instability might increase.[35]

Even the sector of the population that is aware of the national government is more preoccupied with the government's output and its effects on them than with the attempts to influence government. The political attitudes and orientations of this sector of the population are thus more typical of subjects than of participating citizens. They accept the national government as legitimate, although their loyalties are often focused on the person of the president, and feel considerable pride in the Revolution and the presidency. However, their most frequent contacts with government involve the bureaucracy, which they regard as corrupt, arbitrary, and inefficient. These contacts give rise to political cynicism and frustration, which discourages active involvement in attempts to influence government. Furthermore, reverence for the Revolution fuels cynicism, since the oft-repeated lofty goals of the Revolution are still far from fulfillment.

Mexico has had longer to forge its national political culture than have many developing nations. That Mexico is still struggling to create a national political culture after over 150 years of independence and 65 years of the Revolution suggests that the path of national political development may be a long one for those nations just beginning on it.


## NIGERIA: THE POLITICAL HERITAGE

When the British first made political inroads into the area now known as Nigeria, they encountered a diverse set of cultures. The creation of modern Nigeria was an arbitrary act on the part of the colonial masters. Each of the ethnic groups living in the area had its own history, culture, religion, and language. The major communities in the north were Islamic in religion and culture; those in the south were adherents of animistic religions. These various communal groups had no history of political cooperation or integration prior to the arrival of the British.

What the British did find were well-established kingdoms. Among these was the Bornu Kingdom, whose people had migrated centuries earlier from Sudan to the north of Nigeria. To the west of Bornu were the seven Hausa

---

35. See the argument of Samuel P. Huntington that too rapid social and economic mobilization may overtax the existing political structures and lead to political decay. Samuel P. Huntington, *Political Order in Changing Societies* (New Haven and London: Yale University Press, 1968).

FIGURE 1.7
*Some Important Landmarks in Nigerian History*

| | |
|---|---|
| 700–200 B.C. | Nok culture flourishes |
| 1861–1914 | British annex Lagos (1861) and establish control over Nigeria |
| 1914 | Nigeria formally becomes a colony of Great Britain |
| 1952–1954 | Britain takes steps toward African participation in government to prepare for independence |
| 1960 | Nigeria becomes an independent federal state within the Commonwealth |
| 1966 | Two military coups end northern-dominated government: January 1966 Major General Aguiyi-Ironsi overthrows parliamentary system |
| | July 1966 Ironsi is killed and Lieutenant Colonel Gowon assumes control of the Federal Military Government |
| 1967 | May 27, the military government alters the regional governmental structure by forming 12 states |
| | May 30, the Eastern Region secedes and forms the Independent Republic of Biafra; civil war ensues |
| 1970 | Secessionists capitulate; General Gowon announces a general amnesty |
| 1975 | Gowon overthrown by new military coup |

states, seats of Islamic culture straddling trade routes to the north and south. To the south lay the Yoruba Kingdom and its very rich and flourishing cultural offshoot, the Benin Kingdom. To the east were the Ibos and other minority groups that lived in political units smaller than the integrated kingdoms. Each of these groups had developed a rich and variegated culture.

The British did not act with foresight and intelligence in building their colony in Nigeria. It was not regarded as among the most important of Britain's African colonies, and simply grew piecemeal from the annexation of Lagos in 1861 until 1914, when it acquired its present boundaries. Motivated by trade, the British gradually increased their political control. In 1914 they amalgamated the predominantly Muslim north with the southern kingdoms, forming the Colony and Protectorate of Nigeria.

The consolidation of Nigeria under British rule obscured important cultural, political, social, and economic differences among the various communities that composed the colony. The Ibo, in the east, were decentralized, each Ibo village remaining largely autonomous. Political power within the Ibo village was dispersed, and opportunities existed for democratic participation. Positions of leadership were the result of individual achievement rather than birth. The Yoruba community in the west had a complex centralized monarchy, the king claiming descent from the legendary Oduduwa, founder of the capital of Yorubaland. The status of other Yoruba towns was a function of the intimacy of the hereditary link between their leader and the king. In the north, the Muslim Hausa-Fulani system was a highly centralized bureaucratic empire with strong theocratic overtones.

## THE COLONIAL IMPACT

British and other European missionaries sought to introduce Christianity to the peoples of Nigeria, and such other Western values as individualism, education, efficiency, and capitalism were also introduced. However, differing communal group values meant that the impact of colonial rule varied from one region to the next and from one tribe to the next. For example, the Ibo culture was oriented toward granting status on the basis of personal achievement whereas among the Hausa-Fulani status was determined by an individual's birth and/or social ties. Consequently, the Ibos were generally more willing to take advantage of educational opportunities. The Southern animistic religions proved more vulnerable to Christianity than did the highly developed Islamic religion in the north. And the Christianized portion of the population was often readier to accept other Western cultural and economic values than were the Islamic peoples who rejected Christianity.

British colonial governance was based on indirect rule through a colonial bureaucracy and indigenous leaders. In Nigeria, the effect of indirect rule was to perpetuate and accentuate communal and regional differences. The British recognized three regions, each of which had a dominant ethnic group and, more often than not, several dissatisfied minority ethnic groups. By 1914 there had already emerged the basic regional alignments that were later to be a major cause of communal conflict and, ultimately, of civil war: the Northern Region was dominated by the Hausa-Fulani peoples, the Western Region by the Yorubas, and the Eastern Region by the Ibos.

The colony was governed by a British governor-general assisted by a variety of national and regional advisory groups. While the councils sometimes included Nigerian representatives, their influence was limited. For example, under the first governor-general (1914–1918) there was an advisory committee known as the Nigerian Council with forty-two appointed members, twelve of whom were Nigerians. It met infrequently, only seven times in as many years. The governor-general relied more on the two British lieutenant-governors, one for northern Nigeria and one for southern Nigeria. Each had considerable autonomy and developed his own budget. The regional governments provided basic services (health, education, police) and there was little federal coordination. This lack of coordination between regions, especially in the realm of education, aggravated existing regional discrepancies. Some centralized control was exercised by the governor-general, who retained control over mines, telecommunications, railways, judicial functions, the military, and finances.

The lieutenant-governors relied heavily upon native tribal leaders to administer their programs. This practice too tended to perpetuate traditional social, economic, and political structures and to encourage regional disparities due to differences in values. For example, the British collaboration with the Muslim emirates in the north led to the exclusion of Christian missionaries from the north. While southerners were educated in missionary-run schools, the north lacked any significant mass education. In the long run this meant that national politics and the civil service would be dominated by the better-educated southerners and that northerners would be suspicious of political dominance by the less numerous southerners.

In 1922 a constitution was provided for Nigeria by its governor-general. It established a Legislative Council, which included the first popularly elected Africans to sit in a colonial council in all of British Africa. The Legislative Council had its limitations. For one thing the Nigerian population permitted to participate in the election of native members was limited to a few taxpayers. Even more significant for the course of later events was the exclusion of northern Nigeria from participation in the legislative body. Thus, the first governing body with Nigerian membership was oriented toward the south, and the economic and political development of the north began to lag further and further behind that of the south.

While the electorate eligible to vote for the Nigerian Council was small, this did not prevent the emergence of nationalist political leaders and movements. Among the first of the Nigerian nationalist leaders was Herbert Macauley, a civil engineer and journalist trained in Britain. In 1923 Macauley formed the Nigerian National Democratic Party, one of Nigeria's first political parties. The activities of the party were centered in Lagos, and it increasingly found itself more involved in Western regional politics than in nationalist causes. In reaction, dissatisfied educated youth formed more militant nationalist movements, the most important of which was the Nigerian Youth Movement. Among the leaders of the new movement was Nnamdi Azikiwe, who had studied abroad and returned to Nigeria to head a daily nationalist newspaper. The young nationalists used the press to condemn colonial rule and rally support for national self-determination. In 1944 Macauley, Azikiwe, and other nationalist leaders joined in forming the National Council of Nigeria and the Cameroons (NCNC). Nearly all the major nationalist movements, trade unions, and youth groups were associated with this common front for constitutional change and self-rule.

Perhaps the most significant feature of Nigerian politics to this point was the virtual exclusion of northerners from national Nigerian politics. None of the nationalist groups was successful (or genuinely interested) in winning the support of the Hausa-Fulani, and the lack of northern representatives in national politics retarded the development of leadership and political awareness in the north. Furthermore, their exclusion from politics may well have contributed to later fears of domination by the more politically developed south. Not until 1946, when a new constitution was imposed by the British governor-general, did northerners begin to become involved in national politics. The new constitution created legislative councils in each of three regions and a national legislative council, with northern members, in Lagos. This reform was too late to assuage northern fears of discrimination by southerners; the economic and cultural disparities between north and south were by then well entrenched. Furthermore, the peremptory fashion in which the governor-general promulgated the new constitution did little to make it acceptable to the increasingly impatient Nigerian nationalists.

The growing strength and vigor of Nigerian nationalism quickly undermined the 1946 constitution. In 1951 a new governor-general issued yet another constitution, this one somewhat more sensitive to Nigerian nationalist aspirations. The regional governments were further strengthened and endowed with full governmental systems. Representatives to regional legislatures were thenceforth directly elected and representatives to the federal legislature, formerly elected directly by popular vote, were selected indirectly by the regional legislatures. However, the constitution of 1951 failed to establish effective mechanisms for policy-making, and it was dealt a near death-blow in 1953 when the Eastern Region's legislature refused to pass an appropriations bill. The crisis had to be resolved by means of a constitutional amendment allowing the central government to dissolve the recalcitrant regional legislature and hold new elections.

Now that elections took place on the regional level (federal legislators being appointed rather than elected), regional politics became all the more important. The Yorubas decided to form a political party separate from the Ibo-dominated NCNC. The new party, known as the Action Group, competed primarily in the Western Region. In the north the Northern People's Congress, which had been organized in 1948, won control of the regional legislature. Cooperation between these ethnically and regionally based parties in the national legislature was often tenuous. One early sign of the growing political tensions between regions appeared in 1954 when the Action Group and the NCNC jointly supported a resolution in the Federal House of Representatives calling for full independence by 1956. The northerners were reluctant to support such a motion since they felt the need of more time under British rule to prepare for more direct political competition with the more politically astute southerners. Their motion doomed to failure because of northern opposition, the members of the Action Group and the NCNC walked out of the legislature. When the northern delegates departed, they found an angry crowd of proindependence nationalists awaiting them. In retaliation, northerners rioted and revenged themselves on southerners living in northern cities.

Yet another constitution was adopted, with considerable involvement on the part of Nigerian political leaders. This constitution reduced centralized control and enhanced the power of the regions. The central government was assigned carefully and narrowly defined responsibilities, and all other governmental functions were left to the regional governments. In addition, the bureaucracy and court systems were shifted from the central government to the regional governments. It was this constitution that carried Nigeria toward independence. The constitution adopted at the time of independence retained the weak federal links of the 1954 constitution.

## INDEPENDENCE

Nigeria was one of seventeen former African colonies to win independence in 1960. While self-rule was effectuated without conflict, it had long been sought after by ardent Nigerian nationalist leaders. The insistence of these individuals and their counterparts in the rest of Africa had brought an end to the colonial era in Africa. The legacy of colonial rule, however, remained. While the relative merits and faults of colonial rule can be argued, two signal failures characterized British rule in Nigeria. First, the basic British policy that no colony should place an economic burden on the motherland meant that Nigerian resources were exploited for the benefit of Britain without equivalent investment in Nigeria. Not until after World War Two did Britain begin to take seriously the responsibility of providing education, health services, and public works, and fulfilling other governmental obligations in Nigeria. And when these investments finally began to be made, they were not equitably distributed throughout Nigeria. The fact that the southern regions benefitted more than the Northern Region tended to exacerbate regional and ethnic tensions. The second failure of British policy was the rigidification of ethnic differences as a result of indirect rule and loose federalism based on ethnically defined regions. These policies also increased ethnic tensions and paved the way to secession and civil war.

Despite the high expectations of Nigerian nationalists, the achievement of independence was not sufficient to create the authority necessary for governing a nation anxious to develop and plagued with numerous economic and social challenges. Within a few years ethnic tensions had developed into the core of a self-destructive political conflict. This situation led to political coalitions that undermined election results, to ethnic hostilities, and ultimately in 1966 to two military coups. The first coup, in January, deposed the civilian regime; the second, in the summer, altered the military leadership. The ultimate victor in these coups was General Yakubu Gowon, who headed Nigeria's regime into the 1970s. The military regime changed the political format by banning the existing political parties, prohibiting the revival of ethnic parties, and instituting military control in twelve states to replace the regional governments.

# Conclusions

Though this chapter has dealt separately with the historical backgrounds of the six countries, their histories intermingle. As colonial power and colony, as wartime allies and enemies, as economic partners and rivals, they have been involved with each other. For example, the British impact on China and, even more significantly, on Nigeria is clear. In China, submission to the indignities of British imperial trade policies ultimately contributed to the breakdown of the imperial dynasty and the advent of China's modern era of revolution. In Nigeria, the legacy of colonial institutions paved the way to a tragic civil war.

Perhaps equally important, the nations' historical experiences have served each other as patterns to be imitated or as warnings to be heeded. The French Revolution of 1789 may well have helped sensitize British aristocrats to the need to grant moderate reforms in order to prevent comparable events in Britain. It is more clear that the experience of the Russians in implementing the communist ideology alerted the Chinese communists to possible dangers. Mao reacted against Stalin's use of terror, seeking to establish control and conformity through "re-education" and periodic exchanges of life roles to familiarize all citizens with manual labor. Learning from the problems Lenin encountered as a result of his direct political involvement, Mao assured himself of a more reflective vantage-point by withdrawing often from day-to-day politics. In addition, Mao acted to avoid the bureaucratization and the subsequent revival of social privilege and hierarchy characteristic of the Soviet revolution by emphasizing social justice, equality, and participation.

The most obvious point of contrast between Mexico and Nigeria is the length of their independence. Mexico is sometimes treated as an illustration of the length of time political development requires in former colonial areas. It took nearly 120 years for Mexico to proceed very far along the path of development toward the modern nation-state. And it is debatable whether or not Mexico has yet reached the point at which its development is comparable to that of countries universally considered developed. This does not necessarily mean, however, that Nigeria and other new states must go through an equally long period of political turmoil. It is possible that Nigeria and its counterparts will benefit from the experience of older former colonies so as to shorten the development process. The ease with which ideas and people circulate in the contemporary era may facilitate the development process.

The impact of history on contemporary politics cannot be underemphasized. Throughout this text historical factors will be seen to be important in understanding current developments. In Chapter 2, we shall examine the continuing political effects of social cleavages and structures inherited from the past.

**2**

# *Society and Politics*

## Introduction

Politics is one of the many types of activity — political, social, economic, cultural, and religious — that characterize a society, and the political process is intertwined with other social activities and structures. It is affected by these activities and in turn affects them. The concept of the political system outlined on pages 3–4 emphasizes usefully the interrelationship of the political system and its environment. An important aspect of the environment is the social system in which the political unit functions. It would be as misleading to ignore the social setting of contemporary politics as it would be to disregard its historical background. This chapter examines the ways in which society affects the political process. Chapter 9 will explore the effects of political action and governmental policies on society.

Among the most important effects of social structures and activities is their impact on the orderly and stable operation of the political process. Society is the source of conflict and sometimes violence, which the political unit must resolve or regulate. Nearly every political unit has faced the task of resolving social crises that have tested its ability to survive. Such tests occur frequently in the developing world, where ethnic conflict, vast economic disparities and inequities, and conflicting value systems render the functioning of stable political processes extremely difficult. Even mature industrial states face frequent social crises, such as unrest among blacks, Chicanos, and Indians in the United States; peasant discontent in France; conflict between French- and English-speaking Canadians; worker discontent in many Western nations; and the dissatisfaction of intellectuals in the Soviet Union and other communist states.

Society thus presents the political system with problems it must try to resolve in order to achieve and maintain political stability. On the other hand, society also provides supports that help to maintain the stability of the political system. These supports include economic and social structures, established patterns of interpersonal relations, and consensus on the goals of social life. An ethnically homogeneous developing society may experience less difficulty than a heterogeneous one in the creation of a unified and integrated state. Even the much-maligned class and caste structures may sustain certain types of political systems. Class and caste divisions, though inherently inequitable, may promote harmonious relations among social groups by limiting conflict over social rank and scarce economic rewards. However, such a positive result of caste is likely to be the case only so long as the caste system is ideologically validated and widely accepted as inevitable.

## TYPES OF SOCIAL CONFLICT

All societies are divided. Conflict develops among the various sectors of society over many issues and relationships. Conflict is inevitable in all political settings, since no society has at its disposal enough economic wealth, prestige, and social influence to satisfy all who seek these resources. Competition for these scarce resources need not be violent or disruptive: it can be directed, limited, deflected or otherwise regulated, but it cannot be eliminated. Conflict is thus normal in all societies, and under certain circumstances it may even be desirable. Some sociologists argue that conflict tends both to integrate society by creating interdependency among antagonistic groups and to inhibit social stagnation by generating pressure for innovational creativity.[1] And many insist, in the laissez-faire tradition, that conflict and competition are likely to produce the "best" distribution of wealth, prestige, and influence.

Much social conflict can be either ignored or easily managed by the political system. Most governments can, for example, avoid involvement in competition between religious groups for new members, among fraternal organizations over prestige, among doctors over alternative remedies, and other kinds of social conflict with tenuous political implications. Such issues may become politicized, however. For instance, doctors may urge the government to introduce a compulsory vaccination program and pressure groups may insist that fraternal organizations admit members without regard to race or religion. But these areas are ordinarily of minimal political significance.

Other types of social conflict are less easily isolated from politics. There are several kinds of *social cleavages* — or divisions within society — that have proved durable and politically relevant in a variety of systems. At times such cleavages reflect conflicts of such intensity that they polarize society into warring camps. A situation of this sort portends high levels of conflict and possible

1. Lewis A. Coser, *The Functions of Social Conflict* (New York: The Free Press, 1964).

violence. At other times cleavages are simply social differences with political implications but little potential for violence.

The political system is frequently affected by socioeconomic, regional, cultural, and ideological cleavages. *Socioeconomic* or *class* cleavages are social distinctions that reflect the stratification of society according to income and social position. There are, typically, three broad social classes: the working class, or proletariat; the middle class, or bourgeoise; and the upper class. Political scientists have paid considerable attention to the significance of class divisions, and rightly so. The effects of class pervade politics, whether we examine socialization, parties, or leadership. In fact, Karl Marx regarded class conflict as the essential characteristic of capitalist society and politics, arguing that other apparent social divisions were either manifestations of class conflict or nonexistent.

In most Western democracies, class conflict between workers and the middle and upper classes reached a peak during the early stages of industrialization. At that time, Western societies most closely corresponded to the Marxist model of all-encompassing class conflict between the proletariat and the bourgeoisie. Individuals who were totally involved in the defense of class interests were not unusual, and the result was often intense class conflict. In most Western democracies, the subsequent emergence of mass consumption and the accompanying leveling of class differences have eliminated much of the intensity from class conflict. Class differences with political implications still exist, but they are rarely disruptive of the political system. However, class differences, especially as manifested in relative levels of wealth, often aggravate and intensify other lines of cleavage. This is particularly the case when class coincides with racial and regional cleavages, as we shall see.

The classic Marxist view of class conflict (proletariat versus bourgeoisie) was based on an analysis of nineteenth-century European societies. It is not readily applicable to those parts of the Third World where industrialization has not yet occurred and where, consequently, there is no proletariat and no bourgeoisie. Lenin and Mao both recognized the limitations of Marx's arguments and applied them to the developing world by amplifying the definition of the proletariat to include landless peasants and others without property. This broader interpretation of class conflict as occurring between the "haves" and the "have-nots" is clearly of major political significance in much of the Third World, including Mexico and Nigeria.

Communist states are also subject to class conflict, despite their ideological commitment to a classless society. While the communist regimes have eliminated the old capitalist privileged classes — or, more precisely, absorbed them into the working class — new privileged sectors of society have emerged: technocrats, bureaucrats, party officials, military officers. Conflict between these privileged groups and the working class is muted by the regime and the party. But it undeniably exists and occasionally bursts into the open, as in the case of the Polish workers' food riots in 1971, which led to the removal of Poland's party leader.

A second politically significant cleavage is the division of society along *geographic* or *regional* lines. In many modern nations, differing political values and attitudes characterize the different geographic regions. These populations often compete for scarce government resources, such as money, jobs, and development projects. Regional cleavages are likely to be deep, and to become explosive if one region's viewpoint regularly prevails or if it receives a disproportionate share of the government's offerings. If such a cleavage becomes bitter, there is frequently a danger that the deprived region will secede. Disparities in the economic development of the north and the south in the United States were a primary cause of the American Civil War. Similarly, in Nigeria, regional conflicts emanating in part from economic disparities resulted in the secession of Biafra and a tragic civil war.

Closely related to regional cleavages is the cleavage between urban and rural populations. The distribution of political power, and ultimately of government-provided resources, is a source of tension between urban and rural populations. This is particularly true in nations undergoing the transition from a predominantly rural to an urban society. Rural areas are likely to resist the loss of influence and preferential treatment. They are likely to sense that their problems and needs are neglected as a result of the government's shift of focus to the cities and urban problems. Such an urban/rural cleavage is an important source of political tension in France, where the substantial agrarian population feels neglected as government has focused its attention and resources on modernization and industrialization. In some systems, political power remains in the hands of rural sectors though the bulk of the population is urbanized. This situation is also likely to create tension stemming from the government's neglect of urban problems. This was the case in many American state legislatures until the court-ordered reapportionments of the 1960s.

Other cleavages are *cultural* or *ethnic* in origin. Cultural cleavages divide societies along *racial, linguistic* and *religious* lines.[2] They are at least as important in the politics of most nations as are class differences. Only a dozen or so of the approximately 150 independent nations are ethnically homogeneous. Most countries are culturally plural, composed of several groups of peoples with different racial, linguistic, and/or religious heritages. Their political systems must cope with the problems posed by cultural pluralism if they are to maintain their unity and stability.

Among the most important political effects of cultural pluralism is the threat that it can pose to national unity and stability. Creating a sense of belonging to a single political unit among the various cultural groups that inhabit a nation is known as *political integration* or *nation-building*.[3] It is a

2. The terms "ethnic group" and "cultural group" will be used interchangeably to refer to groups characterized by distinctive racial, religious, and/or linguistic traits.

3. For discussions of political integration and nation-building, see Myron Weiner, "Political Integration and Political Development," *Annals of the American Academy of Political and Social Sciences* 358 (March 1965): 52–65; Karl Deutsch and William J. Foltz, *Nation-Building* (Chicago: Aldine-Atherton, 1966); and Clifford Geertz, "The Integrative Revolution: Primordial Sentiments and Civil Politics in New States," in *Old Societies and New States,* ed. Clifford Geertz (Glencoe, Ill.: The Free Press, 1963).

continuing political process, involving agreement on a national language or languages, acceptance of a uniform set of political symbols that evoke emotional support for the state and feelings of patriotism (flag, national anthem, national heroes and martyrs), and the building of political loyalties that transcend the tribe, religious body, or racial group. In short, political integration is the process whereby loyalties and attachments to religious, linguistic, and racial groups are weakened and attachment to a broader political unit (the nation-state) is promoted as the object of the individual's ultimate political loyalty.

In most of Europe and North America, the process of political integration has been continuing for centuries and is not yet complete. In the United States, we are now struggling with the tasks of integrating and assuring equal opportunity and justice for minority cultural groups such as blacks, Chicanos, and American Indians. The current tension between the government of the Soviet Union and Russian Jews and Lithuanians is only the most recent clash between a centralized political regime and nationality groups within its borders; in France, the Bretons plead for a free Brittany; in Italy, the German-speaking Tyroleans would like to be reunited with Austria; in Yugoslavia, the Croats and the Serbs are renewing their ancient enmity; and so on. Often these ethnic political conflicts are potentially explosive and occasionally they burst into open violence as in Northern Ireland and Quebec.

With the problems of political integration so crucial in the mature industrialized states, it is little wonder that the newly independent states of Africa, Asia, and the Middle East have grave difficulty integrating diverse cultural groups into cohesive states. Many of these new states are populated by several racial groups or nationalities. In some cases, this ethnic pluralism results from the perpetuation of boundaries drawn by colonial regimes without regard to human geography. The colonial powers simply drew straight lines or followed rivers to demarcate their colonies. In other cases, cultural pluralism has resulted from the desire to bring together in a single political unit enough people and territory to make an economically viable state. As a consequence, various cultural groups suddenly find themselves encouraged to share their lives and futures with those of other cultural groups with which they have not cooperated in the past. Indeed, it is not uncommon for groups with long-standing traditions of fighting to become citizens of the same state.

Another source of cleavage is competition among various social and political ideologies. *Ideological cleavages* exist where incompatible views of the organization, goals, and values of society are present within a single system. Ideologies, or encompassing visions of the world (*Weltanschauung*), characterize all societies. In some systems there is a consensus on ideology; in other systems, several ideologies compete for the allegiance of the population. Such ideological differences — especially where ideologies are held with great fervor — may produce conflict over ideas and over the political power to implement them.

Two ideological cleavages with massive political consequences are democracy/autocracy and socialism or communism/capitalism or free enterprise.

In most Third World countries, the gap between the few very rich and the masses living at or below subsistence level is large and often increasing. In Nigeria, an elite has benefited from the country's oil wealth and enjoys all the luxuries of the West—including golf— while most of the population struggles for existence with an average annual per capita income of just over one hundred American dollars. China has made strenuous efforts to break down economic and social class distinctions and to prevent their reemergence. To avoid class-based status relationships, in particular among the respected educators, teachers must engage in manual labor as well as their intellectual pursuits. Faculty and students are shown "returning to the countryside" to work on rural development projects. The Soviet Union too aspires to social equality but the intelligentsia there enjoys special privileges and prestige. A few internationally known intellectuals have been able to capitalize on their prominence to publicly dissent from some actions of the Soviet regime. Alexander Solzhenitsyn was one such dissenter whose actions ultimately led to his expulsion from the Soviet Union (he is shown with Heinrich Böll upon arrival in Germany on that occasion); less prominent dissenters are imprisoned or confined in asylums.

Conflict along either or both of these lines indicates a lack of consensus on the basic structures and goals of society. Most of the developed world has experienced conflict of varying intensities over both of these ideological cleavages.

Another ideological conflict of importance in many states is the clerical/anticlerical cleavage. Most countries with a Roman Catholic background and population have experienced division over the proper role of the church in politics and society. The church has traditionally played a prominent, and sometimes dominant, part in the politics and social life of Catholic countries. Efforts by liberal reformers to limit the political, social, and economic power of the church has produced conflict, and occasionally violence, in most Catholic countries.

These three ideological cleavages have lost most of their intensity in Western democracies as a result of a consensus emerging on most of the old issues. The decline in salience of these ideological cleavages has led some to proclaim the *end of ideology*.[4] It is more accurate, however, to refer to the end of these particular ideological cleavages. The new consensus built of compromise on the old conflicts is itself an ideology, and may in turn be challenged in the future. In fact, some argue that the "counterculture" of the late 1960s and early 1970s reflects such an alternative view of the world and represents a new ideology challenging the established consensus.

In the developing world, conflicts over democracy, the nature of the economic order, and the role of religious institutions in society are by no means resolved. Furthermore, there often exists a more nebulous ideological conflict between sectors of the population that accept modernity and change and those that cling to traditional values and the status quo. While these alternative views of society are less clearly defined than the conflict between socialism and capitalism, the cleavage between traditionalists and modernizers is often deep.

There are many other cleavages with political significance — among them generational and sexual divisions. As old cleavages wane in political importance, new ones appear. Change in society generates new divisions, which are inevitably manifested in politics.

We have dealt separately with class, regional, cultural, and ideological differences, but in the real world it is rare that a conflict involves only one such cleavage. Social conflict — especially very intense or violent conflict — usually has several dimensions; it may reflect all four of these major types of cleavages simultaneously. The socioeconomic or class cleavage frequently coincides with other social divisions: ideologies are sometimes little more than manifestations of class conflict, and cultural and regional cleavages may have a class dimension as well. For example, the racial cleavages in the United States between the majority white population and black and Chicano minority populations are aggravated by the fact that whites are generally middle- and upper-class

---

4. Daniel Bell, *The End of Ideology*, rev. ed. (New York: The Free Press, 1962).

and the minority groups are predominantly working- or lower-class. The frequent coincidence of class and other cleavages leads some, especially those influenced by Marxist thought, to conclude that the crucial element in social strife is class division. According to this view, social conflict — even if it appears to be racial, regional, or ideological in nature — is best explained as class conflict.

Others stress the multiple dimensions of most severe social conflict. This position acknowledges the importance of economic disparities, but argues that it is wrong to ignore the other dimensions of a conflict. Whether regional, cultural, or ideological, they are not simply disguises for class conflict but genuine sources of social division.

The violence between Protestants and Catholics in Northern Ireland is an example of a conflict arising from multiple cleavages. The cultural cleavages between Catholics of indigenous Irish stock and Protestants of Scottish ancestry is aggravated by the geographic (certain neighborhoods, towns, and districts are Catholic; others are Protestant) and class cleavages (Catholics tend to be poorer and slightly more frequently working-class than do Protestants).

## THE DYNAMICS OF SOCIAL CLEAVAGES

It is a very intriguing and difficult problem to account for the rise and decline of social cleavages. Such divisions appear and disappear; they become politically important — even critical — and then wane. At times a society will be relatively free of apparent cleavages and then experience an era of social polarization.

Several factors account for the varying intensity of social conflict. The general structure of a cleavage is one important factor. Where several lines of cleavage coincide, social polarization and high levels of conflict are likely. An example of *coinciding* cleavages is a hypothetical society divided into two camps: one lower-class, eastern, urban, of uniform ethnic background, and espousing socialism; the other middle-class, western, rural, of a different ethnic origin, and defending capitalism. Such a society would be sharply divided and prone to conflict.

Where several lines of cleavage *overlap* or criss-cross, conflict may be more easily regulated. A society of this kind might, for example, have a working class composed of easterners and westerners, urban and rural dwellers, both ethnic groups, and both socialists and capitalists. And the middle class would include the same elements as the working class. In such a situation, urban workers may decline to push their class interests to the extreme because they need to cooperate with the urban middle class to attain better housing or transportation for the city. In short, criss-crossing lines of cleavage divide a society into many small camps that agree on some issues and disagree on others, instead of two diametrically opposed camps produced by coinciding cleavages. Where there is a pattern of overlapping or criss-crossing cleavages, therefore, conflict tends to be less intense.

Another factor affecting the intensity of conflict is the general level of economic wealth and future economic trends. Social conflict is heightened and the likelihood of violence greatly increased where scarcity of jobs, housing, education, and other social goods leads to fierce competition among various sectors of society. The individual may blame failure to gain all he or she deserves on the "unfair" competition of other classes, regions, or cultural groups. This is particularly dangerous when one social group does in fact have an economic advantage or a faster rate of economic advancement than the others. Societies in which part of the population is living at or near the subsistence level are likely to experience heightened tension and even violence during times of economic crisis. Conversely, general prosperity and optimism about future economic growth may diminish class, regional, and cultural tensions.

Third, the attitudes of leaders can importantly influence the level of conflict. If national political leaders are responsive to tensions between social groups and work to reduce these tensions, polarization may be avoided. If they are unaware of such tensions or inept in dealing with them, the level of conflict may rise. Similarly, the attitudes of class, regional, and/or ethnic elites are significant. The willingness or unwillingness of leaders involved in social conflict to resort to violence or to exploit social tensions importantly influences the intensity of conflict.

Fourth, the ways conflict situations have been resolved in the past affects the manner in which contemporary cleavages are handled. If there is a tradition of violence stemming from social cleavages, it is likely that contemporary cleavages will assume violent dimensions. Where past social conflict has been peacefully resolved, new conflicts are also likely to be handled without recourse to violence. Traditions of peaceful or violent resolution to social conflict can, of course, be broken with. However, they tend to provide precedents and formulas that are readily available for application to new conflict situations.

Finally, social cleavages may be heightened by international contagion. Periodically, social ideas and conflicts sweep through many countries, dividing them similarly. An example is the liberal-democratic revolutionary spirit that swept Europe in 1848–1849, touching off revolutions against autocracy in nearly every major European state. Contemporary improvements in communication heighten the probability and extent of contagion of social conflict. This is well illustrated by the rapid spread of student revolts in 1967–1969, when major disorders occurred in the United States, Britain, France, Germany, Mexico, and elsewhere. Thus, social conflict and tension in one country spills over into other countries, creating new cleavages or intensifying existing ones.

None of these five factors is alone sufficient to explain the diminution or intensification of social cleavages. Together, they go far toward explaining the reasons for varying levels of social conflict at different times within the same society and in different societies. In the following case studies, we will look at the social cleavages characteristic of the six countries, the political manifestations of these cleavages, and the reasons for rises and declines in social conflicts.

# Britain and France:
## Conflict and Consensus in
### Pluralist Societies

Western democracies such as Britain and France are *pluralist* in the sense that diverse social forces such as labor unions, business groups, civic action movements, political groupings, social clubs, and churches are permitted to develop and act autonomously. Since the free interaction of these social forces is tolerated and sometimes fostered, social conflict is a normal aspect of pluralism. But there are limits to pluralism. Democratic governments sometimes act to restrict the activities of extremist groups, and there is a natural human tendency to conform to the norms of society. Nevertheless, pluralism allows for a considerable variety of social conflict in democratic societies.

The intensity of such conflict is generally at a low level in Britain and France. Since World War Two, both countries have experienced conditions that favor the control of social conflict. The French economy has grown steadily and rapidly; the British economy, though less dynamic and subject to intermittent periods of stagnation, has also expanded significantly. This general prosperity and economic progress has permitted both countries to avoid the extreme scarcity-induced social tensions produced by economic depression.

Nearly all sectors of both societies have experienced real improvements in the overall quality of life. Important social and economic differences still exist, but it is usually no longer a case of the wealthy having and the worker doing without. Workers may have smaller cars, cheaper televisions, and more modest vacation plans than the wealthy, but they are not deprived. This general leveling of society has tended to mitigate most social cleavages without eliminating all their social and political consequences. Opinion surveys reveal that people from different classes express similar degrees of satisfaction with their jobs and their lives. Table 2.1 illustrates this finding in the case of Britain. Economic expansion and growing affluence have made it possible for all parties to social conflict to look forward to improved situations. Social conflict is not a zero-sum game in which one player wins everything and others gain nothing. It need not be the case that one region or social class improves its position only at the expense of other regions or classes. All can expect to gain from an expanding economy.

Social conflict has also been reduced by the spread of a single culture in each country. Mass communications — especially television — have been instrumental in undermining the distinctive lifestyles of classes, regions, and ethnic groups and promoting a single national lifestyle and value system. This phenomenon has lessened some of the differences among sectors of society and may thus facilitate the regulation of conflict within society.[5]

5. This does not mean, however, that Britain and France no longer experience much social unrest. As we shall see, both undergo periodic episodes of intensifying social conflict.

TABLE 2.1

## Survey of Self-Assessment on Class Basis

| Social class self-definition | Total | Working | Lower middle | Middle | Upper middle | Upper |
|---|---|---|---|---|---|---|
| Base: all informants having jobs | 623 | 309 | 85 | 192 | 35 | 2 |
| | % | % | % | % | % | No. |
| How satisfied are you with the sort of job you have? — Very satisfied | 52 | 45 | 56 | 59 | 66 | (1) |
| Fairly satisfied | 38 | 42 | 38 | 32 | 26 | (1) |
| Fairly dissatisfied | 6 | 8 | 1 | 7 | 8 | (—) |
| Very dissatisfied | 4 | 5 | 5 | 2 | — | (—) |
| Base: all informants | 948 | 471 | 129 | 292 | 50 | 6 |
| | % | % | % | % | % | No. |
| How satisfied are you with the sort of house you live in? — Very satisfied | 47 | 44 | 44 | 54 | 52 | (1) |
| Fairly satisfied | 34 | 35 | 37 | 30 | 32 | (4) |
| Fairly dissatisfied | 10 | 10 | 12 | 8 | 10 | (—) |
| Very dissatisfied | 9 | 11 | 7 | 8 | 6 | (1) |
| Base: all informants | 948 | 471 | 129 | 292 | 50 | 6 |
| | % | % | % | % | % | No. |
| How satisfied are you with the people you make friends with? — Very satisfied | 75 | 73 | 75 | 81 | 78 | (3) |
| Fairly satisfied | 22 | 24 | 24 | 18 | 18 | (3) |
| Fairly dissatisfied | 2 | 2 | 1 | 1 | 4 | (—) |
| Very dissatisfied | 1 | 1 | — | — | — | (—) |
| Base: all informants | 948 | 471 | 129 | 292 | 50 | 6 |
| | % | % | % | % | % | No. |
| How satisfied are you with the kind of neighborhood you live in? — Very satisfied | 53 | 49 | 49 | 61 | 56 | (1) |
| Fairly satisfied | 30 | 32 | 33 | 26 | 24 | (3) |
| Fairly dissatisfied | 9 | 9 | 9 | 7 | 14 | (1) |
| Very dissatisfied | 8 | 10 | 9 | 6 | 6 | (1) |

Source: Marplan Ltd., Market Research, The Times, September 29, 1969. Reprinted by permission.

Taken together, economic development and mass communications have tended to promote consensus on the basic ends of society and politics and on the appropriate means to pursue them. In Britain this consensus is well developed and includes acceptance of the established social order and existing political institutions. In France consensus has long been absent; many French citizens still argue the merits of the Revolution of 1789. However, there is still some evidence from public opinion surveys that a consensus on the social order and political institutions is emerging among the general public despite the rhetoric of partisan political leaders.[6]

6. See Emeric Deutsch, Denis Lindon, and Pierre Weill, Les Familles politiques aujourd'hui en France (Paris: Editions de Minuit, 1966).

Notwithstanding the growth of consensus and development that limit the intensity of conflict, there continue to be cleavages with political significance in Britain and France. However, the political manifestations of these cleavages are usually not disruptive, as is well illustrated by the survival of social class divisions. Most British and French citizens see themselves as belonging to a given social class, but there is little evidence of significant class conflict. Public opinion polls indicate that less than half the populations of Britain and France

TABLE 2.2

## Voting Intentions by Socio-occupational Group, France

|  | 1968 % | 1973 % |
| --- | --- | --- |
| Farmers | | |
| Communist | 12 | 8 |
| Socialist | 20 | 19 |
| Centrist | 12 | 16 |
| Gaullist | 48 | 49 |
| Other | 8 | 8 |
| Industrialists & businessmen* | | |
| Communist | 10 | 12 |
| Socialist | 13 | 22 |
| Centrist | 15 | 22 |
| Gaullist | 53 | 36 |
| Other | 9 | 8 |
| Upper management, professionals | | |
| Communist | 10 | 11 |
| Socialist | 9 | 20 |
| Centrist | 23 | 20 |
| Gaullist | 48 | 39 |
| Other | 10 | 10 |
| Middle management, white-collar | | |
| Communist | 21 | 17 |
| Socialist | 15 | 29 |
| Centrist | 12 | 19 |
| Gaullist | 40 | 23 |
| Other | 12 | 12 |
| Workers | | |
| Communist | 33 | 33 |
| Socialist | 18 | 27 |
| Centrist | 8 | 12 |
| Gaullist | 31 | 22 |
| Other | 10 | 6 |

* 1973 data refer to small industrial and commercial employers.

Source: Sondages, 1968, No. 2, p. 102 and 1973, No. 1, p. 21. Reprinted by permission.

TABLE 2.3

## Class Differences in Voting Behavior, Britain

| | 1945 | 1955 | 1964 |
|---|---|---|---|
| **Upper middle class** | | | |
| Conservative | 76% | 89% | 77% |
| Labour | 14 | 9 | 9 |
| Liberal | 10 | 2 | 14 |
| **Middle class** | | | |
| Conservative | 61 | 77 | 65 |
| Labour | 24 | 21 | 22 |
| Liberal | 15 | 2 | 13 |
| **Working class** | | | |
| Conservative | 32* | 41 | 33 |
| Labour | 57* | 57 | 53 |
| Liberal | 11* | 2 | 14 |
| **Very poor** | | | |
| Conservative | 32* | 44 | 32 |
| Labour | 57* | 54 | 59 |
| Liberal | 11* | 2 | 9 |

* 1945 figures for "working class" and "very poor" are combined.

Source: Adapted from Henry Durant, "Voting Behaviour in Britain, 1945–64," in Studies in British Politics, ed. Richard Rose (New York: St. Martin's Press, 1968), p. 123.

believe there is conflict between classes. Thus, Marxist predictions that society would polarize along class lines and that class conflict would intensify have not been fulfilled in these countries. What class-based politics exists takes the thoroughly un-Marxian forms of labor union activities and voter alignments with political parties. Most of those in Britain who identify themselves as belonging to the working class vote for the Labour party, while most who regard themselves as middle- or upper-class vote Conservative. A similar pattern exists in France: the working class is more likely to vote for the leftist parties, and the middle and upper classes tend to support the Gaullists. In neither country, however, is the class basis of parties absolute, and there is evidence to suggest a further weakening of class/party alignments.[7]

The other political manifestation of class is the trade union movement. In both Britain and France, trade unions represent the working class in negotiations with government leaders, bureaucrats, and other interest group representatives over proposed policies. This is class conflict in the sense of competition for influence in policy-making, but it is obviously of very low intensity. Strikes represent a somewhat higher level of union-led class conflict. In Britain labor

7. See David Butler and Donald Stokes, Political Change in Britain, college ed. (New York: St. Martin's Press, 1971), pp. 126–134.

leaders use strikes as a means of achieving economic advances in the form of higher salaries or longer vacations, rather than for political purposes. The avoidance of political strikes and labor's resolve to keep strikes nonviolent have kept even this variety of class conflict at low levels of intensity. However, strikes can manifest growing worker unrest and can be a means of intensifying class conflict. For example, a work slowdown followed by a full strike by coal-miners demanding higher wages forced the economy into a three-day work week in late 1973 and early 1974. Ultimately, the Conservative government of Edward Heath sought a resolution to the crisis by calling new parliamentary elections in February 1974. The Conservatives lost the majority in these elections and a Labour-led government quickly resolved the miners' strike. In France there is a greater tendency toward political strikes, although in recent years communist and noncommunist labor leaders have tried to focus strikes on economic rather than political questions. However, the general strike that paralyzed France during the Events of May 1968 (discussed on pages 81–82) was in the tradition of political strikes, and illustrated the explosiveness of an effective general strike.

Other social cleavages continue to have political consequences. In France the longstanding struggle between clericals and anticlericals has lost most of its potency. There are periodic renewals of the conflict in debates over public subsidies to parochial schools, but these are only shadows of the old battles. The political alignments stemming from this now-resolved cleavage do persist, however, making the best single predictor of how a French citizen will vote his or her religious commitment. The more faithful to Catholicism, the more likely an individual is to vote for the Gaullist; the less devout, the more likely to vote for the leftist.

Regional conflicts of political significance exist in both Britain and France. For one thing, the political, economic, and social pre-eminence of London and Paris has created political division. Those who live outside the capitals feel that they do not receive a fair share of governmental service and attention. Furthermore, the highly centralized nature of both states has generated social tension and demands for greater regional autonomy. There is also, as we have

TABLE 2.4
*Party Preference by Degree of Religious Practice, France 1973*

|  | Regularly practicing Catholics | Occasionally practicing Catholics | Nonpracticing Catholics |
|---|---|---|---|
| Communist | 1% | 14% | 32% |
| Socialist | 10 | 22 | 31 |
| Centrist | 16 | 13 | 11 |
| Gaullist | 70 | 47 | 20 |
| Other | 3 | 4 | 6 |

*Source:* Sondages, *1973, No. 1, p. 26. Reprinted by permission.*

said, a significant urban/rural cleavage in France, which is the source of wide-spread agrarian discontent. Small farmers and peasants have not shared in the general postwar economic boom. The farm population is larger in France than in most other industrialized states, accounting for about one-ninth of the population. Yet approximately one out of three farms is too small to be economically viable. The flight of former peasants to the cities and the continuing low standard of rural living contribute to the malaise of French peasants. This unrest periodically explodes in protest demonstrations and confrontation politics.

Other regional conflicts reflect cultural and ethnic differences. In Britain the Welsh and the Scots demand greater autonomy and respect for their cultural traditions. Scottish Nationalists advocating autonomy for Scotland won nearly 30 percent of the Scottish vote, and Welsh separatists won nearly 11 percent of the Welsh vote in the October 1974 House of Commons' election. In France some Bretons call for an independent Brittany. Ethnic separatism is in part motivated by recognition of the relative economic underdevelopment of the group's regions, but it also reflects fear that the group's distinctive cultural traits are threatened with extinction on account of the emergence of a mass national culture. Thus, some of the forces contributing to social and political consensus — especially economic development, mobility, and mass communications — may provoke a back-to-the-roots reaction on the part of cultural minority groups that perceive threats to their cherished traditions.

Both Britain and France are experiencing growing social strain over immigrant racial minority groups. In Britain the immigration of "coloureds" from East Asian and West Indian Commonwealth countries has produced tensions in the populous centers where the immigrants have congregated. The newcomers compete with each other and with native British workers for jobs, health and education services, and, most importantly, low-cost housing. There have been a number of racial incidents — protests, demonstrations, and some violence — and racist slogans are commonplace on walls and buildings. Some political leaders — especially a faction of the Conservative party led by Enoch Powell until he left that party in 1974 — have sought to exploit these tensions by advocating restrictions on immigration and even the expulsion of the coloureds.

In France the immigration of pro-French Algerians after Algeria achieved independence in 1962, and the influx of foreign workers from Portugal, Italy, Spain, and elsewhere in response to the labor shortage of the 1960s, resulted in an immigrant population of over 3.7 million, or about 7 percent of the total population, by 1973.[8] In industrial areas the immigrant population is often as high as 12 percent of the total. As in Britain, the foreign workers tend to end up with those jobs that the French prefer not to take: street-cleaning, trash-collecting, and other unskilled labor. The foreign workers' dissatisfaction with these jobs and with slums (*bidonvilles*), coupled with French resentment toward them, touched off a series of violent incidents in 1973 and 1974 involving French workers and, usually, Algerians. As in Britain, the housing shortage

8. *Le Monde,* 23 January 1974.

and a tightening job market aggravated the basic intolerance of racially different peoples often exhibited by the lower classes.

## MAJOR SOCIAL CONFLICT IN BRITAIN AND FRANCE

The cleavages described above are more social differences than deep divisions. They have political consequences, but they have seriously threatened neither the overall stability nor the existence of the established regimes. However, this state of affairs does not preclude the possibility of future conflict. Indeed, two recent episodes, the conflict in Northern Ireland and the Events of May–June 1968 in France, illustrate how rapidly serious conflict can disrupt the political system.

The most critical threat to British national unity — and a clear source of present political instability — is the conflict between Catholics and Protestants in Northern Ireland. Northern Ireland is made up of the six northern counties (most of the province of Ulster) of Ireland. When the almost uniformly Catholic south obtained independence in 1921, predominantly Protestant Ulster, most of whose inhabitants were fiercely loyal to Britain, insisted on the partition of Ireland and the continued union of Northern Ireland to the United Kingdom. Over the objections of the Irish, the island was finally partitioned, Ulster remaining a part of Britain and the rest of Ireland gaining independence.

Today Northern Ireland continues to be a major problem for the British political system. The conflict there is essentially a cultural division between the Protestant two-thirds of the population and the Catholic one-third. The Protestants are descendants of Scottish immigrants who colonized Northern Ireland in the seventeenth and eighteenth centuries when others from Britain were colonizing America; the Catholics are Irish whose ancestors were dispossessed by the colonists. There is also a social and economic element in the conflict. Relative to the rest of Britain, Northern Ireland is industrially underdeveloped, and there is considerable economic discontent among both Protestants and Catholics. The Catholics allege economic discrimination in the form of lower salaries and lower-quality public services, such as council (public) housing. However, it is the religious aspect of the conflict that most deeply affects politics.[9] When class loyalty and ethnic loyalty conflict, the ethnic bond usually takes precedence. The Protestant worker joins middle-class Protestants to fight "popery" rather than joining the Catholic worker in a struggle against middle-class exploitation of the proletariat. Indeed, the militancy and extremism of the proletariat on both sides has caused the situation to be described as "the war of the proles": Catholic workers fight Protestant workers.

Unlike Scotland and Wales, Northern Ireland has had its own parliament

---

9. On this point, see the well-documented argument of Richard Rose, *Governing Without Consensus: An Irish Perspective* (Boston: Beacon Press, 1971), pp. 275–326.

and regional government, and considerable local autonomy. The Protestant two-thirds of the population has been able to control the Northern Irish government, and has used its ascendancy to assure continued political, economic, and social dominance over the Catholic minority. In the 1960s, a moderate Catholic civil rights movement, inspired by the civil rights movement in the United States, pressed for an end to discrimination.[10] However, reforms were slow in coming, and those that were instituted at the end of the 1960s were branded as insufficient by key sectors of the Catholic community and as excessive by some Protestants. In 1968 Catholic civil rights demonstrations and counter-demonstrations by Protestants led to rioting.

Once open conflict began, both sides revived the tactics and organizations of earlier confrontations. The memory of martyrs from earlier battles, celebrated in folklore and annual parades, provided models for today's militants. The Irish Republican Army (IRA), a militant Catholic nationalist group that had led the battle for Irish independence in the first few decades of the twentieth century, was revitalized. Growing rapidly in numbers and in activity, the IRA sought an end to British rule in Northern Ireland and the reunification of all Ireland. When the Provisional branch of the IRA began to perpetrate bombings and assassinations, the Northern Irish police proved unable to keep order. Furthermore, the police force is part of the problem, since it is virtually all-Protestant and is consequently distrusted by most sections of the Catholic community. Over 15,000 British troops were sent to Ulster, but they too failed to restore order. Most Catholics view the troops as agents of British domination and protectors of the Protestants.

In 1972 the British government moved to end the violence by dissolving the overtly anti-Catholic Ulster government and appointing a British governor to rule over Northern Ireland. At first the British governor made headway toward peace by adopting a more conciliatory attitude toward the Catholics, and freeing many Catholics being held in "preventive detention" without trial as suspected terrorists. The Protestants, fearing a British sellout of their interests, reacted by mobilizing their own irregular army, the Ulster Defense Association (UDA). The UDA began by taking reprisals against Catholics for IRA terrorism but ultimately clashed with British troops. By the middle of 1974 Northern Ireland had suffered more than 1,000 deaths directly attributable to the conflict and seemed headed toward open ethnic and religious civil war.

The British attempted to find a basis for a compromise settlement to the conflict. Despite the objections of extremists on both sides, elections for a new Northern Irish parliament were held in July 1973. Proportional representation — an electoral system that awards parties representation equivalent to

10. The decade of the 1960s was an era of growing assertiveness among ethnic minority groups in many countries. Northern Irish Catholics often rhetorically asked why, if the oppressed minority can rise in the United States and elsewhere, it cannot do so in Northern Ireland. The thesis of international contagion is supported by the fact that the Catholic civil rights movement was patterned on the American movement and even adopted its song, "We Shall Overcome."

the percentage of the popular vote they win — assured that Catholics would receive a fair share of the seats in the regional parliament. Cautious optimism was widely expressed when over two-thirds of the seats were won by moderates from both communities. While violence (including some bombings in London and other British cities) continued on a sporadic basis, optimism seemed even more justified when the executive was reorganized in late 1973 to share power between Catholics and Protestants. However, in the summer of 1974, Protestant extremists led a general strike that succeeded in toppling the moderate Protestant–Catholic coalition government. The result was the reimposition of direct rule from London, more violence, and a growing threat of civil war.

The government tried again to find a political solution to the dilemma. New elections for a constitutional convention were held in May 1975. The constitutional convention was then expected to draw up a new constitution for Northern Ireland that would incorporate the principle of power-sharing between the Catholic and Protestant communities. To bolster the prospects for success, the British warned that failure of power-sharing this time would lead to the termination of the annual subsidies from London of the nearly billion U.S. dollars that underwrite the Northern Irish economy. Prospects for the success of the new attempt at power-sharing hinge upon the ability of the moderates in both communities to prevail and to counter the anticipated violent reactions of both Catholic and Protestant extremists.

In the early spring of 1968, French political observers were debating whether or not the nation was bored as a result of the political and economic stability insured by the Gaullist regime. A few weeks later, student riots and a general strike provoked the most serious political crisis to confront the Fifth Republic and brought France to the brink of civil war.

Student unrest had a number of causes: seriously overcrowded university facilities, archaic university procedures, aloof professors, limited guest hours in dormitories, and uncertain job prospects for graduates. The French students were also clearly influenced by the student unrest and rioting that beset most Western democracies at the end of the 1960s.

The immediate cause of the student demonstrations was the closing of both the University of Paris at Narbonne and the Sorbonne in response to fighting between extremist groups of the Right and Left. The violence of the police in dealing with the students prompted the labor unions to call a general strike for May 13. In Paris on that day, a procession of 600,000 workers, students, teachers, and other sympathizers marched through the Latin Quarter. The purpose of the demonstration was to express support and sympathy for the students, but it was clear from the workers' placards that the unions were using the occasion to make their own demands. Spontaneous strikes broke out during the next week, followed by the occupation of factories by their workers. Eventually 8–10 million people took part in the strikes, and at the same time university students and many high-school students occupied their campuses. These strikes were spontaneous, resulting from the workers' sense that their problems were being neglected by the Gaullist regime. With the exception of the one-day general strike called for May 13, the national unions did not authorize these strikes. The Communist union and the non-Communist unions attempted to limit the strikers' claims to economic issues, rather than actively politicizing the strikes. In spite of their efforts, however, the strikes rapidly assumed a political flavor at the grass roots. Thus, when union leaders presented strikers the agreement they had reached with government and management, it was rejected. The reason for the rejection was not unsatisfied economic demands but political demands for the resignation of President de Gaulle and Prime Minister Pompidou.

The strikes, student riots, and occupations of factories, universities, and public buildings continued for over three weeks, ending when de Gaulle dissolved the National Assembly and called for new elections. This act shifted the focus of conflict from street politics and strikes to electoral politics. The strikes were quickly ended, student rioting abated, and order was restored as politicians and social leaders concentrated on the election. The overwhelming electoral victory of the Gaullists and the defeat of all left-wing forces even remotely associated with the crisis marked the final chapter in this episode.

The intensification of conflict to the point that it endangered the existence of the regime is explained by the romantic attraction of "revolution" in France. As we have said, many participants consciously patterned their vocabulary, goals, and actions on past revolutionary eras: the Revolution of 1789, the Revolution of 1848, the Paris Commune of 1871, and the General Strike of 1936. Present-day events provided the opportunity to experience firsthand the romance and glory of revolution, which could otherwise be experienced only through books. The implication of this argument is that France will always be vulnerable to periods of rapidly accelerating social conflict and near-revolution because serious conflict has been manifested thus in the past. The Events of May belong to a long history of glorious revolutionary episodes that will doubtless incite similar ventures in the future.

## DYNAMICS OF SOCIAL CLEAVAGES IN BRITAIN AND FRANCE

Democratic pluralist countries such as Britain and France must accept and regulate such conflict, since it is an inevitable concomitant of social pluralism. The free competition of social forces is simply a reflection of a variety of conflicts and cleavages that exist within the society. Consensus on basic issues helps to keep conflict at manageable levels, and such consensus on political and socioeconomic structures is usually the product of decades of conflict and compromise. Once established, it provides a framework for the management of conflict. It is only when this consensus breaks down (as it has in Northern Ireland) or is challenged (as it was during the Events of May) that democratic stability is endangered. Then, the maintenance of consensus is facilitated by willingness on the part of the majority to use force under most circumstances to preserve the status quo. Historical and contemporary evidence about the United States[11] and other Western democracies suggests that the public generally sanctions, and sometimes insists upon, the use of violence to maintain public order and the status quo. The reaction of the typical citizen to the turmoil of the 1960s illustrates this tendency. Black militants and antiwar activists in the United States, student rebels in France and elsewhere, and the IRA in Ireland have all been victims of official governmental violence as the majority rallied to the support of the existing order.

# China and the Soviet Union: Monolithic or Pluralist Societies

Marx and his followers believed that the eventual triumph of socialism would bring about a classless society. Since they considered all cleavages in capitalist societies to be manifestations of class conflict, the development of a classless society was expected to eliminate other cleavages. In practice, this has not proved to be the case. Both China and the Soviet Union provide evidence that social cleavages continue to exist and to affect politics in communist states.

Social pluralism in communist systems confounds not only Marxist ideology but also Western assumptions about the monolithic nature of communist societies. According to many Western critics, pluralism and social cleavages are prevented in communist states by the use of totalitarian controls. The result, they claim, is a monolithic society lacking the "natural" social divisions characteristic of the Western world. This view is not sustained by examination of the Soviet Union and China. Both exhibit far more social diversity and pluralism than is compatible with the monolithic model of communist societies. While this pluralism may be less openly expressed than in liberal democracies, it is present and politically influential.

## SOCIAL CLASS IN COMMUNIST SOCIETIES

The triumph of socialism in the Soviet Union has clearly not resulted in the elimination of socioeconomic class divisions. Soviet officials informally acknowledge the existence of three classes: workers, peasants, and the intelligentsia. Furthermore, there is within the intelligentsia a distinct sociopolitical class composed of party leaders and rank and file.

The peasant, or farm, population accounts for approximately one-third of the total Soviet work force, a much larger proportion than in most other industrial states. The peasantry has been suspect in the eyes of the Communist party elite since the inception of the Soviet Union. The peasant's attachment

11. Hugh Davis Graham and Ted Robert Gurr, "Conclusion," in *Violence in America: Historical and Comparative Perspectives* (New York: New American Library, 1969), pp. 787–788.

TABLE 2.5

## Monthly Incomes of Selected Occupations in the Soviet Union, 1960

| | |
|---|---|
| Top party and state leader | $ 2,220 |
| Scientist (academician) | $888–1,665 |
| Plant manager | $333–1,110 |
| Engineer | $111– 333 |
| Staff physician | $ 94– 111 |
| High school teacher | $ 94– 111 |
| Office clerk | $ 89– 100 |
| Skilled worker | $111– 278 |
| Semiskilled worker | $ 67– 100 |
| Unskilled worker | $ 37– 56 |
| Collective farmer | $ 30– 56 |

Source: Adapted from Vernon V. Aspaturian, "The Soviet Union," in Modern Political Systems: Europe, 3d ed., ed. Roy C. Macridis and Robert E. Ward (Englewood Cliffs, N.J.: Prentice-Hall), © 1972, p. 543. By permission of Prentice-Hall, Inc.

to the land has been regarded as a source of latent bourgeois desire for private, rather than public, ownership of land. Even after nearly all land had been collectivized, the peasants continued to be regarded as poor socialist citizens. Rather than devoting the bulk of their energies to the collective farms, they often spent excessive amounts of time on private plots cultivated for their own use and for sale at town markets.

Communist party membership is less prevalent among the farm population than in any other occupational category. In 1971 approximately 15 percent of the party membership was from farm occupations — about half the farm population's share in the total population. At the level of party leadership, the proportion of peasants or farmers is even lower. The weakness of the party in rural areas exacerbates tensions between the party and the farmers, since the party officials who regulate agriculture are often city-bred and relatively unfamiliar with farm problems.

Though agriculture has been subordinated to industrial development in the Soviet Union, the deliberate neglect of the farmer that was a feature of the Stalinist era has given way to greater concern in the past two decades. However, there remains a large gap between the standards of living of the farmer and the worker. The average annual income in cash and kind of the collective farmer is about 900 rubles, while that of the industrial worker is 1,600 rubles (a ruble is worth approximately $1.10).[12] While the income of the collective farmer has increased since 1953 when the income was about 300 rubles at present prices, the gap between worker and farmer remains large. Certainly

12. John A. Armstrong, *Ideology, Politics, and Government in the Soviet Union*, 3d ed. (New York: Praeger, 1974), p. 152.

Marx's vision of erasing the differences in the standard of living between town and country has not been fulfilled.

The situation of the worker is less enviable than might be expected in a "socialist state of workers and peasants." The worker may be subject to constant pressure from management, the party, and even the trade unions to maximize production. The choice of training, location, and job is often limited, or pre-empted, by the party and state. The early phases of Soviet industrialization were partly "financed" by the workers, who worked long hours under strict discipline. In the long run, though, the workers profited and their standard of living improved. If Soviet workers are still less affluent than their counterparts in western Europe, they are much better off than they or their parents were twenty years ago when the Soviet Union was still struggling to recover from wartime destruction.

Despite party leaders' repeated efforts to recruit workers, the working class appears to be underrepresented among the rank-and-file of the Communist party. At the level of party leadership, moreover, the number of workers is disproportionately low. Even more significant is the fact that in a workers' state ideologically committed to equality, there is an important discrepancy between the income and prestige of workers and those of more privileged social strata.

One of the privileged classes in Soviet society is the intelligentsia, those who perform mental and creative work rather than manual labor: scientists, economic planners, engineers, technicians, medical personnel, students and teachers, managers, bureaucrats, journalists, writers, artists, and the like. As the level of education in the Soviet Union has risen, so has the size of the intelligentsia; it now accounts for 30 million people, out of a total population of 240 million. The intelligentsia is a privileged class in terms of both social prestige and economic advantages. Its members, especially the more prominent scientists and creative artists, enjoy special respect in the eyes of the public and have access to better housing, greater travel opportunities, and higher salaries than do the workers or peasants. Perhaps most importantly, prominent members of the intelligentsia enjoy greater freedom of action and thought than the rest of society.

The Communist party increasingly draws its members, and especially its leaders, from the ranks of the better educated. Thus members of the intelligentsia and their children are more likely to achieve positions of prominence in the party and the state than are workers or peasants. Nevertheless, the intelligentsia too is suspect in the eyes of the party leaders, who fear that it poses a danger to the regime. Scientists are suspected of being more technocratic than ideological, and intellectuals (writers, poets, scholars) of opposing the regime. There is some cause for suspicion in that the intelligentsia is the major source of dissenters and ideological revisionists. Furthermore, control of these dissenters is sometimes difficult because their national and international renown protects them from the punishments meted out to other dissenters. Thus, the

Nobel Prize-winning novelists Boris Pasternak and Alexander Solzhenitsyn and the physicist Andrei Sakharov (who helped develop the Soviet hydrogen bomb) have made public protests that would have caused less prominent individuals to be confined in prisons or insane asylums. There is a price for such dissidence, however: Pasternak and Solzhenitsyn were prevented from participating in the Nobel ceremonies; Solzhenitsyn was eventually expelled from the Soviet Union; and Sakharov faced continual harassment and threats. While there are proportionately more dissenters among the intelligentsia than in other occupational groups, the intelligentsia is by no means seething with dissent. On the contrary, the overwhelming majority unquestionably accept the regime and the special advantages the regime bestows on them.

The party leadership and *apparatchiki* (full-time professional party workers) enjoy approximately the same economic rewards as the intelligentsia, considerable social prestige, and special political privileges. The party dominates all Soviet social, economic, and political activities, and its monopoly on decision-making powers affords its leadership sole control of national policy.

Indeed, the party elite is the ruling class of the Soviet Union. It is not a closed elite, since party members come from all social backgrounds. For a peasant or worker who desires higher social or political status, membership in the party and advancement through its ranks are among the surest means of upward social mobility. However, the sons and daughters of party leaders and apparatchiki (and of the intelligentsia) stand the best chance of receiving the university training that is increasingly valuable for progress through the party hierarchy.

The problem of eliminating social class differentiation has been attacked more energetically and persistently in the People's Republic of China, where the class cleavages inherited by the communist regime were severe. Edgar Snow describes China in the mid-1930s as follows:

> Have you ever seen a man — a good honest man who has worked hard, a "law-abiding citizen," doing no serious harm to anyone — when he has had no food for more than a month? It is a most agonizing sight. His dying flesh hangs from him in wrinkled folds; you can clearly see every bone in his body; his eyes stare out unseeing, and even if he is a youth of twenty he moves like an ancient crone. . . . Children are even more pitiable, with their little skeletons bent over and misshapen, their crooked bones, their little arms like twigs, and their purpling bellies, filled with bark and sawdust, protruding like tumors. . . .
>
> . . . The shocking thing was that in many of these towns there were still rich men, rice hoarders, wheat hoarders, money-lenders, and landlords, with armed guards to defend them, while they profiteered enormously. The shocking thing was that in the cities — where officials danced or played with sing song girls — there was grain and food, and had been for months.[13]

Many of China's major industries were in the hands of foreign investors; they and the Chinese military, merchants, and landed elite composed the upper classes. The pronounced class cleavages provided fertile ground for Chairman

13. Edgar Snow, *Red Star Over China* (New York: Grove Press, 1944), pp. 226–227.

Mao's analysis of the status quo and recommendations for change. One of his followers recalls the nature of prerevolutionary class conflict:

> My fellow students were nearly all the sons of landlords or merchants, as few poor boys ever got to school. I studied at the same desks with them, but many hated me because I seldom had any shoes and my clothes were poor and ragged. I could not avoid fighting with them, when they cursed me. If I ran to the teacher for help, I was invariably beaten by him. But if the landlords' sons got the worst of it, and went to the teacher, I was also beaten.[14]

With the establishment of the revolutionary regime, efforts were made to eliminate class differences. Land reforms undertaken to abolish the system of landlords and tenant farmers were followed by the aggregation of agricultural land into collective farms and, later, agricultural communes. Foreign-owned industries and commercial enterprises were expropriated and all other industry and commerce was gradually converted to state ownership. The regime made a special effort to provide political and educational opportunities to those classes that had previously been deprived of such benefits.

Interestingly, one of the first steps the Chinese took toward the elimination of class conflict was the identification of individuals with clearcut social classes. Peasants were classified as former landlords, rich peasants, middle peasants, or poor peasants. Students were subdivided into three broad classes: (1) "revolutionary classes," consisting of the children of workers, poor peasants, lower-middle peasants, revolutionary martyrs, revolutionary cadres, and revolutionary soldiers; (2) "backward classes," made up of the children of landlords, rich peasants, capitalists, "rightists," and "bad elements" (criminals, thieves, loafers, and former Kuomintang officials); and (3) the middle range or "free professions," including the children of doctors, teachers, technicians, middle peasants, and shop clerks. Once such class ties were identified, the new communist regime could give preference to those who had been disadvantaged under the old regime and limit the influence of those who had exploited others. The middle-range group was regarded as having particular potential, because many of its members had accepted the party's leadership.

Student sensitivity to class origins was encouraged in party and educational activities. One student noted:

> . . . We spent a great deal of time studying the origins and distinguishing characteristics of different social classes.
>
> As a result, the concept of class was very much in our minds. Everybody was evaluated in terms of his social class background. This did not mean that we had outright conflict within the school; actually, everybody continued to get along well enough. It was just that we began to grow more aware of an individual's class background and there was a tendency to explain his conduct in terms of this factor.[15]

14. *Ibid.,* pp. 328–329.
15. Ronald Montaperto, "Revolutionary Successors to Revolutionaries," in *Elites in the People's Republic of China,* ed. Robert Scalapino (Seattle: University of Washington Press, 1972), p. 596.

A major obstacle to the elimination of class differences is the emergence of new classes as the old are destroyed. As Soviet experience indicates, the elimination of classes rooted in capitalism may well be followed by the emergence of classes characteristic of a communist society. In a large state undergoing economic and social change, it is inevitable that social class differences develop between urban and rural residents, government administrators and those they govern, professionals and nonprofessionals, and educated and uneducated people.

In attempting to lessen the consequences of such new social differentiations, Mao utilized several devices. Mass migrations have been undertaken to minimize the differences between urban and rural life. Doctors, teachers, entertainers, and other trained individuals have been moved from the city to the countryside with the aim of providing the rural population (still about 80 percent of the total population) with the cultural attractions, medical care, and educational opportunities once available only in the cities. The regime has also sought to promote equality by requiring those of higher social status to exchange jobs with workers and peasants. Thus, industrial managers work on assembly lines or in the fields at harvest time; students and professors spend part of each year performing manual labor on farms or in factories; farmers and workers join the "revolutionary committees" that make decisions about the operation of their communes or factories.

The most dramatic and far-reaching of the Chinese attempts to disrupt the natural trends towards bureaucratization and class differentiation are the mass revolutionary movements. The Cultural Revolution of 1966–1970 was such a movement. Periodically, Mao sought to destroy the privileged bureaucracies he saw developing in the People's Republic of China, in order to prevent the emergence of new privileged classes and to perpetuate the social and economic equality that existed within the Communist movement during its long struggle for power. Mao has been willing to do so even at the cost of disrupting society and slowing economic development because the revolutionary spirit of equality has taken precedence over stability and economic progress for Mao and his followers.

The struggle against class differentiation divided the party and ultimately culminated in the Cultural Revolution. Liu Shao-chi, head of the government from 1959 to 1969, led a faction seeking more pragmatic approaches to national development that had opposed Mao in several key areas. In 1957 Liu had opposed the *hsia fang* movement to send leaders back to the countryside, arguing that leaders were scarce and needed in their usual positions. He also reintroduced personal incentives and private farm holdings. To promote industrial efficiency, Liu argued in favor of applying cost-benefit criteria designed to result in profits. Mao opposed these deviations from socialism, arguing that they would lead to exploitation by powerful and privileged individuals. A related issue in this conflict was the "red versus expert" debate. Mao sought in the early 1960s to launch a campaign promoting the virtues of expertise and commitment to socialist principles, especially the injunctions against the sins of status. Again, the entrenched urban elites and the experts, including many in high party positions, opposed the campaign. The political conflict over the dangers of class and status was resolved (at least for a while) by the Cultural Revolution, which was a triumph for Mao's egalitarianism. Liu and his followers were expelled from their positions in the party and in the government.

Neither China nor the Soviet Union has abolished social class distinctions. In the Soviet Union the elimination of traditional social classes was succeeded by the emergence of new ones. Even Mao's determined efforts to control status and privilege seem uncertain of success. The reason such distinctions inevitably revive is that any organizational system is characterized by distinct social roles and a hierarchy of authority. The various roles and levels in the organization require different skills, and thus accord different degrees of prestige. At best, a system dedicated to the achievement of equality and social justice can only regulate the distribution of material rewards; it cannot prohibit the natural stratification of society.

## CULTURAL PLURALISM IN THE SOVIET UNION AND CHINA

The most significant social cleavages in the Soviet Union are conflicts among nationality groups. The expansion of the Russian Empire subjected to czarist rule widely diverse ethnic groups, many of which had long histories as independent nations. Russia's cultural pluralism was the source of considerable tensions under the czarist regime: the Great Russian majority enjoyed economic, social, and political privileges not shared by other nationality groups within the empire. The Bolsheviks exploited these tensions at the time of the revolution by promising the minorities political autonomy and better treatment. Even under the communists, however, there continues to be social conflict stemming from cultural pluralism.

The Soviet Union takes pride in its cultural diversity and boasts of more than one hundred different nationality groups. The major nationalities are listed in Table 2.6.

Each nationality group has its own language, culture, and religion. Under Soviet rule distinctive languages have been tolerated to the extent that the language of each geographic area is used in its schools, economic transactions, and governmental affairs. In some cases, in fact, Soviet leaders have encouraged these languages by assisting non-Russian peoples to devise alphabets and written languages where none existed before. However, in accordance with communist ideology, the Soviet leaders have discouraged organized religion and have been particularly hostile to religions with spiritual ties outside the Soviet Union. For example, the Uniate Catholics of the Ukraine and the Lithuanian Roman Catholics were forced to break their ties with the Vatican; Russian Jews are automatically suspected of Zionism and sympathy for Israel; in Latvia and Estonia, special efforts have been made to suppress Lutheranism.

TABLE 2.6

## Major Ethnic Groups of the Soviet Union

| Nationality | Population (in millions) |
|---|---|
| Slavs | |
| *Great Russians | 129.0 |
| *Ukrainians | 40.8 |
| *Belorussians | 9.1 |
| Turko-Tatars | |
| *Uzbeks | 9.2 |
| Tatars | 5.9 |
| *Kazakhs | 5.3 |
| *Tadzhiks | 2.1 |
| Chuvash | 1.7 |
| *Turkmen | 1.5 |
| *Kirghiz | 1.5 |
| Caucasians | |
| *Azerbaidzhans | 4.4 |
| *Armenians | 3.5 |
| *Georgians | 3.2 |
| Baltics | |
| *Lithuanians | 2.7 |
| *Latvians | 1.4 |
| *Estonians | less than 1 |
| Others | |
| *Moldavians | 2.7 |
| Jews | 2.2 |
| Germans | 1.8 |

* Ethnic groups with their own union republics.

Source: 1970 census figures from Robert G. Wesson, The Soviet Russian State (New York: John Wiley and Sons, 1972), p. 309.

As a result of the geographic distribution of ethnic groups, the Soviet Union has — at least theoretically — a federal structure. As is suggested by its name, the Union of Soviet Socialist Republics is a federation of fifteen "union republics," each the home of a major ethnic group. In addition, twenty "autonomous republics" within these union republics allow for the self-determination of smaller ethnic groups. The Soviet constitution guarantees the union republics considerable autonomy and generous rights not matched by the American or Canadian federations: the rights to secede, to conduct diplomatic relations, and to maintain their own military establishments. These terms fulfill Lenin's prerevolutionary pledges to end the czars' "prison of nations" and to assure self-determination for the peoples of Imperial Russia in return for their support of the Bolshevik cause.

The Soviet federal structure is, however, rendered null and void by the highly centralized nature of the Communist party. Since the union republics act in unison under the direction of the party, real autonomy for ethnic groups is lacking. Distinctive social, economic, and political traits of the various nationalities have frequently been suppressed. The party is dominated by Slavs and especially by Great Russians: since 1964 all secretaries of the party's Central Committee have been Great Russians. Furthermore, although the various republics have "native" figurehead leaders, the actual leadership of non-Slavic republics is as a rule exercised by Great Russians and other Slavs who control the party.

The federal framework disguises the party's goal of assimilating all nationalities into a single nation through the creation of the "new Soviet Man." The chief vehicle of mass assimilation is the Russian language, which is used by the national government, the party, the military, nearly all institutions of higher education, and the national mass media. Furthermore, the Cyrillic alphabet of the Russian language has been imposed on nearly all the languages of the Soviet Union. Another means of assimilation is migration. Great Russians and other Slavs have been moved or encouraged to move into non-Slav areas, especially Central Asia and Siberia. As a consequence, all union republics have substantial Great Russian populations; in some cases the Russians outnumber the native population. Furthermore, members of minority groups who receive higher education are usually assigned their first jobs outside their native republics. Finally, the party is a major agent of assimilation, particularly at the level of the elite. By enforcing central discipline and standardizing the political orientation of the elite (whether they be administrators, industrial managers, intellectuals, or artists), the party serves as an important homogenizing agent in Soviet life.

Since Stalin's death, the assimilation process has not been characterized by compulsion. Instead, the regime weakens ethnic loyalties by offering incentives: education, social and economic advancement, general mobility, and political power. This philosophy is well described by one expert on Soviet nationality problems: "Soviet policy is not based on the principle, 'learn Russian or perish,' but rather 'learn Russian and prosper.' "[16] Assimilation has been furthered by Soviet success at industrialization and economic development. While the benefits of development are not always equitably distributed, they have been sufficiently widespread to justify and legitimize cultural assimilation.

The past decade has witnessed a resurgence of ethnic nationalism in the Soviet Union. Most ethnic unrest is still covert, but two groups have succeeded in bringing their dissent to the attention of the world and even of the Soviet citizenry. Jews, chafing under years of unofficial discrimination and official suspicion of their loyalty, have insisted upon their right to emigrate. Such dissent has sometimes been overt: in 1970 there was an attempted plane

---

16. Vernon V. Aspaturian, "The Non-Russian Nationalities," in *Prospects for Soviet Society,* ed. Allen Kassof (New York: Praeger, 1968), p. 163.

hijacking by Jews, and in March 1971 thirty Jews conducted a sit-in at government offices in Moscow to demand the right to emigrate. These tactics and the international attention they aroused have made it difficult to suppress Jewish unrest. As a result, Soviet officials reluctantly liberalized emigration requirements. Despite official efforts to slow the tide of Jewish emigration, the numbers leaving continue to grow; in 1973 nearly 35,000 Jews left the Soviet Union.

The Lithuanians are the other group whose unrest has taken violent forms and thus become public. In 1970 two plane hijackings were attempted by Lithuanians desiring to flee the Soviet Union: one succeeded and the other failed. And there was the case of the Lithuanian sailor who swam to a U.S. Coast Guard cutter only to be returned to his ship against his will. In 1972 there were three political suicides by Lithuanians who set themselves on fire, crying "Freedom for Lithuania." The funeral of one of the victims resulted in a mob of several thousand youths rampaging through Lithuania's largest city calling for freedom. The riots were followed by strikes, and ultimately the army had to be called in to restore order.

Unlike the Soviet Union, China has few major problems deriving from cultural pluralism. In terms of absolute numbers, Chinese ethnic minorities account for only about 5 percent of China's population. Though 95 percent of the population is ethnically uniform, however, linguistic differences divide the Han majority. The Han Chinese speak a number of mutually unintelligible dialects. Most speak one of the northern dialects commonly called Mandarin, and in recent years Mandarin has been promoted as the basis of a new national language. Other important dialects used by Hans, principally in the south, include Wu, Cantonese, and Hakka. In addition, several provinces have their own distinctive dialects. The linguistic diversity of the Hans is rendered somewhat less complex by the existence of a universal script that can be read by all Han Chinese. Language differences often affect interregional social attitudes and relations. For example, note the pleasure some southern students derived from their linguistic advantage over a group of northern (Peking) students: "We were repulsed by the conceit the Peking Red Guards displayed and thoroughly enjoyed putting them on. Peking dialect was commonly used all over the country, so we knew what they said; however, when we spoke in Cantonese, the Peking Red Guards could not understand us. When we cursed them, they simply smiled." [17]

The Chinese have strongly discouraged nationalist cleavages in the interest of pursuing the construction of socialism and modernization. Their goal is to eradicate the minorities' national aspirations without destroying their cultures. Ideally, for example, Tibetans will view themselves not as Tibetans but as Chinese of Tibetan descent. Integration is seen as requiring the establishment

17. Gordon A. Bennett and Ronald N. Montaperto, *Red Guard: The Political Biography of Dai Hsiao-ai* (New York: Doubleday, 1971), p. 134.

TABLE 2.7

## National Autonomous Districts of China

| Districts | National Minorities |
|---|---|
| Yunnan | |
| Te-hung | Thai and Chingpo |
| Hsi-shuang-pa-na | Thai |
| Hung-ho | Hani and Yi |
| Nu-chiang | Lisu |
| Ti-ch'ing | Tibetan |
| Ta-Li | Pai |
| Wen-shan | Chuang and Miao |
| Ch'u-hsiung | Yi |
| Kweichow | |
| Southeastern Kweichow | Miao and Tung |
| Southern Kweichow | Puyi and Miao |
| Szechwan | |
| Kan-tzu | Tibetan |
| A-pa | Tibetan |
| Liang-shan | Yi |
| Sinkiang Vigur Autonomous Region | |
| I-Li | Kazakh |
| K'e-tzu-Le-su | Khalka |
| Ch'ang-Chi | Hui |
| Pa-yin-kuo-leng | Mongol |
| Po-erh-ta-la | Mongol |
| Tsinghai | |
| Hai-pei | Tibetan |
| Hai-nan | Tibetan |
| Huang-nan | Tibetan |
| Yü-shu | Tibetan |
| Kuo-lo | Tibetan |
| Hai-hsi | Mongol, Tibetan and Kazakh |
| Kansu | |
| Liu-hsia | Hui |
| Southern Kansu | Tibetan |
| Hunan | |
| Western Hunan | Tuchia and Miao |
| Kwangtung | |
| Hainan | Li and Miao |
| Kirin | |
| Yen-pien | Korean |

Source: Winberg Chai, The New Politics of Communist China: Modernization Process of a Developing Nation (Pacific Palisades, Cal.: Goodyear Publishing Company, 1972), p. 14. Copyright © 1972. Goodyear Publishing Company. Reprinted by permission of the publisher.

of a uniform political culture and the development of a new Chinese citizen who will be supportive of a communist society.

While China has generally succeeded in integrating diverse cultural groups, it still faces problems originating in cultural pluralism. One such problem is the need to integrate the border-based ethnic groups psychologically with the rest of the nation. Ethnic groups that straddle the nation's frontiers are difficult to integrate successfully into the state, and also pose the potential for international conflict if both states claim the ethnic group and its homeland. It is along the Sino-Soviet border that the most critical problems and dangers of this nature exist. The border is poorly defined and disputed by both China and the Soviet Union. Ethnic groups — notably the Uighurs, Mongols, Kazakhs, Tadzhiks, and Kirghiz — overlap the border. Each side has made claims on territories now held by the other and manipulated ethnic groups to support its claims. The result has been a prolonged border dispute that periodically flares into open military confrontation and battle. So far military clashes have remained limited, but the potential for a major political and military showdown clearly exists.

Another problem for China is Tibet. China has claimed sovereignty over Tibet since conquering it in the eighteenth century. In 1914 Tibet achieved relative independence under British sponsorship in order to serve as a buffer state between British India and czarist Russia. In 1950 the Chinese reoccupied Tibet and announced its integration into China as an autonomous republic. The powers of the Dalai Lama, Tibet's all-powerful spiritual leader, were curtailed; Chinese communist leaders were installed; and immigration of Han Chinese was encouraged. In 1959 the Tibetans revolted against Chinese rule and curtailment of the powers of religious orders. The revolt was crushed and the Dalai Lama fled to India. The Chinese replaced him with the Panchen Lama, who was expected to be more cooperative. He too proved insufficiently compliant, however, and in 1964 the Chinese removed him from office. Further evidence of Tibetan unrest came to light during the Cultural Revolution, when Red Guard activities aroused resentment and upheaval in Tibet.

## THE DYNAMICS OF SOCIAL CLEAVAGES
## IN COMMUNIST SYSTEMS

The rise and decline of social cleavages in communist states is much more directly influenced by government and party than is the case in Western societies. Though neither China nor the Soviet Union is monolithic, the political manifestations of social divisions are subject to stringent regulation by the party. Further, not all social cleavages are manifested politically. At times the party loosens its social controls and divisions become more evident. For example, the Soviet Union has experienced "thaws," characterized by freer expression of pluralist tendencies, during the de-Stalinization drive of the mid-1950s and again during the mid-1960s. At these times social cleavages were more readily apparent and protest, especially among intellectuals, was allowed.

A similar thaw took place in China during the "Hundred Flowers" era of the middle 1950s, when Mao proposed to "Let a Hundred Flowers Bloom and a Hundred Schools of Thought Contest." This official tolerance of diversity encouraged intellectuals and others to criticize the party and to present differing views of society. Eventually, the party concluded it was fostering "poisonous weeds" instead of flowers and reinstituted strict controls to crush re-emergent "bourgeois" or nonconformist thought. During the Cultural Revolution ethnic loyalties resurfaced and class feuds erupted throughout China's countryside. However, this manifestation of latent pluralism was also short-lived.

What the party gives, it can take away. Any expression of political pluralism is subject to the forbearance of the party elite, which places severe limitations on manifestations of social division. They are tolerated only so long as they neither challenge the supremacy and infallibility of the party nor represent bourgeois ideological deviations. China and the Soviet Union both give evidence of continued willingness to use force to suppress such threatening divisions.

Repression is not the only explanation, nor even the primary one, for these nations' success in controlling pluralism. Both have used positive incentives to minimize conflict. The tolerance of ethnic languages and folkways has made integration less distasteful to minority groups. Communication and interaction between social classes have been fostered. Economic development of outlying areas has been undertaken to alleviate regional conflicts. In contemporary China and the Soviet Union, the traditionally deprived groups — workers, peasants, and ethnic minorities — are far better off than they were under the czars and the emperors. Inequities still exist, but economic development, industrialization, and material advantages are far more widely and equitably distributed than in the past. All groups have shared in the advantages of economic growth and industrialization, though some more than others.

# Mexico and Nigeria: Dimensions and Challenges of Integration

Cultural cleavages in developing societies are rendered highly complex by the interaction of traditional divisions — ethnic, religious, regional, and class — with new social identifications. In the traditional rural–agricultural society, individuals belong only to kinship, ethnic, and religious groups. With modernization — the process whereby a society evolves from traditional social, economic, and political structures to new institutions — new social groups emerge. Individuals find themselves to be members of more than one group simultaneously. An individual is a member not only of a family, religious, and regional group, but also perhaps of an occupational group, a civic association, a sports club, a charitable organization, or even a political action group. Thus, a man may be black, Catholic, a chemistry professor, a member of the American Chemical Association, an employee of a large chemical firm, a member of a golf club, an Optimist, a member of a neighborhood association, and perhaps a member of a political party.

At first glance, Mexico and Nigeria appear to represent two distinct configurations of social cleavages: Nigeria with strong ethnic and regional divisions, and Mexico with clear socioeconomic class divisions. However, both societies (particularly Mexico, because of its longer period of industrialization) are developing other cleavages associated with the modernization process. In Mexico and Nigeria social tension emanates from legacies of class, regional, religious, and ethnic divisions, which are often institutionalized into deep social cleavages. The traditional cleavages frequently become so deeply embedded in the newly emergent political institutions — such as parties, interest groups, and policy-making procedures — that they inhibit formation of the new social divisions that usually accompany modernization. To prevent these potentially divisive factors from impairing political stability, developing nations must devise effective strategies of national integration. In the case of China, the government has made efforts at eliminating class and ethnic barriers. Mexico and Nigeria have responded differently to the challenge of controlling traditional cleavages and forging national unity. Let us examine their responses.

## SOCIAL CLASS CLEAVAGES IN MEXICO AND NIGERIA

The evolution of Mexico's class structure is typical of a nation in the early stages of economic development. Since the turn of the century, Mexico's upper class has grown from 1 percent to an estimated 6 percent of the population, and the middle class from approximately 8 percent to around 20 percent; the lower classes, including both urban proletariat and rural peasantry, now comprise about 74 percent of the total population.[18] While the Mexican middle class is growing rapidly for a developing country, the gap between the very poor and the very rich is large and growing. One scholar points out that in 1950 the average income of the wealthiest sector of society was twelve times that of the poorest sector; by 1964 it was eighteen times.[19] These statistics reflect the stubborn persistence of class differences despite industrialization. Mexico's impressive economic development continues to have no effect on many members of the lower classes. In the past twenty-five years, Mexico's gross national product and per-capita income have both more than doubled, but distribution of these benefits remains uneven. Mexico's urban slums contain increasing numbers of persons who exist at the subsistence level, and an even larger percentage of the population ekes out a marginal existence in rural areas.

Urban and rural poverty are two distinct phenomena. Despite subsistence-level income or unemployment, city-dwellers have greater access to opportunities

18. Pablo Gonzáles Casanova, *Democracy in Mexico* (New York: Oxford University Press, 1970), pp. 112–113.
19. Victor Alba, *The Mexicans* (New York: Pegasus, 1970), pp. 242–243.

TABLE 2.8

*Occupational Structure in Mexico*
*(percent of total employment)*

| Year | Agriculture | Industry | Services |
|------|-------------|----------|----------|
| 1940 | 65.4 | 12.7 | 21.9 |
| 1950 | 58.3 | 15.9 | 25.7 |
| 1960 | 54.1 | 19.0 | 26.9 |
| 1964 | 52.3 | 20.1 | 27.6 |

*Source: Roger D. Hansen,* The Politics of Mexican Development *(Baltimore: Johns Hopkins Press, 1971), p. 43, from various issues of Nacional Financiera, La Economía mexicana en cifras. Reprinted by permission.*

and amenities than do the rural poor. Cities offer more and better schools, more cultural diversity, and higher-paying jobs than do rural areas. Sanitation, though poor in urban slums, may be considerably better than is available to those lowest on the rural social scale. Urban slum housing, as bad as it is, often far surpasses the mud adobe huts and mud floors of the rural masses. Running water, health clinics, schools, and movie theaters are all available in the neighborhood of the urbanite; for the rural resident, they may be miles away at best. While there are some relative advantages in urban as opposed to rural poverty, neither is a tolerable norm. In fact, the alienation and psychological isolation that compound the material sufferings of the urban poor suggest that it may be the possibilities rather than the realities of urban life that make cities so attractive to rural immigrants.

Mexico's class disparities have had profound political consequences. During the decade 1910–1920, class tensions led to an anarchic civil war in which peasant armies fought government forces and each other. Eventually, the lower classes were organized into labor and agrarian interest groups. Labor was actively recruited for, and ultimately instrumental in, Carranza's successful 1917 drive for the presidency. Since that time, the peasant and labor sectors have become an integral part of Mexico's politics through Mexico's dominant party (PRI).

The ability of labor and the peasantry to identify with their occupational groups and along class lines has stabilized Mexico's political system — which is essential to political institutionalization — and provided long-term payoffs to both groups. Granted, these payoffs have been minimal, especially for the peasants. However, the elite realizes that its position is dependent upon the support of these groups and takes appropriate action to maintain their support. This dependency pattern, or "patron-client link," is an important integrating structure, reflecting and, in fact, institutionalizing class relationships. It is characterized by hierarchical and unequal reciprocal relations. The patron, who has more resources at his disposal than do the clients, clearly dominates exchanges of material (money, clothes, and food), status (jobs, offices), and votes.

There is a wide gulf — indeed a chasm — between the massive numbers of very poor and the handful of very wealthy people and little evidence that it is narrowing. Furthermore, tensions are likely to increase as more Mexicans move from rural settings, where they were isolated from politics, to urban settings, where they become aware of politics and are accessible to political organizers. This phenomenon might pose a serious threat to the regime should the poor become convinced that the government fails to meet their needs. Thus far the leadership has successfully deflected the blame for economic discontent onto others: the church, greedy, corrupt bureaucrats, and foreigners. The PRI, the presidents, and the Revolution have thus avoided blame for continued inequities. Furthermore, the regime has proved capable of responding to serious threats by enacting reforms that undercut resentment of the regime itself. The future stability of the regime hinges upon the leadership's continued ability to direct blame away from itself and to respond to imperative needs for reform.

Nigerian society is also characterized by class distinctions. However, they have neither become determinants of psychological identification nor given rise to partisan activities, as in Mexico. This is attributable to the dominance of ethnic and regional identifications and of patron-client links that cut across class lines. The strong kinship and village ties that characterize traditional Nigerian society give rise to interdependent patron-client relationships. These relationships are hierarchical, and those who possess valuable property, status, or high office are able to build followings among those of lesser means and status. Thus a propertied Ibo may well be a member, or the head, of the village council. If he also has a relative who is influential in the armed forces or a federal ministry, he will be able to assist villagers of lesser status with, for instance, recommendations for federal jobs. In exchange for such favors, he receives their future support and recognition of his leadership status. While hierarchical relationships persist in both rural and urban Nigeria, social identification remains firmly bound to one's family and, when challenged by other ethnic groups, one's ethnic group. These familial and cultural identifications tend to retard the development of socioeconomic class identifications.

Social mobility may cause the individual to be confronted with conflicting demands on his or her loyalty. In the early stages of mobility, ethnic identity is preserved and reinforced by strong community pressures. Thus the migrant Ibo who leaves his native eastern region for Lagos in the west is likely to choose a residence in Lagos inhabited by Ibos and easterners. Workers studied prior to the 1964 elections were found to prefer the labor party to ethnic-based political parties, but they cast their votes for the ethnic-based parties.[20] This phenomenon suggests the slow emergence of class awareness, and the continued strength of ethnic and kinship–village ties. With the discovery and production of oil from vast reserves, Nigeria's class distinctions are becoming more pro-

20. Robert Melson, "Ideology and Inconsistency: The Cross-Pressured Nigerian Worker," in *Nigeria: Modernization and the Politics of Communalism*, ed. Robert Melson and H. Wolpe (East Lansing: Michigan State University Press, 1971), pp. 581–605.

nounced. Seventy percent of the population still live at subsistence level and are engaged in agriculture, while a very small group of nouveau riche Nigerian business and government elite enjoy newly discovered luxuries.

If class identification is nascent among workers, it is both more advanced and more directly related to political activities among entrepreneurs. As might be expected, middle- to upper-class businessmen play a prominent part in the politics and economics of Nigeria. One study of political parties before the Biafran civil war revealed that businessmen made up a disproportionately large share of the leadership and membership of all three major parties.[21] They are also important sources of financial support for the parties. Furthermore, foreign businessmen involved in the Nigerian economy enjoy special privileges and are often lent a receptive ear by important government policy-makers.

## ETHNIC DIVISIONS IN MEXICO AND NIGERIA

Both Mexico and Nigeria confront problems stemming from cultural pluralism. A century and a half after independence, Mexico is still troubled by the major racial cleavages it inherited from its Spanish colonial past. While approximately two-thirds of the population are mestizos, there are more than 3 million Indians, of whom about one-third speak only their native languages.

A noted Mexican scholar, Gonzáles Casanova, observes that Indians are exploited by a form of internal colonialism. Municipal centers controlled by Ladinos (mestizos) "exercise a monopoly over Indian commerce and credit, with relationships of exchange unfavorable to the Indian communities."[22] These commercial monopolies, he argues, isolate the Indians from other centers or markets and thus result in dependency. Further, Indians are exploited as laborers and sharecroppers, living in virtual peonage in exchange for minimal services. Indians are also distinguished from similarly impoverished mestizos by the unique characteristics of their existence:

> Indian communities have . . . a predominantly subsistence economy, with minimal money and capitalization; lands unsuitable for crops or of low quality, unfit for agriculture because of hilly terrain, or of good quality but in isolated locations; deficient crop-growing and cattle-breeding because of low quality seeds and inferior animals smaller than the average of their kind and pre-Hispanic or colonial techniques of land exploitation; a low level of productivity; standards of living lower than those of peasants in non-Indian areas, exemplified by poor health, high rates of mortality, including infant mortality, illiteracy and the presence of rickets; lack of facilities and resources, such as schools, hospitals, water and electricity; promotion of alcoholism and promotion of prostitution by hookers and Ladinos; aggressiveness among communities, which may be overt, or expressed through games or dreams; magic-religious culture; economic manipula-

---

21. R. L. Sklar, "Contradictions in the Nigerian Political System," *Journal of Modern African Studies* 3, no. 2 (1964): 204–205.

22. Gonzáles Casanova, *Democracy in Mexico*, pp. 85–86.

tion through the imposition of taxes and a status-bound economy; and . . . political manipulation.[23]

Perhaps more important than geographic isolation is psychological isolation, the source of the Indian's reluctance to make demands on government. The Indian regards himself as uninvolved in the politics and economy of the national state, whether or not this is the case. He is usually uninterested in the government's activities and does not desire to know more about them. This apathy derives in part from cynicism about what government can or will do for him, and in part from the sense that the Indian way of life is superior to that of the rest of society. The Indian outlook prompts him not to confront and master his environment but to accept and live in harmony with it.[24] These attitudes explain why the unassimilated Indian population is not often a source of instability in contemporary Mexican politics. As one scholar has noted about the Indian's expectations from the government: "If it is outside his nature to conquer his environment, he will scarcely demand that the government do it for him."[25]

The assimilation process is not easy for those Indians who are caught up in it. Other Indians ostracize those who begin to accept modern culture, and it is often difficult for them to find a place in society once they leave their native villages. Oscar Lewis describes the trials of assimilation in his study *Pedro Martinez*,[26] in which he describes the life of an Indian family living at the subsistence level in rural Mexico. Pedro's primary concern is to adapt to mestizo lifestyles. Spanish is replacing his native Nahuatl dialect. Yet, like other peasants, he is fatalistic and mistrustful, and his attitudes toward government are chiefly awe and fear. Indians and peasant mestizos who are making the transition from traditional village cultures to the national culture may eventually pose a threat to Mexico's racial and cultural harmony. As these individuals are assimilated, their expectations of a modern existence and their desires for the upward mobility of their children may well become serious destabilizing factors in Mexican politics.

There is no governmental obstacle to the integration of the Indians, but the regime has shown little interest in actively promoting assimilation. Periodic efforts have been made to teach Spanish to Indians and to improve communication with remote tribes by constructing roads and installing telegraph or telephone lines. But these efforts have lacked adequate financing and sufficient government commitment to be successful. Similarly, land reforms aimed at fulfilling the Revolution's promise to give land to the Indian and poor mestizo have done little to improve the position of the Indian: only one-fifth of all Indians possess land of their own.

23. *Ibid.*, p. 87.
24. See Robert E. Scott, *Mexican Government in Transition*, rev. ed. (Urbana: University of Illinois Press, 1964), pp. 64–65.
25. *Ibid.*, p. 65.
26. Oscar Lewis, *Pedro Martinez* (New York: Random House, 1964).

The Mexican government's attitude toward the Indian is paradoxical. On the one hand, the Indian is idealized as the oppressed victim of colonization and the tyrannies of the nineteenth century and as a revolutionary hero and chief beneficiary of the Revolution of 1910. Ancient civilizations are praised and studied by one of the world's finest archeological museums. And the cultural richness of contemporary Indian life is highly valued. On the other hand, the Indian is ignored by government. Few efforts are made to improve the quality of Indians' lives or even to fulfill their basic health and nutritional requirements. The government's policy toward the Indians is determined by the Instituto Indigenista (Institute for Natives), which exists to upgrade the Indians' standard of living. However, divergent forces contend within this agency. One group is convinced of the need to "raise the Indians to a higher level of civilization," while another faction argues for the preservation of the Indians' own unique cultural heritage. As frequently happens, such a split results in a minimal policy — in this case, literacy drives and the introduction of the Spanish language. This minimal goal is expected to help make Mexico a unified nation.

Nigeria's basic cleavages are ethnic and regional. There are 18 different ethnic groups and nearly 400 linguistic subgroups among the 60 million people in Nigeria. The three main groups are the Hausa and Fulani of northern Nigeria, the Ibos of southeastern Nigeria, and the Yoruba of southwestern Nigeria. Table 2.9 indicates the relative sizes of the several ethnic groups. Each of the three main groups is centered in a single region, although some members of each

TABLE 2.9
## Major Ethnic Groups in Nigeria

| | Estimated ethnic population (in millions) | Estimated ethnic percentage |
|---|---|---|
| Hausa-Fulani | 15.3 | 29 |
| Yoruba | 10.8 | 20 |
| Ibo | 9.8 | 17 |
| Tiv and Plateu Cluster | 4.8 | 9 |
| Kanuri | 2.5 | 5 |
| Ibibio | 3.2 | 6 |
| Idoma | 1.4 | 2.6 |
| Edo types | 1.7 | 3.3 |
| Ijaw | 1.08 | 2 |
| Bororo (pastoral Fulani) | .975 | 1.5 |
| Nupe | .682 | 1.2 |

Source: Official Nigerian Census, vol. 3 (1963) and New York Times Encyclopedic Almanac, 1972. These selected groups do not constitute the total population.

reside in other regions; there are several minority groups in every region. Figure 2.1 shows the locations of the principal groups. The Hausa-Fulani, the Ibos, and the Yorubas are clearly differentiated from each other by language (each has its own distinctive language and several dialects), by religion (the Hausa-Fulani are mainly Moslem; there are many indigenous religions; and the Christians are mostly Ibos and Yorubas), and by lifestyle (the Hausa-Fulani are nomadic tribes; the Ibos and Yorubas are more sedentary, urbanized, and educated). The generally coincident nature of linguistic, religious, and life style cleavages along tribal lines renders the gulf separating the various cultural groups in Nigeria both wide and deep.

The system of indirect colonial rule employed by the British helped to institutionalize Nigeria's linguistic, ethnic, and regional differences. The British recruited the most respected native leaders, who were often granted considerable political authority, and employed the ethnic unions to administer politics at

FIGURE 2.1
*Nigeria's Main Ethnic Groups*

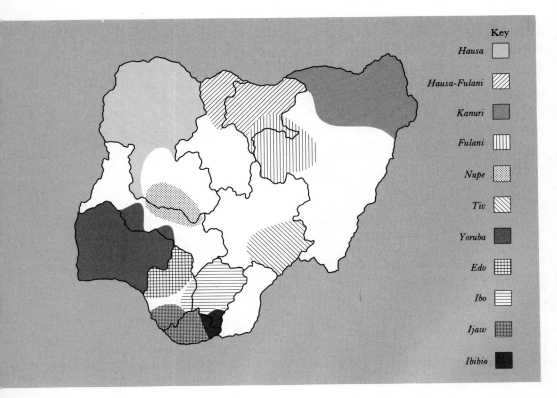

Key

Hausa
Hausa-Fulani
Kanuri
Fulani
Nupe
Tiv
Yoruba
Edo
Ibo
Ijaw
Ibibio

*Source:* Nigerian Politics *by John M. Ostheimer, p. 10. Copyright* © *1973 by John Ostheimer. By permission of Harper & Row, Publishers.*

the local level. The result was that the authority of tribal rulers was enhanced, regional outlooks were perpetuated, and interaction among Nigeria's numerous ethnic groups was not encouraged.

With the achievement of independence of 1960, the need to allocate very scarce resources further intensified ethnic tensions. While the presence of three major ethnic groups, each with its own political network and region, would challenge any new nation, Nigeria's problems were enhanced by large-scale migrations. Under colonial rule considerable numbers of Ibos and Yorubas moved to the north, and Hausa traders moved to all parts of the nation from the north. Each relocated ethnic group founded a "union" to maintain its customs, cultural attributes, and ties to its home region. As is frequently true of those impelled by ambition to relocate, many of the immigrants were more successful than the average inhabitants of the localities to which they had moved. The presence of these immigrant groups outside their own regions — but with firm ties to their kinship groups — was the spark that led to the civil war of 1966–1970.

## RELIGIOUS AND REGIONAL CLEAVAGES

Since Mexico's independence, religion has been a perpetual subject of political debate. While nearly all Mexicans are Catholics (91 percent of the population in 1970), Mexico has shared with other Catholic countries political division over the proper extent of the church's influence on society and politics. Conflict between clerical and anticlerical elements among the crillos and middle-class mestizos played an important part in the turmoil of the nineteenth century, and the struggle to separate church and state was long and bitter. In 1857 the constitution formally separated church and state, but the church continued to wield political, social, and economic power. The 1917 constitution further restricted the role of the church, prohibiting it from acquiring land and nationalizing all former church properties. In the 1920s an attempted revolt by militant Catholics provoked a stern reaction. The government suppressed the political influence of the priesthood and went so far in the 1929–1931 period as to close the churches themselves. President Emilio Portes Gil (1928–1930) was able to reach an understanding with the church that led to a relatively stable relationship with the government.

The church still maintains considerable influence over its followers, and its influence has occasionally taken political form. In the early 1940s many Catholics were considerably attracted to the *Sinarquista* movement, which advocated restoration of the hierarchical religious-led state. This movement succeeded in electing a governor in Guanajuato before its political aspirations were undermined by the rise of Partido de Acción Nacional (PAN), a more moderate conservative Catholic party.

While regional and religious cleavages are both more pronounced in Nigeria than in Mexico, the former have had greater impact on Nigerian political stability. Nigeria's religious character — the predominance of Muslims in the north, a large segment of Muslims amid Christians and animists in the west, and large numbers of Christians in the east — has had less political significance. The exception is the close ties between the Muslim religion and the social and political culture of the north. In that region, divisions between modernizers and traditionalist Muslim leaders have been reflected in political party and pressure group cleavages.

In Nigeria regional divisions reflect and aggravate socioeconomic divisions and ethnic cleavages. The gravity of regional social disparities between regions is evident in the following figures: in 1963 there were some 2.5 million primary students in southern Nigeria and fewer than .5 million students in the north, even though the north contained approximately 30 million people out of a total population of 56 million. Similarly, power consumption was much greater in the south (270 million kilowatt hours in 1964) than in the north (40 million kilowatt hours).[27]

Resources are distributed inequitably in Nigeria, and the more developed regions tend to be reluctant to share their resources with other regions. This problem became acute when the northern region, because of its larger population, succeeded in gaining political control. Resentment aroused by the use of this power, aggravated by coinciding ethnic cleavages, precipitated the military coups of 1966 and the Biafran secession of 1967.

## CIVIL WAR IN NIGERIA

Nigeria's move toward independence caused several ethnically based political parties to emerge, supposedly to promote national unity. The Northern People's Party (NPC) represented the Hausa and Fulani peoples; the Action Group (AG) appealed to a national audience but was primarily based on the support of Yorubas; and the National Council of Nigerian Citizens (NCNC) was the party of the Ibos, despite its desire to appeal to other ethnic groups. Politics quickly acquired a pronounced ethnic or communal orientation. Competition between parties was intense and often violent. By the early 1950s the phenomena that were to characterize Nigerian politics after independence had already emerged: politics steeped in interethnic and interregional tensions and competition, conflict within each region between the dominant group and the region's minorities, and a gradual deterioration of the federal compact.

Federalism was the strategy devised by the Nigerians, with the aid of the British, to cope with their ethnic and regional problems. Each ethnic group was to be politically dominant in its own region. The federal division of powers assigned control of essential governmental services with ethnic ramifications to the regional governments. Among the tasks conferred on the regional governments, and thus on the major ethnic groups, were education, public health, and local economic development. However, Nigerian federalism not only failed to provide an effective means of political integration but actually promoted intensified ethnic conflict. The Northern Region, the least economically devel-

27. Sklar, "Contradictions in the Nigerian Political System."

oped, had a larger population than the other regions combined. Thus, once politically organized, northerners could dominate federal Nigerian politics and use their political control to divert the resources of the other regions for their own use. The Eastern Region, homeland of the Ibos and numerous minority groups, was economically better off than most of Nigeria, and this economic disequilibrium was increased by the discovery and exploitation there of large oil deposits. Many Ibos felt that too much of their revenues was being siphoned off for other regions.

The existing political structures were not the only factors tending to exacerbate the ethnic aspect of this regional conflict. The migrations of ethnic groups to regions where they were minorities also aroused political tensions. In particular, Ibos moving to the Northern Region found themselves in the midst of resentful and jealous hosts. Ibo markets were often more successful than those of the region's native Hausa-Fulani.

These tensions were important background factors in the political strife that resulted in the 1966 military coups. The first coup in January was undertaken by young reformist army officers who apparently found the irresponsible activities of the politicians intolerable. When the dust had settled after the first coup, General Johnson Aguyi-Ironsi was at the head of the new military order. General Ironsi, although an Ibo, was committed to the national unity of Nigeria. Like many others in the military, he put professional and national interests above ethnic loyalties. However, rumors circulated that Ironsi was under the influence of Ibos. These rumors were fed by Ironsi's efforts to merge the civil services of the various regions — a reform that would have undermined regional–ethnic control of the bureaucracy and of civil service jobs. In addition, competition among ethnic groups over markets, land, political positions, employment, educational opportunities, and even language was growing. The tendency was widespread to blame competition from other ethnic groups for an individual's inability to find a job, secure the desired education, or find adequate housing. This high level of ethnic tension made it difficult for the Hausa to accept rule by an Ibo. The northern Hausa feared an Ibo plot to gain national political control, and acted to prevent this from happening. Their first target was the large Ibo population that had settled in the north. In May 1966 there occurred attacks on the Ibo immigrant population in the north. In July a second military coup resulted in the murder of Ironsi and the ascension of General Gowon, a Tiv who had the full backing of the Hausas.

Attacks on Ibo immigrants continued in the north, especially in the city of Kano. By October violence in the north had reached a peak, and the Ibos began to flee to the south. Ibos arriving at Kano's airport in October were attacked by Hausas with automatic weapons. The result was a highly inflammatory bloodbath in which several thousand Ibos were massacred; more than 1 million were forced to flee the north.[28]

28. John Paden, "Communal Competition, Conflict and Violence in Kano," in *Nigeria: Modernization and the Politics of Communalism*, ed. Robert Melson and H. Wolpe (East Lansing: Michigan University Press, 1971).

The Ibos now demanded more autonomy through a confederal formula assuring greater powers for their regional government. Negotiations toward this goal failed, and in May 1967 the Eastern Region seceded, declaring itself the Republic of Biafra. The Nigerian military immediately launched a two-pronged attack on the east; the civil war was under way. After an initial Biafran advance, the Nigerian army was successful in reducing the territory of Biafra. However, decisive victory eluded both sides and there ensued a war of attrition, in which the Nigerian forces cut off the flow of urgently needed food, medicine, and military supplies to the Biafrans. After two-and-a-half years and an estimated 1 million casualties, Biafra surrendered in January 1970.

The former Eastern Region was redrawn and reintegrated into a twelve-state Nigeria. To a certain extent the war exhausted but did not eliminate ethnic tensions. At the present time there is greater ethnic harmony in Nigeria than at any time since independence. Under General Gowon's leadership, economic development proceeded in all parts of Nigeria. However, industrialization and economic progress should not be seen as an automatic solution to the problems of cultural pluralism. In the past, economic development in Nigeria contributed to racial tension by accentuating interregional economic differences and encouraging the migration of ethnic groups from their home regions to the cities.[29] If, as in the past, development is inequitably concentrated in any single region, the disparity between regions will increase. Such uneven economic growth is highly conducive to the type of regional animosity that led to the Ibo independence movement. It also tends to stimulate migration, which leads to concentrations of the ethnic minorities in urban areas and heightens urban tensions. If the government is unable to provide employment opportunities, these ethnic tensions are likely to increase and again to pose a threat to the nation's political stability.

Another potential source of instability is Ibo resentment, and even desire for revenge, stemming from the civil war. The new federal framework of twelve states reduces the area under Ibo control, and the new state boundaries have been drawn in such a way as to remove Port Harcourt, a leading industrial center in "Iboland," from the east central state (the heart of the Ibo region).

Brigadier Muritala Rufai Muhammed's military regime is attempting to remedy weaknesses inherent in the previous governmental structures that rendered nearly impossible the avoidance of civil war. The military regime is encouraging integration through institutional changes, including the substitution of nineteen new states for the former regions. Centralized rule exists with nominal federal structures. Other manifestations of the effort to integrate are multiethnic recruitment for public institutions, the creation of multistate-run firms, promotion of English as the national language, and even-handed social and economic development programs.

The road to ethnic harmony in Nigeria seems likely to be a long one. Let us simply note here that where cultural cleavages coincide with geography

29. See Melson and Wolpe, *Nigeria.*

and where political institutions are fragile, as during a nation's first few years of independence, such cleavages may be a very important variable affecting the course of political development and the stability of the regime. Such is the case in Nigeria. A political artifact such as federalism can hardly be expected to remedy the potentially harmful instability resulting from severe social cleavage.

## REFLECTIONS ON SOCIAL CLEAVAGES IN DEVELOPING NATIONS

The histories of Mexico and Nigeria illustrate the impact that social cleavages can have on three major problems of developing nations: national integration, political development, and economic modernization. The problem of integrating or minimizing ethnic and cultural cleavages does not lend itself to easy answers. At best, nations can allow cultural groups to persist, and simultaneously minimize the political impact of these groups by adopting even-handed nondiscriminatory policies. In the long run, many such ethnic affiliations may be weakened through social and geographical mobility and the acquisition of the multiple memberships characteristic of complex industrialized societies. Respect and tolerance can be furthered by effective use of the mass media, and particularly by exposing all citizens to the nation's cultural diversity.

If, as in Nigeria, ethnic cleavages take a political form and competition over scarce resources is subject more to force than to the criterion of justice, animosities and hostilities will result, seriously impeding the nation's ability to develop stable government. If economic development — which in developing nations often requires considerable governmental encouragement — is also a function of relative political power rather than attempts at equal distribution, the development of certain regions or minority ethnic groups will suffer, and political tensions are quite likely to rise.

In most Third World nations there is a trend toward policies based on social justice, in the sense of promoting political and economic equality and providing for the welfare of the people.

However, degrees of commitment to social change vary greatly. There are, for example, military regimes like that of Nigeria, which seek social justice but not at the cost of disrupting the capitalist-based economic system. In other militarily ruled states, such as Peru and Burma, the leaders are engaged in radical reform. Single-party and competitive-party Third World nations tend to be divided with regard to the pursuit of social justice. Mexico is committed to social justice, but not to the extent of seriously infringing on its capitalist economic structures. Thus both Nigeria and Mexico are confronting an intriguing question: Can private enterprise economic systems generate enough jobs and governmental revenues to cope with rising expectations, population growth, and urban migrations without markedly increasing the material and psychological gap between the lower and upper classes? If this gap widens, it is likely to promote ideological cleavages as well as political instability.

# Conclusions

The political process does not exist in a vacuum; it is intimately affected by society. In the modern era, governments are increasingly expected to respond to and shape their societies. People everywhere expect government to take an active part in directing the economy, eliminating social inequities, promoting equality of the races and sexes, regulating the use of natural resources, improving educational and health services, and so on. The deep involvement of the state in basic social processes heightens the impact of society on politics. Social cleavages affect the nature and degree of governmental intervention in the society and the economy and are simultaneously affected by governmental action. We shall examine this interaction between state and society more fully in Chapter 9, which focuses on governmental performance in socioeconomic matters.

The set of social cleavages that has been most susceptible to violent manifestations in the past two decades is ethnic conflict. The problems of coping with culturally plural societies are particularly acute in newly independent states (like Nigeria), but by no means absent even in the most advanced and highly developed industrial states (like Britain and the Soviet Union).

As long as distinctive cultural groups persist in a state, there is the danger that re-emergent nationalism or separatism will threaten political stability. But there is no easy answer to the problem of ethnic cleavages. Assimilation may seem to some the most promising solution since it aims at the elimination of cultural differentiations. However, there are significant political and social costs to be considered before endorsing assimilation as a solution to cultural pluralism. First, coercion may be required to destroy existing loyalties to ethnic, racial, or religious groups. The use of force is expensive in social, political, and human terms even for an authoritarian government, and it is usually avoided if other means can be found. Furthermore, assimilation may rob a nation of the cultural richness provided by the folklore, traditions, languages, and distinctive artistic achievements of the various ethnic groups. Finally, the elimination of cultural conflict through assimilation by no means assures the advent of social harmony. New cleavages that develop along class, regional, or ideological lines may have equivalent or more severe effects on political stability. In short, political integration is an ongoing process in which states at all stages of development must be involved to assure the maintenance of national unity and political stability.

3

# The Political Framework

## Introduction

They may sit here for years and years in
Philadelphia!
Those indecisive grenadiers of
Philadelphia!
They can't agree on what is right or wrong
Or what is good or bad.
I'm convinced the only purpose
This Congress ever had
Was to gather here, specifically
To drive John Adams mad!
You see we
    Piddle, twiddle, and resolve.
    Not one damned thing do we solve
    Piddle, twiddle, and resolve
    Nothing's ever solved in
    Foul, fetid, fuming, foggy, filthy
Philadelphi.[1]

So sang John Adams in *1776*, the recent musical comedy about the drafting of
the American Declaration of Independence. The American founding fathers,
popular myth to the contrary, were not all godlike heroes, ever careful and
studious in their work; their proceedings were ponderous and at times frivolous.

1. Peter Stone and Sherman Edwards, *1776, A Musical Play* (New York: Viking Press,
1964), p. 6.

The same is true of contemporary efforts to provide modern nations with constitutions.

A constitution articulates the goals of the political unit, describes the institutions for public decision-making, allocates powers, and establishes rules for the selection of officials and the transfer of public offices. However, a nation's constitution rarely offers one an accurate impression of the real nature of politics. For example, the Constitution of the United States says absolutely nothing about political parties, interest groups, or even the president's cabinet, all of which are of immeasurable import to politics and policy-making in the United States. Virtually every nation is characterized by a gap between the formal rules outlined in the constitution and the actual practice of day-to-day policy-making, though the size of this gap varies widely. Some state constitutions have no bearing on actual politics. This is often the case in states whose leaders aspire to radical socioeconomic reforms and do not wish to be restrained by established procedures. Leaders with more modest plans for change sometimes — but not always — find it possible to operate in closer accord with formal constitutional provisions. In some states it matters little whether the leaders' goals are ambitious or limited, since the notion of adhering to constitutional procedures is poorly developed or nonexistent in the minds of the leaders and the general population.

The purpose of this chapter is to describe the basic institutional frameworks of politics in the six countries. An institution that does not perform as the constitution says it should may still be important. For example, the Supreme Soviet does not perform the legislative tasks assigned to it by the constitution, but its meetings do have political significance. In this chapter, which examines political institutions and procedures in order to clarify the framework in which political actors operate and decisions are made, we shall focus on three major areas of concern: (1) how political power is divided vertically, or geographically; (2) how power is divided horizontally, among various branches of government; and (3) how political power is transferred from one set of leaders to the next.

## THE TERRITORIAL DIVISION OF POWER

All political frameworks are characterized by a division of power among political officers at the various levels of government: national, regional, and local. The political framework defines the activities of governmental units at these three levels and the relationship among them. There are three basic patterns: unitary, federal, and confederal.

In the *unitary* system, the national or central government determines the degree of power it will delegate to the provincial and local governments. As a rule, policy decisions are made at the center and implemented by local authorities with only marginal discretionary powers. A hierarchical command structure radiates from the central government to the local political units. In most such unitary systems, the central government maintains its control over politics at the lower levels by controlling their finances. Taxes are centrally assessed and collected, and subsequently reallocated to the local governments. This practice, of course, affords the central government considerable leverage in its efforts to dominate local politics.

Unitary frameworks have been adopted by most developing and developed nations, including China, Japan, Poland, Britain, France, Spain, Belgium, Holland, the Scandinavian nations, Romania, Bulgaria, and most of the African and Latin American nations. There is, though, considerable variation among unitary governments. For example, in some nations provincial leaders are elected, while in others they are appointed.

Where regional or ethnic segmentalism is strong, or where a significant proportion of the population is engaged in subsistence agriculture, a unitary government may well minimize strife and effectively maximize the necessary political control. On the other hand, this system may discourage or restrict the expression of local needs, particularly where communications linkages between remote areas and the capital are weak. Furthermore, the central government may consequently ignore provincial needs. Allocations of resources may be determined by political whim, rather than the exigencies of national economic criteria. But the problem most frequently encountered in unitary states is the overburdening of the center and consequent paralysis of its administrative structure. Where resources are monopolized by the central government, local demands for such services as education, health, and communications often overtax the capacities of the center.

Consequently, there is a strong centrifugal tendency toward the decentralization of government even in highly centralized unitary states. Although the formal rules prescribe a centralized framework, rule is decentralized in practice as national leaders designate local officials to implement policy in their areas. De facto decentralization is also promoted by the national leaders' need to rely upon the cooperation of local officials in carrying out their policy directives. This reliance, however, is often frustrated, since it is easier to constrain local officials' behavior than to ensure their compliance with requests for positive action. The limited capacity of the central government and local political resistance to its directives are the most frequent sources of inaction. Regardless of the constitution's provisions, policy is often modified to suit the needs of the local unit.

The second most frequent form of government, preferred by all but one of the world's six largest nations (the exception being China), is *federalism*. Though there is considerable variation among federal entities, a set of norms that define the characteristics of a federal system can be specified. The first is that "the political authority is territorially divided between two autonomous sets of separate jurisdictions, one national and one provincial, which both operate directly upon the people."[2] Thus a single indivisible state overarches the subunits. Second, the component units retain all powers the constitution has not specifically assigned to the central authority. Third, it is important

2. Ivo D. Duchacek, *Comparative Federalism: The Territorial Dimension of Politics* (New York: Holt Rinehart Winston, 1970), p. 192.

that the territorial division of authority be clear. When federal constitutions are ambiguous about either the distribution of powers or procedures for altering the formula for distribution, the federation's subunits may find their powers subverted by the more powerful central unit. Finally, the federal entity should have exclusive responsibility for diplomacy and defense.[3]

Federal systems are usually forged at the time of independence in an effort to distribute power either to existing units or to groups anxious to assure their cultural, economic, and political status within the new political entity. Pre-civil war Nigeria was an example of a federal system designed to assure traditional political elites that their merger with the new nation would not entail a sacrifice of status. Federal arrangements are often, if not always, a prerequisite to survival for new states troubled by cultural pluralism. Such a system represents a formal assurance to the ethnic groups that they will survive and that their traditions and needs will be fulfilled within the newly formed political framework. A federal system may also be adopted to enhance a nation's capacity to protect itself against foreign threats. Federalism is suited to large nations, and thus makes possible large concentrations of military, diplomatic, and economic assets.

Among the several advantages of federalism, one of the most important is the provision of a clearly defined basis for decentralizing political decision-making. The subunits have independent bases of operation and scopes of activity. Each layer of government has certain tasks to perform, and the independence of the subunits permits flexibility in dealing with local situations. Experimentation is facilitated by the federal structure in that an untried program need not be applied to the whole nation. One or more subunits may try out and perfect such a program before it is adopted nationally. Some commentators also argue that federalism helps a political system to maintain its stability by isolating political unrest. A comparison between the United States and France will illustrate. Student protest and rioting in the United States during the late 1960s posed little serious threat to the national political system because the focal points of protest were state educational systems rather than a national educational program. Riots at the University of California were handled by California authorities, not by a national police force or army. In France, by contrast, the focal point of protest was the Ministry of National Education, which is responsible for all universities and public schools. The challenge was thus directed at the national government, which employed national police and antiriot forces to protect itself. Instead of being isolated, the conflict quickly became a national crisis involving the stability and even the existence of the national government; this outcome is attributable in part to the highly centralized nature of French government.

Despite the advantages of federalism, there appears to be a universal tendency toward the erosion of the subunits' prerogatives, as we have seen in the United States. As new governmental responsibilities have developed, the cen-

3. *Ibid.*, pp. 206–231.

tral government's role has expanded to meet new needs the subunits are unable to provide for. The costs of education, highways, and welfare are often prohibitive to subunits, whose financial resources are limited and fluctuating. Furthermore, many problems — particularly those related to environmental protection — cannot be handled adequately within the boundaries of the local governmental unit. As the national government makes inroads into the activities of the subunits, it tends to disseminate national values and standards to replace local ones. In the United States, for example, the federal government has sometimes promoted racial equality by insisting on school integration and racially integrated workforces as preconditions to the allocation of federal education and building funds.

Federalism does have some significant disadvantages. Rapid social and economic change may be impeded by a federal structure. Federalism may encourage sectionalism and, if the subunits coincide with ethnic boundaries, ethnic conflict. At times sectional and ethnic conflicts may lead to secession and civil war, as was the case in the United States in 1860–1865 and in Nigeria in 1967–1970. Federalism may also foster social and economic inequalities if certain subunits provide more extensive social services than do their neighbors. In short, federalism is by no means a panacea.

The third and least frequent major type of constitutional framework is the *confederation,* a voluntary agreement among political units to form a union. Such a union is characterized by considerable autonomy for the subunits. The subunit allows the central unit to be responsible for foreign affairs, but retains its own executive, legislative, and judicial system, and considerable policy-making autonomy. Many confederations, such as the United States Confederation (1777–1789) and the German Confederation (1815–1866), eventually gave way to federal unions.

## THE EXERCISE OF POWER: ALTERNATIVE FORMULAS

Within the general political framework dictated by the territorial division of authority, political power is allocated to different institutions. The institutions characteristic of the political framework include the executive, the legislature, the judiciary, such major political forces as parties and the military, and the bureaucracy. In practice, there are many ways of organizing these various institutions in order to govern a political unit. However, two patterns are most common in today's world: parliamentary regimes and presidential regimes.

The most widespread form of government among the "democratic" nations is the *parliamentary system,* which locates sovereignty (the legitimate authority to govern) in the parliament. The prime minister and cabinet are chosen from among the parliament's members and are collectively called "the government." The parliament is supreme, and in most systems can force the executive to resign either by refusing to pass vital legislation proposed by the government or by voting to censure the government. The executive, then, is dependent for its position and its continuance in office on maintaining the confidence of the legislature.

Advocates of this formula argue that it is more representative and more efficient than presidential systems. The parliamentary system is claimed to be more representative because the executive is chosen by elected representatives of the people who retain the right to unseat it if it fails to meet popular demands. The leadership's dependence on parliamentary support and favor, it is argued, compels the executive to be sensitive to the people, through their representatives. Those who extol this system's efficiency note that effective coordination and implementation of policy are more likely if the executive and legislative act in concert instead of competing. However, critics of the parliamentary formula argue that it may lead to instability and stagnation in countries where party divisions prevent the development of durable coalitions. The cases used to illustrate the dangers of parliamentary government include Germany's Weimar Republic (1918–1933), in which executive instability facilitated the rise of Hitler; the Fourth French Republic (1944–1958), which had twenty-seven governments in fourteen years; and the contemporary Italian Republic, which continues to be plagued by governmental crises.

Most democratic governments in the world today employ parliamentary systems. Nondemocratic regimes, too, may take parliamentary forms; for example, the Soviet Union and most of the other communist political systems have parliamentary frameworks. In these nations, however, the parliamentary system is usually only a façade that lends the appearance of democracy to political formulas that place effective political power in the hands of a single party or dictator.

*Presidential* systems are characterized by independent executive, legislative, and sometimes judicial branches of government. Presidents are elected directly by the people or by delegates other than the legislature, and the presidential term of office is not subject to the legislature. The United States' presidential system was intended to guarantee certain checks and balances in the hope that excesses of power through consolidation might be avoided by a division of power between the executive, legislative, and judicial branches. Advocates of the presidential framework suggest that it allows for strong leadership and avoids the parliamentary stalemates and governmental instability that frequently occur in multiparty parliamentary polities. However, critics argue that the presidential system may facilitate the rise of potential dictators and may be more vulnerable to "immobilization" than the parliamentary system should the president be of one party while the legislative body is dominated by other parties. In the United States, this has occurred during the Eisenhower, Nixon, and Ford administrations.

The presidential formula can be used by democracies. The chief danger of combining presidentialism and democracy is the tendency toward the unrestrained growth of presidential power, which threatens democratic constraints on the exercise of power. On the other hand, crises require powerful executive action, which may be hindered by the division of power among a president, legis-

TABLE 3.1

## Contrasts Between the Presidential and Parliamentary Frameworks of Government

| Presidential | Parliamentary |
|---|---|
| Division of governmental power among various branches of government | Unity of governmental power in parliament |
| Checks and balances among theoretically equal branches | Supremacy of parliament |
| Unified executive | Divided executive |
| President is head of both the state and the government | President or monarch is honorific head of state |
| | Prime minister (also called premier or chancellor) is head of government along with his cabinet of ministers |
| Independence of the executive | Dependence of the executive |
| President has own mandate through election by the general population | President usually elected by the parliament |
| President can be removed from office only through the difficult process of impeachment | Prime minister and cabinet named by parliament and may be removed from office by vote of censure or by parliament's refusal to pass important legislation desired by the government |

lature, and judiciary each protective of its own prerogatives and interests. Presidentialism has been a problem for many Latin American countries that have patterned their political frameworks on that of the United States. Most of these presidential democracies have very rapidly evolved into presidential dictatorships.

Many states have no established constitutional principles or formal institutions for political decision-making. There may be no constitution, or it may be suspended or ignored. Such a political framework is characterized by ad hoc arrangements of power. A single individual, political party, or group of military officers exercises power and makes decisions without observing any clearly established procedure or set of rules. Most authoritarian systems (including military regimes) are characterized by such ad hoc arrangements.

Ad hoc arrangements are capable of responding efficiently to crisis situations and promoting far-reaching socioeconomic change because the leadership has the flexibility to do whatever it deems necessary to achieve its end. They allow for rapid and efficient decision-making. On the other hand, ad hoc arrangements tend to be unstable due to the lack of regularized forms of decision-making, failure to define areas of competence and responsibility, and the resultant uncertainty about what government will do and how.

# THE POLITICS OF SUCCESSION

One of the gravest crises a regime can face is the transition of power from one leader or set of leaders to another. Unless procedures for the transferral of power are well established and universally accepted, the period of transition may be dangerous. The process of *succession,* the technical term for transferrals of power, has two components: (1) the actual transferral of power to new leaders, and (2) the legitimization of the new leaders, in the sense that the people come to regard them not only as wielding power but also as possessing the right to that power.

In a democratic system, the problem of succession is resolved by constitutional provisions for periodic elections. Political parties take responsibility for selecting candidates, conducting the elections, and thus recruiting new leaders to replace those who retire, die, or are defeated in electoral contests. The legitimization of these leaders is usually a natural by-product of the elections: the leaders chosen are those the majority of voters preferred. As a consequence of these established procedures, crises of succession rarely occur in liberal democracies. However, the sudden death or unexpected retirement of a leader can sometimes create problems, as we shall see in the case of France.

In communist political systems, elections are not ordinarily a component of the process of succession. Leaders are co-opted into positions of authority on the basis of decisions made at the top levels of the Communist party. Both within the party and in the nation as a whole, elections only endorse the party elite's selection of leaders. The Soviet Union experienced serious crises of succession after the deaths of Lenin and Stalin, while the new leaders consolidated their power. However, there are signs that the succession process may have been regularized in the Soviet Union and other communist countries. Khrushchev's removal from office in 1964 aroused little disruption; the death of Ho Chi Minh did not provoke a crisis in North Vietnam; Walter Ulbricht was eased out of power in East Germany without a struggle. In short, some communist countries appear to have successfully established procedures for the orderly transfer of power from one leader to the next. Some communist states may still lack such procedures because their regimes are largely functions of the personalized rule of one individual: e.g., Tito in Yugoslavia, Castro in Cuba, and Mao Tse-tung in China.

In the developing political systems, succession is a major problem. Many relatively new states are still governed by the leaders who guided them to independence. Such leaders are often of the charismatic type, whose authority is based on allegiance to personalized rule rather than a well-defined set of political institutions. As a result, the procedures for succession are poorly established and untried. When the leader dies, retires, or is deposed, a period of uncertainty and instability ensues and the search begins for a replacement. For example, Egypt's Anwar Sadat faced serious difficulty in consolidating his hold on power after the death of Nasser. Within a few months of Nasser's death,

Sadat forced the resignations of his vice-president, six cabinet members, and dozens of other top political leaders and charged them all with high treason.

In some developing countries, such as Mexico, Malaysia, and India, a new leader is chosen by means of elections (the results of which are often rigged or predetermined by negotiations among various national elites). In other developing nations the new leader is selected by a caucus of the military elite or party leaders. In such cases, succession is determined either by a few or by those capable of mobilizing a successful effort to impose by threat or force acceptance of their claim to office.

In the following sections we shall examine formal and actual political frameworks, focusing on differences in the origins of the six nations' constitutions, relative degrees of federalism and centralism, discrepancies between formal structures and norms and their actual functions, and the politics of succession.

# Britain and France

Britain and France are good illustrations of the diverse political frameworks found in liberal democracies. Britain's political system has evolved gradually for nearly a millennium, producing a constitutional monarchy with a parliamentary structure. France has undergone a much more turbulent process of development, experiencing at least a dozen complete changes in the formal political framework over the past two centuries. At present the French Fifth Republic is a mixed presidential and parliamentary system with a tendency toward the growth of presidential power. However, it is by no means clear that this system will be any more durable than its predecessors.

The British regard their "constitution" with the same respect and awe that Americans usually express for their Constitution. However, Britain has no written constitution. Instead, the British constitution is composed of unwritten conventions and norms, acts of Parliament, major historical pronouncements and documents (such as the Magna Carta), and traditions, never codified in a single constitutional document. Most of the informal conventions and practices are not in written form, yet they make up much of the constitution's content and would be legally binding were it necessary to enforce them through the courts.

The French constitution has not been invested with the symbolic values and emotional attachments that characterize the British and American constitutions. This is so because the current constitution, which dates only from 1958, is the latest of a long series of constitutions. Furthermore, unlike the American and British political systems, the French Fifth Republic (like all its predecessors) does not represent a broad-based consensus on the way politics should be organized. Several major political parties pledge wholesale revision of the constitution should they ever win power. Even those who do support the constitution do not adhere to strict constitutional interpretation. President Charles de Gaulle, under whose direction the constitution was drafted, expanded the role

These photos depict the high degree of centralization in France, the Soviet Union, and Mexico. The highly centralized nature of government in France places nearly all political power in the hands of the national government. Attuning centrally made policy to the interests and needs of remote towns is a major problem. Here a cabinet minister and a mayor discuss local issues in a small French town. Unlike the significant roles of the British and French parliaments, the Supreme Soviet, which is the Soviet Union's parallel to these legislatures, has little power and is primarily of symbolic value. It meets briefly once a year to ratify policies adopted elsewhere by the highest Communist party councils. Mexico's president is seen in this photo visiting an agricultural development project. This illustrates his roles as chief policy maker, head of the ruling party, and symbol of national authority.

of the president far beyond the specifications of the constitution and ignored its provisions for amendment when he employed a referendum to open the presidential election to all adult voters.

## THE CENTRALIZATION OF POLITICAL POWER

Britain and France both have centralized, rather than federal, governments. British and French local governments are free to act only in areas where specific authority has been delegated to them by the central government. With only limited independent financial resources, they are dependent upon the central government for grants and loans to provide essential public services. Lacking both financial resources and the authority to enter upon new areas of government action, British and French local governments are unable to take initiatives to respond to new problems and changing public needs. Such new concerns of government as urban planning and renewal, environmental control, and social welfare programs — all of which might have been delegated to local authorities — have in fact been added to the duties of the central governments. Despite the formal limitations on local government, however, local political leaders often enjoy considerable influence on policies germane to their localities. The central government must rely on the cooperation of these local officials. It is difficult both to compel them to do what they do not want to do and to prevent them from doing what they are determined to do.

In both countries, local officials are popularly elected and thus politically responsible for their actions. However, since they are legally subordinate to the central governments, they are not entirely free to respond to the demands of their electorates as they see fit. At times they must feel trapped between the demands of their electorates and their governments' denials of the requisite authority or finances. On the other hand, local officials can use their powerlessness to explain their lack of performance to the electorates. Surprisingly, local elections in both countries elicit greater electoral participation than do similar elections in the United States, where local officials have considerable power.

In Britain centralized control over local authorities is exercised by the minister for planning and local government and the secretaries of state for Scotland and Wales. The functional ministries (e.g., Education and Social Security) oversee the performance of local authorities in their areas of responsibilities. In France, the supervision of local governments by the minister of interior is much more direct. Each of the ninety political subdivisions (called *départements*) has a centrally appointed prefect who oversees the actions of local governments, heads the local police, and coordinates the other ministries in his département.

Despite the strong tradition of centralized control, the French mayor is very powerful and can dominate the political and social life of the community. As the agent of the state in his town, he is delegated to perform certain duties on behalf of the state. In this sense, he is a state bureaucrat. He is also head of the locally elected municipal council. Though the mayor is formally selected by the municipal council, in practice he usually dominates this body. In many cases the mayor is also an elected member of the département's general council (comparable to a county government). He may also be elected a deputy in the National Assembly or a senator. The mayor (and other local elected officials) can thus hold several elected posts simultaneously, and can even serve as a minister in the national cabinet without resigning his local position. This accumulation of elected mandates permits the local official to increase his political power and to speak in parliament not only for his constituency in general but also for local governmental units.

British mayors are less powerful than their French counterparts. The British local authority cannot hold any other elected public office. Local offices sometimes serve as springboards to national political careers, but there are complaints that the limited power of local government dissuades qualified individuals from involvement in local politics. In Britain the powers of the local authorities vary from one town or county to the next, since parliamentary grants of power are often made to a specific local unit rather than to all.

## POLITICAL STRUCTURES

Through the centuries, conventions and tradition have transformed the British political structure from an absolute monarchy to a *constitutional monarchy* with a parliamentary structure. This structure is based upon a Parliament with two chambers: the House of Commons and the House of Lords. The House of Commons, the more powerful branch of Parliament, is the formal source of political power in Britain. Its 635 members are elected by universal suffrage at least once every five years. In theory, the House of Commons is the supreme political body in the British system. All laws and treaties are enacted by Parliament, and the House of Commons is now dominant and empowered to override the House of Lords when necessary. The House of Commons selects from among its members the prime minister, who in turn chooses a cabinet. The prime minister and the cabinet, collectively called the Government, serve at the discretion of the House of Commons. Commons can force the resignation of the Government by voting censure or by refusing to pass a major piece of legislation desired by the Government.

The House of Lords plays a much less important political role. Its membership is composed of titled nobility who have inherited their positions, lifetime peers (named by the Government, usually to honor achievement), and twenty-six Lords Spiritual from the Church of England. During the twentieth century Parliament has curtailed the powers of the House of Lords. It no longer has the ability to block legislation passed by Commons, though it can delay most legislation for a year (financial legislation for only a month). Since its legislative calendar is less crowded than that of Commons, however, the House of Lords can consider legislation at leisure and suggest needed refinements in bills passed by Commons. A bill designed to eliminate the hereditary peers from the House of Lords and to further reduce its legislative power was introduced in 1967 by the Labour government of Harold Wilson. This proposal was

FIGURE 3.1

*Basic Institutions of British Government*

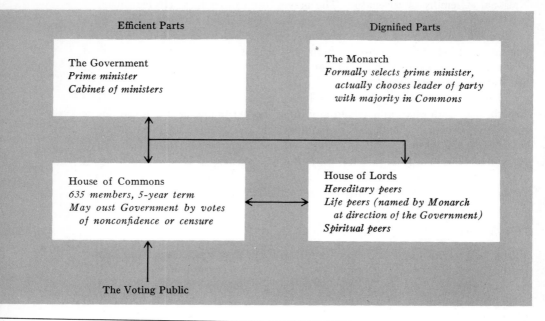

Efficient Parts                                        Dignified Parts

The Government
*Prime minister*
*Cabinet of ministers*

The Monarch
*Formally selects prime minister,*
  *actually chooses leader of party*
  *with majority in Commons*

House of Commons
*635 members, 5-year term*
*May oust Government by votes*
  *of nonconfidence or censure*

House of Lords
*Hereditary peers*
*Life peers (named by Monarch*
  *at direction of the Government)*
*Spiritual peers*

The Voting Public

withdrawn in 1969 but it is likely that similar bills will be introduced in the future. There can be little doubt that a legislative body based on hereditary nobility is an anomaly in a modern democratic state.

Despite Parliament's theoretical supremacy over the Government, the cabinet and especially the prime minister have actual ascendancy over their supposed master. Commons still chooses the prime minister, but this process now amounts to little more than formal ratification of the voters' choice. In the general elections voters elect only the members of Parliament. But because both major parties have made known their choices for prime minister, the outcome of the election determines the naming of the prime minister. If Conservatives win a majority in the Commons, for example, the Conservative party leader will become prime minister. Thus, the selection of the prime minister is no longer a genuine prerogative of the legislative body.

Once selected, the prime minister is free to act virtually as he pleases. He can appoint and dismiss cabinet ministers without ratification by Commons. The Government can shape policy as it desires and be assured that a majority in Commons will support its proposals, and it is also the major source of legislation considered and passed by Parliament. The prime minister can undertake major diplomatic or military ventures without consulting Commons. For example, in 1956 Prime Minister Anthony Eden launched an invasion of the Suez Canal without consulting either Commons or his full cabinet. Though

FIGURE 3.2
## British Cabinet, October 1974

Prime Minister (Harold Wilson)
Lord President of the Council and Leader of the House of Commons
Secretary of State for Foreign and Commonwealth Affairs
Chancellor of the Exchequer (Treasury)
Secretary of State for Employment
Secretary of State for Energy
Lord Chancellor (Justice and Speaker of the House of Lords)
Minister of Agriculture, Fisheries, and Food
Secretary of State for Social Services
Secretary of State for Industry
Secretary of State for the Environment
Secretary of State for Scotland
Chancellor of the Duchy of Lancaster
Secretary of State for Trade
Secretary of State for Prices and Consumer Protection
Secretary of State for Defense
Secretary of State for Northern Ireland
Secretary of State for Wales
Secretary of State for Education and Science
Lord Privy Seal and Leader of the House of Lords
Government Chief Whip
Minister for Planning and Local Government

---

Commons has the formal right to depose the Government, this prerogative has not been exercised successfully since 1895. Once or twice a session, the Opposition will be so incensed by one of the Government's actions that it will introduce a motion of censure. Debate on the motion permits the Opposition to criticize the Government and the Government to defend itself, though the failure of the motion is certain.

The gradual shift of power from the legislature to the executive is not unusual in liberal democracies, and it is commonplace to talk about the "decline" of democratic parliaments. In part, the transfer of power from legislatures to executives is attributable to the changing nature of government in modern industrial societies. It reflects the rapid expansion of the tasks of government; the sheer volume of necessary policy-making is incompatible with the ponderous and unwieldy nature of legislative action, which involves several hundred people. Furthermore, governmental policies tend more and more to require technological and financial expertise not often found in legislatures. The decline of parliaments also results from governments' increasing concern with their foreign and defense policies, which require secrecy and rapid action — requirements that are incompatible with open debate.

In Britain these general trends toward the enhancement of the executive at the expense of Parliament are reinforced by the party system. There are only two parties with a chance of controlling Commons, the Conservative and Labour parties. Party discipline is very strong, and near-perfect unity is reflected in House of Commons' votes. Thus the Government can count on a majority to support its proposals, and effective political power is shifted from Commons to the Government.

Since Parliament's formal powers of restraint on the actions of the Government are ineffectual, one may wonder whether in fact the British prime minister is subject to democratic control. The answer is that he is restrained by informal controls which, though not legally binding, limit his ability to abuse power. One such informal control is the prime minister's need to retain the confidence of the party's backbenchers (members of Commons who do not hold Government or party leadership positions). Backbenchers rarely flout party discipline to vote against the Government, but dissenters can and do work within the party to undermine leaders who act peremptorily. Thus, Anthony Eden's arbitrary intervention in Egypt in 1956 undermined support within his own party and was a major factor in his resignation the following year. In the United States the president and cabinet may be individuals with little or no political experience or commitment to a party (e.g., Dwight Eisenhower). In Britain, however, those who become prime ministers and cabinet members have spent most of their lives working for their party. The typical prime minister has had more than twenty-five years' prior experience in the House of Commons. Such leaders are unwilling to jeopardize the party they have spent years building. They recognize that leadership must be responsive to the rank-and-file if divisions are to be avoided.

Another informal restraint on the Government is its calculation of what will be accepted by the general public. The Government must face the electorate at least every five years, and it recognizes that the Opposition will use any apparent abuse of power to discredit the Government and its party.

Americans are preoccupied with establishing formal institutional restraints on the abuse of power, such as the federal structure, the separation of powers, and the system of checks and balances. The British are no less concerned with misuse of political power, but they have located the means of protection in informal rather than formal institutional restraints. There is no evidence of any serious abuse of power by the British Government, despite the informal nature of restraints on its powers.

In Britain, the executive powers of government are divided between the prime minister, who is the *head of government,* and the monarch, who is the titular *head of state.* A century ago Walter Bagehot, in a classic treatment of the English constitution, distinguished between two aspects of the British government: the dignified parts — those institutions and practices that excite and preserve the reverence of the population — and the efficient parts — those institutions and practices actually responsible for the conduct of government. Chief among the dignified elements is the monarch. More than any other modern state, Britain has preserved the traditions and institutions of its monarchical past, while placing them in a democratic context. There are other constitutional or democratic monarchies, but Britain alone has maintained not only its monarchy but also a full-blown titled aristocracy, elaborate ceremonies, and mass adulation. As the soon-to-be-deposed King Farouk of Egypt said in 1951, "There will soon be only five kings left — the Kings of England, Diamonds, Hearts, Spades, and Clubs." [4]

For the British the monarchy is not an archaic governmental institution. In theory and in law, all acts of government are performed in the name and by the authority of "Her Most Excellent Majesty Elizabeth the Second": she promulgates laws, negotiates treaties, selects a prime minister and a cabinet, names other political and religious leaders, and grants pardons. In actual practice, the queen exercises virtually no political power whatsoever. All the acts performed in her name are actually undertaken by the prime minister and the cabinet. In fact, the political prerogatives of the queen are less extensive than those of the ordinary man in the street. She does not have the right to take a partisan position, she cannot vote, and she cannot express her own political views. Even the conduct of her personal life is subject to approval by the Government that is in theory subordinate to her.

The French political framework is neither parliamentary nor presidential in its formal constitutional aspect, but a mixture of the two. Both the president and the prime minister have extensive political responsibilities and powers. The president is the head of state but, unlike the British monarch, he exercises important political powers. The prime minister is the head of government but, unlike his British counterpart, he is not the leading political figure. It is the president who dominates the political process in France.

According to the constitution of the Fifth Republic, the president is to be an arbiter charged with insuring "by his arbitration, the regular functioning of the governmental authorities, as well as the continuity of the state" (Article 5). The presidency was carefully tailored to suit the political style of the first occupant of the post, Charles de Gaulle; its nature facilitates the arbitration of disputes between narrow political groups by a disinterested and politically uninvolved arbiter. The constitution grants extensive powers to the French president, who is elected by universal suffrage to a seven-year term; he is the only elected official with a national constituency. The president has the power to appoint and dismiss the prime minister and members of the cabinet. He presides over cabinet meetings and controls the agenda and discussions of the Government. He can require the parliament to reconsider the legislation it passes, and if confronted with a hostile majority or a political crisis, he can dissolve the National Assembly and call for new elections. He may propose a referendum on any question he desires. He has the right to declare a state of national emergency and to rule by decree "when the interests of the Republic . . . are

4. Kingsley Martin, *The Crown and the Establishment* (London: Penguin Books, 1963), p. 11.

FIGURE 3.3

*Basic Institutions of French Government*

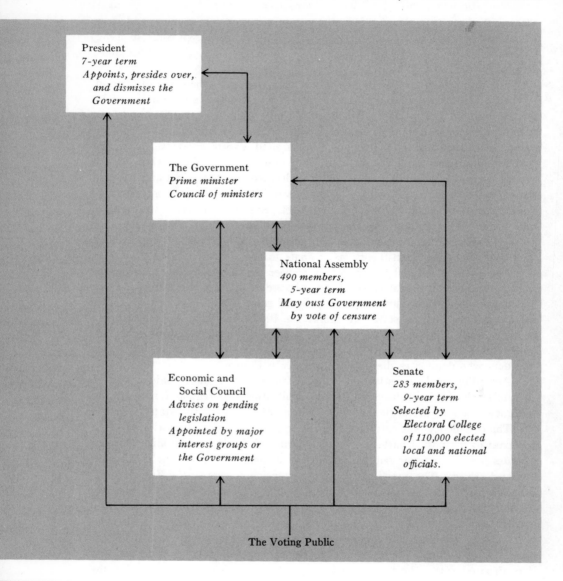

President
7-year term
*Appoints, presides over,
and dismisses the
Government*

The Government
*Prime minister
Council of ministers*

National Assembly
*490 members,
5-year term
May oust Government
by vote of censure*

Economic and
Social Council
*Advises on pending
legislation
Appointed by major
interest groups or
the Government*

Senate
*283 members,
9-year term
Selected by
Electoral College
of 110,000 elected
local and national
officials.*

The Voting Public

threatened in a grave and immediate manner and when the regular functioning of the constitutional public authorities is interrupted" (Article 16).

The Government (the prime minister and cabinet) also has broad powers to "determine and direct the policy of the nation" (Article 20). The Govern-

FIGURE 3.4
*French Cabinet, June 1974*

Prime Minister (Jacques Chirac)
Minister of Interior
Minister of Justice
Minister of Defense
Minister of Foreign Affairs
Minister of the Economy and Finance
Minister of Education
Minister of Cooperation
Minister of Equipment
Minister of Agriculture
Minister for the Quality of Life
Minister of Labor
Minister of Health
Minister of Industry
Minister of Trade and Crafts

ment exercises extensive control over legislative procedures to insure that priority is given to consideration of its proposals. With the authorization of parliament, it may issue as decrees laws that would ordinarily have to be passed by the legislative body. While formally dependent on the National Assembly for its continuance in office, the Government does not have to submit to legislative approval after being named by the president. Furthermore, the process of censure which results in the resignation of the Government, is difficult and cumbersome.

Actual practice has augmented the broad powers granted by the constitution to the two executives. It is the president who has proved more powerful. The role of the president has never been limited to the formal one of impartial arbiter, since de Gaulle immediately assumed direct leadership in broad areas of policy. These areas included the dismantling of the colonial empire, the formulation of foreign and defense policies, and the creation of an independent nuclear force. On these issues the parliament had very little influence, and the Government simply administered the policies determined by de Gaulle.

The powers of the president were significantly enhanced by the 1962 constitutional amendment providing for direct popular election of the president. Previously, the constitution had called for the president to be selected by an electoral college of local and national officials. This change granted future presidents the independent national electoral mandate needed for the exercise of broad presidential powers.

The growth of presidential power was also made possible by the presence in the National Assembly of a cohesive majority strongly supportive of the president's actions. The Gaullist majority, firmly established after 1962, assured the president of the support of the National Assembly. (See Table 3.2.) Con-

TABLE 3.2

## Presidential Majorities in the French National Assembly

| Presidents since 1959 | | Size of presidential majority (Percentage of National Assembly firmly supportive of the president) |
|---|---|---|
| Charles de Gaulle (1959–1969) | 1959–1962 | 80.2–41.6* |
| | 1962–1967 | 55.6 |
| | 1967–1968 | 50.1 |
| | 1968–1969 | 72.7 |
| Georges Pompidou (1969–1974) | 1969–1973 | 74.7 |
| | 1973–1974 | 53.5 |
| Valéry Giscard d'Estaing (1974– | 1974– | 62.5 |

*Figures for the First Legislature (1959–1962) are based on the percentage of deputies supporting the Government in the nine censure motions. Figures for subsequent legislatures are based on the percentage of deputies affiliated with the groups composing the Government.*

sequently, the president could elicit desired legislation from parliament. In addition, he was free to appoint and dismiss prime ministers at his own discretion. When de Gaulle selected Georges Pompidou as prime minister in 1962, Pompidou was a political unknown with no previous ministerial or parliamentary experience. In fact, he had never run for public office. In 1968 de Gaulle abruptly dismissed Pompidou at the height of the latter's popularity and after he had engineered the most impressive electoral victory in French republican experience. When Pompidou succeeded de Gaulle a year later, he further extended the prerogatives of the president. While Pompidou lacked the imperious and aloof style that made de Gaulle's rule appear arbitrary, he extended the purview of presidential power into domestic affairs. De Gaulle had permitted his prime minister to direct the Gaullist political party and coalition, but Pompidou as president performed these tasks himself and was much more willing than de Gaulle to intervene directly in partisan politics. Following his election in 1974, Valéry Giscard d'Estaing acted to maintain and even further extend presidential powers.

Despite constitutional provisions, the French political system is in practice becoming more presidential and less parliamentary. The potential for political crisis is inherent in the emerging pattern, because the prime minister has a dual responsibility: to the increasingly powerful president who appoints him and in practice dominates him, and to the National Assembly, which can force his resignation through a censure motion. So far the threatened crisis has not developed because the Gaullist political coalition has controlled both the National Assembly and the presidency. The threat would, however, become immediate if the political group controlling the National Assembly were hostile to the group whose leader was president. Both de Gaulle and Pompidou indicated that if confronted with a National Assembly unwilling to support the prime minister, they would dissolve the legislative body and call for new elections in the hope of procuring a more favorable alignment in the National Assembly. If this maneuver failed to produce a majority compatible with the president, the next step is uncertain. The president might then be forced either to resign or to accept a prime minister capable of maintaining the confidence of the National Assembly. In either case, the powers of the president would be dramatically curtailed, possibly reducing the post to the mediatorial role assigned by the constitution or to an honorific role. If and when it is encountered, this potential crisis will be an important test of the durability of the present political formula.

The French legislature has two chambers, the National Assembly and the Senate. The National Assembly, the more powerful branch, is composed of 490 deputies popularly elected to five-year terms. The Senate is indirectly elected by mayors, town councillors, and departmental general councillors. This electorate selects a Senate weighted in favor of the less populated (and generally least progressive) areas of France. The two chambers have equal legislative powers. In case of disagreement on pending legislation, the prime minister may appoint a joint conference committee to work out a compromise acceptable to both chambers and the Government. If the joint conference fails, the Government has the discretion to ask the National Assembly to make the final decision.

The powers of the parliament have declined markedly and abruptly under the Fifth Republic, a phenomenon only partly explained by the general trends in that direction affecting all democratic legislatures. Because the legislatures of previous French republics were widely considered to have used their powers in a negative way to block legislation and overthrow cabinets, the framers of the Fifth Republic's constitution deliberately limited legislative power and increased executive power. The parliament's areas of legislative competence are carefully delimited: in some areas it cannot legislate; in other areas it can only legislate broad principles. The constitution specifies that parliament will convene for two sessions of three months each; in the past it had met virtually all year. The committee system was weakened, and the Government's role in the legislative process was enhanced to insure preferential treatment for its proposals. Finally, the president has the right to dissolve the National Assembly at his discretion in order to force new parliamentary elections.

Another reason for the decline of the French parliament, as well as of the House of Commons, is the firm control of the legislature exercised by the same coalition that makes up the Government. Since 1962 the Gaullists have had firm control of the majority in the National Assembly. Tight discipline and strong cohesion have assured close coordination of the parliamentary majority with the Gaullist Government, and the result has been to reinforce the subordination of the National Assembly to the Government.

The powers of the French parliament are in practice no less extensive than those of the British Parliament. French legislators complain more vociferously about their lack of power because they enjoyed (and abused) so much power prior to 1958. It is true that debate in the Palais Bourbon (where the National Assembly sits) is less lively than it once was, but this is attributable to the National Assembly's shift from the very center of politics to the periphery. The National Assembly may even exercise more power than does the British House of Commons: it ousted a government by censure as recently as 1962, and nearly did so again in 1967 and 1968. The House of Commons has not exercised comparable power since 1895.

## SUCCESSION

Succession in democratic states is generally smooth, because who succeeds whom and when is generally determined by the voters in competitive elections. In Britain, for example, successions have been orderly and have rarely given rise to instability or uncertainty. Both British parties have shown themselves willing to accept the voters' decision and even when defeated have worked to ease the transition to new leaders. Both parties have recognized the need for a clear popular mandate. When the results of an election were unclear or the margin of victory was very narrow, both Conservative and Labour Governments have called for new elections sooner than was legally necessary in order to clarify the voters' preference. Nor does any difficulty arise if the prime minister should die in office or suddenly resign. The members of the majority party in Commons elect a new leader, who is named prime minister by the monarch.

A more difficult situation was created by the general election of February 1974, which granted no party a majority in the House of Commons. Edward Heath, the outgoing prime minister whose party had received the most votes, first tried to form a coalition government of his party, the Liberals, and several minor parties. When Heath failed, Harold Wilson, the Labour party leader whose party had won the most seats (301 out of 635), formed a minority government whose existence depended on its ability to draw enough votes from the Liberals and minor parties to maintain an uneasy majority in Commons. This was the first minority government in Britain since 1929. The Wilson government called for new elections eight months later, winning a narrow majority in the House of Commons.

In France the situation is less clearcut, since the same party has been in control for the eighteen years since the establishment of the Fifth Republic. There is some indication, though, that the succession process might be rendered difficult by the polarized nature of French parties. The left-wing parties regard the Gaullists as authoritarian and even fascist; the Gaullists regard the parties of the Left as captives of "totalitarian communism." Interparty hostility has lessened somewhat since de Gaulle left politics, but these strongly negative feelings are likely to make transition tense. Another factor capable of complicating the succession process is that the terms of office of the president and the National Assembly do not coincide but overlap. If a shift in the majority is first manifested in a presidential election, the president can simply call new legislative elections in which his supporters will presumably strengthen their position in the National Assembly. If, however, balance changes first in the National Assembly, the president may confront a hostile parliamentary majority unwilling to accept his leadership or his prime minister.

The first succession problem faced by the Fifth Republic was the replacement of de Gaulle after his abrupt resignation in April 1969. Since France has no vice president, new presidential elections were held two months later. The Gaullist candidate, Georges Pompidou, won the election and transition occurred without incident. Pompidou's death in 1974 was followed by the election to the presidency of Valéry Giscard d'Estaing, leader of a party in the Gaullist coalition. It is likely that there will eventually be a change in the majority, and the nature of the transition will be a crucial test of the Fifth Republic's political framework.

## China and the Soviet Union

China and the Soviet Union have political frameworks that reflect the characteristics of revolutionary societies confronting the challenge of building both communism and modern economic systems. The socioeconomic conditions of both nations in their early formative years — large rural populations, ethnic diversity and tension, and vastly underdeveloped economies — also affected their constitutional frameworks. The ideologies and political values of China and the Soviet Union assigned social justice priority over individual freedoms; the leadership believed that only economic abundance and the satisfaction of such basic social needs as housing, food, health care, and education could assure real freedom for the individual. The means to achieve these social goals — the mobilization of society — was interpreted as requiring that individual liberty be temporarily relegated to a secondary position in the hierarchy of values. Both states' leaders sought maximum centralized control, which they considered necessary for accelerated social and political change. Both perceived that the maintenance of effective political control would require giving priority to party organs over state organs.

The present constitution of the Soviet Union was drafted under Stalin's direction and adopted in 1936. It is the third Soviet constitution since the Bolshevik Revolution, the first having been adopted in 1918 and the second in 1924. During the 1960s a constitutional commission was established to draft a fourth constitution more appropriate to the accomplishment of full communism. The commission met on several occasions but by the mid-1970s no new constitution had been proposed. Unlike France's, the Soviet Union's frequent changes in constitution do not reflect any instability in its internal power relationships; the political institutions defined by the constitution are not those in which real political power is located. Constitutional change is simply window-

dressing for the rule of the Communist party. The constitution sounds democratic and formally guarantees the protection of individual rights, but in practice
it has permitted a tyranny as harsh as Stalin's and has in no way restrained the
conduct of the Communist party and its elite. In recent years, there has been
a trend in the Soviet Union toward greater respect for individual rights, especially in judicial proceedings. But the constitution and the laws that emanate
from it remain tools of the party, not canons of conduct.

The first constitution of the People's Republic of China was adopted in
1954. The preparation of a constitution took five years after the communist victory in China, and according to the Chinese more than 150 million people participated in various stages of the process. The turbulence of Chinese politics during
the 1950s frequently disrupted even the strictly formal functioning of the institutions established by the constitution. The Cultural Revolution of the late
1960s temporarily upset these structures, which were among the chief targets
of the Red Guard drive to eliminate bureaucratic revisionism. In the aftermath
of the Cultural Revolution, a new constitution was drafted by the party and
finally ratified in a modified form by the Tenth Party Congress in late 1973.
Its formal approval came from the Fourth People's National Congress, held in
January 1975. The major modification, the formal merger of party and state
organs at the local level in the form of revolutionary committees, represents an
important attempt to define constitutionally the intimate relationship between
the party and the state in communist political systems. The new constitution
also integrates the military more fully into the decision-making structures.

## FEDERALISM OR CENTRALIZATION?

The constitution of the Soviet Union establishes a federal state composed of
fifteen union republics, nineteen autonomous republics, five autonomous *oblasts*
(provinces), and ten national *okrugs* (areas). Legally, the autonomy and separate powers granted to the federal units seem impressive. The union republics
have the right to their own diplomatic relations and military structures. While
none of the subunits possess independent military bodies, some union republics
do conduct some "independent" foreign relations: the Ukraine and Byelorussia
have their own delegations to the United Nations and occasionally a union republic has negotiated a minor treaty with an adjoining country. In actuality,
Soviet federalism is negated by the centralizing force of the Communist party.
Party hierarchy and discipline assure near-perfect centralization of real political
power in spite of the legal framework of federalism. Central control is also
guaranteed by the federal government's monopoly on financial resources. Union
republics and other subunits do not have independent sources of revenue; they
are allocated money in the national budget. This money may be spent only on
items included in the budget, although the subunits have some freedom to determine the exact location where funds will be spent. While the union republics

have little meaningful autonomy, there is some evidence that governmental officials at the village and city level enjoy some independence. Such self-determination is, however, exercised not by right but at the discretion of the party. The party has permitted, and in some cases encouraged, autonomy at the local level in order to enhance the political system's ability to respond to local needs, and thus to reduce friction at the grass-roots level where government is in direct contact with the people.

China's formal structure is that of a centralized unitary state. Unlike the Soviet Union, it does not even make a pretense of federalism. Both the 1954 and 1975 constitutions clearly articulate the unitary nature of Chinese government. China's administrative structures are designed to implement at all levels of government decisions made at the center. At the apex of local governmental structures are the twenty-nine provinces, five autonomous regions, and three centrally administered municipalities: Peking, Shanghai, and Tientsin. In practice, control has shifted to the provinces, and within them to the counties, cities, villages, and communes. The commune was planned to consolidate the social, economic, political, and military functions in a single new unit. Within the commune, "production brigades" and "production teams" were created to perform political as well as economic tasks. However, initial problems associated with such a radical shift in political institutions caused adaptations to be made. More traditional political units — specifically the provinces and the urban governmental structures — retained many of their traditional functions.

Local government at every level is administered by people's congresses. However, the meetings of these congresses have been irregular. Their standing organs are the revolutionary committees, each elected by and supposedly responsible to the local people's congress. In fact, however, they dominate the parent bodies. After the Cultural Revolution, the revolutionary committees were formed without most of the people's congresses even convening. The responsibilities of the people's congresses are essentially administrative, rather than decision-making.

Despite China's highly centralized formal governmental structures and the centralizing effect of the Communist party, Chinese local governmental units have enjoyed greater autonomy than their Soviet counterparts. Unlike the Soviet Union, China has at times allowed considerable regional autonomy. With the exception of a brief period in the early 1960s, the processes of decision-making have been significantly decentralized in China. Mao's emphasis on greater mass participation and China's revolutionary attempt to merge state and society in the commune have reinforced this trend. The Cultural Revolution, which resulted in the merger of state and party executive organs in the revolutionary committees and in greater military and popular participation, also contributed to decentralization. The local revolutionary committees have shown themselves able to adapt decisions made at the center to local needs and problems. Further, by involving the military in society, the Chinese have minimized potentially serious power conflicts between the party and the military.

## POLITICAL STRUCTURES

In the Soviet Union the basic political unit at all levels of government is the *soviet,* or council. According to the constitution, the "highest organ of state power is the Supreme Soviet of the Soviet Union" (Article 30). The Supreme Soviet is comparable to a parliament or legislative body and has two equal branches, the Soviet of Nationalities and the Soviet of the Union. The Soviet of Nationalities is composed of 767 deputies and accords "representation" to the various ethnic groups; each nationality-based subunit elects a specified number of deputies. The Soviet of the Union has 750 deputies elected from districts of roughly equal populations. Elections of deputies are held every four years, and all adults are eligible to participate. According to the constitution, the Supreme Soviet exercises all political power, naming other governmental officials, enacting all legislation, and ratifying treaties.

The Supreme Soviet elects a Presidium of 36 members, which is theoretically the collegial presidency of the Soviet Union. The Soviets claim that the collegial nature of their presidency eliminates the dangers of one-man rule that threaten most presidential systems. The president of the Presidium — at present Nikolai V. Podgorny — is the titular head of state and performs most of the ceremonial tasks of a president or constitutional monarch: signing treaties, receiving ambassadors, signing legislation, and making official state visits abroad. Though his tasks are largely honorific, the president of the Presidium is nevertheless a powerful figure in Soviet politics. Leonid I. Brezhnev held this post prior to replacing Khrushchev as general secretary of the party. Podgorny, though subordinate to Brezhnev, appears to play an important part in Soviet policy-making. However, his influence is based more on his party offices than his governmental position.

Despite its broad constitutional powers, the Supreme Soviet in fact does very little. It is supposed to meet twice a year, but frequently convenes only once. When it does meet, each session usually lasts five or six days at the most. It elects — unanimously, of course — two key governmental bodies, the Presidium of the Supreme Soviet and the Council of Ministers. Candidates for these high offices are informally nominated by the party leadership, and never face open competition. The Presidium serves as an interim standing committee for the Supreme Soviet and is capable of exercising all the latter's powers when the Supreme Soviet is not in session. The Council of Ministers, which includes the premier and his cabinet, is charged with the actual day-to-day administration of government. When in session, the Supreme Soviet ratifies the actions of the Presidium and the Council of Ministers and adopts legislation proposed to it by its committees and the Council of Ministers. Such ratifications are always unanimous and usually preceded by little or no debate. Much of the Supreme Soviet's legislative output is ceremonial resolutions honoring, for example, party leaders, cosmonauts, and the accomplishments of outstanding workers or mothers.

The reason for the weakness of the Supreme Soviet is that actual political

Figure 3.5
*Soviet Governmental Structures*

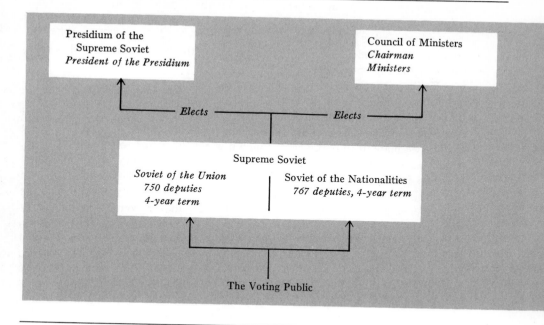

power in the Soviet Union is exercised by the Communist party. Three-quarters of the deputies in the Supreme Soviet are members of the party, and thus committed to follow the party's leaders. The nonparty deputies are notable citizens whose accomplishments are honored with offers of seats in the Supreme Soviet. They, too, willingly accept the party's claim to be the only legitimate voice of the people of the Soviet Union and follow the party leadership's directions. Debate over policy, proposed legislation, or the qualifications of leaders is restricted to party circles and rarely occurs in the Supreme Soviet; it is assumed that the party has already reached the correct decision.

The Presidium of the Supreme Soviet might be expected to play an important part in policy-making: it includes top-level leaders (among them the party's general secretary) and the constitution grants it very broad powers. However, there is little evidence to suggest that this body exercises its formal powers. While more active and influential than its parent body, the Supreme Soviet, the Presidium is not the locus of real political decision-making or debate.

The Council of Ministers, elected by the Supreme Soviet, is somewhat comparable to the cabinets of Britain and France. It is charged with the day-to-day conduct of government and the proposing of legislation for consideration by the Supreme Soviet. The chairman of the Council of Ministers — at present Aleksei Kosygin — is comparable to the British or French prime minister. Unlike his

British counterpart, however, the Soviet premier is not always the leading national political personality, since the single most powerful individual in the Soviet Union is not a government official but the general secretary of the Communist party. At times the party leader has also been the premier; this was true of both Stalin and Khrushchev. But since Khrushchev's fall in 1964, the posts have been held by two different men and the party secretary, Brezhnev, has been the supreme political leader.

Unlike cabinets in western democracies, the Soviet Council of Ministers is not a body organized to act in unison; the various ministries are separately subject to party control. In general, the Council of Ministers implements and administers the policies and decisions of the party. However, it would be wrong to underestimate its importance. Though it is not the major policy-making body, it does have considerable influence on the formulation of policy. Its membership is drawn from the top levels of the party, and thus its personnel overlaps with the party organs that actually do make decisions. Its ability to influence the decision-making process is enhanced by the fact that it conveys to the party information on the needs and interests of the government administration. Furthermore, the Council of Ministers controls the vast state bureaucracy, which gives it a powerful political base from which to influence policy-making. Finally, it can shape policies in the process of implementing them. The party's decisions are often formulated in broad terms, which allows the Council of Ministers considerable leeway in interpretation and implementation. In a similar manner, the chairman of the Council of Ministers is a powerful political leader. The political importance of the post is demonstrated by the fact that, after consolidating hold on power, both Stalin and Khrushchev held this position concurrently with the post of party secretary. Kosygin is regarded as second only to Brezhnev in power and influence.

Following the Cultural Revolution, China's formal structures gave way to ad hoc political groupings like the revolutionary councils. Yet the 1975 constitution reveals that the structural patterns of the 1950s are being institutionalized and adapted to changing conditions. The 1975 constitution describes the emerging role of the rural people's communes, and proclaims the duty to work and the right to such personal private property as "income from labor, savings, houses, and other means of subsistence." It defines procedures for implementing the ideals of social justice in calling for "working personnel of all organs to participate in collective labor"[5] and equal rights for women. The major innovation in the new constitution is the merger of state, party, and military through the formation of the revolutionary committees at each level of political and economic governance.

The highest state structure, under the "leadership of the Communist party of China," is the National People's Congress (NPC). Unlike the bicameral (two-chamber) legislature of the Soviet Union, the Chinese legislative body has

5. Article 7, 1970 draft of the Chinese constitution. Cited in Winberg Chai, *The New Politics of Communist China* (Pacific Palisades, Cal.: Goodyear Publishing Company, 1972), p. 204.

FIGURE 3.6

## Basic Institutions of Chinese Government

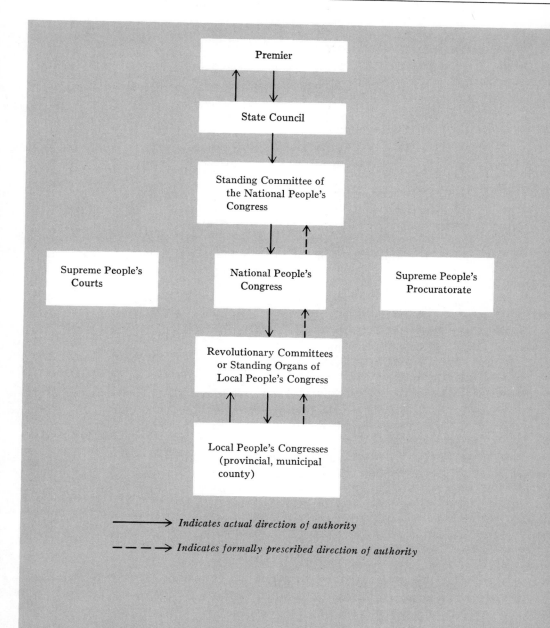

| | Premier | |
| | State Council | |
| | Standing Committee of the National People's Congress | |
| Supreme People's Courts | National People's Congress | Supreme People's Procuratorate |
| | Revolutionary Committees or Standing Organs of Local People's Congress | |
| | Local People's Congresses (provincial, municipal county) | |

⟶ *Indicates actual direction of authority*

--- ⟶ *Indicates formally prescribed direction of authority* only one branch. The NPC is indirectly elected. For example, after the adoption of the 1954 constitution 278 million voters went to the polls to choose more than 5 million deputies to people's congresses at the primary level. They elected deputies to people's congresses at the next level, who in turn chose the deputies for the National People's Congress. Each deputy's term of office is five years.

While the National People's Congress is supposed to be elected every four years and to meet once a year, it had met only four times prior to 1976. Between 1965 and 1975, the NPC met for only one session, held in early 1975. An essential feature of the NPC is the forum it supposedly provides for such major social groups as women, national minorities, religious organizations, and intellectuals.

The NPC's sessions have often been devoted to questions of leadership, rather than deliberation and legislation. Its ability to discharge its formally defined tasks is limited by its size, since there are more than a thousand deputies. It is interesting to note that the most revolutionary restructuring of China's society, the Great Leap Forward's creation of communes, was decreed by the Communist party's politburo without having been presented to the National People's Congress, where there was potential serious opposition to the plan. The formal powers of the NPC are to make and amend the constitution, to make laws, to appoint and remove the premier of the State Council upon the recommendation of the Central Committee of the Communist party, and to examine and approve the state budget. The National People's Congress elects the Standing Committee, which is supposed to assure continuity of state action when the NPC is not in session. The status of this body has not been clear since the end of the Cultural Revolution.

The National People's Congress also initially elected the Chairman of the People's Republic, Mao Tse-tung. He appointed the premier and vice-premier, as well as the heads of ministries and commissions, the Secretary General of the State Council, and the vice-chairman and members of the Council of National Defense. The chairman was also the commander of the armed forces and concurrently chairman of the Council of National Defense. The position of chairman of the People's Republic was thus far more than simply an honorary one.

In 1959 Mao relinquished his hold on the chairmanship, allowing Liu Shao-chi to replace him. Mao counted on his personal authority and position in the party to preserve his influence over China's policy. However, Liu used the chairmanship to control the state bureaucracy, establish his own policies, and gain enough leverage to oppose Mao for more than a decade. Ultimately, Liu was purged during the Cultural Revolution.

The National People's Congress also formally designates the State Council. (Again, it is important to emphasize that in most cases the NPC's appointments are actually determined by the party outside the formal structures of government.) The State Council is the executive organ of the highest state authority. Under the chairman and the premier, it executes and administers the affairs of state. The council is composed of a premier, several vice-premiers, ministers, heads of commissions, and a secretary general. The premier has for the past

FIGURE 3.7

Central Economic Administration in China

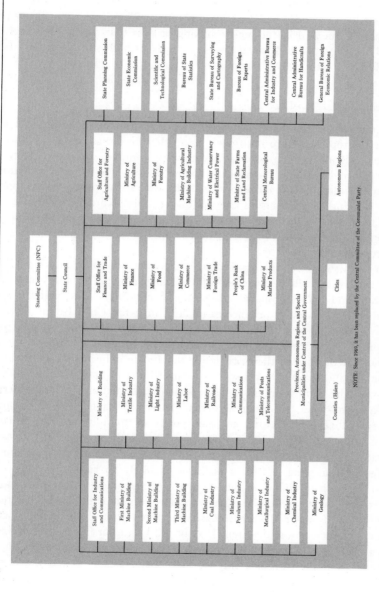

Staff Office for Industry and Communications
First Ministry of Machine Building
Second Ministry of Machine Building
Third Ministry of Machine Building
Ministry of Coal Industry
Ministry of Petroleum Industry
Ministry of Metallurgical Industry
Ministry of Chemical Industry
Ministry of Geology

Ministry of Building
Ministry of Textile Industry
Ministry of Light Industry
Ministry of Labor
Ministry of Railroads
Ministry of Communications
Ministry of Posts and Telecommunications

Standing Committee (NPC)
State Council

Staff Office for Finance and Trade
Ministry of Finance
Ministry of Food
Ministry of Commerce
Ministry of Foreign Trade
People's Bank of China
Ministry of Marine Products

Staff Office for Agriculture and Forestry
Ministry of Agriculture
Ministry of Forestry
Ministry of Agricultural Machine Building Industry
Ministry of Water Conservancy and Electrical Power
Ministry of State Farms and Land Reclamation
Central Meteorological Bureau

State Planning Commission
State Economic Commission
Scientific and Technological Commission
Bureau of State Statistics
State Bureau of Surveying and Cartography
Bureau of Foreign Experts
Central Administrative Bureau for Industry and Commerce
Central Administrative Bureau for Handicrafts
General Bureau of Foreign Economic Relations

Provinces, Autonomous Regions, and Special Municipalities under Control of the Central Government
Counties (Hsien)
Cities
Cities
Autonomous Regions

NOTE: Since 1969, it has been replaced by the Central Committee of the Communist Party.

Source: Winberg Chai, The New Politics of Communist China: Modernization Process of a Developing Nation (Pacific Palisades, Cal.: Goodyear Publishing Company, 1972), p. 73. Copyright © 1972. Goodyear Publishing Company. Reprinted by permission of the publisher.

two decades been Chou En-lai, whose persistence through decades of political struggle suggests both the power of this state position and his own political skills. The State Council's functions include implementation of the national economic plans and the state budget; the direction of cultural, educational, and public health services; the management of affairs concerning national minorities and overseas Chinese; and, finally, national security. The State Council has proved to be more influential in the policy-making process than has the Soviet Union's Council of Ministers, and has at times, through its high officials, found itself an active force in intraparty conflicts.

## SUCCESSION POLITICS

Few communist states have developed and institutionalized patterns of succession for the top leadership positions. As a rule, the formal state and party constitutions call for elections and specify their procedures. However, elections are seldom resorted to unless the aspiring leaders feel assured of success. Otherwise, succession is determined through bargaining within the party organs, and may involve seeking the support of the military (as did Khrushchev in 1953–1957 and Mao in 1960–1968) and the masses. Chairman Mao's mobilization of the Red Guards in the late 1960s was an attempt to use mass support in a battle for succession.

In the struggle for succession that will follow Chairman Mao's death, most of the key actors will be members of the party elite. The dual roles of most high state and military officials make this a certainty. The military and the bureaucracy are likely to produce candidates for what Chou En-lai describes as "the collective leadership which will replace Chairman Mao,"[6] and a political coalition of Mao's closest followers will also be competing. Among those who will undoubtedly utilize their proximity to Mao to gain advantage in the competition for succession are his wife, Chiang Ch'ing; Chang Chun-chiao; Wang Hung-wen, the youthful number-three person in the nation's political hierarchy; and Yao Wen-yuan, a former Shanghai municipal leader. While the military will have the capacity either to seize power or to influence the outcome, it clearly cannot fulfill popular expectations without the support of the state bureaucratic cadres. Among those in the state bureaucratic group are Chou En-lai and Teng Hsiao-p'ing. Thus, a coalition is likely to result.

In the Soviet Union after Lenin's death, the question of succession produced a crisis that lasted a decade. The struggle between Stalin and his real and imaginary rivals reached such intensity at times that the smooth functioning of the entire society was threatened. A brutal battle for power ensued, in which Stalin's unsuccessful rivals were ousted from the party and usually physically eliminated, and the lives not only of the upper echelons of party and government leadership but also of the people at the grassroots were deeply affected.

When Stalin died, a new succession crisis occurred. This struggle, however,

6. *New York Times,* 17 October 1972.

was shorter and less disrupting to the overall political system. Khrushchev consolidated his hold by 1957, about four years after Stalin's death. Unsuccessful rivals were dropped from important governmental and party positions, but were not liquidated or shipped to Siberian work camps. The only exception was Lavrenti Beria, the head of Stalin's secret police, who was executed shortly after Stalin's death. The struggle for power involved individuals and groups from all sectors of Soviet life (the military, industrial managers, and government bureaucrats, as well as party leaders), but it did not deeply affect the lower levels of the governmental and party structures as had the struggle over Lenin's post.

The most recent succession in the Soviet Union was the replacement of Khrushchev by Brezhnev and Kosygin. Though this shift was sudden and unpredicted, it did not produce a dramatic upheaval of the party or the government. The decision to oust Khrushchev was apparently made at a Central Committee meeting. While there was some maneuvering by leaders in the months after Khrushchev's fall, the situation was stabilized within a year. It is unclear whether this pattern will be repeated in future periods of succession or whether the ease of this transition was the product of peculiar circumstances unlikely to be replicated. The mechanisms of succession in the Soviet Union are likely to be tested again soon, as Brezhnev is now in his seventies and there are indications that his health is deteriorating.

## ACTUALITY: THE LONG SHADOW

China and the Soviet Union (and other communist nations as well) are both characterized by a considerable gap between the formal political framework and the actual practice of politics. For the Soviet Union this contradiction is apparent in the statement on federalism, the role of the legislatures at the national and republic levels, and the provisions for elections. For China it is clearest in the national legislature's role and the provisions for elections. In each of these areas, the Communist party's role far exceeds that specified in the constitution. The party sets national goals, recruits public officials, and monitors the state bureaucracies. While the formal state structures oversee the day-to-day administration of public policy, goals are set by the Communist parties of both nations.

The nature of the center of power may vary from party predominance to party coalitions with military, bureaucratic, and even nongovernmental groups (e.g., China's Red Guards in 1966–1968). Industrial development has caused the economic policies of both nations to be based increasingly on the principles of decentralization. In China this process has been accelerated by the Great Leap Forward and the Cultural Revolution. Bureaucracies, state-administered nterprises, and communes all tend to assume initiative in the selection of their policies; these policies must, however, be consistent with national goals. Within both nations, degrees of autonomy vary from region to region and year to year, but the trend is unmistakable.

# Mexico and Nigeria

Whereas China and the Soviet Union have transformed themselves from centralized monarchies to unified single-party structures, Mexico and Nigeria
exemplify a more common pattern in developing nations. Both attained independence as highly segmented societies. In Mexico political allegiance was
divided: the Spanish paid homage to the king in far-off Spain, the mestizos to
the caudillos, and the Indians to the caciques. In Nigeria limited centralization
had been accomplished (particularly in the Northern and Western Regions), but
most citizens' loyalties were to village social and political leaders. The task of
developing a stable political framework without an adequate unifying ideology
or even a common language was a severe challenge to both nations.

Both Mexico and Nigeria turned to foreign models in developing their
constitutions. The Mexicans in 1824, 1857, and 1917 adopted the United
States' presidential system as their model, while Nigeria under British guidance
adopted the British parliamentary pattern. During the formative years of both
nations, federal systems were employed to cope with centrifugal regional forces.
In both cases, the regional forces put too great a stress on the fragile structures,
and the result was military intervention. Mexico's federalist presidential system
exists to this day though it has undergone lapses and considerable modifications;
Nigeria's original framework was cast aside in 1966, but abolition may prove to
be temporary.

## MEXICO: PRESIDENTIAL DEMOCRACY

Mexico's current constitution, promulgated in 1917, is successor to and in-
heritor of a political tradition whose previous manifestations include two formal
constitutions and various adaptations and contributions by a long line of military and civilian leaders. The current Mexican political framework is a federal
presidential system with a bicameral legislature, an independent judiciary, and
exclusive powers for the states. The most powerful forces in the actual political
formula are the presidency and the dominant political party, the Partido
Revolucionario Institucional (PRI). The latter is not specifically provided for
in the formal political framework.

Mexico's constitutions have differed in the degree of powers conferred on
the federal government and the limitations or privileges granted to the church.
For many years the church, the military, and the traditional landed elite were
the major political forces in Mexico. The first constitution (1824) failed to
provide the center the strength it needed during the important early years of
nation-building, and the stress of attempting to unite numerous divisive forces
prompted the first military intervention. (A similar process led to the more
recent military interventions in Nigeria.) The 1857 constitution, also modeled
on that of the United States, was an attempt to remedy these weaknesses. It
incorporated the right of judicial review and abolished some privileges of the
army and clergy.

Many provisions of the 1857 constitution — including the presidential system, bicameral legislature, and parallel executive–legislative structures of the twenty-nine state governments — were incorporated into the 1917 federal constitution. This constitution, still in effect today, was the first modern constitution to posit the government's duty to provide for the social welfare of the people. It further circumscribed the role of the church, prohibiting clerics from working in public educational institutions and enjoining both the church and foreigners from holding land or exploiting subsoil resources. The constitution also granted the president the right to expel foreign companies and individuals from the land. It provided for social rights as well as political liberties, guaranteeing the rights of workers to bargain collectively and to organize labor unions. It also specified principles for land allocations. Like its predecessor, this constitution was not a social contract to which the people had assented. Developed and promulgated by the elite, it reflected a compromise between two weakly held ideologies: the capitalist and libertarian values of the wealthy landed classes, and the stress of social justice and secularization of representatives of peasant and labor groups.

Nominally, Mexico is a federation of thirty-one states. Each state has the right to elect its own governor and legislature. The state governments have the legal power to raise revenues through taxes and to allocate expenditures within the constitutionally defined areas of their jurisdiction. In actual practice, the federal structure has been emasculated. The constitution grants the federal senate the power to appoint a new state governor when it is determined that the government of any state has broken down. In the past this power was used by the federal government to depose state authorities who were unwilling to follow directions from Mexico City. Mexican presidents have called upon the Senate to declare the "disappearance of state powers" some forty-seven times since 1918. In recent years this device has been used rarely because presidents have other means to assure centralized control over the states.[7] The federal system is further weakened by the centralizing force of the PRI, which controls not only the central government but also the governorships and legislatures of every state. Furthermore, while states have the constitutional power to raise their own funds, all are in fact heavily reliant and some virtually totally dependent, upon the federal government for necessary revenues.

Mexico's state and local governments are directly supervised by the Ministry of Interior (Gobernación). The minister of interior has the power through the president to remove local officials. He is represented at the local level by a military commander. Below the state governor and unicameral legislature are the local officials. Municipal governments, each headed by an elected mayor and council, have responsibility over the subdistricts. The municipal council is a deliberative body, presided over by, and considerably weaker than, the mayor; together they approximate the commission-type local government. Local governments usually wait for the central government to develop programs

7. Robert E. Scott, *Mexican Government in Transition* (Urbana: University of Illinois Press, 1964), p. 273.

to solve their problems, and this dependency is reinforced by the federal government's practice of preempting local initiatives and controlling revenues. Local government is further debilitated by the central and state governments' assumption of such functions as education, construction, and public works. The federal government is the source of most of the revenues provided to local government. In fact, federal revenues average around 70 percent of the total, state revenues around 25 percent, and local government collections less than 5 percent.

## MEXICAN POLITICAL STRUCTURES

Perhaps the best explanation for the weakness of the Mexican federal system is the political pre-eminence of the president of the republic. Indeed, the constitutional and real powers of the president make him unrivaled as the dominant figure on the Mexican political scene. Although limited to one six-year term, the president is an extremely powerful leader. Formally, his responsibilities are similar to those of the president of the United States, but his actual powers are much broader. The Mexican president has the power not only to initiate legislation and veto measures passed by congress, but also to delay implementing legislation, and, in the absence of congressional action, to implement policy by decree. In practice, the president can count on the cooperation of the congress to pass the legislation he desires — and little else.

In addition to the generous powers provided by the constitution, the president's ascendancy is enhanced by his control of the PRI and his popular appeal. The PRI controls all aspects of politics at all levels, and the president, as the effective head of the party, uses it to support his actions. While the party is pluralist in composition and lacks the discipline of a governing communist party, it is a powerful political force that can be marshaled by the president for his ends. The president also benefits from the support of the general population. Presidential elections are given considerable attention not because the contest is likely to be close (in fact, the PRI candidate always wins) but because it offers the PRI candidate the opportunity to build an almost personal rapport with the masses. During the campaign the candidate's name and picture are ubiquitous, and he makes an effort to expose himself to as much of the population as possible. For many Mexicans, the president personifies the PRI, the Revolution, and Mexico itself; he is a paternal figure who has replaced the *patrón* of old as the object of total commitment and political loyalty. To these considerable powers of the president must be added control of the military and the capacity to use it for political ends. For example, when a protest movement developed in the Yucatán in 1969 over alleged electoral fraud involving the PRI, the president ordered troops to seize the ballot boxes and restore order.

In short, the president is an elected benevolent dictator for the duration of his six-year term. He can use his position to promote social change, as did

8. James Wilkie, *The Mexican Revolution* (Berkeley: University of California Press, 1970), p. 3.

Cárdenas with rural reforms and López Mateos with programs of socialized medicine, or to maintain the privileges of a few and inhibit social change that adversely affects them, as did Miguel Alemán. In spite of his powers, the president must interact with interest groups, party members, and the formal governmental structures (the judiciary, congress, the bureaucracy, and local and state governments). He is not free of political pressure from these and other sections of society, and his success in achieving his goals depends upon his ability to win the support of at least some of these groups.

The second of the three supposedly equal branches of the Mexican government is the legislature, which has two chambers: the Senate and the Chamber of Deputies. The Senate has 60 members elected for nonrenewable six-year terms. In practice, all are members of the PRI selected for candidacy by the president. The lower house, the Chamber of Deputies, has 231 members, each elected in a single-member district for a three-year term. Nearly all are members of the PRI, but a selected number of *diputados de partido* are chosen from the minority parties to guarantee representation to a variety of partisan interests. Five seats are allotted to each minority party securing a minimum of 1.5 percent of the total national vote, and another seat is awarded for every additional .5 percent to a maximum of twenty-five seats. The participation of the minority parties has led to more enlightened debate.

In terms of actual power, the president clearly dominates congress. Usually more than 80 percent of the president's proposed legislation passes congress unanimously; the rest of his proposals are passed nearly unanimously.[9] Occasionally the president uses the congress as a means of testing public opinion on potentially controversial issues before taking a stand. On other occasions highly controversial and divisive issues with little potential for partisan advantage (e.g., abolition of the death penalty) are left for congress to thrash out without presidential guidance. In spite of its lack of power and independence, the Mexican congress serves to legitimize the regime. As one study of the Chamber of Deputies concludes, "The public understands that the Chamber is subservient to the executive; nonetheless, because of the formal authority of the Chamber in national decision-making it stands as a symbol to assure the public that the government will act in a responsible and responsive manner."[10]

The Supreme Court, a constitutionally independent branch, does in practice manifest a certain degree of independence. In legal disputes involving social rights, laborers and tenants have a slim chance of favorable disposition of their claims to work benefits and land; in cases filed against the president of the republic, the plaintiff's chances of securing a favorable judgment are around 34 percent.[11]

9. Pablo Gonzáles Casanova, *Democracy in Mexico* (New York: Oxford University Press, 1970), pp. 18–20.

10. Rudolph O. de la Garza, *The Mexican Chamber of Deputies as a Legitimizing Agent of the Mexican Government and Political System,* Institute of Government Research Series, no. 12 (Tucson: University of Arizona, 1972), p. 24.

11. Gonzáles Casanova, *Democracy in Mexico*, pp. 21–22.

## PRESIDENTIAL SUCCESSION IN MEXICO

In the past, the transfer of power from one leader to the next was a traumatic event in Mexico. During the nineteenth century most successions were occasioned by military coups or revolts. Since the Revolution, succession has gradually become regularized and in the last thirty-five years it has been accomplished without incident. The focus of the succession process is the nomination of the PRI candidate for the presidency. The nomination procedure involves much elaborate negotiation and maneuvering within the PRI. Needless to say, the incumbent president plays an important and often decisive part in the selection of the candidate. Once the PRI's candidate has been designated, there ensues a brief period of political uncertainty while the candidate builds new loyalties in the PRI and develops a personal bond with the Mexican people. As he does so, he inevitably weakens the incumbent president's authority, and most presidents attempt to delay the nomination of a successor as long as possible to minimize the length of the transition period. Despite the possibility of tension between the outgoing president and the nominee, the process of succession has functioned smoothly since 1940.

## NIGERIA: POLITICAL FRAMEWORK IN FLUX

Between 1945 and 1959, the British in Nigeria were subject to growing pressure from Nigerian nationalists to grant independence to Nigeria as a whole, and to comparable pressure from the major ethnic groups to convey power to them. The British responded by creating a federation of three states — the Western Region, the Eastern Region, and the Northern Region — and the Federal Territory of Lagos.

These early British efforts to supply Nigeria with a political framework contained the seeds of later conflict. By uniting groups with differing political, social, and religious values and no prior history of political cooperation, Britain endowed the new nation with severe ethnic tensions. Because it granted regional autonomy but failed to assure economic equality to the three major groups, the federal solution to Nigerian unity was to exacerbate ethnic tensions. The federal structure strengthened regionalism and allowed differing regional political traditions and institutions to develop. In short, the political framework acknowledged and accentuated ethnic and regional differences. However, it is questionable whether any alternative political framework would have been more successful. The federal structure was a British concession to Nigerian demands for greater regional autonomy, and ethnic tensions were probably unavoidable whatever the political framework.

In 1959, a year before formal independence, a new Nigerian constitution, which retained many of the features of the 1954 constitution, was adopted. At the national level, a bicameral legislature consisting of a House of Representatives and a Senate was established. The constitutional head of state (initially

Dr. Nnamdi Azikiwe) was chosen by an electoral college consisting of members of the Senate and House of Representatives; his term of office was five years. The prime minister, who served as head of the government, was selected from the majority party in the House of Representatives, whose 312 members were elected from single-member districts based on the distribution of population. The Senate had 12 members from each region, as well as 4 senators from the Federal Territory of Lagos and 4 senators selected by the president on the advice of the prime minister. The senators were chosen by their regional governments to represent the regions, but had little power. They could merely delay legislation and vote on constitutional amendments and alterations of constitutional constituencies.

Each of the regional legislatures was bicameral, with an elected House of Assembly from single-member constituencies and an upper chamber called the House of Chiefs. All parliamentary business was conducted in English, except in northern Nigeria, where Hausa was accorded recognition as the second official language. Chiefs were hierarchically classified, with the classes defined differently by each region. First-class or head chiefs were the highest rank. The powers of the House of Chiefs varied by region. In the north, the House of Chiefs established in 1946 was similar to the United States Senate, coequal with the House of Assembly; disagreements were resolved by a joint committee of twenty representatives from each house. The premier was chosen from the House of Assembly in the east, west, and midwest, but could be selected from either house in the Northern Region.

Local government has also varied according to region. In Hausa–Fulani-controlled portions of northern Nigeria, the main local governments are called Native Authorities. *Emirs* (the traditional elite) govern their domains through these councils. The power of the emirs is considerable, and extends even to vetoing council decisions. Through 1967, most of the councils in the north were elected; however, many also had "traditional" members co-opted by the council. The Eastern Region directly elected the provincial assemblies and local councils. When the inclusion of chiefs or "traditional" members was deemed necessary, their numbers were not allowed to exceed one-fifth of the total membership. The Western Region had a third form of local government: at the lowest level were directly elected local councils, which were responsible for electing the divisional councils.

The constitutional provisions never really took root. Structures existed but were not institutionalized; that is, they did not achieve the acceptance and usage necessary for political development, due to strong regional orientations and to the lack of effective socioeconomic interaction and the trust that would have resulted from such interaction. Mistrust was reinforced by abuses of the federal scheme, which was flexible enough to encourage those who would assert themselves at the center, but too fragile without legitimacy and support to prevail against the regional centrifugal forces. The first major abuse was the 1961 effort by the northern regional government to eliminate its political opposition. In a parallel move, federal opposition was reduced when the federal ruling coalition of the Northern People's Congress and the Ibo-dominated NCNC took advantage of a squabble in the western legislature to suspend the western regional government and break up the west's leading party, the Action Group. Subsequent court decisions were influenced to support the move, census figures were falsified, and elections rigged, greatly intensifying southerners' lack of faith in the constitutional system. During and after the 1964 election, anti-Ibo feelings became more pronounced in the north. Following massive riots in the Western Region after the federal election of 1964 and the regional election of 1965, the military intervened in January 1966 and put an end to the federal experiment.

The military's intervention was motivated in part by the need to eliminate regional cleavages as the major source of political conflict. General Ironsi abolished the regions, but did not replace them with any other form of subnational administrative unit. The resulting de facto unitary government, as well as Ironsi's moves to integrate the civil service, further accelerated mistrust and led to another coup in the summer of 1966 that brought General Gowon to power. Gowon, under military auspices, created twelve states, dismissed the parliament, and established in 1967 a constitution that created a government hierarchy organized as shown in Table 3.3.

In place of parliamentary rule, a Supreme Military Council (SMC) appointed ministers to rule at the national level and officials to administer the new state governments. Many of these leaders appointed by the military were civilians with previous political experience, such as Chief Awolowo from the Western Region (who resigned in 1971 to protest proposed higher budgetary allocations to the military).

Although high state officials appoint the local governments, the traditional political elites still hold important positions in the 1970s. Since 1966 the military elite has sought to expand its influence on local political decision-making. There is considerable variation among the states, but the appointed military governor and the state commissioners named by him — often with federal and local elite input — exercise considerable power over the local districts or villages. Furthermore, civil servants representing federal ministries are gaining increasing leverage in local political decision-making.

This military-dominated format has persisted into the early 1970s, though the eventual reinstatement of civilian-elected government has been promised. It is likely that any new constitution will retain the states in place of regions, and that competing political parties — if there are to be rivals to the military–bourgeois-dominated party — will not be regionally or ethnically based. It is also probable that a future constitution will provide for a strongly centralized political authority and will favor the existing political power centers: the military and the emerging business and professional elite. The future power of the traditional elites will depend on their ability to adapt — which has so far been remarkable — and on the rate of economic development in their areas. Development will inevitably give rise to competitive new elites.

TABLE 3.3

## Basic Institutions of Military Rule in Nigeria

| Structure — level | Participants |
|---|---|
| Supreme Military Council (SMC) | Chairman of SMC, heads of air force and navy, and 12 state governors |
| Federal Executive Council | SMC members, attorney-general, inpector-general of police, 15 cabinet department heads |
| Federal Supreme Court | Chief justice, 3 associate justices, and 12 state chief justices |
| State Government Executive Councils (12) | Governor (appointed by SMC), commissioner of police, chief legal officer, permanent secretaries of commissions |
| State High Courts and State Appeals Courts | |
| Village council, village group, council, district council, "native authority" (predominantly in the northwestern and northeastern states) | |

## POLITICAL SUCCESSION IN NIGERIA

The problem of political succession in Nigeria is still unresolved. Thus far the selection of new national leaders has not been regularized, and it is unclear how the military will return power to civilians or how long the military will refrain from new political intervention. The 1966 and 1975 coups may indicate a trend toward military intervention as the means of ousting and recruiting leadership.

## MAJOR CONSTITUTIONAL ISSUES

Mexico and Nigeria have both been plagued by problems arising from cultural cleavages. These conflicts and attempted solutions to them have been manifested in the political framework. Nigeria's first republic (1960–1966) acknowledged these cleavages in the constitution and in, for example, the creation of regional governments, representation of the regions in the federal legislature, and the political party structure. Traditional-modern cleavages were also taken into account in such local governmental structures as the native authorities and the House of Chiefs. While many of these cleavages lost their formal constitutional recognition in the military coups of 1966 — in which the parties, the regional governments, and the federal parliament were all temporarily, and possibly permanently, suspended — the ethnic minority groups have been strengthened by the creation of the twelve new states. Minorities now form informal ruling coalitions, and are no longer subservient to a dominant ethnic group as under the regional system. Traditional elites seem to be declining gradually in influence as impatient educated Nigerian public officials seek to modernize political institutions.

In Mexico, the influence of the church has been a major ongoing constitutional issue. Conflict over the church's political and social power was probably the dominant source of political tension during Mexico's first century of independence. The church's powers were formally and effectively curbed by both the 1857 and 1917 constitutions.

A closely related issue has been the relative powers and responsibilities of the federal government and the regional governments. Though both Nigeria and Mexico have federal frameworks, Mexico is in practice highly centralized and Nigeria is becoming more so under military rule. The Nigerian military government currently exercises jurisdiction over several fields (including education) formerly reserved to the regions. This centralization may well be necessary to integrate new states and to arouse national political loyalties sufficiently strong to minimize sectional and ethnic divisions.

With regard to the overall issue of institutionalization, Mexico is well on its way to developing regularized processes for making and implementing public policy decisions and for transferring power from one set of leaders to the next. Gradually the conditions necessary to the orderly evolution of political rules are being established. Regional and religious cleavages are now minimal in comparison with the past, and the military — formerly a destabilizing factor — has been brought under the control of civilians. However, one debilitating problem remains: Mexico's failure to deal with its serious class cleavages. Class division is the factor most likely to frustrate efforts to institutionalize and stabilize Mexican politics.

With a far shorter history of independence, Nigeria has much farther to go in the pursuit of stable political institutions. Though the coups of 1966 and 1975 were setbacks to political institutionalization, it can also be argued that they contribute to that process. The breakdown of constitutional provisions for policy-making may be seen as detrimental to the process of institutionalization; on the other hand, though, the attempt to alter the conditions that destroyed earlier political frameworks, to regulate ethnic conflict, and to improve social and economic conditions may in the long run contribute to the achievement of appropriate institutions and practices for Nigeria.

# Conclusions

This chapter has demonstrated that constitutions and other descriptions of the political framework are more than inherited documents memorized in civics classes. They are created by individuals and given new life by each generation.

Their substance reflects the values of the prevailing elite and the adaptations the elite must make to existing conditions. Communist and noncommunist nations have faced similar problems in the early period of nation-building: conditions characteristic of minimal development — high illiteracy, unemployment, regionalism, inadequate governmental financial resources, high expectations, and a proliferation of contending factions — place great stress on new political structures. The cases we have examined highlight these problems. The Soviet Union, China, Mexico, and Nigeria all faced the task of integrating strong peripheral forces into the center. The early constitutional formats of Mexico and Nigeria gave way under these pressures, and the inevitable military intervention resulted. The Soviet Union and China, confronting the same conditions, adopted strong organized single-party systems, which, in partnership with the military, acted to institutionalize the state and party frameworks.

In a sense the test of a political framework is its ability to last — not simply to endure statically but to adapt flexibly. The political frameworks of Britain, the Soviet Union, and Mexico have met the test of time. However, a more significant test of their constitutional success will be their ongoing ability to respond to changes germane to the conduct of politics. France, China, and Nigeria still lack universally accepted political frameworks. Time and further development may remedy these nations' political deficiences: China twenty-five years after the advent of the communist regime is at approximately the same stage as was the Soviet Union in the late 1930s; Nigeria may be compared to Mexico in the early years of its independence. However, time alone may not suffice to provide these or other states with institutionalized political frameworks. Over 180 years after the Revolution of 1789, France still lacks consensus on basic political questions; the absence of such a consensus hinders acceptance of a political framework. Severe social and economic tensions may create cleavages that are reflected in political institutions and thus thwart the search for an acceptable political framework.

The political framework, as described in constitutional documents and implemented in actual practice, provides the institutional and procedural context for political action. Even when the framework is little more than a compendium of ad hoc procedures, groups and individuals seeking to influence political decisions must act within or upon the framework to achieve their goals. In the following chapters we shall look at some of the most important political actors: individual citizens, interest groups, political parties, government leaders, bureaucrats, and military officers.

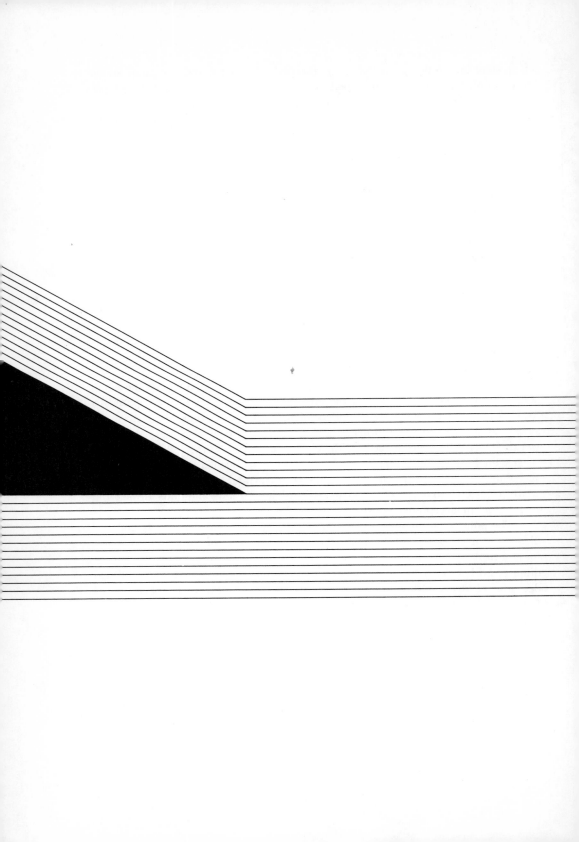

# II

## POLITICAL ACTORS

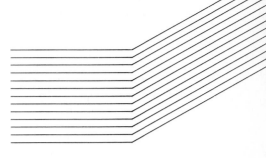

4

# *The Citizen in Politics*

## Introduction

A few days after the arrival in Peking of the Americans accompanying President Nixon on his visit to the People's Republic of China in 1972, the visitors happened to observe a surprising form of citizen political involvement: cooperative snow removal. One press account describes their amazement:

> In their brief time in Peking Americans received a startling lesson in social cooperation. To a man (and a woman), they were stunned at the sight of some 200,000 Chinese pouring onto the streets to remove the snow that had fallen during their visit. A compulsory exercise? To be sure, citizens who neglected their duties would be severely chastised. But the visitors detected a civic spirit and camaraderie that are spectacularly lacking in the present-day U.S.[1]

This voluntary snow removal — a form of political action unfamiliar to Westerners — not only makes unnecessary the expense of paid snow-removal teams and equipment, but also serves as an experience in civic action. The Chinese citizen gains a valuable sense of community participation and civic pride through his involvement in such volunteer work.

From volunteer snow removal to voting, citizens everywhere are involved in political action. Prior to the democratic revolutions of the eighteenth and nineteenth centuries, however, it was not unusual for most of a nation's population to be totally ignorant of and apparently unaffected by the government that ruled it. The individual was a passive *subject,* not a participating *citizen.* To-

1. *Time,* 6 March 1972.

day, the typical individual in nearly all states is aware of and clearly affected by his government. He or she is generally encouraged to participate in some way in the political process. So widespread is the norm of mass political participation that it is regarded as one of the features of the modern political unit, in contrast to the nonparticipatory traditional or primitive state.

One reason for the increase in political involvement on the part of the general population is the widespread acceptance, in principle if not always in fact, of *popular sovereignty* as the basis of legitimate political power. Popular sovereignty is the doctrine that the right to rule belongs to the people and that those who govern derive their authority from the people. With very few exceptions, rulers no longer claim to rule by divine or hereditary right. The general acceptance of the principle of popular sovereignty in both democratic and dictatorial regimes lends support to the norm of mass political participation: if political power is derived from the people, the people should be involved in politics to exercise their sovereignty.

In some states such involvement gives the citizen the opportunity to help shape the state's political future. However, mass political involvement does not necessarily mean that citizens participate in a democratic way by choosing their leaders or setting policy. Authoritarian regimes often have other motives for promoting mass participation. Some traditional authoritarian regimes and some conservative military regimes try to stifle political participation. However, most such regimes, especially those eager to promote social and economic change, find it useful to stimulate mass citizen involvement. Elections can be used to promote the sense of participation even if there is only one candidate for each office or the results are rigged. By means of rigged elections and other forms of controlled participation, authoritarian regimes can enhance their own legitimacy in the eyes of citizens and outsiders. By channeling popular participation into activities it can control, the regime can satisfy those who want to be politically active and give many the feeling of being part of the political process. In addition, authoritarian regimes may encourage voluntary civic action as a means of mobilizing the talents and energies of the masses in the pursuit of goals determined by the elite.

Controls on participation are also found in Western democratic societies. The right to vote may be restricted by poll taxes, literacy tests, property requirements, or registration procedures. Occasionally these restrictions have the effect of limiting the political influence of certain sectors of the population, especially ethnic minority groups and the poor. Blacks in the southern United States were discouraged and often actually prevented from voting by the application of such restrictions. And until recently several European democracies deprived women of the right to vote; as late as 1971, women could not vote in Swiss national elections. Other kinds of restraints are frequently imposed on political participation in democracies. Extremist groups may be barred from political activity and their members jailed or otherwise discriminated against on the basis of their political associations. Protest politics in the form of demonstrations, rallies, picketing, or sit-ins may be outlawed or subjected to severe restrictions. Such informal sanctions as social ostracism or loss of employment may discourage individuals from pursuing political activities deemed unacceptable by the majority.

## Political Participation and Political Stability

The forms of individual political action can vary from reading about political developments in the newspaper to voting to petitioning an elected official or a bureaucrat for a favor to active participation as a campaign worker or party propagandist. Even apparently nonpolitical civic volunteer action is a form of political participation in the sense that it gives the individual a sense of involvement and an administrative part to play in the political system.

No political system has sufficient organizational capacity to endure the stress it would suffer if every individual or group made demands on it at the same time. Unusually high rates of such participation can lead to political instability and even the collapse of the regime. This danger is particularly acute in the developing world, where political institutions are often fragile. However, even the more developed and established states can be endangered by sudden or unexpected increases in participation. They may lack institutions capable of dealing with large numbers of new participants. Furthermore, very high rates of participation are generally accompanied by intense political feelings symptomatic of severe social crisis. Large masses are politically mobilized only when they feel directly threatened by crisis. Consequently, the government's ability to respond to very high rates of participation is often hampered by its need, and sometimes its inability, to deal with the underlying social crisis that provoked such intense political feelings.

In the United States during the late 1960s, for example, a large number of young people became deeply disturbed by American involvement in southeast Asia. Motivated by the belief that the Vietnam War was immoral and by the desire to avoid being drafted to fight what they considered an unjust war, many of these young people sought an effective way to end the war. When normal channels of participation proved fruitless, the antiwar movement turned to demonstrations and street politics, which were perceived by the regime as a dangerous threat to national political stability. However, the government's inability to resolve the underlying social crises — growing public division on the war and the stalemated military situation in southeast Asia — undermined its efforts to respond to the vociferous new participants in the political process.

Too little popular participation can also be a danger to modern political systems. Classical democratic theory assumes a politically interested, informed, and involved public, and considerable participation is obviously important in liberal democracies. If the proportion of the population that participates is small, the goal of governmental accountability to the people will be difficult to achieve. Only authoritarian regimes unconcerned with social change can operate without mass participation. And even they might find their positions undermined by rivals who capitalize on unfulfilled popular desires for participation in order to build a political following.

## WHO PARTICIPATES IN POLITICS

For the overwhelming majority of citizens in most countries, political activities have low priority in rankings of preferred activities. Given the choice of how to spend their leisure time, most would prefer to do something other than engage in politics. Table 4.1 illustrates this finding with data derived from opinion surveys conducted in five countries. No more than 3 percent of those polled indicated that a civic or political activity was a preference in their use of free time. Consequently, the proportion of the population actively participating in politics tends under normal circumstances to be quite low. It usually requires an imminent crisis to draw the masses into voluntary political action. In many Third World countries the portion of the population that is politically aware is very small. The task of mobilizing and involving the rest of the population is rendered difficult by widespread illiteracy and by the virtual absence of past experiences in politics.

There is a wide spectrum of political activities, ranging from nonparticipation through observation of politics to public office-holding, available to the citizens of most states. Generally speaking, the more demanding and time-con-

TABLE 4.1

## Preferred Leisure Activities

| Activity (percentages)* | U.S. | U.K. | Germany | Italy | Mexico |
|---|---|---|---|---|---|
| Civic-political activities | 2 | 2 | 3 | 1 | 0 |
| Economic interest groups | 0 | 0 | 1 | 0 | 0 |
| Other interest groups | 3 | 0 | 0 | 0 | 0 |
| Charitable and welfare activities | 8 | 5 | 2 | 2 | 1 |
| Religious activities | 20 | 7 | 4 | 2 | 4 |
| "Social" activities | 18 | 18 | 8 | 3 | 6 |
| Hobbies, sports, etc. | 70 | 73 | 61 | 42 | 51 |
| Cultural activities (reading, TV, radio, etc.) | 33 | 44 | 52 | 33 | 58 |
| Travel | 0 | 3 | 7 | 8 | 13 |
| Other only | 0 | 5 | 15 | 17 | 4 |
| Nothing | 3 | 6 | 6 | 10 | 2 |
| Don't know | 0 | 0 | 1 | 3 | 1 |

* Percentages exceed 100 because of multiple responses.

Source: Adapted from Gabriel A. Almond and Sidney Verba, The Civic Culture: Political Attitudes and Democracy in Five Nations (Princeton: Princeton University Press, © 1963, published for the Center of International Studies, Princeton University), p. 263. Reprinted by permission of Princeton University Press.

FIGURE 4.1

*Pyramid of Political Involvement*

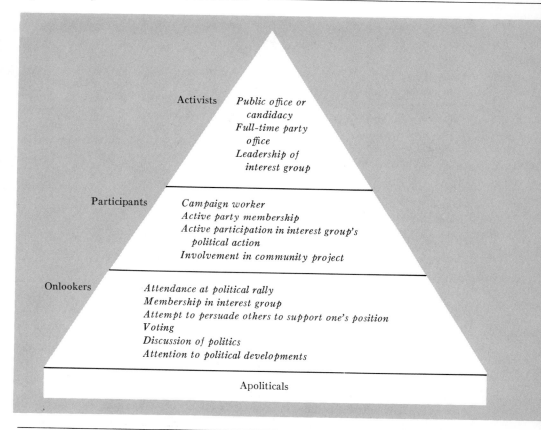

Activists
Public office or
candidacy
Full-time party
office
Leadership of
interest group

Participants
Campaign worker
Active party membership
Active participation in interest group's
political action
Involvement in community project

Onlookers
Attendance at political rally
Membership in interest group
Attempt to persuade others to support one's position
Voting
Discussion of politics
Attention to political developments

Apoliticals

suming a political activity, the fewer people participate. This principle is illustrated by the pyramid of political involvement shown in Figure 4.1. The farther up the pyramid, the fewer participants. At the level of activists, it is unusual to find more than 2 or 3 percent of the adult population.

There are a number of factors that influence the degree of an individual's voluntary political involvement. Some of these are *personal factors* related to the individual's own attitudes, beliefs, and personality traits. For example, the individual's disposition toward social activities, sense of personal efficacy in dealing with government officials, intensity of political attitudes, and perception of civic duties will influence the extent and nature of his or her political involvement. Another set of factors relates to the *political setting,* and includes the amount of exposure to political information accessible through the mass media or personal contacts, the political party structure, the relative accessibility of other organized political action groups, the relative importance of elections,

## TABLE 4.2

### Social Characteristics Correlated with Voting Turnout

| Higher turnout | Lower turnout |
|---|---|
| High income | Low income |
| High education | Low education |
| Occupational groups | Occupational groups |
| Businessmen | Unskilled workers |
| White-collar employees | Servants |
| Government employees | Service workers |
| Commercial-crop farmers | Peasants, subsistence |
| Miners | Farmers |
| Whites | Negroes |
| Men | Women |
| Middle-aged people (35–55) | Young people (under 35) |
| Older people (over 55) | |
| Old residents in community | Newcomers in community |
| Workers in Western Europe | Workers in United States |
| Crisis situations | Normal situations |
| Married people | Single people |
| Members of organizations | Isolated individuals |

Source: Seymour Martin Lipset, Political Man: The Social Bases of Politics (New York: Doubleday Anchor, 1963), p. 189. Reprinted with permission.

and the regime's attitude toward participation. *Socioeconomic factors* also influence participation. Studies of voting behavior have identified a number of social characteristics that correlate with the individual's propensity to vote or not vote. Table 4.2 summarizes the major social factors influencing political participation.

While all these social factors are important, the correlation between level of education and extent of participation is particularly noteworthy. The educated citizen is more likely to engage actively in the political process than is the uneducated citizen. The reasons for this are several: the more educated individual has more political information, a higher income and often more leisure time, and more frequent access to the mass media; he or she tends more frequently to belong to social organizations and to feel a greater sense of personal efficacy. Such a person is more likely to follow political developments, to have opinions on a broad range of political issues, to engage in political discussions, and to become involved in political activities.[2]

2. Gabriel A. Almond and Sidney Verba, *The Civic Culture: Political Attitudes and Democracy in Five Nations* (Boston: Little, Brown, 1965). See also Alex Inkeles, "Participant Citizenship in Six Developing Countries," *American Political Science Review* LXIII (December 1969): 1129–1141.

In communist states, the citizens' role in making policy and choosing leaders is minimized by the dominance of a powerful party elite. However, the proportion of the population actively engaged in political activities is probably larger than in most liberal democracies. The citizen participates in directed discussions of proposed policy, apartment- and commune-governing committees, sanitation teams, militias, volunteer fire brigades, and similar undertakings. Communist party members play the leading roles in all such activities, inspiring their fellow citizens to further efforts by their own dedication. It is incorrect to assume that the high rates of citizen participation in communist states are attributable to outright compulsion. Instead, most communist elites generate voluntary mass participation by strongly emphasizing the norm of community service. In short, the regime attempts to enhance the loyalty of the individual by encouraging civic involvement.

## THE CITIZEN AND POLITICS
## IN THE THIRD WORLD

In developing countries, political participation is a luxury in the sense that it is not available to individuals who live at or near the subsistence level and must devote all their time and energy to the struggle to exist. Since most developing states have low standards of living, few of their citizens have sufficient leisure time for politics. Illiteracy is another obstacle to participation, and often as much as 75–80 percent of the population of a developing nation is illiterate. Some sectors of the population may be geographically isolated from the centers of political power. Clan, tribal, and religious loyalties may also be obstacles to participation in culturally plural states that have yet to achieve national integration. All these factors contribute to widespread political apathy, and sometimes to total ignorance of the existence and operations of a national political unit.

Too little participation may hamper development, since the energy and talents of the population must be engaged if a country is to develop and implement economic programs and social reforms. Furthermore, the creation of effective political institutions is often dependent upon citizen involvement. Political parties, for example, strengthen themselves by recruiting members and involving them in the political process.

Too much participation on the other hand, may be destabilizing. The tensions produced by socioeconomic change and political development may result in protests, demonstrations, riots, violence, and other forms of political activism that are difficult if not impossible for fragile new political institutions to control. Indeed, even low levels of participation may be disruptive if political institutions are not sufficiently developed. If the population is mobilized by means of literacy drives, urbanization, and expansion of the mass media before the political institutions have become capable of directing and responding to the resulting participation, political disorder and instability are all but inevitable. This argument is developed and documented by Samuel Huntington in

*Political Order in Changing Societies* Huntington demonstrates that much of the political instability in the Third World is "the product of rapid social change and the rapid mobilization of new groups into politics coupled with the slow development of political institutions."[3] Too rapid social and economic modernization — in the sense of education, urbanization, mass communications, industrialization, economic growth, and a rising standard of living — may produce *anomie,* or the collapse of social norms and values. Mass political participation in such an atmosphere may result in violence and the destruction of existing political institutions. Thus, priority should be given to political development over social and economic change. Political stability and order will be enhanced if a nation devotes itself first to the creation of political institutions, and makes an effort to expand participation only when those institutions have become capable of handling new participants.

Thus, developing states confront the challenge of maintaining the proper ratio between institutionalization and participation. Too little participation may deprive the regime of human resources useful to the pursuit of its programs and frustrate citizens who want to take part in the political process. Too much participation may threaten the regime's stability and domestic order.

*Patron-client* politics is a mode of political participation common in the Third World that can successfully balance participation and stability. Patron-client relationships bind in unequal hierarchical interdependencies those who control power (patrons) and those who seek status or material benefits (clients).[4] Such bonds facilitate participation by integrating the humblest citizen into the political network and by providing opportunities for upward social and political mobility. The two-level hierarchy of the local patron (usually a prominent community figure) and his personal following of clients may evolve into a network of patron-client bonds in which patrons at a given level are clients of higher-level patrons. Such a network is called a "machine." The ties among the patron-client networks are maintained by mutually beneficial transactions in the form of services and goods. The clients receive jobs, contracts, and financial assistance in times of need from the political machine. In return, they provide political support by getting out the vote to support the machine's candidates, promoting attendance at political rallies, and performing other political chores for the machine. Clients may also provide such personal services to the patron as helping at the wedding of his daughter.

Patron-client politics is an effective means of organizing and controlling participation, and it can offer security, economic benefits, and opportunities for the poor. However, patron-client networks encourage dependence on the part of the clients and are often offensive to those at the bottom of the hierarchy. They are also economically wasteful: contracts are usually awarded for political

3. Samuel P. Huntington, *Political Order in Changing Societies* (New Haven: Yale University Press, 1968), p. 4.
4. René Lemarchand and Keith Legg, "Political Clientelism and Development: A Preliminary Analysis," *Comparative Politics* IV (January 1972): 149–178.

FIGURE 4.2
*A Typical Patron-Client Machine*

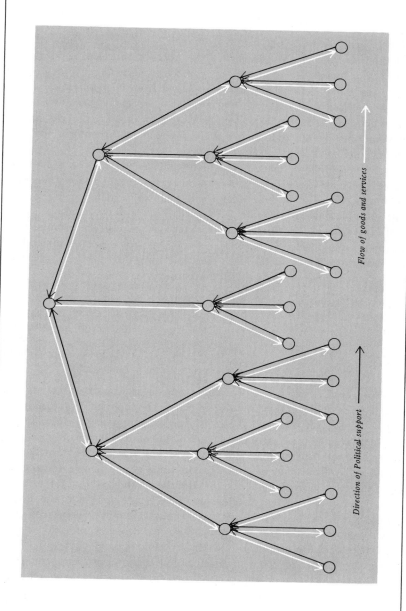

Direction of Political support ⟶

Flow of goods and services

reasons rather than to the lowest bidder, and funds used for individual payoffs to clients would be better invested in pursuit of collective goals.

## POLITICAL SOCIALIZATION

Political participation is not innate in human behavior; it is learned. Political values and attitudes are also learned. The process of developing political values, feelings, and knowledge is known as *political socialization.* Under normal circumstances, values and orientations are passed from one generation to the next through political socialization. Much of this process is accomplished during adolescence. However, political socialization is an ongoing process that persists throughout life as the individual's attitudes change to conform to his or her political experiences.

How the individual learns about political phenomena is an issue as yet unresolved by those who study political socialization. But there is general agreement on the identity of those who teach such political lessons, known as the *agents* of political socialization. The individual's first exposure to political stimuli is through the family. Basic political values, and sometimes party preferences, are developed unconsciously in the home and retained by many individuals throughout their lives. The following description of the socialization of French children delineates the process:

> Growing up, a child learns with what symbols his family identifies itself. Beyond the limits of the family he becomes aware of groups of people, of *cercles,* with which he and his family are either associated or not. He recognizes the associations through many symbols, some small, some important, some obvious, some hidden from all but the initiate. Clothing, food, dress, language, education, profession, all reveal membership in one circle or another.[5]

The school as an agent of socialization is as important as, and in some societies more important than, the family. The political leadership of most countries makes an effort to direct the process of political socialization, and the schools are the most frequent agents of the state's socialization efforts. History and civics courses may be required, and the use of certain textbooks dictated. The classroom may be used to train young people for the kinds of citizenship roles desired by the state. In the United States, for example, flag ceremonies and the pledge of allegiance instill national pride and loyalty. In some countries, military drills prepare students for military service. In others, especially communist states, community service projects undertaken by school groups help inculcate the ideal of voluntary civic action.

Another important agent of socialization is the peer group. As a result of the basic urge to conform, those who surround the individual at school, in the factory, or in the office help to shape his or her political orientations. The individual usually seeks to cooperate with peers and to bring his attitudes into

5. Lawrence Wylie, "Social Change at the Grass Roots," in *In Search of France,* ed. Stanley Hoffmann *et al.* (New York: Harper and Row, 1963), p. 231.

line with theirs. Other agents of political socialization include social groups such as churches, unions, and clubs; the mass media; government; and the individual's own political experience.

Because of the diversity of agents, the process of political socialization is by no means deterministic; that is, the individual's political orientations are not solely the product of outside forces. The individual usually acquires conflicting information and orientations from the various agents of socialization. For example, children in developing countries frequently learn traditional values — service to the family and loyalty to the kinship or ethnic group — in the home and secular values — civic responsibility and loyalty to the country — in school. The choices any given individual makes among the various versions cannot be predetermined. Furthermore, correlation between political attitudes and actual political behavior is not automatic. The fact that an individual has democratic values, for example, does not mean that he or she will always behave politically in a democratic way.

Political socialization provides support for the political system in that it perpetuates political values and orientations. Sometimes, however, the perpetuation of attitudes is detrimental to the regime's goals of political and social change, and a new set of values and orientations supportive of the desired political system is needed. The emergence of such new attitudes may take generations or even centuries. Or the government may undertake direct political socialization to instill the desired new attitudes in the entire population as rapidly as possible.

A brief survey of three of our countries will illustrate alternative means of changing political orientations. In Britain the transition from orientations supportive of a traditional monarchy to those conducive to modern democracy took several centuries. The government avoided overt interference in the process of political socialization, permitting an evolutionary change in attitudes and values. In contrast, the Chinese leadership has actively undertaken political socialization in order to create as rapidly as possible political orientations supportive of their ideological norms. The Chinese have not shrunk from the use of force and have sought to control the contributions of all agents of political socialization. Efforts have been made to eliminate the primacy of the family and to control the content of political socialization in the home. Religious bodies have been virtually abolished as agents of socialization. Massive re-education programs utilizing the mass media and direct person-to-person contact have sought to purge the adult population of traditional political attitudes and to replace them with attitudes in keeping with the new social and political order. Mexico's stance falls somewhere between the two extremes of governmental uninvolvement and total governmental involvement in the socialization process. The Mexican leadership has sought actively to create new political orientations during the sixty years of the Revolution. It has used the schools to inculcate a sense of national identity and to teach norms of political involvement. The revolutionary party uses its control of unions, business groups, and youth movements to organize popular support for the doctrines of the Revolu-

In France, protest is a common form of political involvement. At one time or another, virtually every social group is involved in a protest against government action or inaction. Pictured is a group of winegrowers in southern France protesting against government regulations on the quality of wine.

Women have long been denied access to positions of political power. In the Soviet Union, women have penetrated fields that in other countries are still male preserves, including medicine, university teaching, and the law. (Pictured are two Soviet woman judges alongside a male judge.) But women are still absent from the highest party councils. A major breakthrough for women's political rights took place in 1975 in the British Conservative party when Margaret Thatcher was elected party leader. (She is pictured with the man she defeated for that post, former prime minister Edward Heath.) Should the Conservatives win a majority in the next general election, Mrs. Thatcher would become Britain's first woman prime minister.

tion. The regime has also exploited the mass media as a means of socialization, to a limited degree. Unlike the Chinese, however, the Mexican leadership has not attempted to control certain agents of socialization. There has been no effort to interfere in the family in order to control its political norms and orientations. The church, a frequent target of Mexican revolutionaries in the past, is free of governmental interference so long as it does not intrude in politics. Nor are informal social contacts monitored for their political content.

The Mexicans' moderate approach to the formation of political attitudes is not necessarily to be applauded without criticism. Because more forceful interference in socialization is abjured, contradictory messages emanate from the uncontrolled agents and the government-inspired agents of socialization. Often parochial attitudes are developed in the home and challenged in the schools. Conflict between incompatible patterns of socialization may create problems of national and personal identity that hinder the emergence of a modern participatory political culture. In this sense, the Mexican government's restraint may retard the transformation of Mexican political culture in the directions desired by the leadership. A more radical reformation of political orientations might well have abolished some of the attitudes and norms that still act as obstacles to the political, economic, and social development of Mexico. On the other hand, radical interference in the socialization process has a high price measured in terms of the sacrifice of traditional values and, perhaps, political violence and bloodshed. For those who value both rapid change and human feeling, the choice between the two alternatives may be difficult.

# Britain and France: The People Rule?

Contrary to the implications of traditional democratic theory, most citizens in liberal democracies show little interest in governing themselves. The typical person in the street is generally uninterested in politics, poorly informed about governmental and political developments, and uninvolved in political activities. This pattern of minimal political interest and involvement is typical of most liberal democracies, including our two case studies. Table 4.1 (page 158) indicates that only 2 percent of the British polled chose politics as a preferred leisure activity. A study of French political involvement employed an index of participation ranging from high participation to no participation.[6] French citizens were assigned to the "high participant" category if they voted in national elections and performed any two of the following actions: attended one or more political meetings, read election posters, or attempted to persuade others to vote in a certain way. Even when high participation was defined this broadly (all these activities are attributed to "onlookers" in the pyramid of political involvement illustrated in Figure 4.1), only 18 percent of French respondents qualified as

6. Georges Dupeux, "Citizen Participation in Political Life: France," *International Social Science Journal* XII (1960): 40–53.

high participants. Another study of French political attitudes quotes the following as an example of the feelings and attitudes of politically uninvolved people:

> So far as I'm concerned, everything's fine; I'm not married and I'm looking for a suitable wife . . . I'm putting all my efforts into improving my position . . . As for the general state of France, I'm not really interested, I couldn't care less. Who cares about political debates? The housing situation's bad? Well, let them sort it out then, it's nothing to do with me.[7]

Levels of political information are also low. A cross-national study of political attitudes found that nearly one-third of the British sample *never* followed political and governmental affairs; only 23 percent said they followed such news regularly.[8] In France the evidence is similar. A poll in 1969 found that 38 percent of Frenchmen said that they had little interest in politics and an additional 41 percent said that they had no interest at all in politics.[9] Again, a quotation from a French citizen uninterested in politics exemplifies a widespread attitude:

> I've no time to read the paper, just sports and the local news. And after all if you take different papers they don't tell you the same story. One says black and the others say white and which are you to believe? Radio and T.V. are just the same, trying to throw dust in our eyes.[10]

Voting is the only political act performed by the vast majority of citizens in Britain, France, and other liberal democracies. Other political activities — if there are any — are undertaken only on rare occasions and usually for brief periods of time. Table 4.3 indicates how few British citizens engage in any political action except voting. One expert on British politics suggests that the proportion of the adult population actively participating in politics in England today may be the same or lower than it was before the great extensions of the right to vote in the nineteenth century.[11]

In France the situation is not much better. There are probably more people involved in civic affairs in France than in Britain, due to the larger number of elected local governmental positions. France contains 38,000 communes (local governmental units) — far more relative to the population than any other European state. With each commune electing from 9 to 37 municipal councillors, there are over 470,000 locally elected officials. Consequently, about 1.8 percent of the electorate serves in an elective capacity and an equivalent number runs for public office every six years. However, many of these politicians are involved in politics only at the local level; in fact, the number of local elected officials exceeds the total number of active party members.

7. E. Deutsch, D. Lindon, and P. Weill, *Les familles politiques en France,* cited in *French Politics,* ed. Martin Harrison (Lexington, Mass.: D.C. Heath, 1969), p. 134.
8. Almond and Verba, *The Civic Culture,* p. 54.
9. *Sondages,* 1969, Nos. 1 and 2, pp. 13–14.
10. Deutsch *et al., Les familles politiques,* p. 134.
11. Richard Rose, *Politics in England* (Boston: Little, Brown, 1964), p. 90.

TABLE 4.3

## Political Participation in Britain

| | | Number (in round figures) | Percentage of electorate (approximate) |
|---|---|---|---|
| Size of electorate | | 39,000,000 | 100 |
| Number voting | | 28,000,000 | 72 |
| Membership of political parties | | 3,530,000 | 9 |
| Conservative | 2,500,000 | | |
| Labour | 680,000 | | |
| Liberal | 350,000 | | |
| Active members (e.g., holding office at local or constituency level, attending meetings fairly regularly and assisting with activities, member of or candidate for local council, parliamentary candidate, etc.) | | 1,143,000 | 3 |
| Full-time officials at national level | | 60 | |
| Full-time officials below national level | | 800 | |
| Regions | 100 | | |
| Constituencies | 700 | | |
| Members of Parliament | | 630 | |
| Peers regularly attending the House of Lords | | 200 | |

*Source: T. Brennan,* Politics and Government in Britain *(Cambridge: Cambridge University Press, 1972), p. 81. Reprinted by permission.*

## VOTING

Since it is the only political act performed by the majority of citizens, voting needs further examination. In Britain and France all citizens eighteen and older are eligible to vote.[12] Unlike the United States, where voters must take the initiative to register to vote, Britain and France have made registration automatic; annual revisions keep the lists of voters current. In both Britain and France, election turnouts are generally quite high, and significantly higher than in the United States. (See Table 4.4.) The obligation to vote is successfully and strongly inculcated by the socialization process in Britain and France, and as a result nearly 80 percent of those eligible vote regularly.

At the polls British and French voters encounter a much less complicated ballot than do Americans. In the United States the voter must be prepared to vote for candidates for a long list of public offices — the president, a senator, a congressman, a state assemblyman and senator, judges, and even party pre-

12. Both countries withhold the right to vote from felons and the insane. In addition, the titled aristocracy in Britain is barred from voting in House of Commons elections since it is already represented in the House of Lords.

TABLE 4.4

*Percentage of Eligible Electorate Voting in Britain, France, and the United States*

| British House of Commons elections | | French National Assembly elections | | U.S. Presidential elections | |
|---|---|---|---|---|---|
| 1974 (Oct) | 72.8 | 1973 | 80.9 | 1972 | 54.5 |
| 1974 (Feb) | 78.7 | 1968 | 80.0 | 1968 | 61.0 |
| 1970 | 71.5* | 1967 | 80.9 | 1964 | 62.1 |
| 1966 | 75.8 | 1962 | 69.7* | 1960 | 63.8 |
| 1964 | 77.0 | 1958 | 77.1 | 1956 | 59.9 |

\* Lowest turnouts since 1945.

cinct captains — and to make decisions on a number of complicated propositions. In Britain and France the voter in a general election must make only one decision: which candidate or party to support for the House of Commons or the National Assembly. Municipal elections are held separately, and again there is a single choice. In France additional separate elections are held for the presidency, the general council, and referenda.

The British electoral system for the House of Commons is a single-ballot plurality system. There are 635 districts of approximately equal size — one district for each member of Commons. No primary elections are held, candidates being nominated by the local party units (constituency parties). The candidate winning the largest number of votes, whether or not it constitutes a majority is elected.

In France the electoral system is a two-ballot majority system. Candidates are nominated by the parties for each of the 487 single-member districts. On the first ballot a candidate must receive an absolute majority of the votes cast to be declared elected. (In the 1973 elections 59 candidates were elected on the first ballot.) In districts in which no candidate wins an absolute majority, a runoff election is held the following week. Candidates receiving less than 10 percent of the votes cast on the first ballot are automatically eliminated. Other candidates may withdraw; some endorse one of the remaining candidates upon withdrawal. An example from the 1973 election will illustrate:

| First ballot, March 4 | | Second ballot, March 11 | |
|---|---|---|---|
| Chaban-Delmas (Gaullist) | 49% | Elected | 54% |
| Tran (Socialist) | 19% | | 34% |
| Junca (Reformer) | 17% | | 12% |
| Riviére (Communist) | 12% | Withdrew, supported Tran | |
| Barthélemy (Trotskyite) | 3% | Eliminated | |

Considerable research has been devoted to determining how the voter decides how to vote. The central concern of such research is to ascertain how rational voters are as they make voting decisions. Clearly, the low levels of

TABLE 4.5

**Elections in Britain and France**

| | Type | Frequency | Electing body |
|---|---|---|---|
| Britain | General elections (House of Commons) | Every 5 years or earlier | Entire electorate |
| | Municipal elections* Borough councillors | ⅓ elected each year (3-year terms) | Entire electorate |
| | Aldermen | ½ elected every 3 years (6-year terms) | Borough councillors |
| | Mayors | Every year | Councillors and aldermen |
| France | General elections (National Assembly) | Every 5 years or earlier | Entire electorate |
| | Municipal elections Commune councillors | Every 6 years | Entire electorate |
| | Mayors | Every 6 years | Commune council |
| | General council | ½ elected every 3 years (6-year terms) | Entire electorate |
| | Presidential elections | 7-year terms | Entire electorate |
| | Referendum | At initiative of the president (6 since 1958) | Entire electorate |
| | Senate | ⅓ elected every 3 years (9-year terms) | Electoral college of deputies, general councillors, and delegates of municipal councils (approximately 104,000) |

*\* Municipal elections in the administrative counties and for the Greater London Council are conducted somewhat differently.*

citizens' political interest and information raise doubts about the degree of rationality they exercise in deciding how to vote. Uninformed and uninterested voters are unlikely to be able to select candidates who support their policy preferences. Many voters settle on a party and proceed to vote for that party in every election, without necessarily knowing the candidates' positions or even the party's program. Studies of voting behavior reveal that partisan ties have great stability. In Britain most voters select a party and vote regularly for that party throughout their lives.[13] In France the frequent appearance and disap-

13. Four out of five respondents to one survey claimed they always supported the same party. David Butler and Donald Stokes, *Political Change in Britain* (New York: St. Martin's Press, 1971), p. 27.

pearance of parties makes party loyalties less stable, but the voter usually remains loyal to a general political "family": the Far Left, Left, Center, or Right. Whether determined by parental influence, social class status, acceptance of traditional regional partisan ties, or other factors, partisan loyalties usually persist and are the single most important influence on how the individual votes.

There appears to be only a slight correlation between voting decisions and positions on specific substantive issues. For example, British voters were asked if they would change parties if their habitual party's position on British membership in the Common Market (at the time a crucial issue) differed from their personal opinions. Only 13 percent of Conservative voters and 16 percent of Labour voters said that they would change their votes.[14] Nonissues, such as the personalities of the candidates or party leaders, often significantly influence voters' decisions. An opinion survey at the time of the 1968 elections indicated that most French voters viewed voting as a way of choosing a deputy they trusted or of indicating a favorable or negative attitude toward President de Gaulle (who was not even on the ballot) rather than as a means of choosing representatives whose positions were closest to their own.[15] Furthermore, there is evidence that swing voters — those who change their votes from party to party — are among the least informed and least interested voters.[16] Since small shifts of votes can usually make the difference between victory and defeat at the polls, these uninformed swing voters' whims can determine the outcome of an election.

Low levels of political information and interest and irrational voting behavior bode ill for democratic societies. In part, the vacuum created by the inadequacy of citizen participation is filled by political parties and interest groups that represent special opinions and interests. Political parties can serve to simplify voting decisions. If voters choose parties that accurately represent their class, economic, or regional interests, they need not necessarily carefully evaluate the qualifications of all candidates. They can rely on the party to offer candidates who represent their interests better than the candidates of other parties. In addition, it has been argued that even voters who are not issue-oriented or well-informed are able to assess the performance of the incumbent government. Their votes for or against the incumbents may thus represent rational decisions to affirm or reject the previous performance of one set of candidates. Whether or not they can relate their own specific issue posi-

---

14. Jean Blondel, *Voters, Parties, and Leaders: The Social Fabric of British Politics* (Baltimore: Penguin Books, 1965), pp. 80–81.

15. Only 23 percent thought of elections as a means of supporting the political group closest to their own ideas. *Sondages*, 1968, No. 2, p. 97.

16. See E. Deutsch *et al., Les familles politiques en France* (Paris: Editions de Minuit, 1966). The authors identify a group of voters whom they label the "Marais," or swampland, so uninterested that they have no true political orientation toward the Left or the Right. This group accounts for 30 percent of all voters. While other groups also swing from one party to another, it is the voters of the Marais who are the arbiters of power in elections.

tions correctly with those of candidates or parties, they can make collective judgments of the incumbent government that are basically rational.[17]


## WOMEN IN POLITICS

In Britain women won the right to vote by means of a protracted and sometimes violent struggle. The Suffragette Movement peaked in 1910–1914, when militant suffragettes accelerated their efforts to win equal rights and, especially, the right to vote for women.[18] The suffragettes' tactics included rallies, demonstrations, window-smashing campaigns, heckling of public speeches by government ministers, attempts to destroy the mail, burning slogans on golf greens, hunger strikes, random arson of houses and churches, and even a few bombings. World War One delayed their victory until 1918, when all women over thirty years of age were granted the right to vote; men could vote at twenty-one. Formal political equality was achieved in 1928, when the age of eligibility was reduced to twenty-one for women as well.

In France traditional femininity, not feminism, has been the rule.[19] There was no French counterpart of the British suffragette struggle, and the right to vote was not granted to women until 1945. Even then female suffrage came about not in response to demands by women but as one of the Liberation reforms promulgated by the Provisional Government of Charles de Gaulle. Similarly, equal legal rights for wives vis-à-vis their husbands were only achieved recently. Until 1964 women had to have their husbands' permission to apply for passports, open bank accounts, or conduct other financial affairs. In divorce cases, infidelity on the part of the wife was much more readily accepted as grounds for divorce than was identical behavior by the husband.

Despite formal legal emancipation, women remain politically second-class citizens. Though more than half the electorates of both Britain and France are female, women in both countries are less likely than men to become involved in politics. Women make up a disproportionate share of the nonvoters, and engage in other political or civic activities less frequently than do men. The percentages of women in public office reflect the fact that politics remains a predominantly male pursuit. In France the National Assembly elected in 1973 had only eight women deputies, 1.6 percent of the total. The highest percentage of women deputies ever was 5.8 percent, in 1946. In Britain the February 1974 election resulted in 23 women members of Parliament, or 3.6 percent. At higher levels of government leadership, women are similarly underrepresented. The British Labour Government formed after the February 1974 election in-

17. See especially V. O. Key's arguments in *The Responsible Electorate* (Cambridge: Harvard University Press, 1966), and *Public Opinion and American Democracy* (New York: Knopf, 1961), pp. 472–480.

18. George Dangerfield, *The Strange Death of Liberal England* (New York: G. P. Putnam's Sons, 1961), pp. 139–213, 364–388.

19. See John Ardagh, *The New French Revolution: A Social and Economic Survey of France 1945–1967* (London: Secker and Warburg, 1968), pp. 239–258.

cluded only two women ministers (9.5 percent of the cabinet). In France women first held cabinet-level positions in the Popular Front Government formed in 1936, before they had even been granted the right to vote. However, their numbers have never been high. The Government formed by Jacques Chirac in 1974 included only three women (8.6 percent of the cabinet). Women do not fare much better in local politics. Only about 2 percent of the 38,000 mayors elected in France in 1971 were women.[20]

The scarcity of women in elected positions is due to the infrequency with which women are nominated by the parties: in 1966, for example, the British Conservatives nominated 21 women out of more than 629 candidates for the House of Commons; the Labour Party nominated 30 out of 621 candidates. Women frequently account for a high proportion of the volunteer campaign workers in Britain, but even when they outnumber men as party workers women are less likely to assume positions of party leadership. For example, a study of a local Conservative party unit in England revealed that women accounted for 57 percent of the members but only 25 percent of the officers.[21] In France, women play an even less conspicuous role in party politics. The French Communist party is the most self-conscious in its efforts to attract women members, but in spite of its persistent efforts women make up only 25.5 percent of the party membership.[22] And they are underrepresented in the party leadership, with only 15 women among the 118 members of the Central Committee and 2 women in the 19-member Political Bureau.[23] In 1973, furthermore, only 6 percent of the Communist candidates for the National Assembly were women.[24] In the other two mass-membership parties, the Socialists and the Gaullists, active women members are almost unheard-of. A study of local units of these parties employed a total sample of 400 party members: only 23 were women.[25] Of the more than 450 candidates that each of these groups ran in the 1973 elections, the Socialists nominated only 11 women and the Gaullists only 6.[26]

The small number of women in politics is attributable, by and large, to socialization patterns rather than overt sex discrimination. Political parties are anxious to recruit workers, whatever their sex, and therefore certainly do not formally exclude women. There is little evidence of noteworthy voter antagonism to women candidates for public office. One comparative study of men and women candidates in the same British constituencies indicated that a woman Labour candidate would win as many votes as a male candidate and that a woman Conservative candidate might receive about 200 fewer votes than a man

20. *Le Monde,* 16 February 1974.
21. R. M. Punnett, *British Government and Politics,* 2d ed. (New York: W. W. Norton and Company, 1971), p. 85.
22. Annie Kriegel, *The French Communists: Profile of a People* (Chicago: University of Chicago Press, 1972), pp. 59–70.
23. *Le Monde,* 19 December 1972.
24. *Ibid.,* 16 February 1974.
25. Mark Kesselman, "Recruitment of Rival Party Activists in France: Party Cleavages and Cultural Differentiation," *Journal of Politics* 25 (1973): 23.
26. *Le Monde,* 16 February 1974.

in the same district.[27] Thus, it is not fear that voters will automatically reject women candidates that accounts for the small number of women candidates and officeholders.

Political reticence is only one of many manifestations of the passive social roles prescribed for women. Socialization in the home, among peers, and at school have traditionally emphasized the norms of marriage, childbearing, and homemaking for women. Girls have learned to define their roles in society as housewives and mothers rather than as doctors, merchants, or politicians. Many have learned from their mothers to leave politics to men. The resulting pattern is described by one French analyst who argues that women "have the mentality of minors in many fields and, particularly in politics, they usually accept paternalism on the part of men. The man — husband, fiancé, lover, or myth — is the mediator between them and the political world."[28]

Growing numbers of women are rebelling against these traditional role definitions and insisting upon recognition of their rights to political and social involvement on an equal footing with men. There are counterparts to the American women's liberation movement in both Britain and France, but they have won neither the influence nor the following the American movement has enjoyed. French feminists have had particular difficulty building a following, perhaps partly because France has no tradition of women's clubs, sororities, and other social organizations that have provided American and, to a lesser extent, British women with a sense of solidarity.

Important advances for women's rights were made recently in both Britain and France. In France, President Giscard d'Estaing appointed Françoise Giroud as minister for women's affairs with the responsibility of eliminating discrimination against women in government and society. His government also pushed through a liberalized abortion law despite the opposition of the Catholic hierarchy and many deputies from the Gaullist majority. In Britain, the Labour government issued a "white paper" in late 1974 on the state of women's rights. The government pledged action to remedy the economic, social, and political inequality of women. However, the most dramatic action came from the opposition Conservative party, which elected Margaret Thatcher as its new leader. Should the Conservatives win the next election, Thatcher would become Britain's first woman prime minister. Opinion polls in early 1975 indicated that this was a real possibility, since Thatcher led the incumbent prime minister in popularity polls.

Many liberal democratic states are experiencing a period of transition in which the role of women in society is being reassessed. Britain and France are among those states in which changes may be expected in the next generation. However, because the scarcity of women in politics is the product of people's attitudes and women's self-restraint rather than overt discrimination, changes will probably be gradual and slow. It is one thing to eliminate legal barriers to

27. R. L. Leonard, *Elections in Britain* (Princeton: D. Van Nostrand, 1968), pp. 75–76.
28. Maurice Duverger, *The Political Role of Women* (Paris: UNESCO, 1955).

participation; it is quite another to change the attitudes of men and women toward their social and political roles.

## PROTEST AND DISSENT

Guarantees of the rights of assembly, free speech, and a free press offer individual citizens in Western democracies another means of political participation. The citizen is free within certain, usually reasonable, limits to dissent openly against the positions and policies of the government. While the dissenter may be subjected to informal sanctions for deviating from the dominant consensus, he or she is rarely subject to imprisonment or other punishment simply for dissenting. At times dissent is so widespread and so inadequately represented by the usual political outlets that it is manifested in spontaneous mass protests. Such protest may take the form of sit-ins, boycotts, wildcat strikes, marches, or similar demonstrations. These actions occasionally involve violence, and in extreme cases may be preludes to civil war.

Britain has been surprisingly free of such political manifestations, for several reasons. Britain's broad social and political consensus minimizes conflict and dissent, and its socialization process emphasizes respect for the existing order and hostility to political violence. Furthermore, the adequacy of normal political channels of participation — voting, parties, parliamentary action — makes it unnecessary for the individual or group with grievances to resort to street protest. This was well demonstrated by the labor and economic crisis of 1973–1974. Mineworkers went on a slowdown strike to demand large salary increases and then shut down the nation's coalmines when the Conservative Government offered considerably lower raises. The coal shortage forced a reduction of the work-week to three days and threatened economic paralysis, but both sides remained intransigent. There were threats of violence when the Government hinted that it would use troops to keep the mines operating. However, the resolution of the crisis was a democratic one: Prime Minister Heath called for new parliamentary elections to be held in February 1974. The elections brought the Labour party to power, and the new Government quickly settled the strike and returned the economy to full-time operation. There was no need for further protest or violence because the political system was working.

The major exception to this rule in Britain is ethnic conflict in Northern Ireland. As we have seen, this conflict is the heritage of years of religious intolerance and hatred. What is curious about the Northern Irish problem is that while this conflict has verged on open civil war, it has not disrupted the overall stability of the British political system, largely because few non-Irish Britishers feel involvement or interest in the conflict. Even among the most religious, few non-Irish Britons have taken sides in the conflict. To a foreigner who demands an explanation for the "un-British" chaotic situation in Northern Ireland, the typical Briton will shrug his shoulders and say, "They're Irish." The isolation of the problem has also been facilitated by the fact that Northern Ireland is separated by water from the rest of Britain. The Northern Irish conflict simply has not spread to the rest of Britain, and it is unlikely that it will.

In France protest politics is the norm, not the exception. The Events of May–June 1968 are the most recent manifestation of a long tradition of spontaneous protest and revolt. In addition to major revolutionary or near-revolutionary actions (the Events, Liberation, the Commune of 1871, and the revolutions of 1848, 1830, and 1789), there have been numerous less spectacular but nevertheless disruptive protest actions. Indeed, there is rarely a period in French history when some spontaneous or organized protest was not underway. And at times it appears that there are few Frenchmen who are not protesting in one way or another.[29]

The proclivity of the French to protest is founded in their attitudes toward political participation and authority. An intense desire to safeguard their individual prerogatives and independence tends to make French citizens reluctant to participate in civic action. One French sociologist writes:

> People are very ambivalent toward participation . . . On the one hand, people would like to participate in order to control their own environment. On the other hand, they fear that if and when they participate, their own behavior will be controlled by their coparticipants. It is easier to preserve one's independence and integrity if one does not participate in decision-making. By refusing to be involved in policy determination, one remains much more free from pressure.[30]

By avoiding involvement, furthermore, the French retain their right to protest or oppose whatever decision is finally agreed upon.

There is in the French a certain desire to resist authority, to oppose *le pouvoir*. This impulse to oppose, which is often combined with a strict egalitarianism, has always been an important factor in French politics, especially among those ideologically on the Left. On the other hand, the French are also prone to accept a superior authority, and look to the strong leader to make decisions in normal times as well as crises. This ambivalence was well described by Alexis de Tocqueville over a century ago:

> Undisciplined by temperament, the Frenchman is always readier to put up with the arbitrary rule, however harsh, of an autocrat than with a free well-ordered government by his fellow citizens, however worthy of respect they be. At one moment he is up in arms against authority and the next we find him serving the powers-that-be with a zeal such as the most servile races never display. So long as no one thinks of resisting, you can lead him on a thread, but once a revolutionary movement is afoot, nothing can restrain him from taking part in it.[31]

The principle of popular sovereignty, which Lincoln called "government by the people," is difficult to implement in practice. For the most part, the people

29. Stanley Hoffmann, "Protest in Modern France," in *The Revolution in World Politics,* ed. Morton A. Kaplan (New York: Wiley, 1962).

30. Michel Crozier, *The Bureaucratic Phenomenon* (Chicago: University of Chicago Press, 1964), pp. 204–205.

31. Alexis de Toqueville, *The Old Regime and the French Revolution,* tr. Stuart Gilbert (Garden City, N.Y.: Doubleday, 1955), pp. 210–211.

do not want to govern. The most that can be expected of the general population in liberal democracies is that they vote. At best, their votes will reflect some assessment of the candidates. The relative scarcity of individual participants in democratic politics gives such organized political actors as parties and interest groups added importance. We shall turn to them in Chapter 5.

# China and the Soviet Union: Community Action

In liberal democracies, individual political participation is entirely voluntary — and spontaneous, too, in that the individual is usually not prompted to become involved. The government does little to promote participation except sponsor a "get out the vote" campaign at election time. In communist states, participation is neither spontaneous nor voluntary. The dominant Communist parties are the major stimulants of political involvement. They promote civic involvement and channel individual participation in the direction of such officially determined objectives as sanitation campaigns, production, and political awareness.

The centrally directed nature of mass participation in communist states is readily understandable. For one thing, communist governments are dedicated to the transformation of poor, predominantly rural, traditional societies into modern, socialist, industrialized societies in the shortest possible time. This task requires discipline and central direction to harness and channel human resources. Secondly, many of the prerequisites to spontaneous political participation — notably a literate and affluent population — have been missing in communist states, especially in the critical period after the assumption of power. When the communists came to power in China and the Soviet Union, they inherited traditional societies that did not provide for or stimulate individual involvement. Finally, and perhaps most importantly, the Leninist concept of the party's monopoly on power requires that all political action be directed by the party.

The efforts of the Communist parties of China and the Soviet Union to stimulate mass participation have been successful. Relative to Western democratic systems, a very large share of the populations of both countries is politically involved. In China, for example, workers can be found after factory hours in discussion groups reflecting on the relationship between culture and politics or the roles they can play in national development. Students spend their vacations working alongside peasants in the nation-building process. Elected members of revolutionary committees meet after work to deal with community problems. Women volunteers controlling traffic in towns and cities are a frequent sight.

The extent of participation is determined by the party leadership. The role of leadership has been to define what have at times been the flexible limits of permissible activity, at times expanding them to allow more participation and at other times contracting them. Under Stalin, the use of terror placed severe limits on citizen participation. After de-Stalinization greater mass involvement was stimulated through intensified programs of adult political education. In China the Hundred Flowers Campaign of 1956–1957 was a period of expanded participation; it was followed by a period of tightened control that lasted until 1966. Then, under the aegis of the Great Proletarian Cultural Revolution, China experienced the most extensive participation in its postrevolutionary history. The long-range trend in both China and the Soviet Union is toward governmental decentralization and greater citizen participation.

## FORMS OF PARTICIPATION
## IN CHINA AND THE SOVIET UNION

Acceptable forms of "democratic participation" in communist states include discussion, persuasion, education, elections, civic action, and mass movements. The discussion of public issues is a particularly significant form of participation. Party members present lectures and stimulate discussion of issues deemed important by the party elite. This process gives the party an opportunity to defend its policies and to answer questions that have arisen in citizens' minds. Westerners are prone to dismiss this as political indoctrination, rather than discussion. Indeed, this is often the case. However, there is a genuine two-way flow of communication in these sessions. Party representatives explain policies, but they also hear and report the questions, anxieties, and attitudes expressed by the citizens. The numbers who participate in these political discussions are often phenomenal. For example, some 82 million Soviets attended public meetings at which the 1961 program of the Communist party was discussed. In China equally impressive numbers participate in frequent discussions of policy and doctrine.

In most communist states the regime's interest in shaping the individual's attitudes and values extends beyond the normal school years to a concern for adult socialization. The rationale for socialization and re-education is the assumption that changes in the political and economic systems must endure. To assure this, the political attitudes and orientations that support the social structures must be changed. The party-directed political discussions are one aspect of a concerted program of adult political socialization in China and the Soviet Union. Formal political education programs provide training in Marxism-Leninism, Maoism, and political action. In 1964 over 36 million people participated in these programs of "political enlightenment" in the Soviet Union. The program has since been reduced in scope, but about 16 million were still enrolled in the program in 1971. China too has an extensive program of adult political education. Every adolescent and adult Chinese has been involved in regular political study.[32]

To Westerners these efforts at adult socialization seem anomalous. How-

32. James R. Townsend, *Political Participation in Communist China* (Berkeley: University of California Press, 1968), pp. 174–186.

ever, in both China and the Soviet Union the revolution is still relatively young. Prerevolutionary political values and attitudes persist, and it is believed that they must be changed. These traditional political and social orientations are poorly adapted to the needs of a modern industrial and socialist state. To replace them with values and attitudes conducive to socialism and industrialization requires the socialization not only of the young but also of adults. Hence tremendous resources are invested in programs of political persuasion, discussion, and education.

*Voting*   Elections are taken seriously in communist states even though their outcomes are largely predetermined. The purpose of such elections is not to select political leaders but to provide an opportunity for the citizens to attest to their loyalty by voting for the party's candidates. The party devotes large amounts of time and energy to the pre-election campaign, viewing it as an opportunity to let the people know what the party is doing for them and to explain party policies. Nearly every voter is personally contacted one or more times by the candidates or campaign workers.

In the Soviet Union, elections for national soviets are held every four years and for local soviets every two years. All adults eighteen and older are eligible to vote. And they do vote: the turnout is invariably reported as 99.9 percent. Even those confined to hospitals vote, as election officials carry ballots and ballot boxes to their bedsides. Attention is given by the party to ascertaining a candidate's acceptability to the voters. There is, however, only one candidate for each office. To vote against the candidate, the voter must scratch out the name and, if he or she wishes, write in another name. The ballot is secret, with booths provided at the polling places. However, most Soviet voters simply pick up their ballots, fold them without entering a booth, and deposit them in the ballot box. By spurning the booth, the voter avoids arousing suspicion that he might have voted against the party's candidate. In fact, few vote against the candidates. In the 1966 national election, 99.76 percent voted for the party's candidates. Occasionally candidates do fail to be elected, but only in local elections. In the 1971 local elections 101 candidates were defeated because the number of scratches exceeded the number of votes. At the same time, however, 2,165,000 candidates were elected.

In China there have been several general basic-level elections since 1949, including elections to formal governmental offices and, more recently, to revolutionary committee positions. Elections in urban areas are primarily by secret ballot. However, in rural areas, citizens vote by show of hands. This procedure is provided for in the electoral law to overcome the barrier of illiteracy. Though voter registration, formation of local election committees, and mass mobilization for elections are undertaken and though approximately 85 percent of the eligible voters turn out, they have not been particularly enthused. This is often attested to by delays of up to one year in holding elections, as well as by public comments. Citizen enthusiasm for elections appears to have been undermined by disillusionment with some of the candidates, who in earlier elections were chosen without sensitivity to the citizens' will, and by the failure of the local congresses to fulfill their functions.[33] Thus the Chinese government's role in political participation is simultaneously inhibiting and encouraging, and the net effect is often discouragement.

*Community Service* Voluntary civic action is another form of mass participation. Many basic services, including sanitation, firefighting, and traffic control, are performed by volunteer labor. Committees of volunteers often set or administer policy for such small social units as apartment buildings, collective farms, and factories. Volunteers may also be used for social and political control: in the Soviet Union there are approximately 7 million "people's guards" (*druzhiny*), who are volunteer auxiliary policemen empowered to arrest "hooligans" and petty thieves, settle domestic disputes, and handles unruly or drunken individuals. The druzhiny's counterparts on the judicial side of law enforcement are the comrades' courts and antiparasite tribunals. Manned by volunteers untrained in the law, these bodies hear cases involving hooliganism and other minor crimes and enforce work discipline. The use of these volunteer police and judges serves as an effective deterrent to nonconformity. While the penalties they can mete out are limited, they tend to be more severe than trained police and jurists.

*Mass Movement* A form of political participation unique to China is the mass movement or mass campaign, an attempt to mobilize the emotional and physical strength of the people in order to achieve specific goals established by the leadership. Mass movements are among the most important institutions in contemporary China. They are utilized for education, economic development, morale, the resolution of political competition, the integration of society, party, and government, and, perhaps most importantly, major societal reform. The educational content of each movement is also of great importance. The citizens' total involvement in these campaigns serves to integrate all class, ethnic, and religious groups in pursuit of a common goal. Participation itself, as well as the immediate or eventual rewards of these activities, can readily raise morale.

The most important mass movements have been aimed at transforming the society from its prerevolutionary state to socialism. Among the more notable are the Land Reform (post-1950); the Marriage Law, designed to improve the status of women (1950); the Resist America–Aid Korea Movement (1950–1953); the Three Anti-Movement (1951–1952); and the Five Anti-Movement, which continued the Three Anti-Movement campaign against corruption, waste, and bureaucracy, focusing on tax evasion, cheating the government, bribery, and theft of state property. The latter half of the 1950s witnessed the Hundred Flowers Movement, which allowed open criticism of pernicious party practices, followed by the Great Leap Forward, an attempt at instant socialism and rapidly expanded industrialization. Perhaps largest of all the mass movements was the Great Proletarian Cultural Revolution in the late 1960s.

33. *Ibid.*, p. 117.

The Chinese leadership has frequently resorted to the mass movement to counter apathy and stimulate citizen participation in politics. The mass movement represents a temporary intensification of the pressure to participate and a channeling of citizens' efforts toward chosen objectives. And it is hoped that the experience of participation will change the masses' ideas and behavior patterns permanently. There is considerable evidence that behavior is more likely to change as a result of actual participation than in response to persuasion alone.[34] In a sense, mass participation in the transformation of social institutions is a huge psychodrama aimed at modifying individual and collective traditional behavior. Given the traditional patterns of socialization, which emphasized dependence on authority, it requires an authoritarian political structure to break habits of dependence. The process is slow and there are many setbacks, as is sensitively conveyed by the words of Dai Hsiao-ai describing the early stages of the Cultural Revolution:

> In all of the excitement, it seemed as though the Red Guards were to sprout like bamboo. However, we soon came face to face with the reality that we didn't know how to organize. In the past, we would simply have used the leadership structure that already existed, but that was not possible. We had to decide who was to be eligible to join the Red Guards, what the specific goals should be and what its relationship with the Preparatory Committee established by the work team should be. We pored over the newspapers hoping to find the answers. All that we found, however, were reports in praise of the Red Guards. These kept our enthusiasm at a peak but were of no help in solving the main problem.[35]

It is apparent that China is undergoing an evolution in citizens' roles, which is in turn affecting both political orientations and, ultimately, the political formula. This process is occurring primarily in response to party encouragement and the merger or synchronization of social, economic, and citizenship roles. It is ironic, however, that while the mass movements have stimulated high levels of citizen participation, their format and the overriding organizational necessities of leading the largest population in the world toward modernization have also resulted in reinforcement of the traditional fear of authoritarian government, indifference, and dependence.

## WOMEN IN POLITICS

In czarist Russia women were relegated to secondary social roles and had virtually no place in politics. With the exception of a few individuals in the czar's household, women were expected to serve and obey their husbands, raise children, and care for the household. And the social roles of women in Imperial China were even more circumscribed by the rigid patriarchal family structures. The Chinese woman was completely subject to her husband, and expected to demonstrate her servility publicly by walking a pace or two behind him.

34. See particularly Albert Bandura, *Principles of Behavioral Modification* (New York: Holt, Rinehart and Winston, 1970).

35. Gorden A. Bennett and R. N. Montaperto, *Red Guard: The Political Biography of Dai Hsiao-ai* (Garden City, N.Y.: Doubleday, 1971), pp. 72–73.

One of communists' first acts after acceding to power in both China and Russia was to proclaim the equality of the sexes. Traditional marriage laws granting husbands special prerogatives were replaced by new laws guaranteeing the equality of husbands and wives. Political equality was also assured, and efforts were made to recruit women into political activity. The principle of equal pay for equal work was promulgated, women were encouraged to seek employment, and day-care nurseries were established to permit mothers to work. Needless to say, the leadership's motives were mixed. The desire to eliminate unjust discrimination on the basis of sex was genuine, but so was the leaders' interest in drawing women into the work force. The weakening of traditional family life was also desirable to facilitate development of the new community-oriented values needed for the development of a socialist state.

The results of the liberation of women have been varied. Women now account for about half of China's work force and more than half of the Soviet Union's. During World War Two, women in the Soviet Union were drawn into many traditionally male occupations because the men were needed in the military. Most of those who received higher education during the war were women. As a result, Soviet women have penetrated fields that are still male reserves in other societies: for example, women account for over 70 percent of the physicians, 38 percent of the faculty in higher education, 36 percent of the scientific workers, and 32 percent of the engineers.[36] However, women do not seem typically to be recruited for managerial positions. As one commentator writes: "The farm brigade leader is probably a man, the chairman surely; the pig-tender is probably a woman. Women shovel snow, men run snow-clearing machines."[37]

Women's influence in politics is not great and may even have declined since the early postrevolutionary era, when there were a number of women in conspicuous positions. Today there are none in the two most powerful political bodies, the party Politburo and the party Secretariat. Approximately one-fifth of the Communist party members in the Soviet Union are women; the leaders are nearly all men. Only 3 percent of the members of the Central Committee elected in 1971 were women. Only one woman, Ekaterina Furtseva, has served in the Politburo (1957–1961), in the history of the Soviet Union. Lenin's wife, Nadezhda Krupskaya, was once a member of the party Secretariat. Nor are there many women in the higher ranks of government. A 1971 study found only one woman minister among the 95 men on the Council of Ministers. At the level of the union republics, women fared a bit better, accounting for 9 of the 114 chairmen and deputy chairmen of the 15 union republic Councils of Ministers and 21 of the 538 other union republic ministers.[38]

36. Cyril E. Black, "Soviet Society: A Comparative View," in *Prospects for Soviet Society,* ed. Allen Kassof (New York: Praeger, 1968), p. 38.
37. Robert G. Wesson, *The Soviet Russian State* (New York: John Wiley, 1972), p. 226.
38. Lotta Lennon, "Women in the USSR," *Problems of Communism* (July–August, 1971): 50.

In China, the position of women in politics is comparable. About 10 percent of party members are women, but once again they are rarely found in leadership positions. One study of urban bureaucratic elites found that 94 percent of the elite was male.[39] Women made up only 8 percent of the Chinese party's Central Committee in 1969. The Politburo named in the same year had two women among its 25 members, but one was Mao Tse-tung's wife and the other Lin Piao's. Mao's wife, Chiang Ch'ing, is reputed to be a very powerful leader; her influence has appeared at times to be second only to that of Mao.

In addition, increasing numbers of women are apparent in party and state organs. More than 22 percent of the delegates at the January 1975 Fourth National People's Congress were women.

Efforts continue to improve women's social and political position. The Chinese have been particularly conscientious in their efforts to overcome the traditional oppression of women. In addition to enacting laws guaranteeing equal treatment, they have emphasized the equality of women in their socialization efforts. For example, a study of Chinese films found that many had feminist themes and that women had leading roles more frequently than men.[40] Films play a prominent role in adult socialization in China and by the depiction of heroines the leadership has sought to overcome traditional attitudes toward women.

## PROTEST AND DISSENT
## IN CHINA AND THE SOVIET UNION

Opposition to the Communist party or its leadership is considered antisocial behavior subject to prosecution in China and the Soviet Union. Protest demonstrations, parades, and strikes are regarded as unacceptable direct appeals to the masses over the heads of the party and its leadership. Criticism of individual party and government leaders at the lower and middle levels is, however, acceptable and encouraged within limits. The Soviet press frequently prints letters criticizing party and government leaders for inefficiency or arrogance. Such criticism helps keep the party responsive to the people and combats bureaucratic lethargy. However, the socialist system, the party, and its top leadership are not acceptable targets of criticism.

Open political protest by groups or individuals is extremely rare in the Soviet Union. A few years ago informal circles of intellectuals exchanged mimeographed or hand-written *samizdat* (self-published) political tracts, literary works, and newsletters giving vent to political protest. The numbers involved were never very large, and were too diverse in motivation to be called a protest movement. It is likely that protest by Soviet intellectuals is more widely

39. Ying-mao Kau, "The Urban Bureaucratic Elite in Communist China," in *Communist China: A System-Functional Reader,* ed. Yung Wei (Columbus, Ohio: Charles E. Merrill, 1972), p. 191.

40. John H. Weakland, "Chinese Film Images of Invasion and Resistance," *China Quarterly* XLVII (July/September 1971): 439–470.

known in the West than in the Soviet Union, since it has not been acknowledged in the Soviet press. Although limited and ineffectual, even this form of protest was considered unacceptable. The KGB (secret police) launched a campaign to eradicate the protest and samizdat materials. A number of dissenters were jailed; others were placed under surveillance or interrogated. One prominent dissident, a leading physicist, had his citizenship revoked when he went abroad; others, such as author Alexander Solzhenitsyn, were compelled to emigrate. The repression appeared to have failed; new samizdat materials continue to circulate.

Large-scale protest politics is virtually nonexistent in the Soviet Union. Only six persons turned out in Moscow to demonstrate against the Soviet invasion of Czechoslovakia in 1968. Larger numbers have joined protests against the treatment of Soviet Jews. But there has been nothing comparable to the large-scale protest that is now a permanent factor in the politics of most Western democracies. Soviet citizens who protest are no longer executed, but they do face social ostracism and the threat of prison terms or confinement in mental institutions. Only the nationally and internationally prominent — such as Solzhenitsyn or Nobel prize-winning physicist Andrei Sakharov — escape the harsher penalties for dissent.

Individual citizens in China and the Soviet Union exercise little control over the national political leadership. This, however, does not lessen the importance of their participation in politics. The involvement of the masses in political action is of great importance in sustaining the legitimacy of the regime, bringing manpower to bear in pursuit of social change, and developing and maintaining national pride and loyalty. The notion widespread among Westerners that the citizens of communist states are totally isolated from political action is inaccurate. In fact, though participation is less spontaneous and more restricted, the common citizen is much more likely to be involved in politics than his Western counterpart.

# Mexico and Nigeria: National Consciousness, Alienation, and Mobilization

In former colonies like Mexico and Nigeria, it is frequently during the period immediately preceding independence that citizens with limited awareness of the world outside their village or kinship groups become aware of their membership in a larger political body. At times, they are mobilized to fight for that goal. Following independence, considerable political instability due to regional, cultural, and political competition may ensue. The effects of such instability tend to reinforce the citizens' parochialism and may eventually lead to apathy, alienation, and withdrawal from the uncomfortable new reality. In time, leaders cognizant of the economic and political frustration that often accompanies independence articulate new goals and policies designed to mobilize or draft the citizen into the nation-building process. Nigeria and Mexico have both followed this pattern. Nigerian enthusiasm was very high during the late 1950s — the eve of independence — and the early 1960s. Mexico experienced the same phenomenon in the first two decades of the nineteenth century. Yet both nations' citizens later confronted the bitter realities of postindependence conflict and instability.

The modernization process — urbanization, industrialization, formal education, and the growth of mass communications — undermines traditional orientations toward the world. Education, the mass media, and employment expose individuals to new experiences that broaden their horizons and possibly their extrafamilial social and political involvements. As a result, the individual's predisposition to participate in politics is likely to intensify.

## SOCIALIZATION

However, in many Third World countries — including Mexico and Nigeria — those social conditions that encourage participation are absent or poorly developed. Indeed, the level of education, the mass media, and urbanization are often so rudimentary that they seriously impede mass political participation. This is well illustrated by the case of Mexico. Of Mexico's 28 million citizens aged six or over in 1960, more than 10.5 million were illiterate; the rural population was almost evenly divided between literates (48 percent) and illiterates (52 percent), while 24 percent of the population of urban areas was illiterate.[41] More than 59 percent of urban families and 89 percent of rural families earned less than 85 dollars (U.S.) a month.[42] Though most of the population has traditionally lived in rural areas, by 1970 the urban population accounted for 53 percent of the total. Thus Mexico's population is now slightly more urban than rural. This fact has considerable political significance due to the increased probability of participation by city-dwellers. However, Mexico defines as urban any town with a population of 10,000 or more, and many of these are so remote and impoverished that they totally lack most of the conditions and amenities associated with "urbanism" and participation, including electrification, movies, newspapers, industries, a substantial middle class, and secondary and higher educational opportunities. The trend is encouraging: the high proportion of Mexican citizens living in areas of marginal development is decreasing slightly, and more citizens are emerging into potentially participant areas.[43]

Marginal areas are characterized by certain attitudes unlikely to support political participation. Cross-national studies of these psychological dispositions verify Oscar Lewis' characterization of Pedro Martinez:

He shares many peasant values — a love of the land, a reverence for nature, a strong belief in the intrinsic good of agricultural labor, and a restraint on indi-

41. Pablo González Casanova, *Democracy in Mexico* (New York: Oxford University Press, 1970), p. 72–73.
42. *Ibid.*, p. 240.
43. *Ibid.*, pp. 196–197.

vidual self-seeking in favor of family and community. Like most peasants, he is also authoritarian, fatalistic, suspicious, concrete-minded and ambivalent in his attitudes toward city people.[44]

The investigators who contributed to *The Civic Culture* found that Mexicans often lacked both a sense of personal and political competence and willingness to influence local and national government. About half of the Mexicans polled said they felt they could do something about an unjust local law. However, only 9 percent of those who felt capable of influencing local government had ever in fact tried to do so.[45] Family, school, and job experiences affect the individual's sense of potential efficacy vis-à-vis the government. Those who participate in family and school activities are more likely to have a sense of civic competence.[46] The authors of *The Civic Culture* found that more than half of the Mexicans surveyed felt they had some influence in their families, while 40 percent felt they had none. Often, however, the family acts as a restraint to individual political involvement, counteracting the stimulus to participate of school and peers. Thus, a student who develops a critical consciousness as a result of academic inquiry and discussions with other students may take the step of participating in an antigovernment protest rally. But when he arrives home to tell his parents about his exciting experience they may criticize him for failing to respect or fear the government. Such negative feedback from parents could well discourage and even alter the participatory attitudes learned from the school and other students. (Students in the United States and Western Europe might encounter similar reactions. But in Mexico and other transitional countries familial obligations and controls are often

TABLE 4.6

*Attitudes and Feelings about Voting and Election Campaigns*

| Percentage who report they | U.S. | U.K. | Germany | Mexico |
|---|---|---|---|---|
| Feel satisfaction when going to polls | 71 | 43 | 35 | 34 |
| Sometimes find election campaigns pleasant and enjoyable | 66 | 52 | 28 | 34 |
| Sometimes find campaigns silly or ridiculous | 58 | 37 | 46 | 32 |
| Never enjoy, never get angry, and never feel contempt during campaigns | 12 | 26 | 35 | 41 |

*Source: Gabriel A. Almond and Sidney Verba,* The Civic Culture: Political Attitudes and Democracy in Five Nations *(Princeton, N.J.: Princeton University Press, 1963), p. 146. Copyright 1963 by Princeton University Press. Reprinted by permission of Princeton University Press.*

44. Oscar Lewis, *Pedro Martinez* (New York: Random House, 1964), p. xxxii.
45. Almond and Verba, *The Civic Culture,* pp. 142–143.
46. *Ibid.,* pp. 284–294.

stronger and thus create greater tension in the individual torn between family loyalties and the peer norm of antiregime conduct.)

The Catholic church has also played an important, but less recognized, role in political socialization. For many years, the church has been a unifying influence, a symbol with which many Mexicans could identify as fully as they could with race or nation, and the church's ideas have tended to encourage passive acceptance of one's fate in this life and hope for eternal life in heaven.

In Nigeria there are similar obstacles to participation stemming from existing social conditions and traditional patterns of political socialization. Approximately three out of four Nigerians are illiterate. Per capita annual income is about $130 according to 1973 estimates. The communication system is poorly developed in much of the country: there are only 76,000 telephones for a population of nearly 80 million people, and only seven newspapers for each 1,000 inhabitants. Thus, the social conditions that tend to foster participation are poorly developed or lacking in Nigeria.

During the early years of independence, conflicting socializing forces were operative, and the sum effect was often unconducive to political participation. Indeed, the values taught were often detrimental to the development of a sense of national political loyalty and duty. The family-kinship group inculcated in its members trust of those within the familial context and distrust of those outside, as well as the value orientations of respect for authority. Furthermore, the differing socialization patterns of different tribal units aggravated growing ethnic tension by inculcating dissimilar and sometimes conflicting political and social values. For example, northern children were likely to learn to respect theocratic authority and to manifest unquestioning obedience. They were also likely to observe and internalize the hierarchical relationship, and to apply its norms to potentially participatory situations. On the other hand, Ibos and Ibibios tend to be socialized to individualism, competition, and high parental expectations of excellence and achievement, especially in the marketplace. This orientation has a subtle capitalist component.

Nigerians are in a transitional period as we have seen. Some still retain traditional values, but education, the media, travel, and work experience represent a new set of socializing experiences. Schools orient students beyond the family and village to the nation and the world, and to norms of economic development and social change. They expose children to citizenship roles, voting, discussion, social awareness, and national loyalty. Conflict with traditional values often creates tension between competing patterns of behavior and alternative objects of political loyalty. For example, one study found that while 43 percent of a sample of Nigerian respondents would accept the chief's advice on how to vote, 52 percent would not.[47]

As might be expected, the mass media play a major role in providing information and shaping orientations. It is interesting to note that radio (53 percent) and conversations (43 percent) were cited more frequently as sources

47. John P. Mackintosh, *Nigerian Government and Politics* (Evanston, Ill.: Northwestern University Press, 1966), p. 332.

of information than were newspapers (30 percent) or public meetings (33 percent).[48] Newspapers and the Nigerian Broadcasting Corporation are increasingly important sources of attitudes toward the government and thus toward participation. During the first six years of independence, nongovernment newspapers frequently highlighted personal feuds and governmental corruption. This practice was associated with declining participation in the polls. Since the military coups, government-run newspapers and radio stations have emphasized the government's projects and plans for development in the hope of restoring confidence and mobilizing popular support for the regime's efforts. The state governments too have begun disseminating pamphlets and holding village meetings to promote self-help projects.

Other studies of civic activity in Nigeria point out the important contribution of factory experience in increasing such activity. In 1964 Melson found that 43.2 percent of the workers in his sample expressed verbal support for a labor party, though less than 10 percent actually supported such a party in preference to their communal ethnic party or nonparticipation.[49] This finding indicates that class feelings are beginning to develop during the early stages of industrialization, but suggests that the influence of tradition on the perception of civic role is still strong. While the trend in Nigeria is toward an expanded national conceptualization of the civic role, the existing ethnic parties and interest groups and the military coups of 1966 have partially restrained this trend. However, if education, industrialization, expansion of the mass media, and mass mobilization are accelerated under the military, ground may not be lost in the effort to transcend the existing parochial conception of the civic role. Indeed, there are indications that this is the case.

## FORMS OF PARTICIPATION

In Mexico the level of political involvement is generally quite low, as is illustrated by the difficulty of arousing interest in elections. According to *The Civic Culture,* 45 percent of the Mexicans interviewed said that they paid no attention to election campaigning.[50] Nevertheless, voter turnout is relatively high for presidential elections: 69 percent in 1964 and 64 percent in 1970. (The 5-percent decrease can be attributed to the advent of the eighteen-year-old vote and to a student boycott stemming from the rioting of 1968.) One often-cited explanation for the lack of interest in elections is expressed in Oscar Lewis's study of *Pedro Martinez:*

> . . . everyone knew who was going to win, that is why I say that the public is controlled by the PRI. One can almost say that the votes are not valid, they are only a legal requirement, because it is not the people who decide. Even against

---

48. *Ibid.,* p. 309.
49. Robert Melson, "Ideology and Inconsistency: The 'Cross-Pressured' Nigerian Worker," *American Political Science Review* XLV (March 1971): 167–171.
50. Almond and Verba, *The Civic Culture,* p. 109.

their own will the people say, "Why should I vote for so and so if he is not going to win? The other one will win so we will all vote for him.[51]

However, a recent study of voting patterns in Mexico suggests that the voter turnout is often highest in those areas where competition from the opposition party is *least*.[52] This finding is at odds with the experience of the United States and other competitive systems, in which turnout is highest where competition is greatest. Mexico's variance from this general rule is explained, at least in part, by the fact that the voting is often perceived as a means of expressing loyalty to the regime and group solidarity. It is inculcation of the sense of civic duty, combined with group pressures, that prompts at least this token form of participation. The same influences do not operate to encourage involvement in political organizations, however. Thus the leadership has a difficult time eliciting participation in campaign and party activities, and success is often attributable to the skill of an aggressive and appealing leader at motivating others to join him in undertaking a political action.

In contrast to their low levels of interest in partisan and electoral matters, Mexicans tend to be willing to engage in civic projects for the benefit of the community. Motivated by leaders with visions of social change, Mexicans frequently involve themselves in civic action. In *Pedro Martinez*, we glimpse the extent of this willingness to become involved in voluntary civic service:

> I was always serving my village, as president of the committee on national fiestas, as inspector of the parks, as inspector of charcoal production, as president of the commission to get drinking water for the village and of course, I always volunteered for the *cuatequitl*, the collective working party.[53]

Once involved, the individual's commitment is sometimes total, even to the exclusion of family obligations. Pedro Martinez describes his dedication to a community effort to build a road:

> All through the Lenten season I didn't earn a centavo for my family because I helped build the road. It made no difference to me that my wife and children might starve. It couldn't be helped because I was working for my village, which counted for more. What I aspired to was the improvement of my village![54]

Patron-client links facilitate participation in Mexico's preindustrial society. Thus, as with Nigeria's communal political groupings, participation is encouraged and facilitated by a traditional institution. It is not uncommon for an ordinary individual to seek assistance from the mayor or local PRI leader, the key patrons at the local level. In exchange for his service, the local patron is likely to call upon the client for his and his family's votes in the following election.

51. Lewis, *Pedro Martinez*, p. 265.
52. Barry Ames, "Bases of Support for Mexico's Dominant Party," *American Political Science Review* LXIV (March 1970): 153–167.
53. Lewis, *Pedro Martinez*, pp. 260–261.
54. *Ibid.*, p. 265.

The trend in Mexico is toward more and more citizen participation in organizations and associations, toward transference of the attitudes resulting from this experience to the political arena. This should occur gradually in response to economic development, education, and social change. However, there is an important mitigating factor: the government's frequent use of strong repressive measures to discourage or eliminate potential opposition to the PRI. This situation tends strongly to reinforce negative self-competence attitudes and dispositions not to become involved in formal political competition. It does not, however, seem to affect the motivation to fulfill one's sense of civic responsibility by participating in civic projects.

Political participation in Mexico often takes such violent forms as demonstrations, riots, political assassinations, and occasionally guerrilla warfare. The prevalence of violence in politics, and in society in general, is explained in part by the inadequacy of nonviolent means to resolve conflicts. Since the Mexican is unable to resolve personal and collective problems by legal means or through the normal play of pressure and counterpressure, "he is compelled to resort to drastic expedients that is to express in shouting and shooting what he is unable to express through legal means."[55] Furthermore, the tradition of violence in Mexican history has created a political culture that validates violence as a means of political expression. Finally, Mexican men's *machismo,* or assertive masculinity, is often expressed in violent behavior. By acting aggressively, and sometimes violently, the Mexican male demonstrates his virility.

In Nigeria the impact of ethnicity is evident in patterns of political participation. The different patterns of socialization noted earlier produce differing propensities to participation and differing assumptions about the kinds of participation that are appropriate. Many Nigerians, particularly those from the Ibo ethnic group, gained experience as political activists during the civil war years (1967–1970).

Even before the civil war, the framework for political participation was often regional and ethnic rather than national. National elections might have been expected to enhance citizens' commitment to national political activities. (In Mexico, for example, elections are an important means of expressing national political involvement.) However, Nigerian elections were strongly affected by ethnic and regional considerations. For the Nigerian voter, choosing between national parties and taking stands on national issues was less significant than selecting the candidates most likely to protect one's parochial interests.

After the military coups of 1966, citizen involvement was limited. What little national participation had developed was replaced by communal or ethnic involvement. Traditional Nigerian society offers diverse forms of civic participation. Seldom were these activities relevant to national policies, but they could and do provide experience potentially transferable to the national arena when the government becomes interested in mobilizing its citizens.

Among the Afikpo Ibo of Southeastern Nigeria, age determines one's civic

55. Victor Alba, *The Latin Americans* (New York: Praeger, 1969), p. 44.

role: young men (30–50 years) are members of the village police force; junior men (50–64 years) comprise the executive branch of the Afikpo government, and thus have the most responsibility; and "middle-aged" men (65–83 years) are responsible for legislation and adjudication for the village group. Men 84 years and older are retired and have limited advisory powers.[56] Women are also classified by age, and are responsible for regulations pertaining to women. They may, for example, regulate the number of pots a woman may sell per day at the local market, and make rules for farming women's crops. Men's groups legislate for both men and women. While age directly determines status among the Afikpo Ibo, the Yorubas too practice a form of age grouping that specifies one's civic role. Thus one of the modernizing functions of national and state elections is to extend the civic role equally to all age grades and sexes.

So far the effects of the federal and regional elections — the institutions most likely to promote national integration — have been scant. Regional elections seemed to elicit the interest of more than 60 percent of both men and women polled for a study. When asked why they voted, 45 percent of both men and women said they did so to put their party in power, while 41 percent said they thought it was their civic duty. Approximately 77 percent of the sample polled knew the names of two candidates and the victor.[57]

There is evidence of a contrast between Mexico and Nigeria that is worthy of note. A 1966 study found that 70 percent of the Nigerians surveyed talked about politics often or sometimes, while only 30 percent claimed never to talk about politics.[58] This finding indicates an unusually high interest in political discussion, more typical of highly developed countries such as Britain than of developing states. In comparison, 66 percent of the Mexicans surveyed for *The Civic Culture* study claimed never to talk about politics, and only 32 percent talked about politics often or sometimes.[59] This evidence may be interpreted to mean that Nigeria was overpoliticized by the ethnic and political turmoil that preceded the military coups of 1966. Nigeria's relatively new political institutions may have been overpowered by levels of public participation too high to handle.


## WOMEN IN POLITICS

Perhaps nothing illustrates the dualist nature — both traditional and modern — of Third World countries more succinctly than women's roles in society and politics. While customs prevalent in many parts of Mexico and Nigeria prescribe limited roles for women, modernization is accelerating women's liberation from these traditional norms.

---

56. Phoebe Ottenberg, "The Afikpo Ibo of Eastern Nigeria," in *Peoples of Africa,* ed. James Gibb, Jr. (New York: Holt, Rinehart and Winston, 1966), p. 16.
57. Mackintosh, *Nigerian Government,* p. 309.
58. Mackintosh, *Nigerian Government,* p. 302.
59. Almond and Verba, *The Civic Culture,* p. 79.

Mexico is heavily influenced by a Spanish culture that legitimizes machismo at the cost of women's development. Tradition has assured the male great liberties, ranging from extramarital affairs to the use of force, to realize the macho ideal. Machismo requires that "good" women be treated with outward dignity and ceremony but be restricted to the socially prescribed roles of subservient housewife and pure mother. Thus women have until recently been tacitly discouraged from pursuing education or occupations outside the home. Mexican women did not receive equal citizenship and the right to vote until 1953. They voted in a presidential election for the first time in 1958. Since then women have participated in politics at a much lower rate than men.

*The Civic Culture*'s study found Mexican women to be less informed about politics, less assured in political matters, and less likely to be involved in politics than were men.[60] Only a few women hold public office in Mexico. However, female awareness and participation may be expected to increase as a result of education.

Regional differences in Nigeria make generalizations about the role of women in politics difficult. Historically, women have played important political roles in some parts of Nigeria: conquering, creating kingdoms, importing kola nuts, and acting as chiefs. In other parts of Nigeria their social, economic, and political roles have been severely circumscribed. This is particularly true of the Muslim areas of the north, where women are not encouraged to attend public schools or to involve themselves in politics. In contrast, Ibo women have enjoyed considerable economic and social rights and status, and have exercised political influence. As early as the 1920s, Ibo women organized and fought against a rumored special tax on women. No peaceful battle, the "women's war" of 1929 resulted in the deaths of some fifty women before order was restored.

Women have had the right to vote in Nigerian national elections since 1954. While levels of interest and participation vary from one region to the next, it is not unusual to find women's unions and associations defending their political and social rights. Prior to the military takeover, such groups even existed in the upper echelons of some political parties.


## REFLECTIONS: CITIZEN ROLES IN THE THIRD WORLD

It is apparent that societal conditions, socialization, and political experience interact to shape citizens' roles in developing nations. Economic status, literacy, residence, and sex all influence the form and degree of one's participation. Economic development tends to enhance educational opportunities, mobility, and exposure to mass media, which in theory stimulate political involvement. Such involvement may take the form of political discussion, letter-writing, membership in voluntary associations, or concern with election outcomes. Though not

60. *Ibid.*, pp. 324–335.

always acknowledged in the literature, variations in role socialization are a prominent feature of developing societies. Social norms often tend to restrict female participation: it has long been considered unseemly for girls to discuss politics in Mexico (and much of the Spanish-speaking world), and in many parts of Nigeria, particularly the north. The right to vote has in many places been limited to males with property. These norms and values are changing with exposure to modern educational systems, but if the government does not intervene evolution may be slow. We have noted that in communist systems governmental reform brings about change relatively promptly.

# Conclusions: Citizens and Politics

Few question the value of involving the public in the political process, but agreement on this principle does not solve the attendant problems. Liberal democracies are characterized by too little citizen interest and involvement in a political process supposedly founded on citizen control. The central issue is whether or not democracy — or government by the people — has any meaning if most of the people have little interest in governing. A related problem is to find means of stimulating greater public interest and participation in open pluralist societies. Theoretically, the growing amounts of leisure available in these highly industrialized states should stimulate greater willingness to devote time to political activities. There is, however, little evidence that this is the case. Politics remains a low-priority activity for most citizens in liberal democracies.

In communist states, the dilemma is to broaden participation without losing the central control believed necessary to the achievement of a socialist society. When controls are relaxed in an effort to expand participation, there is a danger that unacceptable protest and dissent will develop. This has, in fact, been the case, which explains the periodic shifts in communist states' policies on participation.

In Third World states, the dilemma is to achieve a balance between the need to stimulate mass interest and participation in politics and the need to protect new and fragile political institutions from unabsorbable pressures exerted by a mobilized and politicized public. The people need to be involved in the national political process in order to develop a sense of loyalty to the new national entity and to minimize regional or ethnic conflicts. At the same time, excessive politicization may create conditions difficult for a new and untried set of political institutions to deal with.

For some, the solution to all these dilemmas can be found in interest groups and political parties. Organized groups can express the interests of special sectors of society. In the process of making policy, governments may even anticipate the desires and responses of such groups as housewives, students, and farmers, whether or not they are represented by formal organizations. Liberal democracies can utilize parties to simplify political decisions for the voter and to mobilize political participation, at least at election times. Communist parties seek to influence and control their own members and to encourage mass participation outside the party. In developing countries, parties are seen as ideal institutions through which to channel and control participation since it is in their own interest to expand participation as they grow. In Chapter 5, after discussing various group forms of political activity, we shall examine parties and their abilities to perform these and other tasks.

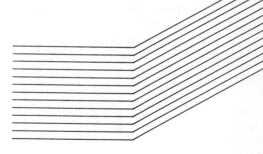

# 5

# *Interest Groups and Political Parties*

## Introduction

In the Western world, political parties are frequently viewed as essential to democratic government. Yet political parties by no means guarantee that politics will function democratically. In fact, they may become tools with which the masses are manipulated for the benefit of an elite. In Ibsen's play *An Enemy of the People,* a doctor discovers that his town's celebrated medicinal baths are dangerously polluted. Rather than suffer the economic hardship of closing the baths, the civic leaders persuade the town's population to declare the doctor a public enemy. Exasperated by the ease with which the party elite manipulates the masses, Dr. Stockmann declares: "A party is like a sausage-machine; it grinds all the brains together in one mash; and that's why we see nothing but porridge-heads and pulp-heads all around." [1]

Whether means of manipulating a gullible population or genuine expressions of democratic alternatives, political parties are major actors in the politics of many countries. As we have seen in Chapter 4, individual participation other than voting is not widespread in most political systems. Individuals who do become politically involved often participate in group activities sponsored by interest groups or political parties. Interest groups and parties serve as important means of organizing political power, either to influence government decision-making or to assure the effective implementation of policy decisions. They can also effectively link the general public to the political process, to the

1. Henrik Ibsen, *Three Plays by Henrik Ibsen* (New York: Heritage Press, 1965), p. 94.

extent that they crystallize and organize popular demands and seek to introduce these demands into the policy-making process. In this chapter we shall look at interest groups and parties from the standpoint of their political tasks, organizational features, political styles, and general relationship to the state.

The distinction between interest groups and parties is not entirely clear, but the most important difference is that parties seek power through elections or other means of gaining public office while interest groups seek mainly to influence those who hold power. Interest groups tend to be "categorical," that is, to represent certain types of constituencies — for example, workers, farmers, or consumers. Parties tend to have more diverse memberships. We will adopt the commonsense approach of designating as political parties those bodies that call themselves parties and as interest groups other bodies that attempt to influence policy outcomes.

# Interest Groups

Americans typically think of legislative lobbying as the major political activity of interest groups. However, lobbying represents only the tip of the iceberg of interest groups' activities in American politics. In other systems, legislative lobbying is much less frequent or nonexistent, but interest groups are nonetheless very important elements in the political process. Indeed, their importance is so great that one school of political thought argues that all politics can be explained as the conflict of interest groups.[2]

The interest groups that are most easily identified are those with *formal organizations,* such as labor unions, farm associations, and business and professional groups. However, *informal unorganized groups* often play important parts in political decision-making too. Among these unorganized groups — variously labeled "latent," "potential," or "nonassociational" — are cultural and ethnic groups, socioeconomic classes, occupational groups without formal structures (peasants, workers, industrial managers, students), and such broad social categories as consumers. Informal groups seldom have political influence comparable to that of organized groups with money, members, and organizations to support their claims. Nevertheless, policy-makers, recognizing the *potential* organizational and electoral strength of these informal groups, are likely to consider their interests even though they lack formal organizations and means of expression.

As a nation develops politically and economically, the formal interest groups tend to grow in power and importance relative to the informal groups. Consequently, workers, farmers, and even ethnic minorities organize formally to influence politics; in some cases governments create formal interest groups as a means of controlling society. However, the informal unorganized groups

2. The "group theory" of politics is stated by David Truman, *The Governmental Process,* 2d ed. (New York: Knopf, 1971).

do not disappear. They remain politically significant, and are often key elements in struggles over policy formulation and implementation even in the most mature political systems.

## THE BASIS FOR INTEREST GROUPS' POLITICAL INFLUENCE

Interest groups have been assuming ever larger parts in the political processes of most states, whatever their stage of development or political system. As governments have extended their regulation of society and the economy, they have become increasingly dependent on nongovernmental groups for both information and cooperation.[3] Social and economic legislation and regulation require technical expertise and precise information about resources and demands often available only from the groups to be regulated. The selective distribution and interpretation of this information permit such groups indirectly to influence the content of governmental policy decisions.

The more deeply involved government becomes in the regulation of people's lives, the more it needs the cooperation of those it seeks to regulate. Of course, governments can seek to compel acceptance of their decisions by means of force or the threat of force. But most regimes, democratic as well as nondemocratic, prefer to avoid coercion, since it indicates lack of public acceptance of their right to rule. Furthermore, the use of force to compel compliance is much less efficient than voluntary acquiescence. As a result, most governments seek the cooperation of affected groups in drafting and implementing policy. Such groups can make their cooperation with governmental policies contingent on the adoption of policies that coincide with their interests. This is true of liberal democratic states, in which voluntary acceptance of laws is essential to the stability of the regime, and as we shall see in our case studies, of communist states as well.

When governments seek to impose policies without winning the cooperation or acquiescence of affected groups, these policies may be sabotaged by the overt or covert resistance of the groups. Such determined opposition will often lead governments to revise their policies rather than coerce acceptance. Again, this is true even in communist states, despite the common stereotype of a "totalitarian" regime that forces implementation of policies over the objections of affected groups. This stereotype is simply inaccurate. Key interest groups in China and the Soviet Union have successfully resisted governmental imposition of policies they believed to be ill-advised or detrimental to their interests.

In sum, since governments need the information and cooperation that groups within their societies have to offer, groups can bargain with their governments to shape policies to meet their needs. Different governments' policies are

---

3. This argument is well developed in the case of Britain by Samuel H. Beer, *British Politics in the Collectivist Age* (New York: Knopf, 1965), pp. 319–331. See also Joel J. Schwartz and William R. Keech, "Group Influence and the Policy Process in the Soviet Union," *American Political Science Review* LXII (September 1968): 840–850.

differently vulnerable to the group pressures we have described. In democratic states, issues that have generated considerable public attention or clearly defined partisan divisions seem to be less vulnerable to interest group influence or sabotage. In communist states, issues with high ideological content are also generally immune from interest group influence.

## INTEREST GROUPS AND THE POLITICAL SETTING

The political activities of interest groups vary from one state to the next. Two factors influencing the nature of their activities are autonomy and access to policy-making circles. "Interest group autonomy" signifies the independence of the group from the state and other political forces.

The interest group's degree of autonomy, and the nature of its ties with government and with other political movements, clearly affect the nature of its activities. Where groups are captives of the state they tend to become means of organizing support for the regime. Where the interest group is linked to a party, its political effectiveness tends to hinge largely on the success of the party.

In some nations, formal interest groups are no more than agents of the government or the ruling elite, charged with assuring popular support for the regime and its policies. In communist states the formal interest groups, such as labor unions, student movements, and professional associations, are all under the control of the Commmunist party and serve primarily as "transmission belts" whereby propaganda is distributed and people are exhorted to work hard to achieve the goals of the ruling elite. Their lack of autonomy makes these interest groups effective tools of the state but inhibits their ability to represent the interests of the sector of society they serve.

In noncommunist states, too, party-interest group links limit the autonomy of groups. In most liberal democracies, each party is loosely linked with a variety of different interest groups, permitting both party and interest groups to act independently. But in other political settings, parties and interest groups are virtually inseparable. Some interest groups, especially labor unions, youth groups, and women's auxiliaries, are almost always strongly tied to political parties. Some are simply specialized branches of the party that exist for the purpose of gaining support from particular sectors of the population. In other cases, the party is the captive of the group in the sense that it is little more than the group's political arm. In either case, the interest group is likely to be in a position advantageous for influencing policy should its party affiliate hold power, and in a disadvantageous position should a rival party hold power. Labor unions have been particularly vulnerable to this problem. In several West European states, for example, the labor movement has been notably unsuccessful in pressing for its interests because Communist party control of a branch of the labor movement has made access to government circles difficult.

For those formal and informal interest groups with sufficient autonomy to seek to influence governmental policy, the key to success is *access* to the policy process. By "access" is meant sufficient opportunity for an interest group to bring its interests, attitudes, and information to the attention of government officials responsible for policy that will affect it. To pursue its interests satisfactorily, the group must have access to policy-makers at crucial points in the decision-making process, and to administrators or bureaucrats during the implementation of the resulting policy.

Success in gaining access and influencing the nature of decisions varies with interest groups' *resources*. Formally organized autonomous interest groups' most useful resources are organizational strength, money, large and cohesive memberships, broad public support, and effective spokesmen. The resources of informal groups are more difficult to enumerate. Since they lack formal organizations, the key to their influence is recognition of their existence and concern for their attitudes on the part of policy-makers. Both kinds of interest groups profit from the presence in the policy process of sympathetic individuals who serve as "brokers" for their viewpoints. This is especially true when the broker has a personal stake in assuring that a group's views are reflected in the policies adopted. In a communist state, for example, the managers of a given industry may find their interests well represented by a party official who serves informally as the broker for their interests because his performance as a party leader will be evaluated on the basis on the industry's production. Thus, his interests (meeting production goals) coincide with their interests (being granted low production goals and the resources necessary to meet those goals). The most important resource for any interest group is the ability to persuade the government that the information and cooperation it alone can provide are essential to the success of the government's goals.

*Points of access* to the policy-making process vary with the political framework. Interest groups quite naturally seek to exert their influence on those who wield the most power over policy. In the United States interest groups resort to legislative lobbying because Congress is strong and legislators are free of party discipline. However, the strength and independence of the American Congress are not typical, and legislative lobbying is not found in most other political systems. Where the party is strong, as in communist states and other single-party systems, the point of access most likely to be fruitful is the party leadership. Where cabinet-level officials control policy, as in many parliamentary systems, interest groups direct their efforts at ministers and their top lieutenants.

In almost all systems, interest groups focus attention on the sectors of the bureaucracy that administer policies directly affecting them. Lower-level bureaucrats are often responsible for interpreting broadly defined policies in the process of applying them to the real world. Such officials are vulnerable to interest groups since they need the cooperation of the governed if they are to look efficient to their superiors. As a result, interest groups can usually operate effectively to encourage bureaucrats to shape policy to correspond to the needs and desires of the groups. In a sense bureaucracies are institutionalized organs for interest groups, e.g., Agriculture, Defense, and Health, Education, and Welfare departments within the United States government.

Industrial nations, both democratic and nondemocratic, are increasingly establishing official and quasi-official "advisory commissions" to regularize interest group access to policy-making and purportedly to represent broader interests. Major interest groups concerned about a particular government policy or activity are invited to approach these commissions in order to advise the government on policy — and sometimes to set policy themselves. Recent American examples are the commissions set up by the Nixon administration in 1971 to formulate and administer wage and price controls. Sometimes labeled "collectivism" or "the new corporatism," the direct involvement of interest groups in the formulation of policy affecting them is often undertaken as a means of assuring their cooperation with the policies finally adopted. But it also provides interest groups with a voice in the decision-making process itself. This *functional representation* (the representation of specific kinds of interests) supplements and sometimes supplants the representation of individuals in certain geographic areas or constituencies provided by the election of legislators.

# Political Parties

Most states have at least one political party, though there are some "no-party" states in which parties have disappeared. In some no-party countries the military suppressed party activity as it supplanted the civilian government. In others, the parties have been absorbed or replaced by government bureaucracies that serve as agents for the regime, not only administering state policies but also maintaining political control. In some places, including some parts of the United States and in the Third World, parties have only a theoretical existence. They exist formally, have members, and may even hold periodic meetings, but their ability to mobilize the citizenry or link government to the people is virtually nil.

Nevertheless, there are movements or forces that call themselves parties in nearly all political systems. They are by no means all the same. The Conservative party of Britain is only superficially similar to the National Council of Nigerian Citizens, though both are clearly political parties. Parties in different political settings differ dramatically in the tasks they perform, their organization, their style of operation, and their relationships to the overall political unit.

It is sometimes argued that the best way to differentiate party types is to determine how many parties operate in a given state. Thus, there are single-party states, two-party states, and multiparty states. However, such a classification neglects some important differences (e. g., the dominant party in Mexico is significantly different from the single party in China) and also obscures similarities between states in different classifications (e.g., the two parties in Britain in some ways closely resemble the many parties in France).

It is also possible to distinguish parties on the basis of their ideologies. There are conservative, liberal, Christian democratic, socialist, and communist parties in many political systems, democratic as well as nondemocratic. But the political context within which parties operate fundamentally affects their natures. For example, the French Communist party is completely different from the Communist party of the Soviet Union, in spite of their common ideology.

A more reliable method of classifying parties is to examine the *tasks* or *functions* they perform in their political systems. These tasks significantly affect their organizations and styles of operation and are reflected in their relationships to the overall political unit.

## PARTIES IN LIBERAL DEMOCRACIES

In the liberal democratic setting, political parties tend to center their activities around the task of conducting and winning competitive elections. Where parties must compete in free elections for public office, they usually become preoccupied with the task of winning elections. The principal criterion by which both party leaders and outside observers measure the effectiveness of a party is its success at the polls. Even parties formally dedicated to the overthrow of the existing political system, such as communist parties, emphasize success at the polls when they operate in liberal democracies. In the hope of such success, they generally abandon clandestine activities and cultivate an air of respectability. A few minor parties may rank other goals, such as the expression of regional or occupational interests, above the electoral objective. Still other parties, having failed in elections, may seek to prevent further decline by giving priority to other tasks. Nevertheless, the vast majority of parties in liberal democracies — and all those of any importance — give precedence to winning elections.

There are many other tasks or functions that parties can or should perform, such as recruitment and training of political leaders, political socialization of the citizenry, communication of political information, the aggregation and expression of interests and ideologies, and the linkage of the state to its people. But in liberal democracies these other functions are secondary to the task of winning elections, and either promote or depend on success at the polls. For example, the provision of information contributes to the party's success at the polls, since such information is generally designed to persuade the public of the party's virtues. The recruitment of national leaders and management of government, by contrast, depends on the party's electoral success. Some functions, such as the aggregation and expression of interests, both contribute to and follow from a party's electoral fortune.

The *organizational features* of democratic parties vary widely. A party's membership may be large or small, and either direct, indirect (e.g., through membership in a labor union), or both. The demands made on members may be heavy or light, although the general trend seems to be toward fewer membership obligations. The party organization may function permanently or only at election times. These variations and others exist because Western parties have diverse political histories and operate in different political contexts. Party organization in political systems with traditions of disciplined party behavior in parliament (such as Britain) differs from organization in systems with traditions of lack of parliamentary discipline (such as the United States). In any case, organizational features tend to be designed in such a way as to maximize the parties' ability to compete effectively in elections.

The *style of party operations* in democracies is also largely determined by the pressures of electoral competition. In recent years, most democratic parties have paid less attention to political doctrines or ideologies than to personalities. Parties seek popular leaders and then emphasize their attractive attributes in attempting to persuade the voters of the parties' virtues and worthiness of support. In addition, parties now make heavy use of the mass media as an efficient means of mobilizing electoral support. The growing personalization of party politics around top party leaders and the use of mass media have the effect in most democratic states of increasing the nationalization of politics. Local party brokers and local issues are of decreasing importance in general elections, since national leaders can now speak to nationwide audiences on national issues.

In the liberal democratic setting, the party is generally clearly distinguishable from the state. The party (or coalition of parties) that wins a majority and places its leaders in positions of government authority may control the political institutions of the state for a given period of time. But it does not merge with the state. It lives with the knowledge that it may be forced to abandon these governmental positions should the electorate reject it in the next election. In the United States, the relationship between party and state is especially weak due to the inability of the president to count on the support of his fellow party members in Congress and in the state and local governments. Hence, the president often selects cabinet members who have no strong party ties or even belong to the opposition party. This is not the case in most other liberal democracies, where party discipline is tighter and the alignment of the majority party with the government is much clearer.

There has been much debate on the contribution of parties to overall political stability. Most agree that where parties are effective they can contribute importantly to the stability of a system. But it is often argued that the number of parties in a system is the key to its relative stability. A two-party system is thought to assure stability, while a multiparty system is likely to create instability. The presence of many parties allegedly brings about instability by making coalition governments necessary; such coalitions may not be durable. There is some evidence to support this contention, since the two-party systems of the United States and Britain have been significantly more stable than the multiparty systems of France and Italy. However, such arguments tend to overlook the existence of such stable multiparty systems as Canada, the Netherlands, and the Scandinavian states.

More important than the number of parties is the ideological distance between the parties.[4] In a state where parties are ideologically polarized, there is no basic consensus on values, attitudes, or goals in the political community. And where parties are polarized, whatever their number, no party will easily accept rule by its rivals. Even if there are only two parties, the outlook for stability is not bright if they are polarized. On the other hand, where parties are not polarized and accept the same values and goals, stability is possible however many parties there may be. We shall examine the effects of polarization on political stability in our discussion of Britain and France.

## PARTIES IN COMMUNIST SYSTEMS

In a communist political system, the primary tasks of the Communist party — the only party with any meaningful existence — are to assure political, social, and economic control over the society and to oversee the implementation at the grassroots of the wishes of the party elite. Since there is no competition between parties, elections are of minor importance. Instead, the party's chief purpose is to serve as an agent of social control. The party leadership makes the key policy decisions, which are then legitimized by governmental institutions, and the party is charged with the task of ensuring the enactment of these policies by monitoring government officials, bureaucrats, and the general public. Party members in the factory strive to make certain that production goals are met; in the military they keep a watchful eye on the officers' loyalty to the party; in the community, they educate the masses in Marxism-Leninism and encourage wholehearted support for the regime. The party, according to one writer, is an organizational weapon to implement the communist ideology as interpreted by its leadership.[5]

Communist parties in communist systems also perform other functions, but in such a way as to contribute to the primary task of social control. For example, political information is communicated by the party not in a neutral way, to create a politically aware populace, but rather to indoctrinate the public with the information the leadership wants it to have. The party also performs the task of recruiting political leaders. However, its recruitment policies are aimed at attracting only those willing to devote their abilities fully to the service of the party and its goals. It thus recruits men and women willing and able to carry out the task of social control.

The *organization* of communist parties is structured to facilitate social control. The party is highly centralized and hierarchical; authoritative decisions are issued at the top and implemented by the entire party structure. At the lowest level, the organizational unit is the *cell*. Unlike the wards or precincts

4. Giovanni Sartori, "European Political Parties: The Case of Polarized Pluralism," in *Political Parties and Political Development,* ed. Joseph LaPalombara and Myron Weiner (Princeton: Princeton University Press, 1966).

5. Philip Selznick, *The Organizational Weapon: A Study of Bolshevik Strategies and Tactics* (Glencoe, Ill.: Free Press, 1960).

of American parties, which are geographically demarcated, cells are occupational in nature, encompassing all the party members who work at the same factory, shop, collective farm, military unit, or school. Cells are usually quite small, and their occupational basis permits constant contact between members, which encourages daily political activity and party solidarity. Beyond the cell, the party's organization parallels that of the rest of society. It permeates other social and political groups, including the governmental bureaucracy, industrial enterprises, collective farms, interest groups, and the military. This form of organization permits the party to monitor the activities of the whole society and ensures acceptance of the party's policies.

Centralized control of the party is exercised through the process of "democratic centralism," whose "democratic" elements include the election of all party officers, from the lowest to the highest, and periodic reports by these officers to the bodies that elected them. The "centralizing" elements are strict party discipline, the subordination of the minority to the majority, and the obligatory acceptance at the lower levels of decisions made by higher party governing bodies. In practice, the centralizing elements have been carefully preserved and the democratic elements frequently ignored. Party officials are formally elected, but since they face no open competition and are nominated at the higher levels the process is more that of co-optation than election. Party officers do report on their activities to the bodies that elected them, but these reports are perfunctory and rarely debated or voted upon. In short, democratic centralism is a device to promote the centralism needed to monitor society effectively.

Discipline is furthered by the encouragement of criticism and self-criticism. Party members criticize themselves and each other in order "to boldly lay bare shortcomings, . . . to combat ostentation, conceit, complacency and parochial tendencies, . . . to resist all actions injurious to the party and state and to give information on them to party bodies. . ." [6] Criticism of the regime, top-level leaders, or their policies is usually not tolerated. Relatively free criticism of middle- and lower-level party officials serves to keep these officials efficient, increase their vulnerability to hierarchical control, and provide scapegoats for party failings.

The *political style* of Communist parties is characterized by acceptance and promulgation of the communist ideology developed by Marx and Lenin. National leaders also claim to have contributed to communist theory: in China, the thought of Chairman Mao is revered; in North Vietnam, Ho Chi Minh and General Giap are regarded as original theoreticians; in Yugoslavia, Tito's contributions are praised. Ideology provides the party with the long-range goal of achieving the pure communist society. In practice, most communist regimes have been highly pragmatic in interpreting and implementing ideology. Like the Bible, the writings of Marx, Lenin, and other theoreticians are subject to

6. Rules of the Communist Party of the Soviet Union, adopted by the Twenty-Second Congress in 1966.

diverse interpretations. The long-run goal of pure communism remains constant, but tactics and short-run goals change with the environment.

Another element of the political style is the high level of activity required of Communist party members. They are expected to be disciplined and professional, and to devote their lives to the service of the party and its goals. Members who fail to maintain discipline or become lax in their performance of party duties are subject to expulsion. There occur periodic "purges" during which the party is "purified" by the elimination of members unwilling to commit their lives to the party's goals. Stalinist purges involving executions, deportation to the hinterlands, and loss of livelihood are avoided in most contemporary communist regimes. The party member who is purged for insufficient dedication or lack of discipline today loses only his or her party membership and the social prestige and advantages that derive from it.

In communist states, the *relationship between party and state* is one of absolute dominance by the party. Although its dominance is sometimes menaced by bureaucratic encroachments and lethargy, the party makes the key political decisions. The formal state institutions simply legitimize them by making them conform to constitutional procedures. Party dominance of the state and society is made possible by the presence of party members in all sectors of society and by widespread acceptance of the party as the only legitimate voice of the people and proper source of political, social, and economic decisions. Distinctions between the party and other social or political organizations are blurred by the presence of party members in key leadership positions. This is especially true of the distinction between party and government. As we have seen, top-level party officials often fill formal government posts. In liberal democracies control of the state is a prize parties seek through competitive elections; in communist systems the state is the permanent captive of the party. It is one of several devices the party uses to maintain control of society.

## PARTIES IN THE THIRD WORLD

It is more difficult to identify the parties' task or set of tasks in Third World countries than to note the primacy of the electoral task in liberal democracies and of social control in communist systems. The variety of political settings in the Third World results in a great diversity of such tasks. In some developing states a single party is the agent of national integration; in others there are several parties, which serve as the political arms of antagonistic cultural groups. The party may be a tool for revolutionary change or maintenance of the power of a traditional autocrat. It may serve to mobilize mass participation or to preserve the political prerogatives of a narrow privileged elite. Unlike liberal democracies or communist states, then, there is no single pre-eminent party task that is performed in all or even most developing states.

Parties are effective devices for regulating and directing mass political participation, and can thus be important tools in overall political development.

For this reason, the establishment of a strong party early in the process of development is highly desirable. An effective party tends to pre-empt anomic and revolutionary mass political action by encouraging participation within the system and by moderating and directing such participation into nondisruptive channels.[7] The party may protect stability during the delicate period when traditional institutions are being replaced by new ones. One of the top priorities in the process of political development is thus the creation of a strong party to manage mass participation.

Evidence to support this contention can be found in communist states, where Leninist doctrine gives the highest priority to construction of a strong party. The comparison between North and South Korea and North and South Vietnam is striking. In both these pairs of nations, the communist state with its strong party has experienced far less turbulence and instability than its noncommunist counterpart, though other factors — political background, economic resources, and foreign assistance — are constant or favor the noncommunist states. The existence of strong parties in the two communist states has prevented the political turmoil, military coups, and general instability that have plagued South Korea and South Vietnam.

As might be expected, party organization varies widely in the developing world. The most nearly universal feature of Third World parties is structural weakness. In developing countries — whether they are newly independent, as in Africa or Asia, or have lengthy histories of independence, as in Latin America and parts of the Middle East — most parties have very weak organizations. There are few genuinely mass-based parties. The parties that do exist meet infrequently, and lack the grassroots organizations necessary to bridge the gap between the rulers and the ruled. The parties generate little interest among the masses and are unable to require much from those who become formal party members.

There appears to be a trend toward the no-party state in much of the Third World. In Africa nationalist movements that fought for independence lost their momentum and sometimes dissolved after the end of colonialism.[8] In Latin America nationalist mass parties, such as the Apristas in Peru or the Peronistas in Argentina, have been unable to resist military takeover and suppression. In some countries, such as Ethiopia, parties have never really existed. Highly organized mass parties are thus rare in the Third World, and a common substitute is a party organizationally based on patron-client relationships. The reciprocal exchange of political support in return for political favors serves as the basis for strong political collaboration on a wide range of issues. In a village or town, party or government leaders often find it useful to work through a local notable (such as a wealthy landowner, merchant, or civil servant) who has developed a following at the grassroots. The local patron be-

7. Samuel P. Huntington, *Political Order in Changing Societies* (New Haven: Yale University Press, 1968), pp. 397–461.

8. See, for example, Immanuel Wallerstein, "The Decline of the Party in Single-Party African States" in *Political Parties and Political Development,* ed. Joseph LaPalombara and Myron Weiner, pp. 201–214.

comes the party's agent in his village and his clients become, in effect, the party's workers. Networks of patron-client bonds link the grassroots with the top of the political hierarchy. The local village patron is a client of a regional patron, who is in turn a client of higher-level patrons and so on up to the national political leader. Thus, patron-client networks not only provide the political leadership with the structure and manpower necessary for its political activities, but also serve to connect the individual at the base to the leader at the top.

Often there are several patron-client networks, each tied to a different political leader. By developing such a network, the aspiring leader builds personal political support. Networks may compete for clients by offering them competing rewards. They may also overlap if an ambitious young leader supports an established leader while developing his own network. His support gives him access to patronage and other material and status benefits with which to reward his own clients.

Patron-client relationships, though a feature of traditional politics, are found in all systems, including modern industrial states. In the United States, for example, the big-city political machine is a form of patron-client network. Patron-client politics is especially common in the developing world, where pyramids of patron-client relationships often form the core of parties' organizations and sometimes serve as substitutes for very weak or nonexistent parties.

Where patron-client relationships are important, they contribute to a distinctive political style in which the party's bond with its supporters is diffuse rather than specifically political. Through its patrons, the party provides a broad range of services to its clients: jobs, educational opportunities, food and medicine during difficult times. In return the patron receives the client's support in such political activities as the distribution of propaganda, elections, rallies, and checking on political rivals, and sometimes nonpolitical personal services such as assistance at a wedding.[9] If the patron-client bond is fragile, this fragility will be transformed to the party. The patron-client bond is highly personal, usually based on face-to-face relationships, and the party's hold on its followers may thus depend on the ability of its patrons to maintain these personal ties. If the patron dies or retires, his clients may be lost to the party. The bond also depends on the perpetuation of reciprocal needs. Should either patron or client no longer feel the need of the other's services, the bond may be dissolved, affecting not only the personal relationship but also the overall strength of the party.

Even in those developing states not characterized by patron-client politics, highly personalized parties are common. The prevalence of personalistic leaders whose authority depends on personal appeal and the reverence of their followers rather than on organizational strength, is another important aspect of a party's

9. James C. Scott, "Patron-Client Politics and Political Change in Southeast Asia," *American Political Science Review* LXVI (March 1972): 95. See also Alex Weingrod, "Patrons, Patronage, and Political Parties," *Comparative Studies in Sociology and History* X (July 1968): 1142–1158.

political style. Personalism is found in the parties of communist systems (e.g., the cults of Lenin, Stalin, and Mao) and of liberal democracies (e.g., de Gaulle and possibly Churchill), but it is especially common in the Third World. Nehru in India, Nasser in Egypt, and Nkrumah in Ghana are examples of leaders whose authority and party strength rested on their personal qualities and attractiveness.

Highly personalistic leadership can be an important asset in political and socioeconomic development if it is accompanied by recognition of the need for change and the ability to mobilize mass support for change by means of personal appeal. Such a leader can become a national symbol, a rallying-point for all citizens, and a powerful advocate of change. However, personalistic leadership may cause the party to become little more than the tool of a single individual who shapes it to fit his personal style and goals. Such a party will have little institutional strength or durability. When the leader is gone, the party, lacking in its own distinctive character, may also disappear. Thus, the first test of a new party's strength is its ability to survive the disappearance of its founder.[10]

*Relationships between party and state* also vary in the developing world. In a few instances a single party is strong enough to dominate the state; Mexico is an example. In some other cases, multiple parties compete for political power; until the Biafran secession, Nigeria had such a multiparty system. More frequently, there is only one party (or a party that clearly dominates its rivals) that has merged with government at both the national and local levels. It is usually not the party that has taken over and dominated the government, but the reverse.[11] The party is "governmentalized" and becomes little more than an agent of the government. In extreme cases, the party merges with the state so completely that it loses its identity and ceases to exist. Such mergers have contributed to the trend toward no-party states in many developing countries.

Genuine party competition is usually lacking in Third World nations. Where competition does exist, whether in the two-party or multiparty pattern, the parties tend to be weak and vulnerable to military coup. Although party competition is viewed as desirable in liberal democracies, it tends in the developing world to promote political instability. The existence of several parties may hinder the integration of diverse social, economic, and cultural groups into the national whole, and may distract attention from the tasks of development. Party competition is divisive and potentially explosive. Whatever the reason, the evidence is clear: there are few examples in the Third World of truly competitive party systems that have succeeded in maintaining political stability. Most competitive systems have fallen victim to coups.

The decline of parties in the developing world portends continued political instability. Perhaps the single most important factor in promoting development and establishing stability is strong parties; the weaker the parties, the more

10. Huntington, *Political Order,* p. 409.
11. Wallerstein, "The Decline of the Party."

TABLE 5.1

## Coups and Attempted Coups in Third World Countries
## (World War Two to Early 1960s)

| Type of political system | Total number of countries | Countries experiencing coups Number | Countries experiencing coups Percent |
|---|---|---|---|
| Communist | 3 | 0 | 0 |
| One-party | 18 | 2 | 11 |
| One-party dominant | 12 | 4 | 33 |
| Two-party dictatorship | 4 | 2 | 50 |
| Two-party democratic | 7 | 3 | 43 |
| Multiparty | 22 | 15 | 68 |
| No effective party | 17 | 14 | 83 |

Source: Adapted from Fred R. von der Mehden, Politics of the Developing Nations (Englewood Cliffs, N.J.: Prentice-Hall), © 1964, p. 65. By permission of Prentice-Hall, Inc.

vulnerable the regime to military overthrow. Overt symptoms of political instability — rioting, violence, political strikes, and the like — are also less likely to occur in systems with strong parties; the strong party serves to control political participation and direct it into channels useful to the regime. Where parties decline, political turmoil becomes more likely. As one writer persuasively argues, "The decline in party strength, the fragmentation of leadership, the evaporation of mass support, the decay of organizational structure, the shift of political leaders from party to bureaucracy, the rise of personalism, all herald the moment when colonels occupy the capitol." [12]

In our case studies, we shall look at the interest groups that participate in the politics of our six states, examining their relationships to their political settings: their relationships with each other, with political parties, and with government. We shall also look at their effectiveness in influencing policy-making and at the ways they seek to exercise this influence.

Our approach to parties will be similar. What parties operate in the system? What is the political setting in which they operate? We shall focus our attention on their tasks, organization, political style, and relationship to the state, and seek to evaluate their contribution to the overall stability of the political system. Our case studies are particularly well suited to investigating the impact of parties on stability. In the democratic examples we can assess the importance of the number of parties, since Britain has a basically two-party system and France a multiparty system. In the communist cases, the Soviet Union has always given highest priority to maintenance of the party's preeminence while China has seen its party subjected to severe attacks. Mexico is an example of a single-party state in which the party dominates the political scene, whereas Nigeria's multiparty system has given way to military rule and civil war.

12. Huntington, Political Order, p. 409.

# Interest Groups and Parties in Britain and France

## INTEREST GROUPS AND DEMOCRATIC POLITICS

Interest group political activity is especially prevalent in the political processes of liberal democracies. Interest groups promote the specific interests of their memberships, which may or may not be compatible with those of the public or the nation as a whole. They are generally free to act as they please within broad legal limits, designed to prevent bribery and corruption, rather than to restrain group political activities. In most democracies, such groups can and do openly oppose governmental policies they find distasteful and seek to influence officials and, if necessary, public opinion.

The dependence of government upon the acquiescence and cooperation of groups is particularly important in the liberal democratic setting. The imposition of unwanted policy on important social groups may require the use of force, which is not likely to enhance the popularity of the government and may alienate voters whose support is needed in the next election. As the British and French governments have sought information and cooperation from groups affected by social policies, interest groups in these countries have played increasingly important and visible parts in politics.

The sheer number of groups attempting to influence policy in these countries is overwhelming. Some groups represent very narrow interests; some are concerned only with local policies; some are active only intermittently, as issues of concern to them arise; some have only fleeting existences contingent on the prominence of a specific issue. Other groups are much more active in politics, attempting to influence policy in many issue areas at the national and local levels. Some of these highly political groups are based in certain sectors of society, such as pensioners, veterans, ethnic groups, or such broader sectors as automobile drivers, taxpayers, or gun-owners. Groups based on occupational interest (such as labor unions, business groups, and professional associations) are among the most politically active, especially since governments have become more involved in regulating economic and social affairs.

Table 5.2 lists the major occupation-based interest groups in Britain and France. The groups listed are the national associations (sometimes called "peak" associations) that federate on the national level smaller associations based in particular regions or industries. For example, the TUC includes the Transport and General Workers' Union, the Amalgamated Engineering Union, the National Union of Mineworkers, and others. While the groups listed in Table 5.2 are among the most powerful in Britain and France, with interests in a broad spectrum of political issues, it should be emphasized that they are not the only important and powerful groups. Smaller groups with narrow interests to defend are often very influential in the shaping of policies that affect them. As a case in point, the General Confederation of Beetgrowers represent-

TABLE 5.2
*Major Formal Interest Groups in Britain and France*

| Type of interest group | Britain | France |
|---|---|---|
| Labor | Trade Union Congress (TUC)<br>  Linked to Labour party<br>  9,500,000 members<br>National Union of Teachers<br>  290,000 members | Confédération Générale du Travail (CGT)<br>  Linked to Communist party<br>  2,100,000 members<br>Confédération Française Démocratique du Travail (CFDT)<br>  Leftist orientation<br>  678,000 members<br>Force Ouvrière (FO)<br>  Moderate leftist orientation<br>  550,000 members<br>Fédération d'Education Nationale (FEN)<br>  Leftist orientation<br>  400,000 members |
| Employers | Confederation of British Industry (CBI)<br>British Employers' Confederation<br>Association of British Chambers of Commerce | Conseil National du Patronat Français (CNPF)<br>Confédération Générale des Petits et Moyens Entreprises (PME)<br>Centre des Jeunes Dirigeants d'Entreprise |
| Farm | National Farmers' Union (NFU) | Fédération Nationale des Syndicats d'Exploitation Agricole (FNSEA)<br>Centre National des Jeunes Agriculteurs (CNJA)<br>Mouvement de Défense de l'Exploitation Familiale (MODEF)<br>  Linked to Communist party |

ing approximately 150,000 beet producers exercised inordinate political muscle for many years prior to the establishment of the Fifth French Republic. Beets were used to make alcohol, and the beetgrowers dictated official policies on the production and use of alcohol. They even succeeded for a while in forcing the addition of alcohol to automobile gasoline, thus raising the cost and inhibiting the performance of the fuel. The beetgrowers' association also meddled in cabinet politics and contributed to the overthrow of cabinets that dared to resist its influence. The political power of this small group stemmed from its financial resources, alliance with other powerful groups in the "alcohol lobby" — winegrowers, bar-owners, and *bouilleurs de cru* (owners of fruit trees entitled to distill alcohol supposedly only for their own use) — and influence over many deputies from rural constituencies.

Several of the major peak associations have close ties with political parties. In Britain, the business and farm interests have informal links with the Conservative party, maintained by Conservative members of Parliament who are businessmen, industrialists, or professionals and retain associations, friendship bonds, and even memberships in employers' associations. Such ties are useful to these interest groups, especially when the Conservatives are in power. The Conservative party and business groups remain formally autonomous, but political cooperation between them is frequent.

The Labour party is a political offshoot of the trade union movement, and remains closely and formally tied to the TUC. Members of unions affiliated with the TUC are automatically members of the Labour party. A TUC member, however, may "contract out" of the party by declaring that he or she does not wish to affiliate with the Labour party. Not all union leaders in the TUC are Labour party members. An estimated 10 percent of the leaders in major trade unions are card-carrying communists. The number of communist trade union officials does not mean that a communist ideology is accepted by the rank-and-file, but instead reflects the workers' feeling that the communists are among the most dedicated and effective labor leaders.

The TUC exercises considerable power within the party, since the unions control five-sixths of the votes in the annual party conferences that set party policy. However, the Labour party members of Parliament enjoy considerable freedom in establishing the policies that the party will pursue in Parliament. And when Labour is in power, the cabinet consciously exercises even more independence from the unions in defining government policy. Sometimes the unions oppose actions taken by a Labour government, and occasionally they are forced by the Government to support policies they might otherwise have rejected. A recent example is the "social contract" of the Labour government in 1974–1975. In exchange for the government's pledge to increase social welfare benefits and to repeal legislation restricting the operations of trade unions, the unions were expected to restrain wage demands in an effort to control spiraling inflation. The unions felt trapped between the need to support the Labour government and the need to respond to the rank-and-file demands for higher salaries to keep up with the rising cost of living. The TUC was clearly unenthusiastic about the "social contract" and supported it only because of the need to back the Wilson government. This example illustrates the problems that can result from too close association between an interest group and a party. The interest group is usually unable to control the party, especially when it is in power; it is obliged to sustain the party even when the party acts against its interests; it is penalized when the opposition party takes over.

In France most interest groups avoid intimate ties with any single party. The sheer number of parties makes it unlikely that any one party will single-handedly dominate politics; thus few interest groups are willing to rely upon one party as a vehicle for their interests. However, some general alignments can be noted. Employers' groups have generally favored centrist and, more recently, Gaullist groups, though fear of de Gaulle's social and economic policies kept them from actively supporting the Gaullists until after de Gaulle's resignation. Labor unions favor the Left on the political spectrum but, with the exception of the Communist CGT, avoid identifying too closely with any single leftist party. Unlike American unions, which gain exclusive organizing rights in a given firm, French unions must compete among themselves for members. As a result, identification with a single party, which might influence potential members with different party loyalties to join one of the competing unions, is avoided. Even the CGT, which is controlled by the Communist party, tries to distinguish itself from the party by including non-Communists on its executive board.

Despite their independence of parties and of the state, French unions are weak and ineffectual. Their weakness stems from division among them: while all are leftist, their ideological differences often prevent joint action against employers or in favor of specific policies. The unions expend a great deal of effort competing among themselves. Furthermore, their leftist orientations and open hostility to the Gaullist regime, which has prevailed for over fifteen years, has made government leaders unresponsive to union demands. Finally, the French unions have been unsuccessful in recruiting members. Only about 20 percent of the work force is unionized in France, compared to more than 40 percent in Britain.

French interest groups have a tendency to emphasize protest, rather than advocacy. Instead of advocating their own interests, groups periodically resort to direct action in efforts to sabotage public policy or undermine the group or regime they view as their enemy.[13] Farm groups have been especially prone to this style of political activity. Scarcely a year passes without a farm group dumping milk on the highway or throwing lettuce in the ocean to protest farm prices or the low standard of living in rural France. But the farmers are not alone in their recourse to protest and direct action. As one analyst points out, "There are times in French history when every social group and political organization seems to be protesting against the status quo. . . ."[14]

Group politics in Britain and France is characterized by activities ranging from attempts to exchange electoral support or campaign contributions for a legislator's support of the groups' interests, to informal contracts between group representatives and government officials, to formal participation in policymaking. These forms of interest group activity will be discussed more fully in Chapter 8, on policy-making. While it would be inaccurate to conclude that interest groups control politics, they do strongly influence the nature and implementation of policy. Political leaders, who are accountable to the electorate, generally determine the general direction and outline of policy. But groups, accountable only to their clientele, actively influence the specific details of policy.

13. Stanley Hoffmann, "Protest in Modern France," in *The Revolution in World Politics*, ed. Morton A. Kaplan (New York: Wiley, 1962).
14. *Ibid.*, p. 69.

The power of interest groups raises important questions for democratic regimes. Where broadly defined policies are passed by elected bodies and then interpreted and applied by bureaucrats and interest group representatives, certain important policy-making powers are in the hands not of elected officials directly accountable to the voters, but of anonymous group leaders and unaccountable bureaucrats. This situation often leads to the regulation of society and the economy by the very groups supposed to be the objects of regulation. As an illustration of the regulated regulating themselves, the British Medical Association (BMA) sits on key governmental committees that define national medical policies and regulate the activities and fees of BMA doctors.

A second problem is that much group activity takes place behind closed doors. Negotiations and compromises between interest groups and government are facilitated by secret meetings. Informal contacts between group spokesmen and government officials are not exposed to the public's eyes. Obviously, such secrecy is detrimental to democratic control by the public, since it is difficult or impossible for the voter to attribute to any individual or group the details of policies worked out in secret sessions.

A third problem is that some sectors of society are unable to participate in this process on an equal footing. The advantage lies with established and well-organized groups. Those elements of society that for a variety of reasons find it difficult to organize — the poor, ethnic minorities, the elderly, the young, consumers — find access to the decision-making process difficult or impossible. Access for such unorganized sections of society comes usually through "public" participants (generally bureaucrats) with strong personal and professional links with the organized groups.

Finally, there is the question of the accuracy with which the spokesmen for interest groups reflect the attitudes of their memberships. It is often alleged, and correctly, that union leaders do not accurately convey the political feelings of their members, and that employers' associations do not know the attitudes of those they represent on any given issue. The problems involved in ascertaining the representativeness of group spokesmen are great. Who is to know, for instance, whether the Royal Automobile Club is correctly reflecting its members' views in urging a new highway?

Interest groups are likely to continue to be prominent participants in the democratic political process. Governments need their information and cooperation, and citizens in Britain, France, and other Western democracies appear to believe that their governments ought to consult groups affected by public policies. Group involvement in politics may also be seen as increasing the representativeness and responsiveness of government by supplementing individual representation by legislators with the functional representation of specific interests by groups. Given the low levels of individual political participation, group politics may be a means of making democracy work despite the inactivity of the masses. In this sense, groups serve as substitutes for individual participation and at least foster political involvement among those interested in and affected by governmental policies.

# THE ELECTORALLY ORIENTED PARTIES OF
BRITAIN AND FRANCE

The political party is another format for organizing and supplementing individual participation. Ideally, in democratic states, parties offer the electorate choices between differing sets of leaders, philosophies, and policy options. Indeed, electoral competition between two or more parties is an essential aspect of the Western democratic process.

Table 5.3 lists the major parties in Britain and France and their electoral and parliamentary strength in recent elections. The most obvious difference between the two nations is the concentration of electoral support in two parties in Britain and its dispersal among many parties in France. In Britain, two parties accounted for 75 percent of the vote and 94 percent of the members of Commons after the 1974 elections. The two elections of 1974 were exceptions due to the large number of voters supporting the Liberal party and other minor parties. In other general elections since 1950, the Conservative and Labour parties alone won between 90 and 98 percent of the vote and 98 percent of the seats in Commons. In France it took six parties to account for a similar pro-

TABLE 5.3
## *Parties in Britain and France*

| | Britain | |
|---|---|---|
| *Party* | *Percentage of vote in October 1974 general election* | *Percentage of seats in House of Commons* |
| Conservative Party | 35.9 | 43.5 |
| Labour Party | 39.5 | 50.2 |
| Liberal Party | 18.3 | 1.9 |
| Scottish National Party | 2.7 | 1.7 |
| Welsh Nationalists | 0.6 | 0.5 |
| Others | 2.6 | 2.0 |
| | *France* | |
| *Party* | *Percentage of vote in 1973 legislative election* | *Percentage of seats in National Assembly* |
| Communist Party (PCF) | 21.3 | 14.9 |
| Unified Socialist Party (PSU) | 3.3 | 0.6 |
| Socialist Party (PS) | 19.2* | 20.4 |
| "Reformers" | 12.5 | 6.3 |
| Union of Democrats for the Republic (UDR) | 24.0 | 37.6 |
| Independent Republicans (RI) | 7.0 | 11.0 |
| Center for Democratic Progress (CDP) | 3.8 | 4.7 |
| Other Gaullist groups | 3.3 | 2.9 |

*\* Including votes for the left-wing Radicals, who were allied with the PS (approximately 1.4% of the vote).*

portion of votes and seats in 1973; the same thing is true of almost every election since the end of World War Two. There is a less apparent but more important difference between the ideological divergence of French parties and the ideological similarity of British parties. In France, parties represent the full political spectrum from the far Left to the far Right; in Britain the two parties have converged at the Center.

In Britain, the Conservative and Labour parties have controlled politics since 1924. The Conservative party tends to represent the interests of the middle and upper social classes, whereas the Labour party defends the interest of the working class and the lower-middle class. However, these class lines are not rigid; a large number of "working-class Tories" vote Conservative and an important sector of the middle and even upper class regularly votes Labour. Both parties attempt to attract voters from all socioeconomic classes, especially those that normally vote for their opponent. Conservatives make special efforts to woo the working-class vote and the Labour party devotes special attention to the middle class. Thus while there are clear differences in the class backgrounds of the constituencies of the two British parties, it would be inaccurate to label them class-based parties since both seek and receive support from all classes.

In terms of policy options, the differences between Conservatives and Labourites are slight. The Conservatives draw support from business and industrial interests, but they have accepted the nationalization of major industries and social welfare programs initially enacted by a Labour government. They have also accepted the notion of governmental management and intervention in the economy. Some have argued that the Conservative party's welfare programs and economic management policies are inspired by upper-class paternalism and a grudging recognition that these policies are vote-pleasers. Nevertheless, whatever its motivations, the Conservative party has often pursued policies that might sooner be expected from a liberal party than from one claiming to defend conservatism and free enterprise.

The Labour party's guiding ideology is socialism, but gradualist or reformist rather than revolutionary. It has supported the nationalization of large industries, governmental economic planning, and extensive social welfare programs. Immediately after World War Two, a Labour government enacted a series of socialist reforms that dramatically changed the economic structures of Britain. Since that time, the Labour party has moderated its socialism and pressed for few additional fundamental reforms. When in power, it has accepted and even promoted the growth of private industry. While seeking to alleviate economic disparities, Labour has tolerated the persistence of the contemporary world's largest and best-developed aristocracy. It has tended to be more aggressive in pushing for social and economic reforms than has the Conservative party, but the two parties' policy or ideological differences are matters of degree rather than direction.

The ideological convergence of the two major British parties is so marked that some British political pundits complain there is but one ideology, "conservo-socialism." This convergence reflects a widely shared consensus among British voters and leaders on the role of government in society and the economy; it does not mean that all party differences have disappeared. The two parties differ over the importance, timing, and specific means of managing the economy, controlling inflation, promoting economic equality, reforming education, regulating immigration, shaping foreign and military commitments, and so forth. In short, the two parties have the same general view of the role of government, but they have proposed different policies on concrete problems.

While the Conservative and Labour parties have long dominated the British party system, there are other parties. The most important is the Liberal party. Once a major political force that alternated in power with the Conservatives, the Liberals were replaced by the Labour party as the second major party after World War One. Since then, the Liberals have remained on the sidelines of British politics. On a Left–Right political spectrum, the Liberals fall between the left-of-center Labourites and the right-of-center Conservatives. In recent years they have campaigned for moderate social reforms and for "community politics" — an attempt to increase "people participation" in making decisions that affect citizens' daily lives. The Liberals scored their greatest electoral success since World War Two in the February 1974 elections, when they received 19.3 percent of the vote. The British electoral system awards a parliamentary seat to the candidate who receives the most votes, whether or not they constitute a majority, and though the Liberals often ran second and third they elected only fourteen members of Parliament. Their relatively large share of the vote reflected voter dissatisfaction with both of the major parties. However, it is unclear whether these results portend a Liberal revival over the long run. Voters tend to support parties they feel will win, in order to avoid "wasting" their votes. The fact that the Liberals win so few seats despite surges of support may eventually result in a decline in their voting strength.

In France party differences are much more pronounced. The variety of political philosophies represented is reflected in the number of parties. These parties are grouped into three loose coalitions: the Gaullists, the Leftists, and the Centrists.

The Gaullists include three parties: the Union of Democrats for the Republic (UDR), the largest party and the one most closely linked to de Gaulle; the Independent Republicans (RI), the more traditional conservatives and followers of President Valéry Giscard d'Estaing; and the Center for Democratic Progress (CDP), centrists who rallied to Gaullism after de Gaulle's retirement. Several smaller groups are also associated with the Gaullists. The UDR defends the legacies of de Gaulle's rule: the institutions of the Fifth Republic, especially a strong presidency; national independence, particularly with regard to alleged violations of French national sovereignty by the United States; and participation, a vague ideal of involving citizens in making the political, social, and economic decisions that affect their lives. The RIs, generally considered to be to the right of the UDR, are defenders of free enterprise and laissez-faire economics. They and the CDP are more favorable to European political and economic unity than is the UDR.

Despite these internal differences, the Gaullist coalition has remained remarkably cohesive, permitting the Gaullists to control politics throughout the life of the Fifth Republic. All the prime ministers from 1958 through 1975 were associated with the UDR; the three men who have occupied the presidency (de Gaulle, Georges Pompidou, and Valéry Giscard d'Estaing) have been Gaullists; and the National Assembly has had a solid Gaullist majority since 1962. While there have been periodic divisions within the coalition, Gaullist unity has remained intact through a series of changes, the most important being the disappearance of de Gaulle, who originally inspired the alliance. The most dramatic division occurred during the 1974 presidential election, when the UDR and CDP endorsed Jacques Chaban-Delmas and the RI supported Valéry Giscard d'Estaing on the first ballot. In a sense, the first ballot was a primary election to determine the Gaullist candidate on the second ballot; and the Gaullist coalition united behind Giscard d'Estaing for the runoff election.

The Gaullist philosophy makes it difficult to place these parties on a Left–Right political spectrum. On the one hand, the Gaullists support political options traditionally associated with the Right: anticommunism, strong executive power, independent military strength, and French nationalism. And they draw support from social groups usually aligned with the Right: the middle class, faithful Catholics, and voters in the north and east of France. On the other hand, the Gaullists are committed to a modernist philosophy of change and adaptation alien to the traditional Right. During the Fifth Republic, the Gaullists completed decolonization; enacted major university, agricultural, and economic reforms; and pressed for fundamental changes in the free enterprise system to provide for the "association" and "participation" of workers in the profits and decisions of industry. Thus, the Gaullists may be labeled rightists, as they usually are, but they are clearly distinguishable from traditional French right-wing groups.

The Left has two major components: the French Communist party (PCF), the second largest communist party outside the Soviet bloc, and the Socialist party (PS). In addition, there are many smaller leftist groups. Some, like the dissident Radical-Socialists (who, despite their name, are neither radical nor socialist), usually participate in the leftist alliances. Others, like the Unified Socialist party (PSU) and the parties of the "New Left," remain outside such alliances.

The left-wing alliance is much more tenuous than that of the Gaullists. Attempts to unify the French Left have been made as long as there have been left-wing parties. The most successful unification occurred during the Popular Front era of the 1930s, when the Communists, Socialists, and Radicals formed a coalition that held power briefly. After World War Two, the Cold War and mutual suspicions made cooperation between the communist and noncommunist branches of the Left impossible. The alliance was renewed briefly in 1965, again in 1966–1968, and most recently in 1972, when PCF and PS agreed upon an electoral alliance and a common program should they win the 1973 elections. The two parties supported a single candidate, François Mitterrand, in the 1974 presidential election on the first and second ballots. Regardless of the outcome of the elections, they were pledged to cooperate in parliament and to oppose the Gaullist regime. However, substantial policy differences — especially in the area of foreign policy — and lingering fear of the communists' intentions continue to compromise the long-range durability of such an alliance. In 1975, the future of the alliance was called into question by new verbal attacks on the Socialists by the Communists. This problem was compounded by the PCF's support for the Portuguese Communists in their suppression of all non-communist newspapers.

The Communists are the largest and best organized party in France, and they enjoy the support of the most powerful labor union. While the PCF verbally advocates revolution, it has done very little to foment revolution or promote subversive activities. The PCF has given priority to winning respectability and increasing its voting strength through political moderation. The party's present strategy is to expand its strength in local and national electoral politics through an alliance with the Socialists. While it remains loyal to the Soviet Union, the PCF has publicly criticized such Soviet actions as the invasion of Czechoslovakia in 1968 and repression of Russian Jews.

The Socialists command fewer votes and have fewer members than the PCF. The Socialist party has had difficulty adjusting its doctrine and style to the postwar political environment. It remains theoretically committed to Marxist socialism and promotion of revolution, but in practice it is pragmatic and thoroughly nonrevolutionary. The party's leader, François Mitterrand, has drawn the party into a coalition with the PCF. The PS, however, remains divided on its ties with the Communists. Some Socialists fear that the Communists will at best use the alliance to cut into socialist electoral strongholds and at worst use it to subvert the regime and install a communist dictatorship. Others believe that the Communists can be trusted, and that Socialists can achieve their desired social and economic reforms only through the unity of the Left. Those favoring the alliance have prevailed, largely because most Socialist elected officials need Communist votes for re-election. The French two-ballot electoral system forces a runoff if no candidate wins a majority on the first ballot. Since few Socialists can muster a first-ballot majority, the Socialist party hopes that the alliance will lead the PCF candidate who is outpolled by the Socialist on the first ballot to withdraw and throw support to the Socialist on the second ballot. Such reciprocal withdrawals proved highly successful in the 1967 and 1973 elections.

The centrists, or members of parties between the Gaullists and the Leftists, appear to be a disappearing political force. The center parties, including the once-powerful Christian Democratic party of the Fourth Republic, have since 1958 steadily lost leaders and voters to the Gaullists. Their voters were attracted by de Gaulle's personality and programs, and their leaders by the possibility of becoming part of the government coalition and possibly receiving ministerial posts. As a result, few centrist parties remain. For the 1973 elections most of these parties formed a loose coalition, which they labeled the "Reformers." It subsumed the main body of the old Radical-Socialist party (under the leadership of Jean-Jacques Servan-Schreiber) and the last remnants of the Christian Democratic party (under the leadership of Jean Lecanuet). The Reformers oppose the authoritarian style of Gaullism, and support efforts to unite Europe and strengthen the European Common Market much more energetically than do the Gaullists.

The gradual movement of centrists toward the Gaullist coalition reached a climax in the 1974 presidential elections. Most centrists endorsed Giscard d'Estaing on the first ballot and nearly all rallied to him for the runoff. After the election the Reformers were rewarded with several cabinet positions and were effectively absorbed into the Giscard-led Gaullist government coalition. The rallying of centrists to the majority was consolidated by the merger of the parliamentary representatives of the Reformers and the CDP (those centrists who had earlier rallied to the Gaullists).

## PARTIES AND POLITICAL STABILITY

In both Britain and France, parties exist in a political setting in which they compete for votes and ultimately control of the government. The competitiveness of this setting is demonstrated in Britain by the alternation in power of the Labour and Conservative parties: between 1945 and 1976 the Labour party held power for fifteen years and the Conservative party for sixteen years. In France, the Gaullists have controlled government without interruption from 1958 through 1976, though the other parties have remained competitive on the national scene and control local politics in much of France.

Because of their highly competitive settings, British and French parties have emphasized the electoral task. Even the supposedly antisystem French Communists have ignored revolutionary goals to concentrate on winning respectability in the eyes of the voter. Party organization, doctrine, and tactics are shaped to maximize voting appeal. For example, when the British Conservative party realized the popularity of socialist reforms introduced by the Labour party, the Conservatives quickly modified their ideology to accept these reforms and even to offer progressive social welfare programs of their own. Failure to make such adjustments leads to defection by voters and the overall decline of the party, as has been the experience of the French Socialists.[15]

In Britain one party usually wins a majority of the seats in the House of Commons, and thus singlehandedly controls government. The majority party names the prime minister from among its MPs and chooses a cabinet. The minority party becomes "Her Majesty's Loyal Opposition" and chooses a "shadow government" to contest government policies. The leader of the opposition even receives a government salary. Thus, the distinction between government and opposition is obvious, and confrontation between the two

15. See Frank L. Wilson, *The French Democratic Left, 1963–1969: Toward a Modern Party System* (Stanford: Stanford University Press, 1971).

PARLIAMENTARY LABOUR PARTY

ON MONDAY, 22nd October 1973, the House will meet at 2.30 p.m.

LOCAL GOVERNMENT (SCOTLAND) BILL; LORDS AMENDMENTS
(Rt. Hon. W. Ross & Team)

**DIVISIONS WILL TAKE PLACE AND YOUR ATTENDANCE FROM 3.30 P.M. IS NECESSARY**


ON TUESDAY, 23rd October, the House will meet at 2.30 p.m.

MAPLIN DEVELOPMENT BILL; LORDS AMENDMENTS
(Rt. Hon. A. Crosland & Team)

**DIVISIIONS ARE EXPECTED AND YOUR ATTENDANCE FROM 3.30 P.M. IS NECESSARY**

Afterwards,   MOTIONS ON NORTHERN IRELAND ORDERS ON LAND ACQUISITION AND
COMPENSATION, AND FINANCE (Mr. Merlyn Rees)
POWERS OF CRIMINAL COURTS BILL (LORDS): (Mr. S. C. Silkin)
MOTIONS ON LEGAL AID ORDERS (Mr. S. C. Silkin)
MOTION TO APPROVE SIXTH REPORT ON THE LANDSCAPING OF
NEW PALACE YARD (Rt. Hon. D. Houghton)

ON WEDNESDAY, 24th October, the House will meet at 2.30 p.m.

DEBATE ON OPPOSITION MOTION ON U.K. IMPORTS OF CANE SUGAR
(Rt. Hon. P. Shore & Rt. Hon. Mrs. J. Hart)

**A DIVISION WILL TAKE PLACE AND YOUR ATTENDANCE BY 9.30 P.M. IS ESSENTIAL**

Afterwards,   MOTIONS ON THE SALARIES OF THE PARLIAMENTARY COMMISSIONER AND
THE COMPTROLLER AND AUDITOR GENERAL (Mr. R. Sheldon)
LOCAL GOVERNMENT (SUCCESSOR PARISHES) ORDER (Mr. G. Oakes)

ON THURSDAY, 25th October, the House will meet at 2.30 p.m.

MOTION TO APPROVE THE WHITE PAPER ON THE CHANNEL TUNNEL
PROJECT (Cmd. No. 5430)
(Rt. Hon. A. Crosland & Rt. Hon. F. Mulley)

**A DIVISION WILL TAKE PLACE AND YOUR ATTENDANCE BY 9.30 P.M. IS NECESSARY**

Subject to progress of Business, PROROGATION will then take place.


BOB MELLISH

NOTE:   The NEW SESSION will be opened on TUESDAY, 30TH OCTOBER.

---

*European political parties tend to be highly disciplined and cohesive in their actions in parliament. In Britain, near perfect voting is attained in House of Commons votes, with all Labour MPs taking the same position on major votes (or "divisions of the House") and all Conservative MPs also voting together. MPs are informed of upcoming debates and divisions by a weekly bulletin known as the Whip (illustrated above). Items which have been underlined three times are of particular importance. The MP is expected to be in attendance for these important debates and to vote in accordance with the party position. Failure to vote with the party, particularly on a "three-line Whip," may entail discipline for the dissident MP, including the ultimate sanction of "withdrawing the Whip," or exclusion from the party. While such stern discipline decreases the independence of the elected representative, it assures party accountability by giving each party a clearly defined position on major issues, and it provides the government with a sure parliamentary majority to enact its proposals.*

groups is institutionalized. The government can be held accountable for its decisions and actions; the opposition can make criticisms and formulate alternative policies. If the government fails to perform its duties adequately, the voters can turn to the opposition for a viable alternative.

This principle of a clearly defined government and opposition was upheld even in the wake of the February 1974 election when no single party had a majority in the House of Commons. The Labour party won 301 seats, more than any other party but short of the 318 needed for a majority in the 635-seat chamber. Rather than form a multiparty coalition, Harold Wilson formed a minority Labour government that was dependent for its continued existence on the informal support or abstention of other parties. This was a stopgap measure designed to provide a government until new elections could be held to elicit another judgment from the voters.

In France, a clearcut division between government and opposition is not always present. The Gaullist government is a fairly cohesive coalition, which allows for a reasonably clear presentation of government positions. However, the opposition is composed of diverse and divided elements. The Left has been the core of this opposition, but it is divided on issues, strategy, and ideology. Thus there is no credible alternative to the Government. The voter is faced with a choice between the Gaullists who — whatever their faults — at least provide stable government, and the Left, which — whatever its virtues — is plagued by disunity. For the voter who is antagonized by Gaullist policies but uneasy about the danger of political instability should the Left win, there is little real choice despite the abundance of parties and their ideological diversity.

In Britain the party system has been a source of strength and stability for the political system as a whole. The two major parties offer the voter reasonably clear alternatives, but are not ideologically polarized. A Conservative voter or party leader does not look on the victory of the Labour party as a total calamity. One party does not regard the other as an authoritarian threat to democracy. The defeated party accepts the voters' decision and begins to prepare for the next election. The intensity of partisan feelings is sufficiently low to make interparty friendships and cooperation possible and common.

In France the party system contributes friction and instability to the overall political scene. Some attribute this instability to the large number of parties, arguing that multiparty systems are inherently unstable and two-party systems inherently stable. However, the number of parties alone is not the crucial factor; other democratic states — Holland, Sweden, Canada, and others — have stable party systems despite the presence of more than two parties. Much more germane to the relative stability of party systems is the degree of ideological or emotional polarization among parties. Where parties are polarized, whatever their number, the party system is likely to be unstable. The degree of polarization between parties is much greater in France than in Britain. The Gaullists claim that the victory of the Left would bring totalitarian communism to power; the leftists denounce the authoritarian and fascist character of Gaullist rule. The intensity of partisan feelings makes interparty cooperation and friendship difficult. While de Gaulle was president, leftist deputies refused to attend even ceremonial functions (such as the annual presidential dinner honoring the National Assembly) if he was to be present. Thus the Gaullists and the leftists offer not just different sets of personnel to operate the government, but wholly different views of governmental organization and goals. There is little chance that political power could alternate between these two blocs unless the political and social institutions of the state changed radically with each alternation.

In summary, Britain and France offer evidence of the importance of parties to the democratic political system. In Britain the party system enhances the stability and efficient functioning of the state as a whole. In France the divided and polarized party scene contributes instability unsettling to the whole system.

# Interest Groups and Parties in the Soviet Union and China

Communist ideology asserts that special interests are anachronisms based on the class differences in capitalist society. With the elimination of class distinctions, the only interests are those of the people as a whole embodied in the Communist party. But these "anachronistic" groups continue to exist in all communist states in forms of formally sanctioned labor unions, peasant associations, youth groups, and such informal groups as intellectual, bureaucratic, or military cliques.

Political parties in communist systems are quite different from parties in liberal democracies. They perform some of the same functions — the recruitment of political leaders and the conduct of elections — but their primary task is the administration and control of society and politics. Competition, which in democratic states takes place *between* parties, occurs in the communist context among factions *within* the single party.

## INTEREST GROUPS IN COMMUNIST POLITICS: TRANSMISSION BELTS OR LIMITED INTEREST GROUP PLURALISM?

For many years Western observers, misled by the model of totalitarian and monolithic communism, tended to ignore the activities of interest groups in communist states. They accepted the notion that the dictatorial powers of the leader and party relegated interest groups to the role of transmission belts that faithfully implement party directives without playing any meaningful part in policy-making. More recently, scholars have challenged this view, arguing that formal and informal groups in communist states influence the nature of policy and can in some cases block policies detrimental to their interests. There are indications that a limited amount of interest group pluralism has developed as the terror of the Stalinist era has subsided and industrialization has given rise to growing technocracy. Groups have become involved in shaping policy, and this situation has been tolerated by the regime so long as it does not challenge the primacy of the party.

## INTEREST GROUPS IN THE SOVIET UNION

In the Soviet Union, the formal interest groups that appear most to resemble Western interest groups — labor unions, professional associations, and youth groups — are either outright auxiliaries of the party or closely tied to it. The party uses these groups to control various segments of society. Thus, the trade unions are used to disseminate party propaganda, stimulate production, and assure discipline among the workers. Unlike Western unions, which use strikes to press their demands, the Soviet unions *prevent* strikes and other work stoppages. Because of their ties to the party, these mass organizations or formal interest groups have severely limited autonomy. Leadership posts are filled by party leaders or nonmembers designated by the party. The group is expected to serve the national interest as defined by the party and to avoid representing narrow special interests.

However, the transmission belt flows in two directions even in the case of these party-dominated mass organizations. The groups provide party and government leaders with information about the interests and needs of their particular sectors of society. Their leadership overlaps with the party's, since party officials are often also leaders of these groups. Such leaders can be expected to articulate and defend their organizations' concerns in the policy-making process. They may express the attitudes of the group and predict its reactions to policies under consideration, thereby informally representing its interests.

Perhaps even more noteworthy for their effect on policy are the informal intellectual and occupational groups, which lack organization but nonetheless exercise important political influence. Among the most important informal groups in the Soviet Union are writers, economists and planners, industrial managers, jurists, agricultural experts, party apparatchiki (fulltime party workers), secret police, and military officers. Some of these informal groups parallel party-dominated formal groups. For example, the writers have an organization under party tutelage that serves as a means of literary control, preventing the publication of questionable writings and disciplining dissident authors. Apart from this formal organization, writers as an occupational group may have influence over policy. They and related informal groups are influential because of their strategic positions in society and relatively easy access to decisionmakers. They form an intellectual elite that strives to participate in policy-making on its own behalf and that of larger interests it feels it represents. Since the cooperation of these informal groups is frequently essential to the success of economic, agricultural, legal, and other programs, policy-makers sometimes seek their informal advice on policies. Even when groups are not permitted to offer advice on policy, decisionmakers often attempt to anticipate their reaction and to take the expected reactions into account.

The Soviet regime's abandonment of terror and preference for persuasion since Stalin's death has made it possible for some groups discreetly to sabotage party-sponsored programs that damage their interests. Such resistance must be carefully camouflaged and avoid a frontal threat to the party or the system. It is unlikely that interest group sabotage would be tolerated if a major program were at stake. However, some large-scale reforms have been abandoned as a result of determined resistance by affected groups. An example is the educational reform proposed by then-party secretary Nikita Khrushchev at the end of the 1950s.[16] Teachers and school administrators felt the reform damaged their vested interests. Rather than overtly attacking the well-publicized program, the teachers and administrators subtly undermined it by indicating their expertise led them to doubt the wisdom of the reform. They raised questions about its effects on the performance of the educational system and its ability to provide needed scientific and technical experts. They also gathered support from other groups, including scientists, industrial managers, and parents. In the end, they appeared to be successful; Khrushchev ultimately abandoned most of the reform.

Groups are also involved in factional jockeying within the topmost strata of the party hierarchy. Aspiring leaders may seek the backing of various interests as they struggle for power, and groups may attempt to barter their support for pledges of favorable policies. Among the groups most frequently involved in factional struggles are the secret police and the military (because of their access to the means of violence) and the party apparatchiki (because of their strategic position within the party).

In exploring interest group activities, it is important to emphasize the context of Soviet politics. Policy-making power resides in the hands of a few powerful party leaders, who can and do make policy without consulting affected groups. When they are so inclined, they can enforce their will upon reluctant groups. Under certain circumstances, groups *may* act to influence policy and the party leaders *may* respond. In no way can Soviet interest groups engage in the open bargaining between government and groups that occurs in Western democracies. Yet there is evidence, as one scholar notes, that "sometimes the decisions of the rulers are taken as a result of the influence of groups and in a milieu of competing and conflicting tendencies."[17]

## CHINESE INTEREST GROUPS: AGENTS OF CHANGE

Formal interest groups in the People's Republic of China are primarily transmission belts. While some have preliberation origins, all are sanctioned and

16. Schwartz and Keech, "Group Influence."
17. H. Gordon Skilling, "Group Conflict in Soviet Politics: Some Conclusions," in *Interest Groups in Soviet Politics,* ed. H. Gordon Skilling and Franklyn Griffiths (Princeton: Princeton University Press, 1971).

monitored by the party by means of the interlocking leadership structure characteristic of all large Chinese organizations. Such groups do, however, also serve to transmit individuals' reactions to policy to the party and bureaucracy. They are encouraged to provide this feedback, within circumscribed limits, but it is clear that their primary role is to help carry out party policy and educate the masses about communism.

Since 1949, interest groups and secondary groups have taken two forms: those based on membership in a common occupational or class category and those based on membership in a residential unit. Examples of the first type are the All-China Federation of Trade Unions, the Women's Federation, the Youth League, and the All-China Students' Federation. Residential committees serve to organize groups that might otherwise be isolated, such as housewives. They are involved in transmitting party policies to the lowest levels of the society. But they are also very active with local problems, such as sanitation, fire and safety services, potable water supplies, and the like. By dealing with these civic problems, they provide opportunities for citizen participation at the lowest levels. In addition, temporary interest groups have formed from time to time around a single cause. Some of these, such as those related to the Great Leap Forward and the Cultural Revolution (especially the Red Guards), developed extensive memberships and organizational structures.

A major dilemma for interest groups in communist states is the difficulty of serving both the party and their clientele. This problem is well illustrated by the Chinese trade union movement. Among the largest and best-known interest groups in China is the All-China Federation of Trade Unions, whose top leadership is appointed by the Communist party of China. While membership is not strictly compulsory, Chinese workers are only eligible to receive social security insurance and other union welfare programs if they are members.

Since the liberation, the union leadership has conducted the labor movement through cycles of considerable autonomy and strict party supervision. First, the leadership sought to promote union professionalism and economic objectives rather than party-favored political tasks. It is interesting to note that though the leaders come from and belong to the Communist party, the immediate pressure of the workers often prevails over the external, if more powerful, political party pressures — that is, in the short run, until the party intervenes to reassert control. This has happened on three occasions. First, in 1952 Li Li-san, the first chairman of the union federation, was relieved for failing to follow party wishes. He was replaced by Lai Jo-yu, who had no previous union experience. An outsider would be expected to be less responsive to workers' interests and more responsive to party directions, but he too eventually succumbed. China was decentralizing and the unions followed the dual rule aspect, or regional party control, which contradicted Lai's visions of a professional and efficient union organization. Here again, workers' interests came into conflict with the party's long-range objectives. This situation created a dilemma for the union cadre, who found themselves caught between party and worker pressures:

We are Party members and according to Party discipline, must subordinate ourselves to resolutions of Party organizations; otherwise we might be labeled "syndicalists," "agitators for independence from the party," or "tailists," etc., and might even be expelled from the party. On the other hand, we are elected by the workers to speak for their interests and should subordinate ourselves to the will of the majority of the workers, otherwise we would be accused by the workers of being the "tail of the administration" and would be discarded by the workers.[18]

Such conflicts occur not only between workers and party, but also among the workers themselves. One of the more serious disputes resulted from the frustration of contract workers, who did menial jobs at factory sites after their work on communes had been completed. They were denied union membership and job security and were poorly paid. Thus during the Cultural Revolution they were readily disposed to join with Red Guards against union workers in fights for control of factories.

Chinese interest groups utilize resources similar to those of groups in Western-oriented political systems. They often have their own press and films, mass meetings, and monetary resources from their memberships' contributions or from the Communist party. Their success is dependent on their leadership and persuasive skills. When these function poorly, as is true of interest groups in open political systems, their cause may well fail.

Because of high illiteracy and low exposure to media (characteristics of more than 80 percent of the Chinese people at the time of the 1949 revolution), voluntary interest group formation is highly unlikely. Yet such groups potentially exist and do have interests that need expression and acknowledgment in public policy. Interest groups' influence on party and government is most evident during times of official governmental encouragement. The party leadership, or portions of it, encourages interest groups to speak out against a given policy or leader, and then uses this "public" protest as a pretext to change the policy or remove the leader. Among the more prominent of such scenarios was the activity of student groups during the Cultural Revolution. In June 1966 students posted large character posters attacking Peking University and party officials. This act led within four days to the dismissal of these officials. This incident was followed by increased student activity throughout the nation to press for changes in policies and in party and government personnel.

In conclusion, interest group activities in communist states are subject to constraints applied by the party. The party frequently uses its powers to control groups in order to pursue ends that may or may not be compatible with the interests of the groups' members. The party also utilizes these groups to mobilize their members for political action. Under certain circumstances the groups are permitted some autonomous action and their contributions to policy-making are tolerated, even encouraged. And these groups gain increased lever-

18. Paul Harper, "The Party and the Unions in Communist China," *China Quarterly* 37, (January–March 1969): 87.

age in times of party factional disputes. More typically, the groups must exercise discretion in bringing their points of view very subtly to the attention of party leaders and decision-makers. It would be wrong to dismiss the influence of groups in contemporary Soviet and Chinese politics, and it would be equally wrong to assume that because groups do participate in policy-making they do so with effectiveness and pervasiveness equal to that of interest groups in Britain and France. The difference between the activities of groups in communist states and those in liberal democracies is attributable to the Communist party's dominance of the political scene.

## THE COMMUNIST PARTY OF THE SOVIET UNION

One of V. I. Lenin's most important contributions to communist ideology was his emphasis on the party as the key to revolution and political power. Expanding on Marx's call for a "dictatorship of the proletariat," Lenin argued that what was needed was the dictatorship of the "vanguard" of the proletariat or, in other words, the party. The oppressed workers might not see the advantages of revolution and communism, or, if they did, might be unable to overthrow an entrenched capitalist society. Therefore, an enlightened elite was needed to carry on the revolutionary struggle on behalf of the proletariat. Since this "vanguard of the proletariat" was a revolutionary weapon, it was of necessity a tightly knit group of totally dedicated militants who could act clandestinely to subvert the existing capitalist political and social order. Lenin and his supporters sought to restrict membership in the party to a narrow elite made up of those who recognized the evils of capitalism, accepted the communist alternative, and were willing to devote their lives to the revolution.

Once in power, Lenin and his successors transformed the party from a revolutionary elite to an organizational weapon for the control of state and society. In Western democracies, the state is independent of the parties that seek access to its leadership. By contrast, the Communist party of the Soviet Union (CPSU) is in many ways a party with a state of its own. In most other political systems, the positions with the most political power are government posts: presidents, monarchs, prime ministers, or chancellors. In the Soviet Union and other communist states, the most powerful official is the general secretary of the CPSU, who may or may not hold formal governmental position; his political influence derives not from government office but from his dominance of the party. Official policy decisions are made by the party leadership, and are sometimes formally legitimized by official governmental bodies such as the Supreme Soviet. Frequently, however, party decisions are not ratified by governmental bodies. Nevertheless, they are accepted as legitimate and binding.

The organization of the CPSU is highly centralized and hierarchical. In keeping with the principles of democratic centralism, each level of the party elects its own leaders and sends delegates to the party congress of the next highest level. This level does the same in turn, until eventually the All-Union Party Congress elects the Central Committee of the Communist party. (See Fig-

Figure 5.1

*Organization of the Communist Party of the Soviet Union*

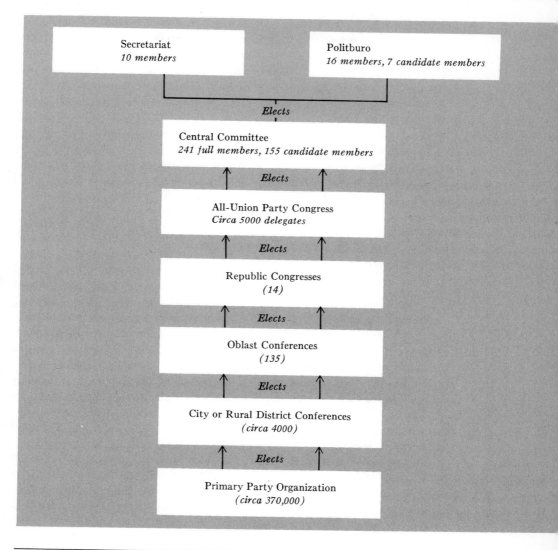

ure 5.1.) The Central Committee elects the Politburo, which is the key policy-making body for the party and the state, and the party's Secretariat, which is responsible for the operations of the party. These elections are by no means open: there is one slate of candidates at each level, prepared informally by the leadership and then favorably voted upon by the general membership.

The two bodies at the apex of the party structure, the Politburo and the Secretariat, dominate the party and the state. The Secretariat is headed by the general secretary, who is the party's official leader and the nation's most powerful political figure. This post, which confers control of the party apparatus, served as the base for Stalin's and Khrushchev's drives to power and for Brezhnev's consolidation of power after Khrushchev's ouster in 1964. Since Stalin's acquisition of this post in 1924, the general secretary has been the key political figure in the Soviet Union.

The party Secretariat controls more than 14 million party members and a vast party apparatus. No longer is the CPSU restricted to a revolutionary elite, as Lenin considered necessary. The party has grown steadily and approximately one out of every ten adults is now a party member.[19] Its transformation from an elite movement to a mass party has caused some dilution of the party's effectiveness. The party has attracted opportunists seeking prestige, social mobility, and other perquisites of party membership. Some are not willing to make the expected total commitment to party affairs. As a consequence, the party has instituted renewal of party membership in order to eliminate the opportunists and other backsliders. These "gentle purges" lack the terror of Stalin's purges, but they do stigmatize those dropped from the party.

The party also has at its service nearly a quarter-million full-time professional party workers (apparatchiki).[20] It is this army of paid professionals, reinforced by hundreds of thousands of volunteer workers, that makes the party a powerful political force. Though its size is sometimes unwieldy and it sometimes falls victim to the bureaucratic lethargy characteristic of any large organization, the CPSU still provides the party elite with an important means of exercising social control.

The primary task of the CPSU is to assure the implementation of policy directives established by the party elite. The CPSU rules state this goal explicitly: "It is the duty of a party member . . . to put party decisions firmly and steadfastly into effect. . . ." In so doing, the CPSU exercises extensive control over Soviet society.

The party's means of exercising social control are varied. Its most important single tool is its monopoly on legitimate authority. The CPSU proclaims itself "the party of the Soviet people as a whole." It has succeeded in instilling the feeling in the Soviet people that the party alone knows the needs and interests of the nation. It is a consequence of the public's acceptance of the party's claim to a monopoly on legitimate authority that there is little questioning of its right to control society. To oppose the party's decisions or top leaders is to oppose the people, and thus to commit treason. The party projects the image of infallibility, although it admits that members and some leaders occasionally have

---

19. When adjustments are made for the lower frequency of membership among women, approximately one out of five adult males is a party member. See Robert G. Wesson, *The Soviet Russian State* (New York: Wiley, 1972), p. 156.

20. In contrast, all three major parties in Britain had a total of only 782 full-time employees in 1973. See Richard Rose, *Politics in England,* 2d ed. (Boston: Little, Brown, 1974), p. 292.

shortcomings. The party's monopoly on legitimate authority is used skillfully by party leaders to squelch opposition to their policies both inside and outside the party.

A second means of social control is the CPSU's use of its powers of persuasion. Much of the party's efforts are devoted to mass propaganda and agitation. Each party member is charged with explaining the party's decisions to the masses and strengthening its bonds with the people. Members present lectures, lead public discussions, show propaganda films, distribute literature, engage in face-to-face discussions, and otherwise promote "the building of communism." The propaganda includes explanations of history, theory, policy and present actions; exhortations to greater personal efforts; and encouragements to meet economic production goals. No Soviet citizen escapes the party's diligent efforts to bring its message to the people.

A third means of social control is the CPSU's power to select key personnel in all sectors of Soviet life: government officials, bureaucrats, plant managers, labor union officials, factory foremen, collective farm work-gang leaders, and others. These leaders make up the nation's *cadres,* or personnel responsible for directing the activities of their organizations. Control of the cadres is essential to the party's maintenance of social and political dominance. Each party unit has a list of positions, called the *nomenklatura,* for which it is responsible. It fills these positions by direct appointment or by nominating a single candidate if the post is filled by election. These leaders (who may or may not be party members) can generally be counted on to heed the party's guidance faithfully in the conduct of their jobs. The CPSU thus seeks to dominate all of society by controlling the selection of virtually all influential leaders inside and outside government.

This control is reinforced by the interlocking of party leadership with leadership structures in other sectors of society. Party leaders are likely also to be leaders in government, industry, or voluntary associations. For example, the Council of Ministers is made up almost exclusively of members of the CPSU's Central Committee. In the military nearly all senior officers are party members, and many hold party leadership positions. Similar overlapping of leadership is evident in all other sectors of society.

Finally, the party exercises control through specific agencies designed to monitor social, economic, and political activities. Among the more important are the Party Control Committee, the People's Control Committees, and the secret police. The Party Control Committee, directly responsible to the Central Committee, monitors the faithful execution of party decisions by CPSU members and government officials. It has disciplinary powers — including the power to recommend censure and expulsion — over party members and state officials. People's Control Committees exist at all levels of the governmental and party hierarchy. There are about 1 million of these committees, manned by volunteers (usually party members) who watch for mismanagement, laziness, unnecessary waste, and administrative inefficiency or unresponsiveness.

The KGB (Committee for State Security, or secret police) no longer exer-

FIGURE 5.2

## Interlocking Party and State Structures in the Soviet Union

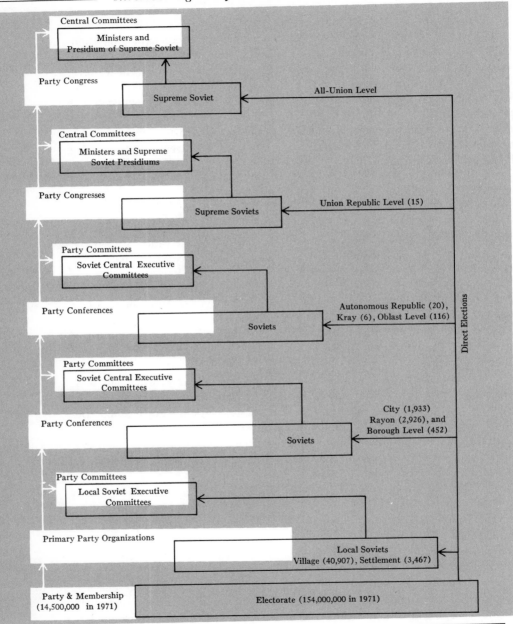

*Source:* Modern Political Systems: Europe, *3d edition, edited by Roy C. Macridis and Robert E. Ward,* © *1972, p. 605. By permission of Prentice-Hall, Inc.*

cises the broad powers it did under Stalin, when it used indiscriminant terror as a means of promoting general acceptance of the regime. However, the KGB still retains responsibility for investigating such political crimes as the dissemination of "anti-Soviet" propaganda, unlawful dissent, espionage, smuggling, and other crimes against the state. Since these crimes are defined ambiguously, the secret police has considerable leeway in pursuing its investigations. Strengthened by an army of informers in all sectors of Soviet life, the KGB exercises important political control on behalf of the CPSU.

We have not exhausted the list of control mechanisms available to the party. The CPSU dominates society through a series of parallel hierarchical structures that monitor each other, the bureaucracy, social groups, and the individual citizen. Ultimately, all these control structures owe allegiance to the party and serve as its agents.

Despite the extensive controls in the hands of the party leadership, the CPSU is not the monolithic tool of an omnipotent dictator. Maintaining control of the party alone is a difficult task for Soviet leaders. Stalin did so by infiltrating the party with secret police spies, ruthlessly eliminating all possible rivals, and terrorizing even the innocent in order to create absolute dependence upon himself. His successors, Khrushchev and Brezhnev, have virtually eliminated terror from the party's repertoire. In the absence of overt means of repression, groupings of leaders representing different viewpoints and linked to specific interests can be discerned in the party. These differences within the party are very discreetly expressed and are not organized, since factions are prohibited by party rules. Such differences — whether over theory, policy, or competing sets of leaders — can cause shifts in policy and personnel not always controllable by the general secretary.

The most dramatic illustration of this phenomenon is the sudden removal of Nikita Khrushchev from the pinnacle of Soviet power in October 1964. Opponents of Khrushchev, who appear to have had a variety of reasons for deposing him, called a meeting of the Central Committee, denounced Khrushchev's leadership, and voted to oust him from his posts as CPSU general secretary and as chairman of the Council of Ministers. The speed and apparent ease with which they removed the national leader, supposedly a well-entrenched dictator, attest to the vulnerability of even the presumably all-powerful party leader to determined rivals.

Another factor that limits the party's real control over society is its size. The CPSUs large membership makes it an increasingly cumbersome body to maneuver and control. A good deal of its members' energy is absorbed in simply making the party work. Its interest in maintaining the status quo and its own privileged position makes it an unlikely tool for major social change.

Another important restraint on the party's ability to control society is the personal ties that inevitably develop between party officials and those they are supposed to control. Officials are in regular contact with those they oversee and their success as party members depends largely upon the performance of those they regulate. Since a cooperative relationship is most likely to result in the highest performance, the party official may develop a sympathetic and co-operative relationship with those he or she supervises. This intimacy may reduce the official's and the party's ability to exercise meaningful control over the group.

In short, there are inevitable pluralistic tendencies at work to prevent the development of the monolithic party desired by party leaders. These pluralistic tendencies are products of the size and complexity of the party and the industrialization of the Soviet Union. While competition between different viewpoints in the party is muted and subject to important restraints, it exists. Differing interests and viewpoints are adjusted and accommodated through informal compromise at the level of the top leadership. Near-universal acceptance of the need for party unity screens much of this accommodation process from public view. In the last analysis, the highest value is placed on unity and the discipline of democratic centralism. Consequently, the Communist party of the Soviet Union remains an impressively united and cohesive agent of social control.

## THE CHINESE COMMUNIST PARTY

In China the center of political power is the Chinese Communist party (CCP). Both the Soviet and Chinese parties have revolutionary rather than parliamentary or electoral origins. This fact is particularly significant in the Chinese case, where the revolutionary experience still colors the political style. During its formation (1921–1928), China's Communist party was subject to the Comintern, a Stalin-led international Communist party movement. Early party congresses were dominated by communists who favored a united front with the Kuomintang and recruitment of an urban base. Mao, who held a minor place in these early years, urged a protracted war that would rely on a peasant base in the countryside. In the spring of 1927, after Comintern delegate M. Roy mistakenly tipped off a Kuomintang official about communist plans to gain a firm foothold within the existing Kuomintang structure, the Kuomintang destroyed the Communists' urban base. Mao filled the resulting vacuum through the organization of soviets (councils) and the development of a peasant movement based on his 1927 Autumn Harvest Insurrection.

Since the party's structure has changed considerably over the years, let us look more closely at post-1949 structures. (Figure 5.3 presents the party's current structure.) In theory, among the most important structures in the party hierarchy is the National Party Congress. It is chosen indirectly by local-level congresses of regional and primary units. There are hierarchical congresses, at the top level of which the provincial party congresses select delegates to the National Congress. Party rules of 1945 called for a national party congress every three years; 1956 and 1969 party rules call for sessions every five years. However, only ten congresses were held between 1921 and 1975. The Ninth Congress (1969) in Peking had more than 1512 delegates, and met for twenty-four days (a record for CCP congresses).

The National Party Congress elects (or ratifies) a Central Committee to meet when the whole body is not in session. While congresses have been in-

FIGURE 5.3
*Formal Structures of the Chinese Communist Party*

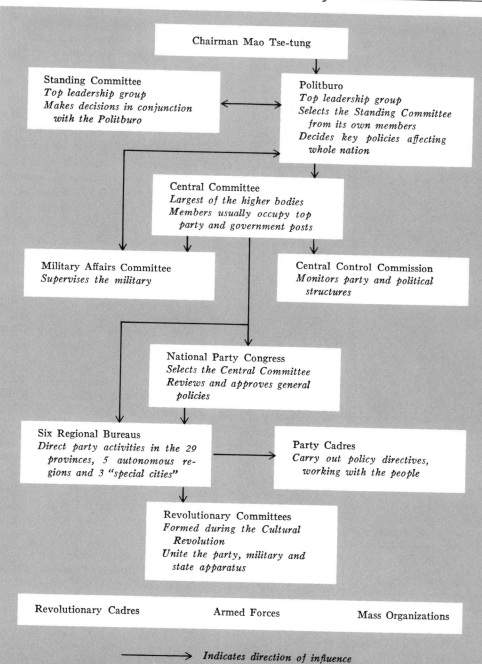

Chairman Mao Tse-tung

**Standing Committee**
*Top leadership group*
*Makes decisions in conjunction*
*with the Politburo*

**Politburo**
*Top leadership group*
*Selects the Standing Committee*
*from its own members*
*Decides key policies affecting*
*whole nation*

**Central Committee**
*Largest of the higher bodies*
*Members usually occupy top*
*party and government posts*

**Military Affairs Committee**
*Supervises the military*

**Central Control Commission**
*Monitors party and political*
*structures*

**National Party Congress**
*Selects the Central Committee*
*Reviews and approves general*
*policies*

**Six Regional Bureaus**
*Direct party activities in the 29*
*provinces, 5 autonomous re-*
*gions and 3 "special cities"*

**Party Cadres**
*Carry out policy directives,*
*working with the people*

**Revolutionary Committees**
*Formed during the Cultural*
*Revolution*
*Unite the party, military and*
*state apparatus*

Revolutionary Cadres        Armed Forces        Mass Organizations

———⟶  *Indicates direction of influence*

frequent, there have been numerous plenary sessions of the Central Committee: it held seven plenums in 1945–1956 and more than ten plenums in 1956–1969. The Central Committee includes most of the party's leaders and meets primarily to ratify or modify decisions made by the Political Bureau (Politburo) or the Politburo's Standing Committee. Both the Central Committee and the National People's Congress are deemed too unwieldly to conduct day-to-day decision-making.

The Central Committee "elects" the Politburo (consisting of twenty-one members and four alternates), which in turn "elects" its Standing Committee (nine members). It was the Politburo, and in particular the Standing Committee, that made most of the important policy decisions in pre-Cultural Revolution China. The Standing Committee of the Politburo was created by the 1956 party constitution to replace the Central Secretariat of the party's Central Committee. Some believe this change represented an institutional agreement for dividing political power between Chairman Mao's followers and a rival group headed by Liu Shao-ch'i. A member of Liu's group was named head of the Central Committee's Secretariat with responsibility for implementing policies established by the Standing Committee. The seven-man Standing Committee was controlled by Mao's group. Chairman Mao had previously been outvoted in the Politburo; the creation of the Standing Committee permitted him to control party policy decisions, if not their implementation. This conflict between Mao's and Liu's groups over control of the party was one of the factors ultimately producing the Cultural Revolution of 1966–1969.

Since the Cultural Revolution the distribution of power in the party hierarchy has been somewhat less clear. The basic change is the formal incorporation of the party-state merger at every level. Each city, commune, production brigade, and production team is governed by a revolutionary committee made up of party representatives, military officers, and representatives of the masses. However, separate party and state institutions still exist below the level of leadership.

There has also been considerable turnover in leadership positions. A new Central Committee of 170 full members and 109 alternates was elected in April 1969, and only 52 of the 170 full members of the previous Central Committee were retained. Forty-four percent of the members of the Central Committee elected in 1969 were military personnel. In 1969 the Politburo and Standing Committee were reconstituted with new members. Since then, however, continuing purges and inactivity due to advanced age eliminated a number of these top-level party officials. Seven full members and one alternate member of the Politburo were purged between 1969 and 1973. (Four military officers, all members of the Politburo, were reported to have died with Lin Piao during an "escape attempt" after their alleged involvement in a plot to assassinate Mao in 1971.) Of the five members of the Standing Committee reconstituted in 1969, only Mao Tse-tung, Chou En-lai, and Teng Hsiao-p'ing were still active four years later. The 270 regional and provincial party secretariats also underwent a thorough turnover of personnel coinciding with the formation of integrated revolutionary committees.

But these changes did not end the turmoil in the ranks of the party's leadership. By the end of August 1973, the Tenth Party Congress had met and selected a new ninety-five-member Central Committee, twenty-one-member Politburo, and nine-member Standing Committee. Five vice-chairmen were named, along with Chairman Mao, in place of the one vice-chairman, Lin Piao, chosen by the Ninth Party Congress. This suggests a decision to institute collective party leadership after the death of Chairman Mao. Among the five vice-chairmen are Chou En-lai; Wang Hung-wen, former Shanghai labor leader and youthful leader of Shanghai's revolutionary committee; Chang Ch'un-ch'iao, a former journalist and Wang's former superior on the Shanghai revolutionary committee; and Yao Wen-yuan, a protégé of Chou En-lai who also occupies a top position with the party's theoretical journal, *Red Flag*. In 1975, Teng Hsiao-p'ing was also named to the party's top leadership organs, the Politburo, and its Standing Committee. He is considered to be closely aligned with Chou En-lai. The composition of the Tenth Party Congress also reflects the party's resumption of ascendancy over the military. Military membership on the Central Committee dropped from 44 percent to less than 31 percent, and among the alternates from 46 percent to 26 percent. Where the military once had a majority on the Politburo, in 1974 they held only six of the twenty-one positions.

Among the other important organs subordinate to the Central Committee are the Military Affairs Committee, which oversees the military, and the Control Committee, whose tasks are investigatory and supervisory. In addition, *party fractions,* or ad hoc working groups, have cells in state and interest group organizations. Their often-delicate job is to monitor and rectify deviations from the party line. When the trade union deviated from the party line in 1952, the party fraction in the union held an enlarged meeting to rectify the deviation. The fraction often finds itself reflecting the parochial interests of those with whom it works. In September 1957 the union party fraction held a lengthy meeting in which its members expressed sharp conflict over the degree of union independence from the party. As in the Soviet Union, the party has organs that coincide and overlap with state institutions. Thus there are six regional party bureaus responsible for political activities in the provinces, autonomous regions, and special cities.

The large number of top-level party institutions, and their shifting tasks, have provided the leadership of the CCP with a flexible, rather than rigid, hierarchical structure for party decision-making. Given the need to maintain a favorably disposed coalition, the leadership may utilize any of these bodies when it seeks a desired policy outcome. Thus Mao's 1958 decisions on the Great Leap Forward were ratified by the Central Committee and bypassed the Politburo. Some Politburo sessions and Central Committee meetings have been expanded to include nonmembers when the leadership deemed this strategically necessary to its policy objectives. Despite intraparty conflict, the policies and political skills of Party Chairman Mao Tse-tung dominated China during the formative years of the revolution — though Mao has not been without opposition, as we shall note.

Unlike the Communist party in the Soviet Union, which is beyond reproach, the Chinese party was publicly attacked by Mao and his supporters during the Cultural Revolution. As a consequence, the CCP emerged considerably altered. The Cultural Revolution was more than an attack on the ideological deviation of some party officials: it clearly reflected severe conflict between Chairman Mao's faction and Liu Shao-ch'i's. The post-1969 purges represented the consolidation and adjustment of the new power configuration. Chairman Mao had clearly prevailed — or had he? The answer is not clear. That Premier Chou En-lai successfully weathered the storm and gradually developed his own policies suggests the possibility of only nominal success for Chairman Mao, and a yet undetermined group within the party holding actual interim control.

## PARTY FUNCTIONS IN CHINA

This intense, if periodic, conflict over control of the party suggests something about the role of the party in China. Its main task is controlling society, which it seeks to do by administering the government, directing the modernization and socialization of the society, and managing social conflicts. The CCP also provides information to the public to encourage support of the party's decision-making role.

In a system in which the state makes most decisions about resource allocation and most firms and agriculture-producing organizations are state-run, the party's responsibility for managing society is indeed massive. Though they are not accountable in elections, leaders are sensitive to the success or failure of their major efforts. Thus, as in the case of Chairman Mao's 1959–1961 temporary eclipse, accountability often takes the form of intraparty competition, a phenomenon also characteristic of noncommunist single-party systems.

In addition to formulating and implementing economic plans, the party is responsible for recruiting public officeholders. This task is performed through its executive committees at the national level and through mass elections at the primary levels. With the revolutionary committees simplifying the managerial structure by including party, state, and military representatives, the selection at the local level is often decided by mass participation. No less important is the party's task of mobilizing the people, creating active citizens, and merging societal roles with citizen roles. Given the near-total organization of the society and its economic structures, there is little room for passive individuals; almost all are involved in the state's activities. Thus, mobilization is a key party function. The party, then, is the bridge between the state and the society.

The party is at once ideological, personalist, and pragmatic. It is ideological in that it advocates a coherent set of ideas and ideals: the development of the nation along socialist lines. It is personalist in that during crises and conflict of leadership, appeals are often made to support the prestige of an individual such as Chairman Mao. It is pragmatic in that when such socialist objectives as equality of salaries or socialization of agriculture conflict with basic needs, such as adequate supplies of food or the need for managerial talent, theoretical ideals are temporarily laid aside.

Yet, on the whole it is most consistently ideological and, with institutionalization, less personalist. No social institution can throw flexibility or pragmatism to the winds in pursuit of principle and long survive. Ideology and pragmatism conflict minimally in China; in fact, they coincide and will probably continue to do so. The process of achieving socialism often requires adaptation. Thus, in 1972 and 1973, major accommodations were made with the United States in order to achieve greater security vis-à-vis the Soviet Union and to acquire the technological inputs necessary for more rapid modernization. Such adjustments bespeak pragmatism in the face of an ideological orientation, since the United States is clearly China's major capitalist adversary.

Both the CCP and the CPSU emphasize maintenance of the party's monopoly on political and social control. The Soviet party leaders have always held the party to be immune from all attack in order to preserve its unity and its aura of infallibility as the ultimate expression of popular will. In contrast, the Chinese leaders have at times themselves attacked the party in efforts to prevent its bureaucratization and loss of revolutionary fervor. The Cultural Revolution's frontal attack on the party left the CCP in shambles. While the Soviets have emphasized effective social control, the Chinese have stressed the need to carry out "permanent revolution" and have therefore on occasion sacrificed effectiveness for militancy.

In part, this difference may be a function of differing stages of party development. The Soviet party is now thoroughly institutionalized, with a stable pattern of decision-making and policy implementation. The smoothness of the transition from Khrushchev to Brezhnev suggests that some progress has been made toward the regularization of succession. The CCP, however, lacks a working party structure for decision-making. Many key decisions are made by ad hoc bodies outside the normal party organization. Perhaps the Chinese party is now at the stage of development the Soviet party passed through during the 1920s and 1930s. It may take several more years, and possibly decades, for the CCP to acquire the degree of institutionalization that characterizes the CPSU.

# Mexico and Nigeria:
## Interest Groups and Parties
## in Developing Nations

The status of interest groups and political parties in Mexico and Nigeria clearly reflects the two nations' respective stages of development. Mexico, whose industrialization dates back to the late nineteenth century, has developed occupationally based groups representing labor, peasants, businessmen, professionals, students, and even, to a limited extent, consumers. Nigeria, with a much shorter history of political and socioeconomic development, has a contemporary history of groups with strong ethnic and regional bases. Yet despite the predominance of ethnic interest groups new organized interests of limited size are developing: business-, labor-, and socialist-based political groupings. In this section we shall examine the emergence of these types of interest groups and parties, and the current and historic relationships between them. Using existing trends, we will speculate on future patterns.

## MEXICO: INTEREST "SECTORS" AND THE DOMINANT PARTY

Mexico's interest groups vary in type and degree of autonomy. Interacting with the government and the dominant PRI are peasant, labor, professional, entrepreneurial, and student groups. Their major activities include organizing individuals with common interests (e.g., workers seeking improved salaries and working conditions) to initiate or modify government policy and serving as channels for communication from government to the society.

Because of its immense political power, Mexico's interest groups have had a close interdependent relationship with the PRI. Indeed, three major associations are formal "sectors" of the PRI, representing portions of the "revolutionary family": workers, peasants, and "popular" or middle-class interests. Each sector has its own organizational voice, but all are strictly limited in autonomy.

*Peasants* The peasant sector is organized as the CNC (National Peasant Confederation). Based in myriad rural labor leagues, the CNC draws most of its support from the *ejiditarios,* small farmers living on land (*ejidos*) they received as a result of government-sponsored land reform, for whom membership in the CNC is mandatory. Because they received their land from the government, the ejiditarios tend to be loyal to the regime. However, they are also highly dependent upon the government. Their plots are small and often only marginally arable, and they depend upon the government-run Ejido Bank for credit to purchase seed and fertilizer and to maintain their farms and families. Political disloyalty to the PRI may result in the withdrawal of credit, and therefore the destruction of one's livelihood. The dependence of the peasants naturally limits the autonomy of their interest group vis-à-vis the party leadership and the government. In practice the leadership of the CNC is designated by the party, and the peasants can be counted on to give loyal support to the PRI and its leaders.

*Labor* The labor movement also has limited autonomy with respect to the PRI and the government. It is divided into two major blocs: The United Workers' Bloc (BUO), which is closely tied to the regime, and an anti-BUO coalition composed of unions favorable to the regime but hostile to the BUO.

The BUO, by far the larger of the two blocs, is dominated by the Confederation of Mexican Workers (CTM), which represents almost two-thirds of all union members in Mexico. The CTM alone has a membership of approximately 2,120,000.

Also within the BUO coalition is the Regional Confederation of Mexican Workers (CROM), the oldest and once the strongest element in the post-revolutionary labor movement. Today the CROM has but 120,000 members. The CROM was founded in 1918 by Luis Morones, who set a precedent of collaboration with the government by accepting government payments to finance CROM's first convention. However, the union did not completely submit to governmental control. Peasants at that time considered a working arrangement with CROM, but in 1920 opted for the formation of a national agrarian party. Both labor and peasants had sizable power bases due to their origins in the revolutionary years, during which time they acquired both arms and control of territory. Both groups rapidly became aware of their potential to influence Mexican politics.

In 1919 Grupo Acción, an activist group within CROM, formed the Partido Laborista Mexicano to support the presidential candidacy of Alvaro Obregón after Obregón had agreed to labor's terms in exchange for its support. In exchange for support, labor would receive important political jobs. The peasant group, the National Agrarian party, also exchanged its support for Obregón's promises. Obregón, however, also set a precedent — one that subsequent presidents have noted. By gaining the support of both groups, he was able to prevent either from controlling him.

Within the official labor sector coalition but opposed to the BUO is a bloc of leftist unions, the strongest of which is the Revolutionary Confederation of Workers and Peasants (CROC), with some 120,000 members. CROC, formed in 1952 when several leftist organizations combined, is many times larger than the four unions allied with it in the anti-CTM-BUO bloc. Conflict within and between the blocs weakens the labor movement and facilitates its control by skillful political leaders.

President Ruiz Cortines' 1952–1958 manipulation of labor to reduce its influence within the PRI offers convincing evidence of its limited autonomy. Cortines purposely encouraged direct competition between the weaker CROC (the anti-BUO labor group) and the usually favored CTM. Uncustomary public attacks on the CTM were allowed to foster the "divide and rule" objective. Other examples of labor's limited autonomy are the government's several crackdowns on the use of the strike. One such is López Mateos' tough stand on strikes called against Mexico's railway system by Demetrio Vallejo, a railroad union boss. The courts found Vallejo's strike illegal, union headquarters were raided, and he was arrested along with several hundred of his followers.[21]

*The Popular Sector* This sector, represented by the National Federation of Popular Organizations (CNOP), is the most heterogeneous of the three official

21. Robert E. Scott, *Mexican Government in Transition*. rev. ed. (Urbana: University of Illinois Press, 1965), pp. 167–168.

sectors. It is primarily middle-class in composition, representing such groups as civil servants, members of cooperatives, small farm proprietors, small merchants, small industrialists, professionals, artisans, women's organizations, youth groups, and even moral movements. Such an organization performs an important function in a preindustrial society, integrating the growing private and state bureaucracies with the single party and the government's policy-making centers.

Unlike the ejiditarios, who must join the CNC, and most workers, who must belong to a PRI-affiliated labor union, the members of most of the groups associated with the CNOP joined voluntarily. This fact gives the popular sector greater autonomy than those groups with respect to the PRI and the government, and causes the CNOP to be more responsive to the interests of its clientele in order to retain their membership. These factors, coupled with the growing tendency of the party and the government to draw on the CNOP for its top leadership, makes the CNOP a very powerful branch of the Revolutionary coalition. Of the three sectors, the CNOP has the greatest access to top-level decisionmakers.[22]

*The Entrepreneurs*  Though not official members of the PRI family of interest group sectors, some business groups have made efforts to join the CNOP. Most business and employer groups, though outside the PRI, are assured of a political voice. They are defined in statutes as "an organ of consultation of the State for the satisfaction of the needs of national commerce and industry." The most powerful of these organizations are the National Confederation of Industrial Chambers and the National Confederation of National Chambers of Commerce. Membership is compulsory for businesses with more than a handful of employees. These groups are often able to influence legislation by commenting on and even modifying legislative proposals that affect their interests. These proposals are submitted to them by government officials and ministries, and their lawyers then evaluate the proposed laws and suggest changes consistent with their wishes. This group, which represents only 0.5 percent of the total population, can effectively utilize its support in the media and among the highest public office-holders, party members, and administrators — often including the president — to achieve its goals.

Because various official interest groups affiliated with the PRI have not always met the expectations of their clients, competing groups have emerged. These groups, which do not belong to the PRI alliance, attempt to pressure the government from without, and often play important parts in Mexican politics. An independent peasant confederation appeared in 1963 and gained support through efforts to eliminate corruption in rural politics and to alleviate the impoverished conditions of Mexico's peasants. Other independent interest groups include dissident workers, students, professionals, businessmen, and the press. During the 1960s businessmen unaffiliated with the popular sector of

22. Kenneth Johnson, *Mexican Democracy: A Critical View* (Boston: Allyn and Bacon, 1971), pp. 67ff.

PRI acted through PAN (a minor party) to protest governmental moves toward the nationalization of industry. Such business groups, the most prominent of which is the "Monterrey Group," continually press the government (and sometimes the right wing of the PRI) to promote conditions conducive to private enterprise. They generally oppose the expansion of governmental economic controls and nationalized enterprises.

## CONTROLLED PLURALISM IN MEXICO

The PRI frequently co-opts groups as they gain significant stature. This practice has both costs and benefits. The groups are assured a hearing and participation in the major political game: competition for resources within the officially sanctioned party. However, if their leaders become too interested in status and official favor, they may sell out their group's interests to a more powerful interest. Labor leaders, for example, have been known to set a price primarily beneficial to a small elite for the termination of a strike. At one point in the late 1930s it was reported that the Mexican Chamber of Commerce distributed to trusted businessmen a list of top labor union officials and the prices they charged to settle labor disputes.[23] Employers and labor leaders benefit, but the workers' movement is weakened. The ensuing resentment has prompted many defections, but rebel groups have a difficult time combatting adversaries that can retaliate with governmnetal pressures, the law, and other sanctions.

The government thus determines the amounts of independent political action it will tolerate. The 1962 peasant uprising over wages and living and working conditions came to an abrupt end when its leader, Rubén Jaramillo, and his family were found killed. When between 1964 and 1965 more than twenty thousand doctors and medical workers struck to protest public health conditions, they were coerced to return to work. Many lost their positions for participating in the protest.

The government's response was even more determined when students mounted a protest in October 1968. As students and other protesters rallied to manifest their grievances against the dominant party and the president of the republic, the embarrassed government responded by firing on them, killing more than three hundred students and injuring close to five hundred. In 1970 a pro-government group of "Hawks" were used to attack students en route to a meeting to which they had been invited by the newly elected president Echeverría Álvarez. (This meeting was supposedly intended to reduce the hostile feelings between students and the new president who, as Minister of Interior, had been responsible for instructing the police to fire on students during the 1968 strike.)

Clearly, the government has used negative sanctions to discourage forms of political behavior it does not favor. Force has been used whenever economic

23. Martin Needler, *Politics and Society in Mexico* (Albuquerque: University of New Mexico Press, 1971), p. 11.

or social protest has caused people to question the PRI's rule. While it is difficult for groups not formally recognized by the PRI to exist, they can and do act to influence government, industry, and landlords to increase their members' wages and to improve working conditions and benefits. But their life spans may be shorter and less fruitful than those of groups within the PRI framework.


## THE MEXICAN PARTY SYSTEM

The emergence of the PRI as the dominant party in postrevolutionary Mexican politics is a result of the amalgamation of the most powerful interest groups in the society. Through the PRI, these groups have access to those who make and implement policy. In turn, the PRI reaps many benefits: political support from all social categories and classes, control of potential competitors for political power, and legitimacy — in that it can claim to represent a broad cross-section of the population.

President Calles realized in 1928 that if the socioeconomic changes wrought by the Revolution were to be maintained, political changes had to be institutionalized. Calles had been made aware of the need for a means to perpetuate the ideals of the Revolution by the threat of military revolt in 1923 when he was named president. The threatened revolt was countered successfully by armed peasants and workers. Calles decided to move beyond personalist leadership cliques by forming a party that would institutionalize the de facto peasant, labor, and military base upon which the Revolution had been built. His concept of an institutionalized party composed of these groups did not foreclose the possibility that those opposed to the Revolution would form their own party. It did involve the consolidation of the "Revolutionary family" into a single ruling political coalition.

These peasant and labor groups provided the basis for Mexico's first "revolutionary" party. In 1934 Lázaro Cárdenas succeeded Calles as president and sought to free himself from what had become the personalist Calles party. Cárdenas thus formed a new revolutionary party, the Mexican Revolutionary party, which was free of the personal control of Calles. The new party, founded in 1938, united the four sectors that supported Cárdenas in his successful resistance to Calles: the peasants, labor, the military, and the popular sector (CNOP). The military sector of the party was merged with the popular sector in 1940. President Alemán in 1946 changed the party's name to Institutionalized Revolutionary Party (PRI), but its style and character had been well established during the regimes of Calles and Cárdenas.

The personality of the PRI is characterized by factional differences between the Left and the Right. The Left favors realization of the Revolution's promise, the Right opts for control and gradual social and economic change consistent with maintenance of the structural status quo. But the influence of competition and interaction among the party's three sectors and associated interest groups prevails over Left/Right polarities. Thus there is a tradition that the PRI nominates to the Chamber of Deputies a representative of the sector that is strongest in each legislative district.[24]

The PRI's structure is personalist and hierarchical. During the regime of each president of the republic, the PRI becomes his personal party. His closest potential rival is the CEN (Comité Ejecutivo Nacional), or party executive committee, and its president. Mexico's current president is Luis Echeverría Álvarez and the CEN is headed by Alfonso Martínez Domínguez. The CEN has seven members: a president who also is president of the party, a general secretary, secretaries for each of the three interest sectors (labor, popular, and peasants), and representatives of the Chamber of Deputies and the Senate. To a large extent, all are dependent for their offices on the president of the republic. The leaders of interest groups associated with the PRI — the CTM, CNOP, and CNC — usually occupy positions on the CEN. An illustration of the president's power even over the party's executive committee is the 1966 firing of the CEN president, Carlos A. Madrazo, who threatened presidential predominance by advocating greater grassroots participation in party nominations.

Formally, the most authoritative party organ is the party's National Assembly, which is supposed to select its candidate for president of the republic. In practice the National Assembly is subordinate to the CEN and the president of the republic. This body ratifies policy decisions made by the CEN and others at high levels; its membership is controlled and its meetings convened by the CEN. The PRI also has a National Council, which represents the party organizations of the twenty-nine states and the three constituent interest sectors. It is through the National Council that the CEN regulates state-level party activities. The CEN, with its power to control state and municipal party membership and policy directions, clearly dominates the party structure, though as we have said its powers are subject to the intervention of the president of the republic. Despite its control of financial resources and its own mass media and propaganda devices, the CEN exercises limited power vis-à-vis the president.

The Mexican political structure is characterized by an advanced version of patron-client relationships. Within the PRI there are numerous cliques. The individual member advances by joining and working for the clique most likely to achieve dominance. If his clique is successful, the aspirant may acquire sufficient financial resources and position to enable him to develop his own following. While this kind of patron-client structure is hierarchical and reciprocal, it is modified in that clients may also be members of occupational interest groups, e.g., the peasants or laborers. Members of cliques may seek collective rewards for the groups they represent rather than the personal rewards sought by participants in the traditional patron-client network.

The patron-client system permeates the process of nominating the party's candidate for the office of president of the republic. The incumbent president's freedom to recruit the cabinet, political resources, and ability to decide when

24. *Ibid.*, p. 12.

the nomination will take place clearly give him the key role in determining the new PRI presidential candidate. However, aspirants for office usually control a network of clients at the federal, state and local levels. These clients may actively seek support from the major and minor interest groups or tactfully work within PRI executive bodies to promote their patron. If the patron is a member of the cabinet, he may use his post to do favors for local elites and groups, or, as López Mateos did with the Ministry of Labor, to gain favors for important sectors of the party. But in spite of such pressures, the nomination of his successor is the president's decision.

## THE PRI AND OTHER GROUPS

The PRI completely dominates Mexican politics. Since its founding it has never lost a presidential, senatorial, or gubernatorial election. The growth of Mexico's middle class, which now constitutes approximately 30 percent of the population, has caused numerous opposition groups to emerge. We have discussed the dissident interest groups outside the PRI that parallel the official interest groups. Opposition is also provided for within the party system by "official parties" affiliated with the PRI network and other parties that are genuinely independent. Among the official parties are "official Left" and "official Right" parties, whose official status is a function of their working arrangements with the PRI. Their role is to attract votes on the extreme Left and Right that the PRI itself could not win and to mobilize these voters behind the PRI presidential candidate, whom they usually support.

Among the parties on the right side of the political spectrum are PARM (the Authentic Party of the Mexican Revolution) and PAN (the National Action party). PARM, the "official Right" party, supports PRI presidential candidates and manages to win a few seats in the Chamber of Deputies. PAN is the only effective opposition party on the Right. Founded in 1939 to preserve the political influence of the church and the private enterprise system, PAN has loose connections with the International Christian Democratic movement. Though PAN's presidential candidates have never won more than 14 percent of the vote, it is the largest opposition party in the Chamber of Deputies. Four of its twenty-five seats were won in the election but the others were granted according to a formula that automatically allocates minority parties a certain number of seats. At times when PAN's candidates have won governorships or other local offices, such as in the Yucatán in 1969, there is always the possibility that the election results will be invalidated and the PRI candidate declared the winner.

On the Left side of the opposition spectrum, the Popular Socialist party (PPS) is the "official Left" party that supports PRI presidential candidates. The small Mexican Communist party (PCM) dates back to Luis Morones' Socialist Workers party of 1919. During the past five decades numerous splinter groups have broken away from the PCM. The PCM attempted in the early 1960s to reconstitute these groups as the National Liberation Movement, but

TABLE 5.4
*PRI's Majority in*
*1964 and 1970 Presidential Elections (Percentages)*

|       | 1964 | 1970 |
|-------|------|------|
| PRI   | 88.8 | 84.3 |
| PAN   | 11.0 | 14.0 |
| Others| 0.2  | 1.7  |

*Source:* Facts on File, *July 1964, July 1970.*

its attempts were frustrated. The failure of this effort was due in part to the existence of an "official" co-opted Left party, the PPS, and to the failure of the National Liberation Movement's front group, the Popular Electoral Front, to amass even 1 percent of the vote (write-ins) during the 1964 election.

Despite the existence and relative freedom of opposition parties, the PRI clearly dominates the Mexican party system. The results of the 1964 and 1970 presidential elections, provided in Table 5.4, illustrate. The domination of Mexico's party system by the PRI is largely due to the PRI leadership's skill at co-opting potentially threatening opposition groups. Its dominance has been a major factor in promoting the institutionalization of political processes in Mexico.


## NIGERIA: COMMUNAL INTEREST GROUPINGS

Nigeria's once active political parties are dormant, and must await military consent to renew their activities and confront the tests of time and popular support. Interest groups still function, and continue to straddle the line between traditional (precolonial) and modern pursuits. Though neither interest groups nor parties function as they did prior to the 1966 military coups, the precoup histories and styles of the political parties contain clues to the roles they will probably play if and when the military returns the country to civilian constitutional rule.

Nigeria's earliest interest groups were ethnic-based, and British colonialism was the main impetus to the development and proliferation of such groups in both northern and southern Nigeria. Among the earliest ethnic-based interest groups was the Egba Society, formed in 1918 to represent the Egba sect of the Yorubas. In the 1930s Ibo emigrés formed unions to maintain their culture and customs in Lagos and other areas outside of Iboland. They collected funds, engaged in politics, and worked to preserve the Ibo language, tribal songs, history, and moral beliefs among emigrés. They provided contact with the home village and such social benefits as mutual aid, financial assistance in case of illness, funerals, and the return of the deceased to his or her ancestral lands. In the north the emirs formed their own organization, the Northern People's Congress, in response to the growing political involvement of the Ibo and Yoruba ethnic associations. Yoruba students in London formed what was to become the base of the Western Region's leading political party, the Action Group party. This London group was known as the Society of the Descendants of Oduduwa, the legendary father of the Yorubas. Most such ethnic associations were multifunctional, serving as a base for social, cultural, religious, political, and financial undertakings.

The political functions of these groups are highly germane to the development of cleavages that contributed to the destruction of the postindependence republic. Some of these ethnic unions served as tax collectors for the colonial government before independence. As pressure groups they prevailed on local authorities for hospitals, dispensaries, better roads, and other public services. They also had a profound political impact in their efforts to democratize village councils, sometimes acting as equivalents of formal governmental bodies in their regions.

Perhaps most important to Nigerian political development is the linkage between ethnic groups and political parties. Ethnic-based interest groups and parties impeded political development and national unity by engendering mutual mistrust, but, on the other hand, the affiliation of ethnic groups with political parties tended to transfer ethnic conflict into the nonviolent arena of political interaction. In some cases, the ethnic unions were the source of the key political factions in regional political parties and their dissident offspring. In other cases, the ethnic unions provided a core of electoral support for the political parties affiliated with them. Such was the case with the Ibo State Union and its affiliates in eastern Nigeria, which preceded the Ibo-dominated National Congress of Nigerian Citizens (NCNC).[25] These ethnic-based associations continue to be active politically, though their party affiliates no longer function.

Urbanization and economic development have caused functional interest groups based on common occupations, tasks, or professions to emerge in Nigeria. There are, for example, labor, medical, student, and farmer groups, though less than 10 percent of Nigeria's 56 million citizens are wage-earners, labor is among the most important of the functional interest groups. The labor movement has been divided throughout the years of independence, despite attempts at unified fronts. The most recent attempt at unity, the United Committee of Central Labor Organizations led by Michael Imoudou, was formed in 1970 to counter inflationary trends and pressure the government to rescind its 1969 decree prohibiting strikes. This coordinating group attempted to bridge the gap between the leftist Independent United Labor Congress and the United Labor Congress of Nigeria (ULC). The United Labor Congress of Nigeria was among the largest until 1971, when it split into two factions.

Tension within the labor movement increased when several of the union's top leaders were arrested and then released by the military regime in early 1973. The government has attempted to promote the unification and control of the

25. Audrey C. Smock, "The Political Role of Ibo Ethnic Unions," in *Nigeria: Modernization and the Politics of Communalism*, ed. Robert Melson and Howard Wolpe (East Lansing: Michigan State University Press, 1971), p. 322.

unions. In November 1973 the Trades Union Decree required unions to be nonpolitical and gave the government the power to regulate and dissolve unions. Although still illegal, strikes and lockouts do occur repeatedly. But, as with the workers in a northern cement factory who futilely sought a larger Christmas bonus in December 1972, such action is usually factory-based and often unsuccessful.

Students are perhaps the most vociferous participants in Nigerian politics. They protest, often successfully, against government interference, increased fees, and the British high officials who still run their universities. But Nigerian students appear less uniformly radical than their counterparts in many developing nations, including Mexico. Through the Nigerian Union of Teachers, teachers press for better working conditions, higher salaries, and job security. Though this group's membership has increased more than threefold since 1950,[26] many of the younger teachers and university graduates consider the union too staid. Dissidents have formed the Nigerian Association of C/S (uncertified) Teachers and the Graduate Teachers Association, both of which have sought to negotiate directly with the government and have used strikes successfully in bargaining with the government.

With a few notable exceptions, such as the Northern Mineworkers' affiliation with the Northern People's Congress (NPC) and the Nigerian Trade Union Congress's affiliation with the NCNC, most of the functional interest groups did not associate themselves with political parties, as the ethnic groups did. When the functional groups tried to form political parties that would cut across ethnic lines, they were unsuccessful. However, the relationship between ethnic interest groups and the ethnic-based political parties was significant: it perpetuated communalism, frustrated national integration, and prolonged political instability. In fact, the nature of political parties in Nigeria — in combination with competitive politics and scarce resources — contributed to retarding institutionalization of a representative form of government.

## NIGERIAN POLITICAL PARTIES: THE SUSPENSION OF INSTITUTIONALIZATION

Unlike many other developing nations that fought colonial powers for independence after World War Two, Nigeria did not develop a single nationalistic and revolutionary independence movement. Nigeria's party divisions reflected its ethnic and regional divisions. Ethnic patterns in Nigerian party politics developed early. The Nigerian National Democratic Party attracted Muslims from Lagos, while the Nigerian Youth Movement recruited from the Yoruba and non-Yoruba (particularly Ibo) working classes. In 1944 the impatient and nationalistic young members of the Nigerian Union of Students were able to convince Herbert Macaulay and Nnamdi Azikiwe to form a united front, the

26. David B. Abernethy, "Education and Integration," in Melson and Wolpe, *Nigeria,* p. 421.

National Council of Nigeria and the Cameroons (NCNC). Of the nationalist groups, only the NYM refused to join.

The NCNC, which at first had been a national party, became "ibonized" (linked to the Ibo tribe) by 1963. In its early years the NCNC opposed ethnic and regional divisions and fought for more self-determination, and ultimately total independence, for Nigeria. But it was not lost on distrustful western Yorubas, long inculcated with cultural ethnocentricism, that the leader of the NCNC was an eastern Ibo. They feared Ibo control of the Western Region via the NCNC. Not long thereafter, also in the mid-1940s, the Society for the Descendants of Oduduwa was formed to protect Yoruba political rights. By 1948 this group had formed a satellite that was to become the main party of the Yorubas, the Action Group (AG). Its original goal was to gain control of the Western Region's government. Later, as was the case with other regional and ethnic-based parties, the Action Group became involved in national politics with the objective of defending its ethnic group's political and economic rights. In 1947 in the north, the emirs formed the Northern People's Congress (NPC), whose declaration of intention stated as its objective the combatting of ignorance, idleness, and oppression.[27] It was primarily composed of civil servants and employees of native administrations.

The political parties claimed to have coherent ideologies, but theory was seldom stressed. The NCNC spoke of "pragmatic African socialism," and the AG of "democratic socialism," but the most socialist in content and intent was the small Socialist Workers and Farmers Party (SWAFP). This party appealed in particular to labor union members and landless peasants, but was relatively insignificant and attracted only a small membership.

The backgrounds of the larger parties' elites reflect their middle-class origins and the clear-cut educational and occupational social divisions between regions. Sklar's 1958 study of NCNC leadership revealed that 27 percent of the top leaders were members of the learned professions (principally law and medicine), 28 percent were engaged in entrepreneurship or finance, while close to 20 percent were educators. Among the NPC, a majority were from the traditional Fulani ruling class in the emirate class.[28]

The cultural backgrounds of the three main parties' leaders suggest more about the dimensions of ethnic conflict. The most cosmopolitan of the former political parties was the NCNC. While some 49 percent of its leadership was Ibo, 10 percent came from other eastern groups and 27 percent were Yoruba. Ninety percent of the NCNC's leaders were Christians. The majority of AG leadership (68 percent) was Yoruba and Christian. The NPC leadership was 34 percent Fulani, 19 percent Habe, 9 percent Nupe, 7 percent Kanuri, and 7 percent Yoruba. All but the Yoruba are northern and muslim.

27. Richard L. Sklar and C. S. Whitaker, Jr., "The Federal Republic of Nigeria," in *National Unity and Regionalism in Eight African States,* ed. Gwendolyn M. Carter (Ithaca, N.Y.: Cornell University Press, 1966), p. 41.
28. Sklar and Whitaker, "The Federal Republic of Nigeria," p. 66.

These three regional and ethnic-based parties — the NCNC, NPC, and AG — became the key actors in Nigeria's electoral and parliamentary system after independence. Given this structure, political conflict was inherently ethnic. Thus Nigeria's political competition was not waged by functional or occupational groups (such as we noted in Mexico), but by ethnic and regional groupings. The parties' primary concerns were succeeding at the ballot box, maintaining political control within their regions, and representing their group's interests in the distribution of national funds and political positions. The competing forces reached a minimal balance in coalitions and pragmatic working relationships in the federal parliament; the winning coalition was comprised of the NPC and NCNC, whose eagerness to control political outcomes prompted them to intervene in western Nigeria's regional politics. This act brought on the first election crisis of 1962, which removed the AG from power in western Nigeria and aroused a good deal of resentment among Yorubas. The second crisis occurred in 1965, after the political parties had adapted in response to their earlier electoral experiences by consolidating political groupings. In the north, the NPC joined with several smaller parties in the Nigerian National Alliance (NNA). This group also gained the support of some small minority-based parties in the Eastern Region. In response, the NCNC, AG, SWAFP, and Northern Progressive Front (a dissident group in the north) formed the United Progressive Grand Alliance (UPGA). A two-party confrontation appeared to be developing, but the SWAFP bowed out soon after the alliance when the UPGA would not allow minor parties to share candidacies in southern urban areas. The 1965 elections were tense, and further accentuated ethnic divisions. The results gave the NNA a majority of 198 seats out of 312. Additional elections were held shortly thereafter in districts where the frustrated electorate had boycotted the formal election, and the result gave an additional 53 seats to the UPGA and none to the NNA. The prime minister, in an attempt to avoid a crisis of confidence and threatened eastern secession, appointed 7 new NCNC members (from the UPGA) to an enlarged cabinet that already had 22 NNA members. The frustration and mistrust engendered by these elections fueled communal violence and increased political haggling, and the growing turmoil prompted the military coups in 1966 that abolished the party system in Nigeria. Political parties were formally proscribed by the military dictatorship and have not re-emerged.

How did the party system give way to "no-party" military rule? Perhaps the outstanding causal factor in the party system's decay was the contradiction between its regional and ethnic basis and the overriding need to achieve nationhood and national integration. The federal constitutional structure, the parallel regional and ethnic-based political parties, the lack of established political norms defining the role of oppositions, and the lack of respect for the will of the electorate all contributed to the chaotic demise of the Nigerian party system. Certainly one can point to the cheating in the October 1965 western regional elections as the nadir in the history of the post-independence party system. But one could also persuasively argue that background factors, especially the weakness of cross-cutting functional interest groups and the tenacity of ethnic identity, were factors of equal importance.

It is clear from this discussion of parties in Mexico and Nigeria that parties originate in and reflect the historical conditions existing at the time of their formation. Neither party system originated as a set of revolutionary weapons, although Nigeria's early political movements did assume the task of nationalist agitation. Mexico's parties emerged after a period of early industrialization during the Díaz regime (1876–1911). Industrialization brought into being the basis of a labor movement. Peasants laid the groundwork for yet another political grouping in armed support of the anti-Díaz revolution. It remained only for the new caudillo to incorporate the groups into the existing authoritarian pattern to create a single-party system based on functional group coalitions. In Nigeria the gradual evolution of national independence and the absence of a feudal agricultural base or a proletarian working class made ethnic cleavages the only possible basis for party formation. The election system fostered the growth of these ethnic-based parties as political weapons in a multiparty system. At the local level the parties' primary task was winning electoral predominance; at the national level it was to win sufficient federal power to protect regional and ethnic interests. Finally, in considering the tragic demise of the Nigerian political party system, one must ask whether or not a developing nation can afford political party competition.

The parties did perform an integrative function, but they integrated regions and ethnic groups rather than the whole Nigerian nation. Parties such as the NCNC served as umbrellas for ethnic unions and minority groups in their regions, and were often able to adapt to minority interests and demands. When the ethnic minority groups developed political awareness, the dominant parties often recruited a few of their members for public or party office. The parties served as bridges between citizens and government paralleling the ethnic associations, which often acted independently in seeking benefits for their members. However, in the marketplace of vote-getting, the financial costs are often as steep as the costs associated with political order and national integration of political party competition. In Nigeria's former Western Region, for example, the government-run Western Region Marketing Board's earnings were invested in political campaigns rather than needed development projects. This and similar situations raise serious questions about the justifiability of such political costs. Financial and human resources might better be devoted to political and economic development than to divisive and explosive partisan elections. Furthermore, party competition in Nigeria reflected and aggravated ethnic and regional cleavages, and thus tended to divide the nation rather than weld it together at the crucial early developmental stage. Thus, Nigeria exemplifies the problems associated with multiparty competition in developing states, and raises questions about its desirability.

Parties in developing nation-states can assume any of the full range of tasks. Nigeria's parties, which concerned themselves primarily with winning elections and managing national and local government, illustrate one possible emphasis. Mexico's dominant party, the PRI, devotes itself to maintaining its winning coalition and managing the government. The maintenance of a dominant coalition is made difficult by the PRI's practice of co-opting and incorporating a highly diverse spectrum of political orientations, but it has so far been extremely successful. The PRI's leadership skills are clearly formidable. Success of this duration and stability cannot be attributed to mere adaptation to crosspressures. The PRI's style has performed an important integrative task, in part because the party offered opportunities for upward social mobility to individuals of strong personality and persuasive skill. It has also integrated various sectors of the economy — peasants, workers, businessmen, and professionals — and regions of the nation. Nigeria's parties also provided opportunities for upward social mobility, and to a certain degree integrated various economic groups, but they did this within regionally segmented, ethnic-based groups.

# Conclusions

Interest groups and political parties are frequently the most prominent actors in a political system. Where they operate effectively, they serve as bridges between the citizens and the state, conveying the needs and concerns of the public to government in a coherent and meaningful way. This task of representation is of paramount importance in Western democratic states such as Britain and France, where several parties compete for the public's allegiance and for political power. However, even in nondemocratic and authoritarian systems — such as Mexico, China, and the Soviet Union — interest groups and parties seek to determine and meet the needs of the public.

Interest groups and parties may also be the means by which government controls and manipulates the public. These phenomena are by no means restricted to the nondemocratic context. The Watergate scandal in the United States is an illustration of an attempt by a governing party in a democratic state to manipulate election campaigns to perpetuate its hold on power.

We have noted the diverse forms and tasks parties and interest groups can assume. One difference between the party systems of different nations has attracted much attention: the number of parties. Many in the West consider the most desirable pattern to be the competition of two or more parties, assuming it to indicate the existence of democratic politics. However, generalizations are risky when dealing with such a complex and vital aspect of politics. Indeed, the Nigerian case suggests that party competition during the early stages of development may be divisive and even explosive. And the French case indicates that party competition may lead to chaos and instability even in states with long histories of political development. The single dominant parties of Mexico, China, and the Soviet Union may not be furthering democracy — this is not their goal — but they have proved successful at integrating their nations, providing effective government, and changing their societies.

Of greater concern than the nature of interest groups or the number of parties is that these important political institutions simply be present and operative in a state. Interest groups provide alternative means of political representation that compensate for the low levels of direct citizen participation in all types of political systems, and serve as informal but essential partners of government in drafting and implementing policy. They are thus important in assuring effective and responsive government.

Even more important is the overall impact of political parties on the political system. The presence of powerful parties is vital to the development of stable political institutions. Where effective dominant parties have prevailed, the course of political development has been eased. The success of the PRI and the CPSU in providing Mexico and the Soviet Union with political institutions and procedures illustrates the role parties can play in the political development and promotion of political stability in developing countries. The failure of the Nigerian parties, and their part in exacerbating ethnic conflict, paved the way for military rule and civil war. In China the CCP had difficulty adapting from guerrilla activity to running a government. It is still in the process of evolving institutions and procedures that may one day provide China with a stable political framework.

Though the stability of party structures is a good indication of the overall stability of the political unit, it would be inaccurate to designate the party system as the only causal factor in the establishment and maintenance of political stability: the party system generally reflects social divisions, leadership skills, political norms and attitudes, and other sources of stability or instability. But the contribution of the party system to overall stability is highly important. Political decay frequently occurs where political parties falter or disappear, because the political system is no longer able to channel or meet the needs of a politically mobilized populace. The failure of parties is thus often a prelude to military rule, bureaucratic stagnation, or both.

*Maps*

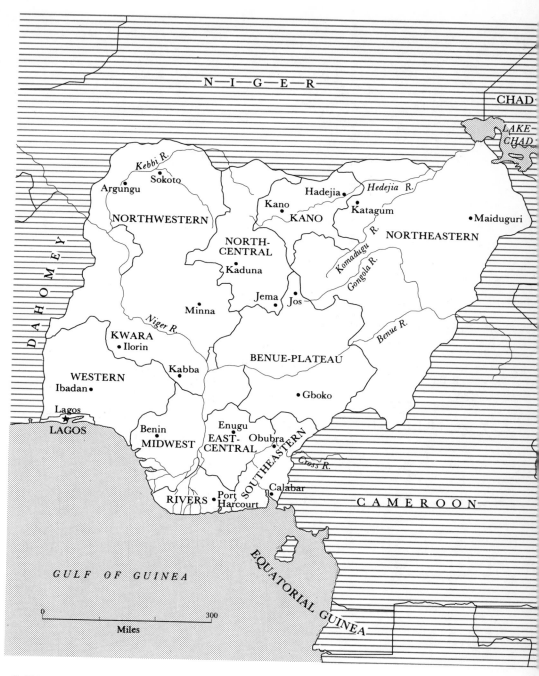

*Nigeria*

*The United Kingdom*

NORTH SEA

ENGLAND

ENGLISH CHANNEL

Calais

Lille
NORD

BELGIUM

GERMANY

LUX

Amiens

PICARDIE

Metz

Le Havre
Rouen
HAUTE
NORMANDIE

Nancy

LORRAINE

Strasbourg

Brest

BASSE
NORMANDIE

Paris

RÉGION
PARISIENNE

CHAMPAGNE

ALSACE

Rhine R.

BRÊTAGNE

Rennes

Seine R.

FRANCHE-
COMTÉ

PAYS DE
LA LOIRE

Loire R.

CENTRE

BOURGOGNE

SWITZER-
LAND

Nantes

Vichy

Lyon

POITOU-
CHARENTE

Limoges

LIMOUSIN

Clermont-
Ferrand

St. Étienne

RHÔNE-ALPES

Grenoble

ITALY

Rhône R.

AUVERGNE

0        100
Miles

BAY OF BISCAY

Bordeaux

AQUITAINE

MIDI-PYRENÉES

Toulouse

Garonne R.

LANGUEDOC

PROVENCE-
CÔTE D'AZUR   Nice

Marseilles
Toulon

SPAIN

MEDITERRANEAN
SEA

Bastia

CORSE
(CORSICA)

## France

*Union of Soviet Socialist Republics*

UNION OF SOVIET SOCIALIS

MONGO

AFGHANISTAN

Tarim R.

SINKIANG UIGHUR
AUTONOMOUS REGION

KANSU

N
H
Yin

Hsini

Lan

PAKISTAN KASHMIR

TSINGHAI

TIBETAN AUTONOMOUS REGION

NEPAL

•Lhasa

SZECHU
Chen
Chu

BHUTAN

INDIA

BANGLA-
DESH

•Ku

YUNNAN

BURMA

VII

LAOS

THAILAND

*People's Republic of China*

EPUBLICS

Amur R.

HEILUNGKIAN

Sungari R.

•Harbin

KIRIN

Changchun

A

ER MONGOLIAN AUTONOMOUS
REGION

LIAONING

Shenyang

SEA OF JAPAN

hehot•

HOPEI

•Peking

Tientsin•

North Korea

J A P A N

w R.

POHAI
SEA

Luta

hih-Chia-Chuang•

•Taiyuan

SOUTH KOREA

•Yenan
SHANSI

•Tsinan •Tsingtao

SHANTUNG

YELLOW SEA

SI

Chengchow

KIANGSU

HONAN

ANHWEI

Nanking•

HUPEH

Hofei

Yangtze

Wuhan

•Shanghai

R.

Hangchow•

EAST CHINA SEA

CHEKIANG

•Nanchang

•Wen Chou

Changsha•

KIANGSI

HUNAN

ng

Foochow

NGSI

FUKIEN

•Taipei

ANG A.R.

KWANGTUNG

Amoy•

FORMOSA STRAIT

g Hsi R.

•Canton

Swatow

TAIWAN
(REPUBLIC OF CHINA)

•Hong Kong (Br.)

Macao (Port.)

•Chankiang

SOUTH CHINA SEA

0                    500

HAINAN IS.

Miles

PHILIPPINES

265

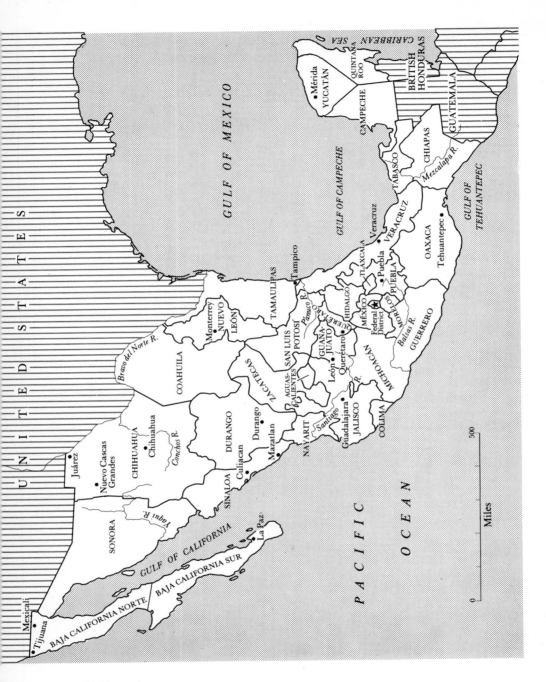

*Mexico*

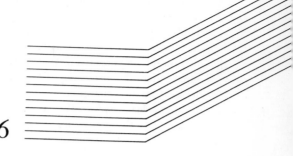

6

# *Political Leadership
and Bureaucracy*

## Introduction

On 15 January 1958 President Ho Chi Minh visited our province. He pointed
out that the province had suffered nine droughts in ten years and *insisted* on the
urgent need for improved water management. He suggested we cut a four-mile
canal. We mustered the population of three districts to carry out the digging, and
the President walked along the proposed line of the canal to indicate the path it
was to follow. It took two months. In the early stages, people's hearts were not
really in the project, and so the output was poor — less than half a cubic yard
per person per day. But after the canal was opened, the paddy fields on either
side yielded two harvests a year instead of one, and we nicknamed it "Uncle Ho's
Canal." There is a little song which runs:

> In Uncle Ho's Canal
> The water is bright and clear.
> The rice and maize grow strong
> The hungry days are gone.[1]

To arrive in an outlying province, identify a major problem, prescribe a solution, and then successfully mobilize mass action to implement the solution is the
mark of successful political leadership. The ability to recruit effective leaders
is of great importance to the overall operation and stability of any system. In

1. Gerard Chailand, *The Peasants of North Vietnam* (Baltimore: Penguin Books, 1970),
pp. 77–78.

many nations the top leader or leaders play such a vital part in the political process that their individual abilities and qualities virtually determine the political fate of millions. We shall define political leaders as individuals who occupy formal public offices and governmental positions, whether elected, appointed, or seized by force, and those who make authoritative decisions affecting large publics. This definition includes both formal occupants of positions of power and those who wield actual influence, whether or not they hold formal governmental positions. This chapter will examine political leadership by looking at the general environment in which leaders operate and at the nature of political leadership. We shall also look briefly at bureaucracies and civil servants — those government agents who administer the decisions of the leaders.

## THE POLITICAL CONTEXT OF LEADERSHIP

No matter how powerful, any leader is constrained by some limitations. Even Stalin and Hitler were restrained by the limitations of their nations' resources, by technological incapacity, and by the need to depend upon others to carry out their orders. Most leaders are also subject to existing political norms and patterns, which they must either accept or try to alter. One important influence on leadership, then, is the nation's political culture. The political culture not only provides the values and norms of citizen, interest group, and political party participation, but also defines norms for leaders and expectations about leadership styles. For example, a nation's political culture may promote deference toward authority, thus fostering the emergence of strong and aloof political leaders. The political culture also determines the types of political power that will be accepted as legitimate. Political leaders must operate within the context of legitimate power or authority. For example, a leader wishing to exercise dictatorial power over society might expect serious obstacles in a political culture whose norms are democracy and limited government. Certain kinds of political action and certain kinds of appeals for mass support may be rendered impossible by existing norms and attitudes toward political authority.

The German sociologist Max Weber delineated three types of legitimate authority upon which leadership may draw: charismatic, traditional, and rational-legal.[2] Charismatic authority is characterized by public acceptance of the sanctity, heroism, or exemplary behavior of an individual leader set apart from ordinary individuals and treated as endowed with exceptional powers or qualities. A crisis environment often gives rise to the emergence of this type of leadership: Hitler, Stalin, de Gaulle, Mao, Nasser, Sukarno, and many other leaders have legitimized their exercise of power by promoting belief in their superhumanity. Traditional authority is justified by established beliefs in the sanctity and legitimacy of tradition, historical institutions, and individuals who occupy traditional positions of authority. Examples are monarchies, aristoc-

---

2. Max Weber, *The Theory of Social and Economic Organization* (New York: Free Press, 1947), pp. 324–429.

racies, and tribal chieftaincies. Rational-legal authority is based on acceptance of the legality of established rules and of the right to govern of those who come to power in observance of these rules. Examples include many of the developed states, both democratic and nondemocratic, in which rules prescribing certain procedures for acquiring positions are observed.

At different stages of development the basis of political authority may vary. During the early stages of political development, the leader's rule may be based on the deference usually accorded either to traditional institutions with rich symbols of authority and respect (such as monarchies) or to charismatic leaders able to generate powerful symbols that obligate their followers to obedience. During the formative years of Indonesia's post-independence period, Sukarno relied heavily on charismatic appeal and the manipulation of political symbols, emphasizing ritual and promising a great and militarily powerful Indonesian nation in the coming years. This was a fruitful tactic, at least for a while, since it offered the prospect of an attractive future, contributed to the development of national unity in an ethnically diverse society, and satisfied the military with whom Sukarno had to share power. At later stages of political development, the leader might rely less on symbolic rewards basing his rule on rational and legal grounds and on a system of particularistic patronage and economic rewards. Sukarno's failure after more than twenty years of rule to make the transition from purely symbolic rewards to economic rewards (and national solvency) contributed to his overthrow in 1965.

In addition to the limits imposed by the political culture and by accepted sources of legitimacy, the leader is often compelled to act within an established political framework. The extent of centralization, the accepted scope of governmental action, the interaction between various sets of leaders (such as the president and congress, the prime minister and the cabinet, the political leadership and bureaucrats), the political party system, the importance of interest groups, and the political activities of the military are among the established patterns that may constrain a leader. Leadership and the characteristics of the system are very deeply interrelated. An achievement-oriented leader like Pierre Mendès-France, former premier of France (1954–1955), can do little in a political system in which power is allocated to a parliament deeply divided by numerous conflicting parties. Such a weak political position obviously minimizes a leader's authority and capacity to act effectively, regardless of personality. American presidents encounter similar frustration when Congress asserts its powers in a system that allocates administrative powers to the president and legislative powers to Congress. Even a highly authoritarian structure can be subject to the same dilemma. Such was the case, for instance, in China between 1959 and 1965, when Mao Tse-tung was kept from asserting his will by political institutions and leaders beyond his influence. The leader must either adapt to the established pattern or expend vast amounts of energy and political credit to change the framework to his specifications. To use China as an example again, it took the turmoil of the Cultural Revolution for Mao to reassert his political pre-eminence.

Finally, the course of political events affects leadership. During an emergency or threatful situation, leaders may be able to exercise more authoritarian rule and to allot less time for consultation and consensus formation. Thus, in the United States, presidential powers expanded dramatically during the Civil War, the two world wars, and the Vietnam War. Periods of relative peace may inhibit otherwise manipulative leaders from reaching their full potential powers. Foreign intervention, natural disasters, and economic depressions also affect the functioning and success of leaders.

## LEADERSHIP CHARACTERISTICS AND SKILLS

Effective leadership is perhaps equally dependent on the leader's personal traits and skills. Among the characteristics that influence leadership performance are socioeconomic background, personality, political ideology, skills and resources, and political style.

The socioeconomic background of a nation's leaders — their occupations, social class, ages, education, and wealth — is an important factor in understanding its leadership. For one thing, the leaders' socioeconomic traits may be important indicators of the nation's level of integration. When individuals from diverse backgrounds are drawn into politics, the political unit may be considered more successful in integrating its society than units that lack leaders recruited from the lower classes or from ethnic minority groups. Also, the socioeconomic characteristics of the leadership may reveal informal linkages between leaders in various parts of the political framework. For example, cooperation and improved mutual understanding among leaders of different parties or between labor leaders and business leaders may be facilitated by similar levels of education and socioeconomic status. Both these forms of integration may bear on the political stability and legitimacy of the system. The integration of elites creates an important possible base of support for the existing political framework.

Another important aspect of leadership is the leader's individual personality. Study of the psychology and personality of leaders has produced some interesting conjectures about the nature of leadership. Harold Lasswell observed that power-seekers are often trying to compensate for low self-images through the recognition and status that accompany political office.[3] Others have investigated traits that distinguish leaders in various occupations — industry, religious groups, labor, and the military. While little cross-national evidence has been found to suggest the existence of a uniform personality type in political elites, the same cannot be said of comparisons within regions and particular stages of development. Thus, among non-Western decisionmakers, the drive for power, achievement, and dominance appears to be less strong than the need for affiliation and status.[4] This configuration can lead to the proliferation of officials who seek office merely for the status associated with it. Once in office, such an

3. Harold D. Lasswell, *Power and Personality* (New York: Norton, 1939), pp. 75–76.
4. John Raser, "Personal Characteristics of Political Decision Makers: A Literature Review," *Peace Research Society Papers* V (1966): p. 39.

official may pursue an adaptive course, reacting only to demands articulated by the influential or necessary to prevent a severe crisis. The need for affiliation and the need to be liked are persistent features of traditional social life, and leadership patterns are thus closely linked to cultural patterns.

Leadership recruitment and leadership structures in typical Third World nations conform to the hierarchical patron-client pattern. The basis of this structure is a leader with a personal following composed of relatives and regional and local associates, each of whom in turn has followers. Such relationships persist as long as the leaders and subleaders can continue to provide rewards in the form of jobs, loans, letters of recommendation, advice, and prestige to their followers.

In industrialized societies, by contrast, leadership linkages tend to be based on horizontal groupings of followers. The political group's members have a common basis for belonging. They may all be members of a labor union, industrial grouping, or religion, or may have a common occupational background. In Europe many political parties originated in such horizontal membership groups. The Christian Democratic parties started as Catholic-based parties; the socialist and labor parties are worker-supported; and the liberal parties have business-bourgeois adherents.

Methods of selecting leaders vary, but personality is always a significant factor where free elections are held. There is much evidence that leaders' attitudes on positions are often less influential than are their personalities in affecting the voters' decision. Mass communications can bring the candidates into the livingrooms of all voters. A candidate's ability to project the image of a confident and amiable leader may be more important than his or her position on specific issues. But voter perceptions and personality interactions are not always left to chance and nature; they may be manipulated. Media experts argue that "print is for ideas," but it is on television that personality and image are exposed and communicated.

Closely related to personality is political style. Political style reflects the leader's ideology and disposition to be active or passive and to be directive or consultative. Those at the zenith of a political system always have more influence than those at lower echelons, but decision latitude — the scope within which leaders can make decisions — varies not only with the system's structure but also with the leader's conscious or unconscious assumptions about the duties of office.

Active and passive leadership styles may reflect personality characteristics. Thus, an individual who is strongly ideological (i.e., one whose outlook on the world reflects consistency, coherence, and comprehensiveness and who feels firmly committed to this view) may be highly motivated to participate in political decision-making. Contemporary ideologies, such as socialism and communism, are schools of thought that offer a vision of an ideal society, a set of norms on how individuals should relate to each other and to government, and a description of the roles government should play in society. Students of political ideology note that among elites in industrial nations there is a trend away from commitment to ideology.[5] Workers' incomes rise, new racial or ethnic groups immigrate and join the population, and class identification commensurately tends to weaken. Technicians replace politicians in bureaucracies and even in cabinets. These changes in socioeconomic conditions and political recruitment patterns tend to reduce the motivation to theorize about social relationships and to lead to a search for new social ideals.

Personality factors other than ideology and beliefs may affect leaders' political styles. Some leaders' dispositions, needs, or achievement-oriented socialization impel them to active roles. Their parents may have been involved in politics: the Kennedys and Indira Gandhi are examples of this tradition. Active leaders tend to have more education, higher incomes, more experience in decision-making groups, and to ask more questions and be more defensive than passive leaders.[6]

Leadership skill involves the successful utilization of available resources. One important resource of leadership is the ability to command respect. The successful leader is able both to elicit the respect of the people and to use this respect as a means of gaining support and of extracting services and sacrifices from lieutenants and followers. In democratic countries, where continued tenure in positions of political leadership requires electoral victory, leaders must expend a great deal of time and energy maintaining the respect of the voters. In most liberal democracies, including Great Britain, France, and the United States, the campaign begins almost as soon as the ballots for the previous election have been counted. Between elections, the leader must seek to maintain a position of respect among the population. The leader who fails to do so may find it difficult to command the respect and cooperation of other leaders.

In communist countries elections have little bearing on the degree of respect the leadership enjoys. In most such political systems, popular respect for leaders results from Communist party efforts to legitimize their authority. Leaders may also enjoy popular respect for making beneficial social changes or delivering the nation from a shameful past (e.g., Castro, Ho Chi Minh, and Mao Tse-tung). More important than popular respect, however, is the respect of party leaders, whose willingness to support the projects of the top leadership is essential to its success. Gaining their respect requires different skills than does the electoral process, notably organizational skill, ideological brilliance, and the ability to forge alliances with key individuals and powerful groups such as the military, bureaucracy, or secret police.

Another important resource for a leader is an innovative mind. The leader who can generate new ideas and approaches to the nation's problems — alone or through advisers — is valuable. However, such ideas must be implemented. Some leaders have ideas but little capacity to perform. The problem of effectiveness is particularly acute in developing countries where leaders often lack

5. Robert D. Putnam, "Studying Elite Political Culture: The Case of Ideology," *American Political Science Review* LXV (September 1971): 651–681.
6. See James D. Barber, *Power in Committees: An Experiment in the Governmental Process* (Chicago: Rand McNally, 1966).

training and skills necessary to success. And yet it is these leaders who face the massive triple challenge of national integration, political development, and economic progress.

Another important skill is the adept use of material and utilitarian rewards to gain the cooperation of others. These rewards include money, goods, services, jobs, administrative capabilities, and technology. Some leaders enhance their effectiveness through coercion: the threat or actual use of force to change or constrain behavior. Others are skilled in the use of symbolic resources to manipulate public opinion. Political symbols are phenomena that trigger emotions of patriotism and devotion, such as the national flag, the national anthem, past heroes, historical events, the military, and national projects. Skillful use of these symbols by leaders can mobilize public opinion and action to serve their ends. The importance of the manipulation of these symbols is apparent in the control over the mass media exercised by governments of all types throughout the world.

Another important skill for leaders is the ability to perceive the needs and demands of the populace. Leaders need to establish and maintain links with citizens, interest groups, and lower-level officials. Where the citizenry is passive, the leadership must determine its needs without waiting for demands to be made. Visitors to a developing state often note that high crime rates, a lack of jobs for college graduates, failing public health services, and inadequate sewage and electric services are accepted without protest by the local populace. The leader who desires change must discern needs even in the absence of demands and must stimulate public interest and support for his or her plans.

## BUREAUCRACIES:
## THE CHALLENGE OF POLITICAL CONTROL

As political systems institutionalize links between those who make policy and those who administer it, bureaucracies emerge. The bureaucracy's task is to carry out policies decided upon by political leaders. Bureaucrats or civil servants may be selected in several ways: the "spoils" or patronage system, in which they are chosen on the basis of partisan service to political leaders or the party; the merit system, in which they are selected on the basis of administrative or technical abilities; or some combination of the merit and spoils systems. The spoils system often (but not always) gives way to the merit system as a state modernizes. (However, the spoils system is still widespread at the state and local levels of government in the United States.) Typically, the top levels of bureaucracies are filled by political leaders whose responsibility it is to assure the bureaucracy's loyalty to the decisions of the political leadership.

A bureaucracy is a complex system, usually hierarchical in structure, with specialized tasks, a body of rules, and a system of records and precedents. It is usually created to fulfill a specific function. Thus, departments or ministries of agriculture, defense, finance, health, and communications are typical government bureaucracies. At the apex of the hierarchy are the department minister and deputies, all political appointees, and frequently one or more senior civil servants promoted to the top for merit rather than political reasons. Subordinate to these officials are subagencies and staffs that perform specific portions of the department's mission. Figure 6.1 illustrates the organization of a typical ministry.

Ideally, bureaucrats simply execute policy decisions made by the political leadership; whatever their own partisan or ideological convictions, they obediently follow the directions of political leaders. In practice, bureaucracies virtually never attain this ideal. In modern governments with extensive social and economic responsibilities, bureaucracies acquire a political influence far greater than organizational charts suggest. Rather than existing to serve the leadership, they themselves make policy on a daily basis. To a degree this is desirable and inevitable, since the execution of laws requires bureaucrats to apply abstract statutes to real-life situations. This means, in effect, setting policy on how to translate the law into practice. However, bureaucracies often act like interest groups, pressing government for policies they want. Bureaucracies can also ignore decisions made by the political leadership: lethargy and outright resistance can delay or sabotage virtually any program.

Studies of bureaucracies tend to cast them as heroes or villains. Those who see bureaucracies as villains argue that they cannot be uncontrolled by their political masters, and pose a threat to democratic values in that expertise re-

FIGURE 6.1
*A Typical Ministry of Health Showing
Political and Bureaucratic Officials*

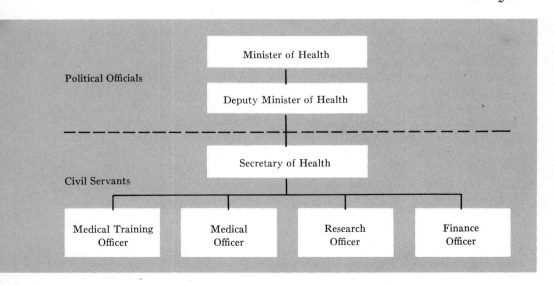

places the will of the people.[7] Among the chief obstacles to political control of the bureaucracy is "the numbers game": the ratio of politicians to civil servants hopelessly overwhelms the politicians. In Britain, for example, some 100 politicians are charged with controlling 800,000 civil servants.[8] Compounding ministerial ineffectiveness is the frequent turnover of ministers. Many political leaders have only a short time in which to become familiar with and gain ascendancy over the bureaucracy. An associated problem is the lack of technically qualified politicians available for ministerial roles. Democratic governments are elected to represent the will of the electorate; they are responsible for the conduct of government during their tenure in office. If they fail to control the actions of bureaucrats, the notion of democratic responsibility is rendered null and void. But the problem of controlling the bureaucracy is not unique to democracies. Authoritarian and dictatorial regimes must also guard against bureaucratic lethargy and sabotage of policies sought by the political leadership.

Those who see bureaucracies as heroes emphasize the rational and efficient administration achieved by the technicians who efficiently implement policy. In contrast to the supposedly inefficient and untrained political hack, the bureaucrat has specialized training for his or her job. Furthermore, the bureaucracy is seen as imparting stability and continuity to government. During periods of political turmoil, the uninterrupted action of the bureaucracy cushions the system from chaos and prevents total collapse. Finally, bureaucracies may be sources of innovation and political initiative, which is particularly valuable in developing countries where interest groups are poorly established and technically competent advice is not readily available to political leaders.

Despite its imperfect realization, the norm of political dominance over the bureaucracy is widespread. Nearly every political system has procedures and mechanisms to promote the loyalty of the civil service to the political leadership. Most political leaders want to see their decisions implemented in the way they were intended, and consequently devote considerable time to surveillance of the bureaucracies' performance.

# Britain and France: Political Leadership in Pluralist Societies

Democracy means government by the people, but in practice some people are more politically engaged than others. Those individuals who are actively engaged and achieve positions of responsibility in the political framework make

7. Wallace S. Sayre, "Bureaucracies: Some Contrasts in Systems," *Indian Journal of Public Administration* (April–June 1964): 219–229.

8. Michael R. Gordon, "Civil Servants, Politicians, and Parties: Shortcomings in the British Policy Process," *Comparative Politics* IV (October 1971): 47.

up the political elite. The word "elite" often carries negative connotations of rule by a closed circle. But this need not be the case. The relative openness and responsiveness of the political elite are of vital importance in democracies, which claim to provide government by and for the people. This section will examine the national political leaders of Britain and France, noting their characteristics, styles, and skills, and also their democratic or elitist tendencies.

Every country has several political elites, each with a number of different levels, but our attention will be focused on the upper levels of the national political leadership. These leaders include members of the government (the prime minister and cabinet ministers) and members of the principal branch of parliament (the British House of Commons and the French National Assembly). Later we shall examine how this top political leadership seeks to control the administrative ranks.

## THE POLITICAL CONTEXT: COMPETITIVE PLURALISM

The limited scope of government in liberal democracies means that the political leadership must share important decision-making with a number of autonomous nonpolitical bodies: unions and private management help set wages and prices; churches and social clubs help establish moral and ethical codes; educators and parents' groups help determine education policy; banks, insurance companies, and other private financial groups help regulate the economy; and so forth. The pluralist nature of Western democratic societies dictates a plurality of leaderships, of which the political leadership is usually the most important. Nonpolitical leaders can make social and economic decisions that have important political effects. For example, a private firm's decision to close unprofitable textile factories or shipyards can have important economic and political effects on the regions in question. The political leadership's ability to control politics is thus limited not only by the difficulty of imposing controls on large and complex societies but also by the fact that many decisions are made by autonomous groups beyond its control.

The setting is not only pluralist, but also competitive, in that officeholders regularly confront rivals who wish to replace them. In Britain the competition between alternative sets of leaders is highly institutionalized. The leader of the Opposition and the shadow government offer a credible substitute for the existing government. In France the opposition is less united, but the competition is nonetheless intense. Though the Gaullists have held office since 1958, they have faced serious challenges from the Left in recent elections, especially in 1967, 1973, and 1974.

## LEADERSHIP CHARACTERISTICS

The socioeconomic backgrounds of the top political leaders in Britain and France suggest that leadership is heterogeneous but by no means a faithful reflection of society as a whole. Leadership in Britain and France tends to be male, upper middle-class in background, and highly educated. Table 6.1 lists the occupational backgrounds of British MPs and French deputies. There are some notable contrasts between the two countries. The large number of Conservative leaders from the business community reflects the influence of business in the Conservative party — an influence not paralleled in France. This difference is explained in part by the mutual suspicions and mistrust between the French business community and the Gaullists (the largest right-of-center party and the most likely recipient of business support). The British Labour party is more successful in bringing workers into parliament than are the French left-wing parties. This difference is a function of political power. Local Labour parties are sometimes dominated by the trade unions and choose candidates from within their midst. In France the unions lack such political influence, and fewer of their members are nominated to public office even by the working-class parties. The medical professions (doctors, dentists, pharmacists, and veterinarians) are an important source of political leaders in France (but not in Britain) due to a tradition of political involvement by doctors and pharmacists and their role as local notables with political and social influence. Teachers are often recruited to political action by left-wing parties in both countries. In France this phenomenon is attributable to the old battle against church-run schools; in Britain, it reflects the Labour party's support of government-run schools and suspicion of private schools. There are many civil servants in the National Assembly and almost none in the House of Commons, reflecting the very strong tradition of nonpartisanship in the British civil service and the politicization of civil servants in France. On the whole, occupational groups well-represented in parliament tend to be those whose practitioners can afford to take leaves of absence for full-time political activity without damaging their careers.

In Britain the political careers of national leaders often begin with election to local offices. The next stage is usually election to the House of Commons. Almost invariably, leaders serve long apprenticeships in Parliament before moving into ministerial positions. In the United States, the president's cabinet frequently includes nonpoliticians, members of the opposition party, or even individuals the president has never met. Such recruitment of outsiders is alien to the British political system. British cabinet ministers are almost always veteran members of the House of Commons or the House of Lords, and are virtually never from the opposition party (except in wartime coalitions). Cabinet ministers are usually also party officers with long histories of service to the party. The prime minister is always a member of Commons, with an average of twenty-seven years of parliamentary service prior to selection as prime minister. He has also usually had several years of experience as a minister in varying posts during previous governments. He is a party loyalist who has earned the position of party leader through years of devoted party work.

The top-level leaders tend to have remarkably similar social, as well as political, backgrounds. Conservative ministers tend to be products of British "public schools," and especially of Eton. ("Public schools" are actually private

TABLE 6.1
## Occupational Backgrounds of British MPs and French Deputies

| | British MPs, 1974 | | | | French Deputies, 1973 | | | |
| | Conservatives | | Labourites | | Gaullists | | Leftists | |
| | Percent | Number | Percent | Number | Percent | Number | Percent | Number |
|---|---|---|---|---|---|---|---|---|
| Legal professions | 21.9 | 65 | 13.3 | 40 | 11.5 | 30 | 5.1 | 9 |
| Journalists | 10.5 | 31 | 9.0 | 27 | 2.7 | 7 | 2.3 | 4 |
| Educators | 1.7 | 5 | 22.9 | 69 | 5.4 | 14 | 31.8 | 56 |
| Medical professions | 1.0 | 3 | 2.0 | 6 | 20.3 | 53 | 5.7 | 10 |
| Civil servants | no data | — | no data | — | 18.8 | 49 | 10.8 | 19 |
| Farmers, landowners | 9.8 | 29 | 0.7 | 2 | 7.7 | 20 | 4.0 | 7 |
| Company directors, brokers | 26.0 | 77 | 1.7 | 5 | 20.3 | 53 | 6.3 | 11 |
| Accountants | 2.0 | 6 | 1.3 | 4 | no data | — | no data | — |
| Managers, executives, etc. | 5.7 | 17 | 9.0 | 27 | 3.4 | 10 | 1.7 | 3 |
| Other business | 14.2 | 42 | 8.3 | 25 | 3.4 | 10 | 2.3 | 4 |
| Clerical and technical | 0 | 0 | 2.0 | 6 | 2.7 | 7 | 11.9 | 21 |
| Engineers | 1.7 | 5 | 9.0 | 27 | no data | — | no data | — |
| Trade union and party officials | 1.4 | 4 | 7.6 | 23 | no data | — | no data | — |
| Workers | 0.3 | 1 | 11.3 | 34 | 0 | 0 | 15.3 | 27 |
| Military officers | 0 | 0 | 0 | 0 | 0.8 | 2 | 0 | 0 |
| Others | 4.0 | 12 | 2.0 | 6 | 5.4 | 14 | 2.3 | 4 |
| Total MPs or deputies | | 296 | | 301 | | 261 | | 176 |

Source: British data from The Times (London), 2 March 1974. French data from Bulletin de l'Assemblée Nationale, Ve Législature, no. 12 (3 July 1973), p. 58. Data on the two nations is only roughly comparable, since the more detailed French classification system was condensed to conform to the British system. Furthermore, some deputies listed more than one occupation.

FIGURE 6.2
## The Road to Ministerial Power in Britain

Prime Minister ⎫
Senior Cabinet Minister ⎬ Cabinet minister
Other Cabinet Minister ⎭

Minister of Cabinet rank
Non-Cabinet minister, e.g., Minister of State ⎬ Minister
Junior minister, e.g., Parliamentary Secretary
   or Under Secretary of State

Parliamentary private ⎫
   secretary to a minister ⎬ Backbencher*
Member of Parliament ⎭

Parliamentary candidate

   * Parliamentary private secretaries are MPs appointed personally by ministers. They are unpaid and are not considered part of the Government.

*Source: Adapted from* British Government and Politics, *2d edition, by Douglas V. Verney, p. 63. Copyright © 1966, 1971 by Douglas V. Verney. By permission of Harper & Row, Publishers.*

elite boarding schools.) They have usually graduated from Cambridge or Oxford and are upper middle-class or upper-class in social background. When Labour is in power, the ministers are generally products of government-run schools. The typical Labour minister either did not attend university or attended a less prestigious university than "Oxbridge" (the popular designation for the two elite universities). The Labour ministers' social backgrounds are more mixed than those of Conservatives; some come from working-class and labor union backgrounds, many from the middle class, and a few from the upper class.

    The leadership development process and the similarity of leaders' backgrounds results in a group of leaders who share experiences and outlooks. They have worked together in the party for years; they have collaborated in Parliament; they may even have served together in a previous Government. Many have social ties from university and boarding-school days. This phenomenon fosters teamwork and unity and contributes to the gentility often noted in British politics. However, it may also stifle initiative and innovation. Too much inbreeding of leaders may accentuate the already unrepresentative nature of leadership and inhibit bold departures from established policies and practices by either party.

    In France the situation under the Fifth Republic is somewhat different.

TABLE 6.2

### Educational and Occupational Backgrounds of Cabinet Ministers in Britain

| Occupation | Conservative November 1959 | Conservative October 1964 | Labour October 1947 | Labour October 1969 |
|---|---|---|---|---|
| Professional | 8 (4 lawyers) | 13 (8 lawyers, 1 educator) | 9 (2 lawyers, 7 educators) | 19 (3 lawyers, 8 educators) |
| Business | 7 | 3 | 1 (small) | 1 (temporary) |
| Manual | 0 | 0 | 5 | 1 |
| Other | 2 | 3 | 2 | 0 |
| (Unknown) | (2) | (4) | (0) | (0) |
| TOTAL | 19 | 23 | 17 | 21 |
| **Education** | | | | |
| Elementary only | 0 | 0 | 7 | 0 |
| State Secondary | 1 | 2 | 2 | 13 |
| Public Schools | 16 | 21 | 6 | 6 |
| Eton | 7 | 11 | 1 | 0 |
| Other fee-paying | 2 | 0 | 1 | 0 |
| (Unknown) | (0) | (0) | (1) | (2) |
| TOTAL | 19 | 23 | 17 | 21 |
| **Education** | | | | |
| All | 16 | 17 (plus 3 at Military Academy) | 8 | 16 |
| Oxford and Cambridge | 15 | 17 | 6 | 11 |

Source: Graeme C. Moodie, The Government of Great Britain, 3d ed. (New York: Thomas Y. Crowell, 1971), p. 142.

While leaders may be drawn from similar socioeconomic backgrounds, the extent of their prior shared political experience is much more limited. Even when a single party has had a majority in the National Assembly (as in 1968–1973), the Government has been a coalition of parties whose leaders have conducted separate and competing partisan activities. Furthermore, under the Fifth Republic, the Council of Ministers has frequently included individuals with little or no prior political experience. Of the twenty ministers in the first Debré government at the start of the Fifth Republic, seven were without elected position or prior ministerial or parliamentary experience. Willingness to appoint outsiders to the Council of Ministers has continuously characterized the Fifth Republic. The first cabinet chosen by Giscard d'Estaing included four political novices out of the fifteen full ministers. These outsiders have generally been senior civil servants, but they have included diplomats, professors, and men of letters. Even at the level of prime minister, outsiders with little political experience have been selected. For example, Georges Pompidou was a political unknown without ministerial or parliamentary experience when de Gaulle selected him as prime minister in 1962. Only three of the six prime ministers since 1958 have had significant prior service in the National Assembly.

The selection of politically inexperienced outsiders as members of the Government and even as prime ministers reflects the primacy of the president in the Fifth Republic. Presidents de Gaulle, Pompidou, and Giscard d'Estaing preferred good administrators and technicians to potential political rivals as top ministers, and especially as prime minister. Politically ambitious prime ministers like Michel Debré, Jacques Chaban-Delmas, and, eventually, Georges Pompidou, can threaten the delicate division of powers between the president and the prime minister required by the mixed presidential-parliamentary system. The relationship between the two executives requires the president to be pre-eminent and the prime minister to acquiesce in taking the blame for failure himself and giving credit for success to the president. Such a delicate balance is difficult to maintain if the prime minister is politically independent and ambitious.

Whether the diversity of men in the top levels of leadership in France obviates the danger of inbreeding is difficult to assess. Many French politicians have personal friendships that transcend party lines, sometimes stemming from wartime resistance activities. The presence of outsiders has a less broadening effect than might be expected because they tend to have served on the ministerial or personal staffs of the leaders they join in the government. In any case, the long-term close political collaboration characteristic of the top leadership in Britain is lacking in France, which may detract from the cohesion and cooperation of French governments. Indeed, there does appear to be greater internal conflict and tension in French than in British governments.

## LEADERSHIP STYLES AND SKILLS

A characteristic common to Britain and France is the absence of ideologically minded political leaders. In Britain leaders from both parties have demonstrated a pragmatic approach to government. Leaders who appear ideologically committed in intraparty debates while out of power generally become pragmatic in positions of national leadership. For example, Harold Wilson was widely regarded as spokesman for the more doctrinaire left wing of the Labour party during the 1950s and early 1960s. Yet little in his behavior as prime minister indicated a firm commitment to a socialist ideology. This is also true of France. Gaullists have often been accused of doctrinaire anticommunism, but Gaullist leaders have successfully implemented a foreign policy of building friendly ties with the communist countries of eastern Europe and Asia. Some members of the opposition, especially leaders of the French left-wing parties, appear more ideologically committed. Whether they would adhere to their ideologies in positions of power is open to debate. The records of earlier socialist governments in France — notably that of Guy Mollet in 1957 — and the behavior of Socialist and Communist local governments suggest that the French Left too would be more pragmatic than ideological once in office.

The parliamentary system of government originally connoted a collective form of leadership in which a cabinet of ministers share power. In Britain the principle of the "collective responsibility" of the Government derives from this notion. While individual ministers are held accountable for their personal conduct and the actions of their departments, the whole cabinet is collectively responsible for decisions made by the Government. Thus cabinet decisions must be accepted and publicly defended by all ministers, even those who strenuously opposed them in the privacy of cabinet meetings. If a minister simply cannot defend a decision, he or she is obligated to resign. While this practice seems strange to Americans accustomed to accounts of disagreements in the president's cabinet, the doctrine of collective responsibility does keep the lines of political responsibility clear. The public knows that the entire cabinet is accountable for all acts of government.

An interesting and rare exception to the principle of collective responsibility occurred in 1975 as a result of the Wilson cabinet's division over continued membership in the European Common Market. The issue of membership in the Common Market had long divided the British people and especially the Labour party. The decision to join the Common Market was made in 1972 by a Conservative government. At that time the Labour party opposed joining and pledged that when it returned to power it would renegotiate Britain's terms of membership or withdraw from the Common Market. Back in power in 1974, the Labour government of Harold Wilson succeeded in negotiating more favorable terms with the other members of the Common Market. The new terms were then submitted to the general public for approval through a national referendum. A majority of the cabinet favored continued membership in the Common Market and urged a yes vote on the referendum. But a powerful minority of the cabinet (7 of the 23 members) supported by a majority of the backbench Labour MPs and the majority of the Labour party outside of Parliament opposed staying in the Common Market. To preserve party unity, Wilson accorded the minority in the cabinet a "license to differ" which permitted them to speak against the referendum issue so long as they did so privately and not as members of the government. When acting officially, even those ministers opposed to the Common Market were expected to support the government position in favor of continued membership. One minister was dismissed abruptly when he spoke against the government position in a debate on the floor of the House of Commons. This deviation from the principle of collective responsibility was clearly exceptional: the most recent precedent was in 1929 when there was a coalition government. It was necessitated by the deep division of the Labour party over the Common Market.

In France the notion of collective responsibility is much less developed, because it is not conducive to multiparty coalition governments. However, under the Fifth Republic the collective action and responsibility of the Council of Ministers has been furthered by the ministers' dependence on the president and by their obligation to support and defend his actions. This is less genuine collective decision-making than it is a well-functioning hierarchical structure committed to the collective defense of the president. But the effect is the same: ministers who publicly disagree with governmental policy are dropped from the cabinet. A recent case is the summary dismissal in 1974 of Jean-Jacques Servan-Schreiber when he voiced opposition to the continued testing of the French nuclear bomb.

The growing powers of the prime minister have enhanced the personalist nature of leadership in Britain. Voters increasingly see the prime minister and a few other top leaders as embodiments of the government and the ruling party. Thus leaders with unattractive images reflect unfavorably on the government and the party. Though the prime minister is not directly elected, there is evidence suggesting that voters often cast their ballots for the candidate of the party whose leader they would like to see as prime minister. Elections are sometimes won or lost on the basis of the impressions made by the leaders.

The British political leader must be concerned with maintaining a solid standing in the public eye because of the electoral implications of declining public approval. Moreover, the leader's ability to control his own party and retain the confidence of his colleagues in government depends upon a favorable public image. Prime ministers whose standings in public opinion polls fall often experience challenges within their own parties. An unpopular leader is likely to be an electoral liability, and may find it difficult to persuade his colleagues to support him or follow his guidance.

In France the personalization of leadership reached an extreme under President Charles de Gaulle. Called to power in 1958 at a time of national crisis and political collapse, de Gaulle's authority was charismatic. He was viewed by many French citizens as having saved France after its defeat in 1940 by the Nazis. His sense of mission and personal mystique led many to believe that he alone could save France from the threat of military rule and civil war in 1958. De Gaulle's regime was permeated by his personal style: his sense of mission, flexibility, aloofness, paternalism, scorn of "intermediaries" such as parties and interest groups, almost regal bearing, self-concept as savior of France — and, above all, the personal mystique he used to win widespread support from French citizens in all walks of life. Many of the French perceived even legislative elections as opportunities to vote for or against de Gaulle through the medium of candidates pledged to follow or to oppose him. Since de Gaulle's resignation in 1969, the charismatic aspect of leadership has dissipated but the president remains the central figure in French politics. His personality and actions pervade nearly all political activities.

Georges Pompidou did not try to adopt de Gaulle's style and instead fashioned his own. While he insisted on retaining or expanding all the presidential powers exercised by de Gaulle, he paid closer attention to public opinion and smoothed some of the rough edges of de Gaulle's style. Styling himself as "one Frenchmen like other Frenchmen," he was less abrasive, more conciliatory, and less formal than de Gaulle. His successor, President Valéry Giscard d'Estaing, set about developing his own distinctive style of leadership in the months after his election in 1974. Moving still further from the regal style of de Gaulle he emphasized his closeness to the people in keeping with his campaign pledge to be "president of all Frenchmen."

The personalization of political leadership has been promoted by the nationalization of politics and political leadership. In the past, the electorate's most immediate contact with the political world was through local officials and the local member of parliament. Now, thanks to national mass media systems and especially to television, voters can more readily see and hear national leaders discussing national issues. The leaders who receive the greatest exposure on the media are the top-level officials and their rivals in the opposition. Increased visibility has tended to enhance national leaders' political powers and to broaden the gap between the top strata and subordinate levels of leadership.

Above all, leadership styles in Britain and France reflect the electoral preoccupations of the leaders, whose tenure depends upon maintaining sufficient public confidence to win the next election. The prevailing pragmatism reflects the public's general lack of interest in abstract political ideologies and concern with specific issues. Personalism follows from the voters' growing tendency to focus attention on the top political leader. And leaders' concern for public opinion and image-consciousness stem from recognition of their dependence on public support in and between elections in order to maintain the confidence and cooperation of colleagues.

## THE DEMOCRATIC CONTROL OF BUREAUCRACIES

The bureaucracy must be subject to the political leaders in a democracy if the people are truly to retain control of their government. Elected officials subject to the voters' sanctions must control the unelected and thus democratically unresponsible bureaucrats. But it is unrealistic to expect bureaucracies to have no say in policy-making. It is also undesirable, since bureaucrats represent not only their own interests but also the interests of the clientele they serve. For example, governmental social workers often defend the interests and needs of their clients, the poor and disabled. However, if the lines of democratic responsibility are to be maintained, it must ultimately be an elected official who regulates the bureaucracy's actions.

In Britain the burden of controlling the civil service falls on a comparatively few politically responsible leaders. This situation contrasts with that of the United States, where each federal department has many — sometimes as many as several hundred — top-level political appointees who oversee the permanent bureaucrats. In the typical British government department, there are only three or four political leaders: the minister and a couple of parliamentary secretaries, all of whom are MPs. The rest of the managerial positions, including the permanent secretary, deputy secretaries, and the minister's private secretary, are all career civil servants removable only on grounds of malfeasance in office.

The ability of the few political leaders to control their departments is limited by other demands on their time: attendance at parliamentary sessions and committee meetings, public appearances and speeches, party leadership obligations, and the need to tend to their own parliamentary constituencies.

Despite this lack of political personnel in supervisory positions, the British civil service remains loyal to the political leadership. Political neutrality and responsiveness to political control are firmly established as norms of the civil service, which explains the British bureaucracy's impressive record of political control and accountability. There have been some abuses, particularly involving bureaucrats' selective use of information to justify a given course of action to a minister. However, the civil service's general record of nonpartisanship and acceptance of political direction is good.

The social backgrounds of senior civil servants tie them more closely to the Conservatives, through "old boy" networks and general social attitudes, than to the Labour party. Thus the key test of the bureaucracy's submissiveness to political leadership occurs when Labour assumes power. Its performance has been surprisingly good. Labour Governments have found senior civil servants not only willing to follow political guidance but almost eager to cooperate in meeting Labour's objectives. For example, when the Labour government came to power in 1964 after thirteen years in opposition, the newly designated chancellor of exchequer (minister of finance) was surprised to find that senior civil servants had studied the Labour program and the economic speeches of Labour leaders and had already prepared a working paper suggesting ways the Labour program could be implemented and possible problems to be encountered.

In France the politically responsible leadership is somewhat more extensive than in Britain. Each minister selects a *cabinet* of personal advisers, varying in size from ten (supposedly the legal limit) to as many as eighty people in the case of former prime minister Chaban-Delmas. The members of the cabinets, civil servants borrowed from other ministries and younger politicians favored by the minister, form a body of advisers that compensates for the lack of innovation endemic in bureaucracies. They also help the minister master the bureaucratic structures and control the bureaucrats who serve under him. In addition, the office of the president has a large staff of senior civil servants and political protégés. Both presidents and ministers have used their cabinets to bypass the bureaucracies so firmly entrenched in the ministries, to avoid bureaucratic sabotage, and to develop innovative ideas. For example, after the Events of May–June 1968, the minister of education used his own staff, rather than the highly conservative and unimaginative senior bureaucrats in the ministry, to draft a thorough reform of the educational system.

A determined bureaucracy, however, can still block or restructure an unwanted reform. A case in point is the French agricultural reform attempted during the early 1960s. Guidelines were drafted by the prime minister's cabinet, in an effort to circumvent the tradition-bound bureaucrats in the ministry of agriculture, and implemented by an energetic young minister of agriculture (Edgard Pisani) determined to destroy established bureaucractic fiefdoms within the ministry. Pisani's efforts met with strong resistance from the bureaucrats, who succeeded in delaying and in some cases thwarting the proposed administrative reforms. When Pisani left government four years later, his successor permitted the bureaucracy to dismantle most of the unwanted administrative changes.

The French civil service adheres much less strongly than its British counterpart to the norm of political nonpartisanship. The recent willingness of political leaders to recruit ministers and other political personnel from among the senior civil servants has made the latter more political. Service in the higher levels of the bureaucracy is now an important route to political careers. At the lower and middle levels of the bureaucracy, however, there are large numbers of socialists politically hostile to the regime and sometimes able to alter or affect government policy. Socialists are particularly numerous in the middle and lower levels of the ministries of interior, national education, and post, telephone, and telegraph.

Open bureaucratic resistance to political leadership is rare in Britain and France. A more prevalent danger is that the range of policy options open to ministers will be restricted by unimaginative thinking, lack of rigorous and open-minded analysis of alternatives, and unsympathetic treatment on the part of permanent officials in their ministries.[9] Of course, an alert, imaginative, and dynamic minister can demand — and probably elicit — better treatment from bureaucrats. All too often, however, the minister is preoccupied with other concerns or simply lacking in the intellectual and technical abilities necessary to tell whether his officials are performing as he desires. Since all British ministers are chosen from among the majority party's members of Parliament, there are usually only about 350 potential candidates. Furthermore, ministerial skills are not always the primary criterion of choice: party factions must be represented and balanced; senior MPs must be rewarded; political debts must be paid. In France the pool of potential ministers is somewhat larger, since ministers can be selected from outside parliament. But the pressure to balance factions and parties, reward the faithful, and pay debts operates there too. Thus, by ministerial default, policy-making powers often slip from the hands of the politically accountable leaders into those of the bureaucrats.

This survey of political leadership in Britain and France makes it apparent that political leaders are clearly differentiated from the general population. In neither nation, however, is the leadership a ruling class or a unified body of individuals whose political decisions narrowly reflect their own interests. The political leaders of Britain and France function within pluralist political and social systems. They share power with autonomous social, economic, and political decision-makers. They compete with rival sets of political leaders for the right to continue in office. They must contend with unwieldy and entrenched bureaucracies. A French sociologist has well described the intermediate nature of democratic political leadership:

9. See Gordon, "Civil Servants."

A unified elite means the end of freedom. But when the groups of the elite are not only distinct but become a disunity, it means the end of the state. Freedom survives in those intermediate regions, which are continually threatened when there is moral unity of the elite, where men and groups preserve the secret of single and eternal wisdom and have learnt how to combine autonomy with co-operation.[10]

It is in this intermediate range that one finds the political elites of Britain, France, and most other Western democracies.

# China and the Soviet Union: From Revolutionary Charisma to "Managerial Modernization"

Leaders in communist states have a much greater impact on their political systems than their counterparts in Western democracies. The top-level leaders of China, the Soviet Union, and other communist states not only define their nations' directions and goals, but also have unusual latitude for realizing these objectives. The broad scope of governmental activity in communist nations gives the leaders much greater control over their social systems than is the case in liberal democracies. Centralized and hierarchical political structures place extensive powers in the hands of a comparatively small group of individuals. Consequently, Western observers devote special attention to the personalities, styles, and skills of top leaders in communist countries.

In most communist states the nature of leadership has shifted over time. Leadership during the period of revolution is often charismatic in nature: the man who led the successful revolt is legitimized by his personal qualities and his revolutionary contributions. Thus Lenin, Mao Tse-tung, Castro, Ho Chi Minh, Tito, and others were accepted as legitimate leaders because of their charismatic appeal. Occasionally this charisma is shared by some of their fellow revolutionary heroes. But as the elite responsible for the revolution dies off, the new leadership must seek legitimacy in other sources. The second- and third-generation leaders are frequently managers and modernizers, who base their power on the party's legitimacy and on their skills at managing the modernization of their societies. Though the man on top may seek to enhance his image and personal appeal, his hold on power typically depends less on charisma than on "managerial modernization."

The apex of political leadership in communist countries is located in the party rather than the official government offices. In the Soviet Union and China, the top-level leadership — the party's central committee, politburo, and secre-

10. Raymond Aron, "Social Structure and the Ruling Class," *British Journal of Sociology* I (June 1950): 143.

tariat — is composed of between three and four hundred individuals. This section will focus on the characteristics, styles, and skills of these members of the political elite and on the environments in which they operate.

## THE POLITICAL CONTEXT OF LEADERSHIP
## IN CHINA AND THE SOVIET UNION

Chinese and Soviet leaders operate in political systems dominated by highly centralized and disciplined Communist parties. In the determination of public policy and in the competition for key political posts, the strategic positions are those that control the party. Chief among these offices is the party secretary or chairman, whose control over the party's apparatus usually gives him an edge over possible rivals.

The top leadership must pay close attention to maintaining the party's strength and discipline, and to training the party's members and leaders. It is believed that among the chief reasons for the ouster of Khrushchev in 1964 was his failure to devote enough attention to the party. When a nation's party stagnates, or when the leaders believe it no longer serves the revolutionary goals they seek, the resultant disruption can be massive. An example is China during the Cultural Revolution, when Mao felt compelled to use the Red Guards to purge "revisionist" elements from the party.

Game theorists refer to competitive situations in which the winner takes all and the loser gains absolutely nothing as *zero-sum* games, and in a very real sense the pursuit of top-level political positions in communist states is a zero-sum game. Those who win join a powerful ruling elite that determines the political fate of the nation. Those who lose are often discredited and relegated to obscure positions without political significance or power. In the past, losers were also subject to imprisonment or death. When Khrushchev denounced Stalin's crimes, he revealed that 98 (or 70 percent) of the 139 members of the Soviet party's Central Committee elected in 1934 had been arrested or shot by 1938 on Stalin's orders in an attempt to consolidate his hold on power. While these severe penalties no longer characterize communist politics, the losers — unlike unsuccessful candidates in Western democracies — do not come back to try again.[11]

Political leaders are generally recruited from within the ranks of the Communist party rather than from industry, science, or other fields, but there is some evidence that increasing numbers of Central Committee members in the Soviet Union have been co-opted into the political leadership relatively late in their careers.[12] By co-opting outsiders into the Central Committee, the party

---

11. However, China has rehabilitated many, such as Teng Hsiao-p'ing, who, after having been disgraced, reappeared in 1972 in a top party position.
12. Michael P. Gehlen and Michael McBride, "The Soviet Central Committee: An Elite Analysis," in *The Behavioral Revolution and Communist Studies,* ed. Roger E. Kanet (New York: Free Press, 1971), pp. 103–24; and Robert H. Donaldson, "The 1971 Soviet Central Committee: An Assessment of the New Elite," *World Politics* XXIV (April 1972): 382–401.

elite can maintain and enhance its legitimacy. Thus there are several alternative paths to positions of political leadership. One route is through the party apparatus: the potential leader develops and demonstrates organizational abilities and leadership skills by serving the party. Another is to develop a technical skill (e.g., expertise in agriculture, engineering, economics, or technology), which permits the aspiring leader to offer substantive knowledge as well as leadership ability. As communist states mature, their leaders tend increasingly to have technical as well as party-based backgrounds. Brezhnev, for example, has an engineering degree in addition to his long apprenticeship in party work.) A third path is ideological training. While the political leadership has few genuine ideologues, there is always a handful who can provide interpretations of the party's ideology.

Formal selection of Central Committee members is the duty of the party congress, but the nominees (who are always elected unanimously) are actually chosen by the top leadership. Since leaders are thus co-opted rather than elected, the aspiring political leader usually seeks a sponsor in the upper levels of leadership. Top leaders are, in turn, looking for potential leaders and for means to reward those who are helpful to them. The ultimate success of the aspiring leader depends on his ability both to establish linkages with sponsors who are rising in the hierarchy and to shift sponsors at the correct time.

There is a degree of ruthlessness in the process as leaders are played off against each other in the struggle for influence and position. The regular sessions of criticism and self-criticism in which individual leaders' performances are evaluated publicly by themselves and their peers provide ready justification should it be decided to eliminate certain leaders. For top leaders, these self-criticism exercises are perfunctory or meaningless. However, they can significantly affect the careers of middle- or lower-level leaders. It not infrequently happens that aspiring leaders turn on the mentors responsible for their co-optation into the inner circle. Thus, Marshal Lin allegedly abused his trusted position at Mao's side by involving himself in an unsuccessful plot to assassinate Mao. Similarly, Khrushchev watched his protégé Brezhnev lead the attack that ended Khrushchev's rule.

Even for a person who has arrived at the very pinnacle of power, the future is by no means secure. Of the thirty-one men who have ruled the various communist countries since 1918, nine were thrown out of office by their comrades; eight died in office; one (Walter Ulbricht of East Germany) retired peacefully; and the remaining thirteen are still in power. The fate of those who are overthrown is total obscurity, as is illustrated by Khrushchev's ouster. One day he was at the head of one of the world's two superpowers; the next day Soviet newspapers carried brief notices that Khrushchev had "retired" from his party and government posts because of age and deteriorating health. Pictures of him were removed from public places; his writings vanished from the shelves of libraries and bookstores. Overnight Khrushchev became virtually a nonperson, banished from the view of the public. His death six years later merited only a one- or two-line notice in the Soviet press.

The uncertainty of the future forces top leaders in communist states to pay close attention to the maintenance of their positions. Although they do not face the threat of being thrown out of office at the next election, communist leaders do devote considerable time and energy to preserving their positions in the party hierarchy. Those who neglect this task may find themselves abruptly disposed of.

## LEADERSHIP CHARACTERISTICS

Studies of Western democratic political elites indicate that as a group they come from higher-than-average socioeconomic backgrounds. It might be expected that in communist societies, where there is greater emphasis on the virtues of the working class, the political elite might include more representatives of the lower socioeconomic classes. However, the available evidence on the leadership of both China and the Soviet Union suggests that this is not the case. The top levels of leadership in both countries are drawn from a relatively small sector of society and are no more representative of its socioeconomic makeup than are the elites in democratic states. The top leaders of China and the Soviet Union are typically cohesive groups of men with remarkably similar backgrounds. They have shared experiences in party service, taken part in similar party political education programs, and engaged in similar party activities.

Political leaders at the levels both of the cadres and the top tend to be of middle-class rather than working- or lower-class origin, and to be considerably better educated than a typical sector of the overall population. At the highest levels of leadership the socioeconomic background of the elite differs even more dramatically from the general population. Studies of the Chinese party's Central Committee and Politburo indicate that many members of the elite have middle- or upper-class backgrounds and most have some college training.[13] Furthermore, present trends suggest that the top levels of leadership in China are becoming increasingly well-educated and middle-class.[14]

Some data is available on the social backgrounds of the top-level party elite selected at the Tenth Party Congress in 1973.[15] There is a large contingent of military officers, though their number has declined since the previous congress. The inner circle of pre-Liberation revolutionaries remains in control. Politburo members now average sixty-five years of age, and the Standing Committee averages seventy-one years as compared to sixty-nine in 1969. Seventy-five percent of the full members of the Central Committee are over sixty years of age. However, there has been a marked change in generational representation. Prior to the Tenth Congress, those who had joined the party during the Long

13. See, for example, Robert C. North and Ithiel de Sola Pool, "Kuomintang and Chinese Communist Elites," in *World Revolutionary Elites*, ed. Harold D. Lasswell and Daniel Lerner (Cambridge, Mass.: MIT Press, 1965).

14. Donald Klein, "The Next Generation of Chinese Communist Leaders," *The China Quarterly* 12 (October–December 1962), p. 64.

15. *Far Eastern Economic Review, Yearbook 1974* (Hong Kong: Far Eastern Economic Review, 1973), p. 119.

TABLE 6.3

*Social Background of the Soviet Political Elite, 1971* _____

| Nationality | Percentage of full members of the Central Committee | Percentage of all members of the Politburo |
|---|---|---|
| Great Russian (53.3%)* | 59.8 | 52.4 |
| Ukrainian Belorussian (20.5%) | 25.0 | 28.5 |
| Georgian, Armenian, Azerbaidzhanin (4.6%) | 3.1 | 4.8 |
| Lithuanian, Latvian, Estonian Moldavian, Jewish (4.1%) | 3.1 | 4.8 |
| Uzbek, Kazakh, Turkmen, Kirgiz, Tadzhik (8.1%) | 5.4 | 9.5 |
| Other minority (9.4%) | 3.6 | 0 |
| *Occupational background* | | |
| Party apparatus | 45.1 | |
| State apparatus | 26.4 | |
| Military and police | 10.2 | |
| Symbol manipulators | 2.1 | |
| Mass organization apparatus (trade unions, etc.) | 2.6 | |
| Economic specialists | 6.4 | |
| Scientific-academic-intellectual | 2.6 | |
| Workers and peasants | 4.7 | |

* Figures in parentheses are the percentage of the total population of the nationality groups.

Source: Robert H. Donaldson, "The 1971 Soviet Central Committee: An Assessment of the New Elite." World Politics XXIV (April 1972): 382–409.

March in 1934–1935 accounted for 80 percent of the Central Committee, whereas at the Tenth they were only 68 percent. In terms of regional representation, southern Chinese have declined from 73 percent of the Central Committee named in 1969 to 64 percent after 1973.

China's patterns of leadership recruitment and mobility have been based on two principles: the patron-client system and administrative or technical skill. Under the first pattern, leaders are recruited and promoted on the basis of their loyalty to some more prominent party or governmental leader. In such cases, the key criterion may well be "redness," or ideological strength. There are times, such as during decentralization periods — 1957–1960 — when expertise becomes important in gaining a leadership position. With China's growing modernization, expertise is increasingly likely to be the basis for the recruitment and promotion of leaders.

In the Soviet Union, the socioeconomic backgrounds of the political elite similarly overrepresent certain groups. Those sectors of society that are over-represented include city-dwellers, Slavs (especially Great Russians), males, middle-aged party apparatchiki, those with higher education, and the intelligentsia. Underrepresented groups include women, farmers, workers, and the young. Some observers have suggested that the dominance of the American political elite by WASPS (white Anglo-Saxon Protestants) has a parallel in the Soviet Union. There, it is suggested, the SRAPPS (Slavic-stock Russian-born apparatchiki) enjoy preferential access to the political elite.[16] In recent years, the number of leaders with technical training and experience appears to be growing. But there is little evidence to suggest a more equitable representation of such groups as women, workers, and farmers. One mitigating factor is relevant, namely, the openness of the education system that gives the sons and daughters of workers and peasants access to the higher education needed for joining the elite. However, education changes the outlooks and values of individuals from lower socioeconomic backgrounds, making them poor representatives of workers and farmers.

There are some interesting contrasts between the political elites of China and the Soviet Union that reflect the different stages of development they have reached in the revolutionary and modernization processes. In China, which is closer in time to its revolutionary experience, the elite exhibits ideological adherence to pure Marxist ideals. Most members of the Chinese elite were revolutionary leaders in the civil war. These revolutionary veterans shared hardship and developed camaraderie during the prolonged struggle. Their political apprenticeships were served under fire, and the training they received was appropriate to wartime. The Chinese elite seems more deeply motivated by the egalitarian and community values embodied in the revolution than does the Soviet elite. There appears to be considerable unwillingness in China to open the elite to experts, who might deviate from pure revolutionary ideals in the interests of greater efficiency and industrialization. Indeed, Mao Tse-tung's determination to avoid sacrificing egalitarian goals even for economic stability is illustrated by his support for economically disruptive but ideologically sound experiments like the Great Leap Forward and the Cultural Revolution.

One study designates the elite of China "revolutionary modernizers" and that of the Soviet Union "managerial modernizers."[17] The revolutionary veteran has long since passed from the Soviet political scene. The Soviet elite appears eager to expand by co-opting specialists. The Soviet revolution is more than fifty years old; the task now is to manage the complex industrial society it has created.

Some argue that the growing number of specialists and experts trained outside the party and co-opted into the Soviet political leadership may be ex-

16. Zbigniew Brzezinski and Samuel P. Huntington, *Political Power: USA/USSR* (New York: Viking Press, 1965), pp. 131–132.
17. Robert H. Donaldson and Derek J. Waller, "Stasis and Change in Revolutionary Elites: A Comparative Analysis of the 1956 Party Central Committees in China and the USSR," *Sage Professional Papers in Comparative Politics* I (1970): 611–622.

pected to broaden the outlook and representativeness of the elite.[18] No longer the exclusive domain of party apparatchiki, the Soviet elite may now include individuals whose prior experience in industry, academic circles, or agricultural work brings the ideas and interests of these groups to the attention of the ruling elite. With time and further economic development, similar trends may well appear in the Chinese elite.

## POLITICAL STYLES AND SKILLS

While the leaders of both China and the Soviet Union are firmly committed to communism and utilize ideology as a guide to action, they are not ideologues in the sense of being constrained by their ideological beliefs. Lenin and his successors warned of the dangers of excessive ideological rigidity and insisted on flexible tactics. The elite, according to Lenin, must apply revolutionary principles to real situations and not simply repeat abstract Marxist slogans. In practice, the Chinese and Soviet elites have on the whole proved remarkably free of ideological constraints. The Soviet Union has modified egalitarian principles to foster economic development; China has made diplomatic overtures and concessions to the United States — the symbol of imperialistic capitalism — to counter what it perceived as the Soviet military threat to China's independence.

Both China and the Soviet Union have experienced periodic variations in ideological rigidity. Often a period of ideological relaxation will be followed by an abrupt reversion to ideological orthodoxy and a forceful reassertion of traditional Marxist-Leninist doctrines. For example, the relatively liberal Hundred Flowers Campaign in China during the mid-1950s was succeeded by the firm imposition of ideological values during the Great Leap Forward a year or two later. Periods of detente, or international relaxation of Cold War tensions during which ideological goals are de-emphasized, will often be accompanied by an internal intensification of traditional ideology and repression of domestic ideological dissidents. This was the case in the Soviet Union during the early 1970s, when the Soviet leadership simultaneously sought detente with the Western powers and conducted a vigorous repression of Soviet citizens who deviated from accepted doctrine. On balance, tactical flexibility rather than doctrinal rigidity is the principal feature of the leadership's current political style in both China and the Soviet Union.

Mao Tse-tung's pre-eminence in China makes it worthwhile to examine his personal political style more closely. Chairman Mao is a revolutionary of vision and impatience, a man of action and skill. His life has been dedicated to achieving and maintaining the power to remold an ancient society toward a single end — the creation of communism. Expressing his impatient modernizing political style in poetry, Chairman Mao wrote:

18. See Frederic C. Fleron, Jr., "Toward a Reconceptualization of Political Change in the Soviet Union: The Political Leadership System," in *Communist Studies and the Social Sciences,* ed. Frederic C. Fleron, Jr. (Chicago: Rand NcNally, 1969).

How many urgent tasks
Have risen one after another!
Heaven and earth revolve
Time presses
Ten thousand years is too long,
We must seize the day
The four seas rise high
The clouds and the water rage
The five continents tremble, wind and thunder are unleashed,
Until not a single one remains.[19]

It was not merely deliberate speed that Mao sought; the content of the changes he made reflected the social ideals he adhered to: participation, egalitarianism, and freedom through human development and industrialization. Some of his ideals conflicted but a strain of romance in Mao's character seemed to assign these contradictions to their natural fate — resolution through human encounter. And so it has been. Order has prevailed over individualism, while bureaucracies have been controlled by periodic critical outcries from their clients. Among Mao's firmest beliefs is the conviction that human potential, once freed and focused, can achieve any degree of social change.

To realize these beliefs, Mao developed a unique style. Realizing that information is one of the most powerful resources of leadership, he cultivated myriad sources to keep abreast of ongoing programs and outcomes. He acted flexibly to maintain political power and promote his policy objective, surviving despite the most awesome constraints and resistance with a success unparalleled in modern leadership. When he deemed a certain decision necessary to keep up the momentum of socialist construction, he submitted it to the decision-making body most likely to provide the needed support. If he felt he would be outvoted by the whole Politburo, he would convene a small group such as its Standing Committee. If he lacked support there, he might convene an expanded meeting of the Politburo with invited nonmembers; alternatively, he would turn to the entire Central Committee or even to ad hoc state conferences. Ultimately, despairing of these groups, he undertook the Cultural Revolution as a means to achieve his goals. Mao's aversion to opportunist careerists reflected a fear that the revolution's leaders might find their status more rewarding than change, and their ambition more compelling than fulfillment of their responsibilities to the revolution's ideals.

Once Mao is gone from the Chinese political scene, his successors may confront a choice between the two leadership styles that have alternated in the Soviet Union and other communist states: collective leadership and one-man rule. Collective leadership is based on the principle that political power should be collegial, or shared among several individuals. Though one leader may act as spokesman, responsibilities are genuinely divided among several, each of whom

19. *New York Times*, 22 February 1972.

has his own power base in the party, the state bureaucracy, the military, or the secret police. Typically, collective leadership involves at least the separation of the tasks of party chief and chief of government. One-man rule is the clear political predominance of a single leader who exercises personal dictatorial powers. There are, of course, other political leaders in such a situation, but they are subordinate to and dependent upon the paramount leader. The dictator usually seeks to imprint his personality on all aspects of politics and society, and fosters dissemination of his public image. The leader's name and picture are everywhere; his sayings and writings are accepted as the latest word in party doctrine; he comes to personify the party and the nation. This "cult of personality," though condemned by Leninist doctrine, recurs frequently. After criticizing Stalin's cult of personality, Khrushchev was guilty of indulging in the same pursuit. Brezhnev decried Khrushchev's cult of personality, but has recently indicated his interest in promoting his own personality.

One-man rule has prevailed in practice much longer than collective leadership. Between 1917 and 1975 in the Soviet Union one-man rule prevailed for forty years and collective leadership for eighteen years. A convincing argument can be made that collective leadership prevails only during periods when a new leader is mustering support for his personal rule. There was a brief era of collective leadership in 1922–1929 when Lenin was incapacitated by a stroke and then died, leaving a political vacuum in which Stalin ultimately triumphed. After Stalin's death there was another era of collective leadership (1953–1957) while Khrushchev consolidated his position. Khrushchev's ouster in 1964 introduced a new period of collective rule. By 1970 it appeared that Brezhnev was achieving superiority over his partners, though he has not yet eliminated his rivals from prestigious positions. Brezhnev has clearly eclipsed his most prominent co-ruler, Aleksei Kosygin, but Kosygin retains his official position as premier and his membership in the party's ruling councils.

## BUREAUCRACIES: CONTROLLED OR OUT OF CONTROL?

Communist states differ from other political systems in the vastness of their administrative tasks. In Western countries, the tasks of government are limited in scope because some or all industrial and commercial enterprises are privately owned. The bureaucracies of these private enterprises are autonomous and loosely interrelated. Organizations such as churches, trade unions, professional societies, and service organizations have separate and independent bureaucracies. In communist states all enterprises are government-owned and controlled, all social organizations are ultimately controlled by the political leadership, and all services are provided by state-controlled bureaucracies. The scope of government activity is thus all-encompassing and includes tasks left to nongovernmental bodies in Western systems.

The tasks of directing and controlling these bureaucracies are massive. They must be centrally directed, since the market forces of supply and demand, free competition, and profit that regulate the economies of noncommunist coun-

In Britain and France, members of the political elite are often drawn from exclusive schools such as Eton or the École Polytechnique With distinctive uniforms and centuries-old traditions, these schools claim to inculcate not only the skills but also the desire for public service. The Etonians are on their way to class at the beginning of day; and the Polytechniciens are being presented in a formal ceremony before the minister of defense. In contrast to emphasizing social elitism, China's Chairman Mao has dedicated his life to the creation of a classless society. The simple garb of the Chinese elite is illustrative of this effort. This photo was taken after Mao's reported nine-mile swim in the Yangtze River, a feat reflecting both his stamina and revolutionary zeal.

tries are absent in China and the Soviet Union. The number of shoes manufactured by a given Soviet plant is the product not of market demands but of a planning decision. The planners must also calculate the manpower, leather, and other materials needed to make the shoes and must make sure that these materials are available at the right time and in the right place. When one realizes that virtually every aspect of the economy and the society is the object of a conscious decision by central economic planners, the immensity and complexity of the planning and bureaucratic tasks become evident.

While the Soviet Union has made periodic efforts to decentralize the bureaucracy and the planning procedure, its structures remain highly centralized and hierarchical. Ultimately, the top-level party leadership in the Politburo and the secretariat oversees the bureaucracy through the Council of Ministers and the appropriate ministries. An illustration will indicate the extremes this centralization can reach. A bakery needed more than its usual allotment of flour. A request for the additional flour was made through the appropriate bureaucratic channels and was ultimately approved by the chairman of the Council of People's Commissars. This is equivalent to the president of the United States having to approve a request for more oil to heat a New York post office substation.[20] This is no doubt an extreme case, but it illustrates the highly centralized nature of bureaucracies in communist states.

In spite of central control, bureaucratic resistance can thwart the desires of the political leadership. Another example will illustrate the problem. After World War Two, the Soviet political leadership decided to disperse industry that had in the past been concentrated in the western parts of the country. Major investments were made to provide the necessary supports for industrial development in the east, including communication and transportation systems, fuel, and raw materials. However, it was apparent by 1955 that the political decision to decentralize had been disregarded by the industrial ministries, who continued to build factories in the west in order to take advantage of the available manpower and the attractions of the more developed western regions.[21] Much of the bureaucratic sabotage that negated the political decision to decentralize took place while Stalin — supposedly the all-powerful dictator — was still in power.

China offers similar examples of overcentralization and bureaucratic sabotage, but of special concern to Mao and his supporters has been the vulnerability of the state bureaucracies to the evils of privilege. Mao has repeatedly demonstrated concern that the bureaucrats will excessively enjoy the privileges of their offices and will acquire social and economic advantages over the peasants and workers they are supposed to serve. He fears that the bureaucrats will fail to be responsive to the interests and needs of these sectors of society, and that their comfortable positions will lead them to forget the ideals of the revolution and weaken their ideological fervor. His apprehensiveness in this regard was

20. David Granick, *The Red Executive* (Garden City, N.Y.: Doubleday, 1961).
21. *Ibid.*

one of the motives for unleashing the Red Guards on the bureaucracy during the Cultural Revolution.

The Soviets have used a variety of techniques to control the state bureaucracy. The principal tool of control is the party; the party is in effect a counter-bureaucracy charged with overseeing the governmental bureaucracies. Its organization parallels that of the state, which facilitates the monitoring of the activities of bureaucrats. Specialized sections of the CPSU Central Committee set national policy on given issues and supervise the administration of these policies by the appropriate bureaucracies. There are twenty-two sections in the Central Committee, which oversee such specific domains as heavy industry, agriculture, culture, and science and educational institutions. There are similar specialized sections in the central committees of each union republic, and at all levels of the party hierarchy individual party leaders are charged with assuring that industrial and agricultural enterprises in their areas meet production quotas and fulfill the desires of the central leadership. Their careers in the party may depend upon their abilities to regulate the sectors of the bureaucracy in their jurisdictions and to meet or exceed expected quotas and standards. Party members occupy strategic positions in the state and economic bureaucracies, and can thus serve as agents to assure that the party's will prevails. The party also controls the appointment and removal of key bureaucratic officials, and those cadres that fail to follow the party's lead or to meet expected standards can be replaced with more reliable officials.

Another means of regulation is the financial control exercised by the central bank. The power of the central leadership to increase or decrease monetary allocations to enterprises and bureaucratic agencies is an important means of control. Perhaps more important are the activities of Gosplan, the state planning agency. The planning process encompasses and seeks to regulate all of Soviet society. Gosplan agents monitor the execution of plans and seek to prevent bureaucratic localism from thwarting planned objectives. In a sense Gosplan serves as the guardian of the national priorities throughout the economic and bureaucratic systems.

Other means of regulation include overt control agencies such as the Ministry of State Control, the secret police, and citizen organizations like the People's Control Committees. All of these agencies can have access to the records of bureaucrats and enterprise managers. In communist states economic blunders, miscalculations, and the misuse of resources are not simply grounds for dismissal but crimes against the state punishable by imprisonment.

As impressive as these controls may seem, the complexity and vastness of the bureaucracy creates opportunities for evading unwanted central direction. One means of minimizing the tensions created by close regulation is "family relations" (*semeistvennost'*) between the controllers and the controlled. Such informal relationships are for the mutual protection of all concerned: since all are evaluated on the basis of their performance, it is in the best interests of the party officials, enterprise managers, and state planning officials in question to cover up for each other's errors and weaknesses. The controllers, whether party officials or state planners, look best when there are no problems in the areas under their supervision. Production quotas may be kept low, access to needed resources finagled, and actual performance misrepresented so that all will look good to their superiors. Despite strenuous efforts to crack down on this and other means of aborting control devices, "semeistvennost' " remain a problem throughout the Soviet bureaucracy.

A means of bureaucratic control unique to China is the mass movement. Mao has used mass movements such as the Great Leap Forward and the Cultural Revolution to shake up the bureaucracy, to emphasize revolutionary ideals, to combat bureaucratic resistance to central direction, and to assure his personal political pre-eminence. One of the principal motives for the Cultural Revolution was to reassert Mao's control over the state bureaucratic structures, which had fallen under the control of his rival, Liu Shao-ch'i, and were being used to circumvent and ignore Mao's leadership. However, the re-establishment of these bureaucracies during periods of consolidation demonstrates Mao's realistic acceptance of their importance in governing and changing society. Other means of keeping bureaucracies "responsive" in China include mass participation in enterprise management, mandatory manual labor by officials and technical personnel, periodic "criticism and self-criticism," and *hsia fang* (return to the countryside) campaigns.

## FROM HEROIC TO INSTITUTIONALIZED LEADERSHIP

Leadership patterns in the Soviet Union and China clearly mirror the two nations' differing stages of revolutionary and economic development. The growing diversity and technical specialization of the Soviet political elite is a function of the Soviet Union's task of having managed the advanced stages of economic modernization and planning that the country has attained. The spread of mass higher education and the availability of time for young people to attend universities have provided the Soviet Union with a highly educated pool of manpower from which political leaders can be drawn. These new leaders tend to base their claim to leadership less on charisma than on skill as "managerial modernizers." The roles and responsibilities of leaders are clearly defined and institutionalized. Even succession crises seem to be readily managed within the elite without serious constitutional repercussions. That the legitimacy of the elite seems to be accepted by the populace no matter who fills the key posts is due to the party's success in winning the acceptance and support of the masses for its leadership. The people seem ready to accept those whom the party chooses as the appropriate national leaders.

China is much less advanced in its developmental process. The leadership elite is a closed circle of revolutionary veterans. Mao's charismatic leadership still prevails as the basic source of the leadership's authority. However, the regime will soon face the task of developing new sources of authority as Mao and other revolutionary heroes disappear from politics. Yet another problem facing China's leadership is the need to institutionalize leadership roles and rules for transferring power. The frequent shifts in the political roles of the top executives will continue. While Chairman Mao has clearly prevailed in the long run, there have been times when his influence over some areas of policy was weaker than that of Liu Shao-ch'i and maybe even of Chou En-lai. Chou's party and state roles have often emanated more influence than others high in the party hierarchy. After Mao's demise, it is likely that power will be shared among groups and individuals at the highest levels. During the Tenth Party Congress in 1973, as we have said, it was strongly suggested that a form of collective leadership would be adopted to replace Mao's personal leadership. It is also likely that decisions on the transfer of power will be made by the Central Committee and Politburo.

# Mexico and Nigeria: Toward the Institutionalization of Leadership

## THE POLITICAL CONTEXT

In Mexico the political leadership is clearly dominated by the personality of the president. In practice, the president (and, in the past, former presidents) has been the key political actor in the system. The president controls 80 percent of the total public budget, makes appointments to the courts and most public offices throughout the country, and exercises direct control over state policies through his power to dismiss state and municipal governments. However, the system of leadership is somewhat more complex than it appears at first glance. Just as each president develops his own autonomy in the shadow of his predecessor, so governors and municipal leaders acquire the political skill and leverage to augment their own powers. Despite the ultimate ability of the president to intervene personally, many lower-level officials exercise important political prerogatives and privileges.

A second major factor in the Mexican leadership system is the dominance of the PRI. As we have seen, the PRI is the only political party with any hope of access to positions of national political influence. Aspiring leaders must pursue their political careers under its auspices or risk near-certain exclusion from top-level political office. Although the PRI remains open to individuals from all socioeconomic backgrounds, it is only through the party that political leadership is developed and recruited. However, the political leadership shares many aspects of its decision-making power with diverse autonomous bodies capable of making important economic and social decisions. Among these social bodies are the church, business and industrial firms, financial concerns, foreign investors, and in some cases local landholders and social notables.

In contrast to the regularized pattern of leadership in Mexico, Nigeria has experienced several rapid and fundamental changes in its leadership system.

These shifts mirror the tumultuous changes in the political system in which Nigerian leaders operate: from colony to independence to civil war to military rule. In the last few decades Nigeria's leadership system has undergone four distinct but overlapping phases. The first phase was characterized by traditional inherited elites in the emirates of the north, the kingdoms of the west and mid-west, and the decentralized lineage systems of the eastern regions. The second or colonial phase brought to the forefront educated professionals and civil servants. This elite of bureaucrats competed with traditional leaders in forming political organizations and helping Britain administer preindependence Nigeria. The independence leadership had roots in the colonial elites. Eventually political power tended to gravitate to those political leaders who could provide goods and services and who succeeded in gaining recognition through the hierarchical patron-client linkages. After the military coups of 1966, a military elite supported by bureaucrats has comprised the leadership. The current system has not completely eliminated traces of preceding systems. Indeed, it tolerates and sometimes encourages minimal input from independence leaders such as Chiefs Awolowo and Enahoro and from a network of traditional regional leaders.

A major difficulty in Nigeria has been the absence of genuine national leaders. Unlike many new states, Nigeria did not have a national charismatic leader who led the nation to independence.[22] Each region and communal group had its own heroes and leaders. After independence, the trend to regional rather than national leadership continued. Some regional leaders who have held federal public office have sought to win acceptance as leaders of the whole country, but they usually continued to be perceived by supporters and opponents alike as regional or communal leaders. Since the end of the Biafran civil war, the military leaders have achieved some success in gaining acceptance as national leaders. They have played down their ethnic origins and loyalties and sought to avoid regional favoritism. While the defeated Ibos were obviously fearful of revenge after the civil war, the military leaders have been basically evenhanded in dealing with different sections and ethnic groups in Nigeria. However, this leadership is supposedly of a temporary nature; whether new political structures will emerge to facilitate national as opposed to regional leadership when and if the military steps down is still an open question.

LEADERSHIP CHARACTERISTICS

The socioeconomic backgrounds of Mexican political leaders are widely varied. In the past a disproportionate share of top leaders were drawn from the military, but since 1940 there has been a decline in military participation at the top levels. It is genuinely possible for individuals of humble peasant origin to reach the highest levels of political leadership, including the presidency. There are indications the leadership is disproportionately drawn from the four most populous

22. However, Nnamdi Azikiwe came very close to being a national leader in the "pre-regional" phase (1940–1950).

states of Mexico: Veracruz, the Federal District, Puebla, and the state of Mexico. Most leaders have had university educations, primarily in law, and most received their higher education at the National University of Mexico. The median age of presidents and cabinet officers is relatively young: forty-five years for the five administrations prior to that of the current president, Luis Echeverría Álvarez.[23]

There are two major patterns of recruitment for top political leaders. In the first pattern, leaders emerge from the competition among the three sectors of the PRI (labor, peasant, and popular sectors). Party workers and government bureaucrats with good party credentials are thus designated for leadership positions. The second path is direct co-optation of leaders from outside the establishment. Promising leaders of dissident groups or political parties are sometimes lured into the system by offers of high-ranking leadership positions. While this procedure is far less frequent, it is important as a way of defusing opposition and preventing excessive inbreeding in the leadership.

An important aspect of both recruitment patterns is the patron-client relationship. A young aspiring politician in Mexico usually begins his career by joining the clique of an established politician. After successfully performing tasks for his patron, he may be promoted to higher positions if his patron is in turn successful in serving those above him. Eventually the young politician may be in a position to develop his own circle of supporters and followers, who will perform tasks to solidify and promote his status. Thus the route to top leadership posts is circuitous, taking the individual in and out of positions in the bureaucracy and government in the service of several patrons before reaching the peak of influence in the president's cabinet or the presidency itself.

A brief sketch of the political careers of two presidents will illustrate the backgrounds and paths to leadership of recent Mexican presidents. Adolfo López Mateos, president of Mexico in 1958–1964, was born into a lower middle-class family whose ancestors had had leading roles in the Revolution. He took advantage of his own talents and educational opportunities, working on a law degree at night while teaching literature during the day. His political career took the route of administrative service to key political leaders rather than elective office. López Mateos' first position of importance was as secretary to the governor of his state. As a result of the exposure this job gave him, he was asked to become private secretary to a man who soon became head of the Revolutionary party. He later served as secretary-general of the party's regional committee in the Federal District and involved himself in social reform projects. These undertakings brought López Mateos to the attention of then-President Cárdenas, who assisted him into other important administrative positions. He fortunately supported the winning PRI presidential candidates in nomination battles prior to the 1946 and 1952 elections, and as a reward for his services he was nominated and elected to the Senate (his first elected position) in 1946. In 1952 he was named secretary-general of the PRI and served as campaign manager

23. Wilfried Gruber, "Career Patterns of Mexico's Political Elite," *Western Political Quarterly* XXIV (September 1971): 467–482.

for the PRI presidential nominee. For this he was rewarded with a cabinet post as minister of labor. His success in that office at limiting strikes and pleasing both management and labor further strengthened his bid for the 1958 presidential nomination, which he easily won.

Luis Echeverría Álvarez, president of Mexico in 1970–1976, was also born into a family closely linked to revolutionary politics. Prior to his marriage Echeverría was an ambitious, bright student of law with no political connections or inherited wealth. He then married the daughter of an influential PRI politician — a well-connected cacique in Jalisco — and within a year he had been recruited into the PRI and begun training for a governmental career. His career too was characterized by administrative service rather than elective position. In 1954 Echeverría was named to the third highest office in the Ministry of Education, in which position he organized the army's occupation of the National Polytechnic Institute in response to "communist-fomented" student riots. In 1958 he was recruited by his new patron, Minister of Interior Díaz Ordaz, to the office of undersecretary of the Ministry of Interior. While his primary duties were to assure PRI victories in congressional and state elections, he was also involved in crushing "communist-inspired" strikes among railroad workers and gathering information on Cuban-inspired political activities in Mexico. When Díaz Ordaz became president of Mexico in 1964, he named Echeverría as minister of interior. Because of the office's important political functions, the minister of interior often becomes the successor to the Mexican presidency. Such was the case with Echeverría, who was nominated by the PRI to replace his old mentor, Díaz Ordaz, in 1970. His nomination, of course, assured his election as president.

In early 1975 a public opinion poll, the first public presidential-preferential inquiry ever noted, recorded the finding that the current secretary of the interior, Mario Moya Palencia, was preferred by almost two to one over his nearest rival, the secretary of the treasury, López Portillo. In September 1975, however, López Portillo won the PRI nomination. This suggests the possibility that a candidate not of the president's choosing, at least initially, was named his successor. Thus López Portillo the person most likely to succeed Echeverría on December 1, 1976.

Each Nigerian region has a unique pattern of leadership recruitment. Though in every region the leaders tend to be better-educated than the general population, there are major interregional disparities in educational attainment; as a group the northern political leaders have had considerably fewer years of formal education than the southern or eastern leaders. Another regional difference is the occupational backgrounds of political leaders: many of the northern political leaders have had administrative careers based on social status rather than on merit, while southerners and easterners are more likely to have had backgrounds in the liberal professions and business.[24]

24. Richard L. Sklar and C. S. Whitaker, Jr., "The Federal Republic of Nigeria," in *National Unity and Regionalism in Eight African States,* ed. Gwendolyn M. Carter (Ithaca, N.Y.: Cornell University Press, 1966), pp. 73–74.

The members of the post-1966 military elite have had various social and economic backgrounds, running the gamut from the humble backgrounds of most military figures to the millionaire family and Oxford degree of Lieutenant Colonel Ojukwu of eastern Nigeria. Upward mobility for military leaders derives primarily from their ties to former classmates and associates of superior military rank. Thus advancement in the military-political elite has been affected by the same patron-client ties that characterize the general society. Furthermore, leadership struggles within the military have not been devoid of ethnic content. There is evidence of the salience of ethnicity in the military, as in other aspects of Nigerian society.

However, one element of the military elite has demonstrated concern for the military's professionalism, discipline, and organizational efficiency, as well as for overall order and national unity for Nigeria. Most prominent among this group was General Yakubu Gowon, former head of Nigeria's Federal Military Government from 1966 to 1975. He was born in 1935, a Methodist by religion and a member of the minority Angas ethnic group. Education was Gowon's initial route to upward social mobility. After a Methodist-run primary school, he attended the government secondary school at Zaria in the Northern Region. After graduation in 1954, he immediately joined the army, then under British control. In recognition of his abilities he was selected for advanced military studies in Britain, which included a period at Sandhurst Royal Military Academy. Following his return to Nigeria, Gowon's promotions in the military were prompt. Between 1960 and 1965 he did two more stints in Britain for additional training and exposure to the problems of African nationalism.

Only a few days after Gowon's return from a third visit to Britain for training, the civilian Nigerian government was overthrown by a military coup. The leader of the coup, General Aguiyi Ironsi, immediately appointed Gowon his Chief of Staff. Resentment of Ironsi grew over the next few months, and Gowon was chosen by his military colleagues to head the successful coup against Ironsi. Gowon's term in office has been marked by many reforms at home and a growing assertion of leadership throughout Africa. Gowon was prominent as the Chairman of the Organization of African Unity and as sponsor of the Second World Black and African Festival of Arts and Culture. On July 29, 1975, nine years to the day after General Gowon came to power, he was removed following a coup led by Brigadier Muritala Rufai Muhammad. Brigadier Muhammad is a Hausa, a Moslem, and comes from northern Nigeria.

## LEADERSHIP STYLES AND SKILLS

A prominent feature of the Mexican political leadership is its freedom from ideological restraints. While the Revolution was socialist in orientation and goals, its leaders were from the beginning more pragmatists than ideologues. Socialist goals and sentiments remain an important part of the Mexican Revolutionary tradition, but mainstream PRI leaders rarely invoke socialist ideology or symbols. Even the more socially concerned leaders who have implemented major economic reforms have been guided less by ideology than by a pragmatic assessment of the consequences of the reforms.

A second pervasive aspect of Mexican leadership is authoritarianism. The presidents' powers are great and holders of the office have proved willing to use them, whether ruthlessly to suppress dissent or courageously to launch major social reforms. Authoritarianism permeates the entire system. The caciques, informal local and regional power-wielders, also exercise considerable powers, and one student of *caciquismo* writes:

> As long as the cacique does not clash with the government in power, his authority sometimes borders on sovereignty. . . . When a cacique actually dominates the local administration, the agents of the central government must obey him if they want to keep their jobs. . . . It hardly matters how strictly they are required to supervise the local administration.[25]

As influential as the caciques have been throughout Mexican history, they are now gradually giving way as local political authorities to institutionalized public officials. The mystery of power and status that has been a keystone of the caciques' privileged position is being eroded by increased education, greater exposure to the mass media, and the growing public awareness of and participation in politics. However, the new public officials are equally authoritarian in their conduct. For example, one author describes the conduct of the municipal president:

> During his period of office the municipal president is supreme in local affairs. He is the community's political leader in every respect; he is the official to whom all citizens turn when they desire services or wish to have a situation corrected; and he is the community's chief broker and representative within the state political system.[26]

Closely related to authoritarianism is personalism. The charismatic appeal of the president as a father image and symbol of the Revolution and of Mexico itself has already been noted; the president's personality dominates the political scene during his six years in office. Like authoritarianism, personalism characterizes all levels of leadership. Indeed, the patron-client system and caciquismo, both well-established Mexican leadership practices, are founded on personal loyalties and traits rather than on loyalties to, and the formal powers of, institutionalized public offices.

A fourth component of the style of Mexican political leaders is skill in balancing contending interests in such a way as to enhance their flexibility and power. The outstanding example of this skill is the performance of Lázaro Cárdenas, president in 1934–1940. Cárdenas had been handpicked by his predecessor, President Calles, and one of his first tasks was to free himself

25. Jacques Lambert, *Latin American Structures and Political Institutions,* tr. Helen Katel (Berkeley: University of California Press, 1967), p. 312.

26. Lawrence S. Graham, *Politics in a Mexican Community* (Gainesville: University of Florida Press, 1968), p. 13.

from his mentor's influence and control. Though sensitive to the frustrations of the lower classes, who were beginning to perceive the illusiveness of the goals of the Revolution, he was not blind to political realities and realized that in order to promote change he would have to free himself from the inherited *Callista* political coalition. This he accomplished by undertaking direct communication with peasants and workers. Cárdenas skillfully laid the groundwork by making a minimum number of political accommodations, e.g., naming Calles' son to a cabinet post and a Calles general as the head of the party. Then he began to take a personal hand in military appointments, promoting those loyal to him. He organized and armed peasants and workers to counterbalance Calles' influence in the military. When the showdown ultimately came, Cárdenas was able with the support of peasants and workers to suppress a military revolt and exile Calles. While Cárdenas' struggle against Calles was unique, the pattern of developing counterforces, arming them if necessary, balancing one interest against another, and building strength through key appointments is characteristic of Mexican politics.

Nigeria's efforts at establishing constitutionally defined leadership was short-circuited by the 1966 military coups and the long civil war, with the result that there is no national political style. Instead, regional patterns still prevail under the military regime of Brigadier Muhammad.

The Northern Region is simultaneously the most important in current Nigerian politics and the most traditional in general outlook and orientation. Its main political subunits are almost independent kingdoms; an illustration of their traditional leadership systems is the Hausa political system in Zaria, a vassal state in the Sokoto empire. The king was appointed from one of three dynasties that rotate in the kingship by the sultan of Sokoto. Each new king would appoint entirely new officials from top to bottom. Rule was autocratic throughout the hierarchy; any official, including the king himself, could be dismissed by the sultan. The rotation of elites made for considerable mobility. The Fulani gradually came to dominate the key elite positions of northern Nigeria. Because public office could lead to personal wealth, officeholding became the most important means of acquiring both wealth and social status.[27] This traditional pattern of leadership, characteristic of the Hausa-Fulani, persists to a considerable extent to this day, although at the upper levels political competition has replaced heredity as the principal means of recruitment to the leadership.

In contrast to Hausa authoritarianism, the Ibo have leadership councils comprised of elders who value and promote group consensus, including the acquiescence of village residents. Among the groups that allocate status are age grades, title societies, and secret men's societies. As in other parts of Nigeria, two leadership systems exist. At the regional, provincial, and now the state

---

27. M. G. Smith, "The Hausa of Northern Nigeria," in *Peoples of Africa*, ed. James L. Gibbs, Jr. (New York: Holt, Rinehart & Winston, 1965), p. 81.

level, there are formal political positions and offices; subordinate to this official structure is the traditional leadership system. Traditional village Ibo leadership is comprised of well-to-do men: those who produce the most yams, own the most property, or can afford to court their neighbors' support by granting favors and holding large social gatherings. Clearly, upward mobility is more accessible in Ibo society than in the system of inherited status and patron-client dependencies found among the Hausas. Economic achievement is the basis of political recruitment among the Ibos, and the group most important in the process is the clan hierarchy. It is the clan organization, rather than the party apparatus, that is most influential in political recruitment. Thus, a former minister in the eastern regional government attributed his appointment to his clan rather than his party membership.[28]

Traditional Yoruba leadership systems were characterized by kings whose prestige derived from divine sources. In practice, however, the king shared power with councils of state whose members included hereditary chiefs and representatives of major territorial and associational groups in the area.[29] Since the Yoruba kings could be removed by their councils, they were not as active or as politically secure as Hausa kings. Nor did the Yoruba kings have accumulations of property or fiefs as did the Hausa kings. Entrepreneurial activity among the Yoruba created a class of individuals as wealthy or more so than the kings.

After 1966, the Nigerian military leadership emphasized national economic development, ethnic reconciliation, and political reform. The military leadership was effective in bringing the war-torn and defeated Eastern Region back into the federal framework. General Gowon was clearly more sophisticated in achieving integrative reforms than his predecessor, General Ironsi. Gowon was able to implement important new governmental structures: the system of twelve states and the ethnic integration of the civil service. At the state level, his leadership relied on military and civilian administrators, most frequently drawn from the dominant ethnic group in a given state. Political concerns such as the formation of coalitions were replaced with administrative concerns. However, this situation did not always lead to political insensitivity. As the governor of a midwest state observed on a recent tour for visitors to his state, "You have noticed that no one is paying any attention to me, that is because I come here every day." His cabinet commissioners noted that they too usually spend two days a week in the countryside. "If we don't the governor has seen for himself things we should have noticed and wants to know why we're not doing something about them."[30] While this approach may represent an attempt to develop a base for political involvement after the return to nonmilitary rule, the style suggests a high degree of administrative sensitivity to public concerns.

28. Audrey C. Smock, *Ibo Politics: The Role of Ethnic Unions of Eastern Nigeria* (Cambridge, Mass.: Harvard University Press, 1971).

29. P. C. Lloyd, "The Yoruba of Nigeria," in *Peoples of Africa,* ed. James L. Gibbs, Jr. (New York: Holt, Rinehart & Winston, 1965), pp. 547–582.

30. Jean Jerskovitz, "One Nigeria," *Foreign Affairs* LI (January 1973): 405.

# BUREAUCRACIES IN MEXICO AND NIGERIA

The emergence of the modern state is characterized by the growth of its bureaucracies. In Mexico the party and the state are the main bureaucratic structures. In Nigeria the military and state are the major bureaucracies. A citizen seeking a public service — whether it be land, irrigation, credit, education, or a new road — might find himself dealing in Mexico with the party or state bureaucracies (or both) in Nigeria the military or state bureaucracies (or both).

The Nigerians adopted the British system for recruiting and promoting civil servants, which stresses the neutrality of the civil servant and seeks to recruit the best possible individuals by offering attractive benefits, particularly to those in the upper grades. These can include inexpensive housing quarters, social security, health benefits, and job security, and regular opportunities for advancement. While political criteria have generally been avoided in Nigeria, nepotism has been a problem. The strength of familial bonds leads many higher-ranking Nigerian civil servants to feel obliged to find civil service jobs for their relatives. The higher an official in the ranks the more "extended" the family, since both near and distant relatives seek jobs from the well-placed. Mexico has a long tradition of the use of public jobs as political payoffs. Supporters of winning politicians are often rewarded for their loyalty with jobs for themselves or their relatives.

At independence Nigeria inherited from its colonial parent a well-developed bureaucracy. Under British indirect rule the bureaucracy was subject to control by the British Colonial Office but was not politically responsible to the Nigerian legislatures, nor in fact to the British Parliament. Furthermore, the scope of the bureaucracy's activities in Nigeria was broad, including the formulation and application of policy and even judicial tasks. As a result, the bureaucracy was more highly developed than such other political bodies as legislatures, parties, and interest groups. But it was "foreign," in the sense that it was tainted with involvement in colonial rule and manned at the upper levels by British civil servants. Thus the task of asserting political control over the bureaucracy was made more pressing by its foreignness and more difficult by its institutional strength relative to other Nigerian political institutions.

The first effort was the "Nigerianization" of the bureaucracy — or the replacement of British colonial civil servants with native Nigerians. This process was slowed in northern Nigeria by the fear that Nigerianization would mean the dominance in the north of the better-educated southern Nigerians. The north was more concerned with "northernization" than with Nigerianization.[31] Elsewhere Nigerianization proceeded rapidly. The result was positive in that it abolished psychological and political dependence on the former colonial power, but negative in that it weakened the civil service by overloading it with young

---

31. J. Donald Kingsley, "Bureaucracy and Political Development, with Particular Reference to Nigeria," in *Bureaucracy and Political Development,* ed. Joseph LaPalombara (Princeton: Princeton University Press, 1967), p. 305.

and inexperienced officers. For example, by 1961 — one year after independence — the median age of administrative officers in the eastern Nigerian civil service was thirty-three years; the average officer had had only three-and-a-half years of previous government experience.[32] Even more importantly is the fact that competition for positions in the civil service heightened ethnic tensions, especially between northern and southern Nigeria. Indeed, fear that General Ironsi's proposed merger of the civil services of the various regions would lead to Ibo dominance exacerbated ethnic tensions in the crucial weeks before the July 1966 coup that produced the secession of Biafra and civil war.

Under military rule, the influence of the bureaucracy has expanded. The military leadership has placed civil servants at the heads of most ministries and in other positions of leadership, while simultaneously reducing or eliminating the influence of past political leaders. Prior to the coups, there were usually only one or two "political" leaders in each ministry;[33] after the coups even these few were replaced with career civil servants. In addition, the bureaucrats' independence has been increased by the disappearance of political parties and the weakness of interest groups. There is thus minimal political pressure on the bureaucrats to make concessions to special interests or to the cronies of political leaders.[34] In these ways, the bureaucracy has seen its powers increase under military rule to the point that it is the chief partner of the military in governing contemporary Nigeria.

Mexico's problem has perhaps been too much politics in the bureaucracy. For the first thirty years of the Revolution, the spoils system prevailed; governmental employees were designated and promoted on the basis of political service to the president, the party, and the various regional bosses (caciques). Not until the Cárdenas administration (1934–1940) were effective steps taken toward the creation of a professional, career-oriented civil service. Even now there is considerable overlap between politics and the civil service. Young people with education who are interested in politics often begin their careers in civil service positions. And former elected officials frequently move into civil service jobs when their terms of office expire. Finally, while the recruitment and promotion of bureaucrats is presumably based on merit, political loyalty and service to the PRI still often influence entry into and advancement within the Mexican bureaucracy.

As is true of many bureaucracies in the Third World, there are widespread allegations of the corruption of the Mexican civil service. One observer concludes that the vast majority of Mexican bureaucrats are "honest":

> Many Mexican career civil servants live almost solely on their biweekly paychecks from the government. Aside from picking up a few pesos here and there by expediting papers, temporarily borrowing minor papers in their charge, and

32. *Ibid.*, p. 311.
33. Joseph F. Maloney, "The Responsibilities of the Nigerian Senior Civil Servant in Policy Formulation," in *Nigerian Administration and Its Political Setting,* ed. Adebayo Adedeji (London: Hutchinson, 1968), pp. 118–126.
34. John M. Ostheimer, *Nigerian Politics* (New York: Harper & Row), pp. 121–123.

accepting gifts at Christmas and before Easter week from middlemen regularly engaged in government work — all in all, totaling less than four hundred U. S. dollars annually — perhaps 90 percent of the bureaucrats are "honest" and thus persons of modest incomes.[35]

However, for the upper 10 percent of the bureaucracy the opportunities and rewards for graft are greater. Top-level bureaucrats — ministers, directors of state-owned industries, and agency heads — are able to accrue immense fortunes:

> The average minister or director finishes his term with two or three houses, a good library, two or three automobiles, a ranch, and $100,000 cash; about 25 directors and ministers hold posts from which they can leave office with fifty times that amount in cash.[36]

## POLITICAL INSTITUTIONALIZATION AND LEADERSHIP IN MEXICO AND NIGERIA

Leadership patterns in Mexico and Nigeria clearly reflect the two states' different stages of political development. With a much longer history of independence, Mexico has developed and institutionalized a pattern of leadership roles that serves to bind the nation together. The public has certain expectations about how leaders will be recruited and how they will act in public office. The transformation from traditional leadership is by no means complete. Traces of caciquismo are still apparent, and patron-client bonds continue to be of vital importance to leadership recruitment and interaction.

In Nigeria, the institutionalization of new leadership roles has not been accomplished. Traditional leadership patterns, which differ from one region to the next, continue to characterize much of the political elite. It is claimed that emergent national political leadership roles were destroyed by the military coups and civil war, but it is equally probable that the military stepped in because of the absence of civilian political leaders capable of unifying a fragmented society. As is true of virtually all aspects of Nigerian society, the leadership system is significantly affected by ethnic and regional differences. Consequently, national leaders — as opposed to regional and ethnic leaders — have not yet established themselves in positions of national political responsibility. Apparently, one of the chief aims of the current military rulers is to provide a set of national leaders — even if they must be "civilianized" military figures.

# Conclusions

In all six countries political leaders are clearly differentiated from the general public by better educations, higher social class origins, and better economic positions. They are more frequently drawn from dominant cultural groups than

35. Frank R. Brandenburg, *The Making of Modern Mexico* (Englewood Cliffs, N.J.: Prentice-Hall, 1964), p. 160.
36. *Ibid.,* p. 162.

from minorities. These findings are not surprising, since these socioeconomic characteristics tend to be associated with greater interest in politics and greater propensities to participate. Thus, leaders are unrepresentative in socioeconomic background because those who are more politically active tend to be unrepresentative of society in general. This does not necessarily mean that underrepresented classes and groups will be slighted by the political leadership in the determination of public policy. Frequently, individuals of upper-class origin are very active in initiating and supporting social and economic reforms that fly in the face of their supposed class interests. Similarly, it is not unusual for leaders from lower-class backgrounds to become insensitive to the concerns of the underprivileged once they have been elevated to the political elite. The point is that elite attitudes and values are not determined by socioeconomic background.

For none of the six countries is there clear-cut evidence of a closed conspiratorial elite. Even the elites of the Soviet Union and China are open to ambitious individuals willing to become politically involved. Certainly, the circle of revolutionary leaders in China is narrow, but this appears to be a product of China's stage of development rather than a permanent feature of Chinese leadership. As the older generation of leaders dies or retires, younger leaders may move in the direction of an elite more open to technical and economic experts drawn from outside the circle of revolutionary heroes. Indeed, evidence of such a trend was seen in the party congress held in 1973.

In several countries we noted the co-optation of outside leaders into the political leadership. In common parlance, "co-optation" often implies a sellout of one's values in the process of absorption by the establishment. This is not necessarily the case. If the co-opted leaders are dynamic and skillful, they may prevail within the system rather than becoming captives of it. Co-optation may be a means of altering the establishment by introducing new ideas and new leadership skills.

Leadership styles and skills differ from one state to the next in accordance with political institutions, traditions, and values. However, two traits were found to characterize the leadership of all six countries: pragmatism and personalism. Even the allegedly ideologically committed communist leaders demonstrate flexibility in applying, and even ignoring, their doctrine in concrete situations. Flexibility is not always a virtue, however. A danger faced by many states — especially the Western democracies — is the sacrifice of principles for the sake of political expediency. If political leaders give in to the demands of powerful interests or voters to make their tasks easier or to broaden their support, they may not be serving the long-range interests of the nation as a whole. What is expedient is not always what is best.

Personalism is a feature of the leadership of all six countries, with the possible exception of Nigeria. While pure charismatic leaders are rare, nearly every top-level leader tries to develop his personality and win sympathy and support for his rule. Whether it be a yachting bachelor prime minister in Britain, a car-loving party secretary in the Soviet Union, or a poet-chairman in China, all leaders to some extent promote the cult of personality. This is not necessarily bad, since citizens' identification with a leader can foster political loyalty and national integration. It is possible that one of Nigeria's most crucial short-comings was the lack of a strong charismatic figure to unify the society after independence.

Finally, we have noted a wide variety of approaches to the imposition of political controls on bureaucracies. None seems to be entirely successful. The size and complexity of modern bureaucracies make such control difficult; it requires trained, perceptive, and powerful political leaders prepared to spend a considerable amount of time and energy mastering the bureaucracies they oversee. Such leaders are unusual even in the more developed states. The need for bureaucracies to respond to local needs and specific situations, and their ability to provide representation for special clientele groups who might otherwise not be represented, may even make total political control of the bureaucracy undesirable.

7

# The Military: Guardians or Gods?

## Introduction

In imperial Rome, the Praetorian Guard gained renown for its role as guardian of the Roman Senate, protecting it against foreign invaders as well as possible rebellion by returning victorious imperial armies. Eventually, the influence of the Praetorians became such that they could control the Senate's selection of new emperors by threatening to deny their protection or to act against the Senate itself. Similarly today, many nations' political institutions are fragile or lack legitimacy and consequently the military stands ready to interfere in politics. Harking back to ancient Rome, the term *praetorianism* is used by political scientists to refer to the condition in which civilian structures lack legitimacy and the military tends to intervene in politics and potentially to control the political process.[1]

While the principle that civilians should control the military is generally accepted, in practice praetorianism is widespread. Of fifty-one states whose origins precede 1917, thirty-two have had military coups. Of twenty-eight founded between 1917 and 1955, thirteen have experienced military coups. Some parts of the world, especially those areas designated "developing," are especially vulnerable to military rule. In the Middle East there is no tradition of civilian

---

1. Amos Perlmutter, "The Praetorian State and the Praetorian Army: Toward a Taxonomy of Civil-Military Relations in Developing Polities," *Comparative Politics* I (April 1969): 382–404.

mastery over the military, and it plays a paramount political role in virtually all the Middle Eastern states. In 1975, nine of the twenty-one Latin American republics were overtly ruled by the military; and in an additional six countries the military was the immediate power base for civilian leadership. By 1975, more than half of the thirty-eight African states south of the Sahara were ruled by military regimes.

In this chapter we will look at civil-military relations. Our attention will be focused on the forms of military involvement in politics, the reasons why the military actively intervenes in politics, and the nature and outcome of civilian attempts to control the military.

## FORMS OF MILITARY INVOLVEMENT IN POLITICS

The military can play many roles in politics, ranging from subtle pressure on private enterprise, bureaucracies, and political leaders to direct control of a nation's political and economic processes. Among the most common military tasks is the maintenance of national security against external threats, which usually involves only minimal domestic political action on the part of the military. However, in times of all-out war, the military's influence in domestic politics may be enhanced by the priority accorded the war effort. Furthermore, the military may become politically involved due to manipulation of public fears about national security by civilian leaders, as is illustrated by the actions of the United States' leaders during the Vietnam War.

The military's role in countering domestic security threats leads more readily to interference in domestic politics. Where police forces are unable to maintain internal security, the military is used to preserve domestic peace. In Third World countries, rebellion by ethnic, linguistic or, regional minorities or segments may be of a magnitude the national police cannot control. Nor is this phenomenon limited to developing nations; several industrialized nations have had to resort to the military in order to maintain domestic order. Repeatedly during the civil rights and antiwar protests of the 1960s, the United States called upon the National Guard to control public dissent. Great Britain sent the military to Ulster, and France during the 1968 uprising alerted national military units for possible duty to restore order.

There is always a latent danger that the military might refuse to protect the regime, or might be more eager to protect it against some threats than others. Military organizations are generally readier to defend the regime against alleged communist threats than against threats emanating from the far Right. Finally, persistent use of the military to control domestic political disorders frequently politicizes the military even if it has a past record of political neutrality. In Chile, for example, Allende's growing reliance on the military to quell civil political disturbances ultimately ended the Chilean military's traditional non-involvement in politics.

Military forces also have other motives for political intervention. They are corporate bodies with their own needs, norms, and objectives. The prime concerns of any corporate body are survival, well-being, and status in the society vis-à-vis other groups. When the military attempts to influence policy-makers, it exhibits behavior characteristic of a pressure group. Pressure may be aimed at augmenting military budgets for investment in weapon systems development, pay hikes, more soldiers, or even particular military policy outcomes; it is directed at those who make policy. In systems with extensive institutionalization, pressure may be put on legislators, such as the members of armed services committees in the United States Congress. In other systems, pressure may be directed at the minister of defense, the prime minister, or other key political leaders. Such pressure group activities are not inconsistent with the norm of civilian control of the military. However, excessive military lobbying may lead to military infringement on the prerogatives of the civilian leadership, particularly in the "grey areas" where civilians must decide but the military claims special expertise. In determining defense strategies and military tactics, for example, military expertise must be balanced by international and domestic political considerations. Examples of recent conflict in such grey areas include the United States military's advocacy of various military tactics during the Cuban invasion in 1961 and the Vietnamese War during the 1960s.

In some countries, military pressure may far exceed the kind of lobbying common in developed, industrialized states. The end result is often overt or covert military rule. One way this might happen is through military involvement in a political coalition. Where political parties are weak, the military may, as the most powerful political group, fill the vacuum. Weak political parties in the opposition may form a coalition with military allies to stage a coup, as was done on several occasions by the Arab Socialist party, predecessor to the Arab Baath Socialist party in Syria. Or the military may form a coalition with labor, as Peron did during his first reign in Argentina in the 1940s.

At a higher level of military political involvement is the military coup to replace civilian leaders. For a variety of reasons the military may come to believe that the existing political leaders should be replaced and act to overthrow the government. This act may be followed by the military's immediate reversion to a nonpolitical stance. Military intervention to block a specific set of policies or leaders is known as a *veto coup*. For example, Peru's military took over in 1962 to prevent the newly elected president from assuming office, and in Guatemala the military intervened in 1963 to forestall the imminent election of a leftist president.

In some cases, the military supplants the civilian leadership (or even another military regime) to enact social and economic reforms. The *reformist coup* may undertake incremental or segmental changes in the political, economic, and/or social sectors. Reformist coups, such as occurred in Indonesia in 1965, Brazil in 1964, and Peru in 1969, usually focus on economic amelioration. Frustrated by stagnant or decaying economies, military regimes initiate attempts to curb inflation, lure foreign industry, and reduce unemployment. Martin Needler points out that reformist military coups in Latin America are declining in frequency: between 1935 and 1944, 50 percent of the successful military coups in Latin America had reformist objectives; between 1945 and 1954, 23 percent had this objective; and between 1955 and 1964, only 17 percent did.[2] The reformist coup is often a response to rising public expectations aroused by mass communications and to the desire for less disparity in the distribution of opportunities.

The *revolutionary coup* differs from the reformist coup in that the goals sought by the new military rulers are much more extreme and broader. They may include land reform, health and education welfare programs, extended political participation, economic change, and industrialization. While revolutionary coups are far less frequent than veto coups or reformist coups, they sometimes occur following disastrous military defeats or in response to widespread despair at existing social, economic, and political conditions.


## WHY THE MILITARY INTERVENES

Some types of political action on the part of the military are entirely appropriate and inevitable. However, in certain countries the military has a propensity to challenge and periodically to overthrow the civilian leadership. The reasons behind such high levels of intervention are a matter of concern for political leaders and scholars alike. The military rarely intervenes in politics in response to an immediate threat of foreign attack or any other stimulus directly related to defense against external enemies. Instead, the military generally intervenes because of domestic political conditions and its own attitudes toward its place in society.

The domestic political context is one of the most influential factors in the military's propensity to intervene. Where civilian political leaders and institutions are regarded by the public as legitimate, the military is unlikely to try to overthrow the regime. An attempted military coup in such a situation would probably either fail, with disastrous effects on the military, or precipitate a civil war, an outcome most militaries are anxious to avoid. On the other hand, where legitimacy is tenuous or lacking, the threat of military coups is severe.

If political institutions able to regulate and channel political activities are lacking, or if they have failed to win general acceptance, praetorianism — the precondition for military intervention — is likely to prevail. In such a society, as one writer points out, "each group employs means which reflect its peculiar nature and capabilities. The wealthy bribe; students riot; workers strike; mobs demonstrate; and the military coups."[3] As politically sensitized groups pursue their goals without an established political format, chaos results, and the military steps in to restore order and preserve the nation. In some states, the decay of political institutions and parties leaves the military as the only organized force

2. Martin C. Needler, *Political Development in Latin America: Instability, Violence, and Evolutionary Change* (New York: Random House, 1968), p. 65.
3. Samuel P. Huntington, *Political Order in Changing Societies* (New Haven: Yale University Press, 1968), p. 196.

capable of governing. And in such a political vacuum, it is almost inevitable that the military will play an important and determining part. For these reasons, military coups are frequent in developing states that lack accepted political institutions and very rare in developed states with institutionalized and legitimized political frameworks.

Another political condition likely to result in military intervention is severe internal crisis brought on by high levels of social or ethnic conflict. When civil war threatens, the military may intervene to avert or control violence. The military may intervene in times of social and political collapse, whether attributable to internal conflict, economic paralysis, defeats dealt the state by foreign enemies, or even severe natural disasters.

The military's disposition to intervene is also influenced by past practices. If in older states there has been no overt military intervention in the past, there is unlikely to be any in the future. If a country has a history of military coups, it is likely that there will be more in the future. Some states have established traditions of military coups as the primary means of changing leaders, periodically cleansing the state of corruption, and resolving social, economic, and political crises. In these countries, it would be unreasonable to expect the military to abstain from politics in the future.

The military's propensity to intervene is also affected by the attitudes of military leaders toward their role in society. Chief among the attitudes likely to induce military intervention is the notion that the military is the guardian of the nation's values and real interests. Some military figures view themselves as the true exponents of the nation's interests, as opposed to the narrow partisan and sectional views of politicians, parties, and interest groups. If the civilian leaders act in ways military leaders feel do violence to the true national values, the military may intervene to defend the nation from the politicians. As one Bolivian president (and military officer) put it, the army should be the country's "tutelary institution . . . watching over the fulfilling of laws and the virtue of governments."[4] The values defended by the military may be the nation's constitutional principles or, more commonly, narrower values such as defense of the status quo and of privileged groups.

Military officers often view themselves as efficient organizers of men and material. The hierarchical command structure of the military may seem to them preferable to the slow-moving and inefficient state bureaucracy. The military may be distressed by the corruption of politicians. In such cases, the military may undertake a coup to cleanse the state by removing corrupt politicians and replacing them with presumably efficient and honest military leaders. Of course, the military's perceptions of its own virtues are often exaggerated, and its ability to perform more efficiently and honestly than civilians is not demonstrated by actual practice in most countries.

Finally, the military is often particularly concerned with economic modernization and expansion. Advanced technology means greater military capacity;

4. *Ibid.*, pp. 225–226.

economic prosperity means more funds for military appropriations. In states where trained technicians are in short supply, the military may want to set its technical personnel to the tasks of economic development. Believing itself to be the best modernizing force in the country, the military may stage a coup to promote economic and social reform.

## THE MILITARY AS MODERNIZERS

Since military intervention occurs most frequently in developing nations, and since coups are often justified on the grounds of social change and reform, one might ask to what extent the military is an effective modernizing agent. There is no clear-cut answer to the question, and it is a matter for debate among experts on military politics.[5] Those who argue on behalf of a modernizing role for the military point to the backgrounds of the military men themselves. Military officers now tend to spring from the new middle class, as opposed to the aristocracy. Since they are able to identify with the middle class in industry, government, and the professions, they tend to represent those interests rather than feudal and repressive aristocratic interests.[6] Junior officers are seen as salaried bureaucrats or corporate personnel seeking personal advancement opportunities and, therefore, reforms in the inhibiting anachronistic societal structure.

Others point to the military's technical orientation and its experience with the latest technology in societies often devoid of technological applications to the environment. It is argued that the military is interested in promoting the technological development of the nation because such improved technical capacity will increase the military's capabilities. Furthermore, the military is sometimes idealized as an effective modernizer because of its allegedly efficient hierarchical organization, which in many developing countries is more highly developed and less prone to corruption than the governmental and private bureaucracies. In short, it is often argued that the military is an important modernizing force in developing countries because of its middle-class orientation, its commitments to nationalism and technological progress, and its organizational features.

Yet other evidence suggests that these expectations are not realized. Essential to political modernization is the development and gradual increase in effectiveness of political institutions, and especially of political parties. When military regimes inhibit the development of political parties, prohibit elections, or prevent other political bodies from operating — as many have done — political institutionalization is retarded. On the other hand, though many of the institutions that process demands to the center and those that make policy at the center are weakened by military intervention, bureaucatic structures may be strengthened. Military governments generally prevent the operation of most

5. For a summary of some major arguments on both sides, see *The Military and Modernization,* ed. Henry Bienen (Chicago and New York: Aldine-Atherton, 1971).
6. Eric A. Nordlinger reviews this argument in "Soldiers in Mufti: The Impact of Military Rule Upon Economic and Social Change in the Non-Western States," *American Political Science Review* LXIV (December 1970): 1132–1133.

political bodies but permit the state bureaucracy to continue functioning. Indeed, bureaucrats are natural allies of the military, and the latter often draws upon civil servants to fill top-level governmental positions formerly held by politicians. The presence of civilians in high positions helps to legitimize the military's rule. The strength of the alliance between the military and the bureaucracy has led one analyst to assert that military regimes are run by "armed bureaucrats."[7]

The military may not necessarily solve the problems of conflicting regional, linguistic, and ethnic groups, but it does prevent them from pursuing their interests through their own parties within the political system. The elimination of party politics may well create an order conducive to eliminating some of the ill effects of such conflict in a developing society. However, regional or ethnic interests in Pakistan, Sudan, Chad, Nigeria, Zaire, and Indonesia have aroused such high levels of conflict that violence has erupted and threatened national unity despite the presence of military regimes.

The effectiveness of military regimes in the pursuit of economic modernization is dubious. Often the military regime, although publicly committed to economic development, expends most of the state's resources on military undertakings and equipment. The much-vaunted organizational skills of the military are not easily redirected from military planning and organization to the tasks of economic planning and modernization. The Spartan qualities that are often cited among the desirable attributes of the military do not persist in practice; military rule has in many developing countries also meant a decrease in austerity. The importation of luxury automobiles rises, as do the salaries of civil servants and other state personnel. A good example is the case of Ghana, where the military ousted the inefficient government of Nkrumah and promised greater emphasis on economic development. In fact, a careful study of the performance of Ghana's first military regime (1966–1969) suggests that it was more concerned with the military's own corporate interests. More was spent for military and defense purposes relative to industry and agriculture than was the case under the Nkrumah regime. As a result, military rule in Ghana has initially resulted in serious unemployment, economic stagnation, and more rapid inflation than under Nkrumah, while per capita GNP remained constant.[8]

Nordlinger's study of some seventy-four nations (1957–1962) suggests that as economic modernizers militaries are deficient at stimulating increased agricultural productivity, investment, and educational expansion. According to his statistical correlation, military rule is only slightly associated with increased industrialization.[9] Only in tropical Africa are there strong positive correlations between military regimes and positive changes in agricultural productivity, industrialization, and educational expansion. In other parts of the world military rule has produced economic decline rather than growth.

7. Edward Feit, *The Armed Bureaucrats* (Boston: Houghton Mifflin, 1973).
8. Robert M. Price, "Military Officers and Political Leadership: The Ghanian Case," *Comparative Politics* III (April 1971): 361–387.
9. Nordlinger, "Soldiers in Mufti," p. 1139.

In general, military leaders are poor modernizers, particularly in the economic sector. However, in some nations (Egypt and Turkey, for example) the military has with the aid of technocrats made a positive contribution toward development. Military regimes can be expected to encourage economic growth and to contribute to political institutionalization only when internal cleavages do not inhibit that end.

Military intervention is also a function of a nation's stage of political and economic development.[10] Nations in the first years of independence face many challenges with weak political institutions. Demands for urban development, housing, sanitation, schools, and jobs are constant, but governmental capacity is limited. Conflict between ethnic, linguistic, and regional groups over the allocation of scarce resources or participation in national policy-making puts immense stress on any government, new or old. Compounding these problems are politicians who often pursue oligarchic goals and ineffective, overstaffed, and underskilled bureaucracies that tempt the military to intervene in the interests of modernization and efficacy. The low salaries of public officeholders and administrators provoke graft and corruption — specifically, the allocation of public resources for private benefit — which tends to inhibit development. It is in a context of fragile institutions and factional disputes among oligarchical political parties that militaries are most likely to intervene.

## CIVILIAN ATTEMPTS
## TO CONTROL THE MILITARY

In order to maintain control over the military, civilian regimes have utilized several tactics, some more successfully than others. Among the more widely used tactics are co-optation of military leaders into civilian politics, budget payoffs and arms modernization, involvement of the military in socioeconomic development, shifts in high command, socialization of the military to inculcate the norm of civilian control, and the formation of rival military and paramilitary groups to counterbalance the traditional military.

In liberal democracies the norm of civilian mastery is usually well established and accepted by the military without question. Furthermore, democractic forms of government rely on a strict hierarchy of authority in which civilians head the military; for example, the president of the United States serves as Commander-in-Chief and appoints civilian secretaries of the navy, the air force, and defense. This system is more likely to work in developed industrialized nations than in developing political entities. Years of socialization have been necessary to produce military leaders willing to accept this pattern.

In Third World countries where the norm of civilian mastery is not as well established, asserting and maintaining civilian control is difficult. One

---

10. See Robert D. Putnam, "Toward Explaining Military Intervention in Latin American Politics," *World Politics* XX (October 1967): 83–110.

approach that has been successful in several countries with past histories of military intervention is to develop political counterforces to offset the natural advantage the military derives from its control of the instruments of force. Political parties, for example, can be powerful counterweights to military power. Parties can be used to organize public support for the regime, and thus raise the specter of civil war in the event of an attempted military coup. The military may be permitted to participate in party politics — as we shall see that it was in Mexico — or it may be primarily an object of party supervision and surveillance — as it has generally been in the Soviet Union.

A similar strategy is to create a rival, quasi-military organization, ostensibly to defend domestic security, as opposed to protecting against external attack. Such a group may take the form of secret police, such as in Nazi Germany, or of a national police force, as in the Philippines. Sometimes civilian control groups dominated by certain classes develop spontaneously. In nineteenth-century Europe, the emerging bourgeoisie thought of itself as the proper instrument of civilian control. This led to conflicts over control of the military between the bureaucracy and the aristocracy, which often domesticated the officer corps. In contemporary Third World nations, such conflict is less verbal. Peasants, who are more prevalent in nonindustrialized developing nations than are the urban bourgeoisie and workers, may develop their own armed guerrilla units (e.g., the Philippines, Vietnam, India) to counter the military forces.

The Mexican case suggests another means of civil control: co-optation. Co-opted military leaders are appointed to civilian policy-making positions in governmental bureaucracies, enterprises, and in the ruling political party, and are thus merged with the bureaucracy and leading party.

Among the long-term factors often considered crucial to the ability of civilians to dominate the military is the size of the middle class. It is argued by some that the larger the middle class, the less likely is direct military intervention, since a dominant middle class is apt and able to insist upon the norm of civilian control of the military.[11] Others dispute this assertion, demonstrating that there is no statistical relationship between the size of the middle class and the frequency of military coups.[12] A related issue is the social background of the military leadership; some argue that the greater the number of officers of middle-class origin, the more likely is the military to intervene in politics.[13]

The size of the middle class is only one in a series of social conditions associated with frequent military involvement in politics. One writer has de-

11. See Samuel Huntington's reply that the size of the middle class nevertheless does affect the impact and significance of military intervention. Huntington, *Political Order,* pp. 220–222.

12. José Nun, "A Latin American Phenomenon: The Middle Class Military Coup," in Institute of International Studies, *Trends in Social Research in Latin American Studies: A Conference Report* (Berkeley: University of California, 1965), pp. 68–69.

13. Manfred Halpern, "Middle Eastern Armies and the New Middle Class," in *The Role of the Military in Underdeveloped Countries,* ed. John J. Johnson (Princeton: Princeton University Press, 1962), p. 295. See also Guy J. Pauker, "Southeast Asia as a Problem Area in the Next Decade," *World Politics* XI (April 1959): 339–340.

scribed the social conditions in societies where the military is most likely to intervene:

> The dominant social forces are the great landowners, the leading clergy, and the wielders of the sword. Social institutions are still relatively undifferentiated, and the members of the ruling class easily and frequently combine political, military, religious, social, and economic leadership roles. The most active groups in politics are still basically rural in nature. Families, cliques, and tribes struggle unremittingly with each other for power, wealth, and status.[14]

To the extent that civilian leaders are able to change their societies and eliminate factors associated with praetorianism, the prospects for mastering the military will be enhanced.

Political involvement on the part of the military takes many forms, but direct military intervention and takeover is much more likely in developing nations. We have seen that there are many factors associated with direct intervention, including economic stagnation, political instability, and *immobillisme*. Nor have we exhausted the list of reasons for political intervention by the military. Others have pointed to threats to the military's professional interests, defense budget cuts, and ascendancy over the military by a rival policy group as grounds for military intervention. Desire for upward mobility and psychological motivations have also been noted in studies of direct military political involvement. The military is clearly an important route to upward social mobility in societies where status roles are dominated by traditional and capitalist elites.

The following case studies offer examples in each category of political system of successful and unsuccessful efforts to control the military. We shall look at the political activities of the military and civilian efforts to control the military in each of the six countries.

# Britain and France:
## The Military in and out of Politics

### BRITAIN: UNQUESTIONED CIVILIAN MASTERY

The most recent military intervention in British politics occurred in the seventeenth century, when the revolt of the army brought about a military dictatorship under Oliver Cromwell. The king was executed; unsympathetic members of Parliament were purged; ultimately Parliament was expelled and the Puritan army became the government of England. Although the interregnum lasted only twelve years, it left in the British a deeply ingrained mistrust of political action by the army and a strong antimilitarism. In the more than three hundred years

---

14. Huntington, *Political Order*, p. 199.

that have passed since, the British have refused to place much political power or trust in the military or its officers.

The primary domestic political activity of the British military is to convey its needs and interests to the government. And even this pursuit is limited in scope: there is no military lobby in Britain, unlike the United States, to press for greater defense expenditures or support military strategic priorities. This circumstance in part reflects the nature of the British political scene; interest groups rarely devote much attention to Parliament since party discipline assures Parliament's acceptance of government proposals. No doubt the military does argue its needs — as indeed it should — within the ministry of defense and related ministries. But most commentaries on interest group politics in Britain do not list the military among the most active and powerful pressure groups.

The British military's lack of politicization is especially surprising in light of the developments of the last thirty years. Once a world power of the first order, Britain is now highly dependent upon other nations for its defense. Britain's navy, long the world's most powerful, has slipped to the rank of a second-rate power. Though loss of the empire and status as a world power has necessitated the abandonment of traditional British military policies, the political leaders have yet to agree upon new policies and strategies. Britain's nuclear weapons program has been curtailed, and other important military procurement programs were precipitously cancelled by politicians. There are far too many high-ranking officers for the military tasks at hand. (For example, in 1964 the navy had eighty admirals and a fleet of fewer than two hundred ships!) Despite these numerous grounds for discontent and politicization, the British military remains politically uninvolved.

The army's long involvement in controlling urban guerrilla warfare in Northern Ireland has also tested the traditional norm of civilian mastery of the military. There are indications that the army and the government differed over the approach to the Protestant general strike that ultimately destroyed the first experiment with Catholic-Protestant power-sharing.[15] The government wanted to use the army to break the strike but the army command apparently argued successfully against this on the grounds that the army was not prepared or equipped to act against the strikers. Then in 1975, the army commander complained publicly that the government's policies were hindering the army's campaign against terrorism. Annoyed by the termination of internment without trial of suspected terrorists and by the reduction of the army's strength in Northern Ireland, the general broke the customary silence of the military and was sternly rebuked for having done so.

Another indication of the military's political aloofness is the near-total absence of former military figures in the political world. It is not unusual in other countries for retired officers to pursue political careers; examples are Eisenhower in the United States and de Gaulle in France. However, in the past

15. *The Times* (London), 14 April 1975.

300 years there has only been one British prime minister with a military background and that was nearly 150 years ago.

The most important means of controlling the British military has been parliamentary control of the army and navy. Members of Parliament recognized early that the military was potentially a weapon the monarch might use against them. As a result, budgetary controls over the military were imposed as a means of assuring not only civilian control but also Parliament's independence from the monarch. In addition to the budgetary powers exercised by Parliament, the legislation authorizing a standing army was of limited duration, requiring renewal by Parliament as frequently as twice a year. In these ways Parliament has been able to maintain constant surveillance over the military's conduct.

Another important factor in the control of the military is Britain's historical reliance on the navy, rather than a land army, as its primary means of defense. The military's political role has been restricted simply because it is harder for a navy deployed on the seas to intervene in domestic politics than it is for an army based in the heart of the country.

More important than formal and legal restraints on the military is the impact of a three hundred-year-old tradition of political uninvolvement. The socialization of military officers informally instills the norms of civilian supremacy and abstention from political action. The informal restraints imposed by such values and orientations make it virtually unthinkable for a British officer to defy civilian authority and seek public support for a political act. If he did so, his fellow officers would repudiate him and the public, also socialized to the norm of civilian mastery, would reject him. The ingrained attitudes of officers and civilians alike serve as a much stronger assurance of military loyalty to political leaders than could any set of laws. If the generals and admirals chose to, they could defy such laws; they will not choose to because of values derived from an antimilitarist tradition dating back to Cromwell.

## FRANCE: THE DEPOLITICIZATION OF A POLITICIZED ARMY

There are two competing traditions of civil–military relations in France. That of the nonpolitical army obedient to the civilian leadership earned the French army the label "the Great Mute" for its quiet acceptance of civilian mastery even in times of political turmoil. While the military made its interests and needs known through political channels, it was subordinate and obedient to civilian leaders throughout most of the nineteenth century and the first forty years of the twentieth century.

The second tradition is that of a politically active army — or at least sections of the army. In part this tradition is based upon the French citizen's receptivity to popular appeals by the "man on the white horse." On several occasions military leaders have offered themselves as saviors of France, sometimes through the normal political process (for example, Louis Napoleon,

The military may well be the source of political leadership even in countries that maintain mastery of the military. Charles de Gaulle as president of France emphasized his military background by frequently appearing in public in his army uniform and by preferring to be addressed as mon général rather than as monsieur le président. Nigeria's two military regimes have been involved in development as well as national security. This photo shows state military leaders opening the Niger Bridge at Onitsha. The model for military involvement in development is the People's Liberation Army of China, engaged here in the construction of the East-West section of the Sinkiang-Tibet Highway. Infrastructure such as highways is important not only for security, but for promotion of economic exchange as well.

Marshal MacMahon, General Boulanger,[16] and Marshal Pétain) and sometimes by imposing their rule in defiance of established procedures (for example, Napoleon Bonaparte and Charles de Gaulle). Recently the tradition of the politicized military has been manifested in the form of quasi-military coups, the first of which occurred in 1940 at the time of France's defeat by Germany. As the legal civilian government capitulated and transformed itself into the Vichy regime, General Charles de Gaulle, a little-known junior cabinet member and second-level military leader, fled France against the orders of his civilian masters and established a "provisional government." However laudable de Gaulle's action, which helped to defeat the Nazis and stirred the resistance and hopes of the defeated French people, it was an instance of political insubordination by a military leader justifiable only on grounds similar to those invoked by generals heading military coups around the world: the political leaders were corrupt and betrayed the nation's trust; therefore the military leader will establish a new government. The only thing that distinguished de Gaulle's action from a typical coup was that it took place in exile and created a government that controlled little territory. (Only a few French colonial territories initially accepted his leadership.) Ultimately, de Gaulle's action was legitimized by success, and his triumphal return to France vindicated his act of insubordination.

Again in 1958, de Gaulle came to power as the result of a near-coup. The French army in Algeria joined a revolt of French colonial settlers to prevent compromise with the Algerian freedom fighters. The rationale for de Gaulle's 1940 action served as a precedent: the army declared that the corrupt and bungling governments of the Fourth Republic were betraying French national interests by considering independence for Algeria; therefore action must be taken to defend France from its politicians. The revolt quickly spread to Corsica, where parachutists assisted civilian rebels in seizing government buildings and communications centers. Amidst threats that troops would be parachuted into Paris, the politicians turned to de Gaulle in the hope of averting military action and civil war. There is no evidence that de Gaulle personally incited the revolt, but some of his supporters were actively involved. The military and civilian rebellion in effect vetoed the leadership of the Fourth Republic and thrust de Gaulle upon the politicians. To be sure, de Gaulle enjoyed considerable independent popularity in France, but his return to power was made possible by illegal action and insubordination on the part of the army in Algeria. Once again, the quasi-coup was legitimized by the overwhelming popular approval accorded the new Fifth Republic. A referendum on the new constitution was approved by nearly 80 percent of the voters; only the communists and a small handful of leftists campaigned against the constitution.

A number of developments since 1945 had politicized the French army.[17]

16. Boulanger's followers contemplated more direct action, but the threatened coup failed when Boulanger chose to spend the evening with his mistress rather than mobilizing the masses milling through the streets of Paris.

17. See John Stewart Ambler, *Soldiers Against the State: The French Army in Politics* (Garden City, N.Y.: Doubleday, 1968); George A. Kelly, *Lost Soldiers* (Cambridge, Mass.:

In contrast to the relatively peaceful dismantling of the British Empire after World War Two, the French became entangled in long and debilitating colonial wars in Indochina and Algeria. Involved in guerrilla wars for fifteen years, the French army had become isolated from the nation. Its new techniques of psychological warfare led the army to take political action first in the colonial territory in question and ultimately in the homeland. The military felt betrayed by the civilian governments that rotated in and out of office with alarming frequency during the Fourth Republic. It sensed accurately the public's withdrawal of legitimacy from the Fourth Republic, and was as a result encouraged to take political action. A poll taken in early 1958 revealed the low degree of legitimacy accorded the civilian leadership: only 8 percent of those polled said they would oppose or even withhold approval of a military coup; only 13 percent would have done as much to oppose a Communist coup.[18]

Once it had become politicized, it was not easy to depoliticize the French army. Thus, when de Gaulle decided to grant independence to Algeria, the military acted against him, once again considering itself the guardian of France's true interests and de Gaulle their betrayer. When the military commander of Algiers, General Massu, was dismissed in 1960 for publicly opposing de Gaulle's offer of self-determination to Algeria, a right-wing civilian revolt took place in Algeria. While the army remained loyal in this crisis, it was the public expression by a military figure of opposition to the government's policy that had triggered the revolt.

A year later, in April 1961, the army was more directly involved in an attempted coup d'état led by four retired generals opposed to Algerian independence. The chief sources of military support for the revolt were the elite paratroop units stationed in Algeria and the French Foreign Legion. In the face of threatened paratroop attacks on Paris, de Gaulle appealed for public help. The revolt was quelled by the rallying of public support for de Gaulle, even including the communists, and the resistance of loyal military units in Algeria to the efforts of the insurgents to expand their control. In subsequent months rightwing extremists (known as the Secret Army Organization, OAS) led by former General Salan, who had been involved in the abortive coup, engaged in acts of terrorism in Algeria and France. But the threat of military rebellion was ended.

The depoliticization of the military was achieved primarily through the Fifth Republic's demonstration of effectiveness and legitimacy. The Fourth Republic's inability to act and declining public acceptance had fatally undermined its efforts to control the military. In contrast, de Gaulle's regime made effective decisions and commanded overwhelming popular acceptance. The very policy that the army had rejected — independence for Algeria — was sustained by the broadest popular consensus. The principle of Algerian self-determination was approved by 75 percent of French voters in the referendum of

MIT Press, 1966); and Paul-Marie de la Gorce, *The French Army: A Military-Political History* (New York: Braziller, 1963).
    18. *Sondages* 1958 No. 3: p. 50.

January 1961, and the actual grant of independence to Algeria was ratified by 90 percent of the voters in April 1962.

Following the abortive coup of April 1961, the government acted to break up the paratroop and Foreign Legion units involved in the coup. It was the professional military rather than the conscript soldiers who had violated civilian supremacy. Since draftees are unlikely to become involved in actions that flout the will of the civil government, the weakening of the elite professional elements of the army helped assure the political reliability of the army. Indeed, the reluctance of draftees in Algeria to join the generals' revolt may have been a key factor in the easy defeat of the intended coup; it serves as evidence for those who see conscription as a means of assuring civilian control of the military.

Perhaps the most important factor in re-establishing military loyalty to civilian leadership was the failure of the Algerian revolt. The leading figures in the revolt were tried and condemned to death or long prison terms (although no executions were actually carried out and all the conspirators in prison had been pardoned by 1968). Thus the 1940 and 1958 precedents of successful military intervention have been supplanted by the decisive defeat of 1961. Such a defeat is unlikely to stimulate further efforts at forceful military intervention in politics.

At present the French military is involved in only the lowest-level political action. No longer as influential in Gaullist circles or in parliament, the army pursues its interests through the appropriate ministerial channels. And it is not very successful there. There are indications of malaise in the military stemming from economic causes: insufficient appropriations for favored weapons, low pay, and low social status. And there are also signs that the military did not participate in de Gaulle's dramatic reshaping of French military strategy. At least some sectors of the military have been unenthusiastic about the emphasis on the development of an independent French nuclear force and about France's withdrawal from the military integration portions of the North Atlantic Treaty Organization (NATO). De Gaulle's firm attachment to his own strategic concepts and disdain for interest group intermediaries appear to have led to the exclusion of the military from the reorientation of French defense priorities since 1962.

Whether the military will remain politically quiescent is uncertain. As long as the regime remains legitimate in the eyes of the public, it is unlikely that the military will act. But it is possible, and some believe likely, that the military would intervene again under certain circumstances. If the communists were to seek power by extralegal means — highly improbable — the military might intervene. However, it is unlikely that the military would act to block legal assumption of power by a leftist government that included communists. In times of extreme political turmoil the military may hold the balance of power. For example, at the height of the May 1968 crisis de Gaulle secretly consulted military leaders to assure himself of their support should it have become necessary to confront the striking workers and rioting students. De Gaulle received the pledge of support he sought, but proved able to control the situation without recourse to military action. In short, the French army has resumed its traditional stance as the Great Mute after experimenting for more than twenty years with an active political role. It seems likely to maintain its aloofness from politics in the normal course of events.

# China and the Soviet Union: Party Control of the Military

It is a major concern of the political leadership in communist states to assure the party's monopoly on political, economic, and social power. In most sectors of society this goal is readily achieved. However, the job of controlling the military presents special problems to the party. On the one hand, a powerful, efficient, and militarily skilled army is necessary to defend the country and the revolution and to pursue revolutionary goals abroad. Eternal vigilance to external military threats is a basic tenet of Marxist-Leninist doctrine, which posits the imperialist drives and natural hostility toward socialist states on the part of capitalist powers. In addition, communist regimes have periodically used their armed forces to "export the revolution," as Trotsky advocated after the Bolshevik success in Russia; to pursue aggressive foreign policy goals, as in the Soviet invasion of Poland in 1939; or to intervene in the domestic affairs of fellow communist states, as in the 1968 intervention in Czechoslovakia. On the other hand, a military force capable of responding to external threats is a potential rival to the party in internal politics. The army alone has sufficient physical force to take over political power should it so wish. The unified and spirited army necessary to external defense might challenge the party's pre-eminence. Consequently, both China and the Soviet Union have devised elaborate means of controlling the military's domestic political activities.

## THE SOVIET UNION:
## PARTY DOMINANCE OF THE MILITARY

There is no tradition of an active political role for the military in the Soviet Union. In contrast to China, the revolutionary struggle was relatively short and the consolidation of political control in the civil war era (1917–1921) did not lead to excessive political dependence on the military. In the years following the Bolshevik Revolution and the civil war, the norm of party pre-eminence has been solidly ingrained through the socialization process and defended by the acts of the party leaders.

Acceptance of the Leninist notion of the party's absolute pre-eminence is accompanied by an evident mistrust of the military on the part of Soviet party leaders. Their suspicion dates back to the early days of the Bolshevik regime, when 75 percent of the new Red Army's officers were former officers in the czarist imperial army. Their loyalty — especially during the civil war — had to be closely monitored. But even after the development of a communist officer corps, the party leadership lacked confidence in the military's political reliability. Even the slightest sign of growing military interest in politics was responded to, sometimes ruthlessly, by the party leaders. For example, Stalin's responses to his perception of military disloyalty were the execution of eight of the highest-ranked officers and a mass purge of the Red Army's entire officer corps. And Stalin did this in 1937 — at the risk of weakening the military when the Nazi threat was rising. (During the de-Stalinization campaign of the late 1950s, Khrushchev claimed that the supposed military disloyalty was entirely imaginary and posthumously rehabilitated the victims of this purge.)

Under Stalin's successors regulation of the military has been firm but less brutal. The means of control have centered on the party and the secret police. The party's controls include the permeation of the military with party members, the use of special organizational structures, and the presence of political officers in each military unit. Nearly all military officers are members of the party; estimates of party membership at the top level of military leadership go as high as 95 percent. Most of the recruits are also members of the party or of Komsomol, the party's youth organization, and thus are subject to party discipline and control. The party's organization for the military membership is linked directly to the Soviet Central Committee, rather than to territorial party units. The head of each party unit in the military is an appointed political officer known as a "zampolit," and unlike the party leaders of nonmilitary sections he is not elected but appointed. There is a zampolit assigned to each company (approximately 150 men). He is charged with the political education of the troops, maintenance of troop morale, sponsorship of social and cultural events, and, of course, the political obedience of both troops and officers.

Alongside the vast party control apparatus in the military is a parallel structure of secret police. KGB agents are assigned to each division in the Soviet armed forces to deal not only with political loyalty and counterespionage, but also with the military's morale, discipline, and effectiveness. They are also charged with watching the party officials assigned to the military by the party. In short, the secret police watches the party watchdogs. Since the secret police is armed (sometimes rather heavily for a police organization), it provides the civilian leadership with an alternative to the military. The tremendous expansion of the secret police and its establishment as a "state within a state" gave Stalin an alternative means of compulsion to check the military as well as other sectors of society. The docility of the army during the purge of 1937 illustrates the success with which the secret police could be used to neutralize the power of the army.

The Soviet leadership also seeks to maintain civilian supremacy through the socialization process. That the party is representative of the people and must have primacy over all other social forces, including the military, is emphasized in public education, in special political education courses for civilians and military personnel, and in military training programs.

Despite the limitations on its activities, the military is by no means without political power. Most of its actions are those of an interest group promoting its own point of view. Like military organizations in Western states, the Soviet army presses for greater appropriations, new military programs, and higher pay. In addition, the centralized state control of the economy leads the Soviet military to seek influence in the determination of national economic priorities. The military frequently speaks out in favor of greater investment in heavy industry and less investment in consumer goods. The Soviet military also often takes a "hard-line" foreign policy stance — opposing policies of detente with the West and China. Given the primacy and independence of the party leaders, the military does not always prevail. Indeed, it often appears that the military's advocacy of certain policies is used to justify the leadership's decisions but is rarely the determining factor in decision-making.

The military has access to the political process through both the state and the party. In most Western states, the defense ministry is headed by a civilian and has a number of other civilian leaders. In the Soviet Union the minister of defense is a professional military officer (currently Marshal Grechko) and the entire staff of the ministry is composed of professional military men. The military is thus represented in the Council of Ministers, and from this point of access can influence government policy.

The army is also represented in party decision-making bodies. Usually between 8 and 10 percent of the members of the Soviet Central Committee are professional soldiers. Representation of this limited magnitude does not threaten civilian control but offers the military an opportunity to voice its point of view. At the level of the Politburo, the military is usually unrepresented. Marshal Zhukov briefly held a full seat on the Politburo in 1957, but he was the first career officer to do so; in 1973 Marshal Grechko became the second military officer to serve on the Politburo. His sudden promotion to full membership in the Politburo without having first served an apprenticeship as a candidate member led to speculation about a possible increase of military influence in the Soviet party. However, by the end of 1975 there was no indication that the military's political influence had grown despite Grechko's presence on the highest party body.

In general, the military's political influence reaches a peak during succession crises, when leaders are contending for top party positions. An illustration is in the period leading to Khrushchev's rise to power. In the wake of Stalin's death, the party leaders were concerned about the potential influence of L. P. Beria, the powerful head of the secret police, and recruited the support of the military, which resented the secret police. Once Beria had been executed and the powers of the secret police reduced, the military was rewarded for its support with, among other things, a seat on the Central Committee for Marshal Zhukov. As Khrushchev squared off against his first major party rival, G. Malenkov, he received Zhukov's support because of his advocacy of greater military appropriations. When Malenkov was removed, Zhukov became minister of defense and the first military officer to be named a candidate member of the Politburo. In June 1957 Khrushchev's position was challenged by the "anti-party" group led by Molotov and other party leaders. Again, Zhukov sided with Khrushchev and the "antiparty" group was defeated, partly because the military supported Khrushchev. Zhukov was rewarded with full membership on the Politburo. However, Khrushchev had by then consolidated his control and could afford to reassert the primacy of the party over the military. Four months later, Zhukov was dismissed as minister of defense and removed from his party posts on both the Politburo and the Central Committee. Khrushchev was enabled to do so without danger by his pre-eminence and his skill in exploiting the jealousies and rivalries aroused in other officers by Zhukov's rapid political ascent.

By focusing solely on the military's role, this description of Khrushchev's rise to power oversimplifies a highly complex political struggle. Other groups and individuals were involved. It is unlikely that Zhukov and the military were determining, or even the most important, factors in Khrushchev's success. By highlighting the military's role, however, we have illustrated how the military may find its political influence heightened during succession crises, how political leaders can manipulate the military in their drive for power, and how once the struggle for power within the party is resolved the supremacy of the party is forcefully reasserted.

The military's role in Khrushchev's removal from office is less clear. There were signs of military discontent in 1963 and 1964 over Khrushchev's reduction of troop levels and military appropriations, and one of the new leadership's first acts was to grant the military larger appropriations and restore higher troop levels. But there is no direct evidence to indicate that the military took an active part in ousting Khrushchev. In any case, when Khrushchev found himself in trouble he could not call upon the military for support in 1964 as he had in 1957. This discretionary withholding of support for the man in power was an important political act on the part of the military, even if it lacked the drama and visibility of military interventions during Khrushchev's rise to power.

Cognizant of the military's unique potential as a rival, the Soviet Communist party is vigilant with regard to military political action. The elaborate mechanisms of civilian control are unparalleled anywhere outside the communist world. Nevertheless, the military still has political influence during times of internal party competition since it constitutes a power base for which rival leaders inevitably compete. Furthermore, even in normal times, the military's professional expertise is needed by the party policy-makers in order to draft defense policies, national economic priorities, and foreign policies. The party's need of the military's expertise enhances the influence of the military on its civilian masters.


CHINA:
CHAIRMAN MAO AND THE MILITARY

In contrast to the rapidity of the Bolshevik Revolution, the revolutionary struggle in China lasted from the early 1920s until the ultimate communist victory in 1949. Throughout this "preliberation" era, the Communist party and its military arm, the People's Liberation Army (PLA), were united and their task was revolutionary victory through military action. After liberation in 1949, the PLA retained considerable power: it was responsible for consolidating political control in the provinces. Not until four years later was the party able to gain effective control over the military in this area of endeavor. Thus, the Chinese communists have a heritage of military–party merger that complicates the problem of maintaining civilian mastery over the military.

Mao Tse-tung has always accepted the Leninist doctrine of party primacy; as one of Mao's slogans has it, "The party commands the guns and guns must never be allowed to command the party." But Mao was also a realist who recognized that the success of the revolution in China depended upon the formation of an army; another of his slogans is, ". . . political power grows out of the barrel of a gun." Given the conflict between the ideal of party control and the reality of military necessities, the PLA has had a prominent role in the politics of the People's Republic of China.

## CIVILIAN CONTROL OF A POLITICAL ARMY

Four factors have prompted continued military involvement in Chinese politics. First, the scarcity and ineffectiveness of party cadres have forced the regime to rely upon the well-organized and efficient military to undertake political control and governmental administration in many parts of China. Second, the military, both before and after liberation, has been called upon by Mao to lead the revolution when the party failed to meet his expectations. Third, the military has been used by Mao as a lever to combat opposition to his rule within the party. Finally, external threats have led to military preparation for potential armed conflicts on several occasions: the Korean War (1950–1953), the Vietnam War (1965–1973), and border disputes with India (1962) and the Soviet Union (1964 to present).

All these factors and the tensions aroused by the Cultural Revolution have contributed to the involvement of the military in domestic politics. Though politicized, however, the military has rarely taken political initiatives on its own. As in many developing countries, the Chinese military has on occasion thrust itself upon the civilian leadership; the most prominent example is Marshal Lin Piao's attempted coup in 1971. It has also been called into politics by the civilian party elite. Unlike many other developing countries, China has so far been successful in integrating and managing the military. Among several means of civilian control, three deserve special attention: (1) the establishment of party control mechanisms, (2) changes in military structures and personnel, and (3) the involvement of the military in the modernization process.

The party's controls start at the top with the Military Affairs Committee of the Central Committee. This committee is headed by Mao, and its members are largely military officers drawn from the party's Central Committee. It oversees the military's actions for the party and advises the party on military policy.

The parallel state institution is the National Defense Council, which is also formally headed by Mao but apparently run by the minister of defense. The party organization permeates the military hierarchy, with party committees at all levels. The Chinese have adopted the Soviet system of zampolits at all levels of the military structure. Day-to-day military operations are regulated by the political officer or commissar assigned to each unit. Theoretically, the political officer has the power to veto politically undesirable action ordered by the unit's military commander. In contrast to the Soviet practice, however, the military commander has at times also been the political officer, limiting somewhat the party's independent control. Disputes between the military commander and the political commissar are referred to the party committees within the PLA for resolution.

The most important single factor in assuring the military's acceptance of civilian and party leadership has been the army's loyalty to Mao. By virtue of his personal authority, Mao has been able to use the military as a pressure group and counterweight to hostile party factions. Once his objectives had been achieved, his skill and the personal loyalty he commanded within the military were apparent in the ease with which he reimposed controls on political action by the military.

A second means of control has been periodic shifts in military structures and personnel. On several occasions during and after the civil war, military commands were radically redefined; military regions were divided or reapportioned; troops and officers were transferred or split up. Such changes weakened the political ties that might otherwise have been established in a given province or between given sets of leaders. In addition, top-level leaders who envisioned larger political roles for themselves than Mao and the party desired have been purged. Those purged have included some of the highest-ranking military figures in China. The most recent case is the death and disgracing of Marshal Lin Piao, formally named as Mao's successor, and officers associated with him following an abortive coup d'état in 1971.

A final means of control has been to combat peacetime stagnation and boredom in the military by employing it in the construction of the socialist state. The military has been involved in farming, industry, education, health programs, and heavy construction. These activities have served not only to assist the nation in its development process but also to incorporate the military into society and to prevent the establishment of wholly distinct military institutions.

## FORMS OF POLITICAL ACTION BY THE CHINESE MILITARY

Mao envisioned a proletariat single-class army whose members would be both producers and warriors. He opposed a military establishment separate from the people. While civilian supremacy has prevailed, it has not gone unchallenged. The first in what would become a series of checks on the military's ascendancy was the 1954 purge of Kao Kang and Jao Shu-shih. At the time China was involved in "support" of the North Korean communists during the Korean War. This war had prompted a shift from the mobile defensive war-of-attrition tactics of Chairman Mao to the creation of a highly professionalized bureaucratic military organization. Kao's defeat resulted from an economic issue with political implications. He sought to apply in China the Soviet model of industrial-managerial responsibility for production, rather than party domination, and in order to do so had sought the assistance of fellow military officers. Kao and Jao believed the army should have a greater voice in its own reorganization. Their mistake was that they not only opposed Mao but also threatened the position of the party group consisting of Liu Shao-ch'i, Teng Hsiao-p'ing, and Chou En-lai. With the support of P'eng Chen, mayor of Peking and a leading Central Committee member, the latter were able to expel Kao and Jao from the party's Central Committee. As rewards for successfully supporting Mao, Liu became chairman of the National People's Congress in 1954 and chief of state in 1959; Teng Hsiao-p'ing was appointed secretary-general of the party; and Chou En-lai maintained his position as premier of the State Council. With this victory, Chairman Mao strengthened his already tight control over the party's Military Affairs Committee (MAC).

A second major challenge to the party occurred during the Great Leap Forward. During the first half-decade of communist rule, the army had emphasized expertise and modernization along the lines of the Soviet model. However, beginning in 1956, the party began to emphasize the need to augment the ideological education of officers and enlisted men. With the Great Leap Forward of 1958 the military's role took a sudden dramatic turn. The massive structural changes accompanying the development of communes caused agricultural production to fall, and declining food production caused morale to suffer and pressures to be felt within the party. Among those expressing opposition to these programs were Marshal P'eng Teh-huai, minister of defense, and General Huang Ko-ch'eng, chief of staff of the army. P'eng opposed not only the Great Leap Forward but also the emphasis on ideology and Mao's strategy of a "people's war" against nuclear attacks. His position, reflecting his military concern for hardware, was stated succinctly after his dismissal: "What's the use of relying on political and ideological work? It can't fly . . ." [19] P'eng also perceived collective leadership of the military as inhibiting its professional capability. In 1959 the Central Committee purged both P'eng and Huang. But their impact on the army has been responsible for the weakening of party control. By 1960 there were no party units in one-third of all PLA companies.

The negative feedback from the initial implementation of the Great Leap Forward convinced Chairman Mao that large sectors of the party elite and cadres were disillusioned with these policies. He chose to remedy their disillusion with new socialist education, and turned to the army to inculcate the necessary ideological spirit. Even during the Great Leap Forward, the army

19. *New China News Agency,* 30 August 1967.

was called upon to assist in agricultural production and construct the communications infrastructure, roads, and irrigation projects. It was also during this period that the military established its own factories to promote self-reliance.

In September 1959, when Lin Piao assumed leadership of the ministry of defense, the role of the army grew dramatically. Among the first of Lin's tasks was to mobilize the political consciousness of the troops. Over 200,000 party members were recruited into the armed forces, and by the end of 1961 party committees were established in most companies.[20] The principle of collective party–military leadership of each military unit was reasserted. Lin Piao is reported to have articulated the following formula to guide the military:

> In the relationship between man and weapons, man is primary; in the relationship between political work and other types of work, political work is primary; in the relationship between ideological and routine work, ideological work is primary; and in the relationship between "book learning" and "practical thought," "practical thought" is primary.[21]

The peak of military influence was the Cultural Revolution. Throughout this period, the military played a leading part in the struggle to reassert Mao's control over the state and party and to renew the commitment to revolutionary ideals. Initially the military trained and directed some parts of the Red Guard Movement. Regional party leaders had also participated in the formation of the Red Guards, hoping to control and limit their antiparty activities. However, when conflict among the Red Guard, Revolutionary Rebels, and Red Workers Guard intensified, appeals were made to the coalition of Lin Piao, Mao, and Chou to support the hard-pressed Red Guard groups. Their response was made in a context of considerable military disunity. The chief of staff, Yang Cheng-wu, had attempted to undermine the regional commanders by filling top divisional and corps positions with men loyal to him. The minister of defense, Lin Piao, was attempting the same thing. Some regional commanders, jealously guarding their own power, occasionally supported Red Guard workers against the commands of the center. In other cases they remained neutral. In only six of the twenty-nine administrative areas did the regional military commanders support the Maoist drive to overthrow existing party leaders. This and a military-party factional revolt in the city of Wuhan forced Mao to reconsider his ability to realize a complete purge of the opposition.

Having succeeded in changing party leadership in the Central Committee, Politburo, and many provincial party ruling bodies, Mao decided to give in to army pressure to suppress the leftist movements. The military rounded up dissident students, sent them to the countryside for re-education, and closed the universities that had been their base of support. In the process of restoring

---

20. Derek J. Wallter, *The Government and Politics of Communist China* (New York: Doubleday, 1971) p. 111.

21. J. Chester Cheng, ed., *The Politics of the Chinese Red Army: A Transition of the Bulletin of Activities of the People's Liberation Army* (Stanford: Hoover Institute, 1966), pp. 66–68.

order after the Cultural Revolution, the military took on important civil and economic functions, including operation of the communication and transportation systems. Eventually its control spread to factories, schools, cities, villages, provinces, and even the highest ruling political bodies.

The Ninth Party Congress in 1969 confirmed the military's role. Among the 21 members of the Politburo, the military had a voting majority (including 4 army marshals, 6 generals, and Lin Piao's wife) and was able to name a military majority to the Politburo's Standing Committee. Forty-five percent of the Central Committee members were PLA party-soldiers. Of the 29 revolutionary committees established at the provincial level, the military held 19 chairmanships and 20 vice-chairmanships. About 60 percent of the regional state officials were military men, and 2,000 of the 2,350 counties were under military rule.

Following the reported coup attempt by Lin Piao and four top military officers in 1971, the party began to assert control over the military. Regional commanders were arrested and/or shifted from one assignment to another, and representatives of the masses and party cadre became more prominent on local revolutionary committees. It is interesting to note the tactics that Mao used to reassert and maintain party control over the military. He first circulated a warning of the impending purge in party and military reports. Then, by expanding the membership of the Military Affairs Committee, he removed Lin Piao and his followers from this important committee. Finally, he reorganized the command of the Peking military region by replacing officers loyal to Lin Piao with others he could rely on.

The decline in the military's influence was evident at the Tenth Party Congress in 1973. Military full members of the Central Committee had dropped from 45 to 31 percent; among the alternates, military membership had declined from 46 percent to 26 percent. But most significantly, the military contingent on the Politburo had decreased from eleven to six. The party has since emphasized that its loyalty is to the masses, who are in turn represented by the party.

## THE COMMUNIST MILITARY: AGENTS FOR STABILITY

In both China and the Soviet Union the army is extolled in films, literature, education curricula, and even ballet and music. Military victories and heroes are important political symbols frequently invoked to stimulate feelings of national pride and patriotism. The military's privileged place in society is matched by its position of political influence. But in both countries the military is subordinate to the civilian party leadership, and threats to the party's preeminence are dealt with firmly.

The Chinese military has been much more politically involved than its Soviet counterpart, but under Mao's guidance and as his tool in combat with his rivals. What is remarkable is that the civilian leadership in China has retained control of the military. Many Asian states near China and at similar levels of political and economic development have faced major challenges to civilian mastery of the military, and in some cases the civil leadership has been replaced by military rulers. The Leninist doctrine of party organization and dominance has provided both China and the Soviet Union with civil political forces capable of mastering and co-opting the military.

Both countries are most vulnerable to the expansion of military influence during succession crises, when new leaders are emerging. The instability of party direction and control and the competition among rivals for the military's backing may open new avenues for military influence. This is likely to be the case in China after Mao leaves politics because of the magnitude of the ensuing power vacuum.

# The Military in Mexico and Nigeria: The Quest for Civilian Control

Seldom does a nation possess effective political institutions at independence. Institutions that can respond to the demands and expectations of both elites and masses often take years to establish. During the initial period of fragile political institutions, the military is often extremely prominent in politics as a result of its control over the technology of force. Neither Mexico nor Nigeria is an exception to these generalizations. Mexico experienced over a hundred years of political instability and incessant military intervention. It is too early to predict whether Nigeria can avoid the intensity and duration of Mexico's era of military intervention. However, Nigeria is currently ruled by a military regime and has been so ruled for more than half of its years as an independent state.

## MEXICO: THE CONTROL OF MILITARISM

Mexico serves as a good example of the extension of civilian control over a politicized military with a longstanding tradition of intervening in politics. In the years after Mexican independence the army, the church, and the mestizo and Spanish upper classes competed for political power. The army prevailed, but not without resistance by civilian groups. Attempts were made throughout the first century of Mexican independence to establish constitutional governments, but each one aroused opposition that more often than not chose the gun over the ballot-box to remove the group in power. So it was that between 1821 and 1917 Mexico had forty-four rulers, thirty of whom were military figures.[22] During the same period of time the army controlled the nation's budget and on occasion spent far more for military purposes than the total revenues collected by the government.

22 Pablo González Casanova, *Democracy in Mexico,* 2d ed. (New York: Oxford University Press, 1970), p. 36.

The first few years of the Revolution of 1911 offered little hope for an end to militarism, characterized as they were by a reversion to the anarchy of the nineteenth century. Although the constitution promulgated in 1917 called for civilian control of the military and prohibited active military officers from holding elected public office, the military continued to play a major part in politics for another twenty years. Since the Revolution, however, the political power of the military has ebbed. Of the fourteen men who have ruled since 1917, only six were former military officers. In the past twenty-five years all of Mexico's presidents have been civilians. The army's claim on the national budget has declined from 44 percent of all federal governmental expenditures in 1925 to only about 5 percent in the 1970s.[23] Whereas military figures once occupied most top-level political positions, since the 1940s they have lost most of their political posts. By 1958 only six of the twenty-nine state governors and two of the eighteen cabinet ministers were military officers.[24] Once the kingmaker and mainstay of politics, the Mexican army is today a model of subservience to civilian members.

Several methods were used to bring the Mexican military under civilian control. First, the creation of effective political institutions was among the most significant developments in the process of mastering the army. By assuring Mexico ongoing political stability, political institutions created the kind of political environment conducive to the abolition of praetorianism. Agreement on rules for governing and procedures for transferring power to new leaders eliminated much of the political uncertainty and instability that had in the past occasioned military intervention. Chief among these institutions were the presidency and the PRI, which proved capable of responding to the interests of a variety of social forces and thus minimized the social discontent that often fosters military intervention.

Mexico's presidents played a major part in extending civilian control over the army; significantly, those who were most successful were former military men. As presidents, former generals enjoyed the confidence of their fellow military officers, who accepted from them budget cutbacks, new civilian controls, and limitations on political activities they might have rejected from civilian presidents. Among the leaders of the effort to control the military were Presidents Calles, Cárdenas, and Ávila Camacho, all former generals. Perhaps most skilled in promoting the transition to civilian dominance of the military was President Cárdenas. Threatened by the ambitions of former President Calles and his military supporters, Cárdenas was able to call on peasants and laborers whom he had armed for support. The president continues to protect the state against renewed military politicization by keeping the actions of the military and its officers under close surveillance. The various state governors, most of whom have been hand-picked by the president, report on the activities of military units in their states; undercover agents for the ministry of interior

23. *Ibid.*
24. Huntington, *Political Order*, p. 257.

also oversee the military, providing the central leadership with a second source of information and control.

The PRI has also contributed importantly to the containment of the military. First, the party has served to channel political participation and prevent excessive political action by mobilized but uneducated masses. The party's status as a symbol of the virtues of the Revolution has helped legitimize and win public support for the regime. Second, as the party grew in membership and absorbed most peasant and labor groups, it became a political counterweight to the military. No longer was the military the only organized political body. Finally, the party co-opted and ultimately absorbed the military. Eventually, as the party came to be organized into sectors, the military acquired its own sector alongside the peasant, worker, and popular sectors. The military sector was an important power in the party for many years, and often determined the party's presidential candidate. However, the tacit acceptance of the party as the proper arena for political action marked an important step in the assertion of civilian mastery. Within the party, skillful politicians could limit the military's influence by developing coalitions among the other sectors. By 1940 the military's political strength had declined to such a degree that President Ávila Camacho abolished the military sector of the PRI and incorporated it into the popular sector.

Another means of assuring civil predominance has been to involve the military in economic and social projects to divert its attention from politics and elicit its commitment to the social aims of the revolution. Thus the military was assigned to manage federal factories producing military arms and goods. Troops were also employed in public works projects. During the past few administrations, the military has been increasingly active in the construction of hospitals, schools, and roads. Teams from the military have also been sent to rural areas to promote adult literacy. Furthermore, military officers have been encouraged to go into private enterprise upon retirement, and the comfortable business positions they are frequently offered serve as an attractive and lucrative alternative to political action.

In the past, Mexican generals developed regional power bases that defied central control and sometimes provided a base from which to undertake a coup. To prevent this in recent years, civilian leaders have periodically rotated commands and officers. Such rotations reduce the generals' ability to develop regional political fiefdoms and foster loyalty to the national political leadership rather than to specific military personalities among the troops and officers.

Finally, Mexican political leaders have attempted to prevent a political vacuum that might foster military intervention by developing alternative political forces. The party, we have noted, is one such countervailing force, and there have been others. Porfirio Díaz, a military dictator who ruled in 1876–1911, formed a rural police force as a counter to the former military organization. President Carranza (1917–1920) recruited labor brigades into the military to oppose the peasant armies of Villa and Zapata. Later, President Cárdenas (1934–1940) won grassroots backing for the regime by undertaking land and social reforms. When confronted by a direct military challenge to his rule, Cárdenas created and armed peasant and labor militias to serve as a countervailing force to the military. His successful resistance to a military threat in 1938 marked the last major political intervention on the part of the Mexican military.

The Mexican military no longer receives special treatment or privileges from the government. It can no longer prevent the government from acting by threatening disobedience or rebellion. While it can and does speak out in defense of its own interests, the military does not always get its way.

The military's main task today is internal security, which frequently involves it in politically relevant activity: antiguerrilla action, riot control, suppression of politically motivated protest (such as that engendered by the invalidation of elections won by the opposition party or by blatant manipulation of election results by PRI supporters), and other such undertakings. However one might evaluate their necessity and appropriateness, the military carries out such political acts at the behest of the civilian leadership. Military defense of domestic security poses the risk that the civilian regime may become dependent upon the military, thereby increasing the military's political influence. The current situation in Mexico is not one of civilian dependence on the military for the maintenance of domestic order. However, the military's role in suppressing student uprisings and rural guerrilla operations illustrates the potential for dependence should the level of social unrest rise precipitously.

After thirty-five years of nonintervention, the norm of civilian supremacy appears to be well established in Mexico. Most observers expect this pattern of civilian mastery to continue. However, there are two recent cases in Latin America of the repoliticization of the military: Chile and Uruguay. In both countries, traditions of military abstinence from politics similar to that of Mexico were destroyed by prolonged periods of social strife, civil disorder, and political instability, leading to military intervention and rule in Uruguay and to a military coup in Chile. It is possible, perhaps even likely, that similar instability and conflict in Mexico might prompt the military to intervene in politics and act independently to restore order.

## NIGERIA: THE MILITARY IN POWER

The Nigerian military lacks the historical tradition and experience of the Mexican army. It is a relatively young army, created by the British during the colonial era. As a product of British colonial rule, it inherited some of the values and norms of British civil–military relations. Officers and troops alike were socialized to accept civilian control over the armed forces.

While the Nigerian military benefited from the organization and training it received from its former imperial masters, the British tradition of military noninvolvement in politics did not last. One reason for its demise is that the Nigerian military had not learned to submit to *Nigerian* political institutions. Prior to independence, the military was of course under the control of the

British. Thus it was not subject to the early Nigerian "home rule" political institutions established by the British as a prelude to withdrawal. Even after independence, until 1965, a British military commander headed the Nigerian army, which meant that Nigerian officers still accepted British political control. Thus when the British intermediary was removed, there was no tradition of military subservience to Nigerian civilian leaders.

Another reason for the rapid breakdown of the norm of civilian control was the Nigerianization of the officer corps. At independence only 18 percent of the officers were Nigerians; within five years all officers were Nigerian. This sudden change in structure involved the promotion to high positions of noncommissioned officers and recruits, who had had little or no previous experience as officers and little time to absorb the British norm of civilian mastery. The effects of this occurrence are evident in the 1966 coups. Of the seven officers who conspired to bring about the first 1966 coup, all but two were commissioned after independence; the two exceptions had been commissioned the year before independence.[25] There was a notable gulf between the new junior officers and the British-trained senior officers, reflecting different backgrounds, training, and values. Lack of respect and even contempt for senior officers on the part of their subordinates was commonplace.

The experience of the Nigerian military after independence also had a politicizing effect. Its main task was to maintain internal security during the increasingly frequent lapses in political and social order. Among the activities of the Nigerian army were the pacification of the Tiv (a minority tribe) in 1960 and again in 1964, the maintenance of essential public services during the general strike of 1964, and control of the widespread rioting in the Western Region after the regional elections of 1965. The last incident was particularly crucial in the politicization of the military, since it involved the army in suppressing politically motivated civil disorders: protests against massive fraud and irregularities in the regional elections. To be sure, the military acted upon the orders of the civilian federal government. However, there was disagreement between the federal president and prime minister on the situation in the Western Region. The confusing political context and the military's part in sustaining election fraud seem to have eliminated any lingering reluctance to intervene in politics on the part of the military.[26] All remnants of the British norm of civilian mastery were destroyed at this time.

Not surprisingly, the ethnic problem that characterized all of Nigerian society was also present in the military, and complicated the maintenance of civilian control. One study describes the Nigerian military structure as a "four-layer sandwich" with different ethnic groups prevailing at each level:

> At the bottom, the bulk of the riflemen were Northerners . . . . The army did not publish tribal statistics, but it is clear that in the General Duty troops the

25. Robert Luckham, *The Nigerian Military 1960–67* (London: Cambridge University Press, 1971), p. 240.

26. N. J. Miners, *The Nigerian Army* (London: Methuen, 1971), pp. 131–158.

FIGURE 7.1

*Military Expenditures as a Percentage of GNP in Nigeria, 1963–1972*

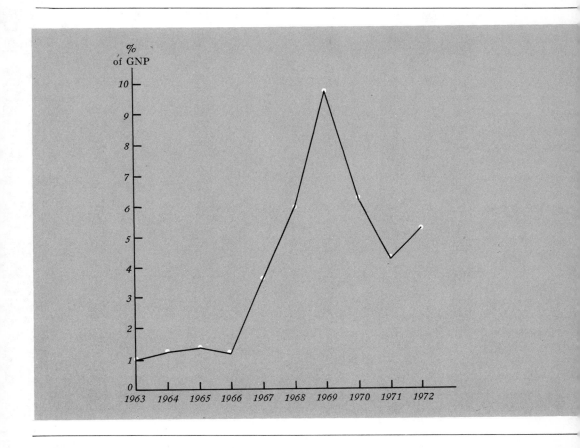

*Source: Data drawn from U.S. Arms Control and Disarmament Agency,* World Military Expenditures and Arms Trade 1963–1973 *(Washington: U.S. Government Printing Office, 1975).*

proportion of Northerners was as high as 75 percent among NCOs and men. Among . . . ancillary soldiers, the proportion of Southerners was much higher. Among the junior officers the representation of the tribes was more or less equal, having been controlled by the quota of 50 percent Northern, 25 percent Eastern and 25 percent Western . . . . Finally in the rank of Major and above the composition of the Officer Corps was the result of the period of open competition and entry by academic qualification introduced by the British in the mid-fifties and continuing until 1961. In this competition Southerners and especially Easterners predominated over the Northerners in the ratio of some seven to one.

Of the 44 officers of the Nigerian army given in the 1960 army list . . . only six were Northern (of those four were murdered in the January 1966 coups, and a fifth, Gowon, escaped by good luck), . . . twenty-three were Eastern and the remainder Western and Midwestern.[27]

The ethnic mix of the officer corps sometimes became a political issue of concern to the ethnic-based political parties. In turn, officers often developed close ties with political leaders from their ethnic groups, especially if they came to feel that ethnic considerations were affecting their careers. The quota system and fears of ethnic discrimination were important sources of internal tension in the army and heightened the politicization of the military.

By 1965 the situation in Nigeria had worsened considerably and was ripe for military intervention. Ethnic tensions continued to mount; there was growing evidence of high-level political corruption and incompetence; the political institutions seemed unable to respond to the prevailing crises; and popular confidence in the government was rapidly eroding. In late 1965 six majors and a captain plotted to seize power by eliminating politicians, from the prime minister down to local ministers, and senior officers. The coup took place on January 15, 1966. Before it was over the federal president, the prime minister, a top cabinet officer, the premiers of the Northern and Western Regions, and many senior military officers had been killed. The younger officers involved in the coup either lost their lives in the fighting or were arrested, and Major General J. T. U. Aguiyi-Ironsi, the former top officer in the Nigerian armed forces, became head of the military regime. Ironsi formed a Military Council to replace the civilian government, and thus brought to an end Nigeria's first republican era.

After the January 1966 coup, the military's political responsibilities outstripped its previous experience and abilities. General Ironsi proposed a number of major reforms designed to reduce some ethnic and political tensions. However, he appeared unaware of or insensitive to the most critical such tensions. Ironsi sought to eliminate the regions but was hesitant to accept the minority ethnic groups' proposal of new states. This hesitation cost him political support, as did his appointment of an Ibo to study unification of the civil service. The regional leaders were fearful that abolition of the regions would reduce their power and status. Northerners were especially concerned about the number of persuasive Ibo advisers around Ironsi. Ibos were said to be getting federal jobs at the expense of other communal groups. Thus, resentments and fears were accumulating faster than the possible positive effects of the reforms. In May 1966, Ironsi proposed a change in the constitution, decreeing a unitary form of government even before the constitutional commission had reported its findings. The decree touched off rioting in the Northern Region and led to talk of secession there and even in the Western Region. Ibos in the north were at-

27. M. J. Dent, "The Military and Politics: A Study of the Relations Between the Army and the Political Process in Nigeria" in *Nigeria: Modernization and the Politics of Communalism* ed. Robert Melson and Howard Wolpe (East Lansing: Michigan State University Press, 1971), p. 371.

tacked and thousands were killed. In early July, Ironsi announced plans to appoint military prefects and provincial secretaries to govern the former regions. Shortly thereafter, a new military revolt led to the arrest and execution of Ironsi. Though the revolt was a military coup, it reflected the deep resentment and fear the Hausa-Fulani masses felt toward the Ironsi regime. The surviving military high command then asked Lieutenant Colonel Yakubu Gowon, army chief of staff, to become the new supreme commander and to head a new military regime.

Gowon acted with greater prudence than had his predecessor, establishing a base of support among the minority ethnic groups by creating twelve new states. He appointed popular local civilian officials or military personnel to head the states. Now, however, it was the Ibos who were fearful and discontented. Murders of Ibos in the north and other areas in May and again in September and October 1966 had aroused bitter enmity and fear among the Ibos in the east. Ultimately the Ibos seceded, forming the new state of Biafra and provoking a long and tragic civil war that lasted two-and-a-half years before the military once again pacified the country.

The civil war further enhanced the importance of the military in Nigerian politics. For one thing, the size of the army ballooned from approximately 8,000 in 1967 to over 260,000 in 1975. The cost of supporting this army rose from a precivil war figure of less than 5 percent of governmental expenditures to as much as one-third of the total budget. Even the end of the civil war did not bring about the expected decline in military expenditures. Between April 1970 and January 1971 defense expenditures totaled approximately 34 million dollars, or more than 2.5 times the initial appropriation for the entire fiscal year.[28] It has proved difficult to demobilize the army. Reduction of the army to its precivil war size would have forced close to 200,000 men onto the already glutted job market. In addition, army pay is often considerably higher than civilian wages. The lowest Nigerian recruit receives a monthly salary of about 51 U.S. dollars, which is about eight times the per capita income of the average Nigerian.[29] The rapid demobilization of these troops is likely to have provoked a grave social and political crisis for the military regime.

The Nigerian military originally pledged to return political power to civilians in 1976 — a decade after its entrance into politics. But in 1974 General Gowon announced that the promise could not be kept because of persistent "sectional politicking."[30] However, Gowon failed to maintain the confidence of his fellow officers. In the summer of 1975, while Gowon was out of the country, a new and bloodless coup overthrew him and brought to power Brigadier Muritala Rufai Muhammad. The coup was motivated by dissatisfaction with Gowon's inability to deal with growing corruption and political discontent. The new Muhammad government acted quickly to remove some sources of tension, notably by pledging to ignore a census taken in 1973 that threatened

28. Henry L. Bretton, *Power and Politics in Africa* (Chicago: Aldine, 1973), p. 232.
29. *Ibid.*, p. 231.
30. *New York Times,* 6 October 1974.

to heighten ethnic tensions, and by removing "corrupt" local and federal officials. The eventual end of military rule may simply involve the "civilianization" of the current military rulers, as the officers shed their uniforms for mufti but retain control of politics. Few efforts have been made thus far to prepare for the reinstatement of civilian rule, and without effective civilian political institutions and such political forces as parties, the return of power to civilians may be short-lived. The chaos caused by inadequate civilian government may in turn provoke new military action. In short, the prospects for the Nigerian military's imminent return to a nonpolitical role do not appear bright.

# Conclusions

It makes little difference whether a state is old or new, communist or democratic, developed or underdeveloped: when civilian political institutions prove unable to perform the tasks expected of them by the people, the armed forces may abandon their normal role as guards against external attack and become the country's political gods, ousting and installing political leaders. Thus, when civilian authorities were unable to cope with grave social and political crises in France during the Algerian war, in China during the Cultural Revolution, and in Nigeria when ethnic tensions reached the point of explosion, the armies intervened politically to install new leaders, fill the political vacuum, or completely replace the civilian government. The transformation of the military from guards to gods is likely to occur during periods of prolonged political instability and/or intense political turmoil, because at such times the military may be the only organized group capable of preventing further decay or civil war.

Once a tradition of military intervention is established, it is difficult to nullify the political pretensions of the military and reassert the norm of civilian control. Having successfully intervened in the past, the military is readier to do so in the future. Furthermore, a military regime often lacks the knowledge and incentive to develop effective civilian governmental structures. Thus, when the officers restore the government to the civilians, such institutions may be lacking and conditions that foster military intervention may quickly recur. The job of imposing civil authority on a politicized military is arduous. That it can be accomplished is demonstrated by the re-establishment of civilian mastery in France, and more dramatically by the abolition of a century-old tradition of praetorianism in Mexico.

# III

# POLITICAL
# PERFORMANCE

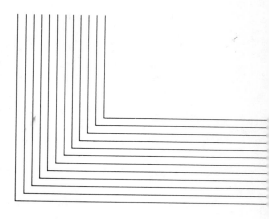

# 8

# *Making Public Policy:*
# *The Prelude to Performance*

## Introduction

One often associates policy-making with smoke-filled rooms where politicians wheel and deal in the exchange of goods and values, including the public offices they covet. But the destruction of a village by raiding bombers, the construction of a school, a judge's decision, and the promise of "a chicken in very pot" are also aspects of the policy process. In the policy process authoritative actors, governmental officials, legislators, and administrators interact with each other, with other individuals and groups, and with other governments to formulate policy that will affect the public. In this chapter we shall examine how political issues are born and why some issues are never submitted to the policy-making process. We shall also explore how political decisions and policies are made: the participants, the settings, and the styles of decision-making. In the following chapters of Part III, we shall deal with the nature and outcomes of such decisions relative to three important areas of political performance: social and economic development, stability, and change.

### THE BIRTH OF POLITICAL ISSUES

The formation of policy is a governmental response to issues or concerns expressed by the political leadership, party leaders, interest groups, or by the public in general. Many aspects of society have the potential to become subject to public policy; however, only a few such matters become political issues that demand policy responses. It is thus important to understand how certain issues develop, move into the forefront of the political process, and become prone to be acted upon.

Many issues arise out of societal needs: the regulation of food processing to protect public health, the construction of superhighways to link industrial centers, the establishment of minimum wage levels to provide protection for salaried workers, the expansion of educational facilities to accommodate more students. Such needs may exist, however, long before they become politically salient. There was a need for controls on environmental pollution long before the environment became a worldwide political issue in the late 1960s; there was a need in the United States for policy assuring racial equality long before this issue emerged politically in the late 1950s.

An explanation of why and when needs become issues and then objects of policy is not easy to provide. Two mediums through which needs are transformed into issues are political leaders and events. Political leaders may see in certain issues a need for action and/or political advantage. It has been suggested that the origin of the American poverty programs of the 1960s can be traced to John F. Kennedy's campaign for the Democratic presidential nomination in 1960. During a primary campaign in West Virginia he became acquainted on a first-hand basis with the problems of the Appalachian poor. His conscience was pricked; he saw an issue with potential political appeal; and he committed himself and his administration to improving the lot of impoverished Americans.

Events may raise issues, as political decision-makers are compelled to deal with current problems and crises. Disasters or crises may reveal or dramatize needs and produce mass pressure for policy action. A train crash may demonstrate the need for governmental action to improve the rail system; student riots may point to the need for university reforms; a power or fuel shortage may lead to greater governmental concern with an energy policy; exposure of scandal or graft may draw policy-makers' attention to reform of the bureaucracy. However, issues that are closely tied to events may lose momentum over time. A good illustration is in gun control legislation in the United States. The clamor for stricter regulation of handguns that occurred after the assassinations of major political figures disappeared once the shock of those events had worn off, with the result that gun control is still minimal.

Almost as important as the ability to influence policy decisions is the ability to prevent issues from emerging. Leaders can accomplish this fairly easily in countries where the government controls the news media. Only those issues approved by the regime are discussed in the media. Even major natural disasters may be ignored in the press if the regime wishes to contain their repercussions. Leaders and groups may also prevent issues from emerging by failing to perceive or refusing to respond to certain needs. American leaders long ignored the pockets of poverty that still persist in this "rich" country. Nigerian leaders failed to respond to the danger signs of regionalism and communalism prior to the civil war. Leaders may also choose to emphasize certain issues or policy areas at the expense of others; the Soviet Union, for example, emphasized industrialization and ignored needed agricultural reforms. They may dodge issues, such as capital punishment or abortion, that are very sensitive and divisive.

In short, out of myriad possible issues relatively few achieve sufficient political importance to become objects of policy. Leaders are often able to choose the issues that emerge, and they tend to emphasize those that are consistent with their goals. The leadership's ideology may dictate a set of policy goals. For example, Maoist ideological principles give priority to the achievement of social justice and equality. Or political parties may have long-standing programs and commitments that they seek to implement. The Gaullists were long committed to an independent French foreign policy.

However, all these explanations of the sources of issues are insufficient. Some issues arise and become politically salient for no apparent reason. The recently emergent concern for the environment is such a case. Though the need for environmental protection had been clear for a long time, the issue had had little political impact. Suddenly it became a major issue, which politicians in many countries talked about and attempted to act on. No single event or series of events was responsible for the intensified interest, nor was there a leader within or outside government whose championing of the issue led to its popularity. The need had finally become apparent to many and had stimulated policy responses. Whether or not they like it, leaders must often make policy on issues such as these "whose time has come."

## STAGES OF THE POLICY-MAKING PROCESS

It is essential to understand the stages in the policy-making process. Policy-makers frequently first establish *goals*. Then specific *acts* must be agreed upon and implemented by the government's or private sector's decision-making machinery. Finally, the results or *outcomes* are observed and evaluated. Thus, a prime minister's promises to win the war and eliminate inflation are illustrations of policy goals. When he sends troops to a far-off battleground and imposes a ceiling on prices, he is undertaking policy acts. When the ministries of defense and finance announce the number of villages captured and a reduction in the rate of price increases, they are describing the third phase in the policy process, policy outcomes.

*Goals* Goals can vary considerably in type and scope. They may involve broad changes in society; goals are termed *radical* if they seek to alter existing social and political institutions and replace them with others. *Reformist* policy goals also seek to alter the existing state of affairs, but in a more limited way and perhaps in a specific area such as old age or medical care. Most policies tend to be *status quo*-oriented adaptations to current demands, with the main objective of satisfying enough clients for the responsible political group or individual politician to maintain power. Or goals may be strictly *political* in that they are intended to reward loyal followers or to build support for re-election.

*Acts*   Goal definition — a process more often than not marred by dispute — is followed by the determination of possible means to realize the goal(s). The first dimension of an act is its *scope,* which may or may not replicate that of the goal. A goal's scope can vary from narrow to total, depending on the leadership's conception of the social needs that require alteration. Similarly, acts or decisions designed to achieve these goals may involve either narrow-in-scope steps or comprehensive steps intended to realize the desired goal in the briefest possible period.

A second dimension of the policy act is its *style.* Some decisions are products of near-instanteous reactions to events or crises. Others are products of the deliberate and rational consideration of alternative courses of action. Still others — the vast majority — result from the consideration of immediate concerns and the political realities of the moment. These decisions are made neither in a crisis atmosphere nor by means of rational deliberation; they are made by political leaders too busy with a multitude of pressing issues and demands to devote much time to any given problem.

*Outcomes*   It is usually part of the policy process to evaluate the outcomes of implemented policies. Policy-makers also look at outcomes to determine whether their policies have created new demands for further acts. A new policy may have unanticipated consequences that necessitate further action. For example, an open immigration policy designed to meet a labor shortage may provoke cultural tensions between the immigrants and the native population. In short, because a policy affects the society in which it is implemented, policy-makers must evaluate its outcome and measure its intended and incidental impact.

## INCREMENTAL VERSUS RATIONAL POLICY-MAKING

Most policy-making is *incremental* — that is, it takes place piecemeal in response to immediate needs and concerns rather than by means of a carefully thought-out rational procedure. Thus policies often emerge from the accumulation of decisions on minor issues, and consequently lack clear identification of overall goals, thorough consideration of all alternatives, and full evaluation of possible outcomes. This is especially true in liberal democracies and Third World countries, where independent economic and social structures make important decisions affecting society as a whole. But it is also true in communist countries, despite the deliberate efforts of their leaders to develop long-term political, economic, and social programs. Not all goals and decisions, of course, involve complex programs. Policy-making also includes such "single-shot" decisions as appointing a lower-court judge to a lifetime position on a higher court, naming a city, and ordering the integration of a public university. Different decisions clearly require varying degrees of rationality, and varying political inputs. They may not necessarily result in efficient decisions or policies that serve the public interest.

While most policy-making is characterized by incrementalism, attempts are made to achieve greater efficiency through a *rational* style of policy-making. We would like to envision our political leaders setting public policy through a well-defined rational process that provides for full examination of all possible alternatives, an assessment of the probable costs and consequences of each, consultation with impartial experts and representatives of affected groups, and an attempt to coordinate each policy with others and with the overall goals of the regime. We would also like to see them put aside such political considerations as the effect of a decision on their ability to remain in office, instead basing their decisions on the good of the country or a broad sector of the public. Leaders should be able to make decisions free of the influence of narrow interest groups, e.g., a medical group wishing to limit the number of new doctors in order to maintain its members' high earnings. In brief, we would want policy-making to be rational.

The methods associated with the rational style are usually intended to maximize the realization of a given social, economic, or political goal while minimizing its costs. Thus far the rational approach to policy has been applied largely to allocative decisions — how much should be allocated where or to whom and when. Specifically, it has been employed in economic planning and government budgeting. In systems characterized by considerable governmental control over the development processes, varying degrees of socioeconomic planning may be utilized. Where governmental controls are less extensive, the rational approach may be limited to attempts to alter existing budgeting for the government's administrative units in favor of financing for new programs.

Planning can typically vary in scope from long-range five- and ten-year plans to short one-year plans. Some nations undertake "sectoral planning," which joins the government and private enterprise in working to achieve given sectoral goals, e.g., industrialization, agricultural production, or improved public health. The more comprehensive plans of communist systems often seek to bring about radical changes in existing social and economic structures and relationships and to accelerate economic development.

Increased governmental efficiency in many liberal democracies and Third World countries may be sought through a technique called "planning, programming, and budgeting" (PPB), which usually involves

1. identifying the existing and needed governmental and nongovernmental agencies and the resources required to implement a given program.

2. identifying the costs of each possible alternative and the values of the expected outputs. These estimates are made by examining together a given alternative input, e.g., given numbers of doctors and hospitals, and its potential output, e.g., a given degree of infant' mortality.

3. the calculation of a cost-benefit ratio for each of the possible combinations.

This process, then, seeks to relate budgeting and expenditures to public policy goals. Policies are to be evaluated in terms of their anticipated costs and prospective social benefits. It also seeks to rationalize performance by minimizing duplication of programs.[1] However, this innovation has encountered many difficulties, including the following, found to characterize one attempt to implement it within a United States executive department:

1. the failure of many agency heads to demand program analysis or to use it when available.

2. the failure of much legislation to stipulate clearly program goals and to provide funds for the collection of follow-up data and other appraisal information.

3. the constraints on substantive and time-consuming policy analysis imposed by the annual budget cycle and process to which the PPB system is tied.

4. a serious scarcity of analytical personnel in the PPB offices of civilian agencies.

5. a basic resistance by many federal employees to economic analysis and the difficult job of program evaluation.

6. the lack of professional agreement on certain basic analytical issues, such as the size of the appropriate public discount rate, the development of shadow prices when outputs are not marketed, and the evaluation of expenditures with multiple objectives.

7. the lack of adequate data from which to develop measures of the benefits of outputs and costs of inputs.[2]

Because human beings have limited intellectual capacities, information, time, and even will power, policies seldom exemplify the hoped-for rationality. Furthermore, in observing rational models of policy-making there is an assumption of simplicity: that a nation has a single set of goals, that one actor's goals prevail and that actions are chosen on the basis of careful examination of all needs. But the policy-making process is complex. National leaders are often unable to account for events, particularly security-related, economic, and environmental events. President Lyndon Johnson was still hoping in January 1968. that he could achieve military victory in Vietnam, not foreseeing that in March 1968 he would announce that he "would not seek, and if offered, would not accept the presidential nomination." There are countless other examples of limited foresight due to human and other factors, which unavoidably affect rational decision-making. Culture may also be a factor, e.g., Ghana's educational system, which for many years utilized the British-imposed model, produced excellent Greek and Latin scholars but few engineers who could run its Volta High Dam. Time perspectives are limited. Leaders of developing nations realize that many industries are difficult to develop because they require technological breakthroughs. Yet as the cost of labor rises — an important input in

1. See particularly David Novick, ed., *Program Budgeting* (San Francisco: Holt, Rinehart & Winston, 1970).
2. Robert Haveman and Julius Margolis, *Public Expenditures and Policy Analysis* (Chicago: Markham, 1970), p. 15.

industries such as shipbuilding — many countries have to opt out of production in favor of those countries with lower labor costs. To foresee the time span and sequence of economic changes, so necessary to realize opportunities for industrialization, is difficult at best. Yet this information is essential for anticipatory planning to provide the necessary preparatory inputs such as education, space, infrastructure, and capital.

In the last analysis, what most often confounds attempts to introduce greater rationality is precisely that these schemes are rational: they assume the rational use of resources to reach objectives, while in actuality ideological and political criteria often outweigh both economic rationality and the overall goals sought by the elite. Thus, in collectivizing all farms during the 1930s, Soviet leaders were willing to accept tremendous economic costs — including massive crop failures and destruction, the loss of half the country's livestock, and widespread famine — because of the ideological benefits: the abolition of private landholding. Political criteria include the degree to which political clients are satisfied with decisions and outcomes. President Nixon's election-year policy to suspend busing to promote racial balance in schools was made not to reject the goal of integration or to minimize social unrest but to satisfy a large segment of the voters. In short, the desire to stay in office often impedes economic rationality and ends–means analysis. Economic losses and temporary compromises of ultimate goals in the interests of retaining power are often justified by claiming that the "national interest" is thereby best served.

In practice, no political system even approximates the ideal rational policy-making process. Public officeholders do not, and really cannot be expected to, put aside calculations of the possible effects of given policies on their political futures. Even the most altruistic leaders concern themselves with retaining their hold on public office and on power. Instead of a rational examination of goals, possible methods, and consequences, the most common form of policy-making is an incremental ad hoc process of reacting to immediate problems, considering limited alternatives, and evaluating possible outcomes in the absence of necessary data. Policy-making usually involves different participants at different times and for different issue areas. The procedures they follow may vary from time to time and are often ad hoc arrangements that develop in the process of discussion. Rarely are all possible policy alternatives considered, and decision-makers often lack information on the costs and consequences of those that are considered. Impartial experts are not always available, and when they are they frequently give conflicting advice. Affected interest groups are more concerned with the special needs of their clienteles than with the overall success of the policy. Related policies are often made separately, as events demand, rather than in coordination with other policies and overall objectives. Objectives are adjusted to available policy options, and a remedial orientation toward handling immediate problems as they arise is often adopted. This orientation generally leads to a "satisficing" style of policy-making, wherein the outcomes are satisfying to those involved rather than being optimal solutions. Sometimes policy is determined by precedent or tradition without anyone having recognized that given actions would set official policy. One author has characterized this kind of policy-making as "muddling through," an apt description of policy-making in most parts of the world.[3]

## THE WHO, WHERE, AND HOW OF POLICY-MAKING

Patterns of policy-making vary from one country to the next, depending upon the established rules outlined by the constitution and defined by precedent and custom. These "rules of the game" for policy-making determine who will be involved, where they will interact, and how their decisions will finally be made.

While there are wide variances among countries and even within a single country, a few general comments can be made on the who, where, and how of policy-making before we turn to the individual case studies. First, who is involved in the policy process? In nearly all political systems, the three major participants are public officeholders (presidents, prime ministers, and sometimes legislators), bureaucrats, and affected interest groups. Public officials are usually responsible for the most important policy decisions because they possess the greatest political power and because their political futures may depend on a "correct" decision. Bureaucrats often must set policy as they administer it, and they can also define policy by manipulating the kind of information they pass on to the political decision-makers. Bureaucrats may also participate directly in deliberations about policy. Interest groups serve as sources of information and sometimes directly influence the policy-making process. Of course, the relative influence of these three sets of actors varies widely from country to country and from issue to issue, but they usually interact with each other and with other participants to reach a policy decision. Other frequent participants are political parties (which dominate the policy process in communist countries), the military (which is especially important in many parts of the Third World and has particularly strong influence over defense policies in all countries), and individual citizens (who sometimes seek to influence particular policies, and whose reactions as a whole are anticipated with concern).

The locales of policy-making are also subject to great variation. Even in those countries that have established constitutional procedures for making policy, ad hoc and informal procedures often rob the formal process of any role other than to legitimize decisions made elsewhere. For example, the lengthy debates and formal votes of the British House of Commons only legitimize policies decided upon in cabinet meetings, party caucuses, or government–bureaucracy–interest-group negotiating sessions. This does not mean that the parliamentary debates are meaningless: they offer the opposition an opportunity to propose alternative policies; they may lead to a better-informed public; they may lead to refinements of the initial proposal. But ordinarily in Britain, France, and Mexico (the three countries among our six whose legislatures genuinely debate policies), real decision-making power on major policies is not found in the legis-

3. Charles E. Lindbloom, "The Science of 'Muddling Through,'" *Public Administration Review* XIX (Spring 1959): 79–88.

TABLE 8.1
*The Stages of a Bill in the British Parliament*   _____

*House of Commons*
1. First reading (A formality)
2. Second reading (An important general debate)
3. Financial resolution in Committee of the Whole (This stage takes place only when money is required.)
4. Committee stage (Bill considered in detail)
5. Report stage (House considers committee amendments)
6. Third reading (Usually a formality)

*House of Lords*
1 – 6 repeated, except 3

Final stages
1. Consideration of Lords' amendments (Interchange of messages)
2. Royal Assent (Bill becomes Act of Parliament)

*Source:* British Government and Politics, 2d ed. by Douglas V. Verney, p. 135. Copyright © 1966, 1971 by Douglas V. Verney. By permission of Harper & Row, Publishers.

lature. In these countries and other liberal democracies, Western traditions of legalism and obedience to constitutional procedures usually enforce formal adoption of major policies by the parliament and other appropriate governmental bodies even when the actual decisions are made elsewhere.

Legalism and constitutionalism are norms absent in many other parts of the world. In some countries, such as Nigeria and China, the near-absence of institutionalized procedures means that ad hoc arrangements are the predominant pattern of policy-making. Practical and political needs will determine whether a decision is made in a party meeting, a military staff session, or a conference between local notables and government administrators. The procedures, setting, and participants may be entirely different for the next policy decision. Shifting patterns of policy-making need not be considered inferior to regularized patterns. Indeed, the improvisational nature of this kind of decision-making may be an asset in countries undergoing rapid change, where the locus of political power is shifting and transitory alliances are necessary to build support for change.

The style of policy-making may take three general forms: elite-dominant, in which a narrow circle of leaders at the very top of the political hierarchy determines policy; closed-bargaining, in which policy is made as a result of bargaining among a limited number of participants; and open-bargaining, in which policy is the product of negotiation among most of those interested in the policy at hand. One might expect the open-bargaining style to characterize the policy process in liberal democracies, but this is not always the case. Issues affecting national security may be addressed by a very small closed group of decision-makers. Other policies, especially those that do not become controversial or visible to the general public, are set by a restricted number of participants. Only a few of the most controversial subjects give rise to open bargaining by large numbers of participants. In communist countries, by contrast, much of the national decision-making takes place at the top levels of the party hierarchy, but large numbers are occasionally drawn into the deliberations on some policy issues — always with strict limits on the nature of their participation. While communist systems tend to be highly centralized, they vary over time, and trends in the large nations indicate gradual decentralization. With economic development, large complex bureaucracies — including the party, the military, and myriad functional ministries and local administrative and economic organizations — begin to support competing goals and policies.

Communist systems seek to maintain efficient communications networks. Thus, though the frequency of inputs from the environment may be as great as in nonpublicly controlled systems, their diversity is considerably narrower. There is greater consensus on goals, though competition clearly exists in that area. Policy goals and acts tend to be rational and broad in scope, and the system tends to be increasingly effective in ascertaining outcomes. Technology and research are emphasizing cybernetic system development — that is, goal determination, followed by evaluation and adjustment of policy in light of outcomes and feedback.

In Third World nations the most common policy-making style is elite-dominated closed bargaining, in part due to the limited numbers of literates, poor communications, masses with low incomes, and traditions that legitimize elite-authoritarian rule. Such traditions may be adopted early by a single party or military regime. Where nonelite participation in policy-making occurs, it increasingly reflects the dualist nature of Third World societies. Professionals, often foreign or foreign-trained, are called in to help with planning and to improve administrative procedures and skills. Outside this modern sector, the masses have access only to the traditional mode of communication, patron-client links. Those of lesser status excluded from the original decision-making process may attempt through this network to affect the application of a policy by petitioning for a favor from the government. Such an individual may want help for the family, a job, a loan, a child's admission to secondary school, or money to visit a doctor. Though such money may come from public funds, it is often disbursed through some local politician or official.

In the case studies, we shall be focusing on the policy-making structures of each of the six nations.

# Britain and France:
## Policy Processes in the Pluralist Context

The policy process in Britain, France, and other liberal democracies is influenced above all by the pluralist nature of the political and social systems. This is evident in the scope, process, and outcomes of policy-making. Pluralism limits the *scope* of governmental decision-making; in that society is informally divided into a public sector, for which government is responsible, and a private sector, where government is not expected to intrude. Important decisions are made in the private sector by numerous autonomous nongovernmental bodies, which usually guard their rights to make such decisions even if they have far-reaching effects on society. The policy-making *process* in Britain and France is pluralist in that political power is dispersed, rather than concentrated at any one point in the government. Important policy decisions are made at various levels and at various locales within the governmental structures. Where and by whom policy is set varies from one type of issue to the next and sometimes from one time period to the next. Policy *outcomes* also reflect pluralism, in that policies are often determined by the pluralist interaction of various political forces, interest groups, and government bodies.

Because of the competitive nature of such interaction, policy goals may appear to be poorly defined. Decision-making in Britain and France has usually lacked an ideological component that establishes goals and priorities. Instead, much policy-making is undertaken in the absence of clear long-range goals. There are, however, some notable exceptions to the general absence of explicit socioeconomic goals. The British Labour party came to power in 1945 with a clear set of goals, which it subsequently enacted in a series of sweeping reforms. De Gaulle's goal of restoring French grandeur and independence of action in world politics guided his foreign policy and that of his successors.

When goals are defined in liberal democracies, they are usually reformist rather than radical in nature. Indeed, radical goals are probably incompatible with the accommodation and compromise that are central to pluralist policy processes. But even clearly enunciated reformist goals are the exception rather than the rule in Britain and France, where for the most part, goals are unstated. To the extent that British and French policies have implicit goals, they usually involve the maintenance and adjustment of the status quo.

We have noted that the scope of governmental policy in Britain and France is limited by the distinction between the private and public sectors. However, both Britain and France have "mixed economies"; that is, their economies are characterized by a private sector of privately owned industry and commerce, and a public sector of nationalized industry, financial institutions, and transportation services owned and operated by the government. Both countries' public sectors include key industries and financial institutions, which permit the government to influence the whole economy profoundly through its management of the nationalized corporations. As a result, the British and French governments have larger parts in economic policy-making than does the United States government. For example, it is not unusual for the French government to play a major role in salary negotiations between management and labor, not simply as a mediator but as an active participant.

Both Britain and France have extensive government-operated social welfare programs, which further broaden the scope of governmental activity in society. Social welfare programs involve both governments in medical care, housing, education, retirement programs, and, in the case of France, official encouragement of a higher birth rate by means of family support payments based on family size.

Present trends suggest that the expanding scope of governmental activity will continue. In the case of most liberal democracies, including Britain and France, the expanding role of government is not attributable to governmental pursuit of new responsibilities. In fact, the opposite is often the case: the public frequently expects the government to broaden its activities to subsume new problems. For example, apparently uninterested governments were prodded by citizen demands to establish automobile safety standards. Another reason for the growth of governmental activity is the complexity of modern economies and societies. Only the government has the power and the legal right to deal with many of the major issues confronting modern societies. Two illustrations are environmental control and energy resource allocation, both of which have necessitated governmental action in areas previously free of governmental interference. Thus, the broadening scope of government policy is not because of conspiratorial forces or "creeping communism"; it is made inevitable by the requirements of modern society and public expectations.

## POLICY PROCESSES IN BRITAIN AND FRANCE

Policy decisions affecting society in general are made in a variety of settings inside and outside government in pluralist systems such as Britain and France. As a general rule, the most important policies are set by the top governmental executive bodies: the prime minister and the Cabinet in Britain and the president and the Council of Ministers in France. Policy decisions made at this level often take the form of broad definitions of principles and goals, which must be interpreted and fleshed out at lower levels. Such lower-level policy-making is clearly important in shaping the actual policy that is ultimately implemented. But, as one former British minister explained, the cabinet is the "center of the web" and "in every decision of importance that affects the country, the threads of those decisions run into the cabinet."[4]

In Britain, the prime minister is the most influential policy-maker. Individual ministers are responsible for policies within the scope of their ministries, but the most important of these policies are agreed upon collectively. And, while most important policies are established collectively by the cabinet, it is the prime minister who decides what is the collective view of the cabinet. Occasionally, too, the prime minister will make important policy decisions on his own or in consultation with an inner circle of advisers.

The cabinet meets on a weekly basis to discuss and make policy. Important decisions are usually subject to long deliberations in cabinet subcommittees and informal meetings. When the time comes for a decision to be made, tradition bars formal voting by the cabinet. In most cases, there is sufficient unity for

4. Iain Macleod, cited by Anthony Sampson in *The New Anatomy of Britain* (New York: Stein and Day, 1972), p. 69.

the prime minister to state the consensus of the meeting for the record. In instances when the cabinet is divided, it may be necessary to "collect the voices." Lord Morrison, a former minister under three prime ministers, describes how this is done without breaking the traditional ban on formal voting. The procedure is

> to go round the table and to get the views of Ministers for and against the proposition under consideration. Somebody is carefully noting the numbers each way and at the end the Prime Minister will declare the predominant view, avoiding the figures if he can. This, of course, is very near formal voting, but we protect tradition by somewhat regretfully collecting the voices and counting them as informally as we can.[5]

In France the situation is complicated by the presence of both a powerful president and an influential prime minister. The president dominates the policy process in areas of interest to him. In areas within the presidential domain, the cabinet may offer its advice to the president but its task is essentially to execute the president's decisions. On occasion, opposition in the cabinet may delay implementation of the president's desired policy. Former ministers have reported spirited and prolonged cabinet debate on issues within the president's jurisdiction, such as granting independence to Algeria — an issue that de Gaulle clearly regarded as within his exclusive domain.[6] However, the final decision in this and other areas of his choosing belonged to de Gaulle. The same has been true in the cases of Pompidou and Giscard d'Estaing within an even broader range of presidential policy-making.

In practice, the French president generally leaves his prime minister and Council of Ministers considerable scope for independent action, especially in domestic economic and social policy. The prime minister plays a major part in defining policy outside the areas reserved by the president. He coordinates the action of the cabinet and arbitrates conflicts among ministers. He may even have ambitious policy goals of his own distinguishable from but not in conflict with those of the president. Jacques Chaban-Delmas, the first prime minister (1969–1972) under President Pompidou, was able to develop and promote his own domestic program for a "New Society." However, the prime minister cannot challenge the primacy of the president.

> When the prime minister utilizes the means of control in a too effective manner, a "dyarchy" tends to develop at the summit. The only manner of remedying such a situation is for the president to re-establish unity of direction by compelling the prime minister to resign.[7]

Thus, de Gaulle replaced Pompidou with a new prime minister in 1968 after Pompidou's prestige grew markedly because of his successful resolution of the

5. Lord Morrison of Lambeth, *Government and Parliament: A Survey from the Inside,* 3d ed. (London: Oxford University Press, 1964), p. 20.
6. See Robert Buron, *Le Plus beau des métiers* (Paris: Plon, 1963), pp. 220–223.
7. Alain Claisse, *Le Premier ministre de la V^e République* (Lille: Université de Lille, 1970), p. 113.

Events of May and his landslide victory in the parliamentary elections of 1968. Four years later, Pompidou, then president, replaced Chaban-Delmas — in part because of Chaban's pursuit of policies and activities he disapproved of.

The French cabinet meets on a weekly basis with both the president and the prime minister in attendance. It is the president who presides over and dominates these meetings. In his memoirs, de Gaulle described how cabinet decisions are reached:

> Each minister may ask for the floor; it is always given him. In the most important cases, I invite all the members of the cabinet to state their views. At any rate, the prime minister presents his arguments and proposals. In the end, I indicate how I see the issue and I formulate the conclusion.[8]

Individual ministers may also shape important policy within their areas of reponsibility. The minister of finance has considerable influence on a broad range of policy decisions because of his control over the financial aspects of most policies. Valéry Giscard d'Estaing held this post throughout much of the Fifth Republic (1962–1966, 1969–1974) and left the imprint of his fiscal attitudes on French domestic policies. In some cases, individual ministers may prevail despite the opposition of their colleagues in the cabinet. Minister of Education Edgar Faure's proposals for sweeping university reforms in the aftermath of the Events of May were implemented despite important opposition within the Cabinet and the majority coalition. In this case Faure prevailed over powerful opponents because de Gaulle sided with him.

In both Britain and France, the parliaments' task is primarily to polish decisions made by the cabinet. Rarely does a major policy proposal originate in either parliament. Amendments to the Government's bills are offered by the legislators and passage of such amendments is usually dependent upon the government's acceptance. Government-sponsored bills are usually assured of passage because of the strict discipline of the majority. When a government proposal meets stiff opposition from members of the majority, it is modified by government-accepted amendments. In some cases it is withdrawn by the government to avoid dividing the majority. Parliamentary debate on policy also provides for a useful airing of divergent views and offers Opposition forces the opportunity to explain how they would perform differently and presumably better. The parliaments, thus, have a place in the policy process but clearly a secondary one compared to the government.

Two other important sets of participants in the policy processes of Britain and France are political parties and interest groups. In both countries, the left-wing parties develop elaborate party programs not only for electoral purposes but to establish policy goals and priorities. Such party-defined policy is often enacted as national policy once the party controls the government. In Britain, the Labour government elected in 1945 faithfully implemented the program of economic nationalizations and social welfare established by the party long be-

8. Charles de Gaulle, *Mémoires d'espoir: le renouveau 1958–1962* (Paris: Plon, 1970), p. 285.

fore the elections. But such fidelity to the party program is not always the case. Harold Wilson's first Labour government (1964–1970) had a much less clearly defined set of goals and failed to enact several of those that had been defined (e.g., the reform of the House of Lords).

Whether or not they formulate programs, most British and French parties contribute to the policy-making process by identifying and crystallizing national concerns. Seeking issues for election campaigns, the parties often initiate policy proposals that are implemented once they reach power. Even parties that do not win office may develop issues that are eventually enacted as official state policy. Parties also lead public debate and discussion of alternative policies. During elections, parties often focus on specific issues thought to be of national interest. In so doing, they publicize different approaches to the issues and thereby inform the public of alternative policies.

Interest groups also play a very important part in the policy processes of Britian and France. There is little legislative lobbying by interest groups, such as is found in the United States Congress and state legislatures, because the British and French parliaments have limited independent power and their members are usually bound to vote as the parties dictate. So, British and French interest groups seek avenues of access to policy-making. The most important points of access are formal governmental institutions created to assure that interest groups have a say in policy-making that affects their clients or followers. These formal governmental institutions include advisory boards, councils, committees, boards of directors for nationalized industries or institutes, and other such. All bring representatives of the government and interest groups together for regular consultation and bargaining. Very often these bodies serve not only to inform government but actually to set official policy. In Britain literally hundreds of these bodies, most established on the initiative of the government or of parliament, provide regular opportunities for interest groups to participate in shaping policy. Occasionally they implement and administer policy, thereby involving interest groups in the enforcement of government policy.

The situation is similar in France. As one commentator points out, ". . . there exist now no less than five hundred 'Councils,' twelve hundred 'Committees,' and three thousand 'Commissions,' all bringing together group representatives and members of the bureaucracy."[9] At the national level, the Economic and Social Council, made up of representatives appointed by major interest groups and the government, must give both government and parliament advice on all bills that will affect economic and social affairs. However, neither the government nor parliament is obliged to follow the Council's advice and both in fact frequently disregard it entirely. At the regional level, Economic and Social Committees made up of representatives from the interest groups advise the regional councils. The effectiveness of these various committees and councils in permitting interest groups to influence policy is variable. In general, they are less effective than their British counterparts.

9. Henry Ehrmann, *Politics in France,* 2d ed. (Boston: Little, Brown, 1971), p. 178.

In addition to these institutional arrangements, informal contacts between public officials and interest spokesmen abound at all levels of the policy-making and implementation process in Britain and France. These informal ties may be the product of "old boy" associations from the prestige schools (in Britain the elite private prep schools and Oxford and Cambridge, in France the Ecole Polytechnique and other *Grandes Ecoles*). Or they may result from careful efforts by interest spokesmen to cultivate ties with selected politicians and bureaucrats. Informal access is usually less visible than the more institutionalized forms of interest group involvement, but it may be equally effective. The informal ties and alliances of convenience or necessity between interest groups and public officials can significantly shape policy.

The influence of interest groups on policy varies widely. Some decisions are made by the political leadership with little or no input from such sources. De Gaulle's disdain for "intermediaries" representing narrow special interests kept his decisions relatively free of interest group influence. For example, interest groups favoring European unification had no opportunity to influence his policy decisions on the Common Market. Other decisions may be strongly influenced, and sometimes even made, by interest groups, this is especially true of governmental policies that require the cooperation of the affected interest groups.

## REFLECTIONS ON POLICY-MAKING IN BRITAIN AND FRANCE

Policy-makers, especially those at the highest political levels, face numerous pressures on their time and abilities. Rarely does a top government official have the time to examine fully and independently all aspects of any single policy, no matter how important. Other policies must be considered and other decisions made. Party matters, electoral concerns, and personal appearances demand his or her attention. Consequently, the president, prime minister, or cabinet minister must rely on the advice of assistants, bureaucrats, and interest group spokesmen in making decisions. The pace of current developments usually leaves little time to plan coordinated approaches to policy-making even on single issues. One former British MP and minister said that in his experience there is

> very little Cabinet policy, as such, on any subject. No one has time to think it out, to discuss it, to coordinate its various elements, or to see to its prompt and consistent enforcement. There are only departmental policies. . .
>
> The whole system is one of mutual friction and delay with, at best, some partial measure of mutual adjustment between unrelated policies. It is quite incompatible with any coherent planning of policy as a whole, or with the effective execution of such a policy. It breaks down hopelessly in a serious crisis where clear thinking over difficult and complex situations, definite decisions (not formulae of agreement) and swift and resolute action are required.[10]

10. L. S. Amery, *Thoughts on the Constitution* (London: Oxford University Press, 1947), p. 87.

In most liberal democracies, as we have said, policy-making takes place on a piecemeal or incremental basis in response to needs for immediate action. Overall goals are poorly defined or reflect the diversity of pluralist societies. In most cases, there is only limited consideration of possible policy alternatives. Decisions are more often than not made in the absence of reliable information about the possible consequences of those alternatives being considered. Coordination of policy is generally lacking, and when it is attempted unexpected events may intervene. Thus, the efforts of Britain, France, and other Western nations (including the United States) to respond to the energy crisis of 1973–1974 were upset by the disruption of petroleum shipments from the Middle East because of the Yom Kippur War between the Arabs and Israelis.

Both countries have attempted to make long-range plans to coordinate development of the private and public sectors of their economies. In contrast to the compulsory nature of economic plans in communist states, the British and French planning is voluntary. Its purpose is to establish national economic priorities in consultations between representatives of government, industry, agriculture, and labor and to coordinate their efforts to achieve these goals. In Britain the National Economic Development Council (called "Neddy") was created in 1961 to develop national economic plans. In operation, Neddy has been undercut by both Labour governments (which sought stronger forms of planning) and Conservative governments (which preferred a less active governmental role in the economy). Planning has generally been more successful in France than in Britain; France has just completed its sixth economic plan (1971–1975). However, there have been times in France when goals and priorities had to be abandoned entirely because of the pressure of events.

Another feature of liberal democracies is the inordinate slowness of policy-making. To build broad popular support and to avoid alienating those whose cooperation is essential to the policy's success often requires many years. For example, eighteen years after initial efforts at decentralization, French regional institutions remained weak though there has been no organized resistance.[11] An absence of policy or "nondecisions" may result from such delays or from government's refusal to act. Nondecisions too affect society. For instance, French university enrollments expanded at very rapid rates during the 1960s, and the government took no action to accommodate the growing university. The absence of reform and the overcrowding of the universities were major underlying causes of the student riots of May 1968.

The disjointed and unplanned nature of policy-making in Britain and France is no doubt a product of the interaction of autonomous social, economic, and political bodies. That the dominant style is "mudding through" is apparent even to the casual observer because of the open and public nature of policy-making in these countries. But, as we shall see, muddling through is by no means restricted to pluralist democracies. It is also characteristic of much

11. See William G. Andrews, "The Politics of Regionalization in France," in *Politics in Europe: Structures and Processes in Some Postindustrial Democracies*, ed. Martin O. Heisler (New York: David McKay, 1974).

policy-making in the supposedly controlled and planned societies of the Soviet Union and China.

# Policy Processes in China and the Soviet Union: Institutionalizing Change

In Western political systems, political leaders change, but in general the procedures of making policy vary only to the extent that each leader introduces his or her own style. A reading of the constitution will generally direct the interested observer to at least some of the important centers of governmental decision-making. This is not the case in communist political systems, where the constitutionally prescribed governmental structures are only the formal façades that legitimize policy made elsewhere, usually at the top levels of the party. Another difference between communist and liberal democratic political systems is the scope of governmental decision-making. There is no distinction between private and public sectors of social decision-making in communist states: the party asserts the right to make any and all policy decisions that affect society.

The making of policy in communist states is elite-dominated, or oligarchic. This is not a matter of embarrassment to communists since Leninist thought explicitly calls for control of the revolution by the party elite. "Bourgeois democratic" forms of decision-making are condemned as shams and poor substitutes for rule by the Communist party, which alone is capable of interpreting the will of the masses. The elite operates in secret as it sets policy. Public sessions of governmental bodies or party units have little importance in the policy-making process and serve primarily to publicize new programs. The numerous discussions and public meetings that preceded the adoption of the 1961 CPSU program had virtually no effect on the content of the program, but did serve to convince rank-and-file party members and the general public of the new program's virtues.

The basically oligarchic nature of policy-making does not exclude the possibility of meaningful participation by nonmembers of the elite. Under certain circumstances, and usually at the party's discretion, formal and informal interest groups may affect policy. One study of Soviet interest groups reveals how an informal coalition of interests forced Khrushchev to change his policy of mandatory work experience and vocational training in elementary and secondary schools.[12] Furthermore, members of the elite often serve as informal spokesmen for outside interests. Marshal Grechko represents the military's views in

12. Philip D. Stewart, "Soviet Interest Groups and the Policy Process: The Repeal of Production Education," *World Politics* XXII (October 1969): 29–50.

the Soviet Politburo. Prior to his purge, Kao Kang, a former military leader, voiced the attitudes of the industrial management in the Chinese party elite.

The tight control over policy maintained by the party elite makes possible gestures of "democratization" that do not endanger its monopoly over decision-making. In both China and the Soviet Union, controlled public discussions of proposed policy are used to give citizens the sense of participation without actually surrendering the party's decision-making prerogatives. There is often mass participation in the implementation of policy at the level of the commune or local industry. General guidelines are established at the center, but local units have some latitude in applying them to the concrete local situation.

The oligarchic nature of communist policy-making does not mean that there is always unanimous agreement within the elite. On the contrary, there is often subtle evidence of genuine conflict at all levels and stages of policy-making. Khrushchev frankly admitted as much to a Western newsman who asked how the party's executive body made its decisions. Khrushchev replied:

> More often than not, when questions are examined at meetings of the Central Committee Presidium, different points of view are expressed, as the members of the Presidium strive to examine the problem under discussion as thoroughly as possible. During the discussions, the members of the Presidium usually arrive at a unanimous point of view. If on some question unanimity cannot be reached, the problem is decided by a simple majority vote.
>
> Of course, very heated debates sometimes arise. But that is quite natural in a democratic discussion.[13]

Evidence from both China and the Soviet Union suggests that even the top leader encounters resistance to his ideas and must sometimes abandon them.

By definition, the initial goals of communist states are radical: the complete transformation of existing social, political, and economic institutions into a new communist society. In the pursuit of these radical goals, novel policies and policy-making procedures are often utilized. China's experiment involves both organizational and substantive innovations. Given this penchant for innovation, policy-making processes could hardly be expected to escape dramatic change. Such substantive changes as the Great Leap Forward and the Great Proletarian Cultural Revolution have been created, in part, by means of ad hoc policy processes and implemented by both the institutionalized formal structures and innovative mechanisms designed especially to realize these programs. In the Soviet Union, where the revolution is older, both policies and policy-making procedures are becoming more stable and more conservative. There is a growing preoccupation with defending existing accomplishments by avoiding adventuresome policies. A growing stability of policy-making procedures first emerged after Stalin's death, and the avoidance of dramatic policy innovation has been pronounced since Khrushchev's ouster.

---

13. Cited in Sidney Ploss, *Conflict and Interest Groups in Soviet Russia: A Case Study of Agricultural Policy, 1953–1963* (Princeton: Princeton University Press, 1964), p. 8.

## POLICY-MAKING STRUCTURES

China's supreme policy-making groups are, in ascending order of importance, the Communist Party's Central Committee, the Politburo, the Poltiburo's Standing Committee, the Military Affairs Committee, and the party chairman. Their policy decisions tend to be broad in scope, and are translated into operational terms by the government's State Council. Premier Chou En-lai and some sixteen vice-premiers and thirty ministers are responsible for developing and implementing plans and policies consistent with party requirements. Among the key policy groups under the State Council are the National Economic Commission, the State Planning Commission, the State Capital Construction Commission, and the Scientific–Technological Commission. Most of the high officials who head ministries and commissions also hold positions in the party hierarchy, which serves to facilitate communication and party control.

Long-term planning, which usually takes the form of five-year plans, is done by the State Planning Commission. Such plans usually focus on selected areas, e.g., the sectors of development (agriculture and industry), and on setting priorities for heavy and light industry, agriculture, consumption, and investment allocations.

Party control over policy persists beyond the planning stage, and is exercised not only through the appointment of party members to top ministerial positions, but also through the party fraction, which assures the implementation of policy in all governmental and economic organizations. Party committees and branches (known as "fractions") permeate the governmental hierarchy and other economic institutions, e.g., industry and communes. A further mode of party control is the party-directed mass organizations: unions, peasant associations, the Young Communist League, and women's associations.

In actual practice, these structures do exist and have persisted with considerable modification. Yet, the most prominent actor in the policy process was Chairman Mao. When Mao went into semiretirement in the late 1960s, the day-to-day decisions were assumed by Chou En-lai; however, Mao has maintained a keen interest in their general direction. The key organizations have been the State Council, the party headquarters, and the party's Military Affairs Committee (MAC), each of which has developed well-defined task areas. The State Council deals with economic policy, education, health, and diplomacy; the party headquarters with ideology, social policy, and international communist affairs; and the MAC with national security and the military's involvement in the society. Each has been headed by a Politburo member with his own style. Lin Piao headed the MAC for much of the 1960s until his purge; Chou continues to head the Standing Committee of the State Council; Liu Shao-ch'i and Teng Hsiao-p'ing were influential in the party headquarters until they too were purged in the late 1960s.[14] Liu's reported confession after being purged suggests the latitude of party leaders in and the impact of their personalities on the policy process:

14. Teng Hsiao-p'ing has since been reinstated.

During a certain period prior to July 18, 1966, when Chairman Mao was absent from Peking, the Central Committee's daily work pivoted around me. I made decisions affecting the conduct of the Cultural Revolution in all quarters of Peking and made reports to the Central Committee meetings . . . At that time, requests came from many quarters for work teams . . . However, at that time, we should not have done anything more than to handle the situation by sending liaison men. At the time, some comrades discovered the work teams were in conflict with the masses, and taking up this issue, proposed that the dispatch of work teams was unnecessary. For instance, Comrade Ch'en P'o-ta made such a proposal. He understood Mao's thinking. Had we also understood Chairman Mao's thought, we would have suspended these activities, and would not have pursued a mistaken line and direction . . . Precisely at this critical moment when I was directing the Central Work Meetings, I committed the above mentioned mistakes.[15]

As we have suggested, the responsibilities of the formal institutions of policy-making have varied depending on their leaders and on the matters at issue. Such variations are considerable. For example, only nine of the fifteen Central Committee plenums convened since 1949 met in the five years between 1956 and 1961. The State Council met often during the 1950s but less so during the 1960s; and the MAC was given center stage in the 1960s following a shadowy existence in the 1950s.

The actual policy process during the first two decades of communist rule was dominated by Mao. Until his semiretirement, Mao was consistently able to combine China's ideologically defined overall goal — the use of human potential and technology to establish a participatory, egalitarian, industrialized socialist society — with skillful leadership tactics. He was particular about methods as well as ends. In developing policy, he sought the participation of individuals, usually party officials, who were involved at various levels. Once he had heard the range of opinions and a debate of the alternatives, he posited his own summary view, which he then expected to be translated into action. Many of these decisions, most notably and vigorously the Great Leap Forward, have been opposed by the party elite and by governmental and mass groups. Policy objectives are then transmitted to the State Council, the party headquarters (Central Committee Politburo), the Military Affairs Commission (MAC), and at times special Central Committee plenums. They are publicized by means of articles and editorials in the mass media, various types of national congresses, and local cadre groups.[16] Implementation is dependent on the reception given these objectives by those in the government ministries and provincial or commune-governing bodies. Further, the availability of resources, material, and manpower, as well as conflicts with local priorities, also affect implementation.

15. *The Collected Works of Liu Shao-ch'i, 1958–1967* (Hong Kong: Union Research Institute, 1968), pp. 357–359.

16. The best commentary on China's policy process is Michel Oksenberg, "Policy Making Under Mao, 1949–1968: An Overview," in *China: Management of a Revolutionary Society,* ed. John M. Lindbeck (Seattle: Washington University Press, 1971). See also Paris H. Chang, "Research Notes on the Changing Loci of Decision in the Chinese Communist Party," *The China Quarterly* (October–December 1970): 169–193.

During the Great Proletarian Cultural Revolution, conflicts over policy-making at the center, between the center and the local party, and between military and Red Guard organizations were readily apparent. Evidence of widespread pluralism and local autonomous decision-making became abundant. The newspapers of the center, the local areas, the party, and the army expressed different views as to who should be admitted to universities and how to motivate workers — two important issues that divided the center and peripheral political units. Commands from the center during and after the Cultural Revolution were often disobeyed by local party and Red Guard units.

In the Soviet Union the primary policy-making organs are the top levels of the party hierarchy, the Central Committee and the Politburo (called the Presidium from 1952 to 1966). In the past, the Central Committee played an active role in decision-making. However, its unwieldy size (396 full and candidate members) and infrequent meetings (about twice a year) have reduced its importance. Now it ratifies the decisions of the Politburo and, in rare cases, resolves issues that have seriously divided the Politburo. It is thus the Politburo that is the most important policy-making body. Meeting weekly, this elite core of the party leadership sets the general policy directions for the nation.

The coordination of party and government is assured by the overlap of personnel at the top levels. Key government officials — such as Foreign Minister Gromyko and KGB head Andropov — are also members of the Politburo and presumably have influence in party circles over issues within the scope of their governmental responsibilities. Official state policy is usually formalized by the Council of Ministers, although some important decisions have been publicly announced as joint decrees of the Council of Ministers and the party Central Committee (or its Politburo). The ministries are often involved in the policy-making process from the earliest stages, but the ultimate power of decision resides in the Politburo. At times, even seemingly unimportant details are decided in the Politburo and imposed on the ministries. Of course, the party monitors the faithful execution of its will in the administrative realm, and has on occasion assumed for itself the task of directly administering policy. Thus, the "virgin lands" policy of farming previously unused and often marginally arable land, initiated by Khrushchev in the mid-1950s, was implemented directly by the party rather than by the state bureaucracies.

Since the death of Stalin no single personality has dominated Soviet decision-making as Mao has in China. Khrushchev's period of pre-eminence was short (1957–1964), and even at the height of his power, opposition compelled him to drop some of his most cherished proposals. His hopes for major agricultural changes were frustrated on several occasions between 1959 and 1963, when the party elite rejected his efforts to shift the priorities of resource allocation from heavy industry to agriculture and consumer goods.[17] Khrushchev's successor, Leonid Brezhnev, seems predisposed (or compelled) to share his

17. Ploss, *Conflict and Interest Groups, pp.* 216–268.

decision-making powers with others despite his consolidation of power in the past few years. Collegial rule has prevailed in principle and practice since Khrushchev's ouster.

## POLICY STYLES IN THE COMMUNIST SETTING

It might be expected that communist regimes would approximate the rational model of policy-making. They have well-defined goals derived from their ideology; they are self-conscious about making policy decisions that will pursue these goals; they are committed to centralized planning and decision-making; and they have the political ability to resist temporary tides of public opinion. In fact, however, policy in communist states seems to be as much the product of "muddling through" as is United States' policy. That this is the case is evident in Soviet attempts to cope with the problems of excessive centralization. The need for greater flexibility and the initiative at the local level led to some decentralization of state functions in the mid-1950s. The resulting rise in localism and problems of coordination and control led to recentralization a few years later. In the last years of his rule, Khrushchev tried again to decentralize state bodies, and this time even the party. One of the first acts the new leaders undertook after removing Khrushchev was to reverse once again his decentralization reforms.

Attempts at developing rational policies are often compromised by the tendency to choose policies for political reasons rather than for their contributions to long-range goals. This is especially true during succession crises, when aspiring leaders seek to rally supporters around various policy stands. Both Stalin and Khrushchev shifted position on major issues to rally supporters and undermine opponents during their drives to the top. Such jockeying around issues continues even when there is no succession crisis as leaders seek to manipulate or accommodate various sectors of society. In addition, vested interests in the party, the state bureaucracy, and elsewhere affect the policy-makers' decisions and sometimes distort their intent in the process of implementation. Thus, as one study suggests, ". . . while bureaucratic efficiency, economic productivity, and social well-being are high on the priority list of the Soviet policy-makers, they are not always the determining ends of policy-making."[18]

Policy is initiated in the top levels of the party leadership. The pattern that characterizes major reforms in the Soviet Union has been described as follows:

(1) several years of growing difficulties and discontent during which the specific groups directly involved presumably tried to make their complaints heard; (2) a formal denunciation of current evils by a top party leader or leadership, with the timing and manner much influenced by the specific power relations within that leadership; (3) an interval of several weeks or months during which pre-

18. Zbigniew Brzezinski and Samuel P. Huntington, *Political Power: USA/USSR* (New York: Viking, 1965), p. 202.

sumably the top leadership formulated and agreed to its basic proposals for dealing with the evils; (4) the official announcement of these proposals in the form of a "memorandum" or "theses" from a top leader or top party body.[19]

The procedure is similar in China, where each of the several decision-making bodies has its own approach to policy-making. As one study points out:

> The agendas, directives, and procedure of the State Council suggest a well-organized pragmatic institution at work; sifting reports, searching for realistic options, calm and unhurrying, competently responding to problems by adjusting ongoing policies at the margins. Reports from Party plenums and the informal Party meetings suggest another policy making style; tumultuous, hurried, concerned with relating means to ideological ends. Finally although the image of the PLA is extremely ill-defined, the PLA *Work Bulletin* as well as PLA actions in 1967–68 reflect an organization that was proud of its tradition and impatient with civilian society, which had relatively good communications channels and a capacity to handle problems pragmatically, but which may have been plagued by inter- and intra-service rivalries.[20]

There are indications that major decisions are accompanied by considerable politicking and persuasion. Position papers circulated by individuals and fractions often give rise to lengthy and lively debates.

Perhaps one of the most important factors in the shifting policy-making structures is Chairman Mao's leadership style and skills. In order to preserve control over the policy-making process, he not only absorbed massive amounts of information, but also skillfully alternated his use of decision-making bodies. This practice prevented any single group from consolidating power and inhibited institutionalization of decision-making mechanisms. Thus Mao utilized segments of the Politburo, the standing committee, or the whole, as he saw fit. He arranged for expanded decision-making meetings of the party bodies, including the Politburo, by inviting nonmembers to attend. He convened ad hoc Supreme State Conferences and conferences of regional party officials. And he kept informed on proceedings at party meetings, performance problems, and results in areas of concern to him, utilizing this information to maintain his influence over the policy-making processes.

Mao's role is also important because, as monitor of the policy process, he was able to use feedback to correct flaws and revise policy, and thus to maintain the system's ongoing ideological objectives. This has been no easy task, and it makes China unique among political entities. Because policies have been heavily weighted with ideological objectives, many have resulted in extensive short-term costs. For example, a decline in food production was partially associated with the dramatic structural changes of the Great Leap Forward, and the disruption of established institutions was one of the costs of the Great Proletarian Cultural Revolution.

One of the distinctive features of policy in both China and the Soviet

---

19. *Ibid.,* p. 207.
20. Oksenberg, "Policy Making Under Mao," pp. 109–110.

Union has been the frequent introduction of dramatic new programs that are implemented and then abandoned, often rapidly. Rather than adjusting existing programs to correct their deficiencies, both appear to have a proclivity to introduce entirely new programs, which are in turn replaced as they prove inadequate. Considerable uncertainty and flux arise as major reforms intended to solve the same problems succeed each other. For example, Khrushchev sought to solve Soviet agricultural problems with a series of major reforms: the virgin lands programs, the reorganization of collective farms, the introduction of new crops such as corn and soy beans, crash programs to develop fertilizers, and reforms in tractor use and deployment. Rapid policy turnover pervades the whole political and economic system, affecting the stability of policy even at the local level. In 1962 the construction plan for one oblast (province) was altered some five hundred times! [21]

The same tumult surrounds policy in China. Successive policies that address the same problem have radically different approaches and goals. The post-Liberation drive to provide China with a modern economy by promoting the development of large-scale heavy industry was followed by a program that called for backyard steel furnaces, the extreme in small-scale industry. Similar instability in the political scene is illustrated by the shift from the liberalism of the Hundred Flowers Campaign of 1956–1957 to the mobilization of the Great Leap Forward of 1956–1960.

There is some evidence of a stabilization of policy in the Soviet Union since the ouster of Khrushchev. The new leadership condemned Khrushchev for his "hare-brained schemes, half-baked conclusions, and hasty decisions and actions. . . ." [22] Under Brezhnev there has been much greater continuity of policy and a lack of major innovative reforms. This change may reflect the aging of the Soviet political system and the stabilization of its policies. But it may simply be a function of the attitudes of the present leaders, and new leaders might revert to the old pattern of rapid policy turnover.

## REFLECTIONS ON POLICY-MAKING IN COMMUNIST SOCIETIES

While the communist policy process is clearly elite-dominated, the leaders are not totally unresponsive to public attitudes. The leaders of China and the Soviet Union are generally reluctant to introduce policies that will antagonize the general public. Though the Communist party's claim that it always knows what the people want and acts in accord with the popular will is at best exaggerated, the party leaders do attempt to keep informed about the attitudes of the people and usually act in such a way as to minimize negative popular reaction to their policies.

The highly centralized policy-making that is a distinctive feature of communist states has both advantages and disadvantages. On the positive

21. Brzezinski and Huntington, *Political Power*, p. 222.
22. *Current Digest of the Soviet Press*, 28 October 1964.

side from the standpoint of the elite, it facilitates the maintenance of control over policy and society. It permits the marshaling of all human and material resources to change society in the desired manner. On the other hand, the high degree of centralization often poses enormous problems because of the scope of planning. All decisions are governmental rather than private, and must be consciously made by central bodies. This requirement tends to overburden the policy-makers and to foster such bureaucratic vices as red-tape, delay, "buck-passing," and the like. Another negative outcome is lack of responsiveness to local needs and problems. There have been periodic gestures toward decentralization in both China and the Soviet Union, but such efforts are handicapped by the elites' insistence on maintaining its monopoly on control. As the Soviet and Chinese societies become even more complex, pressures for decentralization will become increasingly difficult to resist.

The commitment to long range central planning seems likely to endure. The Soviet Union has just completed its ninth five-year plan (1970–1975). The coordination of resources toward the attainment of well-defined economic goals in this and previous five-year plans has been largely responsible for the rapid economic modernization and expansion of the Soviet Union. China is currently pursuing its fourth five-year plan (1971–1976). Though previous plans were disrupted by political developments such as the Great Leap Forward and the Great Proletarian Cultural Revolution, the Chinese five-year plans have contributed to the considerable economic development and progress of China since 1949.

The extraordinary dimensions and complexity of the planning and policy process in communist systems should be emphasized. Since market forces do not operate, conscious decisions must be made on the prices of all goods produced and services offered. What and how much to produce must be determined. The production of various components must be consciously coordinated. Each seemingly simple decision entails a series of further decisions, all of which must be coordinated with each other. The application of this process to a huge modern society makes the problems of central planning and decision-making almost unbelievably complex.

Modern computer technology is of potentially great value to communist planners. So far, however, communist states have lagged in the development of cybernetics and in its application to the planning process. Soviet mathematical economists have developed proposals to rationalize planning by using computers to determine optimal allocations of resources to meet established goals. These proposals have made little headway toward implementation due to the determined resistance of old-style ideologues, who accuse the new-style planners of disdain for Marxist thought. They fear that computerization of planning and decision-making would reduce the party's control and dilute the ideological element in the setting of policies and priorities. Despite this opposition, it is likely that as the Soviets and Chinese develop computer skills and as their societies become more complex, there will be continued interest in applying cybernetics to planning problems.

# Mexico and Nigeria: Toward Governmental Control of the Policy Process

In most parts of the Third World, there is a tendency toward greater demands on governmental decision-makers. The government is expected to provide social welfare, promote economic development, control the influence of former colonial powers, and solve a host of other social, economic, and political problems. In spite of these pressures, the policy-making capabilities of many Third World countries are slight. In nearly all cases, the policy-making process is hierarchical and offers little opportunity to mobilize mass participation in social change. In some cases, powerful forces — committed to the social and political status quo — such as military hierarchies, bureaucracies, "official" churches, business interests, and foreign investors — block change. In other cases, the political leadership has the power to bring about change but is prevented from doing so by its ideological blinders.

There are too many varieties of policy pattern in the developing world for any one or two countries to be typical. However, Mexico and Nigeria do offer contrasting examples of policy-making in the Third World. Mexico's policy-making institutions are older, and hence more developed, than those of Nigeria. Nigeria offers an example of policy-making under military rulers clearly committeed to free enterprise. The Mexican government claims to be committed to a socially just society but, as is the case in many Third World countries, the important private economic sector continues to thrive. Its values, including the primacy of private enterprise and market mechanisms for distribution of goods and services, remain dominant.

## MEXICAN POLICY STRUCTURES

Since the 1917 Revolution, Mexico's policy-making network has developed considerable stability. The major participants in the policy process are the president, his cabinet of ministers, and beneath them the PRI's three active sectors: the peasant sector, the labor sector, and the popular sector. In addition, the military, the church, the agro-industrial elite, representatives of state and local government, and an expanding number of socioeconomic associations are all active in the policy process.

While the policy-making process is characterized by a two-way flow, the dominant direction is from top to bottom. It is an elite-dominated system. Competing elite groups use their leverage with the president to gain concessions in the policy finally adopted. There are both formal and informal channels for policy-making in Mexico. The formal process involves presidential initiative, congressional approval, and ultimately a ministerial or ad hoc commission with members from the affected groups that hammer out the details of implementation. The informal process, based on patron-client relationships and individualism, tends to deal with minor issues and policy requests that flow from bottom to top.

The formal process usually involves presidential initiative, although in some policy areas the inspiration for a given policy may come from the minister of one of Mexico's eighteen federal ministries or departments. If the president has decided on a given policy, he may consult relevant ministers or technocrats about the proposal. Thereafter, modifications may be made in the original proposals, and a law will be proposed to the Congress. It is then always passed by the Chamber of Deputies and the Senate, the PRI deputies voting unanimously in support of the measure.

The actual implementation of the law requires the support of the interest groups involved, and may also require the definition of the law to be sharpened. For this, the president may appoint an ad hoc commission, which will last until its mission of defining the law and gaining the acceptance of the involved groups is complete. In this process, the policy is further modified. The president's guidelines and intent must prevail, but the commission — and the involved groups represented on it — may well define the real content of the policy. An example is President López Mateos' decision in late 1961 to amend the Mexican constitution (Article 123) to allow for profit-sharing for employees of corporate enterprises.[23] He appointed a special commission, whose responsibility was to determine the details of the profit-sharing. This required a decision between two alternatives. The business sector, through the National Confederation of Mexican Chambers of Industry, the National Confederation of Mexican Chambers of Commerce, and the Employers' Confederation of the Mexican Republic, favored a deduction from profits of a percentage of the firm's capital investment; the remainder would then be subject to profit-sharing. The presidentially appointed head of the commission rejected this option in favor of a maximum 5 to 7 percent of the total profits subject to profit-sharing. This decision was more favorable to the unions than to the employers, but both finally agreed. In the case of the 1964–1965 doctors' strike, the higher wages and improved conditions agreed upon by the commission were virtually determined by the doctors. They were rejected by the president after considerable turmoil, and a presidential decree offering lower raises was rejected by the doctors as inadequate. Ultimately, the doctors' movement was suppressed with force.

Among the most powerful sectors influencing the policy processes are the wealthy landed elite, including both the large ranchers and the more successful *ejiditarios* (beneficiaries of the land reform programs), and the wealthy businessmen. The latter's success has been enhanced by the government's role in creating their enterprises. Industrial policies are often made in consultation with the National Confederation of Chambers of Industry of Mexico and the National Confederation of Chambers of Commerce. Although not part of the

23. Susan Kaufman Purcell, "Decision Making in an Authoritarian Regime: Theoretical Implications from a Mexican Case Study," *World Politics* XXVI (October 1973): 28–57.

PRI, they are at least as powerful as the labor and farm sectors of PRI. Their influence is clearly evident in the government's investment priorities, which have strongly favored economic infrastructure and industrial investment over rural and urban education, credit for the ejidos, housing, and agricultural extension. Thus, while policies are influenced by various political interests, they are not influenced equally. Business interests do not always prevail, as we have seen in the case of the profit-sharing legislation. The personality and policy preferences of the president are also very important. Indeed, the president's ability to manipulate interests in order to maximize support for his preferred policies can significantly limit or increase the power of the privileged sections of Mexican society. However, business interests do have considerable influence and success in the competition among interests that is a feature of the Mexican policy process.

Both Mexico and Nigeria have well-entrenched patron-client hierarchies, which are the basis of the informal policy structures. Whether Mexican leaders with followings of peasants, laborers, or bureaucrats or Nigerians who have the allegiance of a village or extended family unit, the effect is the same: a hierarchical decision-making structure. Persons of lower status approach those of higher status to ask for specific favors. If a visitor of high status — for example, the minister of health — visits a village, the villagers may ask for a hospital or clinic for their village. Such requests are sometimes granted, but often the response takes the form of a "symbolic payoff," or verbal assurance that the minister understands the villagers' problem and that action will be taken to respond to their needs. This form of citizen participation is not usually fruitful. Particularistic payoffs are often granted, but loans and part-time jobs do not really constitute a solution to the complex poverty-rooted problems that continue to plague the average villager's life.

There is also considerable subpresidential-level policy-making in Mexico, in part due to the extensive involvement of the federal government in public enterprises. In addition to its control over subsoil natural resources and irrigation systems, the state has a considerable investment in communication and transportation: telegraph, maritime transportation, railroads, commercial aviation, newsprint, motion picture distribution, and even the nominally private telephone company. It also controls or has interests in such other industries and services as electric power, petroleum exploration and production, iron and steel production, petrochemicals, textile mills, truck and auto assembly, the nation's largest meat-packing plants, banking, and consumer distribution. Thus public policy affecting the conditions of large numbers of workers, consumers, and other businessmen is directly related to the decisions of these units. Within these state-owned or -controlled enterprises there is considerable interaction between the PRI sectors and the politicians, particularly over labor conditions and wages.

Policy-making processes at the state and local level are also hierarchical. Here too, the president has considerable influence through the state PRI organization and the option, in most cases, to choose the governor. In some cases, however, the president defers to the state political leader. Further, the president and the executive branch control most of the finances of local governments. Finally, the president can influence the allocation of many other important rewards to individuals, groups, and politicians, including pet projects, credit for business and industry, government jobs, and political appointments and promotions.

The governor, as intermediary for the president, is also in a powerful position. He is the dominant force in local politics. Most municipal governments are limited to the routine administration of such state tasks as collecting taxes, building roads, and providing public services. Thus when a community group seeks a given project, it will often make a courtesy call on the local mayor (municipal president) and council members, but focus most of its efforts on the governor and his assistants.

Local officials are appointed to three-year terms, which gives them little time to gain the administrative experience most lack on taking office. Because there are often no state or local plans to guide expenditures, the door is left open to myriad particularistic demands and an allocation system based on status-influence links. Given this state of affairs, the *diputado* (federal deputy) and his relatives are much more likely to have government projects in their neighborhoods than is a member of a poor *barrio* (neighborhood).

The dispersion of influence and the heterogeneous nature of the political participants make it unsurprising that there is little logic or cohesion to Mexican policy outputs. There are protectionist policies for the wealthy business elite, policies for foreign investors, policies increasing credit opportunities for the wealthy landed elite, and programs for the redistribution of land to the landless. Efforts to rationalize policy-making in Mexico have taken several directions. First, there is growing momentum toward urban and regional planning, which could result in the mobilization of skilled professionals from the private sector to complement the efforts of those in the ministries seeking to further regional and urban/rural balances. A related phenomenon has been the effort by President Luis Echeverría to bring "technocrats" — experts in engineering, industrial management, and economic planning — rather than political loyalists, into his cabinet. The experience of other relatively undeveloped nations suggests that even major improvements in planning are not sufficient to improve performance. In this regard, Mexico is still faltering in the implementation of policy. For example, while there is increased use of mass campaigns in implementing government programs, these usually take the form of propaganda and are seldom followed up by social action as in China. Thus Mexico's weakness in implementing sophisticated socioeconomic plans has severely affected performance.

## NIGERIA'S POLICY STRUCTURES

Nigeria's policy-making processes are best understood by an initial examination of the formal division of political power provided for in the constitution of the Federal Republic (1960–1966). In the First Republic ministers, parliament, regional leaders (politicians and chiefs) and economic and social interest groups dominated the policy process. Planning bodies existed, but they were concerned primarily with infrastructural development. Their plans were merely advisory and were subject to acceptance by the politicians.

Changes in the policy-making process as a result of General Gowon's establishment of the twelve states in 1966 have been more apparent than real. At the apex of the new structure is the Supreme Military Council (SMC) headed by the new chairman, Olusegun Obasanso. Also members are the twelve state governors (mostly military men), and the heads of the navy and air force. The SMC develops policy in the areas of defense, post and telecommunications, and foreign affairs, and has also assumed the dominant role in developmental planning and education. Under the SMC's initiative a new planning group, the Joint Planning Board, has been created to harmonize and coordinate the economic policies of the federal and state governments and their agencies (including local governments). The Joint Planning Board is responsible for evaluating and developing long-range plans, and recently completed work on the plan for the 1975–1980 period. Its activities focus primarily on economic development, with little emphasis on social and political change.

Beneath the politically dominant SMC is the Federal Executive Council, comprised of the fifteen cabinet department heads and the SMC members. The key policy-making body, it is also responsible through the various departments for policy implementation. At the state level, policy-making is dominated by the governors and their executive councils. The commissioners at both the federal and state levels are often former politicians, as in the case of Federal Commissioner for Finance Chief Awolowo. Also being recruited as state and federal commissioners are former civil servants and permanent secretaries of ministries, who have often been responsible for developing and implementing their ministries' policies. As in the First Republic, policy-making under the military regime involves considerable interaction between interest groups and the state and local policy-makers.

During the First Republic there was considerable interaction in most issue areas among the prime minister, ministries, parliament, and regional governments, but today the Supreme Military Council is clearly dominant. It provides general policy guidelines, usually after various commissioners have developed proposals in response to problems upon which they must act. While most major decrees originate in the Federal Executive Council, comprised of the cabinet members and the SMC, each ministry has considerable latitude to develop policies on its own. There is a definite trend towards the centralization of decision-making by co-opting issue areas traditionally left to the regions and states, such as education, health, and planning. As we will note in the ensuing chapters, there is considerable tension between the federal military regime and the states as a result of the former's centralizing efforts. Many of the state governments have youthful, enthusiastic, and ambitious leaders, so eager to expand their powers and resources that the Muhammad regime (1975) has accused governors under the former regime of corruption.

Decision-making at the local level is the responsibility of the district councils, which develop public policy in the areas of public health, sanitation, sewage, road maintenance, cemeteries, and such other public conveniences as streetlights and public safety. District and village governmental decisions are mostly routine. The local leaders must work closely with state governors, and it is at this point, as in Mexico, that groups express their demands and focus their pressures. Many governors are heartily involved in infrastructure and developmental efforts, working closely on a day-to-day basis with local civil servants and, in particular, with the permanent secretaries of state ministries, their counterparts at the federal level, Nigerian and foreign businessmen, and local leaders.

In Nigeria, as in Mexico, there is considerable juxtaposition of governmental commands from above and particularistic interests expressed from below. They do not always interact, and may in fact travel along separate paths of communication. Where they do interact and conflict, as opposed to complementing each other, such as in determining priorities for industrial sites or government credits, the government usually prevails over the interest groups. As in Mexico, if the regime is bent on a certain objective and feels that public demands exceed its will to compromise, it will hold the line against the protesting interest group. Such was the case in early 1973, when students protested the requirement that they serve in the new National Youth Service Corps: their protests were without success.

## POLICY STYLES

After early periods of status quo-oriented policy, Mexico's post-1917 regime and Nigeria's post-1966 military regime have pursued reformist-oriented goals. Mexico's regime has made some radical innovations in land reform, though they have been neither extensive nor systematic. Nigeria too has moved in more dynamic directions. State enterprises have been created in order to provide investment in regions that had previously lacked it. Because both nations give priority to the market system in the allocation of scarce resources and accept the precedence of individual liberty over social justice, most policies tend to develop incrementally. That is, they are limited in scope and tend to emerge in response to immediate needs. Villagers in Mexico or Nigeria approach the local officials to ask for a road to be repaired or for running water to be piped to their area. If they have enough influence or if the local officials are so disposed, their requests may be fulfilled. In most cases, they are told that the request will be considered; then they may hear nothing more until the year when the project they requested becomes part of some national plan. If the pressures from a given area are sufficiently great, e.g., if enough mass and local elite support develops for a doctor to be sent to a village or a clinic to be established, the state or federal officials responsible may respond to their demands. In fact, most projects tend to be allocated in keeping with this format. Once an objective becomes a matter of national policy, particularistic political pressures determine allocations. This process results in incremental changes within the substantive area of concern, the geographical region in question, and the total scope of social change. Such policies, then, result in partial changes, not comprehensive changes in any of these dimensions.

There is a growing awareness in both nations of the need to expand the scope and style of decision-making to allow for more planning of manpower and resource allocations and of regional, town, and national development. If this trend continues, rational policy styles are likely to be more evident. Both nations' policy systems are relatively centralized and tend to be elite-dominant. Mexico's president, cabinet, and single party are the key participants in policy-making, and the president is clearly dominant. Because of the limited number of large group actors and the cleavages among them (e.g., labor and peasants), Mexican presidents and governors have considerable latitude. This is also true of Nigeria's military leaders at the federal and state levels. Yet the policies issuing from the authoritarian superstructures and pluralist substructures often lack continuity. Implementation of policy directives is as significant an arena for policy-making as is the initial stage of goal formation. Thus, while Nigeria's military regime can legislate by decree, and Mexico's president and ministers shape comparable policy-making powers, interest groups are able to influence implementation through pressures on cabinet ministers, committees, state governors, local officials, and bureaucrats. It is during the stages of implementation that opportunities for corruption are prevalent in both nations. Officials who are paid relatively low salaries collect their due from the "users." While this practice tends to improve public officials' salaries, and to incorporate the views of the consumers of public policies into the policy outcomes, it does not always do so justly.[24] Large segments of potential clients directly affected by policies are unable to make inputs because they lack the necessary access and/or financial resources. A further weakness of this system is inadequate evaluation. Because there is little consensus on social and political goals, aside from those related to economic development, evaluation of previous performance — an important ingredient in the policy process — is minimal. The dilemma caused by pluralist policy inputs, ineffective overall coordination, and mass mobilization will become apparent as we look at specific areas of governmental performance.

The Mexican and Nigerian policy-making processes reflect both nations' political forces and states of transition. Mexico's policy processes are authoritarian, dominated by the coalition of functional groups that make up the ruling alliance. Yet tugging at the decision-makers are sets of sub-elites, or patrons and their followers, seeking particularistic favors from the top elite. The task of distributing public goods has been shared by the modern functional group sector and the traditional patron-client sector. Nigeria's elite-dominant

24. See James C. Scott, *Comparative Political Corruption* (Englewood, N.J.: Prentice-Hall, 1972).

system faces a similar set of tensions. While the military and technocrats dominate the policy processes, appointed state commissioners and local leaders, nurture the whims of traditional local elites and their followers, perhaps with an eye to future political competition under a civilian regime. In both systems the leaders have considerable leverage, which springs primarily from their monopoly on coercive force, and from the ability to allocate credits, appointments, governmental contracts, and other important political, social, and economic opportunities. Mexico, like Britain and France, has more of a problem with lack of continuity than do China and the Soviet Union, where planning and persistence tend to prevail. In Mexico, unlike Nigeria, terms of public offices are short and there is little or no chance of being immediately returned to the same office. Thus problems and responsibilities, unfinished though they may be, are passed on to subsequent regimes.

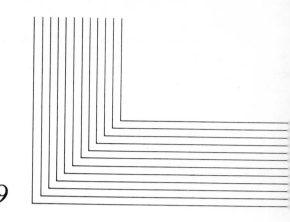

# 9

# *The Government and Society*

## Introduction

Thoughtlessly, the French queen dismissed her protesting subjects with "Let them eat cake!" But their response was more than she had contemplated — loss of the monarchy and her head as well. Though this event occurred in the highly authoritarian and elitist political structure of eighteenth-century France, it has relevance today. Whatever a regime's ability to consolidate political power, there is always a degree of interaction between the government and the society that is not hierarchical. That is, political relationships involving public policy are to varying degrees reciprocal, governmental and societal groups influencing each other. In Chapter 2 we discussed the effects of the society on the polity; in this chapter we shall be emphasizing the role of government in society.

### THE PROBLEM OF EVALUATING PERFORMANCE

One of the tasks of political scientists is to evaluate the success with which political systems meet the needs of their societies; it is rendered difficult by the subjective nature of such evaluations. The values and norms of the evaluator inevitably find their way into his or her evaluations. Even where objectivity is sought by recourse to supposedly neutral and accurate statistics, the very choice of statistics is affected by the evaluator's own biases and in turn affects conclusions.

The choice of areas to evaluate also affects judgments of the performance of a political system. Whatever measure is adopted, it has a built-in bias. To emphasize a system's ability to foster economic development as a measure of political performance is to slight other possible measures. The political system that denies individual liberties in order to devote all of its human and physical resources to the task of industrialization will be judged more successful than a system that posits the individual's right to choose one's own job or operate one's own business.

Given the subjective nature of such evaluations, it is important to state clearly our own basis for evaluating performance. In this chapter, we shall be judging the impact of governments on their societies by measuring their performance in rural development, industrialization, and social welfare and human development (specifically education and medical care). This criterion for evaluating performance necessarily places a premium on a high degree of organization and collective discipline and de-emphasizes other values such as individual freedom, liberty, and equal enforcement of the law. The system that succeeds in promoting economic development, even by means of slave labor, is evaluated higher than a system that develops more slowly but respects the individual's own political and economic choices.

This does not mean that we value freedom less than economic development. It simply reflects our belief that economic measures of performance are less subjective than, for example, estimates of the degree of legal justice and freedom in this or that state. Fairly reliable statistics on a given political system's record of promoting economic growth can be found. But opinions on whether a French worker "trapped in a capitalist economy" is any freer than a Russian worker "caught up in communist totalitarianism" are of necessity impressionistic. Furthermore, freedom is a relative concept. Chinese peasants who share in the fruits of their work through membership in a commune may feel much freer than their ancestors, who tilled the land for a rich landlord, despite greater governmental regulation of their lives. Subjection to a government in which one feels a stake may be freedom compared to the humiliation of subjection and servility to another individual who just happened to inherit property and wealth.

Furthermore, the areas of performance we have chosen to emphasize are increasingly regarded as crucial to effective government. For example, the inability of both the British Labour and Conservative parties to stimulate economic growth and control inflation contributed to the disaffection with both parties expressed by British voters in the two general elections of 1974. And the failure of the Mexican regime to provide for the welfare of its Indians and other rural poor population raises questions about the future stability of that system. The inability of a government to meet the basic economic and social needs of its people may undermine its legitimacy and stability more rapidly than would the absence or limitation of freedom or justice.

## DIFFERING PERCEPTIONS OF
## THE ROLE OF GOVERNMENT IN SOCIETY

While our focus will be on economic development and social welfare, it is important to note that not all political systems give priority to these values. To keep our evaluations in perspective, we need to recognize the priorities, goals, and role perceptions of each political system. Among the factors that determine policy preferences, perhaps the most important is the governing elite's concept of the government's role in society. If the elite considers it necessary to grant small payoffs to the silent majority's few expressive members merely in order to retain power, the government's impact is likely to be *minimal*. This minimalist role may be limited to such activities as law enforcement, maintenance of basic public sanitation, road repairs and construction, and a central banking and currency system. Governments that maintain minimal profiles usually profess ideologies that emphasize protecting individual rights and allowing market mechanisms to regulate and motivate economic development.

As economic development progresses and the politically aware portion of the population grows, conflict among societal groups increases and the government's involvement may be commensurately enhanced. Government may then adopt the role of *referee,* acting — ideally — as an impartial arbiter for autonomous social and economic actors. In deciding among policy priorities, governments committed to the role of referee place a high value on private initiative and sociopolitical freedoms and often limit their own activities to fiscal and monetary policies. Fiscal policies — the control of budget expenditures — may be used to stimulate certain sectors of the general economy through increased governmental spending. Monetary policies are utilized by the government to control the amount of credit and actual monies available. If the money supply increases faster than the rate of production, increased consumer demand and inadequate supplies of goods and services will lead to price increases. In addition to the referee role, governments must concern themselves with policy choices affecting the quality of life.

Governments that adhere to the *planner/protector* role focus on nonmandatory development programs and economic plans. These include the development of infrastructure,* the use of fiscal and monetary controls or investment funds, and the initiation of social welfare schemes. Communist systems often adopt the *controller/supervisor* role. Such governments' plans are mandatory, and the state actively intervenes in most aspects of social and economic change, seeking to assure social justice, economic well-being, and the fastest possible economic development.

The various roles tend to correspond to certain types of policy. The minimal and referee roles are closely associated with allocative and regulatory policy. Allocative policies are expenditures aimed at those individuals who support public services with their taxes, whereas regulatory policies are rules constraining or encouraging certain forms of behavior. Redistributive policy commonly corresponds to the planner/protector and controller/director roles, and is usually accompanied by proportionately greater taxation of the wealthy and the re-allocation of tax receipts to the poorer classes. Unemployment insurance, public

---

* The term "infrastructure" refers to the basic supportive structures of development: roads, electricity, potable water, and irrigation facilities.

health benefits, and public housing are examples of policies that usually involve a redistribution of wealth.

## CONSTRAINTS ON DEVELOPMENT

Most modern regimes are committed, to a greater or lesser extent, to the furthering of economic development. Economic development involves increases in the use of capital and technology, or nonhuman forms of production, for agriculture and industry and in the percentage of the gross national product that arises from industry. However, development is a multifaceted phenomenon with cultural and political, as well as economic, aspects. Despite the near-universal commitment to economic development, development takes place within a set of sociopolitical constraints.

Religion is often detrimental to economic development. Some religious socialization encourages passivity and fatalism, rather than optimism and the sense that one can control one's often oppressive environment. Many religions counsel the individual to endure patiently the trials of this life in the hope of a better life after death. On the other hand, religion may also provide a credo that encourages a "work ethic," savings, and characteristics said to be conducive to capitalist development.[1] Furthermore, religion may well provide a comforting and meaningful set of identifications and associations with which people can sustain themselves during the social changes associated with economic development.

Religion is not the only institution that may inhibit development. The family itself plays a dual role in the development process. Family structures, particularly the extended family and clan system, are the main social units of traditional society. They perform many tasks, including education (training for sex and occupational roles); economic production (trade, farming); food production; entertainment; security in unemployment and old age; and even upward social mobility (when one member of a family achieves higher economic or political status and assists those of lower status). Each of these tasks is subject to considerable variation with economic change. There is currently considerable tension resulting from confrontations between traditional norms of family unity and sex roles — which prescribe that women specialize in childrearing, household chores, and light agricultural duties — and emerging alternative norms that stress individual growth and self-interest.

There are also certain economic obstacles to development. Groups and classes with inherited privileges and political power may inhibit development by opposing the redistribution of social, economic, or political goods and status. They also tend to consume, rather than investing in economic projects necessary for growth. Some governments have removed such elements from privileged positions, but in many countries they remain powerful obstacles to social and economic change.

1. Max Weber, *The Protestant Ethic and the Spirit of Capitalism* (New York: Charles Scribner's Sons, 1958).

A number of other constraints may hinder economic growth and social change. In many Third World nations the traditional culture disdains work, particularly physical labor as opposed to mental labor. The *brain drain* is another important impediment to development: many Third World nations' best students remain in the foreign nations whose schools they attend because their own countries do not offer jobs in the fields for which they were trained or competitive salaries. Another obstacle to development, particularly for nations dependent on a single export product, is the uncertainty of international market conditions. The inelastic demand for many export products means that small fluctuations in market prices may seriously affect such a nation's economy, i.e., jobs, income, and government revenues. The most serious obstacle, however, is rapid population growth (2.0 percent or more), which can undermine governmental efforts to ameliorate difficult conditions. It affects the use of scarce natural resources, education, jobs, income, health, and even ecology, and can wipe out modest gains resulting from economic growth.

Furthermore, development is often uneven. The nations of Latin America, Asia, and Africa are unable to provide enough industrial-based jobs to keep up with the rate of migration to the cities. With more time to develop, the United States and western European nations have been able to do so. Additional complicating factors are regional disparities within nations, a high percentage of the population with low or subsistence incomes, stagnant economies, and high unemployment rates. Vulnerability to decay is reinforced by demands for food, housing, health, education, electricity, water, and jobs greater than the governments of less-developed nations can supply. This problem is less severe in less-developed communist nations, where the masses are mobilized to provide the necessities of housing and food, and savings from agriculture can be used for industrial investment.

## RURAL DEVELOPMENT

Social policy objectives seek to alter conditions affecting the society or political system. Rural development, agricultural production, and improvement of the lot of rural residents are significant problems in more than two-thirds of the world's nations. Industrialized nations have experienced massive rural-urban migration, and with as little as 5 percent of the population employed in agriculture they produce enough food for the entire population by using high-yielding seeds, machinery, irrigation, and fertilizer. The agricultural sector is perhaps even more important for less-developed nations. As many as 80 percent of the populations of Asia, Africa, and Latin America are engaged in agriculture. The agricultural sector is so important that many developing nations seeking to give priority to industrialization have found that they must give renewed attention to the agricultural sector in pursuit of economic development. Others, like China and Mexico, have had to respond to increased political participation on the part of peasants empowered during wars of independence or national revolutions.

The rural situation in many nations is characterized by one of two ex-

In Britain farm population has declined to less than 2 percent of the working population. Yet intensive farming and high productivity have permitted fewer farmers to satisfy more of Britain's food needs today than was the case forty years ago. In Mexico urbanization has resulted in more rural residents migrating to the cities than the urban areas can provide for. Inadequate housing may well breed slums, frustration, unemployment problems, and crime. While oil has brought increased governmental revenues to Nigeria, the capacity to provide services such as education is limited by many factors, most significant of which is the lack of adequate numbers of trained personnel. Because of these constraints, illiteracy still remains high at around 75 percent.

tremes, or a combination of the two. In some countries, such as prerevolutionary China and Mexico and many contemporary Latin American states, large agricultural holdings (*latifundia*) are concentrated in the hands of a few elite landholders. And there are *minifundia* as well: countries such as France and Nigeria have a profusion of small landholders. The inheritance system that divides land among the deceased's children, or male children, steadily reduces the size of holdings over the generations. Small holdings often lead to indebtedness and loss of ownership by farmers barely able to subsist.

Small plots tend to be uneconomical, although they sometimes contribute to political stability by satisfying the peasants' desire for land. Many industrialized states have neglected rural problems in devoting their interest and money to industrial growth. Palliatives such as farm subsidies, high tariffs on food imports, and price supports have been used as substitutes for more thoroughgoing structural reforms of agriculture. In most industrial states farmers' incomes lag considerably behind those of their counterparts in industry. In addition, rural education, cultural opportunities, recreational facilities, and health services cannot compete with these services in urban areas. In short, rural reform is not a concern of the developing world alone; it is an important, though oft-neglected, policy area for industrialized states.

Several strategies for rural change have been employed. Given the nature of the political resistance, the most common approach has been to augment agricultural production through government-funded technological assistance, loans, and subsidies. A related procedure is to attempt to raise the incomes of those employed in the agricultural sector through price supports, subsidies, or high tariffs. Political systems are traditionally most sensitive to landowners, and governmental policy — or lack of policy — has tended to favor them at the expense of farm laborers and tenants. In many countries attempts are being made to eliminate the disparity between agricultural and industrial incomes. The purpose of this undertaking is in part to retard the flow of rural residents from agricultural work to higher-paying industrial jobs, which leads to urban overcrowding. Some countries push rural development one step further by pledging to improve the educational, health, and cultural opportunities of their rural residents with the goal of eliminating urban–rural differences in the quality of life.

Some countries with ambitious rural development schemes have passed legislation to redistribute land, but such efforts have often been frustrated. For example, legislators (many of them from the landed elite) may refuse to authorize funds for legal advice to peasants ignorant of the procedures necessary to obtain land. Thus the reform's intent is frustrated by legislators and their allies in the bureaucracy. In some countries the inheritance system has created such tensions that uprisings have occurred, leading to the advent of revolutionary governments that carry out needed land reform. But land reform is not a panacea, and often results in economically inefficient landholdings. Some countries have responded to this dilemma by creating agricultural cooperatives. Cooperatives can be state-run, as in communist countries, or privately owned by their members. Each member receives a share relative to the land, labor, or other input he or she invests.

Some nations are uninterested or unsuccessful in redistributing land and have attempted to solve their agrarian problems by modernizing production techniques. This process has been greatly aided by the scientific breakthroughs of the "green revolution," notably new high-yielding seeds that enable farmers to increase their output of rice, wheat, and other products up to 300 percent. But such yields require additional inputs, including fertilizers, pesticides, and irrigation, and because the richest farmers are best able to avail themselves of capital-requiring inputs, the disparity between rich and poor farmers is increased. Thus the green revolution may contribute to rural tensions.

Because the frustration of rural policies is a fact of life for many of the nations that have pursued incremental rather than systematic approaches to their problems, urban migration is an important issue. In order to counter this migration, new jobs must be created in urban and rural areas. Thus many countries look to industrialization for its potentially desirable effects: new jobs, increased capital, technological and industrial inputs for agricultural production, a more competitive international position, increased governmental revenues for development, greater productivity, and higher per capita income.

## INDUSTRIALIZATION

Industrialization is high on the list of priorities for most developed, less-developed, and communist nations. If an industrial sector already exists, the emphasis may be on enhancing its competitive position. But industrialization first requires a market — that is, enough persons to consume the mass-produced goods and to make it economically feasible to invest in the needed plant and machinery. For most developing nations, the lack of an adequate market is a serious obstacle to industrialization. More than half of all nations have populations under 6 million persons and gross national products of 200 U.S. dollars per capita or less.[2] Because of high illiteracy rates, the technological training necessary to operate and maintain complex machinery is also missing. But the most essential factor is capital. To raise capital, developing nations attempt one or more of the following: (1) to borrow from foreign sources such as the World Bank, foreign governments, foreign private banks, or foreign financial markets (bonds); (2) to utilize internal profits from agriculture or exports of raw materials, or savings from the expropriation and nationalization of industries; (3) to entice foreign investments, either "unlimited" with tax benefits or "limited" with or without tax benefits (e.g., limited to 49 percent foreign ownership).

Many developing nations have sought to encourage private and foreign investments, with differing degrees of success. Some provide industrial parks, free trade zones (which permit the importation of some raw materials), five-

2. Bruce M. Russett, et al., World Handbook of Political and Social Indicators (New Haven: Yale University Press, 1964), pp. 155–157.

year tax holidays, and low rates of corporate taxation and have been successful in attracting large amounts of foreign capital. Other countries have rejected such foreign investment out of fear of a new form of colonialism. Some with inconsistent policies, fewer tax incentives, and inadequate infrastructure have been less successful in attracting, or benefiting from, foreign private investment: they may have attracted foreign industries but allowed too high a proportion of profits to leave the country for the industrial sector to grow. Much foreign investment is in the processing or extracting industries (food, minerals, raw materials), which do not facilitate domestic technological advance or the growth of heavy industries. Third World nations often find that their limited populations and low per capita incomes act as an important constraint on industrial development, which requires extensive capital investment, and hence a large market in order to minimize costs. The fear of expropriation also tends to discourage foreign investment.

Communist countries have tended to generate capital by utilizing savings from other sectors. Stalin was so bent on industrializing the Soviet Union that he did not hesitate to use violence against the kulaks (wealthy peasants) to bring them into the state-run agricultural network. This decision was consistent with long-range Soviet plans for the socialization of agriculture, with the policy of exploiting the farm population in order to finance industrialization. This may seem an inappropriate means of generating investment capital, but it was consistent with the needs of the time. The Soviet leadership was not interested in permitting foreign financial interests to dominate Soviet industrialization. Thus, low salaries for farmers and industrial workers enabled the regime to raise the investment funds needed for industrial growth.

The challenge of industrialization is not simply to bring into existence an industrial economy. In countries that have achieved industrialization, the government continues to bear the responsibility for managing the economy. The government is therefore expected to assure economic expansion, promote productivity, guide new capital investments, regulate industry and labor, subsidize key industries, and in some cases even assume ownership of all or part of the means of production. Governmental intervention in the economy is expected even in capitalist countries, and is of course much more pronounced in those industrialized countries guided by socialist or communist ideologies.

## URBANIZATION AND POVERTY

For industrialized, less-developed, and communist nations, the urban growth that accompanies industrialization (particularly with industrial centralization) can mean ever-increasing demands for services: water, sanitation, housing, job placements, welfare, and public safety. It also means traffic congestion, pollution, crime, alienation, and new forms of poverty — the poverty of isolation and despair — alongside the old — material and nutritional need. But too few political leaders have been aware of these needs, and the shortage of skilled persons able to respond to them has become increasingly apparent in recent years.

Poverty plagues all nations. Whether widespread, as in the developing nations, or isolated in hard-core pockets, as in the industrialized states, it requires a policy response. Those responsible for developing public policies to deal with poverty generally first seek an understanding of it. Two explanations of poverty currently prevail. The first argues that poverty is part of a syndrome of social activities known as "the culture of poverty." Those taking this approach point to the existence among the poor of social structures, norms, and values different from those in the middle class:

> The economic traits . . . of the culture of poverty include the constant struggle for survival, unemployment and underemployment, low wages, a miscellany of unskilled occupations, child labor, the absence of savings, a chronic shortage of cash, the absence of food reserves in the home, the pattern of frequent buying of small quantities of food many times a day as the need arises, the pawning of personal goods, borrowing from the local money lenders at usurious rates of interest, spontaneous informal credit devices (*tandas*) organized by neighbors, and the use of second hand clothing and furniture.
> Some of the social and psychological characteristics include living in crowded quarters, a lack of privacy, . . . a high incidence of alcoholism, frequent resort to violence in the settlement of quarrels, frequent use of physical violence in the training of children, . . . a trend toward mother-centered families, the predominance of nuclear family, a strong predisposition to authoritarianism, and a great emphasis on family solidarity — an ideal only seldom achieved.[3]

Others argue that poverty is the result not of unique values, norms, and institutions peculiar to the poor, but of social class, economic, and political barriers. For example, institutional arrangements among the poor discourage or restrict upward mobility. The poor lack political influence and are blocked from improving their status, even individually, by economic handicaps. For example, most of the urban poor are confined to slums or public housing. Home-owning provides stability, opportunities for kinship relations and for the establishment of economic enterprises in the home, and a considerable saving in expenses due to the number of persons who share homes. Public housing encourages none of these: quarters are small and overcrowded; residents have to move when their incomes rise, encouraging the breakup of families, and unemployment is high and morale is low.[4]

These two views suggest divergent policy responses. If one assumes the culture of poverty, policy should seek to eliminate or change the values, attitudes, and social characteristics of the poor. The Job Corps in the United States took this approach: Trainees were removed from their "culture"; indoctrinated with "better" values, including job training; and instructed in the use of table manners and deodorants. If one sees poverty as the result of class and other institutional barriers, one would adopt such approaches as organizing the poor

3. Oscar Lewis, *The Children of Sanchez* (New York: Random House, 1963), p. xxvi.
4. See Gerald D. Suttles, *The Social Order of the Slum: Ethnicity and Territory in the Inner City* (Chicago: University of Chicago Press, 1968).

to articulate their needs, plan their alternatives, and act on their own behalf; or redistributing wealth by providing cash subsidies to the poor for food, clothing, and shelter.

## SOCIAL SECURITY AND HUMAN DEVELOPMENT

While the main thrust of developing societies is economic development, the transition from traditional institutions and the social patterns that accompany urbanization and industrialization create other needs. These include the individual's need for economic security, physical well-being, and the knowledge necessary for self-growth.

*Social Security*  The vicissitudes of the economic and life cycles may make large segments of the population unable to provide for themselves and their families. Traditionally, and currently in many less-developed nations, the family has been depended on to assist those of its members unemployed or physically incapacitated by illness or old age; but the extended family is a thing of the past in most industrialized nations. Capitalist societies have recognized that the economic cycle is characterized by slowdowns in production, which result in layoffs; most have responded to this economic defect by legislating unemployment insurance programs, employment services, and even job training. The breakdown of the extended family has also prompted governments in industrialized nations to institute various programs for the elderly and handicapped. Communist nations have confronted the same problems with a commitment to provide basic social needs, including education, health care, and old-age assistance. Full employment is another major concern of policy in communist and noncommunist industrialized countries.

*Education*  Individuals should be able to achieve their potential, whatever that might be, and the principal mechanism for reaching this objective is mass education. Education usually has several functions, including citizenship training, preparation for an occupation, and self-fulfillment. The form it takes depends on national educational policies. Some developing nations emphasize urban educational opportunities, some seek to provide mass primary education, while others try to develop complete systems, primary through university, for the few who have sufficient funds and mental ability. Communist countries emphasize education in citizenship, and attempt to realize the ideal of social justice through compulsory mass education. In the developing communist nations such as China, the emphasis is on mass primary education, whereas the policies of the more industrialized European communist states include free stipends for university students.

*Health Care*  Health is also vitally important to human and societal development. It affects the individual's outlook and ability to work, and in the aggregate affects the performance of the economy (through absenteeism and alertness on the job). Among the major concerns of contemporary government is the provision of health care. Most liberal democracies have left this responsibility primarily to the private sector. Several, however, including Britain, Sweden, Denmark, and, more slowly, the United States, have developed large-scale public health care programs. Some have allowed a private sector to coexist with the public sector. Opponents of public medicine argue that a doctor's quality is based on the incentive provided by the market, and that a free service will prompt abuses of the system. Proponents argue that health care is essential and should be provided by the state, and further that the market economy tends to result in another type of abuse: the misallocation of personnel that results in inadequate medical personnel in rural and remote regions. Third World nations have found that market mechanisms are not local but international in scope, resulting in a massive brain drain of doctors and nurses. The distribution of health services is thus a major issue confronting each of the three types of political systems.

Human development is more than education and health; it involves freeing the individual from such social constraints as sexual or racial discrimination and class barriers. Many governments have adopted policies in these areas (e.g., the United States during the 1960s and 1970s).

# Socioeconomic Policy in Britain and France

## BRITAIN: A MANAGED ECONOMY AND WELFARE STATE

> A woman whose husband was in prison was struggling to support herself and her eight children. The rent was in arrears so a social security officer came to investigate to see if the woman qualified for supplementary benefits such as money for rent and food. The children were scruffy, the house was damp, and there was no hot water. This brought in the school-care people. Prison welfare officers were called in connection with the father's situation. One child was ill and the regular health visitor became involved. The water drains failed and this was the concern of a public health inspector. . .[5]

This summary of one London family's problems and government's role in solving them illustrates the extent of the government's involvement in British society. Even before World War Two, the social and economic activities of government had begun to grow. Wartime needs considerably furthered the expansion of government, and the postwar government of Clement Attlee enacted a series of major political, social, and economic reforms establishing a managed economy and welfare state. Since then, the government's role has been that of a planner/protector actively engaged in many aspects of society.

*Agricultural Policy* Less than 2 percent of the working population is involved in agriculture, but governmental concern for this sector of the economy remains

5. *Christian Science Monitor*, 4 April 1970.

very high. Some 16,000 civil servants annually appropriate 300 million pounds (720 million U.S. dollars) in subsidies, price guarantees, and other services to the fewer than 500,000 farmers.[6] The generous treatment agriculture receives is evidence of the political strength and effectiveness of agricultural interest groups, especially the National Farmers' Union (NFU).

While the farm population is small and declining in size, its productivity is high. Thus, governmental support of agriculture has been well-rewarded. In the last ten years, agricultural production has increased at a rate twice that of industrial production. Whereas before World War Two British farmers provided about 30 percent of the nation's food, fewer farmers now produce about 50 percent of the food. The major challenge facing British agriculture is to adapt to the new conditions brought about by membership in the European Common Market. Its adaptation will be facilitated by the higher productivity, efficiency, and greater mechanization of British agriculture relative to that of other members of the Common Market.

*British Industrial Policy*   The British government attempts to manage the economy by several means. There are of course economic consequences to government statutes on working conditions, minimum wages, maximum hours of work per week, health and safety standards, and labor–management relations. But of much greater impact on the economy are those actions explicitly designed to affect the directions, priorities, and growth rates of industry and commerce. Among the most important are economic planning, wage and price controls, policies in the nationalized industries, and subsidies.

Economic planning is still minimal in Britain. The planning body known as Neddy was not organized until the mid-1960s, and efforts to formulate long-term economic plans, such as four- or five-year plans, have not come to fruition. What planning there has been is based on voluntary participation by industry, labor, and government. Even the Labour party has preferred indirect manipulation to quantitative planning through direct government controls.[7]

The government's actions in the sector of the economy it directly controls influence the economic situation in general. About 20 percent of the working population is employed by the government, either in nationalized industry or in the civil service, and approximately 11 percent of the gross national product (GNP) is derived from the public sector.[8] Among the nationalized industries are those that tend to set the pace for the economy as a whole: coal and steel, railroads, electricity, civil aviation, the Bank of England, and some trucking. The Labour government elected in 1974 was pledged to nationalize about two dozen more large enterprises in order to increase government control over the economy. The government's decisions on investment, wages, and prices in the

6. Anthony Sampson, *The New Anatomy of Britain* (New York: Stein and Day, 1973), pp. 566-567.

7. Samuel H. Beer, *British Politics in the Collectivist Age* (New York: Alfred A. Knopf, 1967), pp. 188–216.

8. Jeremy Bray, *Decision in Government* (London: Gollancz, 1970).

nationalized industries inevitably affect the rest of the economy and are often made with the overall economic effect prominently in mind.

The government also seeks to control the economy through the manipulation of fiscal and monetary policies. If the economy is lagging, fiscal policy is changed to permit greater governmental expenditures in public works, which stimulate the economy. Governmental expenditures are reduced in times of economic boom to cool off the economy and prevent inflation. Similarly, the government's control of monetary policy permits loan interest rates to be lowered to encourage investment during recessions and raised to limit inflation during periods of expansion.

Direct intervention has been another form of government control over the economy. The imposition of wage and price controls by the Heath Government in 1972 marked the first peacetime use of such economic controls in Britain. Another type of direct intervention was engaged in during the late 1960s, when the government promoted mergers of private companies through persuasion and subsidies, with the goal of "promoting industrial efficiency and profitability and assisting the economy of the United Kingdom." Government subsidies have also been used to rescue important private corporations in serious financial difficulty. For example, in 1972 the government pumped massive subsidies into the shipbuilding industry to save it from bankruptcy. The effect was de facto nationalization, although ownership remains formally in private hands. That subsidies are not always successful is demonstrated by the 1971 bankruptcy of Rolls-Royce — one of the three largest manufacturers of jet aircraft engines in the Western world — after the government had provided tens of millions of pounds in subsidies and loan guarantees.

Such direct economic intervention has often aroused considerable opposition from both business and the trade unions. Business interests oppose further nationalization but have supported generous subsidies to troubled industries. Trade unions support a greater government role in managing the economy and further nationalization but oppose government controls on their activities.

The performance of the British economy has not been very impressive compared with other European countries. Between 1958 and 1968 the British per capita GNP increased by slightly less than 50 percent, while France, West Germany, Holland, Italy, Norway, Denmark, and Sweden all increased their per capita GNP by more than 100 percent. In fact, Britain had the lowest economic growth rate for the years 1962–1972 of the twenty-three countries in the Organization of Economic Cooperation and Development (OECD).[9] A partial cause has been lagging capital investments in industry, but British worker productivity has also been outstripped by several other countries, as shown in Table 9.1. Gross value added per employee is an approximate measure of the value of work, and hence of the productivity of the typical worker. Whereas productivity increased by over 50 percent in France, Italy, and West Germany, British worker productivity increased by only 26 percent.

9. OECD figures, U.S. Department of State news release, August 1973.

TABLE 9.1

## Industrial Efficiency and Productivity

|  | Gross value added per worker | | |
|---|---|---|---|
|  | 1962 | 1968 | % change |
| France | $3,800 | $6,100 | +60 |
| Italy | 1,900 | 3,200 | +68 |
| West Germany | 3,100 | 4,800 | +55 |
| Japan | 1,900 | 3,300 | +74 |
| USA | 8,800 | 11,700 | +33 |
| Britain | 2,700 | 3,400 | +26 |

*Source: European Community Press and Information Service,* The Common Market and the Common Man, *rev. ed. (July 1970), p. 15.*

Thus British entry into the European Common Market offers opportunities and challenges. The expanded markets open to British industry may permit a more rapid rate of industrial growth. On the other hand, face-to-face competition with European industry will test Britain's ability to increase industrial efficiency and productivity. The six months immediately following Britain's January 1973 entrance into the Common Market indicated that British industry was meeting the challenge. Then came the energy crisis and severe labor conflicts in late 1973 and 1974 to pose new threats. In 1974 Britain's GNP (after adjustments for inflation) fell by 1.5 percent while the GNP in real terms of her European rivals grew: France and Italy were up 4.75 percent and West Germany was up 0.4 percent. While the economy faltered inflation thrived; in early 1975 the rate of inflation in Britain reached the annual rate of 25.4 percent. However, over the long run Britain's economic prospects look brighter. The discovery of important oil and natural gas fields in the North Sea promises to make Britain less reliant upon increasingly high-priced foreign oil. Along with large domestic coal reserves, the North Sea oil and gas will soon meet Britain's growing need for energy resources more fully than will the domestic energy resources of most of its economic competitors in Europe. By conservative estimates, Britain should be producing between 50 and 75 percent of its own oil needs by 1980.

*Social Welfare and Human Development*   Social welfare is not a recent concern for the British government. As early as 1908 the British government enacted an old age pension program, and in 1911 it passed the National Health Insurance Act providing governmental assistance to meet the medical needs of the poor. However, welfare programs enacted since World War Two now provide government-sponsored services from the cradle to the coffin. Three social welfare programs worthy of note here are those for income redistribution, education, and national health.

Attempts to reduce the gap between the wealthy and the poor have included progressive taxation and the provision of necessary social services to all. A major share of the government's receipts comes from a steeply progressive income tax: the higher the income the greater the tax rate. In addition, estate taxes help to minimize the inheritance of wealth. The government spends heavily on social services likely to help those with lower incomes more than they help the wealthy: housing, health care, education, and old age pensions. In 1971–1972, 54 percent of the total public expenditure was for social services and public housing. Thus income is redistributed by taxing the wealthy to aid the poor. However, a recent cross-national study suggests that inequality in income has not been reduced, and may even be increasing, in Britain and several other western European countries, as shown in Table 9.2.[10]

TABLE 9.2

*Distribution of Personal Income in Selected European Countries* ————

| | Percentage of total personal income earned by | | Ratio of inequality |
| | Wealthiest 10% of population | Poorest 30% of population | (Share of top 10% to share of bottom 30%) |
|---|---|---|---|
| Britain | | | |
| 1954 | 30.4 | 10.0 | 3.0 |
| 1964 | 29.3 | 9.3 | 3.2 |
| France | | | |
| 1956 | 34.1 | 6.2 | 5.5 |
| 1962 | 36.8 | 4.8 | 7.7 |
| West Germany | | | |
| 1955 | 44.0 | 7.5 | 5.9 |
| 1964 | 41.4 | 10.0 | 4.1 |
| Denmark | | | |
| 1953 | 28.0 | 9.0 | 3.1 |
| 1963 | 27.1 | 8.7 | 2.8 |
| Netherlands | | | |
| 1952 | 35.0 | 8.3 | 4.2 |
| 1962 | 33.8 | 8.2 | 4.1 |
| Norway | | | |
| 1957 | 27.6 | 9.1 | 3.0 |
| 1963 | 24.9 | 9.8 | 2.5 |
| Sweden | | | |
| 1954 | 27.3 | 10.6 | 2.6 |
| 1963 | 27.9 | 8.5 | 3.3 |
| Finland | | | |
| 1952 | 28.9 | 8.9 | 3.3 |
| 1962 | 32.5 | 5.9 | 5.5 |

*Source: Data drawn from United Nations,* Incomes in Postwar Europe: A Study of Policies, Growth and Distribution. *Economic Survey of Europe in 1965, Part 2 (Geneva: Secretariat of the Economic Commission for Europe, 1967) pp. 14–17.*

10. See also Harold F. Lydall, *The Structure of Earnings* (London: Clarendon Press, 1968), p. 200ff.

The British educational system has for many years supported an elitist and deferential society. Not until 1879 was public primary education assured to all, and it was 1944 before universal secondary education was provided. There are two sets of schools offering primary and secondary education: state-funded schools and the exclusive private "public" schools. The so-called public schools (really private boarding schools) have provided Britain with its political, social, and economic elite since the fifteenth century; the two oldest and most prestigious are Eton (founded in 1440) and Winchester (founded in 1382). Eton alone has provided eighteen prime ministers to the nation. Despite the elitist nature of the public schools, few efforts have been made to reform them. Those who defend the public schools point to the self-discipline and commitment to public service they supposedly instill in their pupils.

The social and political influence of the public schools has diminished in recent years as well-educated young people have emerged from the state-sponsored school system. At the age of eleven, children take tests to determine whether they go on to a "grammar school" or a "modern school." Grammar schools provide academic preparation for university education and modern schools offer technical and practical training for the less gifted. There is little likelihood that the child who fails to demonstrate academic potential at eleven will be able to attend a university.

The Labour government of Harold Wilson (1964–1970) urged the consolidation of grammar and modern schools into comprehensive schools similar to American high schools, to avoid the ruthless sorting of eleven-year-olds and to reduce social class divisions among children. By 1971 an estimated 35 percent of secondary school students were in comprehensive schools.[11] However, the Conservatives have been less enthusiastic about promoting the transition to comprehensive schools and it seems likely that the three types of school will continue to coexist, depending on the inclinations of local education officials.

Higher education is still dominated by the two prestige universities, Oxford and Cambridge. In the past, graduates of these two universities accounted for the most prominent politicians and nearly all the senior civil servants. Their dominance seems likely to wane in the future as able and civic-minded young people graduate from the newer universities (referred to as the "Redbrick" universities, in contrast to "Oxbridge"). Among the Redbrick universities, the London School of Economics (founded in the nineteenth century) has particular political significance since many of the Labour party's leaders were educated there.

The number of new universities has quadrupled since 1939; the number of students has grown even more rapidly. But the proportion of young people attending universities (8 percent of the relevant age group) is lower in Britain than in most other industrial nations. While British education can be seen as perpetuating social class divisions, the picture is certainly not clear. A 1967 UNESCO survey found that Britain had a higher percentage of students from

11. Sampson, *New Anatomy of Britain*, p. 146.

TABLE 9.3
## Some Statistics on Economic and Social Performance in Britain and France

|  | Britain | France |
|---|---|---|
| Population (1973 estimates) | 56,470,000 | 52,010,000 |
| **Economy** | | |
| Gross GNP (1972) | $152.3 billion | $220.8 billion |
| Average annual growth rate of GNP (1962–1972) | 2.9% | 5.7% |
| Total % growth in GNP (1962–1972) | 33.7% | 73.4% |
| Per capita income | $2,731 | $4,269 |
| Rate of growth of real salary | 2.0% | 4.6% |
| **Education** | | |
| % of GNP spent on education | 6.0% | 4.6% |
| % of young people in higher education | 8% | 16% |
| **Medical care** | | |
| Birth rate (1972) | 16.2 per 1,000 | 17.1 per 1,000 |
| Hospital beds | 103 persons per bed | 150 persons per bed |
| Doctors | 1,059 persons per doctor | 770 persons per doctor |
| Life expectancy | 68.5 years (males) 74.7 years (females) | 71 years |
| **Communications** | | |
| Newspapers (copies per 1,000 people) | 476 | 243 |
| Radio sets | 20,000,000 (1971) | 15,796,000 (1969) |
| Television sets | 16,000,000 (1971) | 10,121,000 (1969) |
| Telephones | 13,958,826 (1972) | 8,114,000 (1970) |

(All dollar figures based on exchange rates in April 1973.)

*Sources: Organization for Economic Cooperation and Development, and the* Associated Press Almanac 1974 (*Maplewood, N.J.: Hammond Almanac, 1974*).

working-class backgrounds enrolled in higher education than any other western European country.[12]

One of the most successful and popular of Britain's social services is the National Health Service (NHS). Founded in 1947, the NHS provides complete medical, dental, and eye care at no charge. Patients may choose their own

12. *Ibid.,* p. 157.

doctors, and the doctors receive remuneration based on the number of patients on their "panels." Drugs, eyeglasses, and other personal medical supplies are subsidized. There are 113 doctors per 100,000 people in Britain, somewhat fewer than the 150 per 100,000 average in the original six members of the European Common Market and the 165 per 100,000 in the United States. There are over 3,000 hospitals owned and operated by the Ministry of Health and Social Security, and about 972 hospital beds for every 100,000 people — higher than comparable figures in the United States but slightly less than the average on the Continent. The cost of operating the system amounted to 2.4 billion pounds (5.8 billion dollars) in 1971–1972, or about 11 percent of total public expenditures. The future of the NHS has been clouded in the past few years by growing financial difficulties. The rapid inflation of health costs during 1974–1975 threatened the NHS with insolvency.

The question remains whether Britain's social benefits and economic controls give its citizens a sense of security and confidence in their future. The evidence is mixed. The British express pride in the social services provided for them, and public opinion polls have regularly found that more Britons are optimistic about the future than pessimistic. However, other signs indicate a lack of confidence in the future, especially in the area of economics. The labor discontent of 1972–1975 reflected this insecurity and tension: with inflation seemingly uncontrollable, entry into the European Common Market causing economic dislocations, and unemployment at the highest point since World War Two (about 4 percent of the working population), many were insecure about the future. Thus, the government's performance in socioeconomic matters is mixed, with continued economic problems offsetting success in agriculture and social welfare.

## FRANCE: A CONCERTED ECONOMY AND "PARTICIPATION"

The Gaullist regime placed priority on foreign and defense policies at the expense of domestic policies. De Gaulle correctly perceived that the French had lost their national pride in a series of humiliating defeats and near-defeats: the two world wars, the Indochina conflict, and the Algerian War. And he was personally much more interested in restoring French grandeur in international affairs and developing an independent defense capability than in pursuing domestic reform. Of course, de Gaulle was interested in maintaining a strong economy — but in part to strengthen his position in international bargaining. Although Pompidou and Giscard d'Estaing paid closer attention to domestic issues during their presidencies, it is important to remember as we assess its performance on socioeconomic issues that the regime's priorities were elsewhere. These priorities were clear to the voting public. The continued electoral success of the Gaullists and their allies of other parties suggests that if the voters supporting the Gaullists did not necessarily endorse these priorities, they at least did not repudiate them.

*Agricultural Policy*  Agriculture remains a very important part of the French economy and society. It accounts for approximately 10 percent of the GNP and about 12 percent of the working population. However, French agriculture has been plagued with serious problems. The basic difficulty is that there are too many farmers working farms that are too small. Traditional French inheritance laws dictated the equal division of land among all sons. This practice created a land-use pattern of very small farms; three-quarters of the arable land is divided into farms of less than 125 acres. Often a single farmer owns several long narrow strips of land a mile or two apart, and this "parcellization" has obviously hindered mechanization and efficiency. In addition, nearly half the farm work force is made up of tenants working for absentee landlords. Farmers have generally not benefited from the postwar economic boom: their average income remains 30 percent below that of the typical industrial worker. In part their poverty is explained by marketing practices, which put the farmers largely at the mercy of the buyers. The gap between the price French farmers receive for their product and the price it brings on the retail market is the largest in Europe.

In the past the government's response to agricultural problems was to subsidize the farmer and impose high tariffs on imported food. Under the Fifth Republic, subsidies and tariffs have been supplemented by attempts at structural reform. First, the government provided social security benefits and health insurance to farmers. It also introduced an old age pension, partly in the hope of encouraging older farmers to retire. It established new and stricter regulations on absentee landlords, and promoted the formation of collective marketing groups to strengthen the farmers' position in negotiations with buyers. Most importantly, the government encouraged the consolidation of small plots so that more farmers would own one large field instead of several scattered plots. In some cases, the government was active in persuading farmers to swap land in order to consolidate their holdings.[13]

While the government's programs have suffered from lack of funds, and sometimes from lack of genuine commitment on the part of top-level officials, progress has been made. The percentage of the population working in agriculture declined from 20 to 16 percent between 1962 and 1968, an annual drop of 3.8 percent in the agricultural population.[14] The size of the average farm has doubled since the turn of the century, and productivity per acre has doubled since 1949. Farm incomes have increased, although the average remains considerably below that of the nonfarm population. Farm prices still fluctuate but the gap between the price at the farm and at the marketplace has declined for many products. But there are still important problems and farmers remain unhappy. A 1966 poll found that over half the farmers surveyed considered the government's agricultural policy bad or very bad; only 4 percent thought

13. John Ardagh, *The New French Revolution* (London: Secker & Warburg, 1968), pp. 74–78.
14. *Le Monde,* 6 January 1970.

that it was good.[15] Farm income is still very low and the gap between rural and urban standards of living is large. Many older farmers resist change in favor of inefficient and uneconomic traditional practices. Finally, there is a striking contrast between the wealth of the large farms on the plains north of Paris and the small impoverished farms in the southwest and Brittany. All of these conditions motivated periodic outbreaks of peasant protest, and occasionally violence. A few years ago the minister of agriculture was kidnapped by a group of farmers in Brittany and held prisoner so that he could be told in full detail of the farmers' grievances.

*Industrial Policies*   There is in France a strong tradition of state intervention in economic matters dating back at least to the nineteenth century, when the development of mines, banks, railroads, and heavy industry was publicly subsidized even though ownership was in private hands. Today the government intervenes importantly in all aspects of the economy, using methods similar to Britain's: fiscal and monetary policies, subsidies, wage and price controls, informal persuasion and manipulation, and economic planning.

The French describe theirs as a "concerted economy" based on the voluntary collaboration of the public and private sectors and of the affected interest groups. Approximately 15 percent of the French working population is employed by the state, and the public sector accounts for about 10 percent of the total GNP. But its economic influence is much greater than its size suggests, because it controls key industries: part of the automobile industry, part of the banking and insurance industries, electricity and gas, tobacco, telecommunications, petroleum, shipping, and part of the housing industry.

A major element in the concerted economy is economic planning. Plans establish goals for increased production and productivity agreed upon by means of intensive consultation between government technocrats and interest group representatives. Approximately 4,000 people are involved in some way in the planning process. Guidelines are indicative rather than mandatory and the participation of private industry is voluntary. As an observer notes: "Knowledge of income and industry projections and faith in the inevitability of expansion are communicated to firms at intra- and inter-industry meetings. This is perhaps the most powerful effect, and one which has a faint resemblance to a revivalist prayer meeting."[16]

Whether the plan works by faith-healing or by actual direction, the French economy has prospered since World War Two. France has the fifth highest GNP in the world (after the United States, the Soviet Union, Japan, and West Germany). In 1972 the GNP was $292 billion or $4,269 per capita. The gross national product grew between 1962 and 1972 at an annual rate of 5.7 percent, higher than any of France's partners in the Common Market and nearly twice

15. *Sondages,* 1966, nos. 3 & 4: p. 66.
16. Charles P. Kindleberger, "The Postwar Resurgence of the French Economy," in Stanley Hoffmann, *et al., In Search of France* (New York: Harper & Row, 1965), p. 155.

the British rate.[17] As indicated in Table 9.1 (page 402), French worker productivity grew by 60 percent between 1962 and 1968. Perhaps the single most important economic problem has been inflation, which was especially critical in 1974–1975 when worldwide "stagflation" pushed the French rate of inflation above 15 percent per annum. As bad as this was, French inflation was less than that of several other industrialized states, including Japan, Britain, and Italy.

The economic development of the past few years has been unevenly distributed through the country. Most industrialists and businessmen prefer to build their plants near Paris or a half-dozen other large cities, where they can be assured of a good labor market, good shipping connections, and the conveniences and culture available in large cities. The result is that industrial growth has been concentrated in a few areas, excluding the rest of the country from the benefits of economic development and prosperity.

*Social Welfare and Human Development*   Despite statistical evidence indicating notable economic expansion, public opinion polls regularly find that more French citizens are pessimistic about the future than optimistic. For example, a poll in December 1973 indicated that 63 percent of the respondents thought things were getting worse and only 16 percent thought things were getting better.[18] The French are also worried about unemployment, though actual rates of unemployment are quite low. (In 1975, the unemployment rate was only 3.5 percent of the potential working population.) [19] In part such findings reflect the political cynicism and critical stance typical of many of the French. But they also suggest personal insecurity and dissatisfaction with the government's perfomance.

The Gaullist approach to social welfare has been to advocate "participation" as an alternative to both totalitarian communism and "savage" capitalism. But participation has in practice been more a political slogan than a concrete program of action. It may presumably be defined as greater involvement by citizens in politics, workers in industrial and business decision-making, and students and faculty in administering education. The practical implementations of this notion have been minimal: some modest employee profit-sharing and greater student influence in the universities. In operation, profit-sharing has provided small bonuses to about one out of seven industrial workers.

Efforts to redistribute income are hindered by the ineffectiveness of income taxes. An estimated one-third of French taxpayers illegally avoid paying their fair share. And, of course, there are legal loopholes as well. A few years ago the prime minister admitted paying very little tax because of a loophole. Thus, the steeply progressive income taxes account for less than 14 percent of the

17. Organization for Economic Cooperation and Development figures, U.S. Department of State news release, August 1973.
18. *Christian Science Monitor*, 4 December 1973.
19. If part-time employees who desired full-time jobs were included, the unemployment rate rose to 8 percent.

government's revenues.[20] In contrast, three times as much money is collected in the form of regressive taxes on expenditures (value-added taxes), which burden the poor more than the wealthy. Furthermore, social benefits are financed largely from employers' and employees' contributions, with only about one-quarter of the costs covered by tax-based public funds. Thus, unlike Britain, the French government is not actively trying to equalize income differences by taxing the wealthy to provide basic services for the poor. Compared with other nations at similar levels of development, France has an unusually high level of income inequality,[21] as shown in Table 9.2 on page 403.

Social welfare and social security benefits are high. National expenditures for social benefits in 1967 amounted to $377 for each person in France,[22] more than in Britain ($214) or in any other Common Market country. A large share of social benefits take the form of family allowances that vary with the number of children. A family with three children, for example, receives monthly benefits of $46.[23] The purpose of these allowances, however, is to encourage large families rather than to aid the needy. The government's actions in the area of social welfare have not always elicited popular support. For example, in 1967 the government was faced with rising social security costs because of the extension of benefits to the farm population. To meet the problem, the government increased employees' and employers' contributions to the social security fund and simultaneously reduced benefits. The resulting anger and discontent was one of the underlying causes of the Events of May the following year.

Education has been a source of particular difficulty for the French government. The very rapid growth of higher education created new pressures for the reform of an already overcentralized and outmoded university system. The number of students in higher education grew from 247,000 in 1960 to 514,000 in 1967 (about 16 percent of the young people between twenty and twenty-four); 160,000 attended the University of Paris alone.[24] There was a shortage of facilities and, more importantly, a need to revise both methods and the traditional student–teacher relationship. Powerful vested interests — professors, administrators, and bureaucrats — blocked meaningful reform. The fact that there were eleven ministers of education in eleven years indicates the frustration of government.

Then came the explosion of May 1968, when student rioting precipitated a general strike and the most serious threat of revolution in recent French history. In its aftermath, a major university reform was enacted. Under the leadership of Edgar Faure, the new minister of education, the University Orientation Law was passed unanimously in both the National Assembly and the

20. *Le Monde,* 7 November 1972.
21. See also Lydall, *Structure of Earnings,* p. 157ff.
22. European Community Press and Information Service, *The Common Market and The Common Man,* rev. ed. (July 1970) p. 28.
23. *Ibid.,* p. 29 (1970 figures).
24. Ardagh, *New French Revolution,* pp. 522–532.

Senate — an extremely unusual occurrence in the divided French parliament. Faure's reforms granted considerable fiscal, academic, and administrative autonomy to the universities, and called for the election of student–faculty committees in each department and for the university as a whole with broad powers to set academic policy.

The success of these reforms is not yet clear. Financial resources to provide new facilities and aid students have been difficult to acquire. Student participation in the election of representatives for the student–faculty committees has been lower than anticipated. And student disorders continue. However, there is some evidence that the reforms are working. The transition to the new organizational units was accomplished with a minimum of disruption. And, while student unrest is still evident, it is directed at the government instead of the university: there are protests against the government's treatment of left-wing extremists, draft laws, and nuclear testing, but there have been very few protests directed at university policy and structure.

By objective standards, the performance of the French political system in the economic realm compares very favorably with its own past record and with the records of other western European countries. Similar positive assessments might be made — albeit more tentatively — of its performance in agriculture and social welfare: important improvements and gains have been made over past performance, and present achievements compare favorably with the records of other European countries at similar high levels of development. Nevertheless, polls continue to suggest a noteworthy current of socioeconomic dissatisfaction and insecurity. For example, a poll in January 1975 found that 70 percent were worried about the future.[25] Perhaps the explanation of this apparent paradox may be found in the French attitudes toward authority we have discussed: the French grant substantial power to government but retain the rights to criticize, to protest violently, and ultimately to threaten rebellion.

# Socioeconomic Policies in China and the Soviet Union

## THE SOVIET UNION: THE ATTEMPT AT TOTAL GOVERNMENTAL CONTROL

Among the fundamental rights guaranteed the Soviet people by the constitution are some that transcend the protection of individual political freedoms to promise social and economic protection. These social rights include guaranteed employment, rest and leisure, old-age maintenance, education, and social, economic, and political equality. In practice the Soviet regime has made efforts to

25. *L'Express,* 27 January 1975.

fulfill these pledges over the long run, although they have at times been subordinated to other priorities. In addition, the Soviet leadership has been committed to rapid industrialization in order to modernize the backward and underdeveloped economy inherited from the czars. Consequently, the Soviet government has been deeply involved in shaping and reshaping society and economics. The role of the Soviet government in society has been that of an activist director/controller pursuing revolutionary social and economic ends.

At times the constitution's pledges of social rights have conflicted with the needs of rapid industrialization. When this has happened, the Soviet leadership has generally given priority to industrialization. However, such key Marxist ideological principles as economic equality, rejection of the profit motive, socialist ownership of the means of production, and strong centralization have generally been adhered to, sometimes at the price of impeding economic growth. Despite conflicts and compromises among ideology, industrialization needs, and social rights, the Soviet Union has made impressive gains in the areas of industrialization, social security, and human development.

*Soviet Agricultural Policy*  A considerably less favorable assessment must be made of the Soviet performance in agriculture. While more than 40 percent of the Soviet population is still rural, and marginal climatic conditions raise the specter of periodic crop failure, agriculture has been the most neglected sector of the Soviet economy. As the Revolution of 1917 drew closer, the Bolsheviks adopted a slogan designed specifically to appeal to the peasants: "Peace, Bread, Land." The peasants had suffered severely during World War One: they made up the bulk of the czar's armies and their lands were torn up in the conflict. In addition, the peasants were mostly small landholders or poor tenant farmers working for wealthy landholders. One peasant expressed the prevailing resentment over loss of land to the rich:

> They were purchasing land when they had enough of everything. Except for them, no one could buy land. They would get other people to work for them, paying fifteen kopecks a day and, during the season, twenty kopecks. They were really skinning us — making us work from dawn to dusk. And with all this they even laughed at us.[26]

The promise of land helped win the peasants' support for the Bolsheviks. Once in power, the Communists made it clear that the promise of land was to be fulfilled not by granting private ownership to the landless but by socializing and collectivizing ownership of farmlands. During the era of the New Economic Policy (NEP), peasants were briefly assured possession of specific plots of land in perpetuity. But because title remained in the state's hands land could not be sold or rented to others. In 1929 Stalin launched the collectivization of farms; the kulaks, or rich peasants, were the initial targets. Millions of kulaks

26. *The Village of Viriatino*, trans. and ed. Sula Benet (Garden City, N.Y.: Doubleday, 1970), p. 25.

lost their land, livestock, and other possessions, and many hundreds of thousands were forced into exile or imprisoned. Ultimately the less prosperous peasants were also deprived of their land and forced into collective farms, and by 1936 more than 90 percent of the peasants were collectivized.

The costs of collectivization were tremendous. Millions lost their lives resisting collectivization and in the famine brought on by the conflict. Agricultural production dropped, and the nation's livestock was reduced by half as peasants slaughtered their animals rather than turn them over to the collective farm. But there were ideological, political, and economic benefits. The collective farm was to be a school of communism for the peasantry; it represented the socialist approach to agriculture. The political benefit was easier supervision of the peasants, who remained suspect in the minds of many Communists. The economic benefits included the forced migration of the surplus rural population to the cities, where people were needed in industry. Finally, the collective farm permitted the exploitation of the peasants to support Russian industrialization. By setting high production quotas and paying low prices, the government could feed the industrial workers and still have sufficient food and grains for export to finance the purchase of industrial equipment. In this way, the peasants financed industrialization through forced "savings."

Today Soviet agriculture takes two socialist forms: the collective farm or *kolkhoz* and the state farm or *sovhoz*. The land in the kolkhoz is owned by the collective. Peasant families belonging to the collective share in the work and divide whatever is left over after the state takes its share. The division of such surplus output is based on time worked and the difficulty of the work performed. Each peasant household in the collective is entitled to a small private plot on which it may grow or raise what it pleases for sale at the village market. The collective has its own kindergartens, hospitals, newspapers, theaters, and recreation facilities. There are about 26,000 collective farms in the Soviet Union. The average kolkhoz has 10,000 hectares of land (25,000 acres), 1,000 head of cattle, 40 tractors, 429 households, and 1,700 people.[27] The sovhoz is an agricultural factory owned and operated by the state. Its workers receive salaries just like industrial workers. Unlike collective farmers, the employees of the sovhoz are not entitled to private plots.

The private plots of collective farmers are among the most productive sectors of Soviet agriculture. The tendency of collective farmers to give better care to their own plots has given rise to a number of popular jokes contrasting the plump cows and well-tended gardens of the private plots with the scrawny cows and weed-ridden fields of the collective. There is some truth in these jokes: while private plots make up about 4 percent of tilled land, they provided 64 percent of the potatoes, 42 percent of the vegetables, 42 percent of the meat, 40 percent of the milk, and 66 percent of the eggs produced in 1966.[28] Earnings

27. Robert G. Wesson, *The Soviet Russian State* (New York: John Wiley & Sons, 1972), p. 229.

28. Roy D. Laird, "The Politics of Soviet Agriculture," in *Man, State, and Society in the Soviet Union*, ed. Joseph L. Nogee (New York: Praeger, 1972), p. 419.

from the private plot account for about 40 percent of the collective farmer's total income.

Long years of neglect during the drive for industrialization have left Soviet agriculture a legacy of problems that are reflected in its uneven and generally lackluster performance. Until recently, funds and expertise for agricultural research, hybrid seeds, chemical fertilizers, and farm equipment were simply not available. Recent five-year plans have devoted greater attention to investments in agriculture and might be expected to contribute to the growth of agricultural productivity. But other problems endemic to the highly centralized Soviet economy continue to plague agriculture. Restrictions on local initiative block adaptation of centrally defined goals and methods to local conditions. The individual collective farmer and sovhoz worker lack incentive to increase productivity. Finally, agricultural production will continue to be hampered by limited arable land, uncertain weather, and a short growing season.

*Industrialization*  Soviet efforts at industrialization have been much more successful. Starting in 1928, a series of five-year plans invested the nation's material and human resources in industrialization. The results are impressive. In the course of three decades, the communist regime transformed a backward and underdeveloped country into a powerful industrial giant. This is readily evidenced by the growth of the gross national product from about $62 billion in 1913 to an estimated $514 billion in 1971. Industry now accounts for three-fourths of the GNP. The pace of this expansion is exceptional. When the Soviet rate of industrial growth between 1928 and 1958 is compared with the American rate at a similar stage of economic development (1870–1900), the Soviet record is much better: 8.6–11.7 percent growth each year as opposed to 6.1 percent in the United States.[29] In fact, in comparison with the growth records of all other industrial nations, the Soviet performance is outstanding.

In recent years the Soviet rate of economic growth has dropped sharply. After two decades of annual growth rates in excess of 5 percent, the rate of industrial growth dropped to 2.3 percent in 1968–1969[30] and has remained low. This drop in part reflects the maturity of the Soviet economy and its arrival at the end of the stage during which very rapid growth is easy. But it also reflects the failure to introduce new economic measures to increase the productivity of capital investments and resource allocation. Soviet prices are arbitrary and do not reflect market pressures of supply and demand. Nor do they reflect some important costs of production, such as rent and interest on the use of capital. Consequently, prices are not always an accurate measure with which to determine the most efficient use of resources. Such measures are essential if productivity is to be improved. Yet efforts to alter the price system to reflect actual cost in resources more accurately have succumbed to ideological

29. Herbert S. Levine, "Industry," in *Perspectives for Soviet Society,* ed. Allen Kassof (New York: Praeger, 1968), p. 292.

30. *Handbook of Soviet Social Science Data,* ed. Ellen Mickiewicz (New York: Free Press, 1973), p. 93.

TABLE 9.4

*Distribution of U.S. and Soviet GNP by End Use (Percentages)* ——————

|  | U.S. | U.S.S.R. |
|---|---|---|
| Consumption | 72.0 | 56 |
| Defense | 7.2 | 10 |
| Investment | 17.8 | 33 |
| Government administration | 3.0 | 1 |

*Source: Robert W. Campbell,* The Soviet-Type Economies: Performance and Evolution *(Boston: Houghton Mifflin, 1974), p. 100.*

considerations, which, for example, bar the inclusion of interest charges in calculating costs.

Like agriculture, Soviet industry is troubled by excessive centralization, lack of local initiative, and ineffective incentives. Finally, industrialization has been uneven. Heavy industry and defense-related industry have had priority over light industry and consumer goods. The Soviet Union builds rockets to transport people into space but it does not fly them comfortably and on time from one city to another. While the Soviet Union claims to produce as much steel as the United States, its citizens still complain about shoes that do not fit, household appliances that will not work or cannot be purchased, and the lack of parts for machinery that breaks down. By concentrating on certain economic sectors and neglecting others, the Soviet Union has been able to match the United States in some areas even though its total output or GNP remains well below that of the United States. Table 9.4 illustrates this point by comparing the end use of GNP in the United States and the Soviet Union in the early 1970s. It can be seen that the Soviet Union has devoted much larger shares of its GNP to investments (principally in heavy industry) and defense to the detriment of consumer goods.

*Social Security and Human Development*  A major feature of the Soviet state's involvement in society is its commitment to assure the well-being and security of the individual citizen. The state provides an impressive array of subsidized or free social services, including free health care, education (including subsidies to cover living and miscellaneous expenses for students in higher education), day care centers, summer camps for children, old-age pensions, and paid annual leaves. These "social wages" are estimated to increase the value of the typical Soviet worker's take-home pay by 34.2 percent.[31] The Soviet citizen also benefits from the state's investment in public housing, educational facilities, sports arenas, and cultural activities.

While these services are pledged, however, their availability and quality varies. For example, there is an acute housing shortage in many parts of the

31. Robert J. Osborn, *Soviet Social Policies: Welfare, Equality, and Community* (Homewood, Ill.: Dorsey Press, 1970), p. 32.

Soviet Union but investment in new apartments has been minimal. In general, the metropolitan areas of European Russia are far better off in terms of the quality and quantity of social services than the rest of the Soviet Union. As an illustration, in 1969 about 45 percent of the children in urban areas received preschool training compared to only 10 percent of the children in rural areas — to say nothing of differences in the quality of facilities and teachers.

Soviet workers need not fear unemployment since there has been a substantial labor shortage since the 1930s. The job insecurity felt by workers in the United States, Britain, and France is virtually absent in the Soviet Union. And the widespread notion that Soviet workers are assigned jobs and prevented from leaving them is not true. There is considerable occupational and geographical mobility, which indicates that the individual in fact has the ability to choose her or his job. The labor shortage makes the theoretical freedom to change jobs real, since workers who are dissatisfied with their working conditions or wages can find suitable jobs elsewhere.[32]

In other areas of human welfare, the Soviet Union has performed impressively. The illiteracy that was so widespread under the czars has been eliminated: the size of the literate population rose from 56.6 percent of total population in 1926 to 98.5 percent in 1959.[33] The number of persons with secondary educations rose from 75.7 per thousand in 1939 to 263.0 per thousand in 1959.[34] Today nearly 80 percent of the children who complete eighth grade go on to secondary schools[35] and 24 percent of young people between 20 and 24 are in higher education (compared to 43 percent of this sector of the population in the United States). Health services have also improved. In 1913 there were only 15 doctors per 100,000 people; by 1968 there were 259.[36] The number of hospital beds has increased from 13 for every 10,000 people in 1913 to 104.1 beds per 10,000 in 1968,[37] significantly better than comparable U.S. figures. Improved health services have resulted in longer life. Life expectancy at birth has risen from 32 years in 1896–1897 to 44 years in 1926–1927 to 70 years in 1965–1966.[38] Finally, the Soviets have made important efforts at increasing recreational and cultural facilities. One area in which their achievement has been extraordinary is governmental support for the fine arts. In the Soviet Union the fine arts are available to and enjoyed by the masses as well as the elite. To satisfy popular demand, there are numerous local orchestras, ballet and opera companies, and folk dancing groups, all subsidized by the government.

Overall, the Soviet regime has an impressive record of performance in meeting social and economic needs. Massive changes in the economy and in the quality of individual lives have taken place within the lifetimes of much of

32. *Ibid.*, pp. 136–186.
33. *Handbook of Soviet Data*, p. 139.
34. *Ibid.*, p. 143.
35. Osborn, *Soviet Social Policies*, p. 111.
36. *Handbook of Soviet Data*, p. 108.
37. *Ibid.*, p. 112.
38. *Ibid.*, p. 102.

the population. To be sure, some of this progress has been costly in human terms, such as the exploitation of peasants and workers to finance industrialization and the continuing shortage of consumer goods and housing. But the early stages of industrialization in the United States, Britain, France, and other Western countries also had high human costs, in the forms of child labor, exploited workers, and underpaid farmers. All in all, the Soviet experience demonstrates the organizational strength and capability of a cohesive political elite determined to achieve economic and social goals.

## CHINA: MOBILIZED CHANGE

Like the Soviet Union, the communist regime in China is committed to revolutionary social and economic goals. This involves the creation of a society in which individuals no longer exploit each other and public goods are distributed according to the principle of social justice. It is a demanding and highly idealistic task, requiring major undertakings in the area of rural development, industrial development, and social welfare. Though industrialization initially had the highest priority, rural development was the most in need of attention. Accounting for more than 80 percent of the population, rural areas were potential markets for heavy industry and, more important, sources of savings for industrial development.

*Rural Development*   Much more than in the Soviet Union, Chinese rural development has been in the nature of comprehensive social, political, and economic change. The communist regime first tried to solve agricultural problems and accumulate large agricultural surpluses to finance industrialization by instituting land reforms, the pooling of machinery, and cooperative farming. But these reforms failed to solve agricultural problems or meet industrial needs. Nor were they ideologically satisfying to a communist regime, since property remained in private hands.

By 1957 the Chinese had moved toward the formation of communes as the ideal form of communist agricultural organization. Thus began one of the boldest and most massive social experiments in history. The commune's functions were to be agricultural and industrial production, trade, education, and defense. The commune's basic units — brigades and production teams — were parallel to the former consolidated and preconsolidated cooperatives respectively. The problems of seasonal employment, the discrepancy between urban and rural standards of living and lifestyles, and the resulting threat of an exodus to crowded urban areas was to be solved by the formation of communes to operate rural industries. Off-season labor would be employed to construct public works, highways, dams, and irrigation projects. Mao pushed through this reform in 1957–1958 in the hope of achieving a socialist society, perhaps even during his own lifetime. He also sought to solve major developmental problems; namely, to raise the needed capital for industrial expansion, to reduce migration to the cities, and to alter the trend toward uneven industrialization. Each of these problems was to be met through the creation of the commune system, and each commune was to be a complete and self-sustaining social, economic, and political unit that would bring the benefits of urban life to the countryside. Schools were provided, as were hospitals, tailor shops, nurseries, and public laundries. Some of these innovations freed women from their households, and thus met the need for additional labor. The communes' socioeconomic functions were performed by banks, factories, stores, and their own militia units. Taxes were paid by the commune to the state. Since all nonpersonal property was to be owned by the commune, residual income after taxes, expenses, and welfare funds would be distributed as wages to the members according to a system of work points.

After years of conditioning to labor for material rewards, the absence of incentives adversely affected productivity. Why work hard when one's needs were being provided for and wages were minimal? Following the 1958 party Central Committee meeting, changes were made in the administration, ownership, and system of distribution on communes to deal with the problem of incentive. Mao appears to have agreed to this retrenchment, realizing that massive reeducation would be required before material incentives could be replaced by social motivations to excellence and effort. Large communes were broken up into production brigades and teams, and the team became the *de facto,* but not *de jure,* owner of land. In 1960 private plots and free markets were again allowed.

This decision led to a retreat from the socialist ideals. By 1965 most farm implements were owned by individuals rather than collectives and more time was devoted to private plots than to communal plots.[39] Within a few years the income differential between farmers increased. This trend away from socialist equality and public ownership of land was reversed by the Great Proletarian Cultural Revolution, in the wake of which communes were reestablished and consolidated. The commune remains today the basic economic and political unit in rural China.

China's rural development can be measured in terms of increased agricultural output. Production has increased steadily between 1962 and 1974, and 1970 was a record year. However, full evaluation of China's rural development requires an understanding of the commune. Communes are designed to fulfill certain ideological ends. They allow for mass participation in structures that are both economic units and political jurisdictions. Communes seek not only to expand production, but also to impart meaning to life by means of direct citizen participation and identification, and provision for the members' health, welfare, education, and culture. These considerations, as well as moderate but adequate gains in agricultural production, merit China's rural development a laudatory and favorable evaluation. Many other developing nations can boast gross statistical increases in food production and commercial crops equal to or greater than China's, but their regional disparities and quality of life often can-

39. Chao Kang, *Agricultural Production in Communist China, 1949–1965* (Madison: University of Wisconsin Press, 1970), p. 67.

not compare favorably. In most developing nations class differences, regional imbalances, and insecurity on the part of the average rural resident are glaringly apparent.

*Industrialization Policy*   Industry is often referred to as the "modern" sector of the economy, to distinguish it from traditional agriculture. However, the agricultural and industrial sectors are closely linked, as Chairman Mao noted in 1957:

> As China is a large agricultural country . . . industry must develop together with agriculture, for only thus can industry secure raw materials and a market, and only thus is it possible to accumulate large funds for building a powerful heavy industry. Everyone knows that light industry is closely related to agriculture. Without agriculture there can be no light industry. But it is not yet so understood that agriculture provides heavy industry with an important market.[40]

This statement emphasizes one of the challenges confronting China's policy-makers: the balance between agriculture and industry. The relationship is reciprocal. Peasants have provided a disproportionate share of the capital used for industrialization, with agricultural taxes accounting on the average for 23 percent of the government's revenues. In return, industry supports agriculture through the production of machinery, chemical fertilizers, electric power, and irrigation and drainage equipment.

The destruction that resulted from the long civil war and World War Two made China's main task in 1949 the reconstruction of its economy. Toward this objective, China undertook four five year development plans between 1953 and 1970. As in the Soviet Union, each of the plans has given priority to heavy industry. Yet China has differed from the Soviets in the implementation of this shared goal. The First Five Year Plan (1953–1957) followed a period of political consolidation and progress toward the conversion of the economy from private to state management. Soviet assistance was an important factor in the period of the First Five Year Plan, particularly in the machine industry, iron and steel production, and oil refineries. Much of the Soviet assistance was in the form of complete factory installations.[41] Some 11,000 Soviet experts worked in China, while approximately 28,000 Chinese went to the Soviet Union for training. At the end of the First Five Year Plan, the party proudly announced that many goals were overfulfilled. China's production not only improved dramatically, but considerably outpaced that of India in a similar period (1950–1961) in the areas of steel, electric power, coal, and automobile tire production; India outpaced China in production of electric motors, bicycles, cement, paper, cotton cloth, sugar, and chemical fertilizers.[42]

40. Mao Tse-tung, *Selected Readings from the Works of Mao Tse-tung* (Peking: Foreign Languages Press, 1971), p. 476.
41. Some argue that complete installations are more valuable than separate capital goods assistance. See Chai Nai-ruenn and Walter Galenson, *The Chinese Economy under Communism* (Chicago: Aldine, 1969), p. 53.
42. *Ibid.*, p. 64.

FIGURE 9.1

## China's Economic Advancement 1950–1975 (Estimated)

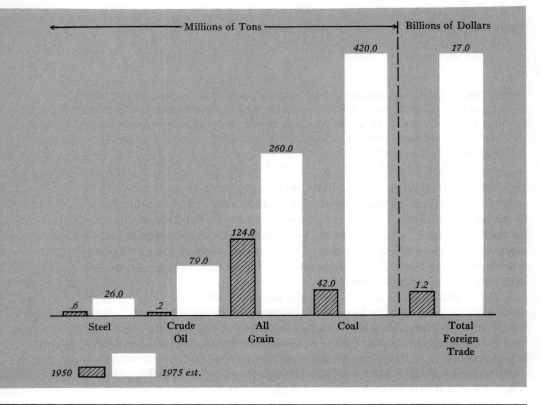

Source: Time *(February 3, 1975), p. 24.*

Enthusiasm was so great that the Second Five Year Plan (1958–1962) articulated even more ambitious objectives. But, as frequently happens with plans, unexpected events intervened and in this case had extremely detrimental effects. First were the disastrous agricultural effects of two years of drought and the poor planning and implementation of the commune policy. In 1960 the Soviets began to withdraw their support, leaving many planned projects incomplete; the lack of spare parts hampered production in other factories. China thus had to make simultaneous adjustments in agriculture, industry, and the political sphere. During the Second Five Year Plan, production declined or stagnated in many areas of agriculture, especially in industry. Delays and the political repercussions of the Great Leap Forward resulted in the postponement of the Third Five Year Plan until 1966.

The Third Five Year Plan (1966–1970) highlighted increased construction and plant modernization. Emphasis was placed on labor-intensive small-scale industry using simple domestic technology and capable of using a surplus work force. It also sought to diversify industrial investment regionally and to prevent its concentration in the coastal areas, which are most vulnerable to enemy attack. Greater attention was given to linking industrial cities with the sources of raw materials, to energy, and to consumption. Production, temporarily constrained by struggles during the Cultural Revolution, soon recovered. The Fourth Five Year Plan was inaugurated in January 1971 with the objective of achieving industrial and agricultural self-sufficiency nationally and at the commune level.

*Social Welfare and Human Development*  Economic modernization is the backbone of the socialist society and the key to the Chinese attempt to cope with the problems of poverty. China's approach to poverty has been to treat its sources — economic underdevelopment and class barriers. But attitudinal changes (changes in motivation and expectations) have by no means been ignored. Socialist development, as it is understood by communist thinkers, is based on human development. This implies more than the elimination of poverty; it means opportunity, freedom from exploitation, and the assurance of basic needs such as food, housing, health, and old-age care.

The best assurance against poverty for the able-bodied is full employment. During the Great Leap Forward there were marked labor shortages, despite the expansion of the labor force brought about by freeing women from their households. While full employment is the main goal in dealing with poverty, China has developed an extensive welfare program. The 1951 Labor Insurance Regulations Act now covers more than 20 million "productive workers, cadres, and government employees." Workers are protected from income loss due to injury, and some medical costs are paid as well. The same legislation provides for such collective welfare services as orphanages, sanatoria, and old-age homes.

Basic to the enhancement of opportunity and the construction of a socialist society is education. The party's objectives have been to eliminate illiteracy, expand public awareness, promote ideological consciousness, and teach skills necessary to a rapidly modernizing society. The essence of Chinese education is summed up in the slogan "Red and Expert." The new socialist person will differ from his or her forebears in that the latter gave priority to traditional norms — kinship groups and individuals — before state and community. The new socialist person is taught that one must not exploit other individuals no matter what one's intellectual or material advantage, and that one owes service to the nation. Only by means of the development of the nation will he or she collectively and individually benefit.

China devotes about 10 percent of its annual budget to education. The formal school system's principal objective is universal primary education. But the school system also includes secondary and university schools, and — unique to developing nations — an extensive kindergarten program for students three–six years of age and a broad network of vocational schools. Furthermore, the ad hoc system includes part-time and correspondence programs and a wide variety of adult courses. These emphasize literacy and job skills to help persons without formal education become qualified for modern industrial and technical jobs.

Clearly, the objective of Chinese education is totally to direct human development. Mao has stressed the need to mix work and study, and mass education includes ideological training, intellectual pursuits, and physical labor. Each person, whether a factory manager who does a once-a-week stint or a party cadre in a rural commune, must partake of physical labor. Students must work part-time and for two years after secondary school in order to be admitted into higher educational institutions. Industrial workers and peasants study after hours. Finally, in an effort to avoid the usual dominance of higher education by the more privileged portions of society, the Chinese have made a special effort to extend the benefits of higher education to workers and peasants. At least 50 percent of those admitted to college in recent years have been from worker or peasant backgrounds.

China's educational attainments have indeed been impressive. In 1949 some 80 percent of the population was illiterate; and it is estimated that today this figure is less than 20 percent. Approximately 80 percent of all primary-age children in rural areas complete primary school (four years), and almost all urban primary-age students do so. Whereas in 1950 there were fewer than 1 million secondary students in all of China, today there are more than 30 million (not including the approximately 5 million special and part-time students in secondary school). Each year some 300,000 pupils enter institutions of higher education, of which there are more than five hundred. Clearly the results would have been even more impressive were it not for the closing of the schools during the Great Proletarian Cultural Revolution. In sum, formal education is aimed at developing a skilled socialist citizen. The stresses inherent in this objective are further intensified by limited resources. Thus, the bulk of China's scarce resources being devoted to universal primary education, many aspiring individuals are frustrated by limited opportunities for secondary and university education.

While education and the elimination of poverty are of vital importance to the modernization of a nation, both efforts would be severely undermined by inadequate health. China on the eve of liberation was suffering. Starvation was not uncommon; the average lifespan was, in Hobbes' words, "nasty, brutish, and short." With less than 30,000 Western-trained doctors and 3,200 persons per hospital bed in 1949, the task ahead was indeed difficult. By the end of 1950 all brothels had been closed, and within a few years venereal disease had virtually been eradicated. By 1953 some 307 million persons had been vaccinated against smallpox, essentially eliminating that disease; over 200,000 midwives had been retrained and 10,000 new maternal and child health workers trained.[43] This effort was followed by major campaigns to eliminate parasitic diseases.

For preventive medicine to become a reality, rural health clinics had to be constructed. This in turn required recognition of those practicing traditional medicine. Chinese medical journals began publishing pharmacological analyses of Chinese herbs, and in 1956 some clinics were turned over to practitioners of traditional medicine. By 1958 every commune had a health center and most production brigades had health stations. After that time, medical students were sent with regularity to the rural health stations for a period up to five years. By 1965 faculty members from leading medical schools were also being sent to help treat rural health problems. The mass migration of students and doctors to rural areas steadily grew.

Over the past twenty years China's health delivery system has vastly improved. The number of doctors increased from 30,000–48,000 in 1952 (11,000 persons per doctor) to an estimated 457,000 in 1972 (3,200 persons per doctor).[44] The ratio of people to hospital beds decreased from 3,200 persons per bed in 1952 to an estimated 350 persons per bed in 1972.[45] The backbone of China's health program is the "barefoot doctor," a paramedic trained to treat less serious medical problems, promote preventive medicine through public health programs, and serve as a communication link with other health centers. China's health delivery system has made impressive progress. Its programs are exemplary for developing nations in that they manifest the important characteristics of developmental policy: clearly stated goals, governmental commitment, coordinated administrative efforts, practicality, public support, evaluation, and adaptation.

# Mexico and Nigeria: Development amidst Diverse Cultures

Mexican public policy responses to social problems have reflected two central strains in its governing coalitions: the drive toward equality, particularly in the poverty-stricken rural areas, and the trend toward enhancing and protecting market mechanisms and profit incentives. The drive toward equality developed its greatest strength among such revolutionary leaders as Emiliano Zapata and President Lázaro Cárdenas, while capitalist views have been espoused by President Miguel Alemán and Gustavo Díaz Ordaz. Nigeria has also shown concern for equality, but with reference to regional rather than individual disparities.

43. Robert M. Worth, "Strategy of Change in the People's Republic of China," in *Communications and Change in the Developing Countries,* ed. Daniel Lerner and Wilbur Schramm (Honolulu: University of Hawaii Press, 1967), p. 223.
44. E. Grey Dimond, "Medicine in the People's Republic of China: A Progress Report," *Journal of the American Medical Association* CCXXII (27 November 1972): 1158.
45. *Ibid.*

The underlying ideology of both nations' economies is reliance on market mechanisms and profit incentives. Though there has been considerable and growing governmental intervention in the economies of both nations, the problems of poverty and human development have not received the governmental attention that is a feature of the communist systems. Table 9.5 illustrates these trends.

## MEXICO: RURAL STAGNATION AND URBAN GROWTH

*Rural Development*  Mexico's rural development policies are very important factors in national development, for more than 50 percent of the population is rural and employed in farming. However, agricultural conditions are not universally good. First, climate and soil conditions vary considerably. Some areas are dry and, lacking irrigation, dependent exclusively on rainfall. The tendency in these areas is to subsistence farming. Other areas are more fertile and enjoy considerable rainfall; in fact, damaging rain storms are not unusual in these areas. Land and income distribution among peasants also reflects dis-

TABLE 9.5

*Average Percent of Federal Mexican Budgetary Expenditure by Type of Emphasis and Presidential Term*

| Years | President | No. of Years in Avg. | Total | Percent Economic | Social | Admin. |
|-------|-----------|--------|-------|----------|--------|--------|
| 1869–1870 | Juárez | (1) | 100.0 | 5.0 | 1.6 | 93.4 |
| 1900–1911 | Díaz | (2)[a] | 100.0 | 16.0 | 6.6 | 77.4 |
| 1911–1912 | Madero | (1) | 100.0 | 17.6 | 9.9 | 72.5 |
| 1912–1913 | Huerta | (1) | 100.0 | 15.2 | 8.9 | 75.9 |
| 1917–1919 | Carranza | (3) | 100.0 | 16.3 | 2.0 | 81.7 |
| 1920 | De la Huerta | (1) | 100.0 | 17.2 | 2.3 | 80.5 |
| 1921–1924 | Obregón | (4) | 100.0 | 17.9 | 9.7 | 72.4 |
| 1925–1928 | Calles | (4) | 100.0 | 24.8 | 10.1 | 65.1 |
| 1929 | Portes Gil | (1) | 100.0 | 23.2 | 12.9 | 63.9 |
| 1930–1932 | Ortiz Rubio | (3) | 100.0 | 28.1 | 15.8 | 56.1 |
| 1933–1934 | Rodríguez | (2) | 100.0 | 21.7 | 15.4 | 62.9 |
| 1935–1940 | Cárdenas | (6) | 100.0 | 37.6 | 18.3 | 44.1 |
| 1941–1946 | Avila Camacho | (6) | 100.0 | 39.2 | 16.5 | 44.3 |
| 1947–1952 | Alemán | (6) | 100.0 | 51.9 | 13.3 | 34.8 |
| 1953–1958 | Ruiz Cortines | (6) | 100.0 | 52.7 | 14.4 | 32.9 |
| 1959–1963 | López Mateos | (5)[b] | 100.0 | 39.0 | 19.2 | 41.8 |

[a] 1900–1901 and 1910–1911.
[b] Data for 1964 not available.

*Source: James Wilkie,* The Mexican Revolution: Federal Expenditure and Social Change Since 1910 *(Berkeley: University of California Press, 1970), p. 32. Copyright © 1970 by The Regents of the University of California; reprinted by permission of the University of California Press. See also* Presupuesto *and* Cuenta Pública *by year.*

TABLE 9.6

## Structure of Production in Mexico
## (Percent of gross domestic product, 1960 prices)

|  | 1940 | 1945 | 1950 | 1955 | 1962 | 1967 |
|---|---|---|---|---|---|---|
| Agricultural Production | 23.2 | 18.6 | 20.8 | 20.3 | 17.2 | 15.8 |
| Industrial Production | 31.0 | 34.0 | 31.0 | 31.3 | 33.9 | 36.7 |
| Manufacturing | 17.8 | 20.8 | 20.7 | 21.1 | 23.3 | 26.5 |
| Mining | 4.6 | 3.5 | 2.4 | 2.2 | 1.6 | 1.5 |
| Electricity | 0.9 | 0.8 | 0.9 | 1.0 | 1.3 | 1.5 |
| Petroleum | 2.8 | 2.4 | 2.7 | 2.7 | 3.2 | 3.2 |
| Construction | 4.9 | 6.5 | 4.3 | 4.3 | 4.5 | 3.9 |
| Services | 45.8 | 47.4 | 48.2 | 48.4 | 48.9 | 47.5 |
| Total | 100.0 | 100.0 | 100.0 | 100.0 | 100.0 | 100.0 |

Source: Adapted from Roger D. Hansen, The Politics of Mexican Development (Baltimore: Johns Hopkins Press, 1971), p. 43. Reprinted by permission. From data originally published in Leopoldo Solís M., "Hacia un análisis general a largo plazo des desarrollo económico de México," Demografía y economía 1 (1967): 73; and Banco de México, Informe annual, 1968.

parities. In 1950 there were approximately 2.3 million farm laborers who did not possess any land.[46] The per capita annual income of these workers is low — approximately $60 a year in 1970[47] — and appears to be declining. A small group of farmers (as noted in Table 9.7) is much more successful: in 1960 it was reported that 54.3 percent of total agricultural output came from only 3.3 percent of the farms. These same wealthy farmers accounted for 80 percent of the increase in agricultural production between 1950 and 1960.[48] In 1960 about 1.4 percent of farm landholders held over 36 percent of the arable land. Even more significant was that half the landholders worked only 12 percent of the arable lands.[49] The proportion of Mexico's national income that goes to the agricultural work force is among the lowest in the world.[50] The government has recognized this situation. In his second State of the Union Message, President Luis Echeverría observed:

> Everyone is aware of the problems found in the rural areas, dramatically expressed in the pressure exerted by man upon the land. . . The Agrarian Reform has distributed land, the means to make it produce and social welfare services, but it has not yet succeeded in achieving an equitable distribution of either income or productivity among farmers. . . Economic progress, population growth, and the need for fair distribution make it urgent to increase the yield of all land

46. Roger D. Hansen, The Politics of Mexican Development (Baltimore: Johns Hopkins University Press, 1971), p. 81.
47. Bank of Mexico, Annual Report, 1971.
48. Hansen, Politics of Mexican Development, p. 79.
49. Ibid.
50. Morris Singer, Growth, Equality, and the Mexican Experience (Austin: University of Texas Press, 1969), p. 142.

TABLE 9.7
## Mexican Land Tenure as Measured by Agricultural Production, 1960 (*in percent*)

| Type of Holding (by value of 1960 production) | Number of Holdings | Arable Land | Irrigated Land | Value of Machinery | Value of Holdings | Value of Production | Change in Value of Production, 1950–1960 |
|---|---|---|---|---|---|---|---|
| 1. Below subsistence, $0–80 | 50.3 | 13.6 | — | 1.3 | 6.7 | 4.2 | −1.0 |
| 2. Subsistence, $80–400 | 33.8 | 24.5 | 3.9 | 6.5 | 13.8 | 17.1 | +10.0 |
| 3. Family, $400–2,000 | 12.6 | 19.2 | 27.0 | 17.0 | 22.6 | 24.4 | +11.0 |
| 4. Multifamily, $2,000–8,000 | 2.8 | 14.4 | 31.5 | 31.5 | 19.3 | 22.0 | +35.0 |
| 5. Large multifamily, above $8,000 | 0.5 | 28.3 | 37.6 | 43.7 | 37.6 | 32.3 | +45.0 |
| Total | 100.0 | 100.0 | 100.0 | 100.0 | 100.0 | 100.0 | 100.0 |

*Source: Adapted from Roger D. Hansen,* The Politics of Mexican Development *(Baltimore: Johns Hopkins Press, 1971), p. 80. Derived from Salomon Eckstein,* El Marco macroeconómico del problema agrario mexicano *(Mexico: Centro de Investigaciones Agrarias, 1968), as cited in Sergio Reyes Osorio, "El Desarrollo polarizado de la agricultura mexicana,"* Comercio exterior *19 (March 1969): 234–235. Reprinted by permission.*

for agriculture, to open new areas to cultivation and to increase employment possibilities.[51]

While the importance of rural problems is recognized, the Mexican government has difficulty finding the means and the will to bring about the needed reforms. The government's rural development policy has had five major thrusts. First, it has experimented with land redistribution and expanded the availability of cultivable land to the landless. Second, it has developed new institutions for rural areas: credit, technical services, marketing, and infrastructure (irrigation, roads and electricity). Third, it has sought to increase the dispersion of industries to the rural areas. In some areas, a fourth focus has been integrated regional development. And finally it has tried to improve rural residents' health and educational opportunities.

The *ejido* movement, which ensued from the Mexican Agrarian Reform Law

51. Luis Echeverría, *State of the Union, 1971* (Mexico City: Government Printing Office, 1972).

of 1921, has been one of the main sources of land distribution. Ejidos, or communal lands, are owned by the village or community and divided up by the village among its inhabitants. The federal government gives the individual title to the land, but it cannot be transferred or mortgaged. The ejido farmer can designate rights of inheritance to those dependent upon him economically. Payment for the land takes the form of a tax approximating 5 percent of the crop per annum. Governmental policy now emphasizes cooperative production rather than the individual plot as the economic base, because individual production proved extremely uneconomical. Individual farmers could not afford the machines, hybrid seeds, irrigation, roads, and electricity essential to the modernization of agriculture.

In addition to promoting cooperatives among small farmers, the government is gradually moving toward the concept of regional development, in which each region's total needs and unique characteristics are considered in economic planning. This approach also allows for consideration of noneconomic needs, such as human development, and recognizes the inherent interrelationship of different aspects of the economy, e.g., rural unemployment and the need for industrial jobs within given geographic regions. Rather than set up new administrative regional units that would ignore state borders, the government has attempted to achieve the same end through "interministerial commissions," such as the one for the economic development of the northern border zone created in 1972. Its job is to "research, study and foster programs to speed up economic integration of the northern border zone and the rest of the country, and to examine matters relative to free ports."

One further governmental response to the needs of rural areas is technical assistance to *ejiditarios*. However, Mexico's record of technical assistance is one of the poorest in Latin America. Through the 1950s and 1960s the ratio of agricultural extension workers to farm families was approximately one to 10,000, compared to one to 3,200 in El Salvador and one to 5,000 in Honduras.[52]

The effect of the government's policies has been mixed. Production of wheat and corn reached the point of self-sufficiency and then tapered off in recent years, necessitating imports again. Between 1964 and 1972 Mexico's agricultural and livestock production increased an average of only 1.7 percent per annum, as opposed to 8.2 percent for industrial production. The standards of peasant life are still low: nutrition is still inadequate for most peasants. Farm income is growing more slowly than in other sectors of the economy. Rural educational opportunities and health services are improving, but nowhere are they adequate to meet needs. Half the agricultural work force is still landless and the number of landless is increasing. There are approximately 350,000 *campesinos* eligible for ejido plots who have not received them.[53] However, from the standpoint of the government the political effects have been generally

52. Hansen, *Politics of Mexican Development*, p. 86.
53. Martin Needler, *Politics and Society in Mexico* (Albuquerque: University of New Mexico Press, 1971), pp. 60–61.

positive. The distribution of land to the peasants — even if partial — has served to meet the political demands of the peasants. And the ejiditarios, who have already received land, form a powerful bulwark of support for the regime.

*Industrialization*  Industrial policies have sought to fulfill nationalist goals by means of "Mexicanization," or restriction of foreign ownership in such key economic sectors as public communications, mines, and other natural resources. The government has also realized the necessity of industrializing in order to increase the incomes of the noncapitalist classes, since industrial incomes tend to be considerably higher than farm labor wages. But industrialization tends to follow capital, skilled labor, and infrastructure to a few urban areas. Thus governmental policy has evolved toward emphasis on the decentralization of industry in the interest of regional balance.

There is sometimes a conflict between the nationalist goal of Mexican ownership of key industries and the desire for industrialization and economic prosperity. If Mexican industry is to compete internationally or survive in an unprotected domestic market, it must utilize the latest in technology. And acquiring this technology means allowing foreign investors to bring it in. To remedy this, the government tries to maintain control of capital, in particular by limiting capital flows out of Mexico.

Mexican industrialization has indeed been impressive, increasing an average of 8.9 percent annually between 1960 and 1970. Industrial production now accounts for more than 37 percent of the gross national product and employs more than 20 percent of the labor force. Industry, however, has been predominantly centralized in Mexico City, Monterrey, and Guadalajara.

Though most of Mexico's early production and extractive industries were foreign-owned, the status of foreign investments has changed markedly in the past two decades. The growth of the governmental sector, which controls public utilities (railways and electric power companies), basic heavy industries (petroleum, part of steel, and petrochemicals) and now even some mining enterprises, has been the primary factor in the transition from foreign to Mexican control of the economy. Foreign investment is still, however, a major factor in the industrial sector. The United States alone has $1.5 billion invested, or approximately 12 percent of all investments in Mexico. The Mexican Central Bank estimated in 1972 that anual inflow of foreign private capital, including reinvested profits, averaged some $105 million over the previous five years, as against an annual $130 million outflow of profits, interest, and royalties to foreign investors.[54]

One of the major decentralization moves has focused on the northern border region, where some 300 plants owned by United States firms and employing more than 40,000 Mexican workers produce some $500 million worth of electronic products, textiles, and other goods annually. Foreign investors are

54. Banco de México, *Informe Annual, 1973*, p. 3.

allowed to bring machinery, parts, and raw materials into the 12.5-mile-deep zone duty-free as long as all finished parts are exported.

Mexican industrial policy prior to 1960 sought to encourage Mexicanization by means of protectionist measures. More recently, the emphasis has been on more equitable distribution of industrial investment throughout the nation and encouragement of export competitiveness through enhanced research and technological innovation by Mexican industry. These policies were formally enacted in July 1970. The legislation on foreign investment establishes three "ranges" of economic activity, with varying degrees of governmental and national control. In range one are five industries under exclusive state control — oil, public utilities, railroads, and basic petrochemicals. In range two are eight sectors restricted to 100-percent Mexican ownership, including radio and television, insurance, banks, and investment companies. The third range is composed of twenty sectors reserved to companies with a majority of Mexican capital (a minimum of 51 percent). Included are mining, steel, book publishing, and secondary chemicals.

The institutionalization of industrial growth requires ongoing support structures. These have been forthcoming from Nacional Financiera, S.A., a state development bank that administers specialized funds. It provides funds for the development of infrastructure (roads, bridges, transportation, electric power, and irrigation), industries, and workers' housing. Smaller firms are provided with financing by the Guarantee and Development Fund for Small and Medium Sized Industries.

*Social Security and Human Development*  Industrialization is associated with the growth of the urban centers. With the breakdown of the hacienda system following Cárdenas' agricultural reform movements, peasants without land moved to the urban areas in ever-increasing numbers. This migration put strains on urban housing, jobs, sanitation, health, education, security, and welfare services. Oscar Lewis characterizes the urban poor as "marginal people":

> In Mexico City, for example, most of the poor have a low level of education and literacy, do not belong to labor unions, are not members of a political party, do not participate in the medical care, maternity and old age benefits of the national welfare agency known as Seguro Social, and make very little use of the city's banks, hospitals, department stores, museums, art galleries and airports.[55]

This description fits approximately one-quarter of Mexico City's residents and a larger proportion of those in other urban areas. Mexico's municipal governments devote most of their resources to public works and make lesser allocations to education and welfare (often less than 5 percent of their budgets). The extent of services and performance varies widely throughout the nation. For those employed in factories (approximately 2.6 million people), unions have been active in gaining higher wages, reduced working hours (a forty-hour five-day week), improvements in retirement and pension plans, and long-term loans

55. Lewis, *The Children of Sanchez*, p. xxvi.

for home purchases. But these benefits apply only to the fortunate wage-earner, not to the marginal human being described above, for whom the government's promise of "a decent house for everyone" is meaningless. The government's policy for wage-earners is implemented only through pressures on large industrial corporations to provide their employees with "decent" housing. Though there is a need for more than 2.3 million housing units, the government is contemplating the production of only 100,000 dwellings a year in nine major urban areas. Government programs affecting Mexico City and the Federal District have produced no more than 20,000 units, less than 10 percent of total need. By 1980 the deficit could reach 3.5 million units.[56] In other areas the government has been more successful. Mexico City's new water and sewage systems, for example, will benefit 450,000 of its inhabitants.

That poverty takes many forms in Mexico is attested to by the urban and rural unemployed and underemployed, and more starkly by the disparity between urban and rural areas. Between 1930 and 1964 the proportion of the working population holding relatively high-paying jobs (industrial and service-related) increased from 30 to 47 percent.[57] Wages are considerably higher in urban than in rural areas, as are opportunities for education, culture, and upward mobility in a society marked by clear class differences. Perhaps two-thirds of the nation's privately held capital is in the hands of only 5 percent of the entrepreneurs. Almost half of the national income is received by one-tenth of the nation's families.[58] Thus there is a clear disparity between the few wealthy and the masses, whose well-being seems to improve painfully slowly. The government's piecemeal approach to poverty focuses on expanded education, encouragement of industrialization, and land redistribution.

Human development through improved health care is made difficult by Mexico's high birthrate, 41.6 per 1,000, though this is partially cancelled out by a relatively high deathrate, 9.4 per 1,000. The three most frequent causes of death — dysentery, pneumonia, and malaria — attest to the effects of poverty on health. Much of the typical Mexican's diet is starch, and the average daily caloric intake ranks in the lower half of the world's nations. More than 35 percent of the population lives in shacks with no sanitary facilities of any kind, and more than half does not have access to safe drinking water. Mexico is training more doctors and establishing more hospital facilities, but few of the poor are covered by medical insurance and thus cannot afford care. There is approximately one doctor for every 1,850 persons and one hospital bed for every 510 persons. Yet their distribution is hardly satisfactory. Furthermore, Mexico's health policies have emphasized curative rather than preventive medical programs, such as in China. And Mexico has been less sensitive than China to the problem of equalizing service in rural and urban areas, largely because the

56. *Christian Science Monitor,* 28 November 1972.
57. Pablo González Casanova, *Democracy in Mexico* (New York: Oxford University Press, 1972), p. 112.
58. John Womack, Jr., "The Mexican Revolution," *Foreign Affairs* XLVIII (July 1970): 680–681.

TABLE 9.8

## Personal Income Distribution in Mexico, 1950, 1957, 1963
### (in percent by deciles of families)

| Deciles | Percent of Families[a] 1950 | 1957 | 1963 | 1950 % of total income | Cumulative income | 1957 % of total income | Cumulative income | 1963 % of total income | Cumulative income |
|---|---|---|---|---|---|---|---|---|---|
| I | 10.0 | 10.0 | 10.0 | 2.7 | 2.7 | 1.7 | 1.7 | 2.0 | 2.0 |
| II | 10.0 | 10.0 | 10.0 | 3.4 | 6.1 | 2.7 | 4.4 | 2.0 | 4.0 |
| III | 10.0 | 10.0 | 10.0 | 3.8 | 9.9 | 3.1 | 7.5 | 2.5 | 6.5 |
| IV | 10.0 | 10.0 | 10.0 | 4.4 | 14.3 | 3.8 | 11.3 | 4.5 | 11.0 |
| V | 10.0 | 10.0 | 10.0 | 4.8 | 19.1 | 4.3 | 15.6 | 4.5 | 15.5 |
| VI | 10.0 | 10.0 | 10.0 | 5.5 | 24.6 | 5.6 | 21.2 | 6.0 | 21.5 |
| VII | 10.0 | 10.0 | 10.0 | 7.0 | 31.6 | 7.4 | 28.6 | 8.0 | 29.5 |
| VIII | 10.0 | 10.0 | 10.0 | 8.6 | 40.2 | 10.0 | 38.6 | 11.5 | 41.0 |
| IX | 10.0 | 10.0 | 10.0 | 10.8 | 51.0 | 14.7 | 53.3 | 17.5 | 58.5 |
| X | 5.2 | 5.1 | 5.0 | 9.2 | 60.2 | 10.1 | 63.4 | 14.5 | 73.0 |
|  | 2.4 | 2.6 | 2.5 | 7.5 | 67.7 | 12.6 | 76.0 | 11.0 | 84.0 |
|  | 2.4 | 2.3 | 2.5 | 32.3 | 100.0 | 24.0 | 100.0 | 16.0 | 100.0 |
| Totals | 100.0 | 100.0 | 100.0 | 100.0 |  | 100.0 |  | 100.0 |  |

[a] Decile I contains the lowest income families; decile X those with the highest income.

Source: Roger D. Hansen, The Politics of Mexican Development (Baltimore: Johns Hopkins Press, 1971), p. 75. For 1950 and 1957, Ifigenia M. de Navarrete, La Distribución del ingreso y el desarrollo económico de México (Mexico, D.F.: Instituto de Investigaciones Económicas, Escuela Nacional de Economía, 1960), table 12. For 1963, Banco de México, Encuesta sobre ingresos y gastos familiares en México—1963 (Mexico, Banco de México, 1967), table 1. Reprinted by permission.

market system operates to influence the allocation of professional medical personnel. Economic incentives have strongly favored urban practices, especially in well-to-do neighborhoods. Yet Mexican policy is changing, and each intern is now required to practice for a while in a rural area. Emphasis is also being given to the educational aspect of public health, which involves considerable person-to-person communication, particularly among the poor, among whom the incidence of illiteracy (51 percent nationally) is extremely high.

Education in Mexico has paralleled the development of other resources in that it is biased toward urban areas and the middle and upper classes. While urban students have a greater chance of gaining secondary and university education than their rural counterparts, opportunities to commence the educational process are in themselves predictive. Rural students rarely complete more than three years of primary school, and typically start late because of agricultural obligations to their families. Urban students are likely to complete six years of primary school, and if they are members of the middle and upper classes even continue on to secondary school.

So far education has done little more than introduce simple literacy to the masses, with few other results conducive to occupational preparation. Demand for greater education is increasing markedly among the masses. In 1965 the Secretary of Education, Agustin Yanez, stated:

> Where there is an elementary school, the people want a secondary school. Where there are both elementary and secondary schools, they demand a preparatory and a normal school. Here there are both, they ask for a technological school or even a university.[59]

In 1971 the government commenced a major effort in school construction. In one year alone, the educational budget increased by 23 percent, and educational expenditures now amount to almost one-quarter of the federal government's budget. Today more than 280,000 students are registered in state universities located throughout the nation.

## NIGERIA: CHANGE THROUGH MINIMAL POLICY INTERVENTION

*Rural Development*  Some 80 percent of Nigeria's population lives and works in rural areas, primarily in agricultural occupations. The importance of agriculture is attested to by the fact that it produces not only ample food for the whole population but also 50 percent of Nigeria's national income and a considerable portion of its export earnings. Yet 60 percent of the total agricultural output is subsistence production consumed by the farmers themselves. The proportion of cultivable lands — estimated at 37 percent of all lands — is much greater than in Mexico, and in fact higher than that in most developing nations. Ownership for the most part takes the form of small individually owned family plots. In many cases the village leader controls the allocation and size of such plots. In addition to this form of land tenure there is a large commercial plantation sector, most of which is foreign-owned; from this sector, Nigeria derives somewhat more than 50 percent of its export earnings. Food crops have been sufficient to national needs (at least through the 1960s). Groundnuts are both an important source of protein in a livestock-short setting and a primary export commodity. Other key exports are palm oil (used in soaps and cooking oils), rubber, cocoa, and cotton.

The predominance of small subsistence landholders has constrained increases in production. Between 1967 and 1972, agriculture's contribution to the gross domestic product is estimated to have risen at an annual rate of 1.5 percent,[60] which is half the rate of population increase and well below the manufacturing sector's growth rate. This stagnation results from the land tenure structure. Small farmers are unable to afford such modern inputs as fertilizers, irrigation, hybrid seeds, and machinery — all of which increase production per acre. Perhaps more ominous are the increased demand for food, unfavorable

59. *Excelsior,* 14 September 1965.
60. I. O. Ebong, "Ways to Increase Food Production in Nigeria." Paper delivered at conference of Nigerian Economic Society, 1972.

long-range climatic changes (particularly droughts in the north), and the absence of rational governmental planning for agricultural development. In lieu of the latter, exploitation of unused land is running its course, and traditional crops such as cocoa continue to be planted despite declining international market prices and the increased demand for food crops.

To correct this sector's weakness, the third national development plan, which runs from April 1975 through March 1980, calls for an allocation to the agricultural sector six times that of the second plan period. The new plan also calls for accelerated fertilizer distribution (960,00 tons) and increased acreage under irrigation (1.4 million). Not apparent in such statistics is the poor quality of life of those who reside and work in the rural areas. This picture is even more bleak. Income, educational opportunities, and upward social mobility are all severely limited relative to urban and industrial sectors. The core of the problem is the limited growth of agricultural production.

The evolution of agriculture — that is, the cultivation of new land and the growth of the labor force — has resulted in natural increases in production. But the growing demand for development revenues and food to feed the growing number of urban dwellers will eventually force the government to adapt by altering existing agricultural practices. Land tenure and distribution has thus far been left to the states because of the considerable variation in regional cultural patterns and land ownership customs. In general, the evolution in land tenure patterns has been from community-owned lands to community-derived rights to land to individual ownership. Experiments with various forms of agricultural cooperatives and even state-run farms have been undertaken, particularly in the north for the raising of livestock. In addition to promoting cooperatives, the government has attempted through the state marketing boards to use price and research findings to augment agricultural production.

The major thrust of the Nigerian rural development program has been to institutionalize and expand the functions of the marketing boards, which are supposed to stabilize prices for the farmers and use any profits from export to stimulate research and improve farming methods. Yet the boards often amount to no more than arenas for political leverage, and as a result their benefits have often been restricted to a few of their clients.

*Industrialization*  As population pressures increase in relation to available farm lands, production limits tend to be realized and the flight to the cities is furthered. The urban-based industrial and commercial branches of the economy are still small, amounting to only 9 percent of gross domestic production. However, industry is growing rapidly and domestic production is now able to meet most of Nigeria's consumer needs. Much of Nigeria's industry, including approximately 1,200 of the 2,000 "modern" firms, is concentrated in Lagos, the capital.

The government is encouraging foreign investments by means of international newspaper advertisements and assurances against nationalization. However, in the oil industry the government is demanding 55 percent of all revenues, and in other industries there is pressure to increase Nigerian participation and to train Nigerian managerial personnel to eventually replace foreigners.

The Nigerian oil industry has boomed following new discoveries, and production is now more than 2 million barrels a day — the same as that of many Middle Eastern oil-producing nations. Yet, ironically, most of the petroleum is exported, leaving Nigeria a shortage that necessitates importing refined petroleum products. Oil discoveries are also making possible increased government investments in industry. Indeed, under the third national development plan, the amount allotted to investment is more than thirty times the amount of the second national development plan. These investments will include development of new refineries, liquified natural gas projects, and construction of cement production capacity. Oil revenues, the largest source of domestic funds, are utilized by the government to realize one of its main industrial strategies — the development of an economic infrastructure. This undertaking, it is hoped, will encourage investment by both foreign and domestic entrepreneurs.

Because industrialization is concentrated primarily in Lagos and such other large cities as Kano, Zaria, and Kaduna in the north and Port Harcourt, Onistsha, Aba, and Enugu in the southeast, the problems of urbanization are of growing concern to Nigerian government officials. Between 1960 and 1965 Lagos alone almost doubled its population, which reached 1 million persons. Each of these urban centers has grown rapidly and become a center for manufacturing, commerce, and administration, leading to problems that local governments are unable to resolve effectively: automobile traffic, inadequate water supply systems and electrical power, slum housing, unemployment, and — even more serious — governmental mismanagement and corruption. The shortage of skilled manpower means that local governments must often call upon foreigners to study and propose solutions for their problems.

The 1975–1980 development plan fails even to recognize urban problems, just as the previous plan did. In fact, the previous plan may well have contributed to these problems by seeking to promote industrialization through augmentation of the infrastructure in areas where industry already exists, rather than its dissemination around the nation. The first development plan set up regional housing corporations, which did build a few middle-class housing estates, mostly for government employees. Some have hopes for the second development plan, which funds town and rural planning for the Western Region. But, on account of administrative shortages, few of the funds allocated for state planning have been spent.

*Social Welfare and Human Development*  Governmental assistance to the aged and unemployed is limited to former government employees, and the major sources of economic security are still the extended family, the clan, and village associations. Human development programs, especially in health and education, are undeniably essential to any effort to overcome poverty and economic insecurity in Nigeria.

Health problems remain as a serious problem for Third World countries, as

TABLE 9.9

*Infant Mortality (per 1,000 population)* _____

| | |
|---|---|
| United Kingdom | 18 |
| France | 16.4 |
| China | Not available |
| Soviet Union | 25 |
| Mexico | 68.4 |
| Nigeria | 68.0 |

*Source:* Associated Press Almanac 1975 *(Maplewood, N.J.: Hammond Almanac, 1974), pp. 478–639.*

noted in the contrast (see Table 9.9) between such countries and countries of the two other political-system types. Inadequately purified water allows many diseases to be passed through drinking and bathing in water polluted by human and animal wastes. The leading causes of death reflect this situation: malaria (19 percent) followed by infectious and parasitic diseases (18 percent). In the north, where the average lifespan is considerably shorter than in the south, vitamins A and C are deficient in the diet. Yet vitamin C, necessary for resistance to disease, is present in palm oils available and heavily consumed in the southern part of the country.

Some comparisons with Mexico are interesting. Although Mexico's population is smaller, its industrial capacity and GNP per capita are greater than Nigeria's, which may be a major factor in comparative health statistics. The high infant mortality rates of both nations are attributable to the weakness of their health delivery systems — particularly Mexico's, because its trained personnel and facilities are considerably more numerous than Nigeria's. In both nations, modern medicine is available to a limited degree for urban residents and infinitesimally for rural citizens. This situation has been aggravated in Nigeria by the decision to relegate responsibility for health delivery to the states.

With regard to education, too, Nigeria faces a severe challenge to distribute educational opportunities justly and provide a meaningful educational experience. In developing nations meaningful education involves far more than self-development; it means preparing individuals for jobs and assuring that precious educated manpower will not be wasted.

In the past education was under regional, and later state, control. This situation was pursuant to the origins of the educational system: religious-dominated Muslim schools for the study of the Koran in the north, and Christian-run missionary schools in the south. Each region sought to preserve its own culture and values by controlling education. But this state of affairs led to disparities: the southern states spent considerably more on education than did the north, and as a result there are more schools and more students at all levels in the southern states than in the northern states.

Less than 30 percent of all primary-age students are enrolled in primary schools. The government's goal is 50 percent by 1980, and in order to achieve it the Federal Commissioner of Education, Chief A. Y. Eke, announced in September 1973 that several changes would be made in the secondary schools. First, the five-year secondary school would be replaced with a six-year primary school and then a choice of a four-year college or professional school. To adapt the curricula to the nation's needs, new courses in science, agriculture, and teacher training would be added.

These are not the only steps being taken by the government. It has also created the National Youth Service Corps, a service program for all college graduates designed to cope with growing unemployment among college graduates and to elicit some public service from graduates who will ultimately end up in private industry. In 1973 almost 2,600 graduates were assigned to a year's compulsory service in rural areas, mostly in the north. This is a small number relative to China's effort to deal with similar problems.

A further step by the federal government is the assumption of greater control over the states' educational programs, which has encountered stiff opposition. There was considerable resistance by the churches — the Catholics in the east, who received state subsidies, and the Muslims in the north — to federal control. They tolerated nothing more than federal determination of academic standards before turning to political pressures. But coherence has been restored under the military regime, and expansion is being pursued by means of direct control of the educational system. To date performance is highly inadequate in terms of facilities, literacy, and communications (a less formal but essential link in the public education system). Clearly, the variance in communication media between Mexico and Nigeria reflects differences in their gross national products, years since independence, and Mexico's proximity to the United States' well-developed communications network.

Reflecting on the government's role in these nations, we note several patterns that are typical of Third World nations. First, the dominant challenge is rural development, which involves the adequacy of food production, rural

TABLE 9.10

_Comparative Statistics on Health in Mexico and Nigeria_

|  | _Mexico_ | _Nigeria_ |
| --- | --- | --- |
| Birthrate | 41.6 per 1,000 | 50 per 1,000 |
| Deathrate | 9.4 per 1,000 | 25 per 1,000 |
| Life expectancy | 60 years | 50 years |
| Infant mortality | 68.4 per 1,000 | 68 per 1,000 |
| Persons per hospital bed | 530 | 1,782 |
| Persons per physician | 1,824 | 36,500 |

_Source:_ United Nations Statistical Yearbook, 1972.

TABLE 9.11

*Comparative Statistics on Education and Communications in Mexico and Nigeria*

| | Mexico | Nigeria |
|---|---|---|
| Combined primary and secondary schools | 46,444 | 16,350 |
| Illiteracy | 49 percent (1970) | 80 percent (1971) |
| Primary and secondary enrollment | 8,648,123 | 3,252,345 |
| Higher education enrollment | 227,692 | 49,198 |
| Telephones | 1,174,945 | 75,900 |
| Newspapers | 116 per 1,000 | 7 per 1,000 |
| TV stations | 47 | 4 |
| TV receivers | 1,850,000 | 57,000 |
| Radio stations | 483 | 6 |
| Radio receivers | 9,897,000 | 1,250,000 |

*Source:* Associated Press Almanac 1973 *(New York: Almanac Publishing Company, 1972), pp. 727, 738.*

incomes, education, health, and opportunities for social mobility. Mexico and Nigeria have both neglected this area of concern until pressures from the neglected elicited government action. The initial response is usually minimal, and only later is full-scale planning undertaken. In many cases, though more in Mexico than Nigeria at this point, greater mass mobilization has also resulted. As population increases, the failures of rural development — increased urban migration and population pressures on land and food supplies that subsistence agriculture cannot effectively meet — become more pronounced. With the government devoting much of its budget to military and administrative costs, little is left for public services, welfare, or investment in research and technological innovations. Both nations became dependent on foreign capital in the push to industrialize, only to attempt to correct this imbalance at a later stage. Unlike China and the Soviet Union, these Third World nations have not attempted to provide for the welfare of the masses prior to developing their economic capacities. It is also evident that both nations are less than completely committed to solving socioeconomic problems. Planning is inadequate; self-generated change and adaptation are the dominant patterns.

# Conclusion

The penetration of society by government has increased in all political systems, whatever their ideologies. Even in liberal democracies with a tradition of clear distinctions between public and private issues, the tendency is to grant a larger role to government. In part, the increased socioeconomic activity of government can be explained by rising public expectations. People no longer expect government to remain passive and allow society and the economy to function on their own. Rightly or wrongly, government is expected to resolve or manage social conflicts and economic difficulties and to take action to prevent their recurrence. Failure to meet these expectations results in the loss of support from the public, the military, or other key political forces.

A second reason for the growth of governmental socioeconomic action is the complexity of modern societies and economies. Many current social problems, such as urban housing, mass transport, education, and public health services, are of no interest to private entrepreneurs. Nor can nongovernmental bodies alone provide solutions to critical socioeconomic problems that must be confronted immediately: the allocation of increasingly scarce natural resources, energy development and utilization, environmental protection, and population control. As these problems come to the forefront, we can expect even greater governmental involvement in society and the economy. The question is no longer whether these are proper areas for governmental action but whether the challenge is best met by governmental or private organizations. The answer most frequently given is that government is better qualified than nongovernmental agencies to face such problems.

The desirability of governmental intervention is, of course, open to question. Can massive bureaucratic machines resolve crises? Will their solutions be worse than the original problems? Will they permit flexibility and responsiveness to local conditions and interests? Can they be controlled by the populace in countries where democratic controls are valued?

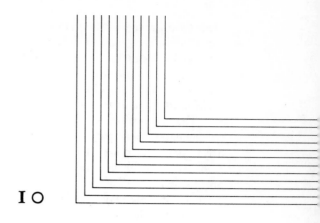

# I O

# *Political Stability*

## Introduction

One of the basic traits of human nature is the desire for security. Among the motivations for the formation of political entities is the desire to provide security by means of collective defense against outsiders and joint action to control the internal environment. People expect their political systems to protect them from invasion by outsiders, assure domestic peace, and prevent uncontrolled change. Consequently, one of the most important elements in a political system's performance is its success in providing overall political stability.

Before we can measure political stability, we must define it and its opposite. For some, political stability is the absence of complete change in the political framework. The country that frequently shifts from one type of regime to another — from monarchy to republic, from civilian dictatorship to military rule, or from one democratic framework to an entirely different one — is regarded as unstable. Another common definition of political stability is the absence of frequent change in government. Thus countries whose prime ministers and cabinets change several times a year are deemed unstable even though the regime does not change. A third common interpretation of political stability is the absence of violence. Countries that are not affected by riots, demonstrations, assassinations, and revolts are considered stable and those that are troubled by such events are unstable.

Each of these common definitions of stability and instability is subject to limitations. The first — regime instability — has the weakness of focusing on the last stages of instability when the political framework collapses and is replaced by another. Many unstable political systems persist for a long time, tottering on the brink of collapse, without actually changing the basic institutions and rules of the regime. The French Third Republic lasted seventy years and was not overthrown, but there are good reasons to question its stability. In some cases a weak political unit will persist and be regarded as stable only because its opponents are inept or unlucky.[1]

The second usage — governmental instability — is only applicable to the parliamentary form of government, in which the prime minister and cabinet are responsible to a parliament that can unseat them. Changes in the government would be an inaccurate indicator of the political stability of regimes that are not parliamentary in structure. In even highly unstable nonparliamentary systems, officials may remain in office indefinitely. An additional weakness of this definition is that rapid turnover in governments may not bespeak instability if the real seat of political power is located elsewhere (for example, in the bureaucracy or a party).

As for the third definition, it is accurate to equate violence with instability in some societies but not in others. Different peoples tolerate different levels of violence. In some societies, even one or two incidents of political violence would indicate serious political instability. In others, widespread violence is tolerable and may not indicate even minor political instability. For example, in the United States — where, as Rap Brown says, "violence is as American as apple pie" — the demonstrations, campus riots, and even sporadic terrorist bombings of the late 1960s and early 1970s did not threaten the overall political stability of the regime. At about the same time in Britain, however, the shooting of two or three policemen in the course of armed robberies was viewed with alarm and provoked a national debate on the breakdown of traditional British nonviolence and the advisability of arming the police.

## COMPONENTS OF POLITICAL STABILITY

As these comments suggest, defining political stability is not easy. A broad definition of political stability that draws upon common usages but seeks to avoid their pitfalls has three components: legitimacy, management of conflict, and durability. The stable political system is one whose institutions and leaders are regarded as *legitimate* in the eyes of the public. Legitimacy exists when the public feels that governmental institutions and personnel have not only the power but the *right* to prevail; the leaders not only can but *ought* to govern. As we have said in Chapter 6, the German sociologist Max Weber identified three forms of legitimacy: traditional, charismatic, and rational-legal.[2] Any or a combination of these sources of authority may provide a regime with a claim to legitimacy. But the problem of determining the extent to which the general

---

1. Harry Eckstein, "A Theory of Stable Democracy," appendix in *Division and Cohesion in Democracy: A Study of Norway* (Princeton, N.J.: Princeton University Press, 1966), p. 228.
2. See pages 268–269 above.

population regards the regime as legitimate is not easy to resolve. In some western countries public opinion surveys offer useful data on public approval or disapproval of the regime. However, even where such evidence is available, it often reflects the public's immediate transitory concerns rather than its general evaluation of the legitimacy of the regime. And in many societies, such surveys are not possible.

The second element in stability is *management of conflict,* or the ability to regulate and control political disruption emanating from social, economic, or political unrest. Every political system is faced with conflict of varying intensity stemming from competition among various sectors of society: ethnic groups, socioeconomic classes, regions, and religions. Political stability need not require economic or social stability or tranquility. The stable system is one that can keep conflict within manageable limits. Definitions of "manageable limits" and acceptable conflict vary from one society to another, depending on past experience and the prevalent political culture. Conflict may be successfully managed in one country despite ongoing guerrilla warfare, while in another country a series of peaceful demonstrations marks the failure of conflict management.

The third element in political stability is the *durability* of the political system over time. As a political system endures it "gathers momentum" and builds support for itself, thus ensuring its continued existence.[3] Each crisis that is encountered and successfully managed increases the regime's ability to overcome future crises. Its past successes have built public confidence and given the political leaders the opportunity to develop skills at meeting crises and institutions flexible enough to respond to crises. However, persistence through time is no guarantee of a regime's stability. In the past century, a number of monarchies that had endured for hundreds of years succumbed to pressures for change and republicanism. Sometimes a system persists by sheer luck, stumbling through crises without really managing them. So accurate measurement of this aspect of political stability is also difficult. There is no set number of years a regime must endure before it can be regarded as stable, but time does seem to be an important factor in political stability. The stable regime does endure and, other things being equal, the longer a regime has existed the safer it is to judge it as stable.

## SOURCES OF POLITICAL STABILITY AND INSTABILITY

As we have noted in Chapter 2, a major threat to political stability is posed by *social conflict* within the society as a whole. Deep social cleavages may polarize the population and produce conflict that cannot be readily managed by the political system. The danger is particularly acute when different kinds of social cleavage (class, cultural, regional, and ideological) coincide, dividing society into warring camps. On the other hand, moderate levels of conflict compatible

3. Seymour Martin Lipset, *Political Man: The Social Basis of Politics* (Garden City, N.Y.: Doubleday, 1963), p. 29. Though Lipset is speaking of democratic political systems, his arguments seem valid for nondemocratic systems as well.

with the maintenance of political stability are most likely to occur when the lines of social cleavage criss-cross or overlap, rather than coincide. The individual who belongs to several social categories is more likely to tolerate diversity and less likely to be polarized into a warring camp.[4] While these arguments are persuasive and accurately describe the nature of social cleavages in most stable political systems, there are divided societies in which stability has been achieved. A good example is Holland, where four social/confessional blocs or "pillars" (Catholics, Calvinist Protestants, secular liberals, and socialists) dominated politics until recently. Despite the fact that the lines of social cleavage coincided more than they overlapped, the willingness of the pillars to accommodate each other and compromise afforded the Dutch one of the most stable democracies in Western Europe.

A particularly important source of potentially destabilizing social conflict is the clash of different cultural groups. Ethnic cleavages are clearly one of the most potent dangers to stability in the early stages of a nation's development, when the task of integrating diverse ethnic groups into a single political entity can easily overwhelm the fragile new political institutions. Many new political systems almost immediately face the task of regulating violent conflict among the racial, tribal, and religious groups under their jurisdiction. The list of developing political systems facing serious problems of cultural pluralism is long, and includes most of the new states of Africa and Asia. Nor is the developed world safe from the destabilizing dangers of cultural pluralism. As we have seen in Chapter 2, serious cultural conflict has challenged the political stability of a number of supposedly developed or mature states, including Belgium, Britain, Canada, the Soviet Union, and the United States.

A second factor that importantly affects political stability is general socioeconomic conditions. Some argue that political stability is more likely to be achieved in the wealthy and economically developed states than in the poor states. Sociologists such as Seymour Martin Lipset[5] and Phillips Cutright[6] have argued that economic development brings about wealth, industrialization, urbanization, improved communications, and education, and that all these factors contribute to stable democracy. As Lipset argues, "The more well-to-do a nation, the greater the chances that it will sustain democracy."[7] There does appear to be some merit in this argument, since the more stable political systems are often the more highly developed nations. However, not all economically developed nations achieve stability, as is attested to by the failure of democracy in Germany between the two world wars and by the chronic instability of Argentina, Brazil, Iraq, Malaysia, and the Philippines, among the more wealthy developing

4. *Ibid.*, pp. 77–79. See also pages 71–72 of the text above.
5. *Ibid.*
6. Phillips Cutright, "National Political Development: Its Measurement and Social Correlates," *American Sociological Review* XXVIII (April 1963): 253–264.
7. Lipset, *Political Man*, p. 31.

states. Furthermore, many of the poorest states — those that have not yet begun the process of economic development — are politically stable.

The relationship between economic wealth and political stability is well articulated by Samuel Huntington:

> Wealthier nations tend to be more stable than those less wealthy, but the poorest nations, those at the bottom of the international economic ladder, tend to be less prone to violence and instability than those countries just above them.[8]

The explanation for this phenomenon is that the process of economic development often produces changes that at first encourage instability. In general, the more rapid the rate of modernization, the more likely it is that instability will ensue. Rapid economic growth creates tensions between those whose economic position is improving and those who are in decline. It tends to weaken traditional social institutions that provide stability and security for the individual and society, e.g., the family and church. And the prospect of a better life may raise people's aspirations beyond present levels of achievement.

A closely related argument is that suddenly uprooting individuals from traditional life patterns and placing them in new and unfamiliar environments creates a *mass society,* described by William Kornhauser[9] as characterized by individual isolation and alienation because of rapid change. Rapid economic development, industrialization, or political change may weaken family ties and undermine such intermediary groups as communal associations, political parties, and interest groups, leaving no buffer between the political elite and the atomized masses. The elite is then vulnerable to the masses and the masses may be manipulated by the elite. In such a situation, *anomie* — the psychological state of a society in which there occurs a breakdown of previously accepted norms — may lead to mass movements, extremism, mob rule, and the collapse of the political system.

Political institutions are a third source of stability and instability. One of the clearest explanations of the importance of institutions as a source of stability is found in Samuel P. Huntington's *Political Order in Changing Societies.* Huntington argues persuasively that the key factor in avoidance of instability is the development of adaptable, complex, and coherent political institutions capable of responding to citizen demands. Where political institutionalization keeps pace with or surpasses socioeconomic modernization, stability will be assured; where socioeconomic development outstrips political institutionalization, instability and vulnerability to military intervention will result.

Others claim that the key to political stability is developing and promulgating the appropriate constitution. This argument is particularly widespread among those who wish to achieve stability in a democratic context. Some believe

8. Samuel P. Huntington, *Political Order in Changing Societies* (New Haven: Yale University Press, 1968), p. 41.
9. William Kornhauser, *The Politics of Mass Society* (New York: The Free Press, 1959).

Ethnic cleavages have been a source of great instability in Britain and Nigeria. The conflict between Catholics and Protestants in Northern Ireland has produced street fighting and near civil war for the past eight years. The socialization of children into this conflict makes it likely that conflict and instability will last for generations to come. The boy holding a club has joined members of a Protestant extremist group manning the barricades in a Belfast street. In contrast to the religious-based cleavage of Northern Ireland, China's conflict is steeped in class differences. Also in contrast to Britain, where the norms of stability and order prevail, China provides a case in which the norm of change predominates. In this photo of "revolutionary fighters" of the Peking Arts School, students are applying their art to criticizing the "handful of top party persons" accused of taking the "capitalist road." In Nigeria, conflict between ethnic groups led to the secession of Biafra, homeland of the Ibos, and to a devastating civil war, which produced hundreds of thousands of casualties before Biafra was forcibly reintegrated into Nigeria. Pictured is a group of Biafrans watching the conquering Nigerian troops during the civil war.

445

that potential sources of political instability can be controlled constitutionally — that, for example, technical procedures restricting the parliament's ability to overthrow a government can be a safeguard against too frequent changes of government in parliamentary systems.

Others believe that broader institutional factors, such as the nature of the party system, affect political stability. It is often argued that a two-party system is more likely to produce stable democracy than is a multiparty system. However, as was pointed out in Chapter 5, several undeniably stable democracies (Holland, Norway, Sweden, and Canada) have multiparty systems, and the crucial factor is not the number of parties but the ideological distance between them. A related line of argument claims that electoral laws affect stability by encouraging or inhibiting the two-party system. Proportional representation, an electoral procedure that distributes seats in strict accordance with the proportion of votes received by each party, is said to foster multipartyism, and hence political instability. Conversely, the election of legislators individually on the basis of plurality votes (e.g., the candidate who receives the most votes wins, whether or not he or she has an absolute majority) is said to produce a two-party system, and hence to contribute to stability.[10] However, in addition to the doubts we have already expressed about equating multipartyism with instability, there are reasons to question the equation between proportional representation and the multiparty systems. Most European multiparty systems developed before the adoption of proportional representation, and other muliparty systems, such as Canada's, thrive in the absence of proportional representation.

A final set of conditions for stability relates to the nature of the *political culture*. Political stability, as Harry Eckstein argues, is most likely to result where the general public assumptions about the nature of political power, its uses and abuses, and its rightful possessors are congruent with the actual patterns of authority in the political system.[11] Authoritarian dictatorship thrives where citizens regard political power as rightfully exercised by a single all-powerful leader. An authoritarian system's stability is enhanced if authority relations in the family, schools, and nongovernmental groups are also authoritarian. Similarly, democracy is most likely to be stable in a society characterized throughout by democratic patterns of authority. Instability will occur where the governmental pattern of authority is different from that of other social groups. A democracy is likely to be unstable if family, school, and other societal authority patterns are nondemocratic.

A similar argument is made by Gabriel A. Almond and Sidney Verba in *The Civic Culture*.[12] They argue that stable democracy requires a particular

---

10. For arguments on the alleged disadvantages of proportional representation, see Maurice Duverger, *Political Parties* (New York: John Wiley & Sons, 1963), pp. 206–255; and F. A. Hermens, *Democracy or Anarchy?* (South Bend: University of Notre Dame Press, 1940).

11. Eckstein, "Theory of Stable Democracy," pp. 234, 240–241.

12. Gabriel A. Almond and Sidney Verba, *The Civic Culture* (Boston: Little, Brown, 1965).

kind of political culture, which they label the "civic culture." The civic culture is founded on a set of political orientations that are supportive of democracy. Where these attitudes are present, stable democracy is likely to thrive; where they are absent, the prospects for stable democracy are at best uncertain. Almond and Verba define the civic culture as a mixed political culture: it includes orientations favoring both active participation and passive acceptance, loyalty to the regime and neutrality, rationality and traditionality, consensus and cleavage. This mixture of attitudes characterizes not only the population as a whole, but also the individual citizen. On the basis of data derived from interviews with citizens of five countries (the United States, Britain, West Germany, Italy, and Mexico), Almond and Verba argue that civic cultures are present only in the United States and Britain, and that their presence explains the success and stability in these countries.

The difficulty with Almond and Verba's approach to political stability is that some successful democratic regimes lack the civic cultures they consider necessary. West Germany failed to meet their standards, but during the past twenty-five years its democratic regime has been at least as stable as Britain's and America's. Perhaps the civic culture is not a requisite for stability in all democracies, but only the Anglo-American pattern. Furthermore, there is no evidence to indicate whether the civic culture is the source or the product of stable democracy. It is possible that the civic culture develops only after many decades of democratic experience. Finally, the correlation between citizens' political orientations and actual behavior is by no means direct. A citizen may have democratic orientations but act in an authoritarian manner politically, and vice versa. Thus the argument that a given political culture is a prerequisite for democratic stability is still open to debate.

In sum, extensive research into the sources of stability has produced a variety of explanations, none of which seems sufficient in itself to account for stable government. Some explanations have severe weaknesses or inaccuracies, but nearly all those summarized above suggest valid ways to promote stability. Unfortunately, the approaches to promoting stability that are most readily implemented — constitutional engineering and electoral laws — are the very ones that seem least promising. Those factors that seem most influential in promoting stability are the least manipulable: political culture, social cleavages, and economic wealth. It is not easy to change people's political attitudes and orientations, eliminate deep social cleavages, or significantly raise the national income. Nevertheless, research into these and other conditions of stability is revealing even if it does not offer guidelines for promoting greater stability.

## DETERMINING POLITICAL STABILITY

In discussing the elements of political stability, we have emphasized the difficulty of accurately measuring stability. The definitions of political stability that seem least readily measureable (regime change, government change, and incidence of violence) are misleading and incomplete, and the more reliable factors (legitimacy, conflict management, and durability) are not readily measured. Because of these problems, the assessment of political performance with regard to the attainment of stability must be impressionistic. Such judgments are subjective (based on personal impressions and opinions) rather than empirical (based on concrete observable facts), and depend upon the analyst's reaction to various and sometimes conflicting indicators. It is important to bear this in mind in evaluating judgments of the stability or instability of a given state — including those of the authors of this book.

Before attempting to evaluate political stability, it is useful to consider some questions relating to the components of political stability: legitimacy, conflict management, and endurance. The first set of questions focuses on *public attitudes* toward the regime and has a direct bearing on the degree of legitimacy the regime enjoys: What kinds of attitudes toward political power do citizens express? Are they generally deferential toward authority or are they frequently rebellious? To what extent do they express pride in their country's political institutions and performance? Are they usually ready to obey the laws and decisions of the political regime?

A second set of questions relates to the *strength of the political institutions* and touches on conflict management: Do the existing political institutions facilitate decisions that are readily accepted as legitimate? Do the institutions allow for decisions to be made under normal and crisis conditions? Are policy decisions made in response to the needs of society and affected interests? Are the political institutions flexible enough to permit new responses to new problems and changing social contexts?

Third, questions should be raised about the *abilities of the leadership:* Do the leaders correctly perceive popular demands and potential conflict situations? Are they perceptive about the political effects of change on society and the economy? If so, do they have the necessary skills to respond effectively to needs and changes? How skillful are they at managing conflict? Do they know how and when to compromise and how and when to use coercion? How skilled are they at anticipating difficulties and recognizing the factors that will affect their policies and actions?

The final set of questions concerns the *extent of unrest* in society: What evidence is there of unrest (strikes, demonstrations, riots, guerrilla activity)? Is unrest widespread, geographically isolated, or restricted to a few groups? What is the nature of governmental reaction to the unrest? Is the level of such conflict within acceptable limits given the country's past record of conflict and violence? Are there potential areas of conflict, as yet repressed or unarticulated, that might pose serious threats in the near future?

Given the subjective nature of such judgments, it is important to state carefully our basis for assessing political stability. Such an explanation of our criteria will enable you to determine the value of our judgments. Furthermore, we hope by posing such questions to encourage you to formulate your own independent judgments.

# Britain and France:
## The Quest for Democratic Stability

## BRITAIN: CHALLENGES TO BRITISH STABILITY

Despite its Northern Irish problems, Britain is the epitome of democratic stability in the eyes of many, including the overwhelming majority of its own citizens. The legitimacy of the British political system is virtually unchallenged. Britons take special pride in the effectiveness of their political institutions: asked what they like about their country, many spontaneously mention their political institutions.[13] They acknowledge that their anachronistic blend of democracy and monarchy is a special form of democracy that only they can make work, but they regard it as more successful than "purer" forms of democracy. There is general satisfaction with the political system's performance is managing conflict and policy-making. Indeed, Britain has been largely free of the serious social strife that has beset other Western democracies in the past decade.

With regard to public attitudes toward the regime, some analysts have argued that the British are endowed with two basic political attitudes that contribute importantly to democracy: a strong respect for individual liberty and deference toward authority. Respect for individual liberty is evidenced by the long and successful battle to limit royal prerogatives and by the protection of individual rights afforded by the English common law tradition. While deference toward authority is found in many political systems, the British are considered more deferential than most other democratic peoples.[14] Evidence of deference is found in British acceptance of social and economic inequality, political privileges accorded to a social elite trained in exclusive private schools, adherence to the upper-class Conservative party by an important sector of the working class, veneration of once-powerful political and social institutions that today have only symbolic value, and profound respect for tradition and custom.

The legitimacy of the British political system is virtually undeniable. Most Britons feel that their government has a positive effect on their lives. Seventy-seven percent of respondents to the *Civic Culture* study said that the national government improved the conditions of life; only 3 percent thought they would be better off without the government.[15] Another sign of legitimacy is the absence of antiregime parties. The February 1974 election took place in a climate of aggravated labor–management–government relations and at a time of widespread public disillusionment with both the major parties. Nevertheless, only 1 percent of the vote went to the Communist party, which is the most stridently

---

13. *Ibid.*, p. 64.
14. Some have questioned whether the British are in fact more deferential than others. See Dennis Kavanagh, "The Deferential British: A Comparative Critique," *Government and Opposition* VI (1971): 333–360.
15. Almond and Verba, *The Civic Culture,* p. 48.

antiregime. Almost 5 percent of the vote went to candidates from Scottish, Welsh, or Irish parties, some of whom advocated separation from the United Kingdom and thus might be regarded as antisystem. However, the bulk of the "protest vote" went to the Liberals (nearly 20 percent of the total vote), a party clearly committed to the institutions and practices of the existing regime. Not since the 1920s has there been a significant challenge from an antiregime party. Public attitudes thus appear conducive to the maintenance of political stability.

The strength of British political institutions is attested to first by their durability: Parliament had its origins over seven hundred years ago; the House of Commons had emerged as a separate chamber by the middle of the fourteenth century. The cabinet dates back to the fifteenth century and had assumed its modern form by the early eighteenth century. The signifiance of their age is not simply that these institutions have survived but that they and other ancient structures continue to prove their utility by adapting to modern circumstances. British political institutions were capable of incorporating new participants and responding to new political demands during the era of rapid social and economic development. The durability of traditional structures, including such anachronisms as the House of Lords and the monarchy, provides the British regime with powerful political symbols that unite Britons and link the present with a glorious past. In so doing, they enhance the stability of the regime.

Britain's institutions are by no means rigid, despite the years of tradition they embody. Confronted with a crisis, the regime has proved highly flexible. During World War Two, for example, all parties consented to suspend partisan politics and elections for the duration of the war.

The process of recruiting political leaders in Britain tends to favor individuals with leadership skills well-suited to the management of conflict. The leaders who gain the top party and government posts have served long apprenticeships in the party and in Parliament, and are skilled in compromise and accommodation. They have already proven that they are sensitive to needs for change and capable of making the required adaptations. British leaders are particularly skillful at balancing contending party and interest group viewpoints in pursuit of a consensus. However, the failure of both Labour and Conservative leaders to resolve the situation in Northern Ireland may indicate that the skills of balance, accommodation, and compromise are ill-suited to violent conflict. Indeed, the search for a democratic solution despite the refusals of both the Protestant majority and the Catholic militants to compromise may have exacerbated the situation: the reluctance of the British leaders to intervene forcefully and decisively to impose a settlement early in the conflict (1968–1970) permitted both sides to become intransigent.

The levels of unrest in Britain seem manageable by the political system. While levels of conflict are generally low and readily managed, there are important areas of social unrest. Two areas of unrest deserve extended analysis: labor-management–government tensions and the situation in Northern Ireland. Between 1971 and 1973 Britain's record of work-days lost due to labor unrest

TABLE 10.1

*Workdays Lost Through Strikes and Lockouts*
*in Selected Countries, 1971–1973 or 1970–1972*

|  | Days lost per 1,000 workers |
|---|---|
| Italy | 3,773 |
| Britain | 2,018 |
| United States | 1,918 |
| Belgium | 995 |
| France | 601 |
| Japan | 456 |
| West Germany | 229 |
| Netherlands | 218 |
| Denmark | 77 |
| Switzerland | 5 |

*Source: Data from* Frankfurter Neue Presse, *6 April 1974.*

exceeded that of all Western industrialized countries except Italy. The unrest stemmed in part from determined governmental efforts to limit inflation by means of wage and price controls. Furthermore, the Conservative government enacted a National Industrial Relations Act that limited trade union activities and established a labor relations court with broad powers to enforce those limits. The unions rejected the legitimacy of the law and refused to participate in sessions of the court. An adverse ruling by the court simply led to a strike.

Labor-government conflict was heightened by the coalminers' slowdown and strike of 1973–1974. Edward Heath's Conservative government refused inflationary salary increases, which the unions insisted on by virtue of the dangerous nature of their work and the fact that they were paid far less than their counterparts in most other European countries. The miners' strike had severe economic repercussions: a drastic reduction in energy resorces at the peak of the worldwide oil shortage, the imposition of a three-day work-week to cut energy consumption, and, ultimately, economic near-paralysis. With negotiations hopelessly deadlocked, Heath dissolved the House of Commons and scheduled new elections for February 1974. The elections resulted in a new Commons in which no single party had a majority — for the first time in forty years. Ultimately, a minority Labour government was formed by Harold Wilson. Among its first actions was settlement of the coalminers' strike on terms favorable to the miners.

At first glance this series of events would appear to be a sign of political instability: a prolonged labor dispute producing economic near-paralysis; a premature election in which no single party wins a majority; and a weak Labour government seventeen seats short of the majority needed to ensure its own existence. However, no real suffering ensued and the majority of the population bore the inconvenience with good cheer. Despite its political effects, the

strike was not a "political strike" but an effort to secure an economic goal —
higher wages, not the overthrow of the Government. Furthermore, despite the
absence of a single-party majority in Commons after the election, the transition to a new Government was smooth and swift. At no time during the crisis
did the public appear to waver in its commitment to or confidence in the regime.
British political institutions, especially the electoral and party systems, proved
their resilience and effectiveness in a time of crisis.

The crisis in labor-management relations clearly reflected the unrest of
British workers. Trapped between rapid inflation and relatively fixed salaries,
workers sensed themselves far less well-off than their counterparts in France,
Germany, and most other Western European countries. At the same time, the
new labor relations law imposed on the trade union movement by the Conservative government restricted union activities and the right to strike. Whether this
unrest constituted a challenge to overall political stability is, however, unclear.
Abstract commitment to the regime on the parts of all groups, including workers,
did not appear to decline. The solution to the crisis of 1974 came about through
resort to normal parliamentary means: new elections and the formation of a new
Government. The conflict did not appear to heighten political tensions, even
during the hard-fought election campaign. Thus, while some might see the
labor unrest as a direct affront to political stability, others argue that it was
an isolated problem created by the intransigence of both the Government and
the labor movement as each sought to cope with inflation and its economic
consequences.

The most serious current challenge to British stability is the conflict in
Northern Ireland. For eight years, the Protestants and Catholics have been on
the verge of civil war and the authorities have been unable to prevent bombings,
assassinations, and other forms of violence. But the strife and violence in
Northern Ireland appear to have little impact on the stability of the British
political unit as a whole, for three reasons. First, Northern Ireland is geographically isolated from the rest of Britain, remote from the areas of densest population and from the center of political power. Attempts by Catholic extremists to
enlarge the area of conflict by means of bombings in London and other cities
failed. Londoners, who had endured the systematic bombings of the Nazi blitz,
were not deeply troubled by the scattered terrorist bombings and in fact seemed
to become more determined to resist extremist demands. Second, since it has
been restricted to Northern Ireland, only 2.6 percent of the total population
is in a position to be directly affected by the conflict.

Third, the conflict is considered by the rest of Britain a Northern Irish
rather than a British problem. Most Britons do not understand why Irish
Catholics and Protestants cannot get along. Both Catholics and Protestants
are dismayed and puzzled by the conduct of their coreligionists in Northern
Ireland; to them, the behavior of both sides in the conflict is "un-British" and
therefore baffling. The sentiment is often expressed that the conflict simply
reflects the Irish temperament, which the English and Scots have never really
understood. The predominant feeling in Britain, then, is aloofness from the

conflict in Northern Ireland, accompanied by a sense of frustration. This feeling was well expressed by Roy Jenkins, who as home secretary from 1964 to 1970 was responsible for Northern Irish problems: "Despite the many attributes of the English, a peculiar talent for solving the problems of Ireland is not among them."[16]

The paradox of the coexistence of near-civil war in Northern Ireland and overall British political stability can be explained by the isolation of the conflict and lack of interest on the part of the large majority of the population. The conflict is acceptable, or at least understandable, to the bulk of the population as a peculiarly Irish problem. Thus Britain as a whole continues to enjoy the solid political stability that is characteristic of the British political tradition.

## FRANCE: UNCERTAIN STABILITY

France has had difficulty blending democracy and stability. Its frequent changes of regime — an average of one every fifteen years or so — have made for a history of instability. Some believe that the Fifth Republic, combining as it does elements of the authoritarian and democratic varieties of previous French experience, may bring new stability. Others insist that the Fifth Republic is inherently unstable since it was tailored to de Gaulle's style of leadership. Clearly, the regime has not yet survived long enough to allow for a definitive judgment on its stability. However, by examining public attitudes, institutional strength, leadership skills, and the extent of socioeconomic unrest, we may make some tentative evaluations.

The attitudes of French citizens toward the present regime and toward power and authority in general are often seen as an important source of potential political instability. As we have seen, the French often distinguish between the nation or fatherland (*la patrie*) and the government. The nation is considered worthy of respect and honor, while the government is thought to be made up of ". . . weak, stupid, selfish, ambitious men. It is the duty of the citizen *not* to cooperate with these men . . . but to hinder them, to prevent them in every possible way from increasing their power over individuals and over families."[17]

Ambivalent attitudes toward authority tend to foster protest rather than positive participation in the political system. We have cited de Tocqueville's comments on the dual nature of French attitudes toward authority: docile acceptance of arbitrary and authoritarian rule combined with periodic revolts against authority.[18] Authoritarian attitudes are reflected in the aloof and often arbitrary rule of French political leaders, whether they be mayors, deputies, or

16. Cited by Richard Rose, *Governing Without Consensus: An Irish Perspective* (New York: Basic Books, 1971), p. 42.
17. Lawrence Wylie, *Village in the Vaucluse* (New York: Harper & Row, 1964), p. 207. (Italics in the original.)
18. See page 178 above. Also see Michel Crozier, *The Bureaucratic Phenomenon* (Chicago: University of Chicago Press, 1964), pp. 204–205; and Jesse R. Pitts, "Continuity and Change in Bourgeois France," in Stanley Hoffmann, *et al.*, *In Search of France* (New York: Harper & Row, 1965).

presidents. The compatibility of these political authority patterns with the authoritarian structure of homes, schools, and other social groups should lead to stability. However, the French citizen's impulse to defy authority and revolt against the powers that be — also expressed in homes, schools, and social groups as well as in the political sphere — obviously threatens stability.

With respect to the legitimacy of current political institutions, there is conflicting evidence. On the one hand, public opinion polls indicate fairly broad acceptance of the institutions of the Fifth Republic. For example, a poll taken in October 1970 indicated that 70 percent of those questioned favored the Fifth Republic's tendency toward increasing the powers of the president; only 13 percent advocated what amounts to a rejection of the Fifth Republic, the reduction of presidential powers.[19] On the other hand, more than 40 percent of the electorate regularly votes for the Socialist and Communist parties, both of which advocate important revisions of the constitution, including reduction of the president's powers. In a sense both parties are antisystem in that they advocate major transformations of the political and economic status quo. The high level of electoral support they receive indicates the uncertainty of consensus on the present regime.

Despite their ambiguous legitimacy, the institutions of the Fifth Republic appear remarkably strong. They have proved sufficiently flexible and durable to manage a variety of social and political conflicts that would strain the abilities of the strongest political institutions: an attempted military coup, terrorist attacks by right-wing extremists opposed to Algerian independence, other tensions and disorders accompanying decolonization, the riots and general strike of May 1968, and the succession crisis provoked by the sudden resignation of the charismatic leader for whom the institutions were created. The regime proved able to handle each threat within the purview of its established institutions. Only once, at the time of the 1961 military putsch, was it thought necessary to invoke the emergency provisions of the constitution.[20] And even then the special powers of decree were used sparingly. It can be argued that, given the French proclivity to sporadic revolt, the institutions of the Fifth Republic are well-designed to control such periods of disruption while retaining the democratic elements of popular control through free elections. Certainly the challenges thus far encountered have proved their strength and value in crisis situations.

As we have noted, the institutions of the French republic have yet to face two predictable challenges: viability in the hands of opposition leaders when the Gaullists are voted out of office, and ability to resolve the problems that will develop when the president is from one party or coalition and the majority in the National Assembly is from another. We discussed the implications of

19. *Sondages* no. 1–2 (1971): 41.
20. The president of the republic is authorized by Article 16 of the constitution to take whatever measures he feels are necessary to respond to grave and immediate threats to the institutions of the republic, the independence of the nation, or its fulfillment of international commitments.

these potential crises in Chapter 3 (pp. 128–129, 130–131). It is possible — indeed probable, given the normal fluctuations of voters — that the leftist opposition will eventually win a majority in the National Assembly and bring about at least the first of these challenges and perhaps the second as well. How well the institutions survive these tests may indicate their prospects for long-term endurance and stability.

The leadership skills demonstrated by the men who have thus far dominated the Fifth Republic have contributed positively to its overall political stability. De Gaulle and Pompidou proved remarkably capable leaders, especially at managing severe crises. In meeting domestic protests and demands they usually responded with the proper mixture of firmness and flexibility. Their sense of political timing — knowing the right moment to act — aided them in responding to serious conflict, as is illustrated by the Events of May 1968. In the early stages of the crisis, de Gaulle and Pompidou seemed to underestimate its seriousness. De Gaulle unwisely proposed a national referendum on the abstract principle of citizen "participation," which did nothing to alleviate the crisis and indeed seemed to many a totally inept response to it. After this false start the leaders waited for the right moment to act. In the meantime the striking workers and especially their families became increasingly uneasy about their missing paychecks; the student rioters became bored with the occupation of their campuses; the general public became apprehensive about continuing riotous conditions; and the opposition leaders pushed themselves into a position in which they appeared to be opportunists trying to take political advantage of a crisis. De Gaulle heightened the growing uneasiness by leaving Paris, supposedly for his country home, which led to speculation and then fear that he would resign. Then he returned to Paris and addressed the nation to announce the dissolution of the National Assembly and the scheduling of new elections, a course of action urged upon him by Pompidou. It was apparent almost immediately that events had run their course and that de Gaulle's action would succeed. The workers quickly dropped their political demands and negotiators reached economic settlements of the strikes. The occupation of public buildings was ended by means of police action, in most cases without resistance. Student riots tapered off and gradually ended. The political parties and the public as a whole shifted their attention from the disorder to preparations for the legislative elections.

As should be apparent from earlier discussions of protest in France, the general level of socioeconomic unrest is high. At times, as we have noted, it seems that everyone in France is protesting something or another. But since protest is commonplace and traditional, high levels of unrest are expected and tolerable. In contrast to the relatively tranquil political scene in Britain, France is accustomed to conflict and crisis. If London were to experience in a year the number of political protests, rallies, and demonstrations that occurs in Paris during a typical two- or three-month period, it would be a sign of serious instability. In France, such activity is normal and not necessarily evidence of instability.

French political leaders have had considerable experience dealing with such protests, and there is a special police force trained in crowd and riot control — the CRS (*Compagnies Républicaines de Securité*). Furthermore, groups that engage in political protests and demonstrations do not necessarily hope for positive outcomes as a result of their actions. They are frequently content simply to manifest their unhappiness publicly. Some see the extent of protest in France as a positive element, claiming that the expression of social tension in a traditional and readily controlled format reduces the likelihood that it will build to dangerous levels. As Stanley Hoffmann argues, "The protest movement is both the safety valve of a society divided by deep conflicts and the traditional French form of democracy."[21]

There is certainly cause to debate the degree of stability of contemporary France. Despite the superficial turbulence of political activity, there is a surprising amount of continuity. The basic public laws that govern the lives of individuals persist even as regimes rise and fall. People visiting France cannot avoid seeing stenciled on public buildings the words *"Défense d'afficher — loi du 29 juillet 1881"* (Post no bills — law of July 29, 1881). The law remains in effect even though the regime that enacted it and two subsequent regimes have disappeared. Continuity is also assured by the persistence of the bureaucracy, whose nature and modes of operation have changed very little despite changes of regime. Taxes are collected and governmental services performed in familiar ways even if the regime crumbles and is replaced by an entirely different political order. Because of these elements of continuity and stability, the surface political turbulence that characterizes France may have little direct impact on the average French citizen.

The mixed nature of the evidence elicits caution in assessing French stability. The Fifth Republic has been more stable in many ways than preceding regimes. It has brought to the fore strong but democratically responsible leaders willing to abide by the electorate's decisions. There has been a slow emergence of consensus on the institutions, if only as a result of public fatigue with institutional debates. It is the general public attitudes toward political power that provoke important reservations about the stability of the regime. Perhaps stability must always be in question in a country like France, whose citizens feel they have a right to revolt and periodically assert this right by rising up against the powers that be.

## STABILITY IN THE WESTERN DEMOCRATIC CONTEXT

In explaining the contrasting experiences of Britain and France in the search for democratic stability, two factors seem crucial. The first is the political attitudes held by both the leaders and the general population. The difference between the trust and deference of the British citizen and the mistrust and latent urge to revolt of the French citizen largely accounts for the greater turmoil of French politics. But elite attitudes are also important. British political leaders

21. Stanley Hoffmann, "Protest in Modern France," in *The Revolution in World Politics*, ed. Morton A. Kaplan (New York: John Wiley & Sons, 1962), p. 79.

have on the whole proved flexible and accommodating rather than dogmatic. The best evidence for this contention is the role that the aristocracy played in democratizing Britain and shifting political power from the hands of a narrow privileged elite to a much broader sector of society. Whatever its motivation, the traditional elite has preferred accommodation to conflict. In France, on the other hand, much of the political elite has been ideologically committed to one stance or another, and has preferred to wait for the opportunity to implement all its ideas rather than compromise. The traditional oligarchy was unwilling and unable to reform itself and had to be ousted by violence. One French sociologist has noted that the French notion of compromise differs from the British and American notion.[22] For the French, compromise does not mean the resolution of a difference by the parties to it but submission of the dispute to an arbiter. French politicians may be as skillful at compromise as politicians elsewhere, but they prefer to avoid it. For them, compromise is in the "non-heroic style of politics."

The second important factor is the nature of the two nations' political institutions. British political institutions were well-developed and institutionalized prior to the industrial and democratic revolutions that mobilized the citizenry. They were able to provide channels for mass participation and to respond to the demands of newly mobilized sectors of the population. In France, meanwhile, debate over the merits of differing sets of political institutions began with the Revolution of 1789 and continues to the present. Traditional institutions were not adapted to changing circumstances. Newly emergent groups frequently found access to the existing institutions difficult or unproductive, and consequently advocated entirely new institutions.

While political attitudes and institutions are probably the most important factors in explaining the different degrees of political stability in Britain and France, there are others. One is a substantial amount of good luck on the part of the British, a facet of which is Britain's freedom from foreign invasion and military defeat. In contrast, the French have suffered military invasions on several occasions and were defeated in 1815, 1870, 1940, and 1945. Each of these military defeats led to the fall of the prevailing regime and its replacement by a radically different political order.

# Stability and Instability in Communist States

Whether or not it is appropriate to expect political stability in societies that define themselves as revolutionary is a matter for debate. A communist regime is initially committed to undertaking a thorough top-to-bottom restructuring of

22. Georges Lavau, *Sociologie de la vie politique française* (Paris: Institut d'Etudes Politiques, 1963–1964), pp. 46–48. Mimeographed.

society when it first takes power. Communist leaders recognize that these revolutionary changes are often incompatible with political stability and are willing to pay the cost of instability in order to progress toward their social and economic goals. The turmoil that accompanies the initial seizure of power in communist states is followed by further disorder as the revolution is applied to society, economics, and politics. This may mean a prolonged period of severe political instability. In the Soviet Union, instability lasted until the death of Stalin. In China, it still persists. Mao has often warned against the declining revolutionary fervor, privilege, and inequality that tend to occur when political and social patterns become stable. Political stability may thus have a much lower priority in communist countries than in liberal democracies, and may even be actively opposed by communist leaders.

## THE SOVIET UNION:
## POLITICAL STABILITY AND LEADERSHIP INSECURITY

Communist rule in the Soviet Union has endured for almost sixty years, but longevity alone is insufficient to prove stability. It can be argued that while the communists have retained control, the nature of the regime has changed dramatically, from the combative stage of "War Communism" (1917–1921) to the relaxed era of the New Economic Policy (1921–1928) to Stalin's reign of terror and forced industrialization (1928–1952) and finally to the post-Stalinist era (1952–present). Each of these changes was accompanied by a more thoroughgoing shift in political procedures, styles, and priorities than characterized the changes of regime in France during the same period. Except during the era of the NEP and the post-Stalinist period, the Soviet leaders did not give priority to establishing political stability. Their major concerns were the radical transformation of society, the consolidation of power, and the defense of the revolution against its internal and external enemies.

A strong case can be made that the Soviet Union has sought and achieved a high degree of political stability since the death of Stalin. Most outside observers credit the Soviet regime with achieving stability. Despite foreign observers' judgments, however, Soviet leaders still act as if the regime would topple if they relaxed their vigil. Soviet citizens are denied access to foreign newspapers and magazines; foreign radio broadcasts are jammed; foreign travel is impossible for all but a select few; and even the slightest public expression of dissent may bring severe penalties. Given the insecurity of the Soviet leaders, it is best to look closely at the various dimensions of political stability before making our own assessment.

In many ways public attitudes — to the extent that they are discernible without the use of public opinion surveys and in-depth interviews of Soviet citizens — seem to support the stability of the current regime. One scholar concludes that the "dominant political culture is the culture of the CPSU, especially of its elite."[23] Marxism–Leninism provides ideological guidelines in economic, social, and political matters for the regime, its leaders, and the general public. While such goals may be utopian, the principles of action call for the concentration of power in the hands of a narrow party elite, and persistent and purposeful efforts at political socialization have succeeded in implanting the party's political culture in much of the population.

Those who reject these political values and orientations generally resort to "internal emigration," manifested in the avoidance of political issues through indifference or apathy, and/or the separation of one's public acts from one's private thoughts. Such a citizen's outward political and social conduct conforms with the regime's expectations, but his or her private political attitudes are at odds with that behavior. It is, of course, impossible to determine how many Soviet citizens resort to internal emigration. But Soviet leaders' repeated denunciations of political apathy suggest that it may be widespread.

Most Soviet citizens do not question the legitimacy of the political system. They have come to accept — usually passively but sometimes enthusiastically — the party's claim to be the sole legitimate spokesman of the national interest. However, there appear to be different levels of loyalty to various aspects of the political system.[24] The notion of a Slavic homeland and Soviet patriotism have the broadest claim on the general public's political loyalty. There is also broad-based loyalty to the communist political and social systems, especially certain of their very popular features: the welfare system, economic development, and scientific and technical achievements. The CPSU's monopoly on political power has the narrowest claim on the public's loyalty.

The fact that the party elicits less loyalty than other features of the Soviet system means not that the public is disloyal to the party, but that it is less positive and more indifferent toward the CPSU than toward other aspects of the political system. Indeed, there is a virtual absence of opposition to the party's monopoly on political power, which is partly explained by habits and fears acquired during the years of Stalinist terror. But this passivity can be only partially attributed to the regime's active repression of protesters. More important is the fact that the public generally accepts (or, at worst, passively tolerates) the party's dominance and the political status quo.

The positive attitudes toward the regime held by most of the public today are attributable to the fact that most Soviet citizens have experienced in their own lifetimes significant improvements in the sense of personal security, relative personal freedom, and material well-being. While Soviet citizens do not have access to the variety and quantity of consumer goods found in Western

23. Frederick C. Barghorn, *Politics in the USSR,* 2d ed. (Boston: Little, Brown, 1972), p. 20. This paragraph is based upon Barghorn's excellent summary of Soviet political culture. See also his "Soviet Russia: Orthodoxy and Adaptiveness," in *Political Culture and Political Development,* ed. Lucian W. Pye and Sidney Verba (Princeton: Princeton University Press, 1965).

24. Raymond A. Bauer, Alex Inkeles, and Clyde Kluckhohn, *How the Soviet System Works* (New York: Random House, 1960), pp. 168–178.

societies, they do enjoy a markedly improved standard of living and more consumer goods than at any point in the remembered past. For example, in 1973 the average take-home pay in the Soviet Union was 129.53 rubles ($180) per month;[25] in 1950 the average monthly salary of industrial workers (a highly paid sector of society) was only 70.3 rubles. Even when an adjustment is made for inflation, the increase in pay is substantial. At the same time, the worker has gained more leisure time: the average work-week declined from 47.8 hours in 1955 to 40.7 hours in 1969.[26]

Even more important is the Soviet citizen's enhanced sense of personal security and freedom. Again, in contrast to the West, Soviet society may seem repressive. However, the average Soviet citizen feels much more security and personal freedom today than during the Stalinist era of absolutist terror, when every individual lived in perpetual fear that he or she was next. De-Stalinization eliminated some of the most serious and widespread sources of public grievance and insecurity. The typical Soviet citizen has thus seen real improvements in the quality of life and often credits the regime for these improvements.

An evaluation of the Soviet Union's institutional strength should focus first on the Communist party. The CPSU has retained most of its discipline, vigor, and organizational strength despite the passage of years since its revolutionary origins. Its monopoly on control over politics is still unquestioned. There is some evidence of a waning of the Marxist-Leninist ideological convictions: technological considerations are often introduced into party deliberations on specific policies, and technocrats who are more concerned with scientific rationality than ideological purity have emerged at the managerial and planning levels. But when economic and scientific rationality tends to infringe upon certain sacred portions of Marxist-Leninist dogma (e.g., in proposals to "decollectivize" farmlands or introduce the profit motive into business dealings), ideology generally prevails over rationality.

Soviet political institutions have proved durable and adaptable. In the past half-century they have successfully managed a series of severe crises, the most challenging of which was the German invasion of 1941–1944. They have been flexible enough to permit adaptation to dramatic social, economic, and political changes: from a vanquished and isolated middle-level world power after World War One to a victorious world superpower at the head of a powerful alliance of fellow communist states after World War Two; from a backward and illiterate people to a well-educated nation capable of sending the first men into space; from an agrarian underdeveloped country to a wealthy industrialized state.

There remains an important question about the ability of Soviet political institutions to provide for orderly succession as leaders retire or are removed from office. The most recent shift in power from Khrushchev to Brezhnev only minimally interrupted the normal political process, causing none of the serious

25. Radio Liberty Dispatch, 17 September 1973.
26. Ellen Mickiewicz, ed., *Handbook of Soviet Social Science Data* (New York: The Free Press, 1973), p. 58.

social imbalances produced by the lengthy battle over succession after Lenin's death. However, it is not clear whether the orderliness of the 1964 succession represents the establishment of agreed-upon procedures for transferring power. It seems unlikely that a future battle over succession will result in a return to the Stalinist pattern of consolidating power. But it is possible that prolonged struggles for top positions might affect future political stability.

As for the contributions of leadership skills to the maintenance of political stability, the evidence suggests some important weaknesses. One is the inability of the party elite to resolve the tension between ideology and rationality. When faced with an apparent conflict between ideological precepts and the dictates of a politically neutral analysis, the party elite is often unable to make clear-cut decisions. It vacillates from orthodoxy to rationality in such a way as to antagonize both the ideological purists and the technocrats. Thus, programs of economic reform and rationalization are implemented by fits and starts as the elite wavers between doctrinal orthodoxy and the advice of economists.

Another source of stress on political stability is the leadership's difficulties adjusting to the elimination of terror as a means of political control. In a sense, both leaders and citizens have since de-Stalinization faced a new political game — in which both sides have been seeking new roles. Leaders have had to find substitutes for terror to assure the obedience of subordinates and of the mass population. And the abolition of terror has also meant that dissent cannot be totally eliminated. The Soviet leaders have simply not found ways to control the expression of dissent now that the use of terror has been abandoned. The forms of repression used against today's political dissenters are severe enough: long prison terms in labor camps, confinement in psychiatric wards, and expulsion from the Soviet Union. But these methods of repression lack the paralyzing effects of the indiscriminate terror and summary executions of the Stalinist era.

When the Soviet leaders have acted against dissenters they have often overreacted to the point of stimulating further dissent. Much of the Soviet intellectual protest of the late 1960s and early 1970s can be traced to individuals who were first prodded into open dissent by the 1966 trials and imprisonment of two unorthodox writers: Andrei Sinyavski and Yuli Daniel. Again, the leadership appears to vacillate, at times tolerating significant manifestations of public dissent, at other times lashing out at the slightest expression of opposition. Such reversals can be abrupt and unpredictable. For example, in the space of a few weeks during 1973, the Soviet leadership first undertook a heavy-handed attack on dissenters and publishers of *samizdat* and then tolerated interviews and even a press conference granted Western journalists by leading Soviet dissenters such as Sakharov and Solzhenitsyn. Such vacillation in the face of political dissent may be expected in open democratic societies where outright repression of dissenters is difficult. In closed authoritarian societies such as the Soviet Union where repression is the norm it reflects indecision or decay of the party's ability to maintain absolute control.

The final dimension of political stability is the extent of discontent. There is discontent in the Soviet Union, but it does not at present constitute a serious challenge to the regime's stability. Three sources of unrest deserve mention: the peasantry, the intelligentsia, and the national minorities. In the past one of the most serious potential sources of discontent was the peasants, whose dissatisfaction stemmed largely from Stalin's collectivization of agriculture in the early 1930s. The collectivization process disrupted the lives of tens of millions of peasants; coercion and starvation were used to force compliance. According to Stalin's own estimates, about 10 million people lost their lives during collectivization.[27] The extreme bitterness of this process is illustrated by one of the "heroes" of collectivization, who has been enshrined as one of the martyrs of the revolution: Pavlik Morozov, a young boy who was killed by his fellow-villagers after he denounced his own father to the authorities for collaborating with those opposed to collectivization.

During World War Two the discontent of the peasants was attested to by the welcome many of them (especially in the Ukraine) initially extended to the German invaders. However, the brutality of the Nazi "liberators" drove the peasants back to the Soviet regime. Most soon rallied to the defense of the Slavic homeland, and in so doing began the process of integration into the system.

At present there is little reason to question the loyalty of the peasantry. Those who have personal memories of the hatreds engendered by collectivization are disappearing. And the attention devoted to farm problems by both Khrushchev and Brezhnev has also aided in reducing peasant unrest. Emigration from rural to urban areas has reduced rural discontent by drawing away from the farms those who are most dissatisfied and giving them more satisfying positions in the cities. There is unrest — or, perhaps more precisely, unhappiness — at the continued discrepancy between the standards of living on the farms and in the cities. But this sort of discontent is neither unique to the Soviet Union nor sufficient to menace overall stability.

Another source of unrest is the intelligentsia. We have already noted the political dissent manifested by certain portions of the intelligentsia. It should be emphasized that the overwhelming majority of the intelligentsia is loyal to the regime and grateful for its special privileges. The attention that Soviet dissenters attract in the West is far out of proportion to their actual political impact in their own country.

The most important source of unrest in the Soviet Union is the national minorities. The communist leadership has not resolved the problems it inherited from the "czar's prison of nations," and there has been recent evidence of unrest among the Jews, Lithuanians, and Ukranians. However, present levels of unrest and indications of future trends do not suggest that these ethnic tensions will pose a serious threat to the maintenance of political stability in the years ahead.

Much of the evidence we have surveyed lends support to the thesis that the

27. Stalin cited this figure in a conversation with Winston Churchill during a meeting in Moscow. Winston S. Churchill, *The Second World War: The Hinge of Fate* (Boston: Houghton Mifflin, 1949), p. 498.

current regime is basically stable. The party's efforts at political socialization have succeeded in instilling public attitudes supportive of the present system. The leaders, although still learning the rules of a new political game, have proven resourceful and responsive. The institutions are durable and flexible. Socioeconomic discontent is within manageable limits and poses no danger to the regime.

Our final assessment of the overall stability of the Soviet political system would be overwhelmingly positive were it not for questions raised by Soviet dissenters and the apparent insecurity of the Soviet leaders themselves. Many of the dissenters within the Soviet Union claim that its supposed stability is in reality very superficial and disguises the decadence of the regime and the seething discontent just below the surface. This position is well stated by Andrei Amalrik, a Soviet writer jailed by the regime for his "defamation" of the Soviet state. For him, "liberalization" is a sign of the growing decrepitude of the regime, a condition that will result in its death, not regeneration. Amalrik uses the following allegory to explain current trends of "liberalization":

> A man is standing in a tense posture, his hands folded above his head. Another, in an equally strained pose, holds a Tommy gun to the first man's stomach. Naturally, they cannot stand like this for very long. The second man will get tired and loosen his grip on the gun, and the first will take advantage of this to lower his hands and relax a bit. In just this way, we are now witnessing a growing yearning for a quiet life and for comfort — even a kind of "comfort cult" — on all levels of our society, particularly at the top and in the middle.[28]

The Soviet leaders often act as if the dire predictions of their critics were true. They seem as convinced of the dangers of creeping capitalism and insidious bourgeois influences as are conservatives in Western democracies of the threats of creeping communism and welfare statism. However, the chronic insecurity of the Soviet leadership is largely produced by Marxist-Leninist doctrine rather than by an honest assessment of its position. Marxist doctrine leads Soviet leaders to take seriously even the slightest sign of unsocialist behavior and to guard carefully against outside influences. Since both the established political elite and its internal critics have reservations about the system's stability, it might be best to avoid hasty judgments on the political stability of the Soviet Union.

## CHINA: STABILITY AMIDST REVOLUTIONARY CHANGE

> Overthrowing the old social system and establishing a new one, the system of socialism, is a great struggle, a great change in the social system and in men's relations with each other. . . . It must not be assumed that the new system can be completely consolidated the moment it is established for that is impossible. It has to be consolidated step by step. To achieve its ultimate consolidation it is necessary to . . . persevere in the socialist revolution on the economic front and to carry on constant and arduous social revolutionary struggles.[29]

28. Andrei Amalrik, *Will the Soviet Union Survive Until 1984?* (New York: Harper & Row, 1970), p. 31.

29. Mao Tse-tung, "Speech to Chinese Communist Party National Conference on Propaganda Work," in *On New Democracy* (Peking: Foreign Language Press, 1967), p. 235.

Mao's dictum that change and consolidation must occur dialectically is the heart of the dilemma confronting the Chinese leadership. It is clear that the norm of political stability is only partially relevant to the People's Republic of China. Stability is desired by the leadership to the extent that it maintains the revolutionary party in power, but nothing else is sacred. The social, economic, and political institutions all undergo change, and even the revolutionary party may be subjected to major transformations. Such was the case when Mao attacked the party during the Hundred Flowers Movement of 1957 and the Great Proletarian Cultural Revolution of the late 1960s.

The twin goals of stability and change often conflict, and when they do preference is usually given in China to social change. The path to change in China has been highly authoritarian in character as the masses have been mobilized for a nonstop drive toward a socialist society. Yet authoritarianism is what the revolution seeks ultimately to destroy in the pursuit of a democratic society. According to Mao, mass participation is the ideal means to realize this goal. This method has frequently been challenged by critics within the party, and the resulting conflict between Mao and his opponents has created pockets of deep political instability. Furthermore, authoritarianism — while useful in limiting dissent and assuring organizational efficiency — produces hostility and frustration, which is in itself another source of potential instability. Finally, the very rapid rate and broad scope of the change taking place in China are destabilizing factors.

With the decline and ultimate overthrow of the monarchy, China experienced considerable political instability until the liberation in 1949. Since then, a communist regime has consolidated control of the polity and slowly evolved a set of political institutions for the transaction of public business. While the regime has been stable in the sense that it has endured, its leadership has been less so. Major purges of leaders occurred as a result of what chairman Mao calls "intraclass contradictions." It should be noted that elite instability and personnel changes revolve about policy issues rather than personalities and coalitional conflict, as is frequently the case in less-developed nations. Finally, the purges of leaders have generally been bloodless. Those purged have simply been removed from positions of power within the party and government, subjected to "thought reform" sessions, and then frequently removed from the public eye.

The first major instance of elite instability, which occurred in the early 1950s, was a major challenge to Mao's leadership by a coalition headed by Kao Kang and Jao Shu-shih. These military heroes and regional administrators believed that party control should be in the hands of the "red" segment of the party, as opposed to the "whites." (The reds were those Communists who prior to 1949 had had most of their experience in the "liberated" or communist-controlled areas; the whites were those involved in Communist party work in Kuomintang-controlled areas.) Further, they favored a close relationship with the Soviet Union, reliance on Soviet aid for development, and professional autonomy rather than party intervention in the management of economic activities. In 1955 Kao Kang, Jao Shu-shih and members of their faction were purged from the party.

During 1957 and 1958, as a result of the Hundred Flowers Movement, the party elite and frustrated cadres undertook another major purge. Those purged were mostly intellectuals, bureaucrats, and their supporters. As a result of frustrations stemming from the 1958 drive to develop the communes, major political shifts occurred in the upper echelon of the party and government structures. The anti-Mao movement was this time headed by Minister of Defense P'eng Teh-huai. When Mao launched his counterattack, P'eng and several of his followers lost their status. Mao himself paid a price for these early frustrations when Liu Shao-ch'i and Teng Hsiao-p'ing became the dominant political coalition during the early 1960s. Also moving to the upper echelons was an ally of Mao Tse-tung, Marshal Lin Piao. It was through Lin Piao's influence with the army that Mao was able to develop a counter-coalition to the prevailing party coalition dominated by Liu. His second move was to mobilize students, and later workers and peasants, to attack the Liu-controlled party apparatus in what became known as the Great Proletarian Cultural Revolution of the late 1960s. Chairman Mao purged Liu Shao-ch'i, P'eng Chen, and most of the Central Committee, but his success was achieved with the assistance of Lin Piao and led to the increased influence of the military. It was only two years later that Lin Piao and several top military cohorts reportedly died in a plane crash after an apparent failure to remove Chairman Mao by coup d'état.

Revolutionary change has its costs, one of which is the likelihood of social unrest. In the early 1950s there was considerable opposition to the Communists among groups that felt they had suffered from their major policy changes. Landlords and rich peasants who opposed land collectivization protested these party policies. Members of the Mongolian minority group and, later, Tibetans protested policies affecting them. In the urban areas, unrest among merchants and industrialists of the former capitalist class over their role in the new society prompted a series of party-sponsored movements to "reform their thoughts."

Dissent increased in the late 1950s, first with the Hundred Flowers Movement and later with the Great Leap Forward. The system having undergone rapid and comprehensive change since 1949, Mao realized that the same potential for violent opposition existed in China that had produced the Hungarian revolt against communist rule in 1956. His solution was to allow the intellectuals, long frustrated by changes in their lifestyle, status, and efficacy vis-à-vis the often less-educated party and government cadres, to express their criticisms. The Hundred Flowers Movement did just that, but to the extent that many party cadres and party elite felt their positions threatened. The reaction was bitter: abrupt suppression of the dissenters.

The major economic dislocations of the Great Leap Forward in 1958 brought more frustration to the surface, this time from peasants, party cadres, and party elite alike. These protestations gave rise to major adaptations, including a change in political leadership in favor of Liu Shao-ch'i's group. Never-

FIGURE 10.1

*Great Proletarian Cultural Revolution,*
*Monthly Chronology of Events (1967–1968)*

1967

| | |
|---|---|
| January | January Revolution erupts in Shanghai |
| | Red Guards exhorted to seize power throughout China |
| | China's *first* revolution committee inaugurated in Heilungkiang Province |
| February | "February Adverse Current" with countermoves by Party powerholders |
| | Chou En-lai issues orders to protect State Council |
| March | Army instructed to support agriculture |
| April | Liu Shao-ch'i officially denounced as "China's Khrushchev" |
| | Red Guards exhorted to love and cherish veteran cadres |
| May | Rectification campaign launched within the army |
| June | China explodes first hydrogen bomb |
| July | Wu Han incidents—Chou En-lai intervenes |
| August | Foreign Ministry temporarily seized by Red Guards |
| September | Mao Tse-tung tours China issuing latest instructions urging rebel factions to reconcile differences |
| October | Drive to establish revolutionary committees accelerated |
| November | Teng Hsiao-p'ing officially denounced |
| December | *People's Daily* editorials stress unity |

1968

| | |
|---|---|
| January | Campaign to support the army |
| February | Army instructed to support the left but not any particular faction |
| March | Leftists regain initiative—army chief of staff purged (Yang Cheng-wu) |
| April | Factionalism of the proletariat lauded in *People's Daily* |
| May | Leftists step up attacks on power holders |
| June | Violence on upswing throughout China |
| July | Mao Tse-tung criticizes Red Guards for lack of discipline |
| August | Chou En-lai announces completion of revolutionary committees throughout China |
| | Army ordered to restore order |

*Source: Winberg Chai,* The New Politics of Communist China: Modernization Process of a Developing Nation *(Pacific Palisades, Cal.: Goodyear Publishing Company, 1972), p. 72. Copyright © 1972. Goodyear Publishing Company. Reprinted by permission of the publisher.*

theless, Mao felt strongly that communism must be achieved in China by means of adherence to a direct nondiversionary path. If any diversions were allowed, he argued, the result would be similar to the situation in Eastern Europe: a return to the "old ideas and practices." This time unrest was promoted by Chairman Mao's group. China soon experienced its greatest postliberation social unrest, the rekindling of "revolutionary fervor and change" by means of the Great Proletarian Cultural Revolution. The Cultural Revolution brought about major changes in policy, which may have represented a compromise. Chairman

Mao's group won some points: the continued ideological socialization of the masses, greater emphasis on the "red" in "red and expert," and greater efforts to recruit the participation of the lower classes in decision-making. On the other hand, pragmatists such as Chou En-lai were permitted to restore professionalism to management and economic practices.

While control and even repression can be utilized to maintain a system, it will ultimately be judged in terms of its legitimacy. China is no exception. There as in the Soviet Union, formal data on public opinion is lacking. But there are indications of popular support for the regime. Morale is certainly one such indicator. China's high morale is evident in the increased modernization of the economic sector and the steady popular cooperation in the difficult process of transition. Other indicators are increases in China's agricultural and industrial output, and the degree of innovation and international competitiveness it is achieving. Throughout China, the visitor is impressed with the results of socialization to render "service to the people." It is not unusual for a student to respond to a question about his or her career plans with the phrase, "wherever the party needs my service"; and with good reason. Years of sacrifice and hard toil to build an infrastructure are beginning to pay off. Life is more secure thanks to massive irrigation, water conservation, and energy projects constructed in the past two decades. Children and adults alike are more relaxed, and their clothes more colorful and varied than in past years. It is not unusual for family ties to be close, and for family members to share afternoon or weekend walks in the local parks.

But not all Chinese citizens have been content. Minority groups such as Tibetans have risen in protest. Students have frequently protested being assigned to dull agricultural tasks after graduation, and being required to work two years before entering the university.

It is hardly likely that any government or party that has undertaken the uncomfortable task of mobilizing large masses of people to maintain a ceaseless effort at social, economic, and political change would not at times incur the hostility of those who misunderstand or are unwilling to participate. Clearly, China is no exception. Yet the adaptive powers of the Chinese Communist party have proven to be rather remarkable. Neither the Great Leap Forward nor the Great Proletarian Cultural Revolution — the latter a direct attack on the party's structures — seriously menaced the party's existence. In fact, it is possible that its strength is greater than before. Its membership has been expanded to include groups that were previously underrepresented: women, minority groups, and members of the lower classes of peasants and industrial workers. Educational campaigns to instill new political orientations and teach technical skills have also enhanced the strength of the party and government cadre. And new mechanisms of governance have advanced political institutionalization. One example is the use of the revolutionary committees to increase the effectiveness of collaboration among the state, party, military, and masses.

Perhaps the key factor in China's institutionalization has been the leadership skills of Chairman Mao, Chou En-lai, and other party leaders. The party and state officeholders, including many who were later purged, put aside their squabbles over leadership posts to develop successful adaptations to a never-ending stream of challenges.

These adaptations have been rendered difficult by several existing socio-economic conditions, principal among which is the pressure of population growth. During the early years, its leaders treated China's huge population as an asset. With many large infrastructure projects to complete and limited capital, the labor surplus was easily utilized. But this large work force had to be fed and clothed, and eventually increases in national wealth will have to be distributed to more persons. It was not long until steps were taken to curb population growth, including campaigns to delay marriage, campaigns to promote contraception, free abortions, and restricted distribution of ration cards to those with more than two children. The uneven distribution of population has given rise to campaigns to return educated and aspiring urban migrant jobholders to the rural areas. The *hsia fang* (to the countryside) campaigns are aimed at stabilizing China's urban population at approximately 110 million persons.

Final assessment of the stability of the People's Republic of China must depend upon one's reading of contradictory evidence. On the one hand, there are signs of the purposeful disruption of society in the Great Leap Forward and the Cultural Revolution; the instability of the leadership, manifested in periodic thoroughgoing purges of top-level leaders; the prospect of further leadership crises arising from the eventual need to find successors to Mao and Chou; and important strains of socioeconomic tension that might well be aggravated should population growth continue.

On the other hand, China compares remarkably well with other countries at similar stages of development. Social tensions have been minimized by successful efforts to equalize material rewards and opportunities. The party has weathered several major crises and emerged a strong instrument for political control and mass mobilization. Perhaps most important is the fact that, unlike many other developing countries, the Chinese regime has successfully countered several threatened military coups. Mao has used the military for his own purposes — sometimes relying quite heavily on it. However, the principle of civilian control has been adhered to in China, while other Asian and African states that achieved independence at about the time of the communist liberation of China have fallen under military rule.

# Mexico and Nigeria: The Search for Stability

When Mexican students took to the streets in 1968, declaring, "The Revolution has brought stability. What we need is more revolution"; and when the Biafrans seceded from Nigeria, provoking civil war, both groups were rejecting

— at these stages of their national development — the norm of political stability. Their actions clearly implied a rejection of the norm that some form of political stability is an essential prerequisite to development. These groups contended that if a regime is stable but neglects the people's needs or is ineffectual, the costs of stability are greater than the returns.

Mexico is at a more advanced stage of political development than Nigeria. While Mexico's first century following independence could hardly be depicted as an example of political stability — marked as it was by frequent alternations between civilian and military regimes, more than 1,000 armed uprisings, and frequent changes in the constitutional format — it has seen the emergence of stable political institutions. The PRI-dominated political system, characterized by a strong executive and relatively weak legislative branches and local governments, has clearly developed roots. In contrast, Nigeria's parliamentary constitutional system, inherited from its colonial past, gave way to a military regime only six years after independence. While this pattern clearly resembles that of the early stages of Mexican independence, Nigeria may well be fortunate enough to by-pass a century of turmoil — albeit under a single-party or military regime. Mexico's first century of turbulence suggests that even a nation with low literacy and an unaware populace can suffer political instability.

With the institutionalization of a single-party system, Mexico has developed considerable elite stability. This accomplishment has not been without costs. While the most important elite position, the presidency of the republic, is smoothly transferred to a new occupant every six years, succession is not always routine in the case of local governmental offices. There is considerable evidence that in an effort to maintain single-party rule, the PRI has overturned many local gubernatorial and mayoralty elections won by opposition candidates. Some officials from opposition parties have even been removed from office on the grounds of minor technicalities.[30]

Nigeria's elite is on the surface quite unstable, but appearances can be deceiving. The first major turnover of key federal elite positions was the military coup in 1966 six years after independence. Although not just the regime but the entire parliamentary-civilian system was replaced, it is notable that the second military executive, General Gowon, occupied the top position for nearly a decade. Regional elites fared less well in the First Republic (1960–1966). There were frequent political interventions by the dominant coalitions — e.g., the western regional fiasco of 1962 — and revolts — e.g., the Biafran elite's withdrawal from the federation in 1967. In the first instance the Northern People's Conference, in alliance with a splinter group from the Western Region, joined to overthrow the existing premier of the region, Awolowo. He was later arrested, provoking considerable communal and political violence. Another such incident is the postelection violence of 1965, which was largely a protest against the fixing of certain local elections.

30. Kenneth Johnson, *Mexican Democracy: A Critical View* (Boston: Allyn and Bacon, 1971), pp. 132–141.

## DETERMINANTS OF POLITICAL STABILITY

The stability of Mexico's single-party system and Nigeria's military regime may well be a function of their degree of popular support. Popular attitudes toward the regime are difficult to measure; certainly, considerable antigovernment feeling is periodically manifest in Mexican politics. In a study of five nations, the Mexicans expressed considerable pride in their political and economic institutions. Yet, while they ranked rather high among the five, the absolute percentages of those expressing such pride were relatively low: 30 percent or less.[31] Much of this pride seems to be identification with the values of the 1917 Revolution. Another indication of apparent support for the regime is the fact that the poorest states of Mexico give the fewest votes to the opposition parties; the same is true of the urban poor.[32]

But these indications of legitimizing support may be deceiving. The poor's support for the PRI is probably attributable to manipulation. For the majority of ejiditarios (small landowners), survival is dependent upon the government's interpretation of the Agrarian Code. There is other evidence of considerable antigovernment feeling, notably frequent outbreaks of peasant, labor, and student unrest. In the early 1960s peasant leaders found Fidel Castro's success an appealing model, and the government spent much of the 1960s and early 1970s suppressing protests and even guerrilla movements. Many were supported by students and intellectuals, notably the famous Mexican painter and communist David Siqueiros, who was arrested in 1962 and charged with supporting student-led demonstrations. Labor has also been restless, engaging in numerous strikes in an effort to gain a larger share of Mexico's growing industrial wealth. While these movements at times sought recognition from PRI, they often went as far as to establish rival peasant and labor movements and directly challenge the PRI. Such was the case in 1968, when a group of forty cocoa workers were slain in a union rivalry; and in the 1950s, when Jacinto López led squatters in an invasion of northern Mexico's large landholdings.

More threatening than Jacinto López was the movement of Lucio Cabañas, who robbed the rich and distributed to the poor before losing his own life in December 1974. The appeal to followers of both López and Cabañas was based on peasant frustrations and the growing gap between the rich and the poor. Professionals, such as the doctors in 1964, also challenged the system, and students between 1968 and 1973 engaged governmental forces in a series of challenges to the governmental system itself. Whenever these movements' demands exceeded the terms the government was willing to grant, force was used to repress them.

In contrast, dissent under Nigeria's First Republic, though a threat to the nation's political stability, was seldom intended to bring about social change or ideological objectives, but rather to protect communal or group in-

31. Gabriel Almond and S. Verba, *The Civic Culture*, p. 64.
32. Barry Ames, "Bases of Support for Mexico's Dominant Party," *American Political Science Review* LXVI (March 1970): 153–167.

terests. But when, as in the case of the Biafran secession, one of these social groups dominates the others, the very legitimacy of the system can be — and in this case, was — brought into question. That the legitimacy of the regime was limited can be argued on the grounds of the low election turnouts under Nigeria's First Republic: as in Mexico, less than half of the eligible voters often turned out. In fact, lack of confidence in Nigeria's First Republic led not only to secession and a major civil war but even to the prior military overthrow of the civilian regime.

If political institutionalization is conducive to perpetuating a political system, Nigeria may well have made little progress since independence. Yet one can argue that any order, even military or single-party stability, that promotes the conditions necessary to the development of viable political institutions is contributing to that end. While Nigeria has discarded its parliamentary constitutional system for military rule (at least until 1978), Mexico has made a major transition to the establishment of flexible political institutions. Since 1917 the Mexican constitution has incorporated many adaptations and concessions to its single party and elite. Decision-making processes within the PRI and the Cabinet are clearly established, as is the regularized transfer of office from one regime to the next. The same can be said of Congress but not of local governments, because of the practice of disqualifying or removing from office members of opposition parties.

Nigeria's military takeover and civil war greatly affected that nation's decision-making process. Some old politicians have reappeared, but in general state and local governments are dominated by new personnel selected by the military rulers. Perhaps the greatest stability characterizes Nigeria's traditional village politicial systems, which remain virtually unchanged even in the wake of colonial, constitutional, and military rule.

Among the key factors in understanding the persistence of Mexico's regime, the "decay" of Nigeria's First Republic, and Nigeria's seven years of political stability under the military, is leadership. Both Mexico and Nigeria have taken positive steps to promote stability. Mexican President Cárdenas' consolidation of the various competing groups into a single ruling party was a major structural contribution to the ensuing political stability. General Ironsi and, later, General Gowon supported the establishment of twelve states to supersede Nigeria's unstable regional framework. While this act in itself has had a less significant effect than the elimination of ethnic-based political parties, it has served to reduce the frustration of minority groups that had felt themselves neglected by regional majorities. Mexican presidents have also skillfully manipulated the symbols and promise of the 1917 Revolution in their efforts to maintain political support.

But the major weapon of both authoritarian regimes is the deterrent effect of repressive physical force. Mexican presidents have mobilized troops on numerous occasions when their offers to settle have been rejected. Nigerian military leaders, more skillful and powerful than their civilian predecessors, have also been able to limit communal and labor unrest by committing their development policies to regional balance and undertaking more direct federal participation in many policy areas, e.g., education and economic development. However, they have not rejected the use of force to quell labor, student, and communal unrest, the most outstanding illustration being the suppression of the Biafran revolt.

Efforts to maintain political stability are complicated in both nations by evolutionary socioeconomic forces, notably the pressure of population on available land, urbanization, increased demands for public services, and Nigerian communal and Mexican class conflict. Population increase, greater than 3.2 percent per annum for both nations, greatly complicates development and political stability. It results in more mouths to feed, more persons to share in a growing national product, and more pressures on local and federal governments for such public services as health care, education, housing, and sanitation. The potential instability of both nations is increased by the plight of urban migrants, who experience high unemployment, squatters' conditions or deteriorating housing, inadequate sanitation, a high incidence of disease threatening to public health, and poor educational opportunities and facilities.

Urbanization is increasing markedly in both countries, particularly Mexico. While urbanization may well tend to increase political participation, an important factor in political stability, it is also a source of discontent for the marginal citizen,[33] whose exposure to higher living standards, a greater variety of consumer goods, educational opportunities, mass media, and the hope of upward social mobility tends to heighten instability. This is particularly the case where living conditions and economic stagnation frustrate the aspirations of marginal citizens. Yet these transitional conditions are temporarily ameliorated by the persistence of extended family ties, which provide subsistence and security. Even so, these ameliorating social conditions are not enough, and frustration had led to increased urban violence in Mexico, in particular in Guadalajara, Mexico City, and Monterrey, during the years of 1974 and 1975.

Clearly the communal rivalries that gave rise to the instability of Nigeria in the early 1960s persists, and will continue to exist until major reforms of the elite and/or mass integration prove successful. During the latter part of the 1960s and the early 1970s, communal tensions tended to be quiescent, while labor and student unrest increased. Laborers frequently strike for higher wages, while students protest European influence over education and other governmental activities. Yet their nationalism is inconsistent. Thus in the spring of 1973 they reacted equally vociferously but less patriotically against the National Youth Corps, which requires a year of their services following university graduation. Each of these forces, particularly labor and student unrest and persistent frustration of civil servants, was present in the July 1975 overthrow of General Gowon.

33. Wayne Cornelius, Jr., "Urbanization as an Agent in Latin American Political Instability: The Case in Mexico," *American Political Science Review* LXII (September 1969): 853.

# Conclusion

Mexico and Nigeria are both experiencing increasing dissent and protest among noncommunal groups. Both systems have authoritarian regimes, but Mexico has succeeded in institutionalizing sectoral participation in the decision-making process, which has yet to be accomplished by Nigeria. The participation of interest groups with cross-cutting cleavages, i.e., agriculture, labor, the professions, and bureaucrats, may well be an effective formula for inhibiting potential instability in a developing nation, particularly where the objective is to limit the scope and rate of change. Mexico's authoritarian regime has also manifested responsiveness to sensitive issues and been able to reinforce widespread mass apathy by depoliticizing local communities. This depoliticization has been achieved by restricting the jurisdiction of local governments and, more importantly, the eligibility of potential participants.

Given this prescription for stability, Nigerian political order may well be more fragile. This is due to Nigeria's failure — to this point — to create viable political institutions, in spite of the fact that the governmental performance has been considerably improved under the military-technocratic regime. Evidence of the latter is apparent in many Nigerian states, where the leadership's motivation to promote efficient economic development is very high.

While Mexico's political institutionalization is impressive, the socioeconomic factors that create a potential for military intervention have been present since 1917. Where fundamental social and economic unrest prevail, there is the likelihood that a civilian regime will become increasingly dependent upon the military to establish and maintain order, and thus that the military will intervene to eliminate the causes of political turmoil. Clearly, if Mexican workers and peasants formed an antigovernmental coalition threatening to the existing PRI triumvirate, the probability of military intervention would greatly increase, particularly if it engaged in open conflict with the regime and the military or police.

As these cases suggest, the nature of stability as an output of government or area of governmental performance is dependent on the government's perception of stability vis-à-vis its other goals. Where comprehensive and immediate changes are sought, societal and economic stability may be less desirable than political stability. The maintenance of political stability is also dependent upon the satisfaction of other needs, both economic and social.

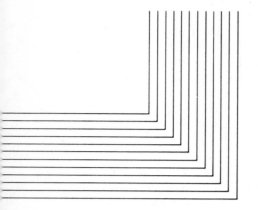

# II

# *The Challenges of Change*

## Introduction

We live in an age when problems are increasingly worldwide — the world food problem, threat of world inflation, the world population problem, world environmental crisis, world drug problem, and so forth.

. . . As rapid population growth in much of the world continues, mankind's backlog of unsolved problems is growing. Questions of global poverty, rising numbers of unemployed and massive rural-urban migration in the poor countries . . . Each promises to worsen in the years immediately ahead.[1]

This passage emphasizes the universality of change and the challenge it poses to develop effective responses. Throughout history, human beings have sought with and without the assistance of government to promote economic development, curb the effects of disease and natural disasters, and control the quality of life by modifying heat and cold. Today, because of mass communications and the general awareness of alternative forms of existence, citizens of liberal democratic, communist, and Third World nations are demanding changes. Whether they want more equitable distribution of wealth, a more effective political voice, improved welfare, or the removal of a disfavored political elite, growing numbers of persons are expecting and promoting more frequent social and political change.

Challenges typically elicit either of two approaches to change. The most common response to goal frustration is *adaptation*. For example, a governing elite recognizes a problem, seeks to develop a response within the existing capac-

1. Lester Brown, *World Without Borders* (New York: Random House, 1972) p. 11.

ity of the government or private groups, and judges the results in terms of their effectiveness. The other approach is to *plan change* in light of perceived needs and/or theoretical or visionary values. This chapter will highlight the interactive relationships between socioeconomic and political changes. We shall initially examine factors that affect the dynamics and types of change, and then turn to an investigation of developmental stages, an important aspect of change. Finally we shall turn to the dynamics of developmental change in Third World, communist, and liberal democratic systems.

## THE DYNAMICS OF CHANGE

We have noted in earlier chapters that communist nations are characterized, at least in their early stages of development, by governmentally induced rapid and comprehensive change. In liberal democracies such societally induced factors as technological change — including communications, modern transportation, industrialization, and the dissemination of mass education — have resulted in comprehensive, incremental changes in both the societal and political spheres. In discussing these phenomena, we shall note at least three factors that affect the dynamics of change: (1) its scope (from limited to comprehensive); (2) its rate (from zero to intense); and (3) its source (governmental or societal). These factors clearly make the dynamics of change multidimensional. Different combinations of the first two factors make for two types of change, revolutionary and evolutionary. Figure 11.1 illustrates the range of possible combinations of these dimensions. The upper end of each pole is in an area of revolutionary change; the intersection is characterized by evolutionary change;

FIGURE 11.1
*Dimensions of Change*

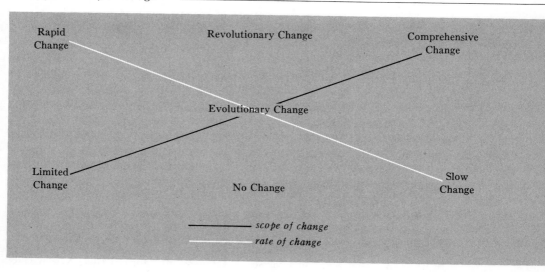

and the area at the lower end of the axes indicates the absence of change, or stagnation. Revolutionary change is thus rapid or intense change affecting a broad scope of institutions and issues. Evolutionary change is more gradual change limited to a few areas of concern. Stagnation is a condition in which change does not occur or does so at a very limited pace and within a limited scope.

The third aspect of social change is its source. Some social change is the result of conscious or unconscious acts of government; for example, the conscious decision to introduce a mass literacy program may have the unforeseen consequence of increasing the political awareness of a previously marginal group. Other changes with important political consequences may come about as a result of natural forces: an extended drought may destroy the crops in a certain region; urban migration may occur because there are too many farmers and not enough land; and population may grow (or decline) despite governmental efforts to control (or stimulate) it.

Many writers[2] treat revolutionary change as invariably governmentally induced; yet marked changes in the societal and economic spheres have occurred without direct governmental intervention. Nongovernmental factors that have accelerated political change include population growth, dynamic entrepreneurship, and rapid technological innovation in the areas of mass communications, industrialization, transportation, urbanization, and mass education. The rate of government-induced change depends to a large extent on the objectives (the scope of change or range of sectors involved), the degree of planning, organization (mobilization), and the commitment of the government and the masses.

The scope of change can vary from attempts at comprehensive social, political, and economic changes — such as in the communist nations where ideology guides policy — to the virtually laissez-faire change that accompanied premilitary coups in Nigeria. In the latter instance, planned change is limited to those levels of government and sectors of society involved in organizing their resources to achieve such limited goals as residential and industrial zoning in urban areas, school construction, or future production goals and markets.

The rate of change can vary from intense or rapid to zero or negative. In a given sector, such as the economic sphere, one subsector's rapid change can be canceled out by another's stagnation. Thus, the gross national product for any given year may reflect a marked increase in agricultural production but major declines in foreign investment, industrial production, and employment. It should be pointed out, however, that once industrialization surpasses agriculture as the main contributor to the gross national product, there is a multiplier

2. The most prominent advocates of party- and government-supported "revolutionary" change are (1) Karl Marx. See David Caute, ed., *Essential Writings of Karl Marx* (New York: Collier Books, 1967); and (2) Chairman Mao. See Edgar Snow's discussion of Mao's thoughts in *Red Star Over China* (New York: Random House, 1968). A second perspective on government-induced revolutionary change can be inferred from the arguments of those who point to political and social change induced by governmental oppression. See particularly Ted Gurr, "A Causal Model of Civil Strife: A Comparative Analysis Using New Indices," *American Political Science Review* LXII (December 1968): 1104–1124.

effect. That is, societally induced changes increase at an incrementally faster rate, and have an increasingly broad impact on the society.

## CONTROLLING CHANGE

In order to control change its processes must be understood, particularly by the national leadership. Among the alternative modes of change are: stagnation or no change; negative change, a return to some previous state; linear change, or a gradual constant increment for a given time period; and exponential change, or a constant percentage of change over a given time period. If we consider that many forms of behavior (e.g., population growth, demands for food and natural resources) have exponential growth patterns, we realize that the period of time during which any given crisis can be anticipated narrows faster than one might expect. Table 11.1 lists the doubling times for exemplary growth or use rates.

TABLE 11.1

*Doubling Time*

| Growth rate (% per year) | Doubling time (years) |
|---|---|
| 0.1 | 700 |
| 1.0 | 70 |
| 2.0 | 35 |
| 5.0 | 14 |
| 10.0 | 7 |

With the present world population rate increasing at 2.0 percent, the doubling time is only thirty-five years.[3] A French children's riddle illustrates another aspect of exponential growth, the suddenness with which it approaches a fixed limit:

> Suppose you own a pond on which a water lily is growing. The lily plant doubles in size each day. If the lily were allowed to grow unchecked, it would completely cover the pond in 30 days, choking off the other forms of life in the water. For a long time the lily plant seems small, and so you decide not to worry about cutting back until it covers half the pond. On what day will that be? On the twenty-ninth day, of course. You have one day to save your pond.[4]

It is easy to imagine the implications of this phenomenon for food, housing, job demand, the family structures, and such other conditions affecting the quality of life as crowding, social welfare, and crime.

Interest is increasing in trying to control change, rather than simply reacting ex post facto to it. To minimize crisis-induced adaptation, which tends to be emotion-laden and often irrational, governmental leaders and social scientists are hopeful that they can plan responses by anticipating future change.

3. Donella H. Meadows, *et al., The Limits to Growth* (New York: Universe Books, 1972), p. 30.
4. *Ibid.,* p. 29.

One traditional way of doing so is by studying history. For example, the experience of the older developing countries of South America may be useful in predicting future political, social, and economic developments in the more recently independent countries of Africa and Asia. At several points in our analysis of Mexico and Nigeria, we have explicitly compared a given stage of development in the histories of both nations to suggest future trends in Nigeria. As valuable as this historical approach may be, there are limitations on its use as a predictor of future changes. The same kind of social changes that occurred in a past era may lead to entirely different outcomes in the present era. For example, during the eighteenth and nineteenth centuries the growing population of Western Europe produced mass migrations to urban areas and provided cheap labor for new labor-intensive industries in the early stages of the Industrial Revolution. Today, however, similar population movements due to rising man-to-land ratios in the Third World lead instead to serious overcrowding of the cities and potential political turmoil, because modern industry is more dependent on technology and skilled labor than on cheap labor. To control these evolutionary factors, sophisticated forms of conjecture and forecasting are utilized in conjunction with planning.

Because contemporary political systems are ongoing dynamic systems, we are concerned with the effects of today's actions on tomorrow's problems. Among the current issues likely to persist into the future are order among nations, or world peace; the disparity in development between rich and poor nations, and its implications for world peace; preservation of the ecosystem's balances; the quality of human life, including social relations, and personal and psychological growth, and the balance between individual growth and the needs of the community. If human beings hope to achieve a balance between, on the one hand, labor-saving technology, innovative products and services, and leisure, and on the other "healthy" psychological growth and a life-supporting ecosystem, some form of planning will be necessary.

This observation suggests a series of crucial questions. Can planning be undertaken and successfully implemented in less-developed societies, which lack such resources as skilled professional administrators and technology? Can plans be implemented democratically in a society characterized by competing and nonintegrated patron-client hierarchies? In developed societies, will a political culture that places a high value on individualism and liberty allow for greater centralized control and the massive information systems required for effective monitoring?

## STAGES OF DEVELOPMENT

These problems will be examined in terms of the stages of development in which different nations find themselves: (1) agrarian, (2) preindustrial, (3) industrial, and (4) postindustrial.[5] Each of these theoretical stages has certain character-

5. Daniel Bell discusses these concepts in *Toward the Year 2000* (Boston: Houghton Mifflin, 1968), which he edited.

tistics that distinguish it from the others. Yet such distinctions are not absolute; some traits overlap from one stage to the next. The boundaries between stages are uncertain. And in the real world it is possible to find characteristics of two or more stages coexisting in the same country. In short, the four stages are ideal types or abstract models rather than descriptions of reality. Table 11.2 lists these stages and their characteristics.

*Agrarian Stage*   During the agrarian stage of development, there is little planned change; individuals and groups are integrated with their political institutions and their environments. Leaders tend to play both religious and secular roles: through them the forces of nature (e.g., the sun and moon cycles) are invoked to explain human events. The family unit tends to be the "stem family," in which many generations live in one household or a common residential compound. This familial unit is also the main economic and social unit, responsible for food, housing, clothing, education, entertainment, and the security of the young and elderly. The primary economic activity is subsistence agriculture. With increased technological change, productivity and organizational effectiveness increases.

The major issues at this stage are adequate food production to provide for a growing population, the improvement of housing, expansion of educational opportunities and public amenities (potable water, streets, sewage), and the initial challenges of nation-building and national integration. For today's liberal democracies, which began this process several hundred years ago, economic development occurred gradually with the emergence of merchants and later small consumer industries. Political order, national integration, and the establishment of state institutions were as much a challenge as they are today. By contrast, Third World and communist states currently at this stage are concerned with mobilizing human capital to create the dams, irrigation projects, roads, and electricity needed for modern agriculture and industry. The priority in communist states is on immediate industrialization, and on heavy industry rather than consumer industries.

Four types of political systems tend to characterize this stage: traditional authoritarian monarchies, authoritarian military regimes, single-party systems, and personal dictatorships. Urbanization, the growth of a modern industrial sector, population pressures, and a more politically attentive and involved citizenry bring about further change.

*Preindustrial Stage*   At this stage the integration of authority, society, and one's environment tends to give way to specialization; there are, for example, separate secular and religious leaders. The economic elite — those with more land and capital — tends to eclipse the religious elite in major issue areas. Family production of food, clothes, tools, and other needs tends to be replaced by specialized economic units engaged in the manufacture of consumer goods in excess of those required by the manufacturer. The savings from such enterprises give rise to industrial and commercial expansion. Urban areas increase in importance.

# TABLE 11.2
## Developmental Stages

|  | Agrarian | Preindustrial | Industrial | Postindustrial |
|---|---|---|---|---|
| Social | Communal; high integration; religio-secular elite; extended family; feudal relations; large rural population; ethnic-residence cleavage; parochial loyalties | Predominantly rural; extended family and nuclear family; emerging urban migrations; differentiation of religious and political elite; landed/capitalist elite; regional, ethnic, class cleavages | Nuclear family; high mobility; atomistic; state-integrated; economic integration; secular belief systems (rationality); high level of education; multiple identifications | Experimental family; high specialization; high mobility; widespread education; professional technocrats; high suburban, low rural population; emerging megalopolis; state integrated; multiple identifications |
| Economic | Subsistence agriculture; village markets; trade/barter; high proportion of GNP from agriculture; high percentage of labor force in agriculture | Dual economies; subsistence and commercial agriculture; monetization of economy; high labor-intensive industry; integration into national markets; increased industrial contribution to GNP; increased blue-collar employees | High industrial; large service sector; service employment; white-collar; capital-intensive industry; international markets; high use of credit | Service industrial; high industry; commercial agriculture; high percentage of labor force in service sector; global markets; high use of credit |
| Political | Elitist politics; authoritarian; patron-client; low participation; legitimacy based on tradition (religion); inherited status; regional, class, ethnic cleavages | Authoritarian single-party; patron-client links; military; some ideologically mobilized parties; low participation, except in mobilized systems; military bureaucracy; ethnic, regional class, traditional-modern cleavages; legitimacy based on tradition, charismatic leadership, and ideological allegiance | Pluralist single or competitive parties; classes occupational cleavages; ethnic/regional cleavages persist to lesser degree; multiple identifications; moderate party identifications; salience of economic issues; high mobilization; high participation; rational-legal basis for authority | Pluralist single or competitive parties; specialized authorities; multiple identification; low party identification; high mobilization; high participation; private-public bureaucratic, professional mass-media; pluralist party coalitions; increased sensitivity to global stimuli (e.g., energy, financial crisis) |

Mobility and technological advances begin to accelerate the processes of change, though not always its scope. Change in these early stages, save in communist countries, tends to affect only an incrementally increasing select few. In both rural and urban areas, social disparities increase markedly; examples are eighteenth- and nineteenth-century Europe and China from the beginning of the twentieth century through the first decade of communist rule. The major issues at this stage are often similar to those of the previous stage: increased food production, population growth, national integration, education, industrialization, increased demands for political participation, and, more recently, environmental problems. In communist nations, the tension between economic development on the one hand and the realization of communist ideals of social justice on the other emerges as a prominent issue. Some nations give preference to economic development, professionalism, and strict centralized control, while others have stressed simultaneous development of communism and the economy, and minimization of the counterideological effects of professionalism and central party control. Many of today's Third World nations, like their eighteenth- and nineteenth-century European counterparts, are developing their economic systems incrementally. The wealthy landed elite and small merchants are accumulating capital for indigenous small industries. However, unlike their European predecessors, these indigenous capitalists are often unable to compete with foreign multinational corporations and imports from the industrialized–developed societies. Political systems during this stage tend to incorporate those of the previous stage, but it is not unusual for institutionalized single-party systems (often encompassing a broad coalition) to gain supremacy over the military and traditional elites.

*Industrial Stage*  With cities attracting the surplus and the dissatisfied among the rural population, pressure increases on urban public services (education, sanitation, roads, and water supplies) as well as on land. Industry now contributes more than agriculture to the gross national product. As a result of this and population mobility, an increasing percentage of the labor force is occupied in higher-paying blue-collar and white-collar jobs. Migration occurs once again, this time to the suburbs, and inevitably tends to accentuate either class differences or communal differences. In societies marked by racial tensions, the migration of one racial group into an area previously inhabited by another race tends to bring about an exodus of the original residents and increased communal tensions. Widespread education, mass communication, and higher per capita incomes lead to greater political participation. Governments are likely to be of the competitive-party representative type, rather than the inherited monarchies, single-party regimes, or military regimes characteristic of the earlier stages. Exceptions to this generalization are the communist states and even some Third World states, which may pass through the industrial stage with single-party systems. However, there is likely to be increased pluralism even within the single parties; the proliferation of professional and occupational groups coincides with modernization to prompt such groups to compete for positions and favored policy outcomes. The major issues at this stage tend to be environmental decay, employment, income distribution, working conditions, urban blight, crime, juvenile delinquency, drugs, and alienation. Continued technological and economic advances give rise to yet another stage.[6]

*Postindustrial Stage*   At this stage, many characteristics of the society and polity have changed. The cities have been eclipsed by suburbia as the center of residence. Most of the population is employed in the service sector, which, along with industry, is the major contributor to the gross national product. Even the nuclear family is increasingly affected by mobility patterns and socialization by the mass media. In competitive market systems, "consumerism" — or the gnawing urge to buy new products — also prescribes dissatisfaction with old products. This socialized dissatisfaction may well be transferred to interhuman relations. Thus an individual conditioned by this steady barrage of advertisements for the new and better may continuously trade in human relationships, as well as new goods or services, in search of excitement. This situation is hardly conducive to stable familial relations. Pockets of poverty exist within a population whose majority is middle-class. Sex cleavages emerge as important political issues; traditional sex roles and relationships first questioned during the industrial stage become subject to political action during the postindustrial stage. Social justice — the equitable distribution of wealth and opportunities — becomes an increasingly important value, joining the quality of life, ecology, population control, allocation of the world's natural resources, and world order as major issues. Alienation resulting from political unresponsiveness or inability to adapt to the rapidity of change creates individuals and groups bent on violent outbursts, e.g., political terrorism such as hijackings, political assassinations, and kidnappings.

Governments tend to be representative. The population is made politically aware and highly politicized by exposure to the electronic media and modern education. Large public and private bureaucracies seem to be engaged in battles over policies the average citizen cannot comprehend. Information overflow further frustrates the citizen, whose party identification tends to have weakened as a result of increased mobility and cross-pressures. Governmental capacity seldom keeps pace with demands, and scepticism prompts frequent turnovers in governments and major governmental reforms. Experiments in decentralization occur with increasing frequency in an attempt to increase government's responsiveness. Specialized private governments, such as large associations, increasingly make decisions formerly reserved by political units.

It is difficult to point to perfect examples of any of these abstract stages of development. The process of development is cumulative in that each stage is built upon earlier stages, and elements of prior stages persist. Thus the United States, which is closest to the postindustrial stage, has a number of traits characteristic of the industrial stage and even some left over from the agrarian stage.

6. For a discussion of the postindustrial stage, see Daniel Bell, *The Coming of Post-Industrial Society* (New York: Basic Books, 1973).

Similarly, development proceeds at different rates in different parts of the same country. So Nigeria, which is perhaps best described as on the threshold of the preindustrial stage, exhibits in some urban areas traits characteristic of the postindustrial stage.

While these stages are useful as theoretical models, it is difficult to establish boundaries between them in the real world. One measure is the nature of the work force. When most of the population is engaged in agriculture, for example, the society is agrarian. Thus China and Nigeria would be at the agrarian stage according to this criterion. When a large percentage but not the majority of the working population is engaged in industry, the society is at the preindustrial stage as in Mexico. The industrial stage is attained when the majority is in industry. This is also the case with the Soviet Union. When the majority of the population is in the service sector (i.e., public administration, trade, finance, transportation, communication), the postindustrial stage has been reached. Britain reached this stage about ten years ago and France has done so in the past few years. But such a mechanical measure oversimplifies the problem and at best provides only a rough approximation of any given nation's stage of development. The fact is that most contemporary societies are a blend of several or all of these stages.

# Change in Liberal Democracies

In most liberal democracies the goals to be achieved through political and social change are insufficiently defined. Rarely is there a dominant ideology that specifies clear-cut overall objectives and the means to attain them. To the extent that such nations have goals, they are defined by a variety of groups and institutions. As a result, the objectives of change are unintegrated and often conflicting. For example, the changes desired by the British trade unions differ from those sought by industrial leaders; and French socialists define goals for the future very differently than do the Gaullists.

Without a well-defined dominant ideology or a general consensus on objectives, change tends to be evolutionary rather than revolutionary. The compromises that result from the competition of different objectives usually lead to gradual changes. Often the most important and far-reaching changes come about only when they are forced on the political system by a crisis. Some examples will illustrate this point. Long after the need for change was evident to all, the French university system was reformed only because the student riots of the Events of May 1968 nearly toppled the regime. In Britain, the United States, and several other liberal democracies, the problem of overconsumption of energy resources was not faced until serious energy shortages occurred in 1973–1974. Though there have been periods of massive change in both Britain and France — most notably in recent times during the first five years after World War Two, when major social, economic, and political changes took place — even these changes are more accurately described as evolutionary than as revolutionary. The general tendency is for change to be very gradual and for decisive changes to come about only in the face of problems that must be immediately resolved. Indeed, it often appears that socioeconomic changes bring about governmental action more than governmental action produces such changes.

Another characteristic of change in liberal democracies is that it tends to be incremental. When it becomes apparent that a policy or institution needs to be changed the prevailing tendency is to tinker with the existing policy or institution rather than to search for entirely new solutions. For example, the collapse of the French Fourth Republic in 1958 resulted in a new constitution that modified the powers of various offices — increasing presidential power and decreasing parliamentary power — without entirely restructuring the political system. Its impact on the lives and acts of most politicians and nearly all citizens was imperceptible. The effects of this change of regime bore no resemblance whatever to those of de-Stalinization on the Soviet Union or of the Cultural Revolution on China.

In liberal democracies, influence over the directions and processes of change is shared by governmental and nongovernmental bodies. Until the 1930s government was largely uninterested in the economic and social systems, except for its regulatory tasks. Since then the governments of most liberal democracies have vastly increased their social and economic responsibilities, and thus increasingly affect and are affected by change in these areas. However, much of the change that takes place is produced by socioeconomic forces apparently beyond the control of either governmental or nongovernmental bodies. Thus important social and political changes can be anticipated to result from the uncontrollable inflation that Britain, France, the United States, and other liberal democracies have experienced over the past few years; from exponential increases in the consumption of energy and other natural resources; from decreasing birthrates (Britain, France, and most other Western democracies are close to zero population growth) and increasing lifespans; and from the decline of religion and the weakening of the nuclear family. Speculation on the possible governmental responses to these looming problems suggests that their political and social consequences will be tremendous.

Putting aside these speculations, some trends can be identified as Britain and France move toward postindustrial societies. Important shifts in political values are taking place. Some students of political attitudes suggest that egalitarian and libertarian issues are eclipsing bread-and-butter economic issues.[7] Western Europe has experienced a twenty-five-year period of unparalleled prosperity, and the resulting sense of economic security has increased public willingness for government to promote civil liberties and social justice rather than preoccupying itself with strictly economic matters. One outgrowth of this concern with social justice is the prominence and success of the women's movements in Britain,

7. Ronald Inglehart, "The Silent Revolution in Europe: Intergenerational Change in Post Industrial Societies," *American Political Science Review* LXV (December 1971): 991–1017.

France, and, especially, the United States. The tendency to give social justice priority over economic security is especially pronounced among the younger generation, who have lived their whole lives during this period of prosperity.

Another form of attitudinal change is a general decline in popular trust of political institutions and leaders.[8] More frequently than in the past, citizens question the effectiveness and responsiveness of parliament, the cabinet, the prime minister or president, and the bureaucracy. "Popular" leaders seem to have difficulty retaining their popularity once in high office. This may be only a temporary phenomenon caused by an era of particularly difficult problems and inept or lackluster leaders. It may be a result of governmental ineffectiveness in handling important but difficult problems such as inflation, pollution, and world peace. But it is also possible that public faith in institutions and leaders is declining because of growing scepticism aroused by better information and by revelations of the ineffectiveness or malfeasance of political figures.[9]

These attitudes lead to shifting patterns of political participation. Since greater participation is a function of higher levels of education, political involvement might be expected to increase. However, partisan attachments appear to be weakening. In the United States a growing portion of the population refuses to identify with either of the two major parties. In the 1974 British general elections many voters demonstrated their dissatisfaction with the two major parties by voting for the Liberals and other minor parties: nearly one out of four British voters supported a minor party, compared to one out of ten who did so in the 1970 election. As one scholar notes: "Unless there is a clear-cut reversal of current trends, however, parties do not appear to be the likely mechanisms for structuring the higher levels of political participation that should characterize post-industrial society." [10] If parties fail to attract the new participants, future forms of involvement may range from politicized professional associations to civic action groups that focus on specific issues to street politics.

There is also a trend toward the increasing centralization of government at the same time that nearly everyone acknowledges the widespread desire for decentralization. Central controls over finances, the need to standardize governmental social services in all parts of the country, and the complexity and non-isolability of many contemporary problems all lead to centralization. The control of air pollution, for example, requires large amounts of money not available to local governments, regional standards, and powers that exceed those of the local government, since walls cannot be erected to keep out pollution from neighboring areas. Thus many contemporary issues are best handled by the central government. But its remoteness and insensitivity to local needs arouse desires for decentralization. France has wrestled with this dilemma since before World War Two without finding a solution. The regional councils put into

8. See the recent polls on American attitudes in 1973 as compared to 1968 and earlier. *Newsweek,* 10 December 1973.

9. Samuel P. Huntington, "Postindustrial Politics: How Benign Will It Be?" *Comparative Politics* VI (January 1974): 182–186.

10. *Ibid.,* p. 175.

operation in 1974 are a step in the direction of decentralization, but their lack of independent power and finances raises questions about their real effectiveness.

As government becomes increasingly remote and unresponsive to local needs, there is a growing tendency toward the revival of separatist sentiments in areas inhabited by distinctive nationality groups. In Britain, many Scots and Welsh are calling for their own legislatures and greater autonomy. Small minorities in Scotland and Wales even advocate independence from England. In France desires for greater autonomy are strongly expressed by the Bretons and Corsicans, and small separatist minorities advocate independence for these two regions also. In Brittany and Corsica, and to a lesser extent in Scotland and Wales, it is felt that the central government has neglected the needs of these regions and withheld fair shares of economic development funds from them. The perception of unequal economic development enhances the desire for decentralized power and greater autonomy for local or regional governments.

Another trend is the bureaucratization of almost all forms of social interaction, including business, commerce, education, and, of course, government. The absence of interest in the individual manifested by supermarkets, automated factory assembly lines, large school classrooms, and impersonal government offices may lead to isolation and alienation. While people have had to contend with bureaucracies and red tape for many years, the growth in size and complexity of bureaucracies has accelerated. For example, within four months of the creation of the United States Federal Energy Office, a government report revealed that the new agency was already unable to meet its responsibilities due to excessive bureaucratization.

Related to the growth of bureaucracies is a trend toward greater governmental regulation, which increases the impact of government on the lives of the citizens. Such regulations now require the use of automobile seat belts, dictate thermostat settings for homes and industry, prevent the use of certain fabrics for children's clothing, control prices and wages, and bar sexual or racial discrimination in housing, education, and private clubs. And it is likely that government's tasks will continue to grow in the years ahead. If the predicted shortages of natural resources occur, government will no doubt be involved in assuring the fairest distribution of scarce products. Some even suggest that the day is not far off when government will regulate the number of children a couple may have, in the interest of limiting population growth.

Despite the arguments that can be made to justify these forms of governmental activity — and good arguments can be made for many of them — the expanding role of government clearly challenges the norm of limited government, so long a key point in the liberal democratic creed. It will be difficult for the government to retain public confidence and support when increased governmental regulation coincides with public mistrust of governmental institutions and officials. The tensions and resentments evident during the energy crisis of the 1970s suggest the political challenge and threat of political instability inherent in these new forms of governmental activity. They need not result in chaos or the decline of democracies. Where institutions are strong and confidence in the leaders can be created, democracies have been able to overcome similar trials in the past. The best example is Britain during the early years of World War Two, when crisis brought out the best in the leaders and the public. On the other hand, where the institutions are ineffective and the leaders discredited, liberal democracy may collapse. Such was the case with the Third French Republic in 1940. It was not the Nazi invasion alone that destroyed the Third Republic; the military defeat simply pointed out that the government had ceased to govern.

# Change in
# Communist Political Systems

Communist states have a comparatively well-defined set of political and social objectives for change derived from their ideology. In contrast to the often aimless nature of change in liberal democracies and in the Third World, the communist ideology specifies the kinds of political, social and economic changes necessary to build a communist society. Furthermore, the ideology prescribes party control over the processes of change so that change tends to be more centrally planned and directed in communist states than elsewhere. Of course, the party is unable to control all change, but its efforts tend in the direction of total regulation of social and political change. It is the inability to achieve complete mastery that raises questions and problems related to the effects of change in communist societies. Our study of the Chinese and Soviet cases have highlighted similarities and differences between these states' approaches to the following shared problems: (1) the challenge of regularizing the processes of political decision-making and the transfer of power or political institutionalization; (2) the challenge of realizing democratic aspirations implicit in the communist ideology, or party–state authority and bureaucratization versus the ideological norm of mass participation; and (3) the challenge of priorities, or rapid economic development versus the creation of a communist society.

After taking power, the Communist party first attempts to consolidate political control by eliminating real and potential rivals. It strengthens its organizational network in order to implement political decisions and to regulate further change. Competing parties are usually banned, although in some cases (such as China) their continued existence is formally tolerated if the party is confident of its ability to regulate them. Social groups such as religions, trade unions, and other associations are brought under party control or eliminated. As consolidation and modernization proceed, conflicts often develop between those who have been members of the Communist party elite since prerevolutionary days and its new postrevolutionary members. These conflicts often prolong the period of political consolidation.

At the same time that political consolidation is proceeding, social and economic changes are promoted. For the most part these changes are intended to create socioeconomic structures and attitudes that will support a communist society. Once the party is assured of its dominance, it usually attempts to promote the rapid industrialization of the economy. This effort is often encouraged by its perception of external threats to the regime. After this period of dramatic change, indirection often ensues as the party leadership adjusts to practical needs and new conditions and seeks to move further down the road to communism. As the communist state matures it may fall victim to organizational conservatism, defense of the status quo, and declining ideological vigor.

In both the Soviet Union and China, the early stages of communist control were devoted to changes in the superstructure. Existing educational, economic, and political institutions were altered under party control to promote the development of communism. China instituted the early mass movement campaigns and the Soviet Union used formal educational institutions, adult education programs, and the mass media to reshape the individual's political and social orientations.

Communist countries are characterized by party-directed social, economic, and political change, the scope of which is limited only by managerial and resource capacities. The rate of change, at least in the early stages of development, is very rapid. The pattern of change is thus clearly revolutionary. There are a number of similarities, but also important differences, between patterns of change in the Soviet Union and China. First, change has been strongly influenced, if not directly dictated, by communist ideological norms. As the revolution has aged, the Soviet Union has exhibited a tendency toward greater pragmatism and a more relaxed ideological climate. But the communist ideology remains the key to an understanding of continuing change in Soviet society and politics. In China political rivals of Mao have often tried to modify his goals to reflect more pragmatic values like the Soviet Union's. However, in the first twenty-five years of communist rule in China they have had only temporary successes. Mao has been able to retain the upper hand politically and to continue to direct change toward the goals of social justice and equality.

The party has taken an active part in dramatically reshaping society and politics in both these countries. Perhaps the most marked government-induced change has occurred in the economic and political spheres. Both nations have been transformed from agrarian societies, characterized by subsistence agriculture, to industrial powers. Their populations are steadily becoming urbanized. The labor force is increasingly blue-collar. Industry is being distributed throughout the nation so as to reduce regional disparities. In China, the merger of agriculture, industry, services, and political authority in decentralized units constitutes a major sociopolitical change. From the quasi-feudal imperial political societies of prerevolutionary days, a single-party mobilizing system has emerged to provide political institutionalization and steady direction.

The party has also overturned the primacy of traditional family and religious loyalties. However, its efforts have not always been successful. The family system has perhaps been affected more by mobility, industrialization, and urbanization than by party or government efforts to undermine it. In fact, family ties are still strong and extended families who reside together are frequently found in China. Religious systems have been under strict party and governmental pressure, resulting in a decline in organized religious activity, particularly in China. However, persistent religious affiliation is still apparent, particularly among the older generations in the Soviet Union.

Political participation is officially encouraged, especially in China where policy-making is becoming increasingly decentralized. Political authority is undergoing major innovations in China, notably the commune and the revolutionary committees with their sectoral representation of the party, the masses, and the military. The frequent mass meetings held by almost every Chinese institution attest to a high degree of popular participation, in striking contrast to the low level of participation in China's prerevolutionary political system. Although there are few data on public opinion, it seems apparent from circumstantial evidence that identification with the Communist party is high in both political systems.

Political cleavages still persist even in these single-party systems. These cleavages have at various times included conflicts among party bureaucrats, state bureaucrats, the military, professionals, students, and over issues (e.g., strategies for modernizing the economy and for defense). As communist countries become increasingly industrialized, and thus more economically and socially complex, incipient political pluralism is likely to increase. Bureaucracies, economic and technical experts, economic managers, and other groups are likely to become more important and more difficult for the party to dominate or manipulate in debates on policy. There is evidence that this trend toward greater pluralism is operative in the Soviet Union. But many believe that it is still weak and can be reversed by a leader who desires greater personal power. In China, where industrialization is increasingly apparent, attempts by technical experts and bureaucrats to increase their influence have been held in check by Mao's insistence on ideological purity and his warnings against the dangers of privilege and inequality. Within the party, the military and the bureaucracy also seek to pursue pragmatic goals, including increased professionalism in the military, increased technological modernization of the army and industry, and corresponding managerial techniques of motivation adopted from the West (e.g., the profit motive and the awarding of reduced work-hours). In addition to these, new groups organized to mobilize the masses, including remnants of the former Red Guard, are active forces in Chinese politics. It may well be that the practice of mobilizing ad hoc mass groups becomes a precedent for future political competition.

In both the Soviet Union and China, the early stages of communist control emphasized changes in the formal political, educational, and economic structures. Over the years these new institutions and political values and orientations have become entrenched in the Soviet Union. Indeed, the formerly revolutionary Soviet Communist party has become a somewhat stodgy and conservative defender of its own monopoly on power and of the social and political status quo. In China, Mao has recognized in the Soviet experience the dangers of organizational conservativism and privilege, and has argued for perpetual interruptions of the process of altering the superstructure so as to purge the party, society, and the bureaucracy of those who seek to prevent the masses from determining how a strict egalitarian evolution toward a communist society will be achieved. The aftermaths of the Great Leap Forward and the Cultural Revolution indicate that the forces that seek pragmatic priorities in the creation of a communist society persistently reappear. Thus Chairman Mao has argued the necessity of "perpetual revolution" and elite and mass re-education programs in an attempt to avoid, or at least delay, the tendency toward decline of a "radical" bent in the Communist party. This fear is based on trends evident in the Soviet Union, particularly the dominance of a pragmatic approach to communist ideological goals.

While the trend in both nations is toward the institutionalization of decision-making by the party's Central Committee and Politburo and their respective standing committees, with intermittent participation by the military and ad hoc mass groups, there are major differences between them in the distribution of power. In the Soviet Union experimental fluctuations between centralization and decentralization occur periodically. In China the trend is toward institutionalized decentralization, represented by the communes and the integrated (party, military, and masses) revolutionary committee network.

# Change in the Third World

A sensitive African author records a villager's wonder at the thought of urban life:

> "There is no darkness there," he told his admiring listeners, "because at night the electric light shines like the sun, and people are always walking about, that is, those who want to walk. If you don't want to walk, you only have to wave your hand and a pleasure car stops for you." His audience (villagers) made sounds of wonderment.[11]

His words clearly reflect the range of development many Third World countries span. They are by and large at the agrarian stage, with most of their population engaged in subsistence agriculture. And yet their economies have modernizing industrial sectors. The scope of their objectives is often broad: economic growth and industrialization without foreign economic domination, elimination of the traditional social structures that bar such economic change, mass education and the development of a national system of higher education, the establishment of effective political institutions, and the end of economic and political dependence on foreign powers. Yet means to achieve these goals are often limited by the lack of sufficient reliable income, indigenous experts and technicians, and capable leaders. The result is a mixture of the traditional and the modern, agrarian and

11. Chinua Achebe, *No Longer at Ease* (New York: Fawcett, 1969), p. 20.

industrial, and often in the most heavily urbanized areas of problems characteristic of postindustrial societies.

Mexico and Nigeria illustrate the transitional and mixed nature of the Third World. Nigeria is still at the agrarian stage of development; most of its population still engages in subsistence-level agriculture. Yet it also has a modernizing industrial sector. Traditional elites, whose roles combine secular political tasks with religious responsibilities, still govern the villages where the bulk of the population resides. In the cities, however, new elites are emerging in the bureaucracies, industries, commercial enterprises, and the military to contend for urban and potentially national political power. Beneath the surface where political parties once existed are firm communal or ethnic ties and identifications. Yet this fabric of traditional communal associations, in which individuals, society, economics, political leadership, and the external world were once clearly integrated, may be slowly giving way to specialization, mobility, and disintegration.

Mexico, where the population is now slightly more urban than rural and where industry is gradually gaining on agriculture as the main contributor to the gross national product, is now at the preindustrial stage of development. Mexico exemplifies the transitional or dual nature of the preindustrial stage. Clear distinctions can be made between traditional patterns characterized by authoritarian and near-feudal conditions (large numbers of landless and illiterates on the margins of society) and the modern urban setting where mass education is a reality and factories utilize the latest technology. Indeed, the larger cities now face many of the problems of postindustrial states — pollution, inflation, political alienation, and disillusionment.

The rate of change in both Mexico and Nigeria has been incremental. The scope of change is often limited, particularly with regard to political changes, notably the expansion of citizen awareness, participation, and differentiation (bureaucracies, parties, and associations). Furthermore, the rate of change has been at the lower end of the scale, and it has been limited in depth to elite groups or those from the upper and middle urban classes. Alienation from "modern" change is widespread among the masses of both countries.

The main sources of change have often been external agents, particularly colonial regimes and, later, foreign threats to postindependence regimes. In Mexico the initial changes were brought on by colonialism. The Spanish brought centralized, albeit hierarchical and authoritarian political power. They created a new Spanish and mestizo land-owning elite and an encompassing cultural system, and in doing so destroyed the traditional culture. The new system was characterized by the dominance of the Catholic church; the *encomienda* system (forced servitude of the Indian population on large privately owned ranches); and European art, language, literature, values, music, and educational institutions. In the political realm, the Spanish brought a European-based set of rules and a constitution upon which the government was supposed to be patterned and developed.

In the years after independence from Spain, the indigenous political elite, such as President Porfirio Díaz, chose to encourage foreign investment in order to accelerate economic change. However, the 1917 Revolution brought about a reversion to nationalist sources of economic change. National pride and "dignity" became the popular norm, and limits were imposed on foreign investment opportunities and land-holding privileges. But it was not always those at the top of the national political system who initiated or brought on change. Clearly, the mobilized peasants, frustrated by Díaz's ambitious attempts at industrial modernization, were not to be ignored. They demanded that change also occur in the rural sector.

The postrevolutionary regime introduced a new set of values in its innovative 1917 constitution. These values emphasized the norm of social justice, which has throughout this century contended with elite forces unwilling to reduce their own vested interests. Post-1917 governments encouraged political differentiation through the formation of voluntary associations of labor, peasant, business, and professional groups. Politically, their major accomplishment has been the amalgamation of these groups. Further, they fostered the institutionalization of political processes, and to varying degrees encouraged the dissemination of land to a small portion of the landless and promoted mass education. Among the major efforts, if not ironies, of the Revolution has been the fostering of industrialization by many of the post-1917 Mexican presidents. This effort has depended — interestingly enough — on foreign investments and the creation of a national capitalist class. Associated with these processes have been a growing middle class, urbanization, increased social and geographical mobility, and the emergence of party identifications.

Nigeria's colonial rulers undertook irreversible processes of political, economic, and social change. Their major contributions included the creation of a single state from various communities, the establishment of an official national language (English), the introduction of European religions and the imposition of European political rules, processes, and institutions (e.g., bureaucracies, parties, a modern military, elections, and a parliamentary political system). The military government has since suspended some of the inherited constitutional legacies, including elections, political parties, the parliamentary system, and regional governments, and has emphasized modern administration and economic development in their place.

Evolutionary agents such as population growth, technology, industrialization, and mass education — and the more aware participatory citizens these phenomena create — also contribute to change. In both nations population growth, often enforced by religious–social values, is increasing the pace of social and political change. Mexico's rate of population increase rose in the 1950s and early 1960s, as compared with 1940–1949. Religious restrictions on birth control and social norms that associate manliness with fertility have contributed to this persistent high birthrate. That it is particularly high among the rural and urban poorer classes compounds their problems. Fertility is also considered a virtue in African families, and sterility is often grounds for divorce in traditional Nigerian societies. Marriage is seen primarily as a means to have children. Surveys made during the 1960s indicated that most women in traditional sectors of the society viewed six or seven children as ideal.[12] Family planning has been acknowledged by government planning officials in both nations as a necessity. Nigeria, however, has made a minimal effort by incorporating family planning into university-sponsored experimental community programs.

Population growth places increased demands on the land, reduces family and individual incomes, and prompts urban migration, which in turn puts further stress on the limited capacities of urban governments. Both countries are experiencing the pressure of demands for housing, public sanitation, water, education, employment, and protection from crime in the large cities and industrial centers. A further dimension of the problem is that both nations' population increases are swelling the dependent sector of the population; more than half the populations of both countries are at the "dependency ages," between birth and fifteen years. Those in these age brackets do not contribute to governmental revenues, but are heavy consumers of public services — education in particular.

Education is a major factor in social and political changes. It trains individuals for roles other than those traditionally taught by agricultural families. It increases exposure to written mass media and to the ideas and values of individualism and achievement, the effect of which is often to weaken family bonds and encourage mobility. When expectations are raised and subsequently not realized, such as among university or secondary school graduates unable to find employment, a potential for political instability might result.

Industrialization and technology accelerate the rate of change. Mass production in both Mexico and Nigeria has increased output and created new social roles — labor and white-collar workers. "Bureaucrats" from the nongovernmental sector are competing with governmental bureaucrats for public allocations. Labor is already a significant political force in Mexico. Indications are that as Nigeria emerges into the preindustrial stage, already existing labor associations will gain additional strength in the political arena. In addition to creating new classes and political forces, technology affects psychological integration. The individual is no longer the master of his or her labor or the creator of the product that results from it. This situation, compounded by the loneliness of urban life, is quite an adjustment for a Mexican or Nigerian accustomed to close family ties and to agricultural work in which one could see and even savor the results of his labor.

Finally, it is important to note that in all systems evolutionary processes can act as a constraint on controlled change. Thus, where population growth exceeds governmental capacity, plans may well end in partial or substantial failure.

12. Harold Nelson *et al., Area Handbook for Nigeria* (Washington, D.C.: U.S. Government Printing Office, 1972).

In November, 1920, after an uneventful election, Alváro Obregon took office as president.

To an observer, the Mexican government appeared then no different from that of the Díaz period with its politicians, demagogues, ambitious generals, big landowners (albeit new, uniformed owners who, as a rule, had seized their lands during the Revolution), small groups who disputed the executive power, and fraudulent elections. All this was too deeply embedded in Mexico by the thirty years of Porfiriate to be conjured away in an instant.[13]

This description poignantly highlights an issue central to the debate between the advocates of noncommunist and communist solutions to the challenges of change in the Third World. On one side are the relatively simple objectives of the Mexican Revolution — land for the landless, uplifting of the conditions of labor, and political reform (in particular, nonre-election of the president). On the other side is Mao's contention that changes in the superstructure without removing their causes in the economic system and political culture will be superficial. Mao could probably use Mexico's and Nigeria's problems in achieving the kinds of rapid change desired by their leaders and people to argue that nothing short of a full-scale effort to alter the political culture and transform the economy will suffice. Leaders of Third World nations often contend, however, that change should not be sought at the price of individual choice. Changing the political culture to embody norms and values determined by an elite would be too high a price, they believe.

There is even disagreement in the communist world over the priorities of change. Soviet leaders argue that communism, or the just distribution of goods, services, and opportunities, must await economic capacity; Mao would not agree. He believes priority must be given to the goals of social justice. Nor would he accept the promise of communist liberation only to see it eclipsed by state–party–bureaucratic oppression. For Mao, change must be guided by values and principles, for if these are sacrificed for certain ends, the ends themselves may well be lost.

Thus the dilemma is to maximize individual choice while maximizing socio-economic progress toward societally determined goals. As we have noted, natural evolutionary forces are at work, along with man's adaptive skills. Clearly each of the systems must make major adaptations to meet its challenges or realize its goals. Many long-cherished theories are now giving way. Third World nations are slowly beginning to realize that the traditional strategies for economic development based on increasing the gross national product will not necessarily result in a more equitable distribution of wealth, or necessarily in political development.

While these problems confronting Third World and communist states appear to be peculiar to them, there are underlying trends that are apparent in all

13. Victor Alba, *The Mexicans* (New York: Pegasus, 1973), p. 147.

three types of political systems. Some argue that communist and noncommunist systems are actually converging.[14] They point to the increasing bureaucratization of all systems, the growth of the state's authority and functions in the welfare societies of the liberal democracies, and the increasing demands for greater participation and less exclusivity in the communist systems. Clearly, the need for greater governmental direction in Third World nations at the early stages of development also supports the argument that different political systems are converging. The same thing can be said of increased governmental involvement in the social and economic problems that confront citizens in each of these systems.

Even the well-developed and affluent liberal democracies face the task of promoting and controlling ongoing social, economic, and political change. At times the slow pace of evolutionary change that tends to characterize these countries seems unconscionable. The spirit of many young people impatient to eliminate persisting social ills is captured by the words of a Frenchman at the time of the Events of May 1968:

> What can possibly be wrong? You are in Paris, the capital of a prosperous country, part of a world slowly curing itself of those hereditary illnesses it used to treat like family heirlooms: misery, hunger, death, logic. You are opening what may well be the most important turning-point in history since the discovery of fire. What troubles you? Are you frightened of Fantomas?
>
> Do you, as they often say, think about yourself too much? Or without knowledge, do you think too much about others? In your confusion you may sense that your destiny is connected to their destiny, that both fortune and misfortune are secret societies, so secret that unknowingly you are members of both, and that somewhere you shelter a voice you do not hear which says:
>
> > So long as there is misery, you are not rich,
> > So long as there is suffering, you are not happy,
> > So long as there are prisons, you are not free.[15]

14. For a critical evaluation of the "convergence" thesis, see Zbigniew Brzezinski and Samuel P. Huntington, *Political Power USA/USSR* (New York: Viking Press, 1963).

15. Cited in Charles Posner, ed., *Reflections on the Revolution in France: 1968* (Harmondsworth, England: Penguin Books, 1970), p. 5.

# INDEX

Britain (*cont.*)

486; immigration, 78; and Tibet, 94; constitution, 117; centralization, 120–121, 485–486; prime minister and cabinet, 121–125, 276–279, 282, 364–365, 368; Parliament, 121–125, 129–130, 309, 323, 325, 360–361, 366–367; elections, 130, 170–172, 177, 217, 219, 224, 388, 400, 449–450, 485; political participation, 158, 168–179; electoral system, 171, 219; protest politics, 177–178; interest groups, 212–216, 366–368; political parties, 217–219, 222–225; opposition in, 222, 224; political leadership, 276–279, 281–282, 283, 286–287, 450, 456–457; civil service, 277, 284–287, 367; leadership compared with France, 284–285; policy-making, 360–361, 362–365, 366–370; economic planning, 368–370, 400; energy crisis, 369; agricultural policy, 399–400, 406; social welfare policies, 399, 402–406, 410; oil, 402; income distribution, 403–404; education system, 404–405; legitimacy of political system, 449–450; at postindustrial stage, 483; change, 484, 485. *See also* House of Commons; House of Lords; Political parties

British Medical Association (BMA), 216

Brittany, 67, 78, 408, 486

Brown, H. Rap, 440

Brown, Lester, 474

Brzezinski, Zbigniew, 9, 375

BUO (United Workers' Bloc–Mexico), 242–243

Bureaucracy: Prussia, 2; China; 42ff, 141–142, 295–300; and interest groups, 201–202; control of, 273–275; Britain, 277, 284–286, 367; France, 277–278, 284–286, 367, 456; Soviet Union, 295–300; Nigeria, 302, 309–311, 493; Mexico, 309–311, 382, 493

Butler, David, 76, 172

Cabañas, Lucio, 470

Caciquismo, 52, 306

Calles, Plutarcho Elías, 246, 306–307, 341

Cambridge University, 279, 280, 368, 404

Campbell, Robert, 415

Canada: French separatism, 63–64, 67, 442; federalism, 90; political parties, 204, 224, 446

Cantonese dialect, 92

Cardénas, Lazáro, 51, 145, 246, 303, 306–307, 310, 341ff, 423, 471

Carranza, Venustiano, 54, 97

Castro, Fidel, 116, 272, 287, 470

Catholic church: in France, 33–34, 176; in Mexico, 50, 98, 103, 142, 150, 168, 189, 491. *See also* Clericalism/anticlericalism

Cells, in communist parties, 205–206

Center for Democratic Progress (CDP), 217, 219–220, 222

Chaban-Delmas, Jacques, 281, 285, 365

Chad, 320

Chai Nai-ruenn, 419

Chai, Winberg, 93, 136

Chang Chun-chiao, 140, 239

Chao Kang, 418

Charles I, King of England, 23

Charles II, King of England, 23

Chartists, 27–28

Cheng, Chester J., 338

Ch'en Po-ta, 373

Chiang Ch'ing, 140, 185

Chiang Kai-shek, 43, 47f

Chile, 315, 343

China: as example of communist system, 5, 6–7; area and population, 10; historical background, 20, 35, 41–49; political culture and socialization, 21, 22, 165–168, 180–181, 421; bureaucracy, 42ff, 88, 141–142, 295–300, 489; land reforms and communes, 48–49, 87, 141, 417–418; civil war, 47–49; languages, 92; ethnic minorities, 92–95; and Soviet Union, 94, 336, 419, 464; social classes, 86–89, 94; succession politics, 116–117, 140, 239, 294–295, 340, 468; ideology, 131, 180–181, 205–206, 240–241, 293, 355, 489; political framework, 131–132, 133, 136–140; local government, 133; military politics, 133, 239, 331, 334–340, 465; centralization, 133, 490; National People's Congress, 136, 138, 337; constitution of 1975, 136; State Council, 138, 140, 372; political participation, 155, 179–186, 391; elections, 181–182; mass movements, 182; women in politics, 183–186; political dissent, 185–186; interest groups, 199, 227–230; political parties, 202, 236–241; labor unions, 228–229; political leadership, 288–289, 290–295, 464–467, 468; and North Korea, 337; policy-making, 361, 371, 372–374, 376–378, 417; planning, 372, 378; economic policy, 417–421; agricultural policy, 417–419; education, 421–422; social welfare policies, 421–423; political stability, 457–458, 463–468; family in, 468, 489–490; at agrarian stage, 483; and change, 487, 488, 489. *See also* Communist party of China; Cultural Revolution

Chirac, Jacques, 175

Chou En-lai, 140, 238ff, 301, 337, 372, 466ff

Christian Democratic party (France), 222

Churchill, Winston S., 17, 210, 462

Civic culture, 446–447

Class cleavages, 65–66, 390

Clericalism/anticlericalism: in France, 33–34, 77; as social cleavage, 67, 70; in Mexico, 103

CNC (National Peasant Confederation–Mexico), 242, 244, 247

CNOP (National Federation of Popular Organizations–Mexico), 243–244, 247

Collective farms and collectivization: in Soviet Union, 37–39, 41, 412–413, 414, 462; in China, 48–49, 87, 141, 417–418

Collectivism, 202

Common Market, 26, 173, 222, 282, 368, 400, 402, 406

Commonwealth of Nations, 26. *See also* Britain, Empire

Communist party of Britain, 449–450

Communist party of China (CPC): in civil war, 47–48, 236, 334–335; Tenth party congress, 132, 290, 291, 339; and political participation, 179–186 *passim;* operations described, 205–207, 236–241; and interest groups, 227ff, 371, 374; central committee, 236–238, 291, 301, 338, 373, 490; Politburo, 238, 239, 294, 301, 338, 376, 490; and Cultural Revolution, 240–241, 288, 464–466; and political stability, 256, 465–467; and political leadership, 288–290, 293; and military, 334–340; 465–467; and policy-making, 361, 371, 372–374, 376–378

Communist party of France (PCF): and women, 175; and labor unions, 213, 215; electoral support, 217, 454; program of, 220–221; and Soviet Union, 221

Communist party of Mexico, 248–249

Communist party of the Soviet Union (CPSU): membership, 84, 85, 86, 184, 232; apparatchiki, 86, 226f, 232, 292; as ruling class, 86, 132, 241; and federalism, 91; secretariat of, 136, 232; and political participation, 179–186; means of social control, 185–186, 232–235; operations described, 205–207, 230–236, 241; organization, 205–206, 230–232; and interest groups, 225–226, 370–371; central committee, 231–232, 289, 291, 299, 333, 374; Politburo, 231–232, 298, 333, 374; and political stability, 256, 458–463; policy-making powers, 370–371, 372–375, 377–378; program of, 370; legitimacy of, 458–459

Comparative politics: definition of, 2–3; study of, 2–5, 9

Confederation of Mexican Workers, *see* CTM

Confucianism, 42–43, 49

Conservative party (Britain): doctrine of, 27, 28, 218, 222; working class support, 27–28, 449; and classes, 75–77; men-

tioned, 123, 202; and women, 175–176; and 1974 elections, 217, 218, 388, 450–452; electoral support, 217–219, 222f; social background of MPs, 277–280; education policies, 404

Constitutions: definition of, 110; types of, 110–115

Cornelius, Wayne Jr., 472

Corsica, 328, 486

Coser, Lewis A., 64

Costa Rica, 6

CROM (Regional Confederation of Mexican Workers), 243

Cromwell, Oliver, 23, 323, 325

Crozier, Michel, 178, 453

CTM (Confederation of Mexican Workers), 242–243, 247

Cultural pluralism: in Soviet Union, 37, 40, 89–92, 108, 462; in Nigeria, 56–61 *passim,* 96, 101–103, 108, 146, 346–347, 468–473 *passim;* defined, 66–67; in France, 67, 78, 408, 486; in Britain, 78–80, 108, 177–178, 442, 450, 452–453, 486; in China, 92–95; in Mexico, 99–101; and political stability, 442

Cultural Revolution (China), 43, 136, 138, 484; as political socialization, 22; motives for, 49, 88, 238, 269, 294, 464–465; and Tibet, 94; and political institutions, 132, 133, 141, 371, 374; as political participation, 180, 182–183; and CPC, 240–241, 288, 464, 465, 466; effects of, 240–241, 418, 468, 490; and ideology, 292; and military politics, 335, 338–339; and five year plan, 378, 421; and political stability, 464–468 *passim. See also* Red Guards

Cutright, Phillips, 442

Czechoslovakia, 7, 186, 331

Dalai Lama, 94

Dangerfield, George, 174

Daniel, Yuli, 461

Debré, Michel, 280, 281

Deference, in Britain, 26–29

de Gaulle, Charles: Algerian independence, 30, 328–330; military rebellion against, 30, 329–330; provisional government of, 30, 174; cited, 33, 366; and Events of May 1968, 82, 330, 455; as president and policy-maker, 125, 127, 128, 129, 220, 225, 281, 363, 365–366, 366–367; resignation of, 131, 219, 220; and voting behavior, 173; and women's suffrage, 174; as charismatic leader, 210, 268, 283; and interest groups, 215, 277; style of leadership, 215, 277, 283, 363, 365–366, 453; military background, 324, 328; relations with military, 329–330; foreign policy of, 330, 406

la Cinquieme République—UDR), 483; and political institutions, 117, 127–131; electoral strength of, 127–128, 129, 217, 222, 276; and women, 175; and interest groups, 215, 277; doctrine and style, 219–220; leadership background of, 277, 278, 279–281; foreign policy positions, 281, 353, 355, 406; social policies of, 409

Geertz, Clifford, 66
Gehlen, Michael P., 288
Germany, East, 7, 116, 289
Germany, Weimar, 114, 322
Germany, West, 21–22, 72, 158, 401, 403, 447, 451
Ghana, 210, 320, 350, 358
Giroud, Françoise, 176
Giscard d'Estaing, Valéry, 125, 131, 176, 220, 281, 284, 365f, 406
González Casanova, Pablo, 96, 99–100, 145, 187, 340, 430
Gordon, Michael R., 275, 286
Gosplan, 229, 299
Gowon, General Yakuba: rule of, 57, 105–106, 305, 307, 308, 383, 469; coup of 1966, 61, 105, 346, 348; overthrown, 347, 472; and federalism, 471
Graham, Hugh Davis, 83
Great Leap Forward (China), 43, 377, 421, 490; how decided upon, 138, 239, 371; as mass movement, 182; and ideology, 292, 465–466; and military, 337; and five year plan, 378, 421; and political party, 465–468 passim
Great Proletarian Cultural Revolution, see Cultural Revolution
Great Reform Act of 1832, 24
Great Russians, 90–92, 292
Grechko, Marshal Andrei A., 333, 370
Gromyko, Andrei A., 374
Group theory of politics, 198
Gurr, Ted Robert, 83, 476

Hakka dialect, 92
Halpern, Manfred, 322
Hamilton, Alexander, 20
Han Chinese, 92–94
Hanson, Roger, 425, 426, 427, 431
Harper, Paul, 229
Haverman, Robert, 358
Heath, Edward, 77, 177, 451
Heisler, Martin, 369
Hermens, F.A., 446
History, impact on politics, 15–62
Hitler, Adolf, 21, 268
Hobbes, Thomas, 422
Ho Chi Minh, 116, 206, 267, 272, 287
Hoffman, Stanley, 178, 215, 453, 456
Holland, see Netherlands, the
House of Commons: history of, 22–25, 450;

powers of, 121–125, 129–130, 360–361, 366–367; membership of, 175, 277–278
House of Lords, 23–24, 121, 122, 125, 277, 360–361, 450
Hsia fang, 88, 300, 468
Huang Ke-ch'eng, 337
Hudson, Michael C., 10
Hundred Flowers movement (China), 95, 180, 182, 377, 464–465
Hungary, 465
Huntington, Samuel P., 8, 161–162, 208–211, 317, 322f, 341, 375, 443, 485

Ibsen, Henrik, 197
Ideology: defined, 20, 67; Britain, 28, 218–219, 281; as source of cleavages, 67–68, 204–205; end of, 70; in China, 131, 180–181, 205–206, 240–241, 290ff, 355, 489; in Soviet Union, 131, 180–181, 205–206, 293, 459, 461, 463, 488; in France, 220, 281–282; in Nigeria, 252; in Mexico, 423
*Immobillisme,* 323
Income distribution in Europe, 403
Incrementalism, 356–360, 369, 484
Independent Republicans (France), 217, 219–220
India, 17, 45, 117, 322, 419
Indians (Mexico), 50ff, 55–56, 99–101, 388
Indonesia, 316, 320, 469
Industrialization, strategies of, 395–396, 417
Industrial stage of development, 478, 480, 481–482
Inglehart, Ronald, 484
Inkeles, Alex, 459
Intelligentsia, 85–86, 185–186, 292, 462
Interest groups: defined, 197–198; role of, 198–202, 360; in U.S., 198, 201f; in Soviet Union, 199, 225–227, 229–230, 370–378 passim, 489; in China, 199, 227–230, 371–378 passim; in Britain, 212–216, 363, 366–368; in France, 212–216, 363, 367–368; in Mexico, 241–246, 380; in Nigeria, 241–242, 249–251
Internal colonialism, 99–101
Ireland, Republic of, 79. See also Northern Ireland
Irish Republican Army (IRA), 80, 83
Ironsi, General Johnson Aguyi, 57, 105, 305, 308, 346, 471
Israel, 89
Italy, 21, 67, 78, 158, 204, 401, 447, 451

James II, King of England, 23
Jao Shu-shih, 336, 464–465
Japan, 20, 45–46, 47, 451
Jaramillo, Rubén, 245
Jefferson, Thomas, 20
Jenkins, Roy, 453
Jews, Russian, 89ff, 186, 462
John I, King of England, 23

ticipation, 172–174, 196; defined, 197–198; and interest groups, 200; organization, style, and tasks, 202–212; in China, 202, 211, 236–241, 255–256; in the Netherlands, 204, 224; in Italy, 204; in Canada, 204, 224; and political stability, 207–208, 210–211, 222, 224–225, 255, 256, 446, 469ff; in Soviet Union, 211, 230–236, 255–256; in Sweden, 224; cross-national comparison, 254–256. *See also individual parties.*

Political socialization: in China, 22, 165–168, 180–181, 421; in Soviet Union, 22, 180–181, 332, 463; in France, 32, 163; defined, 163–168; in U.S., 163; in Britain, 165; in Mexico, 165–168, 187–189; and women, 176; in Nigeria, 189–190

Political stability: in France, 29–32, 34f, 440, 453–457; in Britain, 35, 440, 449–453, 456–457; and society, 64; and social cleavage, 107, 108; and political participation, 157–163; and political parties, 207–208, 210–211, 222, 224–225, 255–256, 446; in Mexico, 256, 468–473; defined, 439–441, 447–448; discussed, 439–473; in U.S., 440; in China, 457–458, 463–468; in Soviet Union, 457–463, in Nigeria, 468–473

Political symbols, defined, 17–20

Political system: defined, 3–4; types of, 6–9

Politics, defined, 1

Pompidou, Georges: and Events of May 1968, 82, 455; as president, 128, 129, 131, 220, 281, 365, 366, 406; as prime minister, 128, 281, 365–366; styles of, 283–284

Pool, Ithiel de Sola, 290

Popular Front government (France), 29, 220

Popular Socialist party, Mexico, *see* PPS

Popular sovereignty, 156, 178–179

Portugal, 45, 78, 221

Postindustrial stage of development, 478, 480, 482–483, 484

Poverty, 396–397

Powell, G. Bingham, 8

PPS (Popular Socialist party–Mexico), 248–249

Praetorianism, 314

Preindustrial stage of development, 478, 479–481

Presidential system, 114–115

PRI (Institutional Revolutionary Party): history of, 54, 97, 246; and poverty, 98; as centralizing force, 142; and political participation, 144f, 190–192; and succession politics, 146; and interest groups, 242–247; dominating position of, 246–249, 301; organization, 247–248; and political stability, 256, 469ff; and political recruitment, 301–304, 310; ideology of, 305–306; and military, 341–343; policy-making role, 379–382

Price, Robert, 320

Proportional representation, *see* Electoral systems

Protest politics and dissent: in Soviet Union, 41, 64, 85–86, 185–186, 461–463; in Britain, 177–178; in France, 178–179, 215, 455–456; in Canada, 185–186; in Mexico, 192, 245, 468, 470, 472

"Public" schools, in Britain, 277, 279, 280

Punnett, R.M., 175

Purcell, Susan Kaufman, 380

Puritan Revolution, 23, 323

Putnam, Robert D., 272, 321

Quebec separatism, 63–64, 67

Radical-Socialist party, 217, 220–222

Raser, John, 270

Red Guards, 92, 94, 140f, 183, 299, 338, 374, 489. *See also* Cultural Revolution

"Reformers," 221–222

Regional cleavages: defined, 52, 65–66; in Nigeria, 58–61, 66, 96, 101–103, 104ff, 254, 304, 307, 320, 346; in Britain, 77–78; in France, 77–78

Regional Confederation of Mexican Workers, *see* CROM

Religion, in Britain, 26

Républicain Indépendents (PI), *see* Independent Republicans

Rolls-Royce, 401

Roman Empire, 314

Rose, Richard, 79, 169, 232, 453

Roy, M.N., 236

Royal Automobile Club, 216

Ruiz Cortines, Adolfo, 243

Rural change, strategies of, 394–395

Russett, Bruce, 395

Russian Orthodox church, 39f

Sadat, Anwar, 116

Sakharov, Andrei, 86, 186, 461

Samizdat, 185–186

Sampson, Anthony, 364, 400

Santa Anna, Antonio López de, 51

Sartori, Giovanni, 205

Sayre, Wallace S., 275

Scalapino, Robert, 87

Schwartz, Joel J., 199, 227

Scotland, 78, 79, 450, 486

Scott, James C., 209, 385

Scott, Robert E., 100, 143, 243

Secret Police, *see* KGB

Selznick, Philip, 205

Semeistvennost', 299, 300

DEFGHIJ–H–79